re Notes in Computer Science   3196

ced Publication in 1973
; and Former Series Editors:
Goos, Juris Hartmanis, and Jan van Leeuwen

tian Stary Constantine Stephanidis (Eds.)

r-Centered
eraction Paradigms
Universal Access
he Information Society

RCIM Workshop on User Interfaces for All
a, Austria, June 28-29, 2004
d Selected Papers

ne Editors

tian Stary
ersity of Linz
rtment of Business Information Systems, Communications Engineering
tädterstraße 315, 4040 Linz, Austria
il: Christian.Stary@jku.at

tantine Stephanidis
dation for Research and Technology-Hellas (FOURTH)
ute of Computer Science
klion, Crete, GR-70013, Greece
il: cs@ics.forth.gr

ry of Congress Control Number: Applied for

ubject Classification (1998): H.5.2, H.5.3, H.5, H.4, H.3, D.2, C.2, K.4

0302-9743
3-540-23375-X Springer Berlin Heidelberg New York

er is a part of Springer Science+Business Media

eronline.com

nger-Verlag Berlin Heidelberg 2004
in Germany

Preface

The 8th ERCIM Workshop "User Interfaces for All" was held in Vienna, Austria, on 28–29 June 2004, building upon the results of the seven previous workshops held in Heraklion, Crete, Greece, 30–31 October 1995; Prague, Czech Republic, 7–8 November 1996; Obernai, France, 3–4 November 1997; Stockholm, Sweden, 19–21 October 1998; Dagstuhl, Germany, 28 November – 1 December 1999; Florence, Italy, 25–26 October 2000; and Paris (Chantilly), France, 24–25 October 2002.

The concept of "User Interfaces for All" targets a proactive realization of the "design for all" principle in the field of human-computer interaction (HCI), and involves the development of user interfaces to interactive applications and e-services, which provide universal access and usability to potentially all users. In the tradition of its predecessors, the 8th ERCIM Workshop "User Interfaces for All" aimed to consolidate recent work and to stimulate further discussion on the state of the art in "User Interfaces for All" and its increasing range of applications in the upcoming Information Society.

The emphasis of the 2004 event was on "User-Centered Interaction Paradigms for Universal Access in the Information Society." The requirement for user-centered universal access stems from the growing impact of the fusion of the emerging technologies and from the different dimensions of diversity that are intrinsic to the Information Society. These dimensions become evident when considering the broad range of user characteristics, the changing nature of human activities, the variety of contexts of use, the increasing availability and diversification of information, knowledge sources and e-services, the proliferation of technological platforms, etc. The 8th ERCIM Workshop "User Interfaces for All" focused on the new HCI challenges arising from this evolution, and on how these affect the continuing efforts towards universal access in the Information Society.

Efforts towards universal access to Information Society technologies have met wide appreciation by an increasing proportion of the international research community, leading to various European and international research and policy initiatives, and to the establishment of forums for the diffusion and exchange of ideas and research results. These initiatives contribute to appropriating the benefits of the increasing international momentum and interest in the topics of universal design and universal access. Among them, the ERCIM working group on "User Interfaces for All" plays a catalytic role in bringing closer researchers and teams working in the different ERCIM organizations (but also organizations beyond ERCIM or the European boundaries), and sharing common interests and aspirations to contribute towards making the emerging Information Society equally accessible to all.

The 8th ERCIM Workshop "User Interfaces for All" attracted the strongest ever interest worldwide, with over 140 submissions from all over the world, covering a wide range of topics that include novel interaction paradigms and contexts of use, innovative concepts of universal accessibility and sociability, new modalities and dialogue styles, user-centered design in mobile application scenarios, late-breaking empirical results with respect to assessing universally accessible applications, and standardization efforts. Contributions addressed not only technological solutions, but also design paradigms and empirical methods for evaluation, as well as policy developments. Reflecting this essential variety of topics, the workshop featured the two keynote speeches "Interface Design Strategies to Promote Learnability for All" by Prof. Ben Shneiderman (University of Maryland, USA) and "Online Communities for All" by Prof. Jenny Preece (University of Maryland Baltimore County, USA).

This volume is organized into five thematic sections:

I Implementing user diversity. Contributions in this section investigate several important issues related to the varying characteristics and requirements of users of Information Society technologies, including cognitive assessment and personality profiling, individual differences and behavioral aspects of Web navigation, automated assessment of clinical populations, information needs of older users, and user requirements related to various types of cognitive impairments.

II Adaptation and personalization. Contributions in this section discuss issues related to user interface and content adaptation for universal access. Addressed topics include adaptive user modeling, interaction monitoring and usage patterns extraction, personalization based on cognitive styles, user interface adaptation for mobile computing devices, and interrelationships between adaptation and accessibility.

III Accessibility and usability of interactive applications and e-services. Papers in this section present methods, design guidelines and tools for accessibility and usability in the context of Web-based applications and services, and in particular in application domains such as education, health, and access to information.

IV Universal access and design for all: guidelines, standards and practice. This section includes papers discussing issues of design inclusiveness, focusing on concrete practice, and standards elaboration and impact.

Novel interaction techniques, devices and metaphors. This section proposes a variety of novel approaches to user interaction, discussing topics such as extended functionality devices, force feedback devices, input rate enhancement techniques, visualization techniques in augmented reality, nomadic speech entry, haptic and audio-based interaction, and multimodality.

We would like to thank all the contributors and participants who made this workshop one of the most successful international events held so far regarding user-centered universal access. The atmosphere was characterized by in-depth and provoking presentations as well as fruitful cross-disciplinary discourse in a socially rewarding environment. We also wish to thank the members of the Programme Committee and all the reviewers for their dedicated efforts to maintain the high scientific quality of the event, as well as the invited speakers Prof. Ben Shneiderman and Prof. Jenny Preece.

June 2004   Christian Stary and Constantine Stephanidis

8th ERCIM Workshop "User Interfaces for All"

Vienna, Austria, 28–29 June 2004

Special Theme: "User-Centred Interaction Paradigms for Universal Access in the Information Society"

Programme Chair

Christian Stary

Workshop Chair

Constantine Stephanidis

Local Organizers

AARIT
Austrian Computer Society

Programme Committee

Dr. Ray Adams, University of Middlesex, UK
Dr. Demosthenes Akoumianakis, ICS-FORTH, Greece
Prof. Elizabeth Andre, University of Augsburg, Germany
Dr. Markus Bylund, SICS, Sweden
Prof. Noelle Carbonell, LORIA (CNRS, INRIA, Université de Nancy), France
Dr. P. John Clarkson, University of Cambridge, UK
Dr. Pier Luigi Emiliani, CNR-IFAC, Italy
Dr. Hans W. Gellersen, Lancaster University, UK
Prof. Andreas Holzinger, University of Graz, Austria
Prof. Michael Fairhurst, University of Kent at Canterbury, UK
Mr. Seppo Haataja, NOKIA Mobile Phones, Finland
Dr. Eija Kaasinen, VTT, Finland
Dr. Simeon Keates, University of Cambridge, UK
Dr. Sri Hastuti Kurniawan, UMIST, UK
Dr. Reinhard Oppermann, Fraunhofer-FIT, Germany
Dr. Fabio Paterno, CNR-ISTI, Italy
Dr. Michael Pieper, Fraunhofer-FIT, Germany
Dr. Thomas Rist, DFKI, Germany
Dr. Anthony Savidis, ICS-FORTH, Greece
Dr. Dominique Scapin, INRIA, France

Prof. Christian Stary, University of Linz, Austria
Prof. Constantine Stephanidis, ICS-FORTH and University of Crete, Greece
Prof. Jean Vanderdonckt, Université Catholique de Louvain, Belgium
Dr. Harald Weber, ITA, Germany
Prof. Michael Wilson, RAL, UK
Dr. Juergen Ziegler, University of Duisburg-Essen, Germany

Sponsors

European Research Consortium for Informatics and Mathematics
(ERCIM – http://www.ercim.org/)

Institute of Computer Science, Foundation for Research and Technology – Hellas
(ICS-FORTH – http://www.ics.forth.gr/)

Austrian Association for Research in IT
(AARIT – http://www.aarit.at/)

Austrian Computer Society
(OCG – http://www.ocg.at/)

Johannes-Kepler-Universität Linz
(JKU Linz – http://www.uni-linz.ac.at/)

Table of Contents

Part I: Implementing User Diversity

Part II: Adaptation and Personalisation

Part III: Accessibility and Usability of Interactive Applications and e-Services

Part IV: Universal Access and Design for All: Guidelines, Standards and Practice

Part V: Novel Interaction Techniques, Devices and Metaphors

Universal Access Through Client-Centred Cognitive Assessment and Personality Profiling

Ray Adams

Middlesex University, School of Computing Science,
Trent Park, Bramley Road, London N14 4YZ
r.g.adams@mdx.ac.uk

Abstract. The demand for universal access to information in the evolving Information Society produces an inexorable move towards complex, powerful and interlinked technological solutions. In this context, user requirements must be captured by more powerful user models, based upon more advanced user centred methods. Traditional HCI techniques may not work well in the new context of future and emerging technologies. Earlier work [1] observed significant dissociations between observed task performance and self report, raising profound and serious problems for user modelling methods. This empirical paper evaluates three different types of method used in user modelling; task performance, self-report and the personality inventory. Four case studies with individuals with acquired disabilities are reported here. The relationships between these three aspects of the user's profile (self report, task performance and the personality inventory) are more complex than expected and provide different, sometimes contradictory, perspectives of user needs. A potential explanatory framework is offered briefly to guide future user modelling work. More importantly, any code of practice for Universal Access must not rely on any one method alone but must combine methods to minimise conceptual and practical errors. User profiles for adaptive technology must also employ multiple methods, if such technology is to be reliable in practice.

1 Introduction

If we are to achieve universal access in the face of emerging technological power and complexity, then we need equally powerful and robust methods of evaluating user requirements and building better user models [3,4,5,6]. We face the challenge of moving beyond simple, desk top applications to more powerful technologies which are embedded in real world artefacts [8,9]. If so, we cannot assume that traditional HCI methods are still adequate [7]. Indeed, recent work [1] demonstrates that different, but equally popular methods may produce different or even conflicting outcomes [10,11].

This empirical paper evaluates three types of method. In a series of case studies; task performance, self-report and personality were all deployed. Task performance was measured by the use of psychometric tests and cognitive tasks. Self report was based upon the use of structured interview methods and questionnaires. Personality was assessed by standard personality inventories (MBTI and 16PF). All procedures

C. Stary and C. Stephanidis (Eds.): UI4All 2004, LNCS 3196, pp. 3–15, 2004.

were implemented by a qualified psychologist as part of a three day vocational assessment for which the individual had volunteered.

2 Case Study 1: Client AB

Client AB received head injuries as a result of a road traffic accident, with resulting frontal lobe damage (right and left lobes). His performance, intelligence (IQ) and other cognitive functions were evaluated by controlled tasks. One was the Stroop test which requires the matching of different colour names in different colour inks according to different rules. His self report, insights and awareness of his problems were evaluated by structured interviews. His personality was assessed by means of two personality inventories (MBTI and 16PF).

2.1 Performance

Pre and post traumatic cognitive aptitude were both measured. Pre-accident ability was measured (the NART test) and produced a pre-morbid IQ of 120. Post-morbid IQ (measured by Ravens Standard Progressive Matrices (RSPM),[2]) produced an IQ estimate of 107. Such an observed reduction is highly likely to be related to his accident. Perceptual speed and accuracy were also measured by means of a perceptual reaction time test. He had no problems with perceptual processes. He carried out the Stroop task as a measure of his higher (executive) cognitive processes. He required significantly much more time to learn each version of the task than is typical, but when he had acquired each task, he performed it well. It appears that he faces significant problems with executive processes, in general and task acquisition / organisation in particular. Clearly, executive functions can be impaired in different ways.

2.2 Self-report

There were significant differences between his comments and his task performance. He reported a poor memory, yet performed well on a simple memory function task. He displayed poor meta-memory but showed no signs of being aware of that fact. He expected to perform poorly on the Stroop task but, after extended practice, did well. He showed no awareness that he had acquired the task slowly, nor that he needed additional practice to do so. Throughout the assessment, it was noticeable than he relied on external instructions from the psychologist to complete tasks adequately. He often remarked that he needed to be told exactly what to do, but could not initiate tasks himself.

2.3 Personality

A comparison was made of his behavior post head injury with his underlying personality. His perceived personality was assessed with the Myers-Briggs Type Indicator, (MBTI) and a 16 Personality Factor Inventory (16PF), [3]. Both inventories provide very similar profiles. There were clear indications that his underlying personality and his post injury behavior were sometimes contradictory. His personality profile pointed towards social correctness, with a very cautious approach to trusting other people. His frontal lobe injuries seem to be related to his passive approach to tasks; his executive function problems; his competent memory and basic attentional processes; lack of drive and observed lack of social inhibition.

2.4 Discussion

It is as if his self-reported personality profile corresponded to a great extent to his pre-morbid self and that his post-morbid personality style was not particularly well reflected. There were clear indications that his underlying personality and his post injury behavior were sometimes contradictory. His personality profile strongly indicated social correctness, with a very cautious approach to trusting other people. His frontal lobe injuries seem to be more related to his passive approach to tasks; his executive function problems; his competent memory and basic attentional processes; lack of drive and observed lack of social inhibition. Both his personality style and his cognitive functioning seem to have changed dramatically as a result of his trauma, but his self report and his reported personality have not changed so much. If so, his ability to reflect on his own personality would appear to be related to his lack of cognitive insight and awareness.

3   Case Study 2: Client AD

Client B is schizophrenic with his condition controlled by medication. When working under direct supervision, it was reported that he appeared to acquire new instructions well, he started the task satisfactorily but when left to work alone, his performance declined very significantly and he often stopped working completely when alone. His overall aptitude (IQ) was measured by Raven Standard Matrices, an allegedly culture-free measure. His self-report and insight were assessed by structured interview and by self report questionnaire. His personality was included by use of a personality questionnaire (16PF). A number of complaints have been reported at his work place, including: brief periods (4 to 5 minutes) when he would sit and do nothing, persistent filing errors and omitting required tasks. These errors have tended to continue and there is now increasing reluctance to continue with his placement. He is, perhaps unsurprisingly, defensive about his performance, agrees that he does make mistakes, but believes that they are minor and can be resolved. However, his personality is now quite labile (see later) and he will often tend to agree with criticisms and comments, even when he himself would never have reached similar conclusions independently. He was able to describe the details of his job, even bringing along a detailed set of notes which set out the parameters of every task. (A employment advisor advised me that these notes, which were prepared for him, do provide sufficient detail).

3.1 Task Performance

He was first given a measure of his overall aptitude (RSPM) [2] which produced a low score with reference to the general population (IQ 83). This suggests serious problems with cognitive skills, so he was given the Stroop test. This task requires the individual to organise and acquire new tasks and to attend and implement them well. He seemed to have no problems in learning and organising the tasks. However, he displayed difficulties carrying out the task and appeared to experience significant negative transfer from one task to another. This result was replicated with a different order of tasks. Whatever the order, he experienced negative transfer from the first to the second task. This suggests he learns better under error free conditions or he will retain errors after training. This hypothesis was tested and supported by a memory test.

He carried out a simple sorting task (MLS), requiring the sorting of chips by colour, by number or letter or by combinations of these dimensions. He was willing to attempt this task as many times as requested. This task indicates the general level of employment that an individual can achieve. It indicates (a) if an individual is actively participating rather than trying to fake poor performance and (b) the individual can learn new work skills.

He performed, without making errors, at a supported employment level on the first, second and third sessions, improving each time, and achieved an open employment level on the fourth session. Thus he shows the ability to acquire a new task of this kind, even though he took a number of trials to reach a satisfactory level. These sessions were relatively brief (by design) and cannot be generalised to much longer tasks. However, they do suggest that he was genuinely attempting to learn the task and was succeeding in so doing. Initial learning of a relatively simple, non-conflicting task does not seem to be the core of any major problem.

3.2 Self-report

There were at least three areas of mismatch between self-report and task performance i.e. self report questionnaire of typical errors, awareness and insight into task related problem and problems in the workplace. First, the Cognitive Failings Questionnaire (CFQ) [2] explores the frequency of everyday mistakes. It requires the individual to report on the perceived frequency of their errors. He reported a perceived low error rate 34 out of 100, indicating a lack of unawareness of mistakes. Second, his self-reports did not correspond with his task performance. Third, he appeared to have no insights or awareness of his inability to maintain performance standards in the work place, suggesting lack of awareness and insight. He estimated that his error rates at work were low i.e. 2–3 %, though his managers estimated a much higher rate.

3.3 Personality

The 16PF contains measures of the extent to which the respondent is attempting to present himself in a favourable or unfavourable manner. His responses indicate that he has answered most of the questions realistically. The following statements are based on his own responses.

His interpersonal style has a tendency towards introversion. He may at times be happier occupied with a task, than dealing with people, and will generally avoid coming forward in social situations, particularly if this places him at the centre of attention. Nevertheless, he can project quite a good-natured personality, putting forward a feeling of warmth when interacting with others. In personal exchanges, he maintains a balance by not being overbearing nor being too easily dominated. He will assert himself or give way as the situation demands.

He has a relatively cynical and questioning nature, tending to often suspect the underlying motives behind the things people say or do. Relatively unpretentious, genuine and rather outspoken, when asked for an opinion, he will on occasion, unintentionally (or otherwise) express himself in a direct and uncalculated manner.

His profile is typical of those who strike a balance between controlling and being controlled by their environment. As such, he is likely to exercise as much initiative as most people. He is a quite self-reliant, non-suggestible individual who is generally quite capable of making decisions and initiating action without group support or approval. He describes himself as a sensitive and creatively oriented person who is usually inclined to feel his way through problems.

3.4 Discussion

There is again, evidence of a double dissociation between, on the one hand, performance and self-report and on the other hand, between performance and reported personality. He showed major problems with performance in both the laboratory and the workplace. He failed to sustain performance at work, but could (or would) offer no explanation. He showed massive negative transfer between tasks with conflicting demand, but showed neither insight nor awareness. In addition, he only learned effectively under error free learning regimes.

His self-reported personality profile contrasted with both his observed and reported work performance, as shown below. These results cannot be explained by simple failure to report, though we cannot rule out cultural influences. His responses indicate that he has answered most of the questions realistically.

In personal exchanges, he feels that he is not too easily dominated, though in practice he was very compliant. He says that he will assert himself or give way as the situation demands, though he never did. He reports but did not show a relatively cynical and questioning nature. Other traits reported but not observed included; overtly critical, dogmatic and opinionated, obstinate from time to time, resentful of being given instructions, doing just the opposite of what he is told, neither feeling bound to conform to societal demands and protocol nor ignoring it. In most situations, he should considers him self to be fairly self-disciplined, relatively unpretentious, genuine and rather outspoken, when asked for an opinion, he will on occasion, unintentionally (or otherwise) express himself in a direct and uncalculated manner.

As well as these observed personality report versus personality expression, there were also at least three areas of mismatch between self-report and task performance i.e. self report questionnaire of typical errors, awareness and insight into task related problem and problems in the workplace. Thus both case studies displayed a double dissociation between (a) task performance and self-report / self-awareness of performance and (b) self-report of personality and observed expression of personality.

3.5 Double Dissociation Between the First, Two Case Studies in Performance

With specific reference to the Stroop task, Client AB had difficulty learning the task but his performance was then good. Client AN, however, showed good initial task learning but his subsequent performance was poor (mainly due to negative task transfer). For example, he often made responses on the second task which were more related to the first task.

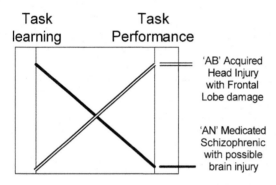

Task learning   Task Performance

'AB' Acquired Head Injury with Frontal Lobe damage

'AN' Medicated Schizophrenic with possible brain injury

Fig. 1. The relationship between task learning and task performance for two individuals tested with the Stroop assessment test.

This is a double dissociation and replicated earlier findings [1]. This is of theoretical importance, since the results cannot be explained in terms of the relative levels of task difficulty. We can be relatively confident that the two individuals are experiencing different types of executive process problem, one task acquisition and two task organisation and implementation.

4   Case Study 3: Client AC

Client AC sustained a head injury as a result of a road traffic accident twelve months previously. The resulting closed head injury involved the left frontal lobe and left parietal lobe (contusions), producing right hemiparesis and mild left hemiparesis. In a structured interview, he suggested that his health was good, as was his concentration and memory. He initially had no insight into his deficits, combined with impaired memory and concentration. After two months, he showed slightly improved insight, better memory but with significant cognitive problems.

4.1 Performance

His overall aptitude was evaluated by means of Ravens Standard Progressive Matrices(RSPM) and double checked by the Ravens Coloured Progressive Matrices (RCPM). They produced an IQ estimate of 69 and 75. The NART test was used to estimate his pre-morbid IQ (a test which is based upon prior knowledge of the pronunciation of irregular words) which turned out to be 105. Clearly his pre-morbid IQ was significantly higher than his currently estimated IQ.

Further analysis explored his numeracy and literacy skills using the Foundation Skills Assessment (FSA) in decreasing order of aptitude as follows: vocabulary (32nd %), reading comprehension (20th %), numerical problem solving (17th %) and number operations (1st %).

In view of his history of memory problems after the accident, his current memory performance was examined, using a simple free recall task for short digit sequences (four digits per sequence, 25 sequences per task). Three tasks were used in all, (i) auditory presentation, (ii) visual presentation and (iii) combined visual plus auditory. He managed 100 % recall in all three tasks for every sequence, so further evaluation of his memory was not undertaken.

To assess his cognitive skills, his performance on a modernised version of the Stroop task was considered (Hartley and Adams, 1974).This task involves the matching of colour names printed in different coloured inks according to predefined rules which vary in different versions of the task. His performance was very slow, completing approximately 25% of the number of items typically completed in the time allowed.

He learned to do each task, but his performance actually declined from the practice session to the main session in every This result is consistent with a difficulty with his ability to organise the demands of the tasks, even though he had been given ample opportunity to learn them i.e. a problem with executive functioning, a predominantly frontal lobe function. This conclusion is supported by the fact that his performance declined significantly across the different versions, suggesting that his ability to organise each task declined with exposure to different variations of the task.

4.2 Self-report

A structured interview was conducted to explore the key issues with him. He responded that his health was good, as was his concentration and memory. He added that he sometimes had problems "with his mind" and added that he sometimes did not think well enough for what he wanted to do, but that this was not a bad problem. Given his background profile of problems, these responses are all consistent with a lack of full insight into his cognitive problems. He also reported that he often experienced only mild headaches, but after each assessment session he reported experiencing significant headaches, requiring him to take rest. During the assessment, he appeared incapable of organising his own timetable and actions without significant prompting and guidance. It was necessary to actively manage him to be sure that he would be in the right place at the right time.

4.3 Personality

He was asked to complete an unpaced personality questionnaire (16PF) which normally takes approximately 45 minutes to complete. Surprisingly, he took over 150 minutes to do it, with breaks, clear evidence of significantly slowed information processing skills.

In his responses, he described himself as active, outgoing (moderate extraversion), independent, tough minded and able to take the initiative. He also reported a high level of self-control. The expression of his personality was markedly different. During the assessment, he appeared incapable of organising his own timetable and actions without significant prompting and guidance. It was necessary to actively manage him to be sure that he would be in the right place at the right time. He appeared to lack awareness of these problems.

4.4 Discussion

Again, there are major differences between his self-report and his task performance, as well as between his self-reported personality and the current expression of his personality through his observed behaviour. An interview or a discussion would not have provided an accurate picture of his strengths or weaknesses. In this case, he significantly underestimates the magnitude of his problems.

Double dissociations are observed not only between his self-report and behaviour, but also between his relative performance on memory and cognition tasks. This individual performed very well in the memory task but very badly on tasks which measure cognitive skills. In contrast, earlier cases described above, showed exactly the opposite profile performing relatively well on cognitive tasks but less well on the memory tasks. This is an important observation, since it means that differences between the two types of task cannot be explained simply in terms of their relative difficulty, suggesting that they measure different sets of cognitive processes.

5 Case Study4: Client JC A(1.4)

This individual was involved in a road traffic accident, with resulting frontal lobe damage and surgical removal of portions from both frontal lobes. No long term physical injuries were sustained. He is reported to exhibit inappropriate social behaviour. He has concerns about his ability to concentrate, his memory and about his lack of career development.

5.1 Performance

His pre-morbid IQ (by the NART test) which produced an IQ of 118. His current overall aptitude was evaluated by means of Ravens Standard Progressive Matrices, in which is produced an IQ estimate of 109. This reduction of ten or more IQ points would only be expected in the normal population in ten percent of cases. The observed reduction is highly likely to be related to his accident rather than being a chance result.

His verbal skills were assessed (DAT test), where his score was at the 50th percentile of the general population and the 78th percentile of the student population. His perceptual speed and accuracy were also measured by means of a DAT subtest. He performed well on this task, completing all items without error. Clearly, he has no problems with perceptual processes. Next, he carried out the Stroop task, as described above, as a measure of his higher cognitive processes. It was observed that he required significantly more time to learn each version of the task, but when he had learned each task he performed them relatively well. This suggests that he faces problems with his executive processes (though not as extreme as earlier cases), whilst his basic information processing skills seem to be intact.

He reported concerns with his memory and so this function was assessed using two versions of a simple word recall task, but no memory problems were found in these tasks (unlike for other individuals), effectively ruling out any significant memory problems. Any problems he experiences are more likely to be due to problems with his executive functioning rather than memory weakness per se.

His metamemory was also tested twice by a simple procedure in which his recall for prior events was tested. In both cases, he was able to recall only one task out of eight that he had actually done. Whilst his basic memory processes seem to be functioning well, his metamemory, a putative frontal lobe function, has been dramatically impaired. This is a striking contrast between working memory and metamemory.

Frontal lobe injury can lead to a number of important dysfunctions, but they can vary from injury to injury, from person to person. In this case study, his basic, low level cognitive skills like simple memory, concentration and attention seem to function well, whilst his higher functions like IQ, executive functions, structuring new tasks and metamemory are significantly impaired. Other traditional consequences of frontal lobe damage were not found (these include; epilepsy, dementia, aphasia, verbal reasoning, verbal performance, attention disorder, distractibility, and poor memory. This individual did not show a wide spread of deficits in this area but he did present problems of acquisition of a cognitive, attentional task (Stroop) as if his executive attention skills were impaired but low level attentional processes were not. As he remarked himself, he takes a very passive approach to work, simply following instructions. Is he relying on intact, low level attentional processes guided by external instruction?

Other features of frontal lobe damage include reduced activity, lack of drive, inability to plan ahead and lack of concern. Again, his passive approach to tasks discussed above, is consistent with these consequences of frontal lobe damage.

Social and cognitive disinhibition is also reported as a major consequence of frontal lobe damage. Whilst no socially inappropriate behaviour was observed here, with a male observer in a relatively formal environment, he has previously displayed socially inappropriate language with a female observer in a less formal setting. If so, this may be explained by recent research evidence that suggests that people with frontal lobe damage, particularly right frontal lobe, will have problems understanding or modelling the mental processes of others. These regions can be critical for understanding the perspectives of other people, leading to a reduction in empathy and sympathy, missing social skills which can lead to inappropriate judgements. For the same reasons, such people may also be poor at detecting deception in others. Interview evidence provided supportive evidence of both lack of understanding and inability to detect deception in this case.

5.2 Self-report

He reports concerns with his memory and so this function was assessed in depth. Despite these claims of a poor memory, he performed well in both versions of the memory task, performing nearly 100% on both, effectively ruling out any significant memory problems. Any problems he experiences are more likely to be due to problems with his executive functioning rather than memory weakness per se. He did not report metamemory problems (remembering what he is doing / has done / plans to do), but testing indicated serious problems in this area. This is a striking contrast between working memory and metamemory.

Frontal lobe injury can lead to a number of important dysfunctions, but they can vary from injury to injury, from person to person. It would appear that the frontal lobes are responsible for a number of functions, perhaps at different locations in the frontal lobes and thus vulnerable to differently located injuries. In this case study, his basic, low level cognitive skills like simple memory, concentration and attention seem to function well, whilst his higher functions like IQ, executive functions, structuring new tasks and metamemory are significantly impaired, though he was unable to report any of his problems in interview.

5.3 Personality

Compare his current behaviour post head injury with his underlying personality. His perceived personality was also assessed (MBTI and 16PF) and there were indications that his underlying personality tendencies and his post injury behaviour were sometimes contradictory (see below). His frontal lobe injuries seem to be implied in his passive approach to tasks, his executive function problems, his competent memory and basic attentional processes, lack of drive and social inhibition.

The MBTI presents him as generally dependable, practical, realistic and with a healthy regard for the facts. He will like everything clearly stated. In such people, their private reactions, which seldom show in their faces, are often vivid and intense. Not until they know you very well do you discover their idiosyncratic view of issues. He would be expected to be hard working, systematic and careful with procedures and principals. He would not enter into things impulsively but once committed they are very hard to discourage. He would be expected to do well in executive roles requiring organisation and control.

In the 16PF, he tended to give socially acceptable answers, so his responses should be treated with some care. He is quite introverted and his marked inhibition with people will make him seem to lack self-confidence and expressiveness. In social interactions, he will be passive and mild mannered, inhibited and formal. He has a cynical and questioning nature, not easily fooled or taken in. He will maintain a careful guard on his own behaviour and the expression of his emotions. This should guard him against taking impulsive action. When he knows people well, he is inclined to be more open and trusting. Conventional in outlook, he will support culturally correct standards and views. At the moment, he has a very high anxiety level and this may be due to his current circumstances. This second measure broadly confirms and complements the first.

5.4 Discussion

In summary, he presents a significant set of contrasts between (a) his performance and his self-report and (b) his behaviour as here assessed and his perceptions of his underlying personality as recorded by two independent personality inventories. Whilst the above statements are only a selection from a bigger corpus of such statements, there is sufficient indication that his personality has been changed dramatically by his head injuries. He is now reported to produce socially unacceptable comments and behaviour, to tell people what he is thinking even when it is unwise to do so, to be impulsive and to let others tell him what to do, passively responding. Current and underlying personality seem to be at odds with each other. This individual present with significant executive function problems as shown by reduced IQ, an inability to organise new tasks, lack of drive, socially inappropriate behaviour, poor metamemory yet functional low level memory and attentional processes.

In conclusion, there are significant differences between his comments and his task performance. He reported a poor memory yet performed well on a simple memory function task, yet displayed poor metamemory. He expected to perform poorly on the stroop task but, after extended practice, did well. His perceptions of his own personality contradicted his own behaviour as observed and reported by reliable others.

6 Discussion

All four case studies reported here, with individuals with acquired disabilities, demonstrate complex inter-relationships between

- task performance (in one case work performance too),
- self report about task performance through structured interview / questionnaire,
- the results of personality inventories and
- personality expression through behaviour.

Summarising the present data, it is clear that significant divergences emerged between the different methods, as follows.

Comparing methods	Observed results
Performance & personality	Divergent for all four cases
Performance & self-report	Divergent for all four cases
Personality and self-report	Weaker evidence of divergence
Personality before & after	Questionnaires reflected pre-injury behaviour

There is considerable complexity in these data. This fact alone point to the need for powerful user modelling methods. Even as summarised above, these results have very important implications for user modelling, since it is clear that we cannot rely on one type of approach to the detriment of others, since they provide different perspectives. Our initial results [1] were explained, in part, by two apparently independent factors. Insight refers to long term knowledge of on-going cognitive problems, whilst we use the term awareness to indicate a shorter term perception of concurrent processing difficulties.

Clearly, we need to now explain why there are striking differences between self-reported and expressed personality as shown in current behaviour. There are several, possible types of dissociation between them. Despite the significant functional differences between our cases in the types of failure of executive functioning, they all seem to show a similar lack of updating of their knowledge of their own personality profile after their traumatic head injuries and frontal lobe damage. It is as if the normal process of self-monitoring and construction of a model of self has been impaired.

This finding can be explained in terms of our own theory of cognition (Simplex Two, see below). In this theory there are eight distinct, semi-autonomous cognitive functions mediated by an executive function which monitors and coordinates. The eight functions are:

- ➢ input / perception
- ➢ feedback management
- ➢ working memory (includes short term memory)
- ➢ emotions and emotional evaluation
- ➢ cognitive modelling
- ➢ long term memory
- ➢ output buffer and
- ➢ complex outputs system.

by supposing that the inter-functionality of the executive module and the cognitive modelling module in Simplex has been disrupted. No doubt other theories will be

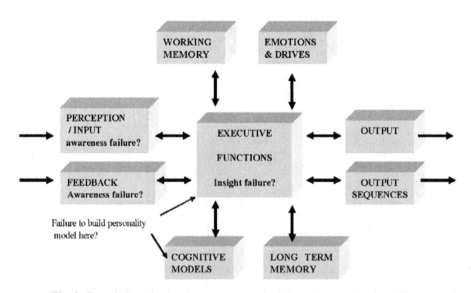

Fig. 2. The relationships between awareness, insight and personality modelling.

able to offer alternative explanations, but, for now, it is sufficient to note that these findings have important implications for universal access, use modelling methods and the design of self-monitoring systems.

Clearly, these data have made a significant impact upon our own user model, but it is also clear that they have equally important implications for codes of practice for Universal Access. These different methods have different strengths and weaknesses, so it will be essential that a code of practice should stipulate that developers deploy judicious combinations of methods, to minimise the effects of such weaknesses.

Finally, user profiles are increasingly used as input to adaptable systems, so that the interface interaction reflect the requirements of the individual. Such user profiles must draw upon a suitable combination of methods if the high standards of universal access are to be achieved.

References

1. Adams, R., Langdon, P., and Clarkson, P.J., (2002), A systematic basis for developing cognitive assessment methods for assistive technology. C6. pp 53-62. In Keates, S., Langdon, P., Clarkson, P.J., and Robinson, P. (Eds.) Universal Access and Assistive Technology. Springer.
2. Raven, J. (2000). The Raven's progressive matrices; Change and stability over culture and time. Cognitive Psychology, 41, 32 47.
3. Lord, W. (1994).a review of item content in the fifth edition of the 16PF. London: ASE.
4. Preece, J., Rogers, Y. and Sharp, H. (2002). Interaction Design; beyond human computer interaction. New York N.Y.: Wiley.
5. Dix, A., Finlay, J., Abowd, G. and Beale, R. (2004). Human-Computer Interaction (3rd ed.). London: Prentice Hall.
6. Nielsen, J. (2000). Designing Web Usability. London: New Riders.
7. Keates, S. and Clarkson, J. (2003). Countering design exclusion: an introduction to inclusive design. London: Springer.
8. Cooper, A. (1999). The Inmates Are Running the Asylum: Why High Tech Products Drive Us Crazy and How To Restore The Sanity. London: SAMS.
9. Norman, D. (1998). The Invisible Computer. Boston, MA.: MIT Press.
10. Newman, W. & Lemming, M. (1995). Interactive System Design. New York, N.Y.: Addison Wesley.
11. Shneiderman, B. (1998). Designing the User Interface (3rd ed.). New York, N.Y.:Addison Wesley.

A Study of Web-Based Information Needs
of Senior Citizens in Singapore

Seck-Pin Chong and Yin-Leng Theng

Nanyang Technological University
School of Communication and Information
31 Nanyang Link, Singapore 637718
seckpin@pmail.ntu.edu.sg, tyltheng@ntu.edu.sg

Abstract. Despite its high penetration rate of information technology among youngsters, most senior citizens in Singapore do not know how to use the Web. This study aims to determine the information needs of senior citizens in Singapore, with particular focus on the use of the Web. It attempts to investigate senior citizens' experience in using computers and the Web, and identify their leisure activities and topics of interests that could be transferred to the Web. The study further explores Web-based services most used by senior citizens and their perceptions of using the Web. It also examined their willingness, as well as their reluctance in learning to use the Web. The paper concludes with a discussion on implications of findings on interface design of Web-based information systems for senior citizens.

1 Introduction

The world population is greying rapidly. According to the United Nations (UN) projections [33], the number of persons aged 60 or older in the world is expected to increase from 629 million in 2002 to over 1,100 million in 2025. By 2050, it is estimated that the figure will grow to 2 billion, by which time the world population of older persons will surpass the population of children (0-14 years of age) for the first time in human history [33]. In fact, in more developed regions, the proportion of older persons had already surpassed that of children (19 percent versus 18 percent) in 2000 [34]. In Singapore, it is projected that the proportion of senior citizens (defined as persons aged 65 and above) will increase from about 7% in 2001 to 19% in 2030, or one in every five persons, making Singapore one of the fastest ageing societies in Asia [17].

In Singapore, although the penetration rate of Internet is high among the younger generation [20], the majority of the elderly do not seem to use the Internet. There appears to be an additional obstacle that may be attributed to the nation's culture, "especially in a work-oriented society that equates retirees as old, unproductive, incompetent, and expendable" [16], where retired people often become the group forgotten by society. Much emphasis is on the development of technology for the children and working adults, but not for the elderly as they are often regarded as of no contribution to the society anymore. This is a serious misconception considering the precious (tacit) knowledge that resides with senior citizens.

C. Stary and C. Stephanidis (Eds.): UI4All 2004, LNCS 3196, pp. 16–33, 2004.
© Springer-Verlag Berlin Heidelberg 2004

2 Our Study

Unlike some countries in North America and Europe, which have recognized information needs of senior citizens and developed many Websites specifically for senior citizens, such Websites can hardly be found in Singapore. Not much research effort has been put into this area as well. There were little published studies in exploring computer/Web literacy of the senior citizens, their information needs and willingness to adopt Web technology; there were also no known Websites that cater to the needs of the local senior citizens. Senior citizens as reported in [4] face numerous Web accessibility and usability problems.

Hence, the main aim of this study is to determine the information needs of senior citizens in Singapore, with particular focus on the use of the World Wide Web. To achieve this overall aim, several specific objectives of the study have been identified:

- Objective 1: To identify the types of information and Web-based services that are of most interest to the senior citizens in Singapore;
- Objective 2: To investigate senior citizens' perceptions of using the Web; and
- Objective 3: To investigate the willingness of the senior citizens to learn and to use the Web.

Approach Taken
The study was carried out in two phases. In the first phase, a general understanding of all aspects of ageing, information needs of the senior citizens, and their perceptions of the Web were obtained through reviewing existing literature of similar topic. With reference to some scientific publications, the second phase of the explorative study employed quantitative research method, namely questionnaire survey to reach a broader population. Information gathered from the two phases were analyzed and contrasted to determine the Web-based information needs of the senior citizens in Singapore.

Terminology Used
The research focuses on senior citizens in Singapore. Similar to most developed countries, Singapore accepts the chronological age of 65 years as the definition of "elderly" or "older persons". On the other hand, the United Nations (UN) criterion for older population is 60 and above.

In the discussion of the literature from the Department of Statistics of Singapore and the UN, respective definitions used in different countries would be adopted. However, this study uses 50 years of age or older as the general definition of senior citizens. Although it was recognized that difficulties may emerge while comparing results with other studies using a different definition of senior citizens, it was deemed necessary to solicit opinions from people in their fifties to gain a wider perspective on both *retirees as well as pre-retirees* as they are approaching retirement soon and their responses will reflect future needs of senior citizens.

In addition, although some scientific publications categorize the senior citizens into the "young-old" (aged 65 to 74), "old-old" (aged 75 to 84), and "oldest-old" (85 and over) [10], or "octogenarians" (aged 80-89), "nonagenarians" (aged 90-99), and "centenarians" (over 100) [13, 34], for the purpose of this study, such distinct classification is not relevant. The terms *senior citizens, elder(s), elderly, senior(s), aged,* and *older person(s)* would be used interchangeably [32, 37].

2.1 Questionnaire Design

Self-administered questionnaire was used in the survey to investigate the information needs of the senior citizens in Singapore. The questionnaire comprises four sections, which are detailed as follows:

- Section I: Demographic Information
  As noted by Vasoo, Ngiam and Cheung [36], when planning and developing programmes for older persons, it is crucial to know the socio-economic profiles of the older population because such information can enable people to shape and to develop programmes appropriate and relevant to the community. The same is applicable to the design of senior Websites. Hence, the demographic information of the senior citizens in Singapore is needed to facilitate the profiling of their information needs. More specifically, the objective is to find out the profile of the general average elderly in Singapore and their corresponding information needs.
  This section consists of seven questions pertaining to the respondents' background information. These demographic details include gender, ethnic group, age group, educational background, labour force participation, spoken and written languages.

- Section II: Physical Health Condition
  This section comprises two questions aimed to understand the subjects' physical health condition. Since age-related disability was identified as one of the main barriers to the adoption of computers and the Web [10, 14, 25, 27, 29, 30], the first question in this section intends to find out the age-related disabilities of the subjects that may affect their abilities to use computer and the Web. These age-related disabilities include dexterity/mobility, vision, and hearing problems. Examples of the most common diseases in each disability category were also included as references for the subjects to ease their understanding. Cognitive disability (such as bad memory or decreased learning ability) was not listed as one of the options because it is generally subjective and difficult to measure. An "others" option was included for the subjects to fill in any other disability.
  Since senior citizens' perceptions of their own health conditions are critical to their willingness in social involvement [6], the second question in this section asked the senior citizens for their self-perception of physical health condition. The physical health rating scale used in this question was adapted from the Older American Resource and Service. To avoid "prestige bias" – a tendency for respondents to answer in a way that put a better light on themselves [21] – the physical health rating scale was modified for this study to "Good", "Satisfactory", "Poor", and "Very bad", with the word "disabilities" in the description changed to "special needs". This was to avoid any possible negative connotation of the words "impaired" and "disabilities" that may inadvertently prompt the subjects to give invalid data or to skip answering this question.

- Section III: Information Needs
  Questions in this section gather the information needs of the senior citizens. There are three questions identifying the subject's leisure activities, topics of interest, and sources of information. For each question, an option was given to the subjects to specify answers not listed in the list of response choices.
  The off-line pastimes of the senior citizens may be translated into Web-based information needs. The list of response choices for leisure activities were derived

from the various studies conducted overseas [9, 10, 11, 24, 26, 27] and locally [6, 12]. Similarly, the response choices for the topics of interest were based on the various studies [2, 15, 19], and all the information sources listed were the most widely used by the senior citizens as shown in previous studies [3, 7, 15, 29], except the option on "World Wide Web", which was actually identified as the most unlikely to be used by older people [3, 29]. The inclusion of this option could help to determine if Web-literate subjects would use the Web as one of their information sources.

- Section IV: Experience and Perception of Computer and the World Wide Web
  This section covers nine questions concerning the senior citizens' experience of using computer and the Web, their willingness in learning computer and the Web, and their perceptions in using the Web.
  All subjects would answer the filter question on computer literacy. For subjects who did not know how to use computer, they would skip the next five questions. For subjects who had used computer before, they would proceed to the next question to indicate their current frequency of computer usage, if at all. This would help to assess the subjects' competency in using the computer.
  The following question would find out if the computer-literate subjects knew how to use the Web. This is another filter question where subjects who did not know how to use the Web would skip the next three questions. For those who were Web literate, their competencies were accessed through the years of knowledge and the usage frequency. The Web-based services that were most commonly used by these Web-literate elderly were also identified.
  For the subjects who did not know how to use computers or the Web, they would indicate their willingness to learn using computer and the Web. Subjects who were reluctant to learn were asked to further pin-point the reasons. Eight reasons were listed as response choices with an "others" option for subjects to specify reasons that may not have been included in the list. The reasons listed were based on the various findings on the main barriers of Web adoption by the senior citizens.
  The last two questions concern the senior citizens' perception of the Web. The subjects were asked if they thought more elderly people should be encouraged to use the Web. The response would determine if the senior citizens had positive or negative feelings towards the Web.

Refinement of Questionnaire
The initial questionnaire contained 21 questions, and it was also translated to the Chinese language since a vast majority of senior citizens understand the Chinese language better than the English language. Given the intended subjects of the study were persons who were 50 years and older, it was crucial that the questionnaire format and wordings were designed in ways that could be easily understood by the people of that age group. To ensure the questionnaire "speaks the user's language", a pilot survey was conducted before the actual questionnaire was administered.

The pilot test was carried out on three test subjects of age range 50-59, 60-69, and 70-79 respectively, using the questionnaire in Chinese version as chosen by them. Based on the feedback from the pre-test, several modifications were made. Sentences were rephrased to provide better understanding for the elderly, additional response choices were added, and format for the questions involving Likert scales were changed from circling to ticking boxes.

2.2 Sample Selection

The sample for this pilot study consisted of persons aged 50 and above who lived in Singapore. The survey employed convenience sampling technique, whereby the samples were collected randomly from channels that were accessible by the researcher [21]. The samples were reached through two channels:

- The first channel consisted of senior citizens from social organizations, namely:
  - Singapore Action Group of Elders (SAGE) – a non-profit and non-religious voluntary welfare organization for the senior citizens in Singapore. Established in 1977, it provides a variety of programmes, services and benefits to promote the continued growth and development of senior citizens in Singapore.
  - A local church with over 3000 church members.
- The second channel was parents of the researcher's acquaintances.

It is acknowledged that the use of convenience sampling does not permit an objective evaluation of the adequacy of the sample as it is a non-probability sampling method, and as such it is hard to determine the probability that any population element has been included in the sample [21]. Nevertheless, the data collected in this pilot study provided some useful insights to the variables of interest which we will highlight in this paper, and could serve as inputs for a bigger study.

3 Findings and Analysis

3.1 Method of Data Analysis

Descriptive statistical analysis was carried out on the raw data using MS-Excel spreadsheet and statistical software Statistical Package for the Social Sciences (SPSS) for Windows version 11.0.0. The results of the questionnaire were mainly analyzed using frequency test and Pearson Chi-Square test for independence.

Incomplete questionnaires were included in the analysis whereby missing data was ignored; questions with missing data were analyzed against smaller sample size according to the total number of answers obtained for that particular question. This was because the omitted questions only comprised a small portion of the entire questionnaire and the available data could provide valuable information to the research questions.

3.2 Profile of Sample

In total, 70 questionnaires (52 in Chinese version and 18 in English version) were given out, and 41 responses were obtained, rendering a response rate of 58.6%. This response rate is considered satisfactory as it is comparable to the National Survey of Senior Citizens in Singapore conducted in 1995, which yielded a response rate of 59.4% [18]. Of the 41 questionnaires returned, one was unusable due to omission in filling in the demographic data. For the remaining 40 responses, 31 were completed fully and 9 were completed partially, all of which are taken into consideration. Therefore, an overall sample size of 40 was achieved.

The sample comprised a mix of both genders, with 62.5% of males and 37.5% of females. The ethnicity of the sample resembled the racial distribution in Singapore, with the majority being Chinese (87.5%), followed by Malay (10.0%) and Indian (2.5%).

There was no person of age 80 and above in the sample group. Only three respondents (7.5%) had lower than primary educational attainment, and 70% had achieved education level of secondary or above. There were equal number of respondents who were still working full-time or had already retired, making up 45% of the total sample respectively, while 10% were holding part-time jobs.

On language proficiency, Mandarin was the most spoken language and its percentage corresponds to the 87.5% of the Chinese respondents. However, not all of these Mandarin-speaking respondents could read Chinese. Most respondents could also speak (72.5%) and read (70%) English. The high level of English literacy among the sample of such age may be attributed to higher educational attainment. In total, all respondents could speak two or more languages, and 35% could even speak up to four languages. However, only 57.5% of the respondents could read two or more languages. There was one respondent (2.5%) who could speak and read Japanese.

65% of the respondents were in good health with no significant health problems and 22.5% of the respondents were suffering from vision problems, of which occurrence was higher than other types of physical problems. The respondents had also specified other health problems that were not in the response choices, such as diabetes, hypertension, heart diseases and liver problem, which did not have direct effect on Web use by the senior citizens. When asked to rate their own physical health condition, 95% of the respondents thought of themselves as having "good" or "satisfactory" health. None of the respondents thought of their health conditions as "very bad". This suggests that despite some physical disabilities, most elderly were still in good health conditions.

3.3 Computer Literacy

With regard to computer and Web literacy, there were 26 respondents (65%) who had used computer before, but only slightly more than half (53.8%) of these people were still using the computer daily or weekly, suggesting the rest were not proficient in computer. For those who knew how to use computer, 11 of them also knew how to use the Web. However, only 6 of these persons still used the Web daily or weekly, and all of them had at least 3 years of Web experience. This implies that only these six persons could be considered as skilled Web users.

Computer literacy was higher for those aged 50-59 compared to those aged 60-69. However, computer literacy did not appear to decrease with age as the computer literacy level for 70-79 age group (66.67%) was greater than that for 60-69 age group (44.44%). Pearson Chi-Square test also yielded a marginal result of $\chi^2(2) = 6.429$, p = .04. This may be attributed to the insufficient sample size for the 70-79 age group. Nevertheless, there was a strong indication that for the age groups 50-59 and 60-69, as the respondents' age increased, their computer literacy decreased. This phenomenon may not be due to biological age per se but the educational attainment of the two age groups. The 50-59 age group tended to have higher educational attainment than the 60-69 age group.

There is a significant relationship between educational attainment and computer literacy, $\chi^2(3) = 24.320$, p < .01. The computer literacy of those with education level of primary or below was significantly lower than that of secondary and above. It could be concluded that educational attainment, particularly the minimum of secondary education, is a strong determinant of computer literacy among the senior citizens. This finding was consistent with the various studies conducted in other countries [1, 30].

The ability of the respondents to speak and to read English was also found to be significantly associated with their computer literacy. Those who could speak and read English tended to know how to use computer. Again, these associations appeared to be due to educational attainment more than English literacy. Those who were English literate were more highly educated than those who were not. Most of the respondents who could speak (93.1%) or read (92.86%) English had education level of secondary or higher, while most respondents who could not speak (90.91%) or read (83.34%) English had educational attainment of primary or lower.

Although the respondents' computer or Web experiences were found to be significantly associated with their age group and English literacy, the main determinant of computer or Web literacy was in fact educational attainment. In addition, unlike studies conducted in the US [1, 28, 30, 35], gender and force participation did not exert any influence on the senior citizens' computer or Web experience.

3.4   Types of Information and Web-Based Services

To identify the Web-based information needs of senior citizens, four factors were examined based on the questionnaire responses:

3.4.1. Leisure activities. This could help to assess the information that would be of most interest to the senior citizens in Singapore;

3.4.2. Topics of interest. Things senior citizens would like to know more about;

3.4.3. Information sources. Sources commonly used by the senior citizens;

3.4.4. Web-based services. Services commonly used by Web literate respondents.

3.4.1   Leisure Activities

Based on the findings, it appeared that senior citizens engaged in a diversity of activities during their leisure times, encompassing sedentary pursuits to active pastimes. The leisure activities of the senior citizens, in the order of pervasiveness, were reading newspaper / books / magazines (92.5%), watching television (90%), listening to radio (65%), chat with family and friends (65%), exercise (52.5%), participation in social / volunteering / religious activities (45%), travelling (37.5%), play computer games / surf the Web (22.5%), and gardening / keeping pets (22.5%). These findings were similar to previous studies conducted in the US [10, 24, 26, 27], Canada [9], the UK [3], and Singapore [12].

Pearson Chi-Square test of independence indicated that senior citizens' demographic profile and computer or Web experience had no significant effects on their overall preferences of leisure activities. However, as one might have expected, there were significant relationships found between the respondents' computer or Web experience and the activity of playing computer games / surfing the Web.

The respondents' computer usage frequency determined if playing computer games / surfing the Web was one of their pastimes, $\chi^2(4) = 12.405$, p = .015. The respondents who used computer daily or weekly selected playing computer games / surfing the Web as one of their pastimes, but those who used computer less frequently did not.

Further association was found between this activity and the respondents' Web literacy, $\chi^2(1) = 12.236$, $p < .01$. Among those who had used computers before, it was more likely for those who were Web literate to play computer games or surf the Web during their leisure time; vice versa, for those who did not know how to use the Web, they were less likely to spend their leisure time on playing computer games or surfing the Web.

3.4.2 Topics of Interest

When asked about the information that they would like to know more about, the responses were diverse. The topics of interest of the senior citizens, in the order of popularity, were news (62.5%), health & fitness (60%), travelling (35%), philosophy / religion (32.5%), arts / music / opera (25%), language (17.5%), computer / Internet (17.5%), history / biography (15%), volunteering / community services (15%), and cooking (15%). None of the respondents were interested in getting more information about housing / nursing homes, which was in concord with earlier studies in Singapore [15]. The findings in Singapore were inconsistent with that in UK [2, 19] and Australia [29] where information on social security benefits and accommodation / nursing homes were the most sought for information by the senior citizens. One possible reason for such disparity may be due to the different cultures between Western and Asian countries. In Asia, it is normally expected that children would provide for their elderly and older people tend to have distaste towards staying in nursing homes. Therefore, it would be likely that senior citizens in Singapore tended to hold less concerns in social security benefits and have no interest in the topics of housing and nursing homes.

A few factors were found to affect some of the senior citizens' topics of interest. Pearson Chi-Square test results showed that the respondents' gender, age, education, and computer and Web experiences had significant effects on the topics that they would like to know more about. Other variables did not show significant associations with the senior citizens' topics of interest.

The senior citizens' topics of interest appeared to be dependent on gender. Male respondents were found to be significantly more interested in information on news, history / biography, and philosophy / religion than female respondents. In contrast, female respondents were interested in information on cooking while none of the male respondents would like to know more about the topic on cooking. No significant differences were found between male and female for the other topic of interest.

Interesting results were uncovered on the interaction between age and interest in information on pets, $\chi^2(2) = 6.984$, $p = .03$. Those in the age group of 60-69 tended to be more interested in the topic of pets than other age groups. This association was unexpected as there was no significant relationship found between age groups and rearing pets as leisure activity, indicating that the hobby of keeping pets was independent of age. Logically, people who keep pets would normally be interested to know more information about pets; yet such logic did not seem to surface in the findings. The findings did not offer any probable explanation for such phenomenon except the possibility of insufficient sample size. Age group was not a determinant for other topics of interest.

The senior citizens' educational attainment was another factor that significantly affected their interest in literary topics. The lower the education level, the less likely the respondents were interested in the topics of history / bibliography and languages. In fact, none of the respondents with primary education or below were interested in these topics at all.

Computer literacy also appeared to be significantly associated with the senior citizens' interest in information on languages, $\chi^2(1) = 4.569$, p = .033. As discussed previously, computer literacy was strongly dependent on the senior citizens' educational attainment. Thus, the association of computer literacy and interest in languages was indirect; educational attainment, rather than computer literacy, was the determinant for the senior citizens' interest in languages.

Finally, not surprisingly, the senior citizens' interest in knowing more about computer / Internet significantly depended on their computer and Web literacy. None of those who were computer and Web illiterate were interested in the topic of computer / Internet. This lack of interest suggested that the computer and Web illiterate senior citizens were not keen in learning more about the computers and Web technology and this may inherently posed a problem in bringing the Web to these senior citizens.

3.4.3 Information Sources

The respondents obtained the information mostly from mass media and informal sources. The most widely-used information sources of the senior citizens were television (90%), newspapers (85%), radio (60%), family and friends (57.5%), books / magazines / journals (45%), and societies / clubs (22.5%). Formal information sources such as the library (15%), the Web (15%) and professionals (10%) were the least used by the senior citizens. This finding was similar to previous studies [3, 7, 15, 29].

The respondents' profile did not show an effect on their use of mass media and acquaintance as information sources. For more formal information sources such as the library, professionals and the Web, elderly of different genders and educational attainment demonstrated differences in their preferences. Male tended to use these formal channels to seek for information more than female. However, none of those with educational attainment of primary or below would use these formal channels to look for information, indicating that the senior citizens' educational attainment was an important factor in determining their selection of formal channels as information sources. This suggests that the gender differences found in the use of formal information sources may be attributed to the male respondents having higher education level compared to female respondents.

With regard to the impact of the respondents' computer and Web experience on their selection of information sources, the result showed that computer literacy was significantly associated with using books / magazines / journals as information sources, $\chi^2(1) = 4.835$, p = .028, whereas Web literacy affected the use of library as information source, $\chi^2(1) = 8.442$, p = .004. However, it was likely that these were indirect associations as educational attainment should be the main determinant, since computer and Web literacy was found to be highly dependent on the senior citizens' education levels.

As for the Web as an avenue for information seeking, computer literacy alone did not dictate its selection by the senior citizens; rather, using the Web as information source was found to be significantly associated with Web literacy, $\chi^2(1) = 10.636$, p = .001. This signifies that the Web could serve as a useful alternative source of information for the Web-literate senior citizens. In spite of that, almost half of the Web literate elderly were still not using the Web to look for information and the reasons for such situation required further investigation.

3.4.4 Web-Based Services

Figure 1 shows the Web-based services most used by the Web-literate respondents. As the number of Web-literate respondents was small (only 11 persons), the frequency (that is, absolute number of respondents) was also shown. Overall, the respondents' main uses of the Web were to seek for information and to surf the net (for no particular purpose). They also made use of the email facility, and two persons joined newsgroup discussion as well. None of the Web-literate respondents used the Web for online shopping, chatting or other purposes (such as online banking or e-learning). This was different from the previous findings in overseas where email was identified as the favourite of the senior citizens, whereas online shopping and banking were popular among the senior citizens too [27, 28].

The small sample size of Web-literate senior citizens did not permit an in-depth analysis of the dependencies between the various variables and the Web-based services most used by the senior citizens. Nevertheless, the results seemed to suggest that there was no association between the respondents' Web competency and the Web-based services used. The senior citizens' Web usage frequency or years of Web experience did not affect the choices of the Web-based services used.

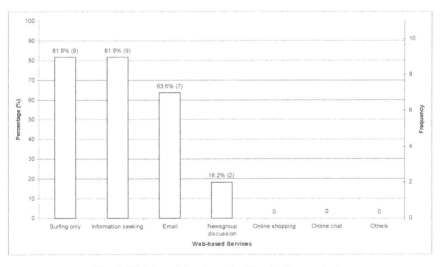

Fig. 1. Web-based Services Used by the Respondents.

3.5 Perceptions of Using the Web

To understand senior citizens' Web-based information needs and their willingness to learn and to use the Web, it is necessary to find out their perceptions of the Web. For the senior citizens who held negative feelings towards the Web, it would be helpful to identify the barriers that might have led to their negative perceptions and look into ways that could help to alleviate their negativity. On the other hand, for those who regarded the Web positively, it would also be beneficial to understand the reasons for their willingness to learn and use the Web, and these positive sides of using the Web at old age could be reinforced to encourage more senior citizens to use the Web.

The responses to the questions on the senior citizens' perceptions of the Web were generally positive, with 75% of the respondents agreeing that older people should be encouraged to use the Web. 15% of the respondents did not agree and 10% did not respond to this question. The respondents' demographic profile and experience of computer and the Web were found to have no influence on their views of encouraging more senior citizens to learn the computer and the Web.

Tables 1 and 2 summarized the respondents' opinions on the statements of the perceptions of the Web. The positive views with regard to using the Web were statements c, d, h, i, and j, while the negative perceptions were statements a, b, e, f, and g.

Table 1. Responses on the Statements of Positive Perceptions of the Web, N=40.

Statement	Strongly Agree	Agree	Don't Know	Disagree	Strongly Disagree	Missing data
c) The Web enables me to keep in touch with my family and friends.	7 (17.5 %)	16 (40.0 %)	6 (15.0 %)	6 (15.0 %)	0	5 (12.5 %)
d) The Web provides a lot of useful information that I need.	9 (22.5 %)	12 (30.0 %)	13 (32.5 %)	4 (10.0 %)	0	2 (5.0 %)
h) Using the Web makes me feel that I am still an active member of the society.	8 (20.0 %)	14 (35.0 %)	6 (15.0 %)	7 (17.5 %)	1 (2.5 %)	4 (10.0 %)
i) Using the Web keeps me mentally active.	9 (22.5 %)	10 (25.0 %)	10 (25.0 %)	3 (7.5 %)	1 (2.5 %)	7 (17.5 %)
j) The Web helps me to bridge the gap with the younger generation.	6 (15.0 %)	13 (32.5 %)	10 (25.0 %)	3 (7.5 %)	1 (2.5 %)	7 (17.5 %)

Table 2. Responses on the Statements of Negative Perceptions of the Web, N=40.

Statement	Strongly Agree	Agree	Don't Know	Disagree	Strongly Disagree	Missing data
a) I have no idea what the Web is and what it can do for me.	6 (15.0 %)	7 (17.5 %)	11 (27.5 %)	10 (25.0 %)	2 (5.0 %)	4 (10.0 %)
b) The Web is for the younger generation and not for elderly people like me.	3 (7.5 %)	11 (27.5 %)	3 (7.5 %)	13 (32.5 %)	6 (15.0 %)	4 (10.0 %)
e) I am afraid of using the Web.	4 (10.0 %)	3 (7.5 %)	13 (32.5 %)	13 (32.5 %)	5 (12.5 %)	2 (5.0 %)
f) I find the Web difficult to use.	7 (17.5 %)	6 (15.0 %)	10 (25.0 %)	11 (27.5 %)	4 (10.0 %)	2 (5.0 %)
g) There aren't many things on the Web that interest me.	2 (5.0 %)	3 (7.5 %)	19 (47.5 %)	10 (25.0 %)	4 (10.0 %)	2 (5.0 %)

Overall, the senior citizens' perceptions of the Web were positive as most respondents agreed to the positive views and disagreed to the negative views. The generally believed that the Web could serve as a good communication tool and information source, and they expected using the Web would promote active ageing and bridge the generation gap. Comparable to the Australia elderly, most senior citizens in Singapore were uninformed consumers of new technology rather than holding negative perceptions towards it [29]. They did not have techno-phobia as commonly believed although perceived difficulties in using high-tech gadget could thwart their enthusiasm.

3.6 Willingness to Learn and Use the Web

The respondents who were computer and Web illiterate were asked to indicate their willingness in learning how to use computers and the Web. Figure 2 shows the possible reasons.

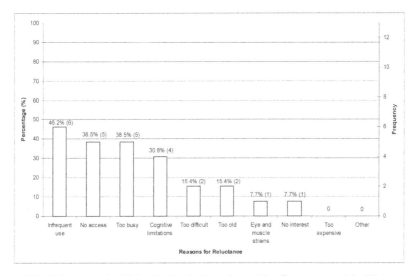

Fig. 2. Reasons for Disinclination in Learning to Use Computer and the Web.

For the respondents who were unwilling to learn how to use computers and the Web, multiple reasons contributed to their disinclination. The major reason was found to be the absence of perceived needs due to infrequent use. Other reasons included no access to computers or the Internet, too busy to learn, lack of memory, concentration and energy needed for learning. Some of the respondents also thought that learning to use computers and the Web would be too difficult and they were already too old to absorb new knowledge. Strains on the eyes and muscles, and lack of interest were also reasons for having no desire to learn. These barriers to Web adoption were similar to that identified in previous studies [10, 14, 25, 27, 29, 30]. However, cost was also found in the previous studies as one of the main factors impeding the senior citizens from embracing computers and the Web, but none of the respondent in this study had identified it as the reason for not willing to learn and to use computers and the Web.

The respondents' physical health conditions were found to have no significant effect on their willingness to learn computer and the Web. Respondents with health problems or lower physical health ratings were not one of the factors for their reluctance in learning.

Perceptions of the Web could be used to identify the reasons for willingness in learning to use the Web. Two perceptions were identified to significantly contribute to the respondents' willingness to learn. Those who thought of the Web as being a useful information source and had the benefit of keeping them mentally active were more willing to learn to use the Web. In addition, those who were reluctant to learn also did not think that older people should be encouraged to use the Web; yet, there were 31.58% of those who were willing to learn did not think that more senior citizens should be encouraged to use the Web. The reasons behind these contradicting views were unclear and further study is needed to uncover the reasons.

With the vast number of baby boomers entering old age in less than a decade, and the majority of these baby boomers are computer and Web literate, perhaps low web acceptance by the elderly population could be a self-regulating problem, as it might diminish as more and more "young elderly" with higher educational attainment and a more technology-oriented socialization are progressively aging.

What is important is for the government to look into ways to encourage active aging, and invest resources to look into the synthesis between information technology and old age.

4 Discussion and Implications for Interface Design

"Design" of any system is seen as both a science and an art [31]. It is a *science* in that it realises an emphasis towards a principled, systematic approach to the creation and production of an artefact (or Web-based information systems for senior citizens, in this case). It is an *art* in the creative conceptualisation, expression and communication of the design ideas with a touch of aestheticism for the intended community of audience or users [31].

Carroll [5] stresses the importance of maintaining a continuous focus on situations of and consequences for human work and activity to promote learning about the structure and dynamics of problem domains, thus seeing usage situations from different perspectives, and managing tradeoffs to reach usable and effective design outcomes. Since designing systems is challenging and demands a more rigorous engineering approach, there is a growing emphasis in the emergent field of "usability engineering" on testing and re-testing with real users [8]. Hence, the study reported in this paper is an initial phase within an on-going project on the design and development of a Web-based information system for senior citizens in Singapore, beginning with a study on understanding the information needs of senior citizens.

We will attempt to discuss in this section implications of findings on interface design in terms of "usefulness" (see Section 4.1) and "usability" (see Section 4.2) of Web-based information systems for senior citizens, hereafter referred to as "systems" for conciseness. Though contentious, "usefulness" refers to the effectiveness of systems in helping users to carry out their tasks, and "usability" refers to the ease of use of systems in helping users to achieve their goals satisfactorily [8]. In Section 4.3, we will discuss pertinent issues that relate uniquely to senior citizens that may have significant influence on "usefulness" and "usability".

4.1 Usefulness

"Usefulness" of systems largely rests on the user group being targeted, and the tasks they support with an understanding of models of task completion [23]. How information is organized "behind the scenes" is just as important because it determines whether various target users do actually find the site both useful [31].

The findings of the study also showed some similarities as well as inconsistencies between the local and overseas senior citizens in terms of their Web-based information needs. Similar to the senior citizens in Northern America, Europe and Australia, majority of the senior citizens in Singapore spent their leisure time engaging in sedentary pursuits such as watching television, reading newspapers and listening to radio. They also enjoyed chatting with family and friends, doing exercises and participating in social / religious activities. The topics of interest of the senior citizens in Singapore also showed some similarities with previous studies, with news and health care being the most sought for information, followed by information about travelling and philosophy / religion. However, unlike those in Western countries, the senior citizens in Singapore did not have interest in the subject of social security benefits and housing / nursing homes. This seems to imply that the contents of the senior Websites that are currently available to the senior citizens on the Internet may not serve the local senior citizens' needs since they were mostly designed for the senior citizens in the US. In designing a Website for the Singapore senior citizens, it might be advisable to gear the contents towards interests that cater to the information needs of the locals.

The Web-literate senior citizens in Singapore used the Web to seek for information, to surf, to communicate through email, and to participate in newsgroup discussions. Among all, information seeking and surfing were the most identified online activities for the senior citizens using the Web. This calls for the attention on the accuracy of the information on the Web. As the senior citizens may search the Web for their favourite topics such as health matters, it is a concern that they must be able to distinguish truth from lies. Hence, in the effort of promoting Web literacy among the senior citizens in Singapore, the importance of information literacy should not be overlooked. As for other online activities such as online shopping and banking, these e-commerce transactions were not utilized by the senior citizens in Singapore and this differs greatly from the Western countries where e-commerce was popular among the senior citizens. The probable reason for such differences may be because Singapore is smaller compared to the Western countries, and grocery stores / markets and banks / ATM are usually more accessible by the residents. There is thus little need for using these services via the Internet.

4.2 Usability

"Usability" as defined in ISO 9241 (see http://www.iso.org/; retrieved April 30, 2004) refers to the "effectiveness, efficiency, and satisfaction with which specified users achieve specified goals in particular environments". The following terms are further defined in ISO 9241 (see http://www.tau-web.de/hci/space/i7.html; retrieved April 30, 2004): (i) *effectiveness* is "the accuracy and completeness with which specified users can achieve specified goals in particular environments"; (ii) *efficiency* as "the resources expended in relation to the accuracy and completeness of goals achieved";

and (iii) *satisfaction* as "comfort and acceptability of the work system to its users and other people affected by its use".

To guide interface design, much work has been done to make explicit usability standards in design, simplifying them to design heuristics, such as well-referenced Nielsen's design heuristics [22]. Imperative to system design is the need to ensure providence of good navigation support and taxonomy so users would not get "lost". While good navigation supports way-finding, good taxonomy ensures user-friendly, intuitive structure of the site [31]. To address navigation problems, the best strategy is to consistently apply basic Web document design principles on every single page in the systems created such as having [31].

Although there was a significant portion of the senior citizens who had used computer before, most of them was not proficient in using computer and even more did not have experience with the Web. This seems to signify that the Web literacy of the senior citizens in Singapore is low and the digital divide between the younger and older ages is apparent. On the other hand, educational attainment of the senior citizens was found to be a significant determinant of their Web literacy. It is highly likely that as the better educated baby boomers enter their old age, the number of senior surfers would increase in big numbers. Even though these future senior citizens may be more net-savvy than the current senior citizens, the age barriers to Web adoption are still present due to the deteriorated functional abilities accompanied by ageing. Therefore, it is necessary to put more emphasis on making the Web more usable for older people.

In addition, unique to senior citizens are also age-related usability issues. The results of the study suggested that senior citizens in Singapore were generally in good health with no major physical disabilities. For those who had minor health impairments, the most encountered age-related problems were the deterioration in eye functioning. In developing Websites for the senior citizens, the designers should take into consideration these age-related disabilities and the associated difficulties for them when using the Web. Appropriate use of fonts, colour combinations, graphics, and page layout were essential in making the Web interface senior-friendly.

4.3 Other Pertinent Issues

The findings of the study seemed to reveal further that the senior citizens in Singapore generally have positive perceptions towards the Web and agreed that more people of their ages should be encouraged to use the Web. They believed that the Web could serve as a useful communication and information seeking tool, as well as an avenue to remain active in the society and to narrow the gap with the younger generations. However, despite their favourable attitudes, the Web illiterate senior citizens did not show overwhelming inclination in learning to use the Web. The reasons cited for their disinclination were mainly lack of needs due to infrequent use, no access to computers and the Web, too busy, and cognitive limitations. From the senior citizens' agreement to some negative views of the Web, it further suggested that other barriers to their Web adoption were unawareness (did not know what the Web was or could do for them), age concerns (perceiving the Web being a gadget for the younger generations only), and perceived difficulties in learning and using the Web.

If more senior citizens were to be encouraged to embrace the Web, these barriers have to be overcome. They should be introduced to the online world through other avenues such as newspapers, word-of-mouth or social clubs. They should be informed of the availability of Web access at public libraries and the benefits that could be gained through Web use. One good way is to have the senior citizens to teach the senior citizens to use the Web so that they can serve as role models to debunk the myth of the Web being a thing only for the young. Finally, it requires effort from the Web design community to make the Web a more senior-friendly place. By bearing in mind the age-related limitations in Web use and develop Websites that cater to the needs of the senior citizens, it is possible to make using the Web easier and an enjoyable experience for the senior citizens.

5 Conclusion and On-Going Work

This paper attempted to determine the information needs of senior citizens in Singapore, with particular focus on the use of the Web. It investigated senior citizens' experience using computers and the Web, and identified their leisure activities and topics of interests that could be transferred to the Web. The study further explored Web-based services most used by senior citizens and their perceptions of using the Web. It also examined their willingness, as well as their reluctance in learning to use the Web.

Certainly, further studies could be done with wider sampling frame and bigger sampling size to achieve greater reliability and generalisability. Future studies could also look at hands-on experiments to identify usability problems encountered by senior citizens when using the Web. A guideline that is applicable to the Singapore context should be made available to aid the Web designers in developing Websites for the local senior citizens.

Nevertheless, the implications of the study were valuable. Firstly, this is a localised study that looked into the Web-based information needs of the senior citizens in Singapore and highlighted the differences from the overseas studies. Secondly, it provided the policy makers and Web designers/developers in Singapore a better understanding of the Web-based information needs of the local senior citizens for narrowing the digital divide in Singapore. Lastly, it could serve as a reference for future studies in Website design for the senior citizens in Singapore.

Acknowledgements

We would like to thank SAGE and Grace Assembly of God for helping us to get participants, and the participants for taking time in providing us valuable feedback.

References

1. Adler, P. (1996). Older Adults and Computers: Report of a National Survey. Retrieved December 31, 2002, from SeniorNet Website:
   http://www.seniornet.org/php/default.php?Version=1&Font=0&PageID=5476
2. Barrett, J. (2000). The Information Needs of Elderly, Disabled Elderly People, and Their Carers. Retrieved on November 26, 2002, from http://freespace.virgin.net/julie.barrett/
3. Boaz, A., Hayden, C. & Bernard, M. (1999). Attitudes and Aspirations of Older People: A Review of the Literature. A report of research carried out by the Local Government Centre, Warwick Business School, University of Warwick on behalf of the Department of Social Security. Retrieved March 12, 2003 from http://www.dwp.gov.uk/asd/asd5/rrep101.html

4. Browne, Hilary. (2000, April 19). Accessibility and Usability of Information Technology by the Elderly. Retrieved November 28, 2002, from the http://www.otal.umd.edu/UUGuide/hbrowne

5. Carroll, J. (2000). Making use: Scenario-based Design of Human-Computer Interactions. The MIT Press.

6. Cheung, Paul & Vasoo, S. (1992). Ageing population in Singapore: a case study. In Phillips, D. R. (Ed.). Ageing in East and South-East Asia, pp.77-104. London: Edward Arnold.

7. Chua, W., Low, C.W. & Ow, S.H. (2000). An investigation of the educational needs of the senior citizens in Singapore. Applied research project, Nanyang Technological University, Singapore.

8. Dix, A., Finlay, J., Abowd, G. and Beale, R. (1998). *Human-Computer Interaction*. Prentice-Hall.

9. Gauthier, A.H. & Smeeding, T.M. (2000). Time Use at Older Ages: Cross-National Differences. Retrieved June 6, 2003 from http://www.oecd.org/pdf/M00019000/M00019554.pdf

10. Hooyman, N.R. & Kiyak, H.A. (1999). Social gerontology: A multidisciplinary perspective (5th ed.). Boston: Allyn & Bacon.

11. Jones, M. (1990). Time Use of the Elderly. Canadian Social Trends. Summer: 28-30.

12. Kua, E.H. (1994). Ageing and old age: among Chinese in a Singapore urban neighbourhood. Singapore: Singapore University Press.

13. Kua, E.H. (1998). The octogenarians in Singapore. In E.H. Kua & S.M. Ko (Eds.), A ripe old age (pp. 1-9). Singapore: SAGE Publication.

14. Leavengood, L.B. (2001). Older People and Internet Use. Generations, 25(3), Fall 2001, 69-71. Retrieved November 26, 2002, from EBSCOhost, Academic Search Premier database.

15. Lim, M. (2001). A study of the information needs of senior citizens in Singapore. Unpublished master's thesis, Nanyang Technological University, Singapore.

16. Ministry of Community Development and Sports Singapore. (2002a). About Elderly, Public Education Initiatives. Retreived October 11, 2002, from MCDS Website: http://www.mcds.gov.sg/web/indv_publicedu.asp?szMod=indv&szSubMod=publicedu

17. Ministry of Community Development and Sports Singapore. (2002b). About Elderly, The Ageing Population. Retrieved October 11, 2002, from MCDS Website: http://www.mcds.gov.sg/web/indv_abtageing.asp?szMod=indv&szSubMod=ageingmain

18. Ministry Community Development, Ministry of Health, & Department of Statistics, Singapore. (1996). The national survey of senior citizens in Singapore 1995. Singapore: Department of Statistics.

19. Monroy, T. (2000). Web Sites Courts 50-And-Older Crowd. Interactive Week, September 25 2000. Retrieved November 28, 2002, from EBSCOhost, Academic Search Premier database.

20. National Office for the Information Economy (NOIE). (2002). Current State of Play – April 2002, A NOIE information economy statistical report. Retrieved June 6, 2003, from http://www.noie.gov.au/projects/framework/progress/ie_stats/CSOP_April2002/index.htm

21. Neuman, W.L. (2003). Social Research Methods: Qualitative and Quantitative Approaches. (5th ed.). Boston: Allyn and Bacon.

22. Nielsen, J. (2002). Jokob Nielsen's Alertbox, April 28, 2002: Usability for senior citizens. Retrieved October 10, 2002, from the useit.com Website: http://www.useit.com/alertbox/20020428.html

23. Norman, D. (1988). The Psychology of Everyday Things. Basic Books.

24. Ogozalek, V.Z. (1994). A Comparison of the Use of Text and Multimedia Interfaces to Provide Information to the Elderly. Human Factors in Computing Systems, April 24-28, 1994, 65-71. Boston, MA: ACM.

25. Pinder, A. (2002, June 27). Help to bridge the digital divide. Computer Weekly, p.24. Retrieved November 28, 2002, from EBSCOhost, Business Source Premier database.

26. Polyak, I. (2000). The center of attention – Courting today's older consumers requires a multi-dimensional strategy. American Demographics, November 2000, 30-32. Retrieved November 26, 2002, from EBSCOhost, Academic Search Premier database.
27. Roberts, P. (2001). Electronic media and the ties that bind. Generations, 25(2), Summer 2001, 96-98. Retrieved November 26, 2002, from EBSCOhost, Academic Search Premier database.
28. SeniorNet. (2002). SeniorNet Survey on Internet Use, November 2002. Retrieved December 31, 2002, from SeniorNet Website:
http://www.seniornet.org/php/default.php?Version=1&Font=0&PageID=6880
29. Scott, H. (2001). "Old dogs learning new clicks" – older Australians in the information age. Paper for E-Commerce, Electronic Banking and Older People Seminar, 22 May 2001, Victoria University. Retrieved November 28, 2002, from
http://www.cota.org.au/ecommerc.htm
30. Silver, C. (2001, August). Internet use among older Canadians. Connectedness Series. Ottawa, Ontario: Minister of Industry, Statistics Canada. Retrieved June 6, 2003 from
http://collection.nlc-bnc.ca/english/research/56F0004MIE/56F0004MIE01004.pdf
31. Theng, Y.L. (2004). Design Lessons for University Portals. Accepted to 7th International Conference on Work With Computing Systems, WWCS 2004, June 29- July 2, 2004, Kuala Lumpur, Malaysia.
32. United Nations, Division for Social Policy and Development. (2000). United Nations Principles for Older Persons. International Year of Older Persons 1999. Retrieved June 6, 2003, from http://www.un.org/esa/socdev/iyop/iyoppop.htm
33. United Nations Secretariat, Population Division of the Department of Economic and Social Affairs. (2002a). World Population Ageing 2002 Wall Chart. Second World Assembly on Ageing. Retrieved June 6, 2003, from
http://www.un.org/esa/population/publications/ageing/Graph.pdf
34. United Nations Secretariat, Population Division of the Department of Economic and Social Affairs. (2003b). World Population Prospects: The 2002 Revision Highlights. New York: United Nations. Retrieved June 6, 2003, from
http://www.un.org/esa/population/publications/wpp2002/WPP2002-HIGHLIGHS.PDF
35. U.S. Department of Commerce. (2000, October). Falling Through the Net: Toward Digital Inclusion. A Report on Americans' Access to Technology Tools. Washington, DC: U.S. Department of Commerce. Retrieved March 12, 2003, from
http://search.ntia.doc.gov/pdf/fttn00.pdf
36. Vasoo, S., Ngiam, Tee-Liang, & Cheung, Paul. (2000) Singapore's ageing population, social challenges and responses. In Phillips, David R. (Ed.). Ageing in the Asia-Pacific region: issues, policies and future trends, pp. 174-193. New York: Routledge.
37. Yadav, S.S. (2001). Disability and Handicap among Elderly Singaporeans. Singapore Medical Journal, 42(8), 360-367. Retrieved November 18, 2002, from
http://www.sma.org.sg/smj/4208/4208a4.pdf

Strategies for Finding Government Information by Older People

Paul Curzon, Suzette Keith, Judy Wilson, and Gill Whitney

Interaction Design Centre, Design for All Group
Middlesex University, London
{p.curzon,s.keith,j.wilson,g.whitney}@mdx.ac.uk

Abstract. Governments increasingly expect web technology to become their major way of exchanging information with citizens, replacing existing methods. They also give accessibility a high priority. Older people are a major user of government services. We describe a pilot study comparing attitudes of older people to e-government with other ways of obtaining information. We examine what individuals consider important in an information search strategy, and the relative effectiveness of each for achieving an individual's personal aims. We do this in the light of research on the effects of aging on cognitive skills.

1 Introduction

All areas of government are being encouraged to put information on the web. It provides important access to services for older people including information on what help is available, who is eligible, and forms to apply for services and support. It is not inconceivable that the internet will soon be used as the main, if not only, route for giving out and collecting information. Millions of pages of government information are now available online. Despite this they are little used. Pinder [6] argues that this is due to the poor usability and poor accessibility of the information.

We start from the premise that improvements in information and communication technologies have the potential to give extra-added benefit to an increasingly aging western world population. Design philosophy often treats their needs as an add-on at the end of the design process or simply ignores issues pertaining to the elderly; they are not seen as part of the potential audience. By contrast, proactive design philosophy stresses the need for ensuring that the broadest possible end-user population is incorporated from the outset [1]. The European Design for All e-Accessibility Network[4] also stresses the need for a methodology which includes elderly people in all areas of research and design so that developed products are not simply catering for a mainstream audience. It is very important to have an inclusive design process to ensure, if universal functionality is at the core of a system's design, that the needs of all clients are catered for. This demands an early consideration at the beginning of the development process as to whether a central design will fit all potential users possibly with adaptations of the interface for different user groups. Development should therefore take account of research on aging.

Rabbitt [8] gives a good overview of neurological and psychological research on aging. The first point of note is that whilst peak performance at a variety of physical and mental activities occurs at a relatively young age, people can retain extremely high levels of competence at a variety of skills throughout their lifetime. At well-practiced skills, whilst competence does drop with age, older people can still perform at levels much higher than unpracticed young individuals. Furthermore aging only accounts for a small proportion of cognitive variability (20% across cohorts between 56 and 85 years of age). Research suggests further that the best model of the decline in cognitive ability is that the incidence of major cognitive impairment increases with age, rather than that of a model of a whole population increasingly being affected. Cognitive impairment does not affect everyone equally as they age.

The second result of particular note is that aging affects some cognitive skills more severely than other skills. In particular, aging has little effect on problem solving skills that have been practiced over a lifetime, nor on skills dependent on knowledge about the world built up gradually. These are known as "crystallized" mental abilities. Older people are likely to be able to continue to perform such mental tasks at a high level if they have performed them throughout their lives and continue to practice them. On the other hand, "fluid" mental abilities are likely to degrade. In particular, where aging is having an effect, working memory capacity is likely to be reduced, information processing speed is slowed, ability to access previously learned information is reduced, as is the ability to solve novel problems. An exception to this is that crystallized skills that depend on fluid skills are not affected by degradation even where the fluid skills do show degradation as part of other similar activities. Freudenthal's [5] experiments suggest that elderly people have more trouble than their younger counterparts in internalizing and applying recently provided foreknowledge. He consequently promotes the incorporation of current knowledge into system development.

This has relevance to the agenda for achieving both accessibility of information for an aging population whilst also pushing forward an e-government agenda. It suggests that older people who have developed information-seeking strategies over a lifetime will continue to be extremely effective at finding information using them. On the other hand a proportion that increases with age will have problems learning and using new information seeking strategies based on electronic sources of information. This will be especially so if these new methods require fluid skills. Poor performance in fluid skills will not similarly degrade existing performance in previously developed information seeking skills. Older people may thus have difficulties accessing e-government web sites in part due to the effect of aging. However the same people may be extremely effective at finding information in more traditional ways. It is this issue that we explore here in an exploratory pilot to locate the major issues.

2 Methodology

A qualitative research methodology was followed. People using e-government web-sites are neither customers in the sense described in Contextual design [2] nor employees as described in Participatory design [9]. Currently they may have no great interest in accessing information in this way, although it may become an essential communication channel in the future. The requirements for a proactive design methodology were met by starting from a Contextual design process, observing users in an environment that was as close to their natural setting as possible.

A scenario-based approach was chosen [3]. Participants were asked to think-aloud performing a web-based e-government information-seeking task. They were asked to find information and an application form for a housing benefit claim. Thereafter they could look for other information of interest. The observer took written notes of the major actions performed and statements made. No tape recording was done to maintain the relaxed nature of the observations. Follow-up questions explored how people would normally find information, their feelings about using a computer to do this, their criteria for choosing a strategy and their feelings about participating in the study. Participants were aged between 62-82. Table 1 gives summary details.

Where possible the observations were carried out in the person's own home using their computer, or in other cases at the home of someone they knew well (possibly the researcher). Lave [6] highlights the importance of natural settings to investigate cognitive phenomena. The setting affects the cognitive processes involved. Indeed, one of our participants left the computer to find personal resources from another room.

A major issue was the sensitivity of issues surrounding aging on the one hand and the use by novice users of possibly difficult to use technology. Technology can fuel people's feeling of inadequacy. Participants may worry about breaking the computer or feel generally stupid. It was therefore ethically important that a sympathetic approach be taken to such issues and the pilot study aimed to use subjects that were well-known to the researcher undertaking an interview. The levels of trust already in existence possibly meant that even when subjects felt inadequate or disadvantaged they were willing to continue with the exercise and discuss their problems. It also ensured that participants were willing to allow the researcher into their own homes that in turn possibly made the participants more comfortable. However, this possibly extended the halo effect in so far as subjects seemed willing to persevere for longer periods than had been anticipated resulting in a successful outcome which possibly would not have occurred in a more natural setting. However, this does not negate the usefulness of this research. The next stage will include using subjects that do not have a personal relationship with the researchers.

Table 1. Details of participants.

Person	Male/ female	Age	Computer user	Ownership of PC used for test	First Language English
A	M	75	Yes	Family pc	Yes
B	F	73	No	Family pc	Yes
C	M	67	Yes	Researcher's	Yes
D	F	62	No	Researcher's	Yes
E	F	70	No	Researcher's	No
F	F	67	Yes	Own	Yes
G	F	82	No	Researcher's	Yes
H	F	79	No	Researcher's	Yes

3 Use of Existing Strategies

The reliance on existing strategies was shown both directly through activity and also anecdotally. For example, **B**, when asked about how she would search for such information recounted the following

> "I would have given up in 2 minutes and gone to the phone book. We tried it [using the internet] with train times once and it took so long I went to the phone [leaving husband on the computer] and I found it all before he got anything on the computer".

A similar position was adopted even more strongly by **G** who stated

"I would never use this in a million years I would use the 'phone!"

C similarly suggested he would use a different approach.

"I would have gone to the council offices and asked to see someone"

Overall the participants could perceive no immediate advantage in using the web for their searches although they were generally keen to understand more about using the computer. They felt their tried and tested methods for searching for information were often quicker and less frustrating or simply fitted in with their lifestyle and re-quirements for reassurance.

C noted that the internet would be really useful if he was physically incapacitated in some way, but as he was not he would be able to solve the problem by talking to someone: the inference being that this was a more desirable approach.

"If I found it difficult to get about then yes but as its not a problem I wouldn't have thought about it [the web]"

He recounted an anecdote to support this:

"It has arisen before with a planning application. I went in. 'What do I have to do'. I was sent to a room. A woman sat me down and got the actual papers out of a series of filing cabinets"

He also noted that he went to the local town several times a week, and given he was retired his pace of life was such that it would be an easy approach. This physical aspect was clearly important. Whilst being observed searching for family tree information he came across the home page of the local records office:

"The difference is I actually went there. I rang up and arranged to go and sit there and I went to [...] library. I went to the actual records office. I rang that office [looking at details online]. You book a seat. I'd do the same again as I actually got hold of the records. They're probably on here [the website]. I wouldn't know. I go to the cabinets and find the records myself."

A provided more direct evidence of the importance and effectiveness of existing search strategies. Having spent much time typing various versions of search terms into the search box of the web browser and finding no links considered worth following, he turned from the computer and looked to his shelf:

"No its downstairs"

He left the room and returned with a telephone directory and in a few seconds found the relevant whole page advert giving all the details of numbers for different council departments. He quickly scanned down the page and found the entry "Housing Benefit Enquiries". He then turned back to the computer and typed in this term as a search term together with "London Borough of ...". He was using the phone book, not to find the phone number or a web address (it did not contain one but he gave no indication that had been what he was looking for), but to find out what the council called its housing department. It was thus an elegant, fast and relatively successful method of finding out about the government view of how their services were structured and so find the appropriate search term.

This information was found in minutes, including finding the relevant resource in the first place as part of a process taking far longer using the web to find equivalent information (the web address as opposed to a phone number). This fact is indicative of how existing life-learnt skills can be much more effective than apparently better, more modern approaches. In fact the information was found faster than the time taken to switch on the computer. Of course having a phone number or address may then lead to a much slower phase in comparison to the web of finding the actual information in that source. However, in this case had the phone book contained web addresses as well as phone numbers for businesses it is plausible that the whole process could have been much faster and less frustrating – using a paper local information resource to find the place to look on the web for the actual information. As a result of this observation, later participants were given a local paper telephone directory at the end of the interview and asked to show how they would find the same information using it. All found a telephone number within a few minutes, often searching in several places in this time before finding the appropriate place. All retained sophisticated search abilities with resources they normally used.

A also appeared to attempt to transfer search strategies from the physical environment directly to the computer. When typing in search terms, he first typed the council name. Due to a spelling mistake that brought no results so he added, "housing benefits" to the query. This gave no satisfactory results so he swapped the order of the search term to "Housing benefits" followed by the council name. In a paper local directory getting the correct ordering can be of vital importance and switching term orders is an effective thing to do.

4   Measures of Information Seeking Effectiveness

The most obvious measure of effectiveness of a search strategy is speed at obtaining the desired information. Indeed this is clearly the measure used by **B**.

> "I found it all [in parallel on the phone] before he got anything on the computer".

However, by this measure the subjects seemed to rate the web poorly. This could of course perhaps be overcome with practice.

However, speed is not always the most important criteria. **C** was happy to wait several days before next going into town. His personal measure of effectiveness was not speed. This was reinforced by a later anecdote. He would not use directory enquiries to find a phone number but would wait until the next time he went into town when he would go to the library and find the number in a full set of telephone directories himself. Being able to do it directly by manipulating physical objects, and talking to actual people seems to be an important factor. **C**, claimed his main criteria for doing things the way he did was familiarity – he had a lifetime's worth of experience using physical libraries, card catalogue systems etc and valued the option of asking a librarian. He finally noted that using physical approaches you gained a confirmation that whatever you were trying to do had been done, citing the example of a bank where a cashier would actually tell you "That's done", reinforced presumably by the fact that you could actually see them do it. He used ATMs for obtaining cash and phone banking when convenient. However, with phone banking he always went straight to the option of speaking to someone for similar reasons.

All subjects had a vague understanding that you could search on some criteria. Even **G** with no computer experience input a valid term as a search keyword having been presented with Google by the researcher. A total lack of computer experience rendered the use of the computer extremely difficult as they did not know the possibilities provided such as what search engines were available, how to locate them, or the importance of the URL. Beyond these conceptual entities are the problems of navigation. The Windows environment offers its own means of moving backwards and forward through the search and scrolling up and down the page. Generally web pages offer their own navigational and hypertext facilities. An extra layer of navigational complexity is added when long pages require the use of the scroll bar. Without assistance for **G** the navigation would not have been possible. Not only was the experience of traversing a virtual space totally alien but the physical requirement of holding down say a mouse to manipulate the scroll-bar was a huge barrier. **G**'s instinct was to try to move the scroll bar on the screen as this appeared physically possible – a whole hand movement rather than a finger depress as well as a controlled hand movement.

Furthermore physical inhibitions meant that though **G** recognized that an A-Z listing would for instance require her to access "H" for housing she did not try to click the mouse on it despite understanding what she should do. **G** (as with others) was also deeply attracted and diverted by the adverts that successfully drew on her attention.

Overall, if we are to provide information to elderly, novice computer users we would need to deal with the physical components and streamline the whole navigational process. The whole area of touch screen and clear navigational components requires serious research. The search concepts that link with users previous search activities, like a telephone directory's A-Z listing aid the cognitive processes required. However, the physical barriers and the modern culture of multiple activity on screen (e.g. adverts) appears to work against the requirements of elderly people with decaying physical abilities. For them it is potentially very demoralising.

In direct contrast **F,** who frequently accesses the web, located the requested information from an e-government information site in less than 5 minutes.

5   Reasons for Choice of Information Seeking Strategies

C who went to his local town to solve information seeking problems noted:

> "Some of this is I'm used to going to libraries. I've spent my life going to libraries. There must be 50 computers there now. I would not go to the computer first. I would go to the catalogue index and see what they had on the shelves in the stacks, but that's what I am used to. If I couldn't find it I'd go to the librarian 'I cant find this have you got it?' "

This supports the conjecture that people with good information seeking strategies developed over their lifetime would naturally prefer to continue using those.

One of the key strands of the government's approach to accessibility is to make internet accessible computer's available in public places such as libraries. Statements from subjects that touched on this suggested a certain amount of ambivalence. **E,** who had no little practical computing experience and no computer at home, on being told that internet connections were available at libraries grimaced and pointed out that she did not want to make a fool of herself in public and expressed concern about breaking the computer. Even **C** whose main information gathering processes revolved around libraries, whilst noting there were now lots of computers in the library, was not interested in using them as seen in the quote above. Those with computers at home such as

F do not generally require this facility but it is those without computer access or experience that seem immediately worthy of further investigation. How can we make information, which they may be required to access, more accessible to them.

6 Losing Track of Location

Frequently the subjects lost track of which site they were currently looking at. Repeatedly adverts were clicked on and comments made by the participants suggested they believed they were still in the original government sites. This led to wasted time and confusion. For example, **D** started to fill in a form for information about mobile phones until she realized it was not relevant. She had clicked on a phone advert "More information". **G** who has no computer experience found navigation almost impossible. If we are considering public provision of information sites, the problems of turning on the PC and possibly even linking to a search engine could be reduced but the navigation of virtual space and the conceptual underpinnings of the search need to be carefully researched.

7 Conclusions

Subjects had strong strategies for information seeking. Some of their current strategies complimented their web searches, (e.g. the use of the telephone directory). Others were misapplied (e.g. swapping the order of search terms). However there were clear indicators that users had a natural propensity towards using their crystallised problem solving skills. If proactive design is an aim then ways need to be found to support the use of existing search strategies and skills. This may mean supporting use of combinations of traditional information seeking approaches with web based ones, rather than seeing the latter as a replacement for the former. Novel interface design based on traditional search strategies may help. More research is needed in this area.

All the participants showed a keen interest in learning to use computers to search for information, however, even with help, finding information about housing benefits was not trivial. The major obstacle was in finding an appropriate site in the first place. There were also both software and hardware related problems such as not knowing what a search engine was and not knowing how to use a mouse. Such skills are not easily gained even with help and require the use of more fluid and responsive mental capabilities. Suggestions that these problems are only with the current generation seem misguided. Several of the subjects had used computers as part of their jobs (e.g. BBC micros), including one who taught their use. The technologies had moved on, however, so that information searching was still problematic. The current generation of workers may be proficient with Google, but that may be of little use after retirement when completely new information technologies and interfaces have replaced it. Future work should consider the incorporation of well used search strategies into interface design in order to reduce the burden on fluid mental resources that may be heavily overburdened in a spiral of technological advancement.

The participant's strategies for effective information searching were based on various criteria for positive satisfaction. Speed of access was often surpassed by other concepts of value as exemplified by the subject who was willing to wait until a next trip to town. Other aims are important such as getting out, socializing, and actually talking to humans. Such issues are vitally important if social exclusion and isolation is to be avoided. E-government can provide a vital additional source of information to older people. However it appears from this study that it is best seen as complementary to other sources of information rather than as a replacement therefore e-government strategies should work to this end if an aim is truly to serve the interests of this group of society. This study was only a pilot and as such is best seen as raising important issues that now need more detailed investigation.

References

1. Akoumianakis,D. and Stephanidis, C: Universal Design in HCI: A critical review of current research and practice in Proc. of Universal Design: Towards universal access in the info society, CHI workshop (2001).
2. Beyer, H. and Holtzblatt, K: Contextual design, defining customer centered systems. Morgan Kaufmann (1998).
3. Braille, L: Future Telecommunications: Exploring methods, in Proc. of HCI 2003: Designing for Society, the 17th British HCI group Annual Conference (2003).
4. European Design for All e-Accessibility Network Statement of Objectives, Retrieved July 8th 2003 from http://www.e-accessibility.org/design_for_all.htm
5. Freudenthal, D.: The role of age, foreknowledge and complexity in learning to operate a complex device. Behaviour and Information Technology, Vol 20, No 1, 23-35 (2001).
6. Lave, J: Cognition in Practice. Cambridge University Press (1998).
7. Pinder, A. Politics and Usability: The digital divide, Keynote presentation at Designing for Society, HCI 2003, the 17th British HCI group annual conference (2003).
8. Rabbitt, P: When age is in, the wit is out?, Chapter 11 of Mind Myths: exploring popular assumptions about the mind and brain. Wiley (1999) pp 165-186.
9. Schuler, D. and Namioka, A: Participatory design, principles and practices. Lawrence Erlbaum Assoc Inc (1993).

Towards Universal Access Through Automated Assessment of Defined Clinical Populations

Michael C. Fairhurst, Sanaul Hoque, and Mohamed A. Razian

Department of Electronics, University of Kent, Canterbury,
Kent CT2 7NT, UK
{mcf,sh,mar}@kent.ac.uk

Abstract. Specific clinical populations often display behavioural characteristics which can seriously impair the ability to engage in a variety of activities taken for granted in other social groups. If the principle of universal access is to be rigorously pursued it is essential that assessment and understanding of the capabilities of the individuals concerned can be effectively and efficiently achieved. A typical example – and the one considered here – is the condition of dyspraxia in younger children. This paper develops a child-centred paradigm where assessment and individual profiling of dyspraxic children can be carried out within an automated computer-assisted scenario. It is argued that the approach described can both facilitate a characterisation and improved understanding of the condition itself and point to strategies for developing rehabilitation programmes, both of which are crucial in achieving a genuine degree of inclusivity for this group which is a key feature of the principle of universal access.

1 Introduction and Background

Writing and drawing tests play an important part in assessing a range of capabilities [1] which might underpin the development of appropriate interaction strategies for individuals with varying forms of neurological dysfunction. A good example of this is to consider the case of visuo-spatial neglect in patients who have suffered from CVA (cerebral-vascular accident) or stroke [2]. In fact, a novel way of assessing conditions such as this involves the on-line acquisition of writing/drawing data and subsequent analysis, and this has provided some important information to further our understanding of this condition. Another typical example is that of dyspraxia in children, where very similar tests and assessment procedures can likewise illuminate our understanding of the condition. Indeed, this is the specific example which will be the focus of this paper, as described below.

However, the key point at issue here is to note that in implementing the evaluation procedures referred to above we require a specific interaction through a specific interface where, by monitoring the interaction process itself, we are able both to generate diagnostically useful information and also point towards the possibility of eventually establishing subsequent effective therapeutic processes [3]. Thus, the automatic monitoring of information exchange at the user interface both directly provides data which subsequent analysis can exploit for clinical evaluation, and also helps to define procedures which might underpin a more generic paradigm for understanding user access mechanisms in the longer term.

C. Stary and C. Stephanidis (Eds.): UI4All 2004, LNCS 3196, pp. 42–49, 2004.
© Springer-Verlag Berlin Heidelberg 2004

Thus, it is appropriate in the context of "User-centred interaction paradigms for universal access in the information society" to consider some of the important issues underlying this approach to testing and evaluation of particular skills, especially in the context of clinical populations, and to begin to analyse the data which can be extracted to support an appropriate profiling of performance of individuals. The primary aim of this paper is therefore to outline the general principles underlying this type of test and evaluation procedure, and to illustrate the potential value of such approaches in the universal access context by presenting preliminary results from a study of dyspraxic children in a typical established drawing test.

The following sections will outline the procedure proposed, will present some initial experimental results to demonstrate the nature of the investigation which is facilitated by the procedure, and will then draw together the basic ideas which collectively identify the ability of this type of study to contribute to the ongoing development of the principles of universal access.

2   Dyspraxia and the VMI Test

Dyspraxia, or developmental coordination disorder, is a condition in children which is associated particularly with difficulty in planning and carrying out complex movements. The condition is also linked to a variety of other possible symptoms, including problems with comprehension, generally slower response times, and a variety of emotional and behavioural factors [4].

However, it is the specific feature of poor fine motor skills which is of particular interest here and, especially, performance in essentially "pencil-and-paper" tests as a means of evaluating the specific nature and severity of the condition. One of the standard tests commonly adopted is the Beery Test of Visual Motor Integration (the VMI test) [5]. In the VMI test the participant is presented with a series of geometrical shapes (24 in total) in an increasing order of complexity, which he/she is required to copy. Performance is generally not limited in time, though not all children will copy all shapes, and defined criteria for terminating the testing process are set out. Evaluation of the outcome of testing requires the tester to compile a raw score which is then generally converted to standard scores and to age equivalent scores. The higher the scores according to the predefined criteria, the more competent the performance. Specific shape-based scoring criteria are defined and adopted universally by all test evaluators.

The test is traditionally administered by trained Occupational Therapy staff using a standard test booklet. The child's performance is assessed by applying the defined scoring procedure to the output generated, on the basis of which the performance indicators noted above can be established.

Figure 1 shows some examples of the individual shapes which form the VMI test sequence, the numeric tag indicating in each case the position of the respective shape in the 24-element sequence.

3   Data Collection and the User Interface

The key to the performance assessment methods under consideration here is the capture on-line of information about the execution of the drawing on-line, so that subse-

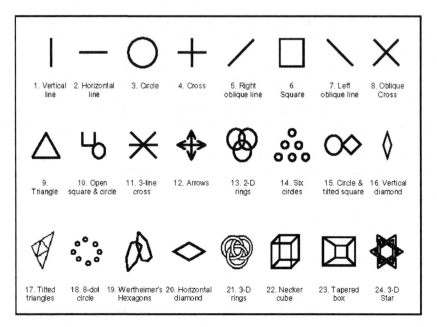

Fig. 1. Shapes from the Beery developmental test of visual-motor integration (VMI).

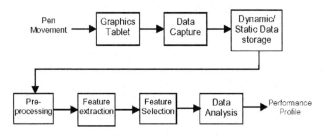

Fig. 2. A schematic of the capture process.

quent (automated) data analysis can extract appropriate diagnostic or profiling characteristics. Specifically, the interface adopted for the collection of data during the figure copying process is a standard computer-linked graphics tablet. In this practical scenario the paper-based test sheets can be placed on top of the tablet surface and positioned in front of the child on a table. The use of a cordless pen of conventional design allows the child to copy the shapes directly on to paper and gain the familiar visual feedback from the drawing process. Thus, the experimental set-up is made to parallel almost exactly the data collection conditions prevailing when entirely manual testing is undertaken. Thus, the interface for on-line data collection remains standard, but allows the capture and analysis of relevant data automatically.

Figure 2 shows a schematic of the capture process, indicating further processing stages involving the extraction and possible selection of performance-related features which might contribute to diagnostic or therapeutic protocols post-capture.

In adopting this testing environment the child is placed at the centre of a test – performance profiling – performance analysis framework which is both transparent to the child within the clinical setting, but also potentially a very powerful means of exploring diagnostic aspects of performance and laying the foundations of appropriate subsequent therapy and rehabilitation [6].

It is clear that a variety of fundamentally different types of performance data can be acquired within this framework. For example, performance features can be readily extracted from the captured drawing which relate directly to the features used in the non-automated form of testing and assessment. Such features are essentially assessable indicators of the quality and form of the finished drawing (generally denoted static features), examples of which might include particular quantitative measurements of geometric properties, completeness of the drawing, relative positioning of drawing components, and similar indicators of the ultimate quality of the finished copied shape as executed by the child.

More importantly, however, this novel on-line data capture approach offers the potential also to extract a much richer set of features which could not readily be extracted through conventional testing, and which relate specifically to the characteristics of the drawing execution pattern [7]. Such dynamic features would typically include measurements which relate to timing information, to pen velocity or acceleration profiles, number of strokes, pen up/down times, and a variety of similar measurements which can provide insights into the fundamental physical mechanisms of drawing execution. These dynamic features are an especially important aspect of our approach. Additionally, we might identify a third fundamental feature type (though strictly speaking a subset of the dynamic feature set already described) which could be characterised as strategy features, encompassing aspects of performance such as specific stroke sequencing, start/end points of drawing element construction, and so on, though such features are not considered separately here.

It is also worth recording that many commercial graphics capture systems also allow the collection of other pen-dependent data relating, for example, to the pressure applied in the writing process and, in many cases, information about the angle and tilt of the pen as it moves across the writing surface.

4 Performance Characterisation and Profiling

Though a detailed clinical assessment is not the focus of this paper, it is instructive to indicate, at least in a preliminary way, some of the indicators of performance which are readily extractable directly from the data-capture process described.

We will consider briefly three comparative populations. The first is a population of children with diagnosed dyspraxia referred to a local Paediatric Assessment Centre. The second population is a group of children (non-screened) with no known disability attending a local Primary School. Both these populations comprise children with a "biological" age of seven years. The third population consists of a group of diagnosed dyspraxic children of varying biological age, but for whom the VMI test (as assessed by a qualified occupational therapist) returns an indicative score corresponding to an age equivalent of seven years.

It is possible by means of even a small number of examples to indicate very simply some immediate aspects of the children's performance which are readily determinable from automated VMI testing, as follows.

Figure 3 shows a plot which illustrates the pen movement time (i.e. total pen-down time) during the execution of two different shapes (Shapes 2 and 3 in the VMI sequence) across each of the three populations. A number of interesting characteristics of performance immediately become apparent. First, in general, the drawing execution by the control subjects is largely characterised by the longer movement times (i.e. the slower execution of the drawings) compared with the dyspraxic children. This simple observation can both provide the sort of information which could contribute to a more complete later diagnostic analysis and performance characterisation, but can also clearly suggest an embryonic framework for a rehabilitation strategy (though, of course, a much more extensive clinical investigation would be essential, and the results presented here are intended only to be illustrative of broader issues).

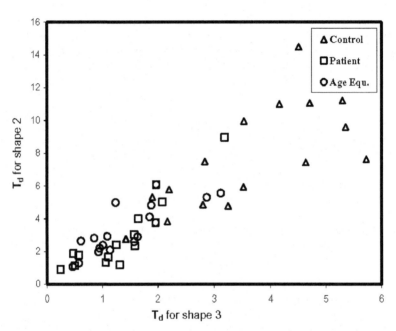

Fig. 3. Pen movement times (of shapes 2 and 3) for different categories of 7 year olds.

Interestingly, however, this Figure also raises a further important issue. The age equivalent population – that is, those for whom the VMI conventional testing predicts an age equivalent comparable to the biological age of the controls tested here – seem to generate a performance profile with respect to the parameters measured here which does not align well with the control population. In other words, there is immediate evidence both that the age equivalent prediction is not applicable to this particular aspect of performance (itself a useful outcome of this type of testing), but also shows more generally that even this simple study can point to the value of adopting a testing framework which can extract the dynamic performance characteristics excluded from analysis based on conventional testing.

This initial observation can be followed up with a second example. Figure 4 shows a plot of two extracted performance features – number of strokes plotted against movement time (pen down time) – in the execution of Shape 6 (Square) in the VMI sequence. Here again there is a significant distinction between controls and patients, though in this case the age equivalent measure is less predictable than in the previous example, and greater dispersion of individual characterising features with respect to the 7-year old patient/control groupings is noted.

No. of Strokes / Pen Movement Time

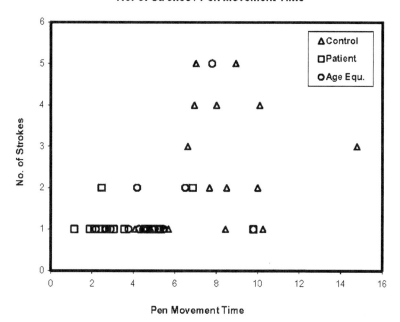

Fig. 4. Pen movement times for shape 6 against number of strokes.

Finally, Figure 5 shows mean pen velocity (measured only in the pen-down segment of the execution cycle) for all subjects tested across all biological age ranges available (5 to 11+ years) with respect to their copying of Shape 1 (Vertical line) and Shape 3 (Circle) in the VMI test sequence. The immediate characteristic of interest here is seen to be the development of a particular behavioural trait with increasing age.

Specifically, this graph confirms the tendency of patients to draw faster than controls of a similar age, and also shows that older patients tend to develop a strategy of slower execution, a tendency much less immediately apparent in the control population. The implications of these simple results are self-evident in relation to an intuitive understanding of the clinical condition and of approaches to therapy, but the effects noted would not be discernible from a conventional application of the VMI test procedure.

These results should be taken as illustrative of a general approach to testing and analysis of subject data (they are not, of course, intended to be interpreted in this form as a formal statistical analysis), and in this respect they usefully point to the potential value in the present context of a structured interaction through an appropriate interface to extract and analyse information to characterise performance in a way which can provide important practical insights into the behaviour of specific clinical populations.

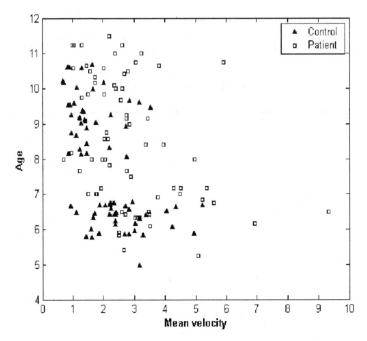

Fig. 5a. Examples of behavioural changes in strategies with age (for shape 1).

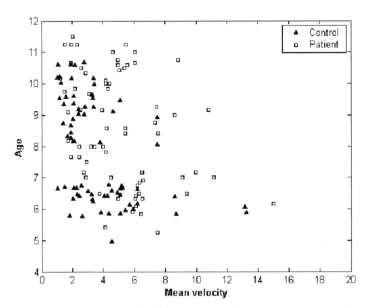

Fig. 5b. Examples of behavioural changes in strategies with age (for shape 3).

Most importantly, however, the nature of the clinical condition under consideration here (as in many other cases) is such that it has a direct impact of the ability of the specific group of affected children to integrate into and interact with their environment. Increasing an understanding of the general nature and particular features of dyspraxia is an essential prerequisite to developing strategies to address the issues of rehabilitation and inclusivity which are the essential foundations of the principle of "universal access". This is a fundamental justification for undertaking this type of study in the context of strategies to enhance the universal access principle.

5 Conclusion

This paper has introduced an approach to the assessment and performance profiling of children affected by the condition of dyspraxia. It is argued that the approach described supports two important contributions to the principle of universal access. First, the technique proposed exploits the potential for structured child-centred interaction with an automated testing system in order to extract and analyse information to characterise aspects of performance relevant to diagnostic and therapeutic understanding of this particular clinical condition. Second, the nature of the condition under investigation is such that it inherently impairs the ability of a sufferer to engage in many meaningful social and behavioural interactions, and this can only be addressed through the development or enhancement of skills and capabilities which are inherently tested and identified in this type of testing framework.

From both points of view, the approach outlined here has an important role to play in supporting the development of strategies to encourage and facilitate those aspects of integration and engagement which reflect the fundamental principles of the universal access paradigm.

Acknowledgement

The authors acknowledge the support of the UK Engineering and Physical Sciences Research Council, and the help of colleagues Mrs Wendy Clarke, Mrs Marian Bond, and Dr Roger Bradford in the child testing and data gathering phases of this work. The cooperation and assistance of the staffs and children of the Blean school, the Vernon Holme school, and the Mary Sheridan Centre, Canterbury, UK are also gratefully acknowledged.

References

1. Sitton, R., Light, P.: Drawing to differentiate: flexibility in young children's human figure drawing. British Journal of Developmental Psychology. 10 (1992) 25–33
2. Fairhurst, M.C., et al.: Extraction of diagnostic information from hand drawn images for the assessment of visuo-spatial neglect. In Proceedings of the 7th International Conference on Image Processing and Applications, vol. 1 (1999). pages 387-391, Manchester, UK.
3. Clar, C. Evaluation of a computer-based method for the analysis of a geometric figure copying test in learning disabled children. MSc Thesis. University of Kent, UK. (1994)
4. Smyth, T. Impaired motor skill (clumsiness) in otherwise normal children. Child: Care, Health and Development, 18 (1992) 283-300
5. Beery, K.E. Developmental test of visual-motor integration VMI: Administration, scoring and teaching manual (4th edition). Modern Curriculum Press. (1997)
6. Potter, J. et al. Computer recording of standard tests of visual neglect in stroke patients. Clinical Rehabilitation, 14 (2000) 441-446
7. Guest, R.M. et al. Diagnosis of visuo-spatial neglect using dynamic sequence features from a cancellation task. Pattern Analysis and Applications, 5 (2002) 261-270

Sc@ut: Platform for Communication in Ubiquitous and Adaptive Environments Applied for Children with Autism

Miguel Gea-Megías, Nuria Medina-Medina, María Luisa Rodríguez-Almendros,
and María José Rodríguez-Fórtiz

GEDES Group. Dpto. Lenguajes y Sistemas Informáticos, ETSI, Informática,
University of Granada, 18071 Granada, Spain
{mgea,nmedina,mlra,mjfortiz}@ugr.es

Abstract. Augmentative and Alternative Communication Systems (AAC) are an emergent technology for improving the social integration of people with temporary or permanent communication difficulties. One problem which arises is the need to adapt these systems to the different users and situations by taking their capabilities, skills and progress into account. In this regard, we propose an adaptive architecture on a ubiquitous computation paradigm, which is being applied for children with autism. This paper proposes a two-tier architecture consisting of a communicator and a context meta-model. It allows child communication to be represented and controlled using a PDA device by means of a wireless network. The main aim of the architecture is to facilitate communication, adapting to changes in user and scenario.

Keywords: autism, PDAs, hypermedia, augmentative and alternative communication, adaptability.

1 Introduction

The focus on people with disabilities and in particular on people with communication difficulties is an area of growing social interest in the spirit of Universal design. In this sense, the new technologies prove extremely useful for the rehabilitation and social integration of such people. Augmentative and Alternative Communication Systems (AACs) [1] are a kind of technical aid for people with physical, psychological or cognitive disabilities which hinder conventional conversation. Various AAC systems have been used among different communities in order to improve communication. Examples of these are sign language (used mainly by deaf people), pictorial languages [2], templates [3], and communicators. Communicators are devices with programmable software, based on an array of cells, to enable the creation of picture templates and programming voices by combining cell touches. Minspeak [4] is an example of a communicator-based language.

Difficulty in communicating with others causes fear and anxiety. This often occurs when the situation/activity is new, frustrating, uncertain, or difficult. In this field, therapeutic researchers have focused on reducing behavioural symptoms, anticipating future events, and creating controllable situations.

Taking this into account, each communicator should be programmed for each person considering their user profile and the environment in which the communication and personal activity are performed. Consequently, communicators should be adaptable [5].

C. Stary and C. Stephanidis (Eds.): UI4All 2004, LNCS 3196, pp. 50–67, 2004.

The engineers must provide mechanisms to allow the communicators to be changed and adapted, and their software to be developed in unanticipated way. In this sense, we can help detect the modifications that are necessary to adapt the communicator, learning from the previous user's interaction with it and from the user's reactions.

The aim of our work, therefore, is to create a communicator which can be adapted to each person by considering their disabilities, user profile and the world around them. We have tested our communicator on a special group of individuals (i.e. children with autism) who require the aid of the ACCs because of the special characteristics which vary from child to child [6]:

- Autistic children have difficulty with social relationships and with verbal and non-verbal communication. A large percentage of them either do not speak or make meaningless sentences. In such cases, in order to know what the children need and to communicate with them, it is essential to use AACs since these enable children to be stimulated so that they may begin and continue a conversation.
- Each autistic child is special and different from the others. As the autism pathology and its manifestations vary from one child to another, each child therefore behaves differently and has different attributes and expectations. This is the main underlying reason for the creation of AACs which can be adapted to each child's abilities and communication needs.
- Autistic children are strongly influenced by their environment and dislike change. The children need to know their environment and the order in which the tasks will be performed. If the child's environment or the order of the tasks changes, the child's behaviour could change in an unpredictable way. The autistic child's behaviour could also change for no apparent reason. The ACC represents a predictable world for the child. However, if changes arise during communication, the child needs the AAC to be adapted to the new behaviour or to environmental changes in real-time.
- Autistic children do not learn by imitating others. Their educators must therefore teach new concepts or how to carry out specific tasks by means of constant repetition and the addition of emotional reinforcement. Teaching and learning must also be adapted to the child's capabilities, abilities and feelings. Although autism symptoms have been studied, there is not enough information about how much an autistic child can learn and adapt. Educators attempt to establish learning objectives, but if these are not reached as the educators hope, then the teaching level must be lowered to adapt to the child's limitations.

The following section explains the user model on which the communicator is based. Section 3 will present the architecture of the communicator. Section 4 will analyse adaptation and evolution processes. Section 5 will put forward a proposal for anticipation on the concept. Finally, conclusions and future lines of research will be described.

2   The User Model

Our approach for an adaptive and unanticipated AAC is called Sc@ut. This is based on adaptive hypermedia, which is an application and extension of our previous work in this area [7].

The most useful tools which are suitable for communicating with people with cognitive disabilities are pictorial templates (see Figure 1). While communicators are based on pictorial templates, they represent different levels of concepts and are static, user-dependent and not adaptable.

Fig. 1. Template of activities for a particular case.

A template can be represented by means of a hypermedia document. Pictures of the template represent concepts and are modelled by means of items in the hypermedia document. The hypermedia links model the relationships between templates and concepts. The hypermedia may include items adapted to each person and these can be easily changed. Taking these ideas into account, we propose the Sc@ut communicator for autistic children with the following features [8, 9]:

- A hypermedia model is used by an individual (the child with autism in our case) to express their desires by navigating through the templates and selecting items. The person creates phrases and is communicating while navigating.
- The user profile and knowledge domain (communication scenario or context) are represented and considered in the hypermedia design.
- Adaptation mechanisms are incorporated so that the communicator can be developed and adapted according to each person and to changes in scenarios.

The user model provides knowledge about the person and his/her interaction abilities and comprises the following components: user profile, knowledge domain, and user interaction. Each of these components is described in the subsections below.

2.1 User Profile

The user profile contains the particular characteristics of each person that will help with the adaptation of the hypermedia model. In the case of a child with autism, this information is collected by the child's educators and relatives. Initially, it is presented informally using natural language. At a later stage, it will be used to model the knowledge domain, and will be structured in behaviour rules on the hypermedia model. The user profile may change over time because of changes in the individual's achievements, motivations and aptitude. There is a history of user profile versions for each person.

By way of example, the information about the user profile of an autistic girl called Ana at a particular time is shown in Figure 2.

(1) Communication habits
- *She is 8 years old and her name is Ana.*
- *She does not talk much and does not read. She has previously used templates to communicate and she is able to create simple phrases with them.*
- *She needs to express her emotions and feelings (love, sad, happy, angry and bored).*

(2) Nutrition scenario
- *She likes fried eggs and watermelon a lot.*
- *She also likes chocolate but she should not eat it.*
- *She drinks a lot of water and has a green cup to drink it with.*
- *Sometimes she drinks milk and juice.*
- *She needs a fork to begin to eat, otherwise she will be furious.*
- *She likes the music of TV advertisements.*

(..... other scenarios)

(3) Objectives of her educators
- *She should learn that her hands must be washed before eating.*
- *Her parents want to gradually introduce new foods into her diet.*

(4) Interaction preferences
- *As she frequently goes to the WC, the item representing this must be accessible in each template.*
- *An item to be returned to the initial template must be added in each template.*
- *An item which allows Ana to indicate if she wants something new that is not in the template must also be added.*
- *If she has not washed her hands before eating, the item relative to this must appear in the nutrition template.*

Fig. 2. Ana's user profile.

It can be seen that the information used is heterogeneous. The success or failure of the communication depends on the selection of characteristics which identify and motivate the person.

2.2 Knowledge Domain

It is necessary to model the world perceived by the person in a way that is friendly and close to them. Consequently, in the case of autistic children, the active participation of educators in the representation of the knowledge domain is essential. The knowledge domain is built to be completely personalized to the user profile. It integrates the different scenarios (and the activities that can be carried out in each) which will later be situated in the communicator. Once the knowledge domain has been built, the system will be able to automatically generate the interaction templates from it. These templates constitute the medium that is used to establish communication with the person and are represented in hypermedia format.

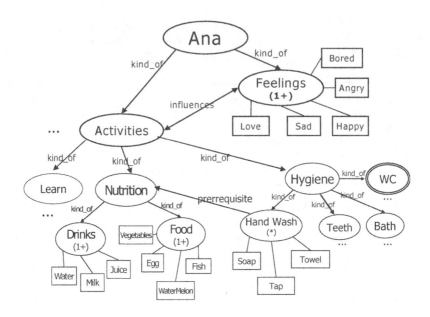

Fig. 3. Knowledge domain for Ana's profile.

The knowledge domain is represented by means of a semantic network. The network clearly and visually represents the different concepts that are part of the person's world and the relationships between them. Figure 3 shows the partial semantic network built for Ana's world. As can be seen, the network reflects an important part of the information about Ana collected in her user profile.

The initial node represents Ana. There are always at least two nodes connected to it: a*ctivities* and f*eelings*. Depending on the user profile, different activities will be added. In Ana's case, there are nodes for *Learn*, *Nutrition*, *Hygiene*, etc. At any moment, by using the system's evolutionary capabilities, nodes and relationships can be added, removed or modified in the network.

We can distinguish two kinds of concepts in the network: basic concepts (c_b) (i.e. *Water*, *Milk* or *Juice*) and complex concepts (c_c). A concept is complex, and represented by a circle, if it has a set of associated basic concepts (as in the case of *Drinks*) or if it can be divided into other complex concepts (as in the case of *Nutrition*). Each concept, whether basic or complex, has associated one or more representations, specially chosen for the person. We name these "item", and they could be audio, video, text, etc. In addition, a complex concept has at least one relationship with other complex concepts. These relationships, called conceptual relationships (r_c), are represented with an arrow and must be semantically labelled. In Figure 3, there is a bi-directional relationship, labelled "influences", between the concepts *Activities* and *Feelings*. This relationship reflects the repercussion that an activity has on the person's feelings, and vice versa. There are two predefined conceptual relationships with a precise meaning: "kind_of" and "prerequisite". The "kind_of" relationship is used to specify the division in parts of a complex concept. In Figure 3, there are two "kind_of" relationships with origin *Nutrition* and destination in *Food* and *Drinks*, which means *Nutrition* is divided into these two complex concepts. The "prerequisite" relationship establishes a necessity relationship between two complex concepts. In Figure 3, a "prerequisite" relationship has been created from *Hand Wash* to *Nutrition*, indicating that it is necessary to wash hands before consuming food. This prerequisite will be inherited by the concepts *Drinks* and *Food* in which *Nutrition* is divided. The *Hand Wash* prerequisite could be that it immediately precedes *Nutrition* or it could be enough for it to happen at any previous moment.

The goal of the basic concepts, shown as rectangles, is to describe, structure or instantiate the complex concept to which they are associated. The association from the basic to the complex concept is carried out by means of a functional relationship (r_f), represented by a line. In Figure 3, for example, the concept *Feelings* has a basic concept for each considered mood: *Angry*, *Happy*, *Sad*, etc. Basic concepts are leaves in the semantic network.

The decision about whether a concept is complex or basic will depend on the detail level which is represented by the knowledge domain and will differ according to the child. It is possible to develop the network by changing a complex concept into a basic concept, and vice versa.

It is also possible to identify concepts in the semantic network that must be accessible to the person at any moment and which are called permanent concepts. This is the case of the *WC* concept, which is surrounded by a double circle in Figure 3. In addition, the type of association between a complex concept and its basic concepts is specified, and there are three types:

- Association (1). The person can only choose one of the basic concepts associated to the complex concept. This would be the case, for example, of a didactic unit where a child is asked to choose the correct option.
- Association (1+). The person can choose one or more of the associated basic concepts. This is the case of the *Food* concept, where the person is allowed to have more than one meal.
- Association (*). The person must choose all the basic concepts and in a specific order. This is the case of the *Hand Wash* activity, in which the child's educator must define a partial or total order among the basic concepts, for example, firstly *Soap*, then *Tap*, and finally *Towel*.

2.3 User Interaction

One important aspect is to determine how the person must interact with the communicator in order to communicate. Because some people, and a large proportion of autistic children, need alternative forms of speech, the way of expressing their intentions may depend on their ability to use different devices. The quantity and extension of the knowledge domains influence the use of more complex mechanisms to represent these.

We use a formal approach to represent the person's interaction. It is based on a direct manipulation style in order to highlight relevant system features and properties [10,11]. This approach allows us to formally describe the system objects (interaction objects), their relationships and the interaction (the user's manipulation process) with them. Our model also enables us to define and check usability properties, which are deduced from the formal representation of the model. We have designed a specification method (MOORE) and a formal language (MORELES) to specify the manipulation process of the user, the child in this case.

Continuing our example, using MORELES, the specification of the scenario *Nutri-tion* (a subset of the semantic network), which includes the templates (complex con-cepts) *Food, Drink* and *Hand Wash,* is divided into several modules. There is one module to specify each object domain (basic concepts and complex concepts in the semantic network) *Hand Wash, Drink, Food, WC, Feelings, Back, Soap, Tap, Towel, Water, Milk, Juice, Vegetables, Egg, Watermelon* and *Fish.* We also define a control object used by the person to interact with the hypermedia: in the example, the object domain *Finger.* There is another module to specify the system: in the example, the scenario *Nutrition.* This division into modules facilitates the specification of the com-plex systems, provides independence during construction and adaptation and enables the reuse of the specification of an object domain in different systems. For each ob-ject, the features, states, graphical representation, topological relationships, manipulative processes and actions are described. The control object is also an object of the system and it therefore has a set of features, states and images, relationships, manipulative processes and actions. Figure 4 shows the description of the object domain *Soap.*

domain *Soap;*
import *Finger;*
features   *position (x,y), mode (normal, selected, ended), sound (active, desactive);*
states   *state_normal = (position (x,y), mode (normal), sound (desactive)),*
               state_selected = (position (x,y), mode (selected), sound (active)),
               state_ended = (position (x,y), mode(ended), sound(desactive));
graphical_representation   *state_normal → image_normal(soap1.jpg),*
                    state_selected →image_selected(soap2.jpg, musicS.wav),
                    state_ended → image_ended(soap3.jpg);
actions   *select: state_normal → state_selected;*
gesture_relationships $\mathfrak{R}_{select}(soap);$
topological_relationships *(fingers on soap);*
manipulative_processes
          $\mathfrak{R}_{select}(soap):= \exists! \ s \in domain(Soap), \ \exists! \ f \in domain(Fingers):(f \ on \ s);$

Fig. 4. Specification of the interaction of the object domain *Soap.*

The object domain *Soap* has three features which describe its relevant characteris-tics: position, mode, and sound. Position gives the situation of the object inside the PDA device, represented by its coordinates; mode can have the values "normal", "selected" or "ended"; and sound can be "active" or "deactive". The values of these features determine the states of the soap object at a given time: "normal" (normal state of the object), "selected" (the soap has been selected by the person and some music is played) and "ended" (the person has finished by using the soap). Each state of the soap object is associated with a single image, a graphical representation of the object in each state. The person selects the soap object when they wash their hands. Therefore, the soap object has the action and gesture relationships "select". The posi-tion of the soap object before and after the action is carried out remains the same; only the mode and sound of the object change.

When a gesture is produced in the system, an action is carried out. Therefore, the specification of a manipulation process means describing the objects, the relationships and their logic and temporal dependencies that intervene in the carrying out of an action. In this example, we have defined the manipulative process "select", carrying out the select action on the soap, which implies the control object (*finger*) is over the soap image (topological relationship *on*).

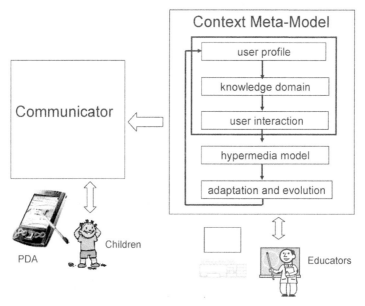

Fig. 5. The Sc@ut architecture.

3   Architecture

Sc@ut is not only a communicator. As Figure 5 shows, the S@ut architecture has two tiers: the *communicator* and the *context meta-model*. This division allows us to analyse the communication and the adaptation processes separately. In addition, it facilitates the development of a distributed architecture for the design of ubiquitous computation spaces. The architecture comprises the following components:

- user model (user profile, knowledge domain and user interaction)
- hypermedia model
- adaptation and evolution process

The benefit of this architecture is that the concerns are separated. Firstly, there are two kinds of users who use it with different purposes and activities. The communicator is used by people with disabilities, and in our experiment children with autism, and the meta-model is used by the therapist, the autistic child's educators in our experiment. Secondly, the cognitive, interactive design and adaptation aspects must be differentiated in order to avoid coupling. Consequently, evolution/adaptability can therefore be carried out more easily and safely as the architecture components are independent [9,12].

This architecture is implemented by connecting different devices. The context meta-model runs on a PC, and a PDA device has been selected for the communicator due to its portability, versatility and ease of use (by means of a tactile screen). Communication between both devices is performed using wireless technology. This implementation is flexible and extensible, because new devices can be added to the user interface to help the child's interaction (screens, switches, sound and voice devices, etc.) independently of the representation model. In addition, devices adapted for other disabilities with a smaller capability of movement (for example, brain paralysis) can be used.

3.1 Hypermedia Model

The hypermedia model is created by taking the user model into account. The knowledge domain and the specification of the interaction are translated to the hypermedia. The hypermedia comprises templates and links. The templates include the items (images, text or sounds) associated with each of the concepts which appear in the knowledge domain. The hypermedia navigation order, given by the links associated to certain items, depends on the kinds of associations established in the knowledge model. There are navigation order constraints to restrict the navigation depending on the previous user's interaction. New items can be added to allow the person to go to the previous template, to a main template, or to represent *"What I want is not here"*.

In the communicator, touching an icon is considered equivalent to writing a word as part of a sentence [13]. Other ACC projects, for example [14], have tested whether a sentence is syntactically valid by considering the order in which the words have been selected, but we can also test the semantic validity of the sentences due to the semantic relationships established in the semantic network and propagated to the hypermedia.

The interaction with the hypermedia system is specified using the same formal language as that used for the objects. The module which specifies the system imports the object domains, including information about the container object (templates) and actions of the system. Topological and property relationships and manipulative processes are also specified. The specification for our example is shown in Figure 6.

The specification of the system "Nutrition" (scenario "Nutrition") defines the object domains of the system (*hand_wash, food, drink, wc, feelings, back, soap, tap, towel, egg, vegetables, watermelon ,fish, water, milk, juice, fingers*) which represent the concepts (basic and complex) that appear in the knowledge domain. The templates describe the complex concept in the knowledge domain. Each template defines the objects with their initial state and position. In this example, all the templates contain the objects *wc, feelings* and *back*, because the concept *wc* is a permanent concept and *feelings* is a conceptual relation (*influences*) in the knowledge domain. The *back* object links to the initial template.

The specification describes all the actions (*s_ hand_wash,do_ hand_wash, s_food,s_drink, have_watermelon, have_egg, have_fish, have_vegetables, have_water, have_juice, have_milk, s_wc, s_feelings, s_back*) that the person can carry out in the system. Each action changes the object states that it affects, implying a change in the state of the system. Moreover, the specification defines the gestures of the system ($\mathfrak{R}_{s\_hand\_wash}$ (*hand wash*), $\mathfrak{R}_{do\_hand\_wash}$ (*soap, tap, towel*), $\mathfrak{R}_{s\_food}$ (*food*), $\mathfrak{R}_{s\_drink}$ (*drink*), $\mathfrak{R}_{have\_watermelon}$ (*watemelon*), $\mathfrak{R}_{have\_egg}$ (*egg*), $\mathfrak{R}_{have\_fish}$ (*fish*), $\mathfrak{R}_{have\_vegetables}$ (*vegetables*), $\mathfrak{R}_{have\_water}$ (*water*), $\mathfrak{R}_{have\_juice}$ (*juice*), $\mathfrak{R}_{have\_milk}$ (*milk*), $\mathfrak{R}_{s\_wc}$ (*wc*), $\mathfrak{R}_{s\_feelings}$ (*feelings*), $\mathfrak{R}_{s\_back}$ (*back*)), because each of the defined actions in the system must have at least one associated gesture which allows the person to carry out the action.

//Specification of the scenario Nutrition"

system *Nutrition;*

import_domain *hand_wash, food, drink, wc, feelings, back, soap, tap, towel, egg, vegetables, watermelon ,fish, water, milk, juice, fingers;*

templates

- *template_nutrition { hand_wash (hw(state_normal(x:10, y:10))),*
  food(f(state_normal(x:10, y:50))), drink(d(state_normal(x:80, 50))),
  wc(w(state_normal(x:10, y:80))), feelings(fe(state_normal(x:50, y:80))),
  back(bc(state_normal(x:100, y:80))))};

- *template_ hand_wash { soap(s(state_normal(x:10, y:10))),*
  tap(t(state_normal(x:10,y:50))}, towel(tw(state_normal(x:50,y:10))),
  wc(w(state_normal(x:10, y:80))), feelings(fe(state_normal(x:50, y:80))),
  back(bc(state_normal(x:100, y:80))))};

- *template_activities {food (f(state_normal(x:10, y:10))),*
  drink(d(state_normal(x:10,y:50))), wc(w(state_normal(x:10, y:80))),
  feelings(fe(state_normal(x:50, y:80))), back(bc(state_normal(x:100, y:80))))};

- *template_food {watermelon (wm(state_normal(x:10, y:10))),*
  egg(e(state_normal(x:10, 50))),
  fish(fh(state_normal(x:50,y:10))),vegetables(v(state_normal(x:50, y:50))),
  wc(w(state_normal(x:10, y:80))), feelings(fe(state_normal(x:50, y:80))),
  back(bc(state_normal(x:100, y:80))))};

- *template_ drink {water(d(state_normal(x:10, y:10))),*
  juice(j(state_normal(x:10, y:50))), milk(m(state_normal(x:50, y:50))),
  wc(w(state_normal(x:10, y:80))), feelings(fe(state_normal(x:50, y:80))),
  back(bc(state_normal(x:100, y:80))))};

actions_system

- *s_ hand_wash:(hand_wash(state_normal) → hand_wash(state_selected)),*
- *do_ hand_wash:(soap(state_normal), tap(state_normal), towel(state_normal)*
  → soap(state_ended), tap(state_ended), towel(state_ended)),
- *s_food:(food(state_normal) → food(state_selected)),*
- *s_drink:(drink(state_normal) → drink(state_selected)),*
- *have_watermelon:(watermelon(state_normal) → watermelon(state_selected)),*
- *have_egg:(egg(state_normal) → egg(state_selected)),*
- *have_fish:(fish(state_normal) → fish(state_selected)),*
- *have_vegetables:(vegetables(state_normal) → vegetables(state_selected)),*
- *have_water:(water(state_normal) → water(state_selected)),*
- *have_juice:(juice(state_normal) → juice(state_selected)),*
- *have_milk:(milk(state_normal) → milk(state_selected)),*
- *s_wc:(wc(state_normal) → wc(state_selected)),*
- *s_feelings:(feelings(state_normal) → feelings(state_selected)),*
- *s_back:(back(state_normal) → back(state_selected));*

gesture_relationships_system

$\mathcal{R}_{s\_hand\_wash}(hand\ wash)$, $\mathcal{R}_{do\_hand\_wash}(soap, tap, towel)$, $\mathcal{R}_{s\_food}(food)$, $\mathcal{R}_{s\_drink}(drink)$,
$\mathcal{R}_{have\_watermelon}(watemelon)$,, $\mathcal{R}_{have\_egg}(egg)$, $\mathcal{R}_{have\_fish}(fish)$, $\mathcal{R}_{have\_vegetables}(vegetables)$,
$\mathcal{R}_{have\_water}(water)$, $\mathcal{R}_{have\_juice}(juice)$, $\mathcal{R}_{have\_milk}(milk)$, $\mathcal{R}_{s\_wc}(wc)$, $\mathcal{R}_{s\_feelings}(feelings)$,
$\mathcal{R}_{s\_back}(back)$;

Fig. 6. Specification of the system, scenario "Nutrition" of Ana.

manipulative_processes

- //Manipulative process: select wash hand

$\mathcal{R}_{s\_hand\_wash}(hand\ wash) := \exists!\ hw \in domain(hand\ wash):\ \mathcal{R}_{select}(hw) \wedge$
link(template_hand_wash),

- //Manipulative process: select food

$\mathcal{R}_{s\_food}(food) := \exists!\ f \in domain(food):\ (\mathcal{R}_{do\_hand\_wash}(hand\ wash)\ S\mathbf{7}\ \mathcal{R}_{select}(f)) \wedge$
link(template_food),

- //Manipulative process: select drink

$\mathcal{R}_{s\_drink}(drink) := \exists!\ d \in domain(drink):\ (\mathcal{R}_{do\_hand\_wash}(hand\ wash)\ S\mathbf{7}\ \mathcal{R}_{select}(d)) \wedge$
link(template_drink),

- //Manipulative process: wash hand

$\mathcal{R}_{do\_hand\_wash}(soap,\ tap,\ towel) := \exists!\ s \in domain(soap),\ \exists!\ t \in domain(tap),\ \exists!\ tw \in$
$domain(towel):\ ((\mathcal{R}_{select}(s)\ \theta\mathbf{7}\ \mathcal{R}_{select}(t))\ \theta\mathbf{7}\ \mathcal{R}_{select}(tw)) \wedge link(template\_activities),$
. . . .

- //Manipulative process: select back

$\mathcal{R}_{s\_back}(back) := \exists!\ bc \in domain(back):\ \mathcal{R}_{select}(bc) \wedge link(template\_nutrition);$

Fig. 6. (continued)

In this example, the manipulative process "s_hand_wash" implies that the person selects the object *hand_wash* (gesture relationships $\mathcal{R}_{select}(hw)$ of the *hand_wash* object) and the system links to the hand wash template (*link(template_hand_wash)*), which describes how the person must wash their hands.

The manipulative process "do_hand_wash", describes the pre-established navigation order for the *do-hand*_wash action. Firstly, the person selects the *soap* object (gesture relationships $\mathcal{R}_{select}(s)$ of the *soap* object). They then select the *tap* object (gesture relationships $\mathcal{R}_{select}(t)$ of the *tap* object). Finally, they select the *towel* object (gesture relationships $\mathcal{R}_{select}(tw)$ of the *towel* object). This navigation order $((\mathcal{R}_{select}(s)\ \theta\mathbf{7}\ \mathcal{R}_{select}(t))\ \theta\mathbf{7}\ \mathcal{R}_{select}(tw))$ is specified with the operator $\theta\mathbf{7}$, which means "only previous". The system then links the activity templates (*link (template_activities)*).

The manipulative process "s_food" (select a food) means that before the *food* object is selected, the person has washed their hands $((\mathcal{R}_{do\_hand\_wash}(hand\ wash)\ S\mathbf{7}\ \mathcal{R}_{select}(f)))$. Operator $S\mathbf{7}$ means "only since and not now". This prerequisite is defined in the knowledge domain. Afterwards, the system then shows the food template (*link(template_food)*).

Figure 7 shows a possible interaction of Ana with the communicator that could be obtained from the formal specification of the interaction. It shows the involved hypermedia templates.

In the building process of the hypermedia, an interaction template is generated for each complex concept according to the following guidelines:

- If basic concepts are associated with the concept, its template shows the corresponding item for each of these. In 7.5 we can see the created template for *Food*. When the association is of the type "(*)", as in *Hand Wash* (Template 7.3), the items are shown in the pre-established order.
- If the concept is divided into other complex concepts, as in the case of *Activities*, its template in 7.1 shows the item corresponding to each of these concepts.

If it is contemplated in the person's profile:

- The template of a concept that has not satisfied the prerequisites shows the items of the concepts needed. We can see that when choosing *Nutrition* in Template 7.1, the new Template 7.2 shows in its upper part the item associated to *Hand Wash.*
- A concept's template can show the item associated to every related concept by a conceptual relationship different to "kind_of" and "prerequisite". Consequently, the concept *Feelings* is included in the lower part of every activity template (Figure 7).

In addition, in every template there is:

- An item for every permanent concept. We can see how in Figure 7 the concept *WC* appears in each template.
- A *Back* item to return to the initial template.
- A *"What I want is not here"* item, which is selected by the person when the desired option cannot be found.

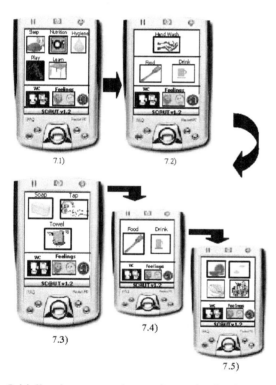

Fig. 7. Hypermedia templates.

Initially, the communicator shows Ana's photo or a symbol that is nice for her in order to make the communicator a familiar object. The first template corresponds to the initial node and shows the items associated to the first level concepts: *Activities* and *Feelings*. When the person touches a complex concept's item, the generated template for the selected concept is obtained. In the example, the first template (7.1) is obtained when selecting *Activities*. The *Back* item links to the previous template or to the initial template depending on what has been specified in the person's profile. If a concept's prerequisites are not satisfied, its selection has no effect. For example, when pushing *Food* in Template 7.2 nothing happens.

In a basic concept template, navigation will vary according to the kind of association: if it is "(1)" only one item in the template can be selected, if it is "(1+)" one or more items can be selected in any order, and if it is "(*)" all the items must be selected in a pre-established order (this kind of navigation is called scanning).

In addition to this use, the therapists are interested in using the communicator to define agendas for the person. An agenda consists of a list of activities and an order in which these are to be performed. In this case, the initial template shows an item for each programmed activity, of course in the indicated order (for example Template 8.1 in Figure 8). Every time the person finishes a task, the communicator goes back to the initial template, where the performed task will be crossed out (Template 8.4). In this way, the person knows what he/she has done and what is left to do, which is very important for children with autism or people who have lost part of their memory. In the example, the child solves the second task in the agenda (*Learn*), by performing a didactic unit about shapes (Template 8.3).

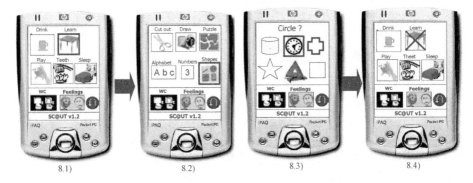

Fig. 8. A possible agenda for Ana.

The following table shows the correspondence between the different models used to represent the knowledge and helps to understand the construction of the communicator.

Table 1. Correspondence between models.

Autism	Semantic net	Interaction	Hypermedia
Scenario	Subset of the semantic network	System	One or more related templates or pages
Template	Complex concept	Container-object	Document or page
Concept	Concept (complex or basic)	Interaction-object	Concept
Relationship	Relationship (functional or conceptual)	Relationship and action	Link
Pictogram	Item	Object representation	Item

4 Adaptation and Evolution

The context meta-model tool is in charge of monitoring and learning from user inter-action, anticipating system changes in order to adapt the hypermedia model used by the user. During interaction, it collects measurable information about the person's navigation through the hypermedia. All of this information will be used to improve the communicator, evolving the user profile and the knowledge domain with the pro-posal of new tasks and educative strategies. These modifications are propagated to the hypermedia model, guaranteeing its consistency and integrity. Figure 9 shows the adaptation and evolution processes.

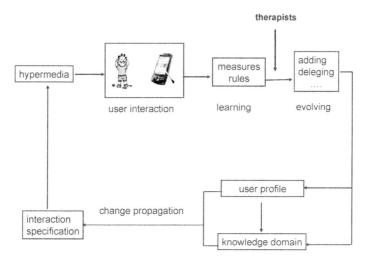

Fig. 9. Adaptation and evolution process.

	Learn	Drinks	Food	
Learn		10	12	
Drinks	7		21	
Food	5	(47)		
Bath	(0)	14	34	
.....				

Fig. 10. Transition matrix.

In order to perform the adaptation process, it is necessary to represent and update the user model with meaningful information about the person and their learning. Both the user profile and knowledge domain (examined in previous sections) are part of the user model. The elements used for adaptation are described as follows:

- *Feelings history:* This stores the succession of moods selected by the person over time. This history is divided into days, and for each annotated mood, the system stores the time at which it was selected and the task the person was performing. This information can be analysed by educators and therapists in order to find out which tasks the person does not like, the times of the day they prefer, etc.
- *Activities history:* This stores the succession of performed and finished tasks by the person through time. If the task corresponds to a "(1+)" association, the system saves all the selections performed during the task. If the task is "(*)", the system stores information about whether the person has finished the task properly or whether it was left unfinished. If the task is a didactic unit "(1)", the system stores information about whether the person chooses the correct option or not. This history is used to check if the person has satisfied the prerequisites of a certain task. In addition, it permits the deduction of information such as didactic units with a high level of failure, tasks that are rarely performed, tasks that are frequently left undone, options in a task that are never selected, etc. From this information, the educator can develop the semantic network and consequently add, delete, modify, or rearrange the items in the templates.
- *Transition matrix:* This captures the conceptual relationships followed by the person during navigation. The matrix has a row and a column for every complex concept represented in the knowledge domain. The cell $M_T[c_c^1, c_c^2]$ counts the number of times that after performing task c_c^1, the person has chosen task c_c^2. For example, taking the matrix in Figure 10 into account, it is possible to deduce that after a meal a child usually drinks something, and that after having a bath the child is not very willing to learn. Based on this analysis, the child's educator can identify conceptual relationships that are needed or not in the knowledge domain. For example, if *Food* and *Drinks* are related in the semantic network in Figure 3, the child will be able to access the template *Food* from the template *Drinks* faster, and vice versa.
- In addition, for each template the number of times the person has pushed the *What I want is not here* button is stored. Comparing this information with the frequency of access to the template, the need to modify the item associated to a concept or to incorporate new concepts (basic or complex) can be detected.

The children's educators or the person's therapists who use the communicator can also observe (and sometimes quantify) the person's reactions while they are using the hypermedia, and the causes of these reactions. All of this information can also be used to improve the communicator. For example, if an autistic child is furious when an item is presented, the educators must make a decision to avoid that feeling. They can choose whether the item must be deleted, changed for another, or if the concept represented by that item must be eliminated. In this case, item and concept are part of the user profile and of the scenario because the child accepts and recognises them. Because the child changes his/her behaviour, his/her profile and/or scenario must be modified, and again, the changes propagated up to the hypermedia. The child can observe the changes in the hypermedia and modify their attitude, changing from furious to calm, or at least, the next time that the child uses the communicator, they will not find the item that made them feel furious. In the same sense, backing techniques could be used when the child carries out a correct action (adding sounds such as clapping, music of their favourite song, their mother's voice, etc.) taking the resources and preferences included in the user model into account.

The following are evolution operations on the knowledge domain:

- Adding an item
- Adding a simple or complex concept
- Deleting an item
- Deleting a simple or complex concept
- Modifying the associations and relationships

Similar changes are carried out to evolve the user interaction and the hypermedia modifying templates, items and order navigation. Modifications may be propagated and consistency must be verified during the adaptation process. In previous work [15] we have used mechanisms and tools (Petri nets and temporal logic) to verify and update the rules used in the adaptation of hypermedia systems.

5 Anticipation on the Context

Another adaptation technique is anticipation based on the context. We can help the communication process if we anticipate the kind of conversation that is most probable according to the person's location (see Figure 11).

The way of determining the context or scenario is to recognise the person's location using their PDA and wireless technologies. The person can interact with their environment (lights, electrical appliances, instruments, devices, etc.) in a predictable context. In this case, the communicator recognises in what scenario the person is at each moment. New temporal and spatial concepts and relationships can be captured, recognizing the person's gestures as inputs to the communicator, and responding to them. For example, if the person goes to the kitchen and signals or looks at the fridge, the communicator knows that the person has selected the *Nutrition* template and recognises that the person wants to eat or to drink.

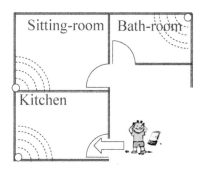

Fig. 11. Anticipation based on the context.

6 Conclusions and Future Lines of Research

In this paper, we have reviewed Augmentative and Alternative Communication Systems (AAC) as a promising technology to enhance the communicative ability of people with speech impediments. From our experience of dealing with children with autism, we know that potential AAC users are a heterogeneous population with nota-

ble differences in sensorial, physical or psychical skills. Anticipation of child requirements might not always be possible or even required. There are two main reasons for this: the child's requirements are defined by their parents and educators, and
the autistic child's behaviour could be unpredictable or variable depending on their
environment. Therefore, an efficient approach to designing an AAC system should be
based on an adaptive approach, allowing the system to be adjusted to each user's
needs in order to fit in with the best treatment for each person. Another advantage of
our approach is that the person's evolution can be monitored and it is possible to control whether they are learning, and communication with their educators or therapists is
being improved.

Although the universal design principle has been applied to this work in a particular context (users with communication and learning problems), this can be extended to
other user models and situations. Adaptability, evolution, context awareness and user
changes in preference have been considered. The same model may be applied to other
groups with minor constraints, other educative systems [16] or those which imply
memory schedules, based on images to obtain knowledge and rules to predict correct
paths or selections.

Acknowledgements

Our thanks go to Manuel González, a teacher from the Special Education School
"Santa Teresa de Jesús" in Granada, Spain, for his help and comments during experimentation with the Sc@ut communicator with his pupils.

References

1. Schlosser, R. W. Y Braun, U. (1994). Efficacy of AAC interventions: Methodological issues in evaluating behavior change, generalization and effects. AAC Augmentative and Alternative Communication, 10, 207-223.
2. Bliss, Semanthography (blisssymbolics), Sydney Semanthography publications. 1965.
3. W. Lynas. Communication Options in the Education of Deaf Children. Whurr publications.
   1998.
4. B. Baker. Minspeak. Semantic Compaction Systems. http://www.minspeak.com/
5. C. Stephanidis, A. Savidis. Universal AACess in the Information Society: Methods, Tools
   and Interaction Technologies. Universal Access to Information Society. 2001.
6. K. Dautenhahn, Design Issues on Interactive Environments for Children with Autism. Humans & Automation Seminar Series. 2002
7. N. Medina-Medina, L. García-Cabrera, M.J. Rodríguez-Fortiz, J. Parets-Llorca. Adaptation
   in an Evolutionary Hyperpedia System: Using Semantic and Petri Nets. Adaptative Hypermedia and Adaptative Web-Based Systems (second international conference, AH 2002).
   Lectures Notes in Computer Science. Vol. 2347 . pp: 284-295 . 2002.
8. M.J. Rodríguez-Fórtiz, P. Paderewski-Rodríguez, M. Rodríguez-Almendros, M. Gea-
   Mejías. An approach for evolving an adaptive and unanticipated system: a communicator
   for children with autism. Electronic Notes in Computer Science. Elsevier. (To be Published). 2004.
9. M.L. Rodríguez-Almendros, M.J. Rodríguez-Fórtiz, M.J.; Gea-Megías, M. A Framework
   for modelling the user interaction with a Complex System. Lectures Notes in Computer
   Science, SpringerVerlag. Vol. 2809, pp. 50-61. 2003.
10. L. García-Cabrera. M.J. Rodríguez-Fórtiz. J. Parets-Llorca. Evolving Hypermedia Systems:
    a Layered Software Architecture. Journal of Software Maintenance and Evolution: Re-
    search and Practice. Wiley. Vol 14. pp: 389-406. 2002.

11. Albacete P. L., Chang S. K., Polse G. 1982. Iconic language design for people with significant speech and multiple impairments. Assistive Technology and Artificial Intelligence:
Applications in Robotics, User Interfaces and Natural Language Processing.
12. VanDyke J. A. 1991. Word prediction for disable users: Applying natural language processing to enhance communication. Thesis for honors bachelor of arts in cognitive studies,
University of Delaware, Newark.
13. P. Paderewski-Rodríguez , J.J. Torres-Carbonell , M.J. Rodríguez-Fortiz, N. Medina-
Medina, Fernando Molina-Ortiz. A Software System Evolutionary and Adaptive Framework. Application to Agent Based Systems. Journal of Systems Architecture. Elsevier. (in
printing) 2004.
14. M. Ortega, M.A. Redondo, M. Paredes, P.P. Sánchez-Villalón, C. Bravo, J. Bravo: New
paradigms of interaction for the XXI centenary. (in Spanish). Interacción (Conference on
Interaction) 2001.

A Question of Realism

Richard Hetherington, Alison Crerar, and Phil Turner

School of Computing, Napier University
Edinburgh EH10 5DT
{r.hetherington,a.crerar,p.turner}@napier.ac.uk

Abstract. We present the results of an exploratory study investigating the feasibility of using multimedia software to teach life skills to adults with learning difficulties. As a precursor to determining whether the clients would benefit from the software, we needed to address the issue of realism in visual displays, to discover if photorealistic images of a familiar kitchen and utensils were essential, or if the clients would be able to abstract and apply information from generic cartoon-like representations. The level of realism was varied in two sets of tasks: object recognition exercises and problem-solving scenarios. Realistic versions of each task contained photorealistic images, and the problem-solving scenarios used images and speech of a support worker known to the participants to supply feedback and prompts. Unrealistic versions used clip art images and a cartoon-style character instead of the support worker. Contrary to expectations, measurements of errors and reaction times revealed the level of realism to have a negligible effect upon user performance in both sets of tasks. What has emerged is the overwhelming effect of individual differences on the design and evaluation of learning software.

1   Introduction

Gates [1] has argued that for adults with learning difficulties the nature of the representation should reflect an adult approach, i.e. be age-appropriate. Indeed the received wisdom is that real-life materials and situations should be used whenever possible. Adults with learning difficulties learn more easily if learning is based on real-life (i.e. realistic) because transfer of learning from artificial teaching situations is limited [2]. This is the basis of the research question we address in the study reported here. There is, of course, a tension between the demands of the learning theorists and the role of realism. Observational learning [3] or learning by imitation – patterning behaviour after an observed model, is a salient feature of human behaviour and provides a very appropriate means of facilitating learning for people with learning difficulties. Attention to the learning materials has been shown to be improved by a display that is novel, interesting and includes a variety of human-based models which are seen as competent, powerful, high in status, and of the same sex and age as the observer. Models should also be seen to be rewarded for any appropriate behaviour they perform. Successful conditions for observational learning in children termed as 'mentally retarded' are highly structured settings in which attention can be directed easily, incorporating simplified displays so that important features are emphasised and the opportunity is given for rehearsal to aid retention [4]. However, this departs from real-life where the use of realistic photographic images or video footage might be considered more appropriate in order to facilitate the successful generalisation of learning into the real world. Similar conflicts are likely to occur when considering the use of other media elements (e.g. sound). In this study we investigated the importance

C. Stary and C. Stephanidis (Eds.): UI4All 2004, LNCS 3196, pp. 68–76, 2004.
© Springer-Verlag Berlin Heidelberg 2004

of realism in visual displays by examining adults with learning difficulties using complementary versions of software whose interfaces differed in the level of realism they exhibited. Below we outline the user-centred design (UCD) approach taken in the development of this software, present the experimental method and results, and discuss the considerable diversity found in the performance profiles of these 'extraordinary users' [5].

2 Method

This study was conducted in collaboration with the Edington Centre – a training centre in North West England for adults with varying degrees of learning difficulty and special educational needs. Liaison was through one of the senior support workers at the Centre.

A strong emphasis on user-centred design in the software development process led to the adoption of the Star lifecycle [6]. We began with a semi-structured interview with a senior support worker and collected data on the available hardware and software, any computer-assisted learning in current practice and so forth. The interview was conducted at the training centre and revealed that software was already being used to teach the trainees life skills, but was considered to be problematic as it was not age-appropriate. A competitive analysis of this software ("Safety Scavenger Hunt", Softkey Multimedia Inc., 1995) following Nielsen [7] was then conducted. The major issues identified were:

1. The content was not age-appropriate – the interface being presented as a cartoon targeted at 3 to 8 year-olds.
2. The choice of characters for the user to interact with were North American animals that spoke quite quickly with American accents.
3. The buttons were quite small and users with co-ordination problems might have difficulty using them. The functionality of the buttons was not consistent.
4. On monitors larger than 14 inches a white border appeared around the screen which made it easy to lose the mouse cursor.
5. Tokens were used as part of the rewards given to participants – this is unsuitable for people lacking numeracy.
6. The use of American phrases in prompts and reward statements may not transfer well to British users.
7. The wording of prompts was device-specific, always referring to the mouse. Consequently confusion could arise if a (frequently preferred) trackerball was used with the software.

However, what was considered useful by both researchers and the support worker was the narrative structure used to describe a particular home safety scenario, and the following verbal praise and reinforcement of a particular safety issue when the user had correctly identified it. From this evaluation, it was decided that the application to be developed to examine the role of realism should contain some problem-solving scenarios designed to educate in life skills.

2.1 Envisionment

The envisionment of the interface designs, object recognition tests and problem-solving scenarios were arrived at through a series of highly iterative brainstorming sessions involving a researcher and the support worker. Initially, pencil and paper storyboards were produced with annotations written on Post-it® notes. This was soon abandoned in favour of Microsoft PowerPoint, which in conjunction with various clip-art libraries and sound files, proved to be effective for generating high-fidelity interface designs. The design of the interface for the problem-solving exercises occurred after the object recognition tests had been conducted and analysed. The software was developed using the multimedia development environment Macromedia® Director™ and was designed to encourage trainees (the subjects of this study) to progress through the various tests with as much independence as possible. However, it was realised that assistance from either the researcher conducting the test, or the support worker may be required. The final software suite consisted of a familiarisation exercise, two object recognition tests and three problem-solving scenarios relating to kitchen safety. It was possible for subjects to pause between tests before continuing on to the next.

2.2 Familiarisation

The familiarisation exercise was the easiest, and its purpose was to determine the range of subject abilities in performing the action of pointing and clicking on an image. All subjects had experience of using a computer at the training centre and familiarity with using a mouse as an input device. A mouse was therefore chosen as the input device for the present study. A picture of a common object was presented randomly in one of six placeholder positions of an invisible 2x3 grid on the screen, and a computer-delivered spoken prompt was given to point and click on that object e.g. "Point and click on the ball". Throughout the application, spoken prompts were programmed to repeat every 25s. On clicking the picture, the next prompt/picture combination was presented. The time taken between issuing the prompt and clicking the picture was logged by the software for pictures of five common objects (viz. house, tree, ball, dog, and bananas). The objects were presented in random order and position each time, and no object was repeated within a single trial. The size of the object pictures was the same as those shown in the subsequent exercises (140 x 140 pixels), and was large enough to minimise the problem of anyone with co-ordination problems having difficulty clicking on them. After the five objects had been clicked, positive reinforcement as verbal praise ("good!") was given and the pause screen shown.

2.3 First Object Recognition Test

The first object recognition test designed to assess the importance of realism consisted of two pictures: one was the 'target' and the other the 'distractor'. The user was verbally requested to identify the target picture by pointing and clicking on it (e.g. "Point and click on the spoon"). If the choice was correct, the next two pictures were presented. If the distractor was clicked, the user was verbally requested to "try again". Twelve pairs of pictures were presented randomly (both in order and left-to-right orientation). Six pairs had a realistically depicted kitchen object as the target, while the other six had an unrealistic kitchen object as the target. In both cases the sets of target objects were the same: fork, spoon, mug, pan, toaster and cooker. The corresponding distractors were different kitchen objects that could be either realistic or unrealistic. The realistic target pictures were photographs of the objects taken from the adult training centre kitchen. While the unrealistic target objects were stylised pieces of clip art. Distractors were drawn randomly from a pool of 40 images consisting of roughly equal numbers of photographs and clip art of other kitchenware. The software logged which picture the user selected and the corresponding reaction time. After completing the twelve object-pairs, verbal reinforcement was given ("well done!") and the pause screen shown as before.

2.4 Second Object Recognition Test

The second object recognition test consisted of a set of six different pictures: one was the target and the remaining 5 were distractors. The user was again prompted to identify the target by a verbal command to click on it. If the choice was correct, the next set of six pictures was presented. If a distractor picture was clicked, the user was verbally requested to "try again". A total of twelve sets of pictures were presented in random order, with each set of six pictures randomly assigned to six placeholders of a 2x3 grid on the screen. Six of the 12 tasks had a realistically depicted kitchen object as the target, and six an unrealistic kitchen object as the target. The corresponding distractors were different kitchen objects that could be either realistic or unrealistic. The sets of realistic/unrealistic target objects and the distractors were the same as used in the previous test. Again, the software logged any image selected and the corresponding reaction time after issue of the prompt. After completing the 12 picture sets the user was given verbal praise as "well done, you've finished!" and taken to the concluding screen which featured pictures of subjects, sound and a simple animation sequence.

2.5 Problem-Solving Scenarios

In these scenarios, some of the domestic objects seen before were now part of the larger context of the kitchen and contributed to a series of scenarios where subjects were required to recognise several safety issues and rectify them. Three scenarios were developed: Tidying up the kitchen to make it safe, making the cooker safe and turning the cooker's ring off. Realistic and unrealistic versions of each scenario were developed and added into the application taking advantage of existing functionality and the familiarity users had gained with the software during testing. The problem-solving exercises were accessible from a hidden menu made available to the researchers and the support worker. Realistic versions of each problem-solving scenario contained photographic images taken in the adult training centre kitchen with the model used to speak prompts being the senior support worker. Unrealistic versions contained corresponding clip-art images with a 'gingerbread man' model whose voice was unfamiliar to the subjects. The verbal content of prompts was identical in both versions of the problem-solving scenarios, which were always presented in the same order. For all scenarios, the software logged which images on the screen participants clicked and the time taken to solve the particular problem. Black and white depictions of screen shots for the first realistic and unrealistic problem-solving scenarios are shown in Fig. 1. The actual screens were developed in colour which considerably improved the visibility. Each scenario was presented along with the prompt "This kitchen is dirty and dangerous, point and click on what is wrong". In order to complete this exercise successfully, subjects were required to identify two safety issues: On identifying the bottle of bleach left out on the table, the subject was informed "Good! Bottles of dangerous chemicals should be put away in the cupboard". The bottle was then animated into the kitchen cupboard. On identifying the floor spillage, the subject was informed "Good! Anything spilled on the floor should be cleaned up, or someone might fall and hurt themselves". If subjects were unable to identify the salient features and clicked on some other part of the interface they were encouraged to "try again". When both tasks were accomplished the subject was praised further and prompted to try the next scenario when they were ready. It was recognised that some users might not complete every scenario, in which case either the researcher or support worker would abandon the scenario and proceed to the next at their discretion. In the second problem-solving scenario, subjects were required to recognise an unsafe pan on the cooker (Fig. 2); and in the third, to identify the knob controlling one of the cooker's rings that had accidentally been left switched on (Fig. 3). The narrative patterns used were similar to that of the first scenario namely a description of the problem, followed by encouragement to try again if unsuccessful, or verbal praise and reinforcement of the safety issue if it was correctly identified.

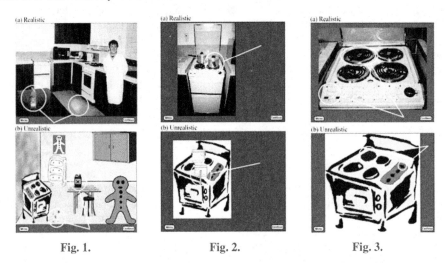

Fig. 1.   Fig. 2.   Fig. 3.

Fig. 1–3. Screen shots showing (a) the realistic interface and (b) the unrealistic interface for the first problem-solving scenario (Fig. 1), the second problem-solving scenario (Fig. 2) and the third problem-solving scenario (Fig. 3). Salient features are circled. Colour was used in the application.

Originally, 15 adults with a range of learning difficulties volunteered to take part in the trials. However, some of the subjects who originally consented refused to participate in certain tests at the last minute. Consequently, nine participants (5 men and 4 women) participated in the initial object recognition tests, while 12 people (the original nine plus an additional man and two women) participated in the problem-solving scenarios. The 12 subjects were aged 22-50. All trials were conducted by the first author using a single desktop computer located in one of the training centre's rooms. Individual trials started by the researcher introducing himself and trying to make the subject feel at ease. At the end of each trial, each participant was thanked and congratulated on their performance. Any observations by the researcher were noted after the subject had left the computer room and the software log recovered for later analysis. In the object recognition tests a subject would typically take less than 10 minutes to complete a trial and all subjects were tested during the course of a morning. In the afternoon of the same day the opportunity was taken to repeat the trials with 7 of the subjects (5 men and 2 women). Due to the low number of available participants, the realistic and unrealistic scenarios were evaluated by within-user testing. People were divided into two groups, ensuring there was no bias of age or gender in either group. For purposes of comparison, object recognition tests were conducted with five age- and gender-matched expert users.

3 Results

All the participants successfully completed the point-and-click familiarisation exercise, with a mean reaction time (RT) of 11.4s (range 1.5 to 54.6 seconds). This compared with a mean RT of 1.6 (range of 1.2 to 2.6 seconds) for five age-matched, non-learning-disabled, expert users performing the same exercise. All learning-impaired participants also completed both object recognition tests without requiring any assistance. Histograms of reaction times for each recognition test revealed a complex multimodal distribution with a large spread of reaction times (Fig.4). As the data were not normally distributed, a Wilcoxon signed-rank test was used to test for differences in reaction times. No reliable differences were found (p=0.374).

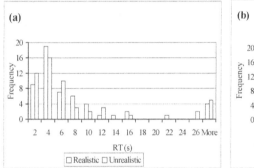 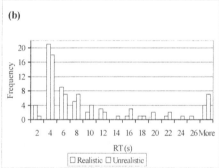

Fig. 4. Histograms showing the frequency of subject reaction times for realistic (open bars) and unrealistic (closed bars) target images for (a) the one-from-two object recognition exercise, and (b) the one-from-six object recognition exercise.

Analysing individual performances for these two tests revealed that 4 of the 9 participants had RTs where the difference between realistic and unrealistic targets was one second or less. Three participants had reaction times around 4s faster for realistic target images; one participant had reaction times on average 4s faster for unrealistic targets; and one individual had faster reaction times for unrealistic images in the first object recognition test, but faster times for realistic targets in the second. When realistic target images were used, there was no significant difference in reaction times when selecting one object from two compared with selecting one object from six (p=0.124). When unrealistic images were the targets, participants took on average 4s longer to recognise one target from six compared with one target from two, which was statistically significant (p<0.05).

Participants made varying numbers of errors in the object recognition tests. Three of the nine participants made no errors at all, whilst one user recorded 70+ erroneous clicks whilst performing the more difficult object recognition test. The nature of such errors was also highly variable. In some cases participants clicked on images that were closely related in some way to the target. Examples include, choosing a cup and saucer when the target was a mug, choosing a food mixer instead of a cooker, choosing a fork instead of a spoon (or visa versa), or choosing a percolator or kettle when the target was a pan. In one trial, a participant appeared to behave deliberately mischievously selecting all other objects before finally choosing the target. Consequently, statistical analysis revealed that the use of realistic versus unrealistic target images had no significant effect upon the numbers of errors produced by participants in either object recognition test (p=0.332). When trials were repeated with seven participants in the afternoon, reaction times were significantly faster than those recorded in the morning for the easier object recognition test (p<0.005). This was the case regardless of whether the target images were depicted realistically or unrealistically (p<0.05 for both image types). The improvement in individual reaction times ranged from 0.15s to 4.4s. In the more difficult object recognition test there was no significant improvement in reaction times (p=0.353).

As for the object recognition tests, considerable variation in participant performance was found in relation to the problem-solving scenarios. The data were not normally distributed, again necessitating the use of a non-parametric form of analysis; a summary of the participants' performances is presented in Table 1.

Table 1. Average reaction times and number of errors recorded for realistic and unrealistic versions of three problem-solving scenarios.

Scenario	Reaction Time (s)		Errors*	
	Realistic	Unrealistic	Realistic	Unrealistic
Tidying the kitchen	68.2	73.6	2.8	3.3
Making the cooker safe	24.1	19.4	0.3	0.5
Turning the cooker's ring off	40.6	37.4	4.18	3.92

* Errors: The number of clicks made on an incorrect object(s) during a trial.

The first problem-solving scenario involved identifying the floor spillage and chemical bottle as safety issues in the kitchen. Ten of the twelve participants successfully completed this exercise. There was no statistically significant difference in participant performance as measured by reaction time or number of errors between the realistic and unrealistic versions of this scenario (p=0.45).

The second problem-solving scenario involved the correct identification of a pan positioned unsafely on the top of the cooker. All participants successfully completed this scenario, with the range of reaction times being around 54s. There were no statistically significant differences between the realistic and unrealistic interfaces in terms of either reaction times (p=0.48) or the number of errors produced (p=0.41). Observations of the participants revealed that different errors were produced depending upon whether the interface was realistic or unrealistic: In the realistic interface most error clicks (75% of the total) were made on the other pan that was positioned safely on the cooker. Whilst in the unrealistic version, all error clicks were made on the background. The reason for this behaviour is unclear. One possibility may be differences in visibility of the salient parts of the screen between the realistic and unrealistic versions.

The third scenario required participants to correctly identify the cooker's knob controlling a ring that had accidentally been left switched on. Of the twelve participants, eleven successfully completed the unrealistic version and ten successfully completed the realistic version of this scenario. In both versions of this scenario over half of the erroneous clicks were made on the background. Of the remainder, 36% of errors were made clicking on the hot cooker ring and 11% from clicking on the incorrect control knobs in the realistic version. This was the reverse in the unrealistic version, with 36% of error clicks being made on incorrect control knobs and 6% on the hot cooker ring. Participants found this mapping exercise significantly more difficult than the second problem-solving scenario, recording significantly more errors and producing longer reaction times ($p<0.005$). However, there were no statistically significant differences in participants' performances between the realistic and unrealistic versions of this scenario as determined by either reaction time ($p=0.17$) or number of errors produced ($p=0.17$).

4 Discussion

Unexpected results are always welcome. We set out to investigate the role of realism on learning and much to our surprise found little or no effect. What was surprising was the effects of individual differences between the participants in this study which were so large as to overwhelm any effects our manipulations might have had. This finding has potentially significant consequences for designing for those with learning difficulties. In this instance we had adopted a fairly conventional UCD approach, but UCD has a number of largely unspoken prerequisites which were dramatically foregrounded. One of these prerequisites is that of generalising from the requirements of the small group of user participants in a UCD intervention. Typically we invite a group of users / stakeholders to act as representatives of the larger group of intended end-users. Choosing such people requires a little care – avoiding self-selection while ensuring that their jobs and experience match our expectations of what is typical of the group. There is an underlying assumption that the intended end-users are homogeneous. This is demonstrably not the case with the people who participated in this study. Indeed the support workers on being introduced to new clients are given a one-word assessment of their disability, namely, mild, moderate or severe. This, in itself, is a recognition that the population of those with learning disabilities is – at least – stratified or at the very least, heterogeneous.

The problem has no easy solution and further work is required to articulate its extent and range. This being so, we then need to revisit the underlying principles of UCD to create a more appropriate approach for those with learning difficulties.

Acknowledgement

We would like to thank the staff and service users of the Edington Centre, Penrith, Cumbria for their collaboration in this work.

References

1. Gates, B.: Understanding learning disability and service provision. In Gates, B. (ed.). Learning Disabilities. Churchill Livingstone, New York (1997) 3-54
2. Sutcliffe, J.: Adults With Learning Difficulties: Education For Choice And Empowerment. National Institute Of Adult Continuing Education in association with the Open University Press, Buckingham (1990)
3. Bandura, A.: Principles of behaviour modification. Holt, Rinehart and Winston, New York, (1969)
4. Robinson, N.M., Robinson, H.B.: The Mentally Retarded Child 2nd edn McGraw-Hill, New York, (1965)
5. Edwards, A.D.N.: Computers and people with disabilities. In: Edwards, A.D.N. (ed.). Extraordinary human-computer interaction. CUP, Cambridge (1995) 19-43
6. Hix, D., Hartson, H.R.: Developing user interfaces: Ensuring usability through product and process. John Wiley, New York (1993)
7. Nielsen, J.: Usability Engineering. Morgan Kaufmann, San Diego (1993)

Individual Differences and Behavioral Aspects Involved in Modeling Web Navigation

Ion Juvina and Herre van Oostendorp

Center for Content and Knowledge Engineering
Institute of Information and Computing Sciences, Utrecht University
Padualaan 14, 3584 CH Utrecht, The Netherlands
{ion,herre}@cs.uu.nl

Abstract. This paper presents an empirical study aiming at investigating individual differences and behavioral aspects involved in modeling web navigation. Factors that have an influence on web navigation behavior were identified with the aid of task analysis and their relevance in predicting task outcomes (performance, satisfaction, disorientation) was tested with the aid of multiple regression analysis. Several types of navigation metrics were calculated based on web logging data and used as indicators of user characteristics and task outcomes. Results show that spatial-semantic cognitive mechanisms seem to be crucial in adequately performing web navigation tasks. The fact that user characteristics and task outcomes can be estimated with reasonable accuracy based on navigation metrics suggests the possibility of building adaptive navigation support in web applications.

1 Background

Navigation is a major part of user experience on the web [1]. This particular type of behavior is triggered by a specific type of applications, which has become very common nowadays, namely *web-based applications*. The user interface of these applications (web interface – WI – as called in [2]) has some characteristics that differentiates it from other types of interface as: common language interface (CLI), graphic user interface (GUI), direct manipulation interface (DMI), WIMP interface (windows, icons, menus and pointing devices), speech user interface (SUI), virtual reality (VR) etc. Unlike in GUI, DMI and WIMP interfaces, where mainly the functionality of an application is explored, WIs prompt the user to explore the domain knowledge. In fact, web users face two different interfaces: the browser interface, which remains consistent in daily use, and the site interface, which changes from site to site. While the browser interface is rather easy to learn, it is impossible to provide adequate training on how to navigate through the many thousands of websites that the user may visit [1].

Web interfaces and the facility of navigation through large information spaces brought new problems for application designers and usability specialists; *cognitive overload* and *disorientation* are the main ones [3]. Interfaces have been traditionally designed with the function of providing users with information and means so that they can perform their tasks. In the case of WIs, this function has so much developed that has almost become a burden for the user. Therefore, adequate ways to filter the information that is offered to the user and to guide her/his navigation through the in-

C. Stary and C. Stephanidis (Eds.): UI4All 2004, LNCS 3196, pp. 77–95, 2004.
© Springer-Verlag Berlin Heidelberg 2004

formation space are necessary. The user must also be assisted in deciding what information is relevant, trustworthy, useful etc. In order to achieve these functions WIs must be aware of the user; in other words, they must incorporate a model of the user.

There is a vast amount of literature showing and analyzing individual differences involved in web navigation. Thus, Eveland Jr. and Dunwoody [4] notice that novices tend to make use of a linear structure in hypermedia systems when it is made available, while experts tend to navigate non-linearly. MacGregor [5] demonstrated that students who had greater *domain knowledge* evidenced more purposeful navigation and allocated time more variably to different information nodes when they were studying using hypertext environments. And novices who possess less *domain knowledge* do not benefit from menu choices as much as experts [6]. *Spatial ability* is an important determinant of hypermedia navigation performance, as reported in several studies [7]. It has also been shown that individuals with low *spatial abilities* have difficulties in constructing, or do not use, a visual mental model of the space [8] and they are more directed to the semantic content [9]. Students with an internal *locus of control* are better able to structure their navigation and take advantage of hypertext learning environments [5]. Aging is associated with decreases in *working memory capacity* [10] and *computer confidence* [11]. Women report higher levels of spatial anxiety, which is negatively related to the orientation way-finding strategy [10].

Research attempting at modeling cognitive mechanisms involved in web-navigation gains increasing influence in the HCI community [12-16]. A cognitive model of Web navigation should be able to simulate the navigation behavior of real users. For instance, such a model, called CoLiDeS, is proposed in [16]. It explains how users parse and comprehend the content of a Web page and then select what action to proceed. This model uses Latent Semantic Analysis (LSA) [17] to estimate the semantic similarity between user goals and semantic objects on web pages (e.g. link anchors). CoLiDeS constitutes the theoretical base of a usability evaluation method, Cognitive Walkthrough for the Web (CWW) [18], which is used to identify and repair usability problems related to navigation in web sites.

A relatively different line of research aims at modeling the user's navigation behavior in order to provide adaptive navigation support in web applications [19]. A user model can include (relatively) stable characteristics as gender, age, education level, and dynamic (changing) characteristics as goals and preferences. Stable characteristics do not pose any difficult problem for the designer of a personalized web application. The dynamic navigator's model is more challenging and more useful for the goals of personalization. A dynamic navigator's model could include:

- Syntactic information about navigation behavior (which links are followed, in which order, how does the navigation graph look (e.g. linear or nonlinear).
- Semantic information (what is the meaning of the information that the user encountered during navigation, which of this information was processed/found relevant by the user).
- Pragmatic information (what is the user using that information for, what are the user's goals and tasks).

The distinction between syntactic/semantic/pragmatic information applied in the analysis of web navigation behavior is analogous with the same distinction in the field of linguistics. A related distinction in the field of psycho-linguistics is presented in [20] cited from [21]. Thus, three levels of representation are involved in text comprehension: *surface*, *textbase* and *situation-model* levels. The surface code reflects features of the surface text (e.g. noun, determiner, verb etc.), the textbase captures the meaning relations among elements within a text, and the situation model captures the referential meaning of the text, that is the situation in the world that the text describes. As we will use this distinction in the context of modeling web navigation, 'syntactic' means structural, topologic information, 'semantic' refers to the content of visited pages, and 'pragmatic' information indicates what are the reasons and gains of visiting certain pages.

1.1   Research Objectives and Questions

The study presented in this paper is aiming at building a model of web navigation with applicability in web usability and design of personalized web applications.

First, we intend to identify factors that are able to predict task outcomes such as performance, satisfaction and reliability. Some of these factors are person-related (user characteristics) and others are interface and context related.

Then, navigation data will be used to estimate person-related factors (user characteristics) and predict task outcomes. We focus on data that is automatically recorded as a byproduct of a navigation session (web logging data), because it is easy to collect in real time and unobtrusively.

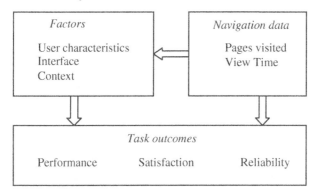

Fig. 1. Overview of objectives.

An overview of the objectives is presented in figure 1. The following are research questions derived from those objectives:

- Are the hypothesized factors indeed significant as predictors of task outcomes? Which ones are the best?
- What is the relative importance of each factor in predicting task outcomes?
- How well can each of the task outcomes be predicted?
- Is it possible to predict user characteristics based on navigation behavior? For example, how accurately can we predict *spatial ability* based on navigation metrics?
- Is it possible to predict task outcomes based on navigation behavior? For example, how accurately can we predict user's *perceived disorientation* based on navigation metrics?
- How accurately can task outcomes be predicted based on both user characteristics and navigation metrics?

2 Methodology

2.1 Task Analysis

Published research shows that *domain knowledge* is a key factor in successful use of web applications [7] and other factors could also be domain dependent. Consequently, a task domain had to be defined in order to capture the influence of those factors that are domain specific.

A valuable source of insight in what types of activities significantly impact people's decisions and actions was found to be [22]. Looking at the collection of incidents mentioned in [22], one can notice that there are some activities that seem to be frequent and specific enough to constitute a domain and that this type of activities has received insufficient attention in research and application so far. The following is an example of such an incident:

I accessed Netscape's financial site to check my credit card balance and how long it would take to pay it off. I'm now MUCH more fiscally aware of my spending habits and am trying to pay off my balance more actively.

We will call this domain Web-assisted Personal Finance (WAPF). It includes using the web to setup personal financial goals, keep a personal budget, decide to save or invest, do financial transactions, finance life events as studying, etc. Three websites were used in this study; two of them are dedicated to WAPF, they provide users with advice and tools (such as planners, calculators, educators) to deal with their financial problems and the third one, an e-commerce website, was used as a reference, being known as a reasonably well-designed web application.

An exploratory task analysis within this domain allowed us to understand which are the most relevant success factors and to build a hypothetical model. Some results of task analysis that determined the composition of the hypothetical model are:

- Some subjects are capable of deploying a fast, elaborated and effective web navigation behavior. Consequently, a factor concerning Internet expertise was considered.
- Although tasks were conceived in such a way to require previous knowledge as little as possible, it was noticed that a certain familiarity of users with the financial domain was an advantage.
- Spatial ability was included in the hypothetical model based on the high frequency of spatial terms used in subjects' verbalizations even when they were dealing with completely nonspatial issues. Examples of verbalizations with spatial connotation: "where am I", "let's go in another place", "I'm stuck in these analyzers", "I saw it somewhere".

Another goal of task analysis was to collect realistic task instances. Real life tasks do not require only finding information but also problem solving and decision-making [23]. Tasks in WAPF include:

- Information search (e.g. „What is the definition of financial goal?");
- Personal life planning (e.g. „Setup a personal budget");
- Problem solving (e.g. "How much do I need to save monthly in order to buy a car in 4 years?");
- Personal decision-making (e.g. „What kind of car can I afford?").

2.2   Variables and Indicators

2.2.1. Task Outcomes. Criteria for task outcomes were specified during task analysis. We wanted to find a small number of criteria to cover as many task outcomes as possible. *Effectiveness, efficiency* and *satisfaction* were taken from [24] and effectiveness and efficiency were grouped under the label *performance*. *Performance* denotes task success (effectiveness) obtained with minimum resources (efficiency). Satisfaction refers to users affective experience toward task execution and task results.

Besides *performance* and *satisfaction*, another criterion was considered necessary to cover the undesirable aspects of task outcomes. There is a vast literature showing that models of human performance are incomplete if they consider only correct performance and neglect the human error or, more general, the human fallibility. For example, Reason [25] states that correct performance and error are like *active* and *passive* sides of a cognitive balance; each *debit* has a corresponding *credit*. For instance, skills development increases performance but also the risk of error by turning off the conscious control mechanisms. In the field of human-computer interaction, van Oostendorp and Walbeehm [26] argue for the necessity of (and propose some modeling techniques for) considering errors, inefficiency and problem-solving processes in modeling human behavior in interaction with direct manipulation interfaces. Since not only errors are dealt with, but also other undesirable aspects of task execution as stress, cognitive workload, disorientation, frustration, violations of privacy etc., a more generic term was chosen, namely *reliability*, which is the antonym of 'fallibility'. In this context, reliability refers to avoiding or minimizing negative outcomes of task execution.

2.2.2. Predictors. As already announced in section 1, among potential predictors we considered navigation metrics, user characteristics, and interface and context factors. They will be described in more detail in this section.

2.2.2.1. Navigation Metrics. An important amount of behavioral data about web navigation is available in web logs. Besides its availability, using this data in modeling web navigation is justified when one has the aim of personalization in mind: web logging data is collected unobtrusively and in real time; analysis of this data can be automated; and adaptive reactions of the application can be based on analysis results.

Interaction events that can be logged during a navigation session are quite numerous: page downloads, view time, use of buttons etc. Some data about the web structure being navigated is also available: page title/URL, number of words per page, number of outgoing/incoming links etc. This constitutes the *raw data* of web navigation, which progresses toward *information* and *knowledge* via analytic and interpretational undertakings during the modeling process.

A number of analyses can be performed on the raw data in order to extract some useful *information* out of this data. We will refer to the results of these analyses as *navigation metrics*. Extracting information out of navigation data by the aid of various navigation metrics is the way toward acquiring *knowledge* about the user.

Different types of information can be derived from navigation data: syntactic, semantic and pragmatic (see section 1 for a description of these types). Within this study, we calculated, based on raw web-logging data, two types of syntactic metrics (first-order and second-order metrics) and one semantic metric (path adequacy) as it will be presented below. These metrics will be used as predictors in the analyses presented in section 3.

The raw data consisted of:

- Interaction events. For each *navigation session*, the following data was collected: Page visited and link followed; Time of visit; Page load time and length of visit; Navigation action (e.g. link, address bar, refresh, back button).

- Site structure data. For each *page* the following data was collected: URL and host; Size in bytes; Number of words and images; Number of outgoing links; Title and author; Source code. For each *link* the following data was collected: Source and target page; Text associated with the link; Type of link (internal, external).

First-Order Metrics. A first set of navigation metrics was labeled first-order metrics, because they were derived directly from the raw data, without taking into consideration any usage matter. For example, Average Connected Distance (ACD) is calculated independent of Back Button Use (BBU), and does not take into consideration the fact that usually low values on ACD are associated with high values on BBU and vice-versa (r=-0.49). This latter information was used in calculating second-order metrics.

After successive trials a number of 19 metrics were selected to be used in further analyses. They will be shortly described below (short labels in brackets). For a more detailed discussion about these metrics see [27].

- *Path length* (pathleng) is the number of pages that the user has viewed during the navigation session.
- *Relative amount of revisits* (revisits) is calculated as the probability that any URL visited is a repeat of a previous visit.
- *Return rate* (return) indicates the average number of times that a page will be re-visited. The return rate is calculated by averaging the number of visits to all pages that have been visited at least twice.
- *Back button usage* (backbutton) indicates the percentage of back button clicks among the navigation actions, including backtracking multiple pages at once using the back button.
- *Relative amount of visits to the homepage* (homepage) is a self-descriptive label. "Relative" refers to a correction of home page visits based on path length.
- *Average view time* (meanview) is calculated by dividing the total time spent on viewing pages by the number of pages visited.
- *Median view time* (medview) is the median of the view times spent on each page, calculated like this: with a list of n page accesses and corresponding view time in increasing order, the median is the view time of page $n/2$.
- *Difference between the average and the median view time* (difview) indicates the extent at which the average view time is overly influenced by a minority of pages that are viewed carefully.
- *Deviation in view time* (devview) indicates how much the view time varies between pages.
- *Other view times*:
  o *time spent on larger pages* (viewlarg): number of words is larger than the average plus the standard deviation

o *time spent on smaller pages* (viewsmall): number of words is smaller than the average minus the standard deviation

o *time spent on index pages* (viewindx): pages with a large number of outgoing links

o *time spent on reference pages* (viewref): pages with a small number of outgoing links.

- *Relative Structural Complexity ('fan degree')* (fandeg) represents the ratio between the number of links followed and the number of distinct pages visited. A large fan degree indicates that users tend to follow more than one link from each page.
- *Number of Cycles* (cycles) is the difference between the number of pages and the number of links, corrected with a constant of 1. It indicates the number of non-linear navigation steps.
- *Path Density* (density) measures at what extent users make use of the links of the site structure. A high path density indicates that a user makes use of short navigation sequences and regularly returns to pages visited before.
- *Compactness* (compact) is a measure similar to path density except that it takes into account the actual site structure (density was relative to all possible links in the site).
- *Stratum* (stratum) is a metric designed to capture the linear ordering of user navigation [28]. Calculation is based on the following idea: pages that are hard to reach, but can easily reach other pages, receive a high 'status'; pages that are easy to reach, but from where it is hard to reach other pages, receive a high 'contra-status'. A *page prestige* is calculated as the difference between *status* and *contra-status*. The stratum is formally defined as the sum of absolute prestiges divided by the highest possible form of linear ordering. A lower stratum indicates less linear navigation, as the 'hierarchical' distance between any two nodes is quite low.
- *Average Connected Distance* (ACD) indicates the average length of a path between any two connected pages. A higher ACD indicates that users do not return to a page very soon, but only after having browsed for a while. They also return using a link rather than using the back button.

Second-Order Metrics. As it is most likely that patterns in the first-order metrics occur quite often simultaneously, second-order navigation metrics – linear combinations of the first order metrics – were calculated. They will be described in section 3.2.

Path Adequacy. A semantic metric, called Path adequacy, was calculated based on navigation data and the task descriptions that subjects were provided with at the beginning of the navigation session. This metric will also be described in section 3.2.

2.2.2.2. User Characteristics. Some user characteristics were hypothesized (based on task analysis and previous research) to have an influence on task outcomes. They were grouped on a conceptual basis in: cognitive, affective, conative and demographic factors.

The distinction between cognition, affection and conation is well-founded in psychology; all human behavior involves some mixture of all three aspects [29-32]. *Cognition* refers to the process of coming to know and understand; the process of encoding, storing, processing, and retrieving information. It is generally associated with the question of "what" (e.g., what happened, what is going on now, what is the meaning of that information). *Affect* refers to the emotional interpretation of perceptions, information, or knowledge. It is generally associated with one's attachment (positive or negative) to people, objects, ideas, etc. and asks the question "How do I feel about this knowledge or information?" *Conation* comes from the Latin verb *conare* meaning to strive. It refers to the connection of knowledge and affect to behavior and is associated with the issue of "why". It is the personal, intentional, deliberate, goal-oriented, or striving component of motivation, the proactive (as opposed to reactive or habitual) aspect of behavior [33]. It is closely associated with the concept of volition, defined as the use of will, or the freedom to make choices about what to do [34]. Some of the conative issues one faces daily are: what are my intentions and goals; what am I going to do; what are my plans and commitments? Conation is absolutely critical when an individual is successfully engaged in self-direction and self-regulation [35].

2.2.2.3. Interface and Context Factors. Given the scope of this study, only a few of the interface and context factors that could have an influence on task outcomes were possible to be investigated. Others were randomized or kept constant. By choosing three different websites to be used as research material, we attempted at randomizing factors pertaining to site structure or interface design. Sites' usability was explicitly measured as an interface factor.

With regard to different usage contexts that could have an influence on task outcomes, we kept constant as much as possible the room, the type of computer and all the other contextual factors that could influence users' navigation behavior, except *Time constraints* that was experimentally manipulated. By trying to induce the feeling of time pressure in a half of our subjects we attempted at simulating part of the 'mobile context' of web navigation.

2.3 Operationalization

The operationalization of the hypothetical model consisted in expressing each factor in measurable variables and indicators.

Thus, the cognitive factor *expertise* was first divided in *Internet expertise* and *Finance expertise*. An *Internet expertise* measure was constructed based on users self reported frequency of Internet use and their self-assessed level of knowledge and skills in web navigation. *Finance expertise* was measured with items such as: "Have you ever used a personal finance website (Yahoo Finance, MSN Money etc.)?".

The variables *spatial ability*, *episodic memory*, and *working memory* were measured with computerized cognitive tests provided by TNO – Human Factors Institute. The 'Spatial ability test' uses the classical mental rotation task, and the spatial ability score is the number of correct solutions obtained by rotating three-dimensional objects. The 'Episodic memory test' presents 3 lists of 60 images each; subjects must loudly name the images in the first 2 lists; between lists 2 and 3 there is a distraction task (we used the 'spatial ability test' as a distraction task, to efficiently use the testing time); list 3 contains images that were presented before in lists 1 and 2 together with new images; the subjects have to recognize the images that were presented in list 1. The 'Working memory test' uses a reading span task [36]: subjects are presented with series of phrases, the size of series increasing progressively from 2 to 7 phrases; the subjects are asked to loudly read the phrases and try to understand their content; after each series, the subjects are asked to recall the last word of each phrase in that particular series; for one random phrase in the series subjects are asked to fill in 2 missing words, to ensure that they really treat the whole content and not only the last words. The working memory score is calculated based on correctness of recalls. This test is more complete and more adequate than digit span tests for working memory capacity, since it takes into consideration not only information storage but also information processing that is normally associated with working memory capacity.

Locus of control refers to the individual's belief regarding the causes of his or her experiences, and those factors to which an individual attributes his or her successes and failures. Research shows that users with an internal locus of control are better able to structure their navigation and take advantage of hyperspace features [5]. Locus of control was measured with a 20-item scale [37]. The *sequential-holistic* cognitive style was measured with items such as: "I like to break down large problems into smaller steps" and "I like to look at the big picture" [38].

A measure of users' affective disposition at the beginning of the navigation session was built based on users ratings of different affective states that they considered appropriate to describe their current disposition. Subsequently, users ratings were factor analyzed and grouped in three basic *moods*. Thus, *active mood* is composed by the following affective states: Determined, Calm, Alert/vigilant, Sluggish/lethargic/lazy (negative sign), and Blue/Depressed (negative sign); *Enthusiastic mood* is mainly composed of Enthusiastic, Excited, and Strong states; and *irritable mood* contains mainly the states: Irritable, Sluggish (lethargic, lazy), Nervous, Sleepy, and Relaxed (negative sign).

Subjects' *propensity toward trust* [39] was measured with items such as: "People always can be trusted" and "People always take care only of themselves".

The factor called 'Motivation' was included in the model based on observations during the experiment and inspections of students' answers to some questionnaires items. A dichotomous variable that differentiates between participants from Utrecht University and Twente University is a strong predictor of user satisfaction in task completion. Besides, the students in the two universities reported consistently different types of interests, e.g. students from Utrecht University declare higher levels of interests in entertainment and personal development, whereas students from Twente University declare higher levels of interests in personal and professional businesses. This variable was hypothesized to pertain to students' motivation and goal orientation. The differences between the two groups of students (Utrecht vs. Twente) seem similar to the difference between mastery and performance goal orientation. *Mastery* oriented students perceive new tasks as an opportunity to learn or to acquire new skills, whereas *performance* oriented students perceive tasks as opportunities to demonstrate already existing competence and skills [40]. This hypothesis must be checked in further research, but, for the moment, the new dichotomous variable is used with the temporary label "Motivation".

Self-efficacy was measured with a questionnaire, adapted from [41], containing items such as: "I could perform better using these websites if I had a lot of time to complete the job for which the sites were provided".

The *interests* factor of the hypothetical model was operationalised based on principal component analysis. Participants were asked to indicate what do they use the Internet for. Answers were factor analyzed and the 2 components that resulted were called respectively 'Interest entertainment and personal development' (for brevity, *interest entertainment*) and 'Interest personal and professional business' (for brevity, *interest business*).

Perceived usability of the three sites used in the study was measured with a selection of items from questionnaires [42] and [43], consisting of items such as: "It was easy to use this website" and "I could effectively complete my tasks using this website".

The factor *time constraints* was experimentally manipulated. Half of the subjects (15) were instructed that only 30 minutes are available to complete the navigation tasks, while the other half did not receive any time indication. In fact, all subjects were given a maximum of 40 minutes to execute the navigation tasks. No clock or other time indication was available.

The criterion *performance* was operationalised only in 'effectiveness' (attaining of task goal). The degree of success for each task was rated from 0 to 4 based on correctness and completeness of answers. The 'Efficiency' side of performance was not directly considered because the time of the navigation sessions was kept constant for all subjects. In this case, 'efficiency' of task execution is implicitly considered in 'effectiveness'. Other non-temporal metrics of efficiency (e.g. number of steps taken in solving a task) are more or less captured by some of the navigation metrics (e.g. path length); including them as criteria would have artificially inflated the predictive power of the model.

Satisfaction as a criterion was measured by items such as: "It was an interesting experience to perform these tasks" and "Overall, working to accomplish these tasks was satisfying". It refers not to the satisfaction of users toward the websites used; the latter is captured by the *usability* factor. By separating satisfaction toward the tools used (web sites) from satisfaction toward task execution and results we aimed at avoiding the 'common measure bias'.

Reliability as a criterion was operationalised in this study by variables *perceived disorientation* and *frustration*. *Perceived disorientation* was measured with items adapted from [44] such as: "It was difficult to find the information I needed on this site" and "It was difficult to find my position after navigating for a while". *Frustration* was measured with items such as: "I felt frustrated when I encountered difficulties in completing the tasks" and "I felt angry when I couldn't find what I needed to complete the tasks".

2.4 Subjects and Procedure

The study was run with 30 participants in a single session lasting approximately 2½ hours. 15 participants (7 females and 8 males) were registered as students in the Information Management Department at Twente University, and the other 15 participants (8 females and 7 males) were students in the Information Science Department at Utrecht University. Participants were selected randomly out of students' catalogues of both universities. Half of the participants were randomly assigned to the 'Time constraints' condition in which the participants were instructed to finish the navigation tasks in 30 minutes.

The first part of the sessions was dedicated to questionnaires and cognitive tests aimed at measuring user characteristics. The second part consisted in execution of web navigation tasks. This part lasted maximum 40 minutes for all participants (including those in the 'time constraints' condition). No clock was available, participants were asked to put away their wristwatches, and the computer clock was disabled. During the navigation task, navigation behavior and task performance were recorded. Subjects were informed that their navigation behavior was recorded. Task performance was recorded by the participants on a dedicated form and coded afterwards by the experimenter. The third part of the sessions consisted of administration of usability and satisfaction questionnaires. Each participant received a compensation of Euro 20 at the end of the session.

3 Results

Results will be presented in the same order as suggested in the overview of objectives (fig. 1). Multiple linear regression analysis was used to investigate the significance of hypothetic factors in predicting task outcomes as well as the possibility of using navigation metrics as estimates of user characteristics and predictors of task outcomes. Including predictors in regression models was based on the *stepwise method*, thus the predictive power must be seen as the best one can get with the minimum number of predictors. Only significant predictions are presented here.

3.1 Predicting Task Outcomes Based on Hypothesized Factors

All task outcomes can be predicted based on a limited number of predictors with various effect sizes[1] (table 1). However, even the smaller R squared (0.22) corresponds to a medium-large effect size according to Cohen [45].

Table 1. Predictions of task outcomes based on the hypothetic factors.

Task outcome	R square	Predictors	Beta
Performance	0,39	Spatial ability	0,496
		Finance expertise	0,385
Satisfaction	0,67	Motivation	0,612
		Usability	0,506
		Interest business	-0,319
Disorientation	0,42	Usability	-0,505
		Working Memory	-0,344
Frustration	0,22	Time constraints	0,471

Task performance is best predicted by *spatial ability* and *finance expertise*. In other words, the user ability to represent the structure of the sites and their domain knowledge are the most important determinants of task success. *Satisfaction* is best predicted by *motivation, usability* and *interest in business*. Users who are motivated, not interested in business and perceiving the websites as usable are more likely to be satisfied with task completion. *Interest business* negatively correlates with *satisfaction* (r = −0.38). A possible interpretation is that subjects with interests in personal and professional business have higher expectations and they are more vulnerable to be

---

[1] The effect size for regression is calculated with the following formula $ES^2 = R^2/(1-R^2)$. 0.02 is considered a small effect, 0.15 a medium one, and 0.35 a large effect size.

dissatisfied when task execution and results do not meet their expectations. *Disorientation* is best predicted by *usability* and *working memory*. Low working memory capacity and low perceived usability are associated with increased probability of users perceived disorientation. *Frustration* is predicted by *time constraints*. Users in the 'time constraints' condition reported a higher level of frustration than users in the control condition.

3.2 Predicting User Characteristics Based on Navigation Metrics

As presented in section 2.2.2.1, several types of navigation metrics were calculated: *first-order, second-order* (navigation styles and reading time) and a semantic metric called *path adequacy*. Few details about how second order and semantic metrics were calculated are presented below.

Two different data analysis approaches were employed in deriving second-order navigation metrics: *unsupervised learning* (principal component analysis) and *supervised learning* (regression). In the unsupervised learning approach, only patterns of covariance in the first-order metrics are considered, regardless any outside criteria. The second-order metrics resulted in this way were called *navigation styles*. They are completely specified (numerically) by first-order metrics. However, interpreting their meaning and labeling them was based on their correlations with user characteristics and task outcomes. In the supervised learning approach, the task outcomes defined in sections 2.2.1 and 2.3 were used as outside criteria in the attempt to combine the first-order metrics. A second-order metric was derived in this way and it was called *reading time*. It is a combination of several view time metrics weighted in such a way to ensure a significant correlation with *task performance*.

Navigation Styles. A principal component analysis with *equamax* rotation was run on the 19 first-order metrics presented above. A 4-components solution that accounts for 85.95% of the initial variance has been selected. Each component accounts for 27.3, 23.8, 22.8, and 12.0 % of variance, respectively. Component loadings in first-order metrics and the correlations between factors and user characteristics and task outcomes were used to interpret the content of each factor in terms of navigation styles as follows:

Component 1. Flimsy Navigation. High scores on this component are associated with small number of pages visited, high density, high view time per page, low average connected distance, low number of cycles, high rate of home page visiting, and high frequency of back button use. It appears to be a parsimonious navigation style. The navigation path is not very elaborated, most of it happens around the homepage. Time is wasted by processing content instead of figuring out the hyperstructure that shows where the relevant information is. A high score on the flimsy navigation style is associated with low Internet expertise ($r=-0.5$), low active mood ($r=0.48$), low working memory ($r=-0.38$), external locus of control ($r=-0.37$), and high perceived disorientation ($r=0.46$).

Component 2. Content Focus. This component groups together all the view-time metrics, which basically indicates that there is a general consistency in users' view-time allocation. In other words, users are consistently 'slow' or 'fast'. High values on this component indicate high view time on a rather small set of pages. Within this style, navigation is a means for reading. Users goal is to find those pages that ought to be read and then read them. This style is not associated with any user characteristics or task outcomes.

Component 3. Laborious Navigation. High scores on this component are associated with high number of links followed per page, high revisitation rate, high number of cycles, high returning rate, high use of back button, high density, high number of pages visited, low average connected distance (short returns). This style involves intensive use of navigational infrastructure provided by the site. Users seem to employ a trial and error strategy. They follow links just to see if they are useful or not. They figure out quite fast when paths are not leading towards their goal and return. Revisits are quite numerous but they are not redundant: once a page is revisited a different link if followed than before, it's just another trial. This navigation style is associated with high episodic memory (r=0.49), low spatial ability (r=-0.40), and low interest in entertainment (r=-0.38). This style indicates the type of revisitation that does not relate to disorientation. The user needs to look around for a while until s/he has a good representation of the site structure, because s/he has a weak spatial ability. Her/his memory though prevents her/him of making redundant revisits. This component shows how people compensate the lack of spatial ability by effort and memory, and do not necessarily decrease performance (no correlations with task performance, although spatial ability and task performance are positively correlated). It also shows why revisitation is not always associated with disorientation.

Component 4. Divergent Navigation. High scores on this component are associated with low compactness, high stratum, low homepage use, high connected distance (long returns). This navigation style is rather explorative. Users are not that eager to revisit pages but rather to explore new directions. This navigation style is only associated with a high propensity to trust (r=0.43).

Reading Time. Another second order-metric was constructed by trying to get meaningful combinations of first-order metrics that would significantly correlate with task outcomes. One such trial that proved to be successful is the following:

$$\text{readtime} = 230.1 + 4.2 * \text{viewlarg} + 1.56 * \text{viewref} - 3.73 * \text{viewsmal} - 4.77 * \text{viewindx} + 2.04 * \text{devview} . \tag{1}$$

It was labeled *reading time* since it positively weighs view time on large and reference pages (presumed to be content pages) and negatively weighs view time on small and index pages (1). High *reading time* is significantly associated with low *flimsy navigation* (r=-0.5), low *divergent navigation* (r=-0.36), high *Internet expertise* (r=0.35), high *performance* (r=0,43), and low *disorientation* (r=-0.39). These correlations show that *reading time* is a more relevant combination of various first-order view times than the navigation style *content focus*.

Path Adequacy. This semantic metric was calculated as a measure of semantic similarity between a navigation path and a task description. A navigation path is a concatenation of semantic objects that the user has encountered in her/his way toward a specific location. As semantic objects, one can consider, link anchors, page titles, page contents, URLs, clickable icons, banners and images etc. We have used navigation paths composed of page titles.

For example, if the user visited the pages titled 'Should I finance or pay cash for a vehicle? Calculators', 'How much will my vehicle payments be? Calculators', 'Glossary', and 'What vehicle can I afford? Calculators', then his/her navigation path is *represented as a string of all words in these titles: <should, I, finance, or, pay, cash, for, a, vehicle, calculators, how, much, will, my, vehicle, payments, be, calculators, glossary, what, vehicle, can, I, afford, calculators>.*

Navigation paths were compared with task descriptions. The following is an example of task description:

Suppose you want to buy a car in 2 years. You have already saved $ 500. How much do you need to save on a monthly basis in order to make a down payment of $ 8000 for the car? Assume that the savings and tax rates are as listed. What is the most expensive car you can afford if you will be able to pay 40 monthly payments of at most $ 150 after the down payment?

In order to measure the semantic similarity between navigation paths and task descriptions we have used the technique called Latent Semantic Analysis [17]. High *path adequacy* significantly correlates with low *return rate* (r=-0.48), high *spatial ability* (r=0.36), high *self efficacy* (r=0.40), and high *performance* (r=0.47).

Table 2 shows that a considerable number of user characteristics can be predicted with reasonable accuracy based on navigation metrics. For example, 25% of the variance in *Internet expertise* can be predicted based on *flimsy navigation style*. This result has a direct implication for providing adaptive support in web navigation. As *Internet expertise* is virtually impossible to be measured in real-time use of a web application, it can be estimated based on user's navigation path.

Table 2. Predictions of user characteristics based on navigation metrics.

Characteristic	R square	Predictors	Beta
Internet expertise	0,25	Flimsy navigation	-0,50
Spatial ability	0,195	Revisits	-0,442
Episodic memory	0,245	Laborious navigation	0,495
Working memory	0,28	Flimsy navigation	-0,83
		Median view time	0,58
Locus of control	0,398	Flimsy navigation,	-0,704
		View reference	0,874
		Deviation view	-0,553
Active mood	0,258	Path density	-0,508
Trust propensity	0,233	Average connected distance	0,483
Interest entertainment	0,147	Revisits	-0,383
Interest business	0,254	Compactness	1,500
		Divergent navigation	1,189

3.3 Predicting Task Outcomes Based on Navigation Metrics

Two of the task outcomes, *performance* and *disorientation*, were significantly predicted based on second-order and semantic metrics (table 3). These results show that second-order and semantic navigation metrics are better predictors of task outcomes than first-order metrics. There are no significant predictions for *satisfaction* and *frustration*, which means that searching for navigation metrics is not finished.

Table 3. Predictions of task outcomes based on navigation metrics.

Task outcome	R square	Predictors	Beta
Performance	0,299	Path adequacy	0,385
		Reading time	0,298
Disorientation	0,213	Flimsy navigation	0,462

3.4 Predicting Task Outcomes Based on Hypothetic Factors and Navigation Metrics

When both factors and metrics are entered in the regression analysis, the selection of the most significant predictors generates slightly different results (table 4). This is due to correlations among predictors. For example, *number of cycles* appears among the significant predictors of disorientation instead of *flimsy navigation*. This is because the amount of variance in disorientation explicable by *flimsy navigation* is explained better by *cycles* and *working memory*, which are correlated with *flimsy navigation*. Two first-order metrics appear as significant predictors of *satisfaction* which can be interpreted as follows: the amount of variance in *satisfaction* left unexplained by *motivation, usability* and *interest for business* can be explained by *view time per large pages* and *view time per small pages*. Note that the *beta* coefficients have opposite signs: users were more satisfied when they spent relatively long time on large pages and relatively short time on small pages than vice versa. In other words, spending relatively long time on large pages (presumed to be content pages) leads to that part of *satisfaction* in task completion that is not determined by *motivation, interest for business* and *sites usability*.

Table 4. Predictions of task outcomes based on hypothetic factors and navigation metrics.

Task outcome	R square	Predictors	Beta
Performance	0,515	Spatial ability	0,399
		Finance expertise	0,340
		Path adequacy	0,216
		Reading time	0,318
Satisfaction	0,793	Motivation	0,754
		Usability	0,619
		Interest business	-0,277
		View large	0,491
		View small	-0,302
Disorientation	0,57	Usability	-0,496
		Cycles	-0,388
		Working Memory	-0,305

Another effect of considering factors and metrics together as predictors of task outcomes is a considerable increase in predictive power: R square is higher than 0.50 for all criteria except *frustration*. This result shows that user characteristics, interface and context factors, on one hand, and navigation metrics, on the other hand, are rather complementary in predicting task outcomes. In other words, navigation metrics cannot completely explain task outcomes by themselves, but they are able to indicate facets of task outcomes that are not explained by the hypothesized factors.

4 Conclusions, Discussion and Further Research

We have shown in this paper that user characteristics such as *domain expertise, spatial ability, working memory, motivation*, and *interest* are important determinants of task outcomes. Interface and context factors such as *sites' usability* and *time constraints* have also an influence on some of the task outcomes.

However, user characteristics as determinants of task outcomes are only possible to be measured in experimental settings. We have also shown that some of the user characteristics such as *Internet expertise, spatial ability, working memory, episodic memory, trust propensity*, and *interests* can be estimated with a reasonable level of accuracy based on web logging data that can unobtrusively be collected in a real-world navigation session.

Our attempt to calculate different types of metrics based on navigation data was proved to be profitable. We have seen that different types of knowledge about the user can be inferred based on the kind of information that is extracted from this data: *syntactic* (structural) information indicates mainly users' navigation styles, for example, if they rather revisit pages than viewing new pages, if they return using the back button or just by following links, etc.; *semantic* information indicates if users are effective in pursuing their goals, somehow regardless their navigation styles; and *pragmatic* information will probably be indicative for users needs, interests, goals and tasks. Only syntactic and semantic metrics were used in this study; extracting pragmatic information from navigation data is one of our intentions for further research.

The predictions of task outcomes based on user characteristics, interface and context factors appeared to be more accurate than those based on navigation metrics. This difference suggests that there is still enough work to be done in searching for accurate and relevant indicators of navigation behavior. However, both categories of predictors are important, one from a more theoretical perspective and the other from an applied one.

From a theoretical perspective, it appears that spatial-semantic cognitive mechanisms are crucial in adequately performing web navigation tasks. In this study we have only identified some individual differences that are consistently associated with specific task outcomes. It is our intention for further research to investigate cognitive mechanisms that are responsible for these individual differences and for their influence of task outcomes.

The results of this study have important practical implications. A web application can be designed in such a way that it takes into consideration (or compensates for) those factors that proved to be significant in predicting task outcomes. For example, since *spatial ability* is one of the determinants of *task performance*, some interface features (e.g. maps) should be designed to compensate for low spatial ability. The indicators of navigation behavior that are automatically calculated during a navigation session and are able to predict relevant user characteristics and also task outcomes can be used to model the user in real time by a personalized application. For example, the application can be programmed to provide additional navigation aid when users are diagnosed 'at risk of disorientation' and to hide useless hints when users are assessed as 'doing well'.

Obviously, there are not yet strong grounds for a large generalization of our results. They apply to situations when goal-directed and performance-oriented tasks are performed. Moreover, our results are valid in the *Desktop* paradigm. Under a *Mobile* paradigm with different site structures and navigation support available, *Flimsy navigation* style, for instance, might not necessarily be associated with *disorientation*. The navigation sessions were restricted to 40 minutes, which could have prevented some of the users to form an adequate mental model of the web sites used. The number of subjects (30) was rather limited and relatively homogenous, as they were students. This might have had an impact especially on factor analysis results. Despite these limitations, there are enough confirmations of previous research [5, 7, 11, 44, 46, 47] to support the reliability of our results.

References

1. Lazar, J., The World Wide Web, in J. Jacko & A. Sears (Eds.): The human-computer interaction handbook: Fundamentals, evolving technologies and emerging applications, 2003, Lawrence Erlbaum: Mahwah, NJ. p. 714-730.
2. Ivory, M., & Hearst, M., State of the Art in Automating Usability Evaluation of User Interfaces. ACM Computing Surveys, 2001. 33(4): p. 1-47.
3. Conklin, J., Hypertext: An introduction and survey. IEEE Computer Magazine, 1987. 20(9): p. 17-41.
4. Eveland Jr., W.P., Dunwoody, S., Users and navigation patterns of a science World Wide Web site for the public. Public Understand. Sci., 1998(7): p. 285-311.
5. MacGregor, S., Hypermedia Navigation Profiles: Cognitive Characteristics and Information Processing Strategies. Journal of Educational Computing Research, 1999. 20(2): p. 189-206.
6. Draper, S.W., Supporting use, learning, and education. Journal of computer documentation, 1999. 23(2): p. 19-24.
7. Chen, C., Individual Differences in a Spatial-Semantic Virtual Environment. Journal of The American Society for Information Science, 2000. 51(6): p. 529-542.
8. Stanney, K.M., & Salvendy, G., Information visualization; assisting low spatial individuals with information access tasks through the use of visual mediators. Ergonomics, 1995. 38(6): p. 1184-1198.
9. Westerman, S.J., Computerized information retrieval: Individual Differences in the use of spatial Vs nonspatial navigational information. Perceptual and Motor Skills, 1995. 81: p. 771-786.
10. Sjolinder, M., Individual differences in spatial cognition and hypermedia navigation, in Towards a Framework for Design and Evaluation of Navigation in Electronic Spaces. 1998, Swedish Institute of Computer Science.
11. Neerincx, M.A., Pemberton, S., Lindenberg, J., U-WISH Web usability: methods, guidelines and support interfaces. 1999, TNO Human Factors Research Institute: Soesterberg.
12. Pirolli, P., & Fu, W.-T., SNIF-ACT: A Model of Information Foraging on the World Wide Web. 2003.
13. Byrne, M.D., Cognitive Architecture, in J. Jacko & A. Sears (Eds.): The human-computer interaction handbook: Fundamentals, evolving technologies and emerging applications., 2003, Lawrence Erlbaum: Mahwah, NJ. p. 97-117.
14. Card, S.K., Pirolli, P., Van Der Wege, M., Morrison, J.B., Reeder, R.W., Schraedley, P.K., & Boshart, J. Information Scent as a Driver of Web Behavior Graphs: Results of a Protocol Analysis Method for Web Usability. in SIGCHI'01. 2001. Seattle, WA, USA.: ACM.

15. Kieras, D.E., Meyer, D.E., An Overview of the EPIC Architecture for Cognition and Performance with Application to Human-Computer Interaction. Human-Computer Interaction, 1997. 12: p. 391-438.
16. Kitajima, M., Blackmon, M.H., & Polson, P.G., A Comprehension-based Model of Web Navigation and Its Application to Web Usability Analysis, in People and Computers XIV. 2000, Springer. p. 357-373.
17. Landauer, T.K., Foltz, P.W., & Laham, D., Introduction to Latent Semantic Analysis. Discourse Processes, 1998. 25: p. 259-284.
18. Blackmon, M.H., et al. Cognitive Walkthrough for the Web. in CHI 2002. 2002. Minneapolis, Minnesota, USA.: ACM.
19. Jameson, A., Adaptive Interfaces and Agents, in The human-computer interaction handbook: Fundamentals, evolving technologies and emerging applications, J.J.A.S. (Eds.), Editor. 2003, Lawrence Erlbaum: Mahwah, NJ. p. 305-330.
20. van Oostendorp, H., & Goldman, S.R. (Eds.), The construction of mental representations during reading. 1999, Mahwah, NJ: Lawrence Erlbaum Associates, Publishers.
21. van Dijk, T.A., & Kintsch, W., Strategies of discourse comprehension. 1983, New York: Academic Press.
22. Morrison, J.B., Pirolli, P., and Card, S. K., A taxonomic analysis of what World Wide Web activities significantly impact people's decisions and actions. 2000, UIR Technical report UIR-R-2000-17, Xerox PARC.
23. Pirolli, P., Card, S.K., Information foraging. Psychological Review, 1999.
24. ISO 9241 - 11 Ergonomic Requirements for office Work with VDT's - Guidance on Usability. 1991.
25. Reason, J., Human error. 1990, Cambridge: Cambridge University Press.
26. Oostendorp, H.v., & Walbeehm, B.J., Towards modelling exploratory learning in the context of direct manipulation interfaces. Interacting with Computers, 1995. 7(1): p. 3-24.
27. Herder, E., & Van Dijk, B., Site Structure and User Navigation: Models, Measures and Methods. 2003.
28. Botafogo, R.A., Rivlin, E., & Shneiderman, B., Structural Analysis of Hypertexts: Identifying Hierarchies and Useful Metrics. ACM Transactions on Information Systems, 1992. 10(2): p. 142-180.
29. Hilgard, E.R., The trilogy of mind: Cognition, affection, and conation. Journal of the History of Behavioral Sciences, 1980. 16: p. 107-117.
30. Atman, K.S., The conation phenomenon. 1982, University of Pittsburgh School of Education: Pittsburgh.
31. Hershberger, W.A.E., Volitional Action: Conation and Control. Advances in Psychology, 62. 1989, Amsterdam: Elsevier Science.
32. Wechsler, D., Cognitive, conative, and non-intellective intelligence. American Psychologist, 1950. 5: p. 78-83.
33. Emmons, R., Personal strivings: An approach to personality and subjective well-being. Journal of Personality and Social Psychology, 1986(51): p. 1058-1068.
34. Mischel, W., From good intentions to willpower, in P. Gollwitzer & J. Bargh (Eds.): The psychology of action, 1996, Guilford Press: New York. p. 197-218.
35. Huitt, W., Conation As An Important Factor of Mind. 1999, Educational Psychology Interactive. Valdosta, GA: Valdosta State University.
36. Linderholm, T., Predictive Inference Generation as a Function of Working Memory Capacity and Causal Text Constraints. Discourse Processes, 2002. 34(3): p. 259-280.
37. Pettijohn, T., Locus of Control Scale. 2002, Web Survey.
38. Peak Performance, Brain Dominance Questionnaire. 2002. http://www.glencoe.com/ps/peak/selfassess/integrate/
39. Egger, F.N., From Interactions to Tranzactions: Designing the Trust Experience for Business-to-Consumer Electronic Commerce. 2003, Eindhoven: Technische Universiteit Eindhoven.

40. Miron, E.A.M. Analyzing the role of students' goal orientation during their interaction with an ILE. in HCT2003 - The 7th Human Centred Technology Postgraduate Workshop. 2003. Falmer, Brighton, UK.: HCT.
41. Compeau, D.R., and Higgins, C.A., Computer self-efficacy: Development of a measure and initial test. MIS Quart., 1995. 19(2): p. 189.
42. Wammi, Web Usability Questionnaire. http://www.wammi.com/
43. Sumi, The Software Usability Measurement Inventory. http://www.ucc.ie/hfrg/questionnaires/sumi/
44. Ahuja, J.S. and J. Webster, Perceived disorientation: an examination of a new measure to assess web design effectiveness. Interacting with Computers, 2001. 14(1): p. 15-29.
45. Cohen, J., A Power Primer. Psychological Bulletin, 1992. 112(1): p. 155-159.
46. Cockburn, A., & McKenzie, B., What Do Web Users Do? An Empirical Analysis of Web Use. Int. J. Human-Computer Studies, 2000.
47. Rouet, J.-F., Ros, C., Jegou, G., Metta, S., Locating Relevant Categories in Web Menues: Effects of Menu Structure, Aging and Task Complexity, in Human-Centred Computing. Cognitive, Social and Ergonomic Aspects. HCI International 2003 - Conference Proceedings. Crete, Greece., D. Harris, Duffy, V., Smith, M., Stephanidis, C., Editor. 2003, Lawrence Erlbaum Associates, Publishers: Mahwah, NJ. p. 547-551.

Enabling Access to Computers for People with Poor Reading Skills

Albrecht Schmidt[1], Thorsten Kölbl[2], Siegfried Wagner[1], and Walter Straßmeier[2]

[1] Media Informatics Group, Ludwig-Maximilians-Universität München,
Amalienstr. 17, 80333 München, Germany
{albrecht.schmidt,siegfried.wagner}@ifi.lmu.de
http://www.medien.ifi.lmu.de/

[2] Department of Pedagogic and Rehabilitation, Ludwig-Maximilians-Universität München
Leopold Str. 13, 80802 München, Germany

Abstract. Access to information and communication using the Internet is still very limited for people with poor reading skills. Current mainstream web-applications such as email or web-shops are designed for people that have good reading skills. In our research we investigated the use of a web based email system by people with poor reading and writing skills. As literacy is not an absolute concept and people's abilities differ by a great extent. Recent reports suggest that even in developed countries up to a quarter of the population have only elementary reading skills. In our research we investigate how web applications can be designed to be usable by this group of people. In this paper we report an analysis of a password based logon procedure and suggest an alternative. The development method use is based on the idea of participatory design, includes investigations and studies and lasted over about 4 months. In a study we could show that the login time can be significantly reduced for those users using an image based authentication method. Furthermore it showed that this method can be used by the users without help. For our experience with working with users we suggest general design guidelines for building UIs for people with a low level of literacy.

1 Introduction

Information access appears to become ubiquitous. Access to Internet and email communication is available to everyone. Infrastructure is in place to allow people to use these technologies virtually everywhere. Looking closer it becomes apparent that the usage of information and communication technology is ubiquitous but mainly for the well educated ones, see [Cps00] for figures in the US; similar figures can be found for other countries. For many people with lower education or less intellectual abilities access to communication and information is often still very difficult. The research described in this paper investigates how the user interface design can help to create universal access for all and how to include people with lower education and less intellectual abilities.

In our work we looked especially at people with poor reading and writing skills. In our case these people also have a lower overall educational level. To our knowledge it is fairly common that reading skills and educational level are linked. Our study con-

C. Stary and C. Stephanidis (Eds.): UI4All 2004, LNCS 3196, pp. 96–115, 2004.

centrates on young people but many of the conclusions we draw are also applicable to other groups that have difficulties with written language.

1.1   Reading Skill and Computer Usage

Literacy and the ability to write is not just a binary state. The ability of people differs to a great extent. Recent reports show that even in well developed industrial countries we can not assume that everyone is able to read and understand a book. As summarized in a recent large scale study "this means that almost one-quarter of young people in Germany can only read at an elementary level (OECD average: 18%)" [Pisa00, p8]; see also [Oecd03]. For the purpose of our work we discriminate groups of people with different levels of literacy:

- Group A: people who can read and understand a whole book
- Group B: people who are able to read a multi-page article in a magazine
- Group C: people who can read a short article in a popular daily newspaper
- Group D: people who can read a newspaper headline
- Group E: people who can read their name
- Group F: people who can not read at all

The capacity to write is from our experience closely related to reading skills and therefore it is clear that many people also have problems creating written text. However in most cases people can not clearly be assigned to one group. The effort people have to put in to read must be also taken into account. Some people may be able to casually read an article or pick up a headline of a newspaper passing someone reading on the train; whereas others may need a significant amount of time and effort to read a heading or a single sentence.

The group we are working with and for which we have designed the systems are young people in group C and D. For most of the users reading a headline or a short article will require that they concentrate and put in significant effort into the task. However all of them are very interested in the use of email and the WWW.

Looking at recent figures [Cbs00] it shows that people with less education and lower personal budgets are the group of people which is least active with regard to using computers for information access and communication. This fact has to be taken into account when considering solutions. Options that are expensive and would require a special computer or specific hardware peripherals are at current not practical.

1.2   Designing an E-Mail Client

At the department of pedagogic and rehabilitation at the University of Munich a computer course for young people from a school for children with special needs is offered. The course is once a week two hours and runs over 4 months. In the course there is a one-to-one ration between students from university and young people from the school. The students explain the programs and help with doing the tasks. The objective is to give the young people a basic knowledge of text processing, Internet browsing, and email communication. Within this group of users email is one application that is of great interest. Email allows communication with friends and family, is used to coordinate leisure activities, and gives an opportunity for requesting information. These issues are important reasons for the young people to take part in a computer course.

One of the initial aims of the course was to enable participants to use particular applications unsupervised after the course. During the course it became apparent that the most popular application – a web-based email program – was very hard to use by the participants if they had no help. Many of the problems seen are due to the poor reading and writing skills of the young people on the course. At first it seemed obvious that using a program of which the main function is to write and read texts is difficult to use for someone having little skills in this domain. However when observing the users and talking to them during the course it became clear, that the problems are very much related to the way these applications are designed and implemented. In many cases the actual texts in the emails were short enough to understand for the users but the process of getting to the point where they could read the email (login and navigation) involved a lot of reading. If people have little competence in reading they can not spot the right word to click on – they have to read over the screen to find it.

The observation that web based email programs have on one hand a great appeal to people but are on the other hand hard to use prompted us to look into design options to improve such applications. We identified 4 areas:

- User authentication
- Navigation within the application
- Reading text
- Writing text

In our research we followed a human centred iterative design process. Based on observation, brainstorming, and contextual enquires we sketched scenarios, developed paper prototypes, and implemented functional prototypes for user studies.

When considering our design options we kept close watch on economic constraints for this user group. In most cases these people will not have their own specific computer – they will rather use terminals in Internet cafés or at a friends place.

In this paper we concentrate on user authentication in the context of a web-based email program. First we discuss the problems people with poor reading skill encounter when using traditional authentication methods. Based on this we will discuss options and alternatives. In the user study we report on a comparison of a traditional login as widely use in the WWW and an image based authentication (an adapted version of [Dha00]) in the context of our user group. Additionally to the findings reported in [Dha00] we can show that the time for authentication using the images is significantly faster and that users find it much easier. Finally we discuss some general issues and findings for the implementation of web based applications for people with a low level of literacy.

2   Authentication for People with Poor Reading Skills

Authentication is one of the basic requirements for many web applications ranging from access to restricted material to applications such as email. There are many different ways how authentication can be implemented. In particular we discriminate in our analyses the following

- Password based Systems (e.g. user name and password, PIN access)
- Token based systems (e.g. access using a smart-card or RFID access systems)
- Biometric systems (e.g. finger print scanner, face recognition)
- Image based systems (e.g. Deja Vu [Dha00])

2.1 Analysing Authentication

The obvious requirement of an authentication mechanism is to ensure the system the user is the one he tells he is. This is either done by sharing a secret between the system and the user (e.g. password or sequence of images), by checking a unique biometric feature, or by checking the presence of a physical device. In the following we analyse different methods with regard to users with poor reading skills.

2.1.1 Password Based Systems

During the course the participants used an account with a free web-based email provider [Web03]. This system uses a common authentication method with user name and password. The observation showed that the users had great difficulties to think of a password in the first place. In many cases they chose an obvious password (e.g. their own name or their pet). Furthermore we could observe that logging in to the system provided great difficulties as the password does not show on the screen and hence it is rather difficult for the users to check what they have typed. This resulted in many cases that they got lost within the word and misspelled the password. The frustration when access failed was high, as they could not easily determine why it failed – as they did not see the password. In some cases they misspelled the password and in other cases they also misspelled their user name. Some found it frustrating to type the password again and asked the student helping them to log them in.

It was interesting to observe that the problems with password login persisted over the time of the entire course. Even after 12 training sessions users had great difficulties with logging on to the system. From the observations and the informal interviews we can conclude that typing in a password that is not readable on the screen is a general problem to users with poor reading skills. Workarounds like writing the password in a text editor and pasting it into the entry box seem obvious solutions but are against the basic principle of a hidden password.

2.1.2 Token Based Access and Biometric Systems

An immediate and obvious solution to us was the use of smart cards, iButtons, or a USB-memory with extra software as physical tokens for authentication. A major advantage is that via the device user name as well as password is provided to the system without action by the user other than inserting the device or even just by proximity [Con02].

In a university and school environment this solution seems easily feasible to do. Relying on extra hardware (e.g. card reader) or specific software (accessing a USB memory device) that enables authentication however does limit the applicability. Many participants in the group of users we worked with are from a social background where money is rather limited. Few of them would be able to afford their own computer and if they can there should be no specific requirements to the system.

Token based access is hard to realise in scenarios where users use systems in an Internet café, a public terminal, or a computer at a friend's place. Using physical tokens to authenticate is defiantly a very useful method if the context of usage is limited. For example for giving people with poor reading skills access to computers in their work environment this is a very efficient solution.

Similarly to token based access biometric systems seem to be quite attractive at a first glance [Rat01]. However the problems are similar to the ones stated above. As most systems (in private use as well as for public access) do not have biometric access devices this solution is limited to a specific environment. Again giving users with poor reading skills access to terminals in a school or work environment the use of a finger print scanner is certainly attractive and can make login much quicker. Similar to token based access here too the user name and password is provided in one step.

Both of these solutions seem not practical at current for general use of applications such as a web-based email system. From our enquires and work with the users we can conclude that limiting access to specific machines for main stream applications such as web browsing and email is not desirable.

2.1.3 Image Based Authentication

In our investigations for potential authentication methods we came across an image based approach, called Déjà vu, described in detail at [Dha00]. Further examples are shown on at [Dha03]. The idea of the approach is that people select and remember images instead of a password. Dhamija and Perrig studied their system with computer science students and could show that these people could remember the images better than passwords. However as their user group was literate and well trained computer users the time difference for login was not significant. To us the idea of using images instead of words was compelling as our user group has much less difficulties handling photos and graphical representations than writing.

With our user group the idea on relying on recall rather than on remembering was a further issue that made the idea attractive to us. From our observations we saw that users had great difficulties in remembering abstract concepts in general and passwords in particular.

An important aspect for us was that this method did not rely on any additional hard- or software to be installed on the client machine. The mechanism can be implemented as a standard web page based on HTML and images. The security can be increased by providing a connection using HTTPS.

2.1.4 Minimal or No Authentication

One option that we discussed was to minimize authentication or to work without authentication at all. Here the idea is that a user name that can be typed in as text is enough to access the web based application. This may be an option in a trusted environment such as a small workplace or in a family but seems not applicable in a wider context. If the user is working always from the same machine it is possible to restrict access to a specific machine and have no authentication or only minimal authentication.

We think however that telling people who can not read well that they need no authentication and hence no private access to data violates the idea of universal accessibility.

Giving people means to access data without help from others and hence without supervision is certainly an important goal. From our informal interviews and observations we can see that people would like to have the opportunity to have private non-supervised access to email and the WWW. Using current systems and mechanism this is however not possible for most of our users. Authentication is one major issue to this. The following study shows that there is real potential of achieving unsupervised access to information and communication given the tools are designed in the right way.

3   Comparing Authentication Methods – An Empirical User Study

Our experience with working with the users showed that the acceptance for systems or the ability of people for performing a certain task is very hard to predict. During the course some tasks in text processing that we regarded simple provided great difficulties to the users whereas other – to us rather complex tasks – were done easily. A lot of assumptions that we make are targeted towards users with good reading skills and not easily transferable to users who can read poorly.

To evaluate the potential of using image based authentication for users with poor reading skills and a general low educational level we decided to do an empirical user study. We decided to compare a password based authentication system with a system using images. The password based system was used by the users throughout the course. The new images based system was introduced in the experiment.

3.1   The Participants in the Experiment and the Environment

The participants in the experiments were children and young people between the age of 14 and 18. All of them visit a school in the centre of Munich (Germany) that is specialized on pupils with special needs. The central problem most of these young people have is poor reading skills and generally low educational level. Some of them are very slow when performing cognitive tasks; others are hyperactive (Attention-Deficit/Hyperactive, ADHD). Some are from immigrant families and have never developed their German language skills properly. Besides these intellectual problems the users formed a lively group of young people interested in the use of computers and keen to go on the Internet and to communicate via email. It was particularly interesting to see that they wanted to communicate via email as everyone else using written text and not audio attachments. Using the same communication channel as others they saw a chance to for communication without standing out. The overall group was 12 people, on average about 10 of them attended the course.

The computer course is run as cooperation between the University of Munich and the school. It provides a one-to-one teaching situation where one student (most of them study for a teacher degree) helps one pupil, see figure 3. It is held at the University in a standard computer lab, equipped with 12 PC that have Internet access and word processing programs installed. The course that runs over 15 weeks aims to teach the pupils' basic skills for using a computer for text processing, Internet access and email communication. For email communication each pupil gets an account with a big German Web-Mail service [Web03]. The accounts are created by the people running the course.

Two of the authors were supervising the course. They regularly observed the young people throughout the course and conducted informal interviews. Using these methods general problems with using computers by this user group are identified. The knowledge gained triggered the search for alternative solutions. In cooperation with the other authors and with students from Media Informatics and Pedagogic alternatives have been developed and analysed. In particular the design of a Web-mail software for users with poor reading skills was at the centre of our interest. In this experiment we concentrate on the authentication process. Further issues with regard to an email client are discussed later.

3.2 Experimental Setup

In the experiment two authentication methods are compared. The overall process is of great interest to us, but we especially looked at the following parameters, considering them as dependent variables in the experiment:

- time needed to log on to the system
- number of retries needed to log on
- the help needed for performing the authentication
- performance in remembering how to log on
- performance in remembering username and password
- subjective level of frustration when authentication fails

We compared two different systems. The first system is a password based login and the other is an image based login. Both are implemented as web applications and are linked from the browser homepage. This home page is already selected at the start of the experiment.

3.2.1 Condition A: Password Based Login

Condition A was the standard login procedure using a web form, see figure 1. The user name is the email address. The passwords selected by the users are generally short and are real words. Using more complicated words (and hence providing more security) would have made it impossible for many of the users to remember their password. Some of the browsers performed word completion for the user name input box.

The accounts were initially created for the users. Authentication consisted of the following steps. Entering the user name, the password and then pressing the login button.

3.2.2 Condition B:
Image Based Authentication

Condition B was to login using an image based authentication mechanism, as depicted in figure 2. This method is implemented as described in [Dah00] with minor modifications.

Authentication is a process that involves the following steps. First the user enters his or her user name. Inputting the name is checked against a database containing all user names. A list of names matching the already typed part of the name is displayed. This list contains the user name and a picture. If the part of the name is unique the user name is auto-completed. If the part already typed is not a sub-string of any user name the list is empty and users can recognize that there is a misspelling.

WEB.DE als Startseite einrichten

Profi-Suche   Hilfe

Handy   **WEB.DE FreeMail**
Spiele   WEB.DE Nutzer
ften
ıenKlick   Passwort

ngebote

nzeigen   Login   ohne SSL

ufgeben   E-Mail, SMS, Fax,
             Voicebox, Telefonieren
             Jetzt registrieren!
                      Fragen/Status

Fig. 1. Screen shot of the web mail login.

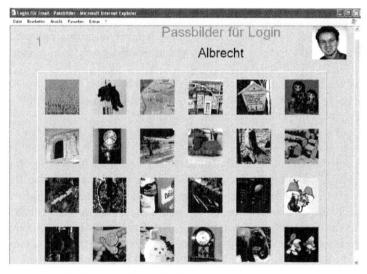

Fig. 2. Screen shot of the image based authentication.

In a second step the user is presented with a set of 24 images – he or she selects one of them by clicking on it. This is repeated two more times with two more sets of images. There is no overlap between the images in three sets. The images that the users select are their password and have been selected by the users themselves from the same sets. After all 3 images have been selected the user is authenticated or authentication has failed. The security achieved by this system (13824 options) is similar to a 4 digit PIN, for details see [Dah01].

3.3 Experiment

Over a period of 8 weeks before the experiment the users worked with the password based web mail system. By the beginning of the experiment they were familiar with this system and had practiced authentication for at least 8 times (most of them much more often).

In the first week of the experiment we introduced the users to the image based authentication system. They selected their pictures that serve them as password by them self. This took place at the beginning of that lecture. At the end of the lecture (about 60 minutes later) they practiced again to log in using the pictures they had selected at the beginning. After this all pupils were asked to remember their pictures as they would need them for login in the following weeks. We also asked them to choose a 4 digit PIN at the beginning of the lecture and repeated this PIN an hour later. They were also asked to remember the PIN. We did not follow up the PIN in the experiment as nearly all users chose trivial PINs (e.g. 1234) and had even problems remembering them over the time of the lecture.

In the second week of the experiment the participants were asked to login to both systems. Half of the group did password based login first. The other half started with image based login. The groups were chosen at random. Additionally to authentication we also investigated further issues in using an email client that was specifically designed with the target group in mind. In this session we recorded the time needed for authentication, whether or not help was needed, number of retries needed; furthermore we asked after the test a number of questions investigating further (subjective) parameters.

In the fifth week (leaving intentionally a gap of 3 weeks) we asked the participants again to log on to both systems. They did not use image based log in the time between. Here we recorded similar parameters as before.

As there was a one-to-one relationship between pupils and students we asked the students to record the parameters of interest. Each of them had a form that described the tasks to carry out in the experiment and also which parameters to record and which questions to be asked. Additionally we used a proxy server to log the user's interaction with the web site of the web-mail provider. On the experimental email client that we prototyped on our server we used a user tracking mechanism (a click stream log) to see how long certain steps took. The data recorded on the server and on the proxy was also used to validate the manual recordings done by the students.

Throughout the experiment we conducted informal interviews with the pupils and the supervising students on the issues they liked and on problems that have occurred. We asked the participants for suggestions what they feel could be made more suitable for them. Figure 3 depicts the one-to-one relationship during the experiment (pupils wear headphones).

3.4 Results of the Experiment

We made quantitative measurements after two weeks and after 5 weeks in the experiments. The results from both measurements show that using image based authentication is significantly faster and that the level of help required is much higher for using traditional password based login. In the following we discuss the results for both sessions separately.

Fig. 3. One-to-one relationship between students and pupils during the course and experiment.

3.4.1 Experimental Results After 1 Week

10 participants took part in the experiments; 2 were ill and did not attend the course on that day. All participants remembered the login procedure for both methods; even so they had practiced the image based method only in the previous lecture.

In table 1 the figures are shown for the first login to both systems after one week. More pupils could login without help at the first try with the image based method compared to the well trained password based method. Under condition B it was interesting to observe that pupils who did it wrong at the first try understood immediately what they did wrong (e.g. selected wrong picture, clicked to fast and selected by accident a picture on the next screen) and performed the second try mostly without help and succeeded. Under condition A many of the pupils were frustrated when authentication failed as they did not see what they typed wrong as the password text was hidden.

Table 1. Comparing logins after 1 week. The figures show the number of occurrence under each condition.

	Condition A password	Condition B image-based
Pupils could log in without help at the first try	3	5
Pupils needed help to login or required more than one try	7	5

Figure 4 shows the time needed for login by the participants. The overall time needed to login was recorded by the supervising students and validated against the log-files. 8 data pairs were gained and could be used, for 2 participants the data was incomplete (students did miss to record the time, the proxy was not set, or cached pages were accessed and hence no log entries were available).

Time required to login after 1 week

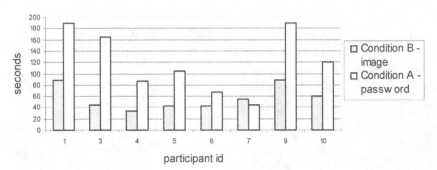

Fig. 4. One-to-one relationship between students and pupils during the course and experiment.

The average for Condition A (password login) is 121 seconds with a standard deviation of 56 and for condition B (image login) it is 57 seconds with a standard deviation of 21. Comparing the average of the login time within the group using the student's t-test showed that image based login is significant faster than password based login (calculated value for p is 0.011).

All of the pupils could remember the pictures they had selected the week before. Some of the pupils however even did not remember their password (used in Condition A) which they had practiced over 9 weeks by then. The subjective level of frustration was much lower with the image based login as the effort for repeating the procedure (selecting images on three successive screens) was considered by the participants as much less than retyping the password.

Asking the pupils as well as the supervising students which of the methods they think the participants could perform on their own without help nearly all voted for the image based authentication scheme. 3 out of 10 pupils however said they would prefer the password based system as they did not want to learn something new, even so the method they already know may be more complicated. Asking the pupils which authentication systems they would be comfortable using at home without help 8 voted for the image based method and only 2 for the trained password based system.

3.4.2   Experimental Results After 5 Weeks
9 participants took part in this session, 3 did not attend class at this day due to various reasons. Again all participants remembered both login procedures. All pupils remembered their images and could log in without help. Using the password based system less than half of the pupils managed to login without help, see table 2 for details.

The difference between the times needed for login between the two methods was similarly to the experiment after 1 week. All but one of the pupils could log on even faster than after one week – without training in between, see figure 5. The average time for authentication was reduced to 36 seconds, with a standard deviation of 22. This indicates that if people use the system more often they are likely to increase the speed.

Table 2. Comparing logins after 5 weeks. The figures show the number of occurrence under each condition.

	Condition A password	Condition B image-based
Pupils could log in without help at the first try	3	7
Pupils could log in without help with two tries	1	2
Pupils needed help to login	3	0
Data for pupils missed under the condition	2	N.A.

time to login, comparing two sessions

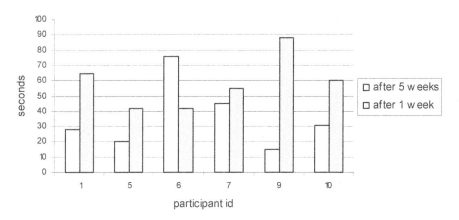

Fig. 5. Time needed for image based login at different times.

From the log files we could also observe that a second try did not cost a lot of time. This is similar to people with good reading and writing skills – for them retyping the password does not cost too much time either. This also reflected in the subjective frustration felt by the participants. Using the image based login they did not feel very much frustrated when they had to do a second try. Having to repeat the password login procedure they tended to ask the student working with them for help because they found it frustrating.

The overall feedback we got in the interviews with the students and pupils was that they liked the image based system and preferred it over the password based system. Especially the pupils gained a good mental model of the image based authentication. To them it was clear how it worked, what could go wrong, and how they could correct their action. They indicated that this gave them the confidence that they would be able to use it by themselves.

There was some discussion about the images we used in our prototype, see figure 2. We used natural images taken from our large collection of digital images. In the paper by Dhamija and Perrig they suggest additionally the use of random pictures

[Dah00]. We decided against random pictures as we assumed that the pupils will remember natural pictures easier. The pupils ask for more interesting pictures. We then asked how they felt about using product pictures, brand name symbols and company logos. To our surprise all of the pupils replied very positive and found it a great idea. They mentioned that this would be very "cool" and that they would like such pictures better than the ones we presented. The domain most often identified was pictures and logos of mobile phones, some also suggested symbols of well known fast food chains or logos from a major car manufacturer. This may be an interesting option for introducing advertising partners in such systems without losing the clarity of the user interface.

4   Designing for People with Poor Reading Skills

Authentication is only one issue in the redesign of a web mail client for people with poor reading skills. However as we saw with authentication it is important to study closely what issues are relevant for this group of users. For us the feedback from the pupils as well as from the students helping the pupils proved extremely valuable. Even so the intellectual capabilities of some of the pupils are limited their taking part in a user centred design process worked very well and the findings reflect their needs.

In the following we introduce briefly the prototype of a web mail program and then conclude a set of general design rules for building applications for people with low levels of literacy.

4.1   Towards a New Web-Mail Program

Our observation showed that there are several areas that need to be addressed when designing a new web-mail client for our target group. These issues are introduced to give the reader an understanding how we carried out our investigations.

4.1.1   States and Navigation Complexity

Analysing the use of email programs for our target audience showed that those products offer a great number of functions that are hardly used and that on the other hand make it rather difficult to use the software. In particular the number of different states one can be in made the use more complex. In our approach we attempted to reduce the number of states and thereby minimize navigation.

In our prototype we combined the two most important states of a standard email program into one. Reading an email and reply to an email is not separated. When reading an email there is always a field attached that allows to directly replying to the sender without further navigation, see figure 6 for a screen shot. The top part of the program indicates who is logged on and provides access to all functions. The middle part shows the email text and the bottom part offers a form for replying to the sender.

The navigation (top part of the screen) does not change throughout the application. The upper frame always stays the same and offers access to the functions offered.

Fig. 6. Screen shot of the email prototype.

4.1.2 Written Words Are Precious

After having seen how slow the participants typed and how much effort they had to put in creating text we came to recognize how precious each word is that they have typed. For our design it became important that all written text is persistent – even when there is navigation in between.

Conceptually we attached a reply data record to each email. Whenever someone would read an email this reply record would show too. Initially this is empty but as the user writes a reply it is kept in this record attached to the email. This record exists persistently; it is only cleared when the user sends the email or when the user chooses to delete the reply. For example when the user start answering an email, then navigates to another email and comes back later to the first one the reply text is as it was before. We applied this approach to all text input fields in the application. All text that is entered is persistent.

4.1.3 Avoid Making the User Read

Again after having observed how much time and effort the users have to invest to read a single sentence we realized that we should avoid making them read if we can. Providing a warning or an error message is already annoying for standard computer users [Cop03] but makes applications extremely hard to use for people who have difficulties in reading.

In our design we avoided the use of confirmation requests, warnings, and error messages by consequently designing the application in a way that actions are reversible. The previously mentioned approach of making text input persistent was one result of this design choice. Instead of asking the user whether or not to keep the started email we just keep it. If the user wants to have it again she can go back and if it is not required there is no great expense in storing the data.

4.1.4 Offer Output Alternative

In a first design session – without the users – we anticipated a system that would read the text to users instead of making them read their emails. However when talking to the users we realized that they wanted to read their email.

In our prototype we included both options, see figure 6. The text is displayed and each sentence can be read by clicking on the sentence or on the loudspeaker icon next to it. In our observation we saw that users combined both modalities in use.

To ease reading we introduced a mechanism that highlights a sentence when the mouse is move over that sentence. For our target audience this helps to keep the focus on the current sentence they were reading. We also discussed a mechanism where when the text is read to the user the word that is read is highlighted. This could help users to improve their reading skills while using the program. This feature is not yet evaluated.

4.1.5 Visually Design and Fonts

One main criticism of standard web mail programs articulated by the users was that the interfaces are too packed with information and that they found it very hard to find the actual email without reading all the news and adverts around. People with good reading skills scan the page and find the area of interest – for users with poor reading skills this does not work in the same way. They have to read their way to the relevant part.

In our design we chose a clear layout, a school font, and spacing between sentences. This proved to help people reading and understanding.

It is obvious that to run a free email system there has to be a way of getting the money for it – and advertisements are one of the most common ones. The users we work with do not object having adverts, in fact they are probably more receptive for advertising than many other user groups. However advertisement as it is used so far (e.g. pop ups on user actions, cluttered screens) does not reach them. It increases just the level of frustration when using the system. A design alternative for the inclusion of adverts would be a box at a fixed position in the design of the application or as earlier suggested pictures related to a brand in the image based login procedure.

4.1.6 Results Form a First User Test

At this moment we have not fully analysed the user study of the web mail prototype. From the interviews we conducted we conclude that users subjectively like the approach. More than two third of the users preferred the new application after one session. They especially valued that they felt they would be able to use it independently. The measured productivity (reading email and replying) of the newly developed prototype was at the first use similar to the productivity with the web mail program that users had practiced for 10 weeks.

4.2   Guidelines to Design for People with Low Competence in Literacy

In this section we summarize the experience gained in our user centred design experiment and the user studies conducted with people who had little competence in literacy. Some of the issues we could underline with quantitative results (in particular with respect to authentication), others are obvious rules in HCI but their application for this user group may be different, some further issues appeared from anecdotal evidence and may lead to discussion.

4.2.1   Authentication

Password based authentication is a source of frustration for people with little competence in literacy. The main problem is that they can not see what they type when typing the password and that spell-checking is not possible in this domain. If passwords are used and people are free to choose them – they will most likely select trivial passwords.

From our experiments we recommend to avoid password based authentication for this user group when possible. Furthermore it is advisable to check the spelling of the user name as the user types and give notification on misspelling of the user name as early as possible. This is hard to implement on a system with millions of users, on local systems this is fairly easy. If the number of people is fairly small images of the user's can replace user names (as common in many operating systems available nowadays).

Alternatives for Authentication:

- Image based authentication as introduced in [Dah00]
  As we showed in our user study this method is highly appropriate for people with poor reading skills. It is generally applicable to applications on the WWW as well as for local applications.
- Token based access
  In a controlled environment such as a workplace or school the use of tokens for authentication is a possible alternative. Depending on the technology there may be requirements for modifications of the computers (e.g. an additional card reader). Using USB-tokens avoids additional hardware however software modification is required on each system. A further problem, especially when considering the users we worked with, is the fact that users may lose or forget the token.
- Biometric access
  Again in a controlled environment such the use of biometric systems provides an alternative. Here additional hard and software at each terminal is required. However not tokens can be lost.

4.2.2   Messages, Warnings and Errors

As a foremost goal in the design one should avoid creating extra text that has to be read by the user. This applies especially to confirmation boxes but also to warning and error messages. In many domains this requires a general redesign of the applications as these messages are included for a reason.

Our experience with the design of the email client showed that if actions are reversible and information is persistent the need for messages to the user can be significantly reduced.

4.2.3 Text and Visual Appearance

There are plenty of rules and guidelines on how to optimize the layout for text on the WWW. However these findings do not necessarily apply to people with poor reading skills. Most recommendations assume users with a fairly high level of reading literacy. We took inspiration from school books for children that start to learn to read and are designed accordingly. These design concepts have then been validated our experiments with the users.

In particular the following issues are of interest

- **School fonts**
  In our prototypes we used fonts that are clearly readable and similar to fonts used in school books for the first years. We realize that there are significant differences between regions and countries so it is hard to give a general recommendation. For our users it proved valuable to have these easy to read fonts.
- **Screen layout**
  In our observations we realized that users have great difficulties finding elements on the screen (e.g. where do I put in the user name). Therefore it is an important consideration to have a consistent and simple page layout that does not change throughout the application.
- **Proximity and distance, gestalt**
  Similarly to the page layout it is important to design the text layout carefully. Especially it is important to ensure that users understand what belongs together. Keeping Gestalt perception in mind is very important. Having structured the layout in effective groups makes orientation without reading easier.
- **Text and information**
  Considering the difficulties users have with reading the choice of words and the structure of sentences is of great importance. Here it is important to write in clear and short sentences avoiding complicated and long words.
- **Pair images and text**
  Where applicable we paired text and photos or images. This makes reading easier and at the same time provides an educational benefit. The users may learn to read new words by using the applications.
- **Combine audio and text**
  If texts are longer it can be beneficial to provide text in written form as well as the option to play it. Here it is important that the junk size of the audio that can be played is appropriate. For our email program using sentences as chunked proved useful. Giving a visual feedback which word is read can also help to educate the users and improve their reading skills by using the system.
- **Never lose a written word**
  As mentioned earlier users put great effort into writing therefore losing words is not acceptable. The design should be persistent.

- **Help to create written words**
  There are various options to help the user to write. One way we explored is to auto-complete their writing when only one option is left (e.g. we used this for user names). Other options are to provide the user with wizards that help to create text in a certain domain (e.g. creating an email text explaining that you are late by only providing the time). Here the advantage is that the result of the operation is text of good quality (the receiver will not notice the poor writing skills of the sender). However the effect may be that the ability to write will even more degrade.

Besides the issues mentioned above it is important to look at the basic HCI guidelines [Shn97] with regard to users that have little competence in literacy. We had the experience that it is of great value for the users if the cost of failure is minimal and if system states are clear and visible.

4.3   Expert Evaluation of UIs for People with Poor Reading Skills

In the process of designing together with the participants we realized that our experience and expertise in user interfaces does not necessarily help us to predict how people with poor reading skills will perform in the task. In many cases we just had difficulties imagining what the problems could be.

The obvious issues to look at when doing an expert evaluation [Nie90] is to carefully assess the reading and writing tasks involved in using the interfaces. For writing this is fairly easy however for reading this becomes more difficult. Experts usually have very good reading skills and have acquired a way of scanning web pages or texts without really reading them. It is therefore important to specify which reading task has to be performed in order to do an expert evaluation of a UI.

One method that helped us to determine how hard or how easy to read a page is was to typeset the page in a font with symbols and also type out the word we are looking for in the same font. The effort we had to put in to find the word seemed very comparable to the tasks some of the users with very poor reading skills performed. This helps especially to structure the layout and to determine the amount of text acceptable.

The following example is to illustrate the approach, see figure 7. In the clear text we will not feel much difference when asked to find the word "Subject" but when looking at the text in symbol font and we are asked to find "♦♦♌℮ℳℳ♦" (again Subject) we see that a clear structure does really help.

5   Conclusions and Further Work

In our research we realized that access to information and communication using computers is very difficult for people with poor reading and writing skills. In a user centred design approach we investigated problems related to the domain and explored solutions that ease the path for people with a low level of literacy for using information technology.

Text in a symbol font:	Text in a symbol font (structured):
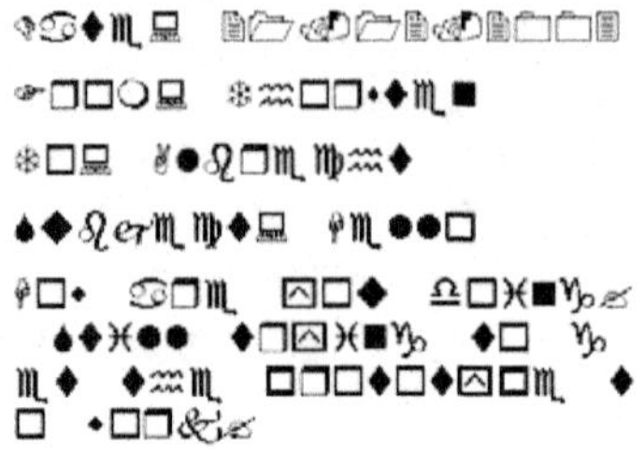 *(symbol font text)*	 *(symbol font text)*
In clear text	In clear text (structured):
Date: 21.12.2003 From: Thorsten To: Albrecht Subject: Hello How are you doing? Still trying to get the prototype to work?	Date: 21.12.2003 From: Thorsten To: Albrecht Subject: Hello How are you doing? Still trying to get the prototype to work?

Fig. 7. Structured and unstructured text in symbol font an as clear text.

To our user group email is an important and interesting application. Considering design issues an email application includes many concepts that can be generalized for other applications on the web. In the first stage of the project we were particularly interested in authentication. Here we looked especially for methods that would allow the user to access information systems without external help.

Comparing different methods for authentication we could show that for people with a low educational level and difficulties in reading and writing image based authentication is significantly faster than using passwords. In our study we found also that people could deal better with that system and did at large not require help. Additionally it was interesting to observe that all participants were able to remember their pictures, even after several weeks without problems. In comparison most of them had great difficulties to remember a password or a PIN.

Based on our study with a prototypical email application we found several design issues. Such as that screen layout and fonts used are even more important than for people with good reading skills. Furthermore we realized that persistence of written text is a foremost goal as it is a great effort for this user group to create text – even if it is just a single word. Beyond that we could observe that there is a chance for educational benefit for the users if interfaces are designed multimodal (e.g. audio and written text) or when pictures are used together with words.

Working with people with poor reading and writing skills we realized how difficult it is to image how they perceive a layout. We used a method where we rendered pages with a symbol font and made ourselves search for a word (also rendered in the same symbol font) to evaluate how well structured pages are for people who have great difficulties reading.

Some of the users we worked with had a very low educational level; however this did not complicate the user centred design process. Observing them and there participation in the experiment shaped decisions from an early stage in the project.

In future work we explore more issues related to the email client mentioned here only briefly. In particular we compare the impact of different decision on productivity and performance. Furthermore we started to implement a general library for image based authentication for web applications.

Acknowledgment

We like to thank the students at the pedagogic institute that volunteered to take part in the course an act as one-to-one tutor for the pupils. We like to acknowledge the participation of the pupils and their willingness to explore new ideas together with us. We like to thank Volker Behringer and Heiko Drewes for the software implementation of the prototype. We are grateful for the help of Heike Flammensbeck in organizing the course and the experiment. Many ideas were contributed by the students of the HCI class at the media informatics group at the University of München held by one of the authors.

References

[Con02] Corner, M., Noble, B. (2002). Zero-interaction authentication. In Proceedings of the Eighth International conference on Mobile Computing and Networking (MOBICOM 2002), p 1-11.

[Coo03] Cooper, A., Reimann, R.M. (2003). About Face 2.0: The Essentials of Interaction Design. John Wiley & Sons; 2nd edition (March 17, 2003).

[Cps00] CPS August 2000. Home Computers and Internet Use in the United States: August 2000 (P23-207). http://www.census.gov/prod/2001pubs/p23-207.pdf

[Dha00] Dhamija, R., Perrig, A. (2000). Déjà Vu: A User Study. Using Images for Authentication. proceedings of the 9th USENIX Security Symposium, August 2000, Denver, Colorado.

[Dha03] Dhamija, R. (2003). Déjà Vu: Using Images for User Authentication. Project Homepage, visited 2004-02-15. http://www.sims.berkeley.edu/~rachna/dejavu/

[Nie90] Nielsen, J. & Molich, R. (1990). Heuristic evaluation of user interfaces, Proceedings of ACM CHI'90 Conf., Seattle, 1-5 April 1900, pp 249-256.
(additions at http://www.useit.com/papers/heuristic/)

[Oecd03] The OECD international program for student assessment. Homepage, visited 2004-02-15. http://www.pisa.oecd.org/

[Pisa00] Stanat, Artelt, Baumert, Klieme, Neubrand, Prenzel, Schiefele, Schneider, Schümer, Tillmann, Weiß (2000). PISA 2000: Overview of the Study. Design, Method and Results. http://www.mpib-berlin.mpg.de/pisa/PISA-2000_Overview.pdf

[Rat01] Ratha, N. K., Connell, J. H., Bolle, , R. M. (2001). Enhancing security and privacy in biometrics-based authentication systems. IBM Systems Journal. Volume 40, Number 3.

[Shn97] Shneiderman, B. (1997). Designing the User Interface: Strategies for Effective Human-Computer Interaction, 3rd Edition, Addison-Wesley.

[Web03] Homepage of WEB.DE FreeMail (2003). visited 2004-02-15. http://web.de

Personalisation Meets Accessibility:
Towards the Design of Individual User Interfaces for All

Anita H.M. Cremers[1] and Mark A. Neerincx[1,2]

[1] TNO Human Factors, P.O. Box 23, 3769 ZG Soesterberg, The Netherlands
{cremers,neerincx}@tm.tno.nl
[2] Delft University of Technology, Fac. EEMCS, Dep. Mediamatics, Mekelweg 4
2628 CD Delft, The Netherlands

Abstract. Current accessibility guidelines are composed to allow users with special needs to more easily and comfortably access the Internet. However, most of the guidelines are written with both a 'standard' device and a 'standard' use context in mind, which is the user sitting in front of a desktop computer, in a non-mobile situation at home or at work. This approach does not take into account the likely possibility that an individual who happens to have a certain limitation may also have other personal needs, a certain type of behaviour or activities that require a specific type of support. In this position paper, we plead for a more fundamental approach of dealing with Internet accessibility for people with special needs. We claim that a person with a special need does not differ from a 'regular' individual, in the sense that they are both users who are trying to accomplish a certain task in a certain use context using a certain device, who may have their own personal requirements for support. One could state that in this way accessibility and personalisation are intertwined to result in an optimal, individual user experience, thereby making optimal use of technologies that are currently available ((dedicated) devices, user interface technologies and assistive technologies).

1 Introduction

Current accessibility guidelines are composed to allow users with special needs to more easily and comfortably access the Internet. Users with special needs are generally divided into four groups, namely people with visual, auditory, motor and/or cognitive limitations. Specific guidelines have been drafted to support each of these four groups. Most of the guidelines are written with both a 'standard' device and a 'standard' use context in mind, which is the user sitting in front of a desktop computer, in a stationary situation at home or at work.

Indeed, the guidelines are suitable for most or at least many of the situations in which Internet use by people with special needs is currently being carried out. In general, if web sites adhere to accessibility guidelines, they can be accessed by people who belong to each of the four groups of limitations. It is, probably rightly, assumed that these people mainly use desktop computers that are placed at one specific location, in particular when these computers are equipped with additional assistive devices.

C. Stary and C. Stephanidis (Eds.): UI4All 2004, LNCS 3196, pp. 119–124, 2004.

The possibility to access the Internet has provided people with special needs with a means to more actively participate in the information society, by allowing them to access information resources, communicate with others (for instance people with similar limitations) and carry out commercial transactions. Many of the users report that these possibilities have significantly improved the quality of their lives.

Although the current situation is definitely a large improvement over the situation before, there are still fundamental improvements that could be made. In the current situation people with special needs are basically seen as people belonging to a special group that requires specific provisions. This approach does not take into account the likely possibility that an individual who happens to have a certain limitation may also have other personal needs, a certain type of behaviour or activities that require a specific type of support. Using a desktop computer to access the Internet may not always be the most optimal solution.

In this position paper, we plead for a more fundamental approach of dealing with Internet accessibility for people with special needs. We claim that a person with a special need does not differ from a 'regular' individual, in the sense that they are both users who are trying to accomplish a certain task in a certain use context using a certain device, who may have their own personal requirements for support. Although many of the user needs may become satisfied by using the Internet, this does not necessarily mean that providing Internet access is a goal in itself. Instead, the starting point should be that users are offered electronic *services* (for instance information, communication or transaction services) that support them in meeting their needs in an effective, efficient and satisfactory manner. In this user-centred approach accessibility guidelines should be involved at an early stage in the user interface design process. One could state that in this way accessibility and personalisation are intertwined to result in an optimal, individual user experience, thereby making optimal use of technologies that are currently available ((dedicated) devices, user interface technologies and assistive technologies).

This paper first provides a brief overview of existing accessibility guidelines. Subsequently, issues with respect to personalisation of user interfaces are briefly discussed, in particular the role of user profiles. The next section provides a sketch of the proposed user-centred approach to attain individual accessibility of electronic services. Finally a brief scenario is provided, illustrating the possible application of the approach in a specific case (travel information for persons with cognitive limitations).

2   Current Accessibly Guidelines

The World Wide Web Consortium (W3C) have drafted a set of guidelines for Internet accessibility, called Web Content Accessibility Guidelines 1.0 (version 2.0 is currently a working draft). The guidelines explain in detail how to make a web site accessible for people with a variety of disabilities. Also, a W3C working group has composed so-called User Agent Accessibility Guidelines (version 1.0). They are intended for software developers and explain how to make accessible browsers, multimedia players, and assistive technologies that interface with these. In addition, an expert committee of the European Telecommunications Standards Institute (ETSI) have composed 'Design for All' guidelines for ICT products and services (ETSI, 2002). Although existing guidelines serve a clear goal in advocating Internet access for all, still a number of improvements can be distinguished. First, most of these guidelines have been composed with a desktop environment in mind or are specifically aimed at traditional (telecommunication) products and services. This illustrates a need for additional 'User Agent Accessibility Guidelines' for novel handheld devices and (multimodal) user interfaces. Second, since these guidelines are aimed at people with a variety of limitations, they do not take additional personal needs and requirements into account. Also, in many cases accessibility guidelines are only applied *after* a web site has already been constructed and are consequently not integrated with possible other personalisation and support concepts. Finally, most guidelines aim at Internet access in general and as such do not explicitly support the use of electronic services.

3 Personalisation

The term personalisation is used to indicate the process of online gathering user and context information, which is then used to deliver appropriate services and content, in a format tailor-made to the user's needs. The aim is to offer the user a highly personal experience of the service (Bonett, 2001).

User profiles play a central role in personalised systems. A user profile is a data-record describing the user with his characteristics, abilities, needs and possibly his interaction history (Lauer et al., 2002). User profiles are usually composed and managed at the start and/or in the course of using the system, either by the user or the system or both. They form the basis for presentation of content, choice of interaction modalities and styles that are optimally suited for the individual user. In addition, in the case of location-based services, content, presentation and interaction can be dynamically adapted to create user interface varieties that are optimally suited for the user, his momentaneous information needs, current location, use context and device. In a situation where multiple devices are used consecutively, the interaction history should be kept in order to ascertain continuity of use over different devices (Lindenberg et al., 2003).

Until now, the community working on personalisation of user interfaces has mainly aimed at serving the individual user, and no explicit attention has been paid to people with special needs. Also, the emphasis mainly lies on mobile use in different use contexts, in which access to different services is supported (location-based services). In general, user-centred design has been widely adopted in this community. Even new methods of enhancing user involvement have been developed, such as 'body storming', a method for collecting user requirements at the location where the system supposedly will be used, for instance in public areas (Oulasvirta et al., 2003).

4 Accessibility for All Individuals

In addition to current user-centred design methods, a fundamental approach for developing accessible user interfaces is based on a generic technological framework enabling the application of adaptive techniques. That is, from the early development stages on, the requirements and design specifications should address the capability of a system to manifest the functional core in alternative interactive embodiments suitable for different users, usage patterns and contexts of use (Stephanidis, 2001). In this way, personalisation is "designed into the system", establishing a large design space for adaptation instances (pluralism), reducing the risk for narrowing the focus to typical uses cases of classical desktop settings for Internet access, and supporting the development of Internet services accessible by diverse of users, at diverse times and diverse places.

This approach takes characteristics of the user, the service and the use context into account. These characteristics should be stored in a personal user profile. A well-designed user profiling system may form the key for intertwining personalisation and accessibility requirements. Several aspects of a service may be personalised based on information in the user profile (Cremers et al., 2002). This user profile may be partly generic, and partly service-specific. Which aspects are actually relevant for a certain service depends on the characteristics of the service and the specific goals of the service provider. In addition, the user can indicate which aspects are relevant to him or her, or they may become clear from the way he uses the service (both at the content and the interaction level). Categories of relevant characteristics are:

- personal details of the user (e.g., name, address, sex, year of birth, credit card number, social/cultural affiliations);
- personal characteristics of the user (e.g., capabilities (e.g., memory, sight), personality (e.g., locus of control);
- personal interests of the user (e.g., topics of interest, information sources of interest or topicality of information);
- interaction settings the user prefers (e.g., which devices are being used to access the service, the location at which certain information should be provided, contextual aspects that should be taken into account (e.g., background noise, lighting), timing preferences of providing certain information).

All categories of characteristics may include information related to accessibility. For instance, the personal details may include medical information of the user. The personal characteristics may include requirements for people with special needs, based on W3C guidelines or research on physical and/or cognitive (Neerincx et al., 2001; Lindenberg & Neerincx, 2001) factors that influence performance in web environments. Based on their personal needs, users should be allowed to accept these 'standard' accessibility settings and/or support concepts, or make alterations or additions. Personal interests may also be related to accessibility. For instance, a user in a wheelchair may indicate that he always wants information on physical accessibility of public buildings he is planning to visit. The interaction settings may include information on assistive devices the user may want to use.

5 A Case: Public Transport Information for Persons with Cognitive Limitations

An example of a possible service in which accessibility and personalisation require-ments are combined in one user profile is a system for public transport travel infor-mation for people with cognitive limitations. The profile contains personal details of the user (for instance his address, which is used for planning the trip), personal char-acteristics (including cognitive limitations, which are used to present the travel infor-mation in a way the user can understand, for instance by using simple text, graphical symbols, images and speech support), personal interests (for instance, information on the location of the information desk at a railway station and contact details of a hu-man travel guide), and interaction settings (both for the desktop application to prepare the trip and a handheld device to use during the trip). The profile may even contain a number of default travel descriptions for trips the user regularly takes.

A person with a cognitive limitation who is making use of this service is supported in planning his trip at home using a desktop application. This desktop application adheres to Web Content Accessibility Guidelines that are specifically targeted at people with cognitive limitations (Pijl, 2002). In addition, the service offers personal support to organise the trip (for instance, to select a default travel description or to contact the travel guide). After having planned the trip, the user actually leaves the house, taking with him a handheld device that provides access to the travel informa-tion, which adheres to User Agent Accessibility Guidelines for handheld devices. Using a location-based service (Knaap et al., 2003), the user receives up-to-date travel information as well as additional information, such as information on the loca-tion of the information desk at the station where he is currently located and a possibil-ity to directly contact the personal travel guide.

6 Conclusion

We propose a fundamental approach for developing user interfaces, in which person-alisation meets accessibility. In this approach, accessibility is not a separate, addi-tional aspect or objective of development processes, but integrated into the design and test of personalisation mechanisms for the user interfaces. For example, background noise in the work environment can provide similar constraints to the interaction as the auditory limitations of specific individuals. As another example, lack of experience and/or cultural differences might lead to similar support needs as the cognitive limita-tions of some people. The objective is to establish individual user interface instances for a diversity of users and usage contexts.

References

1. Bonett, M. (2001). Personalization of web services: opportunities and challenges. *http://www.ariadne.ac.uk/issue28/personalization/intro.html.*
2. Cremers. A.H.M., Lindenberg, J. & Neerincx, M.A. (2002). Apples or oranges? A user-centred framework for co-operative user profile management. *Proceedings 7th WWRF meeting, Eindhoven, The Netherlands, 3-4 December 2002.*

3. ETSI (2002). Human Factors (HF): *Guidelines for ICT products and services; "Design for All"*. Final draft ETSI EG 202 116 V1.2.2 (2002-07). Sophia Antipolis, ETSI.
4. Knaap, R. van der, Egeter, B., Giezen, J. en Haastregt, T. van (2003). *Individueel Reizigers Informatie Systeem voor ouderen en gehandicapten: aanpassing dienstverlenings- en systeemconcept (Individual travellers information system for the elderly and the handicapped)*. TNO, Van Haastregt Bedrijfsadviezen en OC Mobility Coaching. Uitgebracht aan: Ministerie van Verkeer en Waterstaat.
5. Lauer, H., Droegehorn, O., Dargie, W., David, K., Kranenburg, H. van, Arbanowski, S., Postmann, E., Busboom, A., Hjelm, J., Charlton, P., Feichtner, C., Heer, J. de, Raatikainen, K., Yanosy, J. (2002). Personalisation: definition of mechanisms and needed service elements for an efficient use of personal information. *White paper WWRF, WG2*, http://www.wireless-world-research.org/.
6. Lindenberg, J. & Neerincx, M.A. (2001). The need for a 'universal accessibility' engineering tool. *ACM SIGCAPH Computers and the Physically Handicapped*. Issue 69. New York: ACM Press, 14-17.
7. Lindenberg, J., Nagata, S.F. & Neerincx, M.A. (2003). Personal Assistant for onLine Services: Addressing human factors. In: D. Harris, V. Duffy, M. Smith, & C. Stephanides (Eds). *Human-Centred Computing: Cognitive, Social and Ergonomic Aspects*. London: Lawrence Erlbaum Associates, 497-501.
8. Neerincx, M.A., Lindenberg, J., Pemberton, S. (2001). Support concepts for web navigation: a cognitive engineering approach. *Proceedings Tenth World Wide Web Conference*. New York: ACM Press, 119-128.
9. Oulasvirta, A., Kurvinen, E. and Kankainen, T. (2003). Understanding contexts by being there: case studies in bodystorming. *Personal and Ubiquitous Computing* 7(2), 125-134.
10. Pijl, D.J. van der (2002). *Criteria voor websites voor verstandelijk gehandicapten: eindrapport van de literatuurstudie, fase 1 inventarisatie (Criteria for websites for the mentally handicapped)*. Hoensbroek, iRv, Kenniscentrum voor Revalidatie en Handicap.
11. Stephanidis, C. (2001). Adaptive techniques for universal access. *User modeling and user-adapted interaction* 11, 159-179.
12. World Wide Web Consortium. *Web Content Accessibility Guidelines 1.0; User Agent Accessibility Guidelines 1.0*. http://www.w3.org.

Interfacing the Interface:
Unification Through Separation

David Crombie[1], Roger Lenoir[1], Neil McKenzie[1], and Klaus Miesenberger[2]

[1] FNB Netherlands, accessible information for people with a print impairment
Molenpad 2, 1016 GM Amsterdam, The Netherlands
projects@fnb.nl
http://projects.fnb.nl/
[2] University of Linz
"integriert studieren - integrated study" (i3s3)
Altenbergerstrasse 69, A-4040 Linz
klaus.miesenberger@jku.at
http://www.integriert-studieren.jku.at/

Abstract. This paper addresses the modeling of user-centred interaction paradigms at a fundamental level. Interfacing can be described as defining and specifying 'connection' points for communication. By providing interactive means of relating flows between these connection points, we can achieve a dialogue. A dialogue becomes a Dialog if a sufficient level of understanding *both ways* is achieved. We consider this to represent the level of accessibility an environment, whether virtual or real, requires. A well balanced design in any information system provides an architecture with built-in accessibility features. To this end, a high level of flexibility and accessibility can be achieved by separating the various entities that are of importance in the communication process. This paper provides an explanation of this approach and an example of its implementation.

1 Introduction

The history of the relationship between people and technology has always been somewhat problematic, which is perhaps unsurprising when one considers the tensions inherent in any interface which seeks to provide a level of communication between the two. This paper suggests that many of these problems stem from poor communication, a situation which arises because technologists and system users often seem to use different languages while essentially working towards common goals. Nevertheless a common language actually does exist as the common elements in the analysis of computer programming and creative thinking are those of structure and form. At this point interfaces provide connection points for enhancing levels of communication.

The potential unleashed by developments in ICT [1, 2] for people with impairments is remarkable, combining as it does the flexibility and power to meet complex needs and complex situations [3, 4]. In many ways this paradigmatic shift [5] can be considered to embody the modern equivalent of common sense. If a suitable level of abstraction is pursued, it can provide archetypes of implemented practical knowledge which can then be accessed by a user and specialised to their personal requirements.

C. Stary and C. Stephanidis (Eds.): UI4All 2004, LNCS 3196, pp. 125–132, 2004.

The Design For All [6] approach is now familiar to most software designers but in many instances this approach is only followed at a relatively superficial level. There remains a need to communicate information to designers and innovators to enable them further to think about an inclusive world, with recent initiatives such as EDeAN [6] and EUAIN [6] pointing the way forward. Naturally, this activity cannot be performed in isolation, as there is a parallel need to educate system users to make their demands more explicit.

Following research into accessibility solutions for print impaired people [7] we have investigated many complex communication problems following the principles of universal design. Accessibility is a word which we are careful to use in its widest sense. The easiest way to understand this is to consider the requirements for accessible solutions as being the same as the requirements for extreme communication solutions.

2   Communication Through Interface Design

2.1   Well-Balanced System Design

A communication network can be described by the common process model shown below. Modelling information can be separated into three phases; information retrieval, information representation and information reproduction. Retrieval concerns the perception of the information: once perceived, this perception is represented in some manner and can then be reproduced for the consumer. This continuous loop is the same for any producer/consumer relationship, where all consumers are also producers and vice versa.

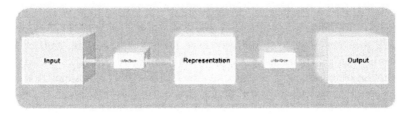

Fig. 1. Simplification of an information processing system.

Different users of the same content necessarily have different perspectives on that content. For example, to academics a book (even a work of fiction) is a reference source for their field. To a layman, reading a book is a leisure activity. To an author, the same book represents a means to communicate concepts. To a publisher, this versatile object is a unit of production in a wider supply chain. Given these multiple perspectives on something as familiar as a book, it is clear that one person's output medium is another's input medium.

When considering physical entity interfaces (tactile, aural or visual), how can we understand the ways in which someone uses sensory information to monitor the external world? How can we understand the techniques used to construct a strategy to achieve their desired goals? If we were able to represent this behaviour (or at least build in some of these notions in 'real world' applications), would this then provide sufficient flexibility to enable different groups of users' groups to use the same piece of software? When considering software user interfaces, we must consider both fixed characteristics (for example a button which cannot be changed, moved or linked to a different action target) and dynamic ones (for example the size, colours, location or semantics of GUI entities). In the latter case, the manifestation of a controller hints at its meaning but how do we parameterise these software controller entities to tie them into the software consistency?

In short, if the design of an information system is well-balanced, it should provide an architecture with built-in accessibility features. By separating the information processing domains we can achieve greater unification by focusing on the points of interaction; that is, the interfaces between the common interface layers.

2.2 Interfacing and Communicating

By addressing the issue of opening up content and its structure for any user, we intro-duce a fundamental question. How does one connect a computer application (which is a dynamic set of concepts with dynamic inter-relations) to the experience of an end user? If we are to design interfaces between the external world and the mental picture of that world which the end user handles to achieve his or her objectives, we go be-yond the level of providing buttons and windows to a computing model. The same pattern of interactions[1] that occur between the end-user's goals and the means of achieving these goals through a computer application, also occur between the soft-ware components of the computer application itself.

If we were able to specify an interfacing paradigm which could be aggregated throughout all of the system design, the opportunity would arise to grant the end-user an intuitive level of interaction between themselves and the computer application at a fundamental level. In order to formulate the basics of such a design, and for us as developers, content providers and distributors to learn from such a design, we must build the notion of multiple perspectives into the design. This implies that all interac-tions between the individual software components, as well as the messages to the end user, should facilitate personalisation. This very much resembles localisation of soft-ware, where important user interface terms are available in various languages and where the preferred language can be selected 'on the fly'.

In order to manage such a design and convey the generic thoughts behind it, we need a metaphorical way of expressing these concepts. Whereas the interaction be-tween an end user and a software application does not (yet) resemble the level of communication between humans, human communication provides the fulcrum for software design processes, the people involved in these processes and the end users. Both groups of users – and many more – can then relate to this set of symbols and concepts. If we build into the design an expression of the processes that can occur

---

[1] Also known as Topic Maps, first fully described in ISO/IEC 13250:2000: various entities in any system that – from any user's perspective - mean something.

(actions, reactions, events and so forth) which mimics communication, we provide a shared framework of concepts. This shared framework could mean more or less the same things to the different groups of participants. We would be able to explicate the communicated entities and, to a certain point, represent the communication process. As we would be able to represent communication, we could control and modify the configuration of this process from both sides of the communication line. We could build in consumer preferences alongside producer, distributor and provider preferences, all the time ensuring that all participants 'talk' by using the same fundamental building blocks. Real communication – as in a dialogue between the various interest groups - could manifest itself as emergent behaviour. Emergent behaviour, however, within a frame of reference.

Naturally, there are numerous advantages to such an approach. The software would be able to rely on a framework of classes that include entities which represent Users, User behaviours and Providers actions, as well as entities that represent production processes and so forth. As these backbone classes exist, the opportunity would arise to personalise the behaviour of these classes. In this way the end user, as well as the producer, would be able to set up the software as preferred. The social impact – for instance - could be the sense of respect that the end-user experiences because the producers have facilitated insight into the content and content provision procedures. For those user groups dependent on accessibility features, this would provide a very definite sense of inclusion, one which might invite many other types of users to participate in the market segment.

3 Building Communication Partnerships

A high level of flexibility and accessibility can be achieved by separating the various entities that are of importance in the communication process. Various groups of users and entities are involved in the dialog between an application and an application user. An application ideally should be seen as a communication partner. Categorising the constituent parts in such a communication process, can be based on three abstract levels of processing as discussed above: Information Retrieval, Information Representation and Information Production. Each processing phase can be represented by its own processing model. Explicating relations between these models enables communication. Rendering the explication of the relations between the three models dynamic facilitates a high level of flexibility in controlling, administrating and personalising this communication. Ideally a well-balanced configuration of such a processing architecture provides accessibility from scratch [7].

3.1 Modelling User Interfaces : Separating Presentation, Content and the User

Following the line of thought described above, we will describe an approach that captures this behavior in an abstract system design. One basis for such a stratification is the idea of separation. If separation occurs between the various elements, the dynamics of the system modules can be contained in such a way that altering or extending any element can take place without causing destruction or compromising the design of another interface or module. An extended diagram of such a system model is provided in Figure 2. The user requirements are detached from the representation system modules. This not only means that the system can support extensibility to itself and to the user requirements, but also that multiple user requirements can be supported through harnessing the inherent dynamism of a well designed interface system.

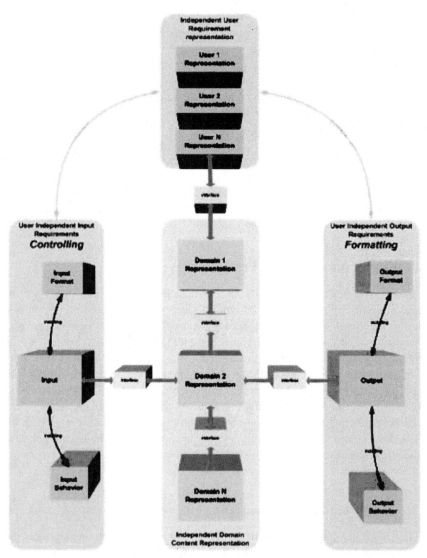

Fig. 2. Separation between layers of accessible information processing components and interfaces between the individual layers and the individual components.

3.2 Presentation: Domain Independent Interaction Models

A further source of separation is through domain independence. This is one good outcome of an extensible system, where any aspect or interaction within the system can function in a different domain. This becomes a difficult task because while it is straightforward and intuitive to make some elements of a system domain independent, the system will be incomplete if time is not taken on making the more difficult elements domain independent. Thus far, the system being described is highly abstract. Such a system comes into fruition when specific behaviours are given to the various parts of the model upon which the system is based.

3.3 Perception Seen as an Interactive Behaviour

Much of the work in defining interaction protocols for all levels of such a system stems from perception. It is important to understand how the environments of the beholder affect the perception of the communication or interaction. Ultimately the system should support communication which allows users to add their own focus on the content. This moves some way towards the interactions being modelled by the users themselves, where the options are sufficiently implicit that a user can choose what to focus on at any given point or during any interaction. By explicating perception models, we provide explicit anchor points in the interaction model, that can function as a 'virtual controller' or 'virtual information point' for producers and providers of information. Modelling perception as an entity enables anticipation behaviour.

3.4 Representing Interfaces for the Underlying Information Domain Model

Application Programming Interfaces (API) that specify how software components talk to each other should cover more than just the 'messages' these API send to each other. Ideally, the messages the components send to each other also contain contextual information. The collection of contextual information that is added to the message as redundant information can be used to communicate this information as parameters that will influence the level of accessibility in the processing that specific information processing components perform. With modern IT solutions in Enterprise Modelling Environments like Application Servers and knowledge management envionments these notions are already in use (Simple Object Access Protocol, SOAP). This is what we mean by design *from scratch* [7] [8].

In order to enhance accessible communication, we require trees of models starting at very abstract levels, but specialising through inheritance and transformational behaviour into particular domains. The most abstract level would have a built-in software interface to facilitate non-destructive and cognition-based information retrieval. Through the definition of a growing and learning class tree representing metamodels, we can ensure a high level of interoperability *between* different information domains. We can also ensure uniform access to all the different information domain models. In this way we can ensure accessibility standards on the level of non-destructive information pre-processing. As communication implies two different participants – the transmitter and the receiver and the creation of a dialogue between them relies on *interaction* between both participants, the pre-processing of information can be considered to be the *interface* to accessibility on the content representation side.

3.5 Expandability

The content provision and transformation model is not based on static entities that only represent the end-result. It also represents the way relations between these end-result entities are treated, presented, transformed and so forth. In this manner we create a context for adding new functionalities and technologies at a later date. The design has a built-in notion of expandability, because the level of representation includes the notion of *changes* in the model. In addition to the newly added technology itself we have a description of the behaviour of that newly added technology. We connect the *description* of the existing technology and the *description* of the new technology to one another and in so doing achieve a high level of accessibility and flexibility.

4 Implementation of Concepts

Alongside the main requirement to provide software frameworks which capture the users' requirements, four important aspects must be borne in mind: scalability, interoperability, adaptability and maintainability. To achieve a harmonious balance, a sufficiently abstract framework is required which provides structures that can be used to group functional modules and the associated consumer and producer requirements. The notion of non-destructive filtering needs to be engrained into the system design.

In a recent project to design a production tool for the automated creation of accessible music formats, an abstract model for the representation for musical content was created. Specialised musical structures can be added through the addition of new subclasses. Each abstract class that describes musical structures, also contains accessibility related methods and the implementation of these accessibility related methods are mandatory. The implementation of these feature happens on the level of use. Specialistic structures can override default (minimal) accessible behavior. This aggregation of accessibility related methods and accessors is distributed throughout the architecture; from content entities to GUI control entities. Accessibility related behavior on the level of content, is also applied on the level of GUI applications. Demonstrating interoperability, the same accessibility requirements were implemented in the development of an accessible maths production tool.

In these projects a clear separation was made between dynamic and static information that models access to the content. Parameters that are used to adapt the behavior of both tools related to end user requirements, producers requirements and distributor requirements are stored in XSL files. These aspects of the software that explicitly require dynamic parameterisation provide associated XSL-(FO) files. This way the adaptability and maintainability of the tools – in their configuration, the storage of sets of preconfigured settings, is ensured. Because these concepts are software design methodology concepts, they can apply to all kinds of information modelling environments.

5 Summary

This paper has argued that the easiest way to approach complex accessibility problems is to consider the requirements for accessible solutions as being the same as the requirements for extreme communication solutions. By considering user centred interaction paradigms and describing these in a set of design patterns, it is possible to extrapolate notions of accessibility to the level of data structures.

References

1. ICT Standards Board Project on "Design for All and Assistive Technologies in ICT, How ICT standards can enable all people in daily living", CEN/ISSS Open Meeting on Design for All and Assistive Technology, Draft Report:
   http://www.cenorm.be/isss/Workshop/Design-for-All/Default.htm
2. IMS (2003). IMS Learner Information Package Accessibility for LIP Version 6.0. Available at: http://www.imsglobal.org/accessibility/index.cfm
3. Miesenberger, K., Klaus, J., Zagler, W. (eds): Computers Helping People with Special Needs - 8th International Conference, ICCHP, Linz, Austria, July 2002, Proceedings, Springer Heidelberg, 2002
4. Winograd, T (2001), Interaction Spaces for 21st Century Computing, in John Carroll (ed.), Human-Computer Interaction in the New Millennium, Addison-Wesley, 2001.
5. Stephanidis, C. (2001) User Interfaces for All: New perspectives into Human-Computer Interaction in C. Stephanidis (Ed), User Interfaces for All – Concepts, Methods, and Tools (pp 3-17). Mahwah, NJ: Lawrence Erlbaum Associates.
6. www.design-for-all.org, www.e-accessibility.org, www.edean.org, www.euain.org
7. Crombie, D., Lenoir, R,, McKenzie, N, (2004) "Accessibility from scratch: How an openfocus contributes to inclusive design, Proceedings ICCHP, Lecture Notes in Computer Scinece Vol. (*forthcoming*). Springer-Verlag, Berlin Heidelberg New York.
8. Kurniawan, S.H., Sutcliffe, A.G., Blenkhorn, P.L. How Blind Users' Mental Models Affect Their Perceived Usability of an Unfamiliar Screen Reader. In M. Rauterberg, M. Menozzi, J. Wesson (Eds.) Human-Computer Interaction (Proceedings of INTERACT'03). Zurich.

Learning Usage Patterns
for Personalized Information Access in e-Commerce

Marco Degemmis, Oriana Licchelli, Pasquale Lops, and Giovanni Semeraro

Dipartimento di Informatica – Università di Bari
Via E. Orabona, 4 – 70125 Bari
{degemmis,licchelli,lops,semeraro}@di.uniba.it

Abstract. The World Wide Web is a vast repository of information, much of which is valuable but very often hidden to the user. Currently, Web personalization is the most promising approach to remedy this problem, and Web usage mining, is considered a crucial component of any effective Web personalization system. Web usage mining techniques such as clustering and association rules, which rely on offline pattern discovery from user transactions, can be used to improve searching in the Web. We present the Profile Extractor, a personalization component based on machine learning techniques, which allows for the discovery of preferences and interests of users that have access to a Web site. More specifically, we present the module that exploits unsupervised learning techniques for the creation of communities of users and usage patterns applied to customers of an on-line bookshop. To support our work, we have performed several experiments and discussed the results.

1 Introduction

In 1999, Ray Oldenburg proposed in [12] three essential places in people's lives: the place we live, the place we work, and the place we gather for conviviality. Although the casual conversation that takes place in cafes, beauty shops, pubs, and town squares is universally considered to be trivial, idle talk, Oldenburg makes the case that such places are where communities can come into being and continue to hold together. These are the unacknowledged agorae of modern life. When the automobile-centric, suburban, fast-food, shopping-mall way of life eliminated many of these "third places" from traditional towns and cities around the world, the social fabric of existing communities started shredding.

The World Wide Web might not be the same kind of place that Oldenburg had in mind, but so many of his descriptions of third places could also describe it. Perhaps the Web is one of the informal public places where people can rebuild the aspects of community that were lost when the malt shop became a mall.

No single metaphor completely conveys the nature of the Web. Virtual communities are places where people meet, and they also are tools; the place-like aspects and tool-like aspects only partially overlap. Some people come to the Web only for the community, some come only for the hard-core information, and some want both. If you need specific information or an expert opinion or a pointer to a resource, a virtual community is like a living encyclopedia. Virtual communities can help their members, whether or not they are information-related workers, to cope with information overload. The problem with the information age, especially for students and knowl-

C. Stary and C. Stephanidis (Eds.): UI4All 2004, LNCS 3196, pp. 133–148, 2004.
© Springer-Verlag Berlin Heidelberg 2004

edge workers who spend their time immersed in the info flow, is that there is too much information available and few effective filters for sifting the key data that are useful and interesting to us as individuals.

Programmers are trying to design better and better software agents that can seek and sift, filter and find, and save us from the awful feeling one gets when it turns out that the specific knowledge one needs is buried in fifteen thousand pages of related information. On the Web the first software agents are available (e.g., Archie, Gopher, Knowbots, WAIS, and Rosebud are the names for different programs that search through the vast digital libraries of Internet and the real-time feed from the news services and retrieve items of interest).

The Web is used to find information and any product that the user needs. In particular, the e-commerce Web sites offer millions of products for sale and a user must choose among so many options. In this situation, the user can easily feel frustrated because he/she receives inaccurate recommendations. To solve this problem, in literature, there are three major categories of recommendation systems: manual decision rule systems, collaborative filtering systems, and content-based filtering agents. Manual decision rule systems, such as Broadvision (www.broadvision.com), allow Web site administrators to specify rules based on demographics or static profiles (collected through a registration process), or session history. Rules are used to affect the content served to a particular user. Collaborative filtering systems, such as Firefly [18], and Net Perceptions (www.netperceptions.com), typically take explicit information in the form of user ratings or preferences, and, through a correlation engine, return information that is predicted to closely match the users' preferences. Content-based filtering approaches such a those used by WebWatcher [9] rely on content similarity of Web documents to personal profiles obtained explicitly or implicitly from users.

Recently, Web mining [21], a natural application of data-mining techniques to the Web as a very large and unstructured information source, had a great impact on Web personalization. Through Web mining techniques, such as the discovery of association rules or sequential patterns, clustering, and classification, we are able to gain a better understanding of Web-user preferences, a knowledge that is crucial for mass customization. At this point in the process, the results of the pattern discovery can be tailored toward several different aspects of Web usage mining. For example, Spiliopoulou et al. [16], Cooley et al. [5], and Buchner and Mulvenna [4] have applied data mining techniques to extract usage patterns from Web logs for the purpose of deriving marketing intelligence. Shahabi et al. [19] and Nasraoui et al. [11] have proposed clustering of user sessions to predict future user behaviour. Sarwar et al. [14] described a method that partitions the users of a collaborative filtering system through a clustering algorithm, and the partitions are used to identify a set of neighbourhoods. Other recent studies have considered the use of association rule mining [2, 20] in recommender systems [8, 10]. For the most part, however, these studies have relied on discovering all association rules prior to generating recommendations (thus requiring search among all rules during the recommendation phase) or on real-time generation of association rules from a subset of transactions within a current user's neighborhood.

In this paper we present a system, the Profile Extractor (PE), that uses information learned from users to construct accurate, comprehensive user profiles [15] and usage patterns. In particular, we present and evaluate the results of the *Usage Pattern Extractor module* that exploits unsupervised learning techniques for the creation of communities of users and usage patterns (clusters and association rules respectively) that can be effectively applied to customers of an on-line media bookshop.

The paper is organised as follows. Section 2 provides analysis of the Profile Extractor system and in particular of the Usage Patterns Extractor module. Section 3 describes how to extract usage patterns. Section 4 describes an experimental session carried out to evaluate the best clustering algorithms to integrate in the Usage Pattern Extractor submodule, and the best parameters to obtain useful association rules. Finally, conclusions are drawn in Section 5.

2   The Profile Extractor System

PE is a highly reusable module that allows to create user profiles to support *one-to-one* marketing actions, and user communities to address clusters of users by means of *mass-marketing* campaigns. It employs both supervised and unsupervised learning techniques. The former are exploited to induce a set of rules, used by a classification module, while the latter are exploited to group users into communities (clusters) and discover association rules used to identify common trends underlying the dataset. The system is able to analyse data gathered from different sources, data-warehouse and transactional systems in order to infer rules describing the customer/user behaviour and more general usage patterns. The complete architecture of the module is shown in Figure 1. The *Profile Rules Extractor* and the *Profile Manager* are the modules mainly involved in the profile generation process, the *Usage Patterns Extractor* implements both a clustering algorithm and a technique for extracting association rules. PE is built upon an intelligent component, called Learning Server, developed in the context of a digital library service [17]. The core of PE is WEKA [22], a machine learning tool developed at the University of Waikato. WEKA provides an implementation of state-of-the-art learning algorithms, which can be applied to a data set expressed in a tabular format called ARFF.

In PE, we developed XWEKA, an XML compliant version of WEKA, that is able to represent input and output in XML format. The *XML I/O Wrapper* is responsible for the integration of the inner modules with external data sources (using the XML protocol) and for the extraction of data required for the learning process.

2.1   The Usage Patterns Extractor Module

The *Usage Patterns Extractor* is composed by three submodules: the *Clustering submodule*, the *Association Rules Extractor submodule* and the *Validator submodule*. The input of the *Usage Patterns Extractor* is an XML file containing the training examples. Notice that the data used to represent the examples are the transactions extracted from the analysis of the log files of an e-commerce Web site. Transactions contain few personal data about the users, due to privacy problems, and browsing and purchasing history of the users. In the area of e-business services, in particular in Business to Consumer (B2C) e-commerce, items are grouped in a fixed number of categories. For this reason the transactional data are related to specific categories in which the items are grouped. The complete set of attributes used to represent the examples (each one representing a single customer of a German virtual book shop) is listed in Table 1.

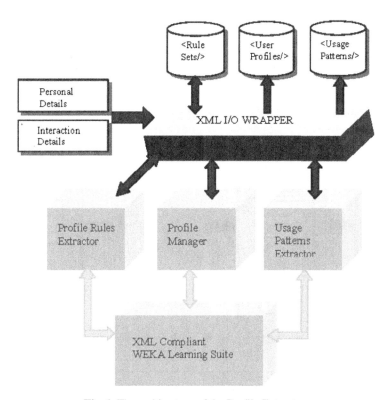

Fig. 1. The architecture of the Profile Extractor.

Table 1. Description of the attributes used to represent examples. *<CategoryName>* denotes each one of the 10 book categories of a German virtual book shop: *Belletristik (Fiction), Computer_und_Internet (Computer and Internet), Kinderbucher (Children's Book), Kultur_und_Geschichte (Culture and History), Nachschlagewerke (Reference Books), Reise (Travel), Sachbuch_und_Ratgeber (Monographs and GuideBook), Schule_und_Bildung (School and Education), Wirtschaft_und_Soziales (Economics and Law), Wissenschaft_und_Technik (Science and Technique).*

Attribute	Description	Type
User_id	Unique identifier of each user	NUMERIC
Access_date	Identifies the date of the last access performed by the user	NOMINAL
Connections_num	Total number of connections to the site performed by the user	NUMERIC
Search_num*<CategoryName>*	Number of searches for a specific category	NUMERIC
Search_freq*<CategoryName>*	Frequency of searches for a specific category	NUMERIC
Purchase_num*<CategoryName>*	Number of purchases for a specific category	NUMERIC
Purchase_freq*<CategoryName>*	Frequency of purchases for a specific category	NUMERIC

The output of the *Usage Patterns Extractor* is translated in XML format and stored in a repository. The purpose of the Clustering submodule is to extract clusters representing the communities of users sharing the same interests within the Web site [13]. The complete clusters extraction process is depicted in Figure 2: data about users is arranged into a set of unclassified instances (each instance represents a user), validated according the Document Type Definition (DTD) shown in the Figure 3. The unclassified instances are processed by the Usage Patterns Extractor, which infers a set of clusters as depicted in Figure 4: each cluster is described by means of the number of instances covered and the mean and the standard deviation of the attributes.

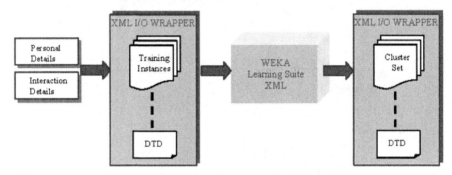

Fig. 2. The process for extracting clusters.

```
<!ELEMENT DATASET_ARFF (USER_ID, ATTRIBUTES_LIST, DATA_INSTANCES_LIST)>
<!ELEMENT USER_ID (#PCDATA)>
<!ELEMENT ATTRIBUTES_LIST ((ATTRIBUTE)+, CLASS)>
 <!ELEMENT ATTRIBUTE (ATTRIBUTE_NAME, ATTRIBUTE_SPECIFICATION)>
 <!ELEMENT ATTRIBUTE_NAME (#PCDATA)>
 <!ELEMENT ATTRIBUTE_SPECIFICATION (NOMINAL_ATTRIBUTE | NUMERIC_ATTRIBUTE)>
      <!ELEMENT NOMINAL_ATTRIBUTE (ATTRIBUTE_VALUE)+>
       <!ELEMENT ATTRIBUTE_VALUE (#PCDATA)>
       <!ELEMENT NUMERIC_ATTRIBUTE  (#PCDATA)>
 <!ELEMENT CLASS (CLASS_NAME, NOMINAL_ATTRIBUTE)>
   <!ELEMENT CLASS_NAME (#PCDATA)>
<!ELEMENT DATA_INSTANCES_LIST (DATA_INSTANCE)+>
 <!ELEMENT DATA_INSTANCE ((ATTRIBUTE_VALUE)+, CLASS_VALUE)>
      <!ELEMENT CLASS_VALUE (#PCDATA)>
```

Fig. 3. The DTD for the input of the Clustering submodule.

The second module of the Usage Patterns Extractor is the *Association Rules Extractor*. The main purpose of the submodule is to extract a set of rules for representing users behavior. The input contains transactional data extracted from the Web server log files, while the output is represented by an XML file containing the set of association rules extracted. Figure 5 depicts a set of rules visualized using an XML style sheet. The figure shows information on large itemsets (see section 3 for itemset definition), and the set of association rules extracted.

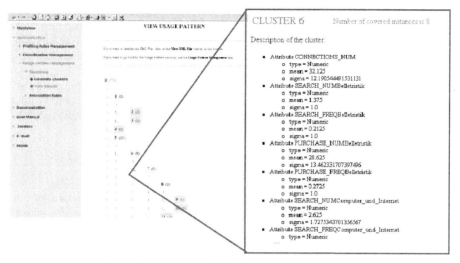

Fig. 4. Example of the XML file representing clusters.

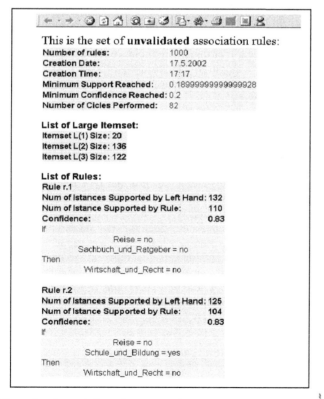

Fig. 5. Example of association rules extracted by the Association Rules Extractor.

Due to the huge number of association rules that could be extracted, it is necessary to provide the domain expert with a tool to examine multiple rules at the same time and then separate "good" rules from "bad" ones. The *Validator submodule* is the module responsible for that. The expert may examine the association rules extracted and accept or reject them using *template-based filtering* operators.

The input to the Validator submodule consists of an XML file representing a set of association rules. The output of the Validator submodule is a set of unvalidated rules (the complete set of rules discovered by Association Rules Extractor, not validated by an accept or reject operator) and a set of accepted and rejected set of rules.

3 The Extraction of Usage Patterns

The purpose of the Usage Patterns Extractor is to extract, from a set of training instances, a set of *common usage patterns*. The main aim of usage patterns is to support marketing decisions in order to improve user's satisfaction in purchasing products and using services of an e-commerce Web site.

3.1 Clusters

Clustering techniques apply when there is no class to be predicted but rather when instances are to be divided into natural groups. Clusters presumably reflect some mechanisms at work in the domain from which instances are drawn, a mechanism that causes some instances to bear a stronger resemblance to one another than they do to the remaining instances. The output of the clustering process is a description of all the clusters extracted. The cluster description is provided with the *cluster centre,* that in turn is represented as follows:

- for each nominal attribute, by the list of all the values (for that attribute) of the instances which lie in that cluster;
- for each numerical attribute, by the mean and the standard deviation.

The algorithm used to cluster users on the basis of their interests is COBWEB [7]. It is an *incremental* clustering algorithm, because the type of run is *instance by instance*. In each step of the process, the algorithm builds a tree where the leaves are the instances and the root is the entire dataset; at the beginning of the run the tree is composed of just the root. Then, instances are added one by one and the tree is updated at every step. During the updating with a new instance, it can happen that the exact position for the leaf, representing the new instance, is found or a re-engineering of the tree is needed in order to insert the new instance. The reason to decide how and when re-engineering the tree depends on a feature called *category utility* that measures the total quality of a part of instances into the clusters.

COBWEB manages the instances positioning into the tree by using one of the four following operators:

- Putting the instance in an existing cluster
- Creating a new cluster
- Merging of two clusters
- Splitting of a cluster

For each new instance, the algorithm runs the four operators and selects the one that maximises the category utility.

3.2 Association Rules

One of the most commonly used data mining technique for e-commerce is finding association rules among a set of co-purchased products. Essentially, these techniques are concerned with discovering association between two sets of products such that the presence of some products in a particular transaction implies that products from the other sets are also present in the same transaction.

The quality of association rules is commonly evaluated by looking at their *coverage* and *accuracy*. The *coverage* is the number of instances for which it predicts correctly – this is often called its *support*. The *accuracy* – often called *confidence* – is the number of instances that it predicts correctly, expressed as a proportion of all instances it applies to. It is usual to specify minimum coverage and accuracy values and to seek only those rules whose coverage and accuracy are both at least these specified minima. We are only interested in association rules with high coverage. We seek combinations of attribute-value pairs that have a prespecified minimum coverage. These are called *item sets*: an attribute-value pair is an *item*.

The algorithm integrated into the Usage Pattern Extractor to extract association rules is APRIORI [2, 3].

As shown in Figure 6, the first step of the algorithm simply counts item occurrences to determine the large 1-itemsets. A subsequent pass, say pass k, consists of two phases. First, the large itemsets L_{k-1} found in the $(k-1)$-th pass are used to generate the candidate itemsets C_k, using the apriori-gen function (this function takes as an argument L_{k-1}, the set of all large $(k-1)$-itemsets and returns a superset of the set of all large k-itemsets). Next, the database is scanned and the support of candidates in C_k is counted. For fast counting, we need to efficiently determine the candidates in C_k that are contained in a given transaction t.

```
1) L_1 = {large 1-itemsets};
2) for ( k = 2; L_{k-1}≠0; k++ ) do begin
3)      C_k = apriori-gen(L_{k-1}); // New candidates
4)      forall transactions t ∈ D(atabase) do begin
5)              C_t = subset(C_k , t); // Candidates contained in t
6)              forall candidates c ∈ C_t do
7)                      c.count++;
8)      end
9)      L_k = {c ∈ C_k | c.count ≥ minsup}
10) end
11) Answer = U_k L_k;
```

Fig. 6. APRIORI algorithm.

The Apriori algorithm is able to find a very large number of association rules. Several of the discovered rules are useless or redundant and they should be discarded. The validation operators [1] allow the expert to specify in general terms the types of rule that he/she wants to accept (using the *accepting* template) or reject (using the *rejecting* template). All rules discovered by Apriori are collected into one set and they are considered unvalidated (Runv). The human expert selects the validation operator and applies it successively to the set of unvalidated rules. Some rules get accepted and some rejected (sets Oacc and Orej in Figure 7) by the operator. Then, a further validation operation could be applied to the set of the remaining unvalidated rules.

Input: Set of all discovered rules Rall.
Output: Mutually disjoint sets of rules Racc, Rrej , Runv, such that
Rall = Racc $\cup$ Rrej $\cup$ Runv.
1. Runv := Rall, Racc := $\varnothing$, Rrej := $\varnothing$.
2. while (not TerminateValidationProcess()) begin
3.   Expert selects a validation operator (say, O) from the set of available
4.   validation operators.
5.   O is applied to Runv. Result: disjoint sets Oacc and Orej .
6.   Runv := Runv - Oacc - Orej , Racc := Racc $\cup$ Oacc, Rrej := Rrej $\cup$ Orej
end

Fig. 7. The algorithm for the rule validation process.

When the validation process is stopped, the set of all the discovered rules *(Rall)* is split into three disjoint sets: accepted rules *(Racc)*, rejected rules *(Rrej)*, and possibly the remaining unvalidated rules *(Runv)*. As shown in Figure 7, several validation operators are successively applied to the set of the unvalidated rules until the stopping criterion TerminateValidationProcess is reached. The stopping criterion of the validation process can be specified by the expert and may include conditions such as (a) only few rules remain unvalidated, (b) only few rules are validated at a time by one or several validation operators, and (c) the total elapsed validation time exceeds the predetermined validation time.

4   Experimental Results

In this section we propose some experiments performed in order to evaluate the most suitable learning system to integrate into the Usage Patterns Extractor.

4.1   COBWEB vs. EM

The first experiment concerns the comparison between COBWEB and EM, a *probability-based* clustering algorithm.

The Expectation Maximization (EM) algorithm [6] is a parameter estimation method which falls into the general framework of maximum-likelihood estimation, and is applied in cases where part of the data are incomplete or "hidden". It is essentially an iterative optimisation algorithm which, at least under certain conditions, will converge to a local maximum of the likelihood function.

The goal of clustering is to determine a set of clusters within which the *inter-cluster dissimilarity* is maximized, while the *intra-cluster* one is minimized. The experiment performed in order to compare the two algorithms consisted in measuring these dissimilarities. The dissimilarity measures have been computed on the output of the two clustering algorithms, using as input files containing 100, 200, 300, 400, 500 instances, respectively.

The *total intra-cluster dissimilarity* is the sum of the intra-cluster dissimilarities of each cluster extracted. For each cluster, *intra-cluster dissimilarity* is the sum of the distances of each instance belonging to the cluster from the cluster centre.

$$D_i^{intra} = \sum_{j=1}^{n_i} d(x^i_{\ j}, v^{(i)})$$

where n_i is the number of instances belonging to the *i-th* cluster, $x^i_{\ j}$ is the j-th instance belonging to the *i-th* cluster, $v^{(i)}$ is the *i-th* cluster prototype.

The distance is the sum of distances computed for each instance attribute, as follows: for each nominal attribute, the distance is the relative frequency of the attribute value concerning the instances belonging to the cluster processed, rendered inversely proportional; for each numeric attribute, it is the Hamming distance between the value in the instance attribute value and the average value, normalized to a value between zero and one;

$$d(x^i_{\ j}, v^{(i)}) = \sum_{x^i_{js}\,nom.} (i - f^i_s(x^i_{js})) + \sum_{x^i_{js}\,num.} \frac{\left| x^i_{js} - v^{(i)}_s \right|}{x_{s\,max} - x_{s\,min}}$$

where s is the number of the attribute.

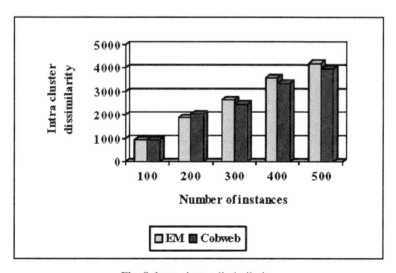

Fig. 8. Intra-cluster dissimilarity.

Comparing the intra-cluster dissimilarity (Figure 8) of the two algorithms, it can be noticed that COBWEB outperforms EM (with large sets of examples).

The *total inter-cluster dissimilarity* is the sum of distances between the prototypes of the k clusters extracted. For each cluster, *inter-cluster dissimilarity* is the sum of distances between the cluster prototype and the other clusters prototypes:

$$D_i^{inter} = \sum_{i \neq j} d(v^{(i)}, v^{(j)})$$

where i is the number of clusters processed and j moves between the other clusters numbers.

The distance between clusters prototypes is for nominal attributes, the sum of the differences of the frequency values of the prototypes distribution; for numeric attributes, the difference of the prototypes values, normalized to one;

$$d(v^{(i)}, v^{(j)}) = \sum_{x_r^i nom} \left| f_s^i(x_s^i) - f_s^j(x_s^j) \right| + \sum_{x_s^i num} \frac{\left| x_s^i - x_s^j \right|}{x_{s\max} - x_{s\min}}$$

Comparing the inter-cluster dissimilarity of the two algorithms, it can be noticed that COBWEB maximizes this value assuming a better performance than EM (Figure 9).

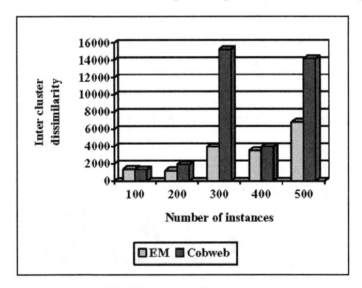

Fig. 9. Inter-cluster dissimilarity.

The *total dissimilarity* is the ratio between the intra-cluster dissimilarity and the inter-cluster dissimilarity. Comparing the two algorithms on the total dissimilarity, it can be noticed that COBWEB has a better performance than EM. In fact, it minimises mainly the total dissimilarity measure, as shown in Figure 10.

We can conclude that COBWEB outperforms EM.

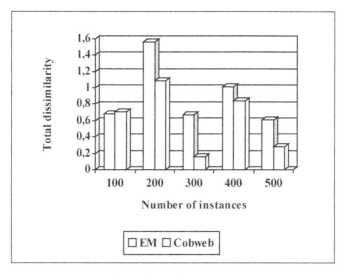

Fig. 10. Total dissimilarity.

4.2   Test on Association Rules

We performed several experiments to define the best parameters to be used for increasing the effectiveness of the discovered association rules.

Table 2. An example of the rules extracted from the analysis of Users' Preferences.

Preferences (Support 0.2, Confidence 0.5)
1. Sachbuch_und_Ratgeber=no 201 ==> Wirtschaft_und_Soziales=no 159 (0.79)
2. Kultur_und_Geschichte=no 244 ==> Wirtschaft_und_Soziales=no 193 (0.79)
3. Reise=yes 209 ==> Schule_und_Bildung=no 165 (0.79)
4. Reise=no 291 ==> Wirtschaft_und_Soziales=no 227 (0.78)
5. Computer_und_Internet=no 246 ==> Wirtschaft_und_Soziales=no 191 (0.78)

Test on Preferences
A first test has been performed on 500 instances, concerning the Preferences attribute classes. The rules found (see Table 2) in the course of the experiment provide good results: they are meaningful rules to describe the users behavior.

Test on Clusters
Another test has been performed on the clusters extracted from the COBWEB algorithm, concerning the Preferences attribute classes as in the previous experiment. We have chosen 4 clusters containing respectively 22, 45, 133, 500 instances.

The cluster with 45 instances provided the better result: it was the one containing the most meaningful rules (a subset of these is shown in Table 3), with a large number of items in the body containing attribute values = *'yes'*. The tests performed were a partial success. In fact, the problem of the large number of zeros into the rules has been solved and the association rules extracted appear in the following form *"if at-*

tribute = value | category = (yes/no) then attribute = value | category = (yes/no)", so they could supply useful information to a marketing expert.

Table 3. An example of the rules extracted from the cluster containing 45 instances.

Preferences (Support 0.2, Confidence 0.8)
1. Kultur_und_Geschichte=yes Sachbuch_und_Ratgeber=yes 16 ==> Computer_und_Internet=yes 15 (0.94)
2. Computer_und_Internet=yes Reise=no 24 ==> Wirtschaft_und_Soziales=no 22 (0.92)
3. Reise=no Wissenschaft_und_Technik=yes 19 ==> Computer_und_Internet=yes 16 (0.84)

Test on User Transactions

The next step was to consider individual user logs on the Web site. To perform the test, 3125 transactions have been simulated. The attributes for each transaction are:

Attribute	Type	Description
date	transaction	Access date
User_id	transaction	Id of the user
product_category	transaction	Purchase category
quantity	transaction	Purchase products quantity for a category

In the following, some of the rules obtained are presented:

1. category=Computer_und_Internet 360 ==> quantity=1 201 (0.56)
2. category=Belletristik 384 ==> quantity=1 213 (0.55)
3. category=Wissenschaft_und_Technik 332 ==> quantity=1 164 (0.49)

Tests on transactions have generated good results (meaningful association rules with a low support value), although the large number of purchase quantities with value = '1' influenced negatively the association rules extraction.

Test on Single User Transaction

Another test performed has been the extraction of association rules from transactions of a single user. The attributes used in this test are shown in the following table:

Attribute	Type	Description
date	transaction	Transaction data
product_category	transaction	Purchase category
dayOfWeek	transaction	Transaction day of week
timeOfDay	transaction	Transaction time of day
quantity	transaction	Purchased products quantity for a category

In this experiment we used 8 users with different number of transactions (user with 115, 39, 25, 20, 15, 10, 5 transactions), in order to provide a guideline for the selection of this value over/below whom the algorithm is not effective.

It has been observed that with less than 20 transactions, the extracted rules reach the maximum confidence value.

Final Considerations
Tests performed show that better results can be gathered starting from:

– preferences attribute classes that supplies rules about behaviors for all users or user communities;
– transactional data for the extraction of rules concerning each single user.

The two processes are not exclusive but it will be interesting to discover a method to merge these two kinds of rules.

4.3 Test on Validation Operators

The last experiment concerns the use of validation operators (templates) to accept/reject the association rules discovered by the APRIORI algorithm. For this test we considered an XML file containing 1000 rules obtained by preferences attribute classes regarding 500 users, and we applied the accept/reject template to select a subset of the validated rules.

The template we used accepts all the rules with a *Body* containing the attribute "*Computer_und_Internet*" with value = "*yes*". It can be noticed that the validated rules are 54 out of 1000 (Figure 11). Then we applied a template that rejects all rules whose *Head* part that contains the attribute "*Reise*". It can be noticed that the rules validated (Figure 12) are 56 out of 946 remaining invalidated rules.

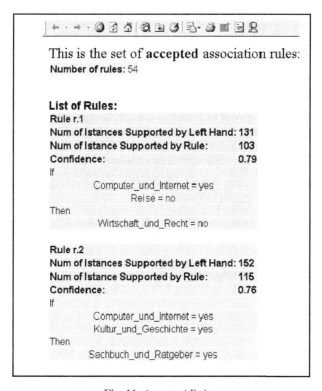

Fig. 11. Accepted Rules.

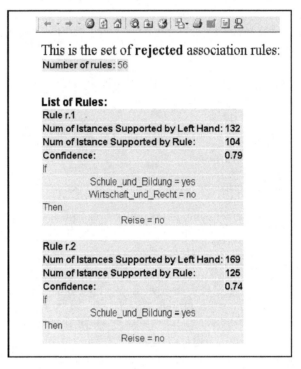

Fig. 12. Rejected Rules.

5 Conclusions

The practicality of employing Web usage mining techniques in recommender system is directly related to the discovery of effective user profiles and usage patterns.

In this paper we have presented a system that builds the usage patterns (user communities and association rules). The construction of the user communities (clusters) was achieved by using unsupervised learning techniques. In particular, we used the COBWEB clustering algorithm because we examined the dissimilarity measure on COBWEB and EM algorithm and we observed that COBWEB results in better performances as compared to EM. Moreover, we used the APRIORI algorithm to discover the association rules and we performed several experiments to define the best parameters to be used for increasing the effectiveness of the discovered association rules. This test showed that it is more interesting to use as attributes the categories of interests of the users and their transactional data.

References

1. Adomavicius, G., Tuzhilin, A.: User profiling in personalization applications through rule discovery and validation, in Proceedings of the Fifth ACM SIGKDD International Conference on Knowledge Discovery and Data Mining, August (1999) 377–381
2. Agrawal, R., Srikant, R.: Fast algorithms for mining association rules in large databases, in Proceedings International Conference on Very Large Databases, Santiage, Chile: Morgan Kaufmann, Los Altos, CA (1994) 478-499

3. Agrawal, R., Imielinsky, T., Swami, A.: Mining association rules between sets of items in large databases, in Proceedings of the ACM SIGMOD Conference, (1993) 207–216
4. Buchner, A., Mulvenna, M.D.: Discovering Internet marketing intelligence through online analytical Web usage mining, ACM SIGMOD Record, 27(4), (1998) 54-61
5. Cooley, R., Mobasher, B., Srivastava, J.: Data preparation for mining World Wide Web browsing patterns, Journal of Knowledge and Information Systems, 1(1), (1999) 5–32
6. Dempster, M. M., Laird, N. M., Jain, D. B.: Maximum Likelihood from Incomplete Data via the EM Algorithm, Journal of Royal Statistical Society, Series B, 39, (1997) 1–38
7. Fisher, D.: Knowledge acquisition via incremental conceptual clustering, Machine Learning, 2(2), (1987) 139–172
8. Fu, X., Budzik, J., Hammond, K. J.: Mining navigation history for recommendation, in Proceedings of the 5th International Conference on Intelligent User Interfaces, New Orleans, ACM, (2000) 106–112
9. Joachims, T., Freitag, D., Mitchell, T.: WebWatcher: A tour guide for the World Wide Web, in Proceedings of the International Joint Conference in AI (IJCAI97), 1997 770–777
10. Lin, W., Alvarez, S. A. Ruiz, C.: Collaborative recommendation via adaptive association rule mining, in Proceedings of 6th International Conference on Knowledge Discovery and Data Mining Workshop on Web Mining for E-Commerce, WebKDD-2000, Boston, 2000
11. Nasraoui, O., Frigui, H., Joshi, A., Krishnapuram, R.: Mining Web access logs using relational competitive fuzzy clustering, in Proceedings of the Eight International Fuzzy Systems Association World Congress, 1997
12. Oldenburg, R.: The Great Good Place: Cafes, Coffee Shops, Bookstores, Bars, Hair Salons, and Other Hangouts at the Heart of the Community, 3rd ed. New York: Marlowe & Company, (1999)
13. Paliouras, G., Papatheodorou, C., Karakaletsis, V., Spyropoulos, C., Malaveta, V.: Learning User Communities for Improving the Service of Information Providers, Lecture Notes in Computer Science, LNCS, No. 1513, Springer-Verlag, (1998) 367–384
14. Sarwar, B. M., Karypis, G., Konstan, J., Riedl, J.: Recommender Systems for Large-Scale E-Commerce: Scalable Neighborhood Formation Using Clustering, in Proceedings of the Fifth International Conference on Computer and Information Technology, East West University, Bangladesh, (2002)
15. Semeraro, G., Abbattista, F., Degemmis, M., Licchelli, O., Lops, P., Zambetta, F.: Agents and Personalisation for Developing Intelligent e-Business Applications, in Corchuelo, R., Ruiz Cortés, A., Wrembel, R. (Eds.), Technologies Supporting Business Solutions, Part IV: Data Analysis and Knowledge Discovery, Nova Sciences Books and Journals, Chapter 7, 2003, 163-186
16. Spiliopoulou, M., Faulstich, L.C.: WUM: A Web Utilization Miner, in Proceedings of EDBT Workshop WebDB98, Valencia, Spain, LNCS 1590, Springer Verlag, (1999)
17. Semeraro, G., Ferilli, S., Fanizzi, N., Abbattista, F.: Learning Interaction Models in a Digital Library Service, in M. Bauer, P. J. Gmytrasiewicz, and J. Vassileva (Eds), User Modelling 2001 - Proceedings of the 8th International Conference. Lecture Notes in Artificial Intelligence, LNAI, No. 2109, Springer, Berlin, (2001) 44–53
18. Shardanand, U., Maes, P.: Social information filtering: algorithms for automating "word of mouth.", in Proceedings of the ACM CHI Conference, (1995) 210–217
19. Shahabi, C., Zarkesh, A.M., Adibi, J., Shah, V.: Knowledge discovery from users Web-page navigation, in Proceedings of Workshop on Research Issues in Data Engineering, Birmingham, England, (1997) 20
20. Srikant, R., Agrawal, R.: Mining generalized association rules, in Proceedings of the 21st International Conference on Very Large Databases, VLDB95, Zurich, Switzerland, September (1995) 407–419
21. Srivastava, J., Cooley, R., Deshpande, M., Tan, P-T.:Web Usage Mining: Discovery and Applications of Usage Patterns from Web Data, SIGKDD Explorations, 1(2), 2000 12-23
22. Witten, I. H., Frank, E.: Data Mining: Practical Machine Learning Tools and Techniques with Java Implementations, Morgan Kaufmann Publishers, San Francisco, CA, (2000)

Adaptive User Modelling in AthosMail

Kristiina Jokinen, Kari Kanto, and Jyrki Rissanen

University of Art and Design Helsinki
Hämeentie 135 C FIN-00560 Helsinki Finland
{kjokinen,kanto,jyrki}@uiah.fi

Abstract. In this paper we discuss the adaptive User Model component of the AthosMail system, and describe especially the Cooperativity Model which produces recommendations for the appropriate explicitness of the system utterances, depending on the user's observed competence levels. The Cooperativity Model deals with the system's dialogue control and explicitness of the given information: these two aspects affect the system's interaction capabilities and thus naturalness of the dialogue as a whole. The model consists of an offline and an online version, which use somewhat different input parameters, due to their different functionality in the system.

1 Introduction

In recent years, the notion of adaptivity has become more important when building spoken interactive systems. The systems are to be used in mobile and versatile environment, by various users with different skills, abilities, and requirements, and the system's usefulness and usability are thus increased if its functionality can be tailored according to preferences of the various users. In interface design, adaptivity is often realised in a static way as a form of personalization whereby the users personalise their interfaces according to different colour or sound choices, and provide a list of preferences for their personal profiles so as to enable preferred filtering and rating of incoming information. Online, dynamic adaptation can be realised in the system's ability to classify users into appropriate categories, e.g. on the basis of their navigation choices or a list of specific keywords, so as to produce personalised access to information sources (e.g. InfoQuest), filtering of interesting news e.g. [1, 11] and recommendations for web-browsing [13] or TV programs [4]. Recommendation systems [5] track preference information of a group by comparing the selected items of one user to similar items selected by the other users.

In the dialogue management research, the focus has been on dialogue strategies, and the system's capability to adapt its initiativeness according to the dialogue situation seems to result in more successful dialogue systems. For instance, [10] compared a user-adaptable and non-adaptable version of an information retrieval system, and concluded that the former outperformed the latter. [3] compared an adaptive dialogue system to two non-adaptive versions of the same system (one with a system initiative and the other with a mixed-initiative dialogue strategy), and found that the adaptive system performed better than the others in terms of user satisfaction, dialogue efficiency (number of utterances), and dialogue quality (ASR performance).

The user may be given an explicit option to change system properties, e.g. the system-initiative dialogue strategy to the user-initiative one, depending on the situation

C. Stary and C. Stephanidis (Eds.): UI4All 2004, LNCS 3196, pp. 149–158, 2004.

[10]. This increases the system's transparency, and the user's feeling of being in control of the system adds to user satisfaction. However, from the point of view of interaction, it is important that the systems also exhibit capability to adapt and adjust their behavioral patters automatically according to various types of users, various situations, and various user actions. For instance, [17] observes that it is safer for beginners to be closely guided by the system, while experienced users like to take the initiative which results in more efficient dialogues in terms of decreased average completion time and a decreased average number of utterances. People also tend to adapt their behaviour to the speech partner, which suggests that a system that adapts itself to the user's behaviour could make human-computer interaction more natural, too. [13] investigated adaptivity and adaptability in a spreadsheet application, and ended up proposing a system that suggests adaptations to the user: he observed that the users wanted to influence the timing and content of adaptations, but the controlling of adaptivity was too demanding a task for the user alone, so the system should provide assistance and be helpful in cases where adaptation is possible. In the small experiment conducted by [7], the users' interaction patterns were visualized using a reinforcement-based learning strategy for the action chains that have occurred in the previous dialogues. Although the corpus was not large enough for statistical conclusions, there were a few examples which can be considered as indications of the patterns that can vary across individual users, and which could be learnt by the system in its attempts to adapt and anticipate the user's behaviour.

In spoken dialogue systems, the User Model (UM) component takes care of this kind of adaptation: it records the user characteristics and allows the system to tailor its responses so that expectations about natural and enjoyable interaction could be fulfilled. From early on, the UM research focused on providing information that would be appropriate to the user's level of expertise, i.e. the new information is presented in the form that the user is most likely to understand correctly [2, 14].

The main goal of the EU-project DUMAS is to develop a prototype interactive email system, AthosMail, with components that would make the user's interaction with the system more flexible and natural. The purpose of the User Model component in AthosMail is three-fold:

1) to provide flexibility and variation in the system utterances,
2) to allow the users to interact with the system in a more natural way,
3) to allow developers to implement and test machine learning techniques.

These goals are exemplified by the User Model design which takes into account:

1) Flexible representation for encoding the system utterances and using this for utterance generation,
2) System functionality that records the user's actions and behaviour, and estimates the user's competence levels that will be further used to give recommendations on the appropriate way of responding,
3) Machine-learning module that provides views to the user's mailbox by classifying messages on the basis of their content and the user's interest.

In this paper we focus on the goals (1) and (2): the system's ability to support natural interaction according to the user's perceived competence levels. Section 2 discusses User Modelling in the AthosMail system, and Section 3 describes the adaptation in the Cooperativity Model in detail. We will conclude with a summary of the first expertise evaluation in Section 4, and views for future research in Section 5.

2 User Modelling in AthosMail

The following sub-components have been considered relevant to the AthosMail system:

1) Message Prioritization. This allows the system to sort out incoming messages so that the messages that the user most likely finds interesting and important are in the beginning of the list. The importance of a message is a function of user actions: what the user has done earlier with the same kind of messages. For instance, if the user has always deleted messages from 'Frank' without reading or listening those messages first, it is pretty obvious that the messages from 'Frank' are not very important for the user. The message priority component analyses message features such as the sender, received group, subject, keywords and topics, and gives a score from -1 to +1 to each of these pieces of information separately. The importance of the whole message is a weighted sum of the scores of message features.

2) Goal Guessing. This allows the system to make educated guesses about the user's goals and behavioural patterns in the interaction situation. The main benefit of the suggestions is to help dialogue management to decide what to do when there is uncertainty of the user action because of bad speech recognition. The goal suggestions can also be used to help e.g. online tutoring system to give more relevant guidance to the user.

3) Cooperativity Model. This component allows the system to give recommendations on the explicitness level of the system utterances depending on the user's competence level, and the level of dialogue control exerted by the system depending on ASR success. If there seems to be a dialogue problem which originates from limited user expertise, the user will be given more explicit guidance, and if the fault is in speech recognizer or in language understanding, the system assumes a more active role and takes more initiative. The two variables involved are dialogue act specific explicitness (DASEX) and initiative (INIT). The component consists of an online and offline parts.

4) Message Categorization. This component allows the system to compare the incoming messages to the existing ones, and to cluster messages according to their topical similarity with the existing messages. The content-based categorization is based on the Random Indexing vector space methodology [15], which accumulates semantic representations of words based on co-occurrence statistics.

5) User Preferences. These are fixed properties of the user dealing with aspects like the preferred speaking style, speed, and voice, or the preferred message senders and topics.

Figure 1 gives an overview of the various User Model components in AthosMail. The components produce recommendations for the Dialogue Manager Module which uses the recommendations in its own planning and generator components to decide on the next action. The recommendations concern the appropriate level of explicitness in the responses (DASEX), whether the system should assume dialogue control (INIT), and how the message list is best presented to the user when she logs in (ViewList). The recommendations are combined in the system's response planner that produces an utterance plan which can be realised in different languages using the system's presentation components. For instance, when the user is a novice, the Cooperativity component recommends the system to produce longer and more explicit utterances than when the user is familiar with the system and its functionality. The UM recommendations can also be used in the interpretation of the user utterances in order to propose expectations of the user's vocabulary and likely next actions. In the beginning of the interaction, the default user preferences are loaded into the system from the UM.

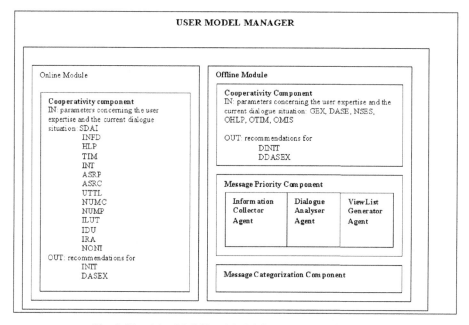

Fig. 1. The AthosMail User Model Component Architecture.

The system monitors and records the user's actions in general, but also specifically on each possible system act. Thus the system can provide help tailored with respect to the user's familiarity with individual acts. For instance, the user may need more help with commands that she does not use so often like CONFIRM or REPEAT. The users may, of course, be familiar with similar commands, but unless the users have tried the commands as part of the current system's functionality, it is controversial whether their skill with respect to the whole system can be said to be comprehensive, or whether part of it is extrapolated via adaptation from some earlier experience. The current UM model does not take into account the user's earlier experience with speech-based systems, but only their experience with AthosMail.

Explicitness in the system replies goes down when the user is more familiar with the commands, i.e. the replies become more implicit concerning the information the user needs to know at each dialogue point. However, explicit confirmation is always given whenever the user attempts to perform some of the destructive actions like cancelling the previous command or deleting a message, regardless of the user's familiarity with the system. It should be noticed that some users might want to opt out from this choice, but the choice was motivated by practical consideration of the present-day speech recognizers: to make sure that the user command was correctly interpreted, an explicit confirmation is the safest option for irreversible actions.

3   Examples of the Cooperativity Model

The User Model component is based on the existing views of what a user model should contain and on project specific requirements of how the user model can be used in the system. For instance, the Cooperativity Model is seen as a continuation of the refinement and filtering mechanism where the system's communicative goal is filtered through communicative obligations [7]. While the obligations are expressed as rules according to which the system's utterance is generated, the Cooperativity Model uses two parameters, explicitness and control, based on the system's knowledge of the current dialogue situation and user expertise.

The support for adaptive performance is motivated by the fact that the users vary in their knowledge and experience with speech-based interactive systems; they need help in learning to use a new system, and often need additional information about the various commands of the system. The two variables involved in specifying recommendations to the Dialogue Manager are dialogue act specific explicitness (DASEX) and dialogue control or initiative (INIT). The higher the explicitness value, the more explicitly the system dialogue act will be presented. The value range is: 1 = taciturn, 2 = normal, 3 = explicit. The higher the initiative value, the more the system controls the dialogue; the value range is: 1 = passive, 2 = declarative, 3 = guiding, 4 = directive. Since the effects of explicitness and initiative on the surface generation of utterances often overlap, the effect of the two variables is integrated into a unified Cooperativity Model. Table 1 gives a summary of utterance level integration.

Table 1. The effect of Initiative and Explicitness value combinations on the surface generation of utterances.

PROMPTS			
INIT/DASEX	(1) TACITURN	(2) NORMAL	(3) EXPLICIT
(1) PASSIVE	options: **none** extra options: **no** prompts: **none**	options: **short** extra options: **no** prompts: **none**	INIT =+1
(2) DECLARATIVE	options: **short** extra options: **no** prompts: **none**	options: **medium** extra options: **no** prompts: **open**	options: **long** extra options: **no** prompts: **open**
(3) GUIDING	DASEX =+1	options: **medium** extra options: **no** prompts: **question**	options: **long** extra options: **yes** prompt: **question**
(4) DIRECTIVE	DASEX =+1	options: **medium** extra options: **no** prompt: **chunk by chunk**	options: **long** extra options: **yes** prompt: **chunk by chunk**

The division of the dialogue control levels is partly based on that of [16], who established a categorization of four initiative modes: a) directive, where the computer has full control and recommends the next subgoal needed to proceed with the task, b) suggestive, where the system still holds the initiative and makes suggestions about subgoals but is willing to change the course of the dialogue according to stated user preferences, c) declarative, where the user is in control, but the system may provide relevant unsolicited information, and d) passive, where the user has complete dialogue control and the system does not recommend subgoals. The parameters that contribute to the initiative value, as well as the respective weights of the parameters, are in part based on those introduced in [18] and [9].

The User Model consists of two modules: the online and offline modules. They use somewhat different input parameters due to their different roles in the system functionality. The offline module keeps track of relevant dialogue history and, based on that, calculates default values for explicitness and control. The offline parameters include the number of help requests (OHLP), timeouts (OTIM), and speech recognition problems (misunderstandings, OMIS), and the module weighs them according to their frequency and recency. In addition, the module tracks the number of sessions the user has had with the system (NSES), and then calculates the user's general expertise level (GEX), default initiative and dialogue act specific explicitness (DDASEX). At the beginning of each session, the default values are passed from the offline module to the online module, and placed as the values of the active explicitness and initiative parameters. The online module modifies the default values according to the changing circumstances in the current dialogue. The online component calculates the explicitness and initiative values, based on parameters that deal with the number of help requests, timeouts, interruptions, ASR Confidence (ASRC), utterance length (UTTL), number of cancels (NUMC), etc. The dialogue events that take place during a session are recorded and relayed to the offline component at the end of the session. This way, the offline module tracks long-term developments, whereas the online module reacts to specific situations at runtime. Accordingly, the offline parameters change more slowly in order to round off coincidental fluctuation, while the online module reacts rather quickly to the user's actions, so that the user's adaptation to the system functionality can be addressed runtime immediately. The parameters and their values are described in more detail in [8].

Each system utterance type has three different surface realizations corresponding to the DASEX values. The higher the DASEX value, the more additional information the surface realization will include. The value is used for choosing between the surface realizations. The following two examples have been translated from their original Finnish forms.

Example 1: A speech recognition error message.

DASEX = 1: I didn't understand.

DASEX = 2: I'm sorry, I didn't understand. Please speak clearly, but do not over-articulate, and speak only after the beep.

DASEX = 3: I'm sorry, I didn't understand, I may have misheard what you said. Please speak clearly, but do not over-articulate, and speak only after the beep. To hear examples of what you can say to the system, say 'what now'.

Example 2: Basic information about a message chosen from a listing of messages from a particular sender.

DASEX = 1: First message, about "reply: sample file".

DASEX = 2: First message, about "reply: sample file". Say 'tell me more', if you want more details.

DASEX = 3: First message, about "reply: sample file". Say 'read', if you want to hear the messages, or 'tell me more', if you want to hear a summary and the send date and length of the message.

The examples show the basic idea behind the DASEX effect on surface generation. In the first example, the novice user is given additional information about how to try and avoid ASR problems. In both examples, some possible commands are hinted at.

The effect of dialogue control or initiative (INIT) to the surface realizations is described by way of an example depicted in Table 2. Detailed parameter calculations have been substituted by verbal descriptions.

Table 2. An example dialogue demonstrating the effect of control and explicitness values on utterance generation.

utterances (U = user, S = system)	relevant parameter values, notes
U: Read Tim's message.	ASR output = "read John's message"
S: There are no messages from John. You have messages from Abdul, Tim, Jaana, and Horst.	The system misheard the sender's name. Since there are no messages from John in the current mail folder, the system suspects an ASR error and raises the INIT value by one (to two).
U: Read Tim's message.	ASR output = "read John's message"
S: Sorry, I didn't understand. The senders in the current folder Inbox are Abdul, Tim, Jaana, and Horst. Whose message would you like to read?	The system hears the same thing again, which is a further clue (although tiny) that the ASR conditions are poor. The speech recognizer also reports a low confidence value. Since a problem was suspected in the previous round as well, there is enough evidence for the system to raise the dialogue control (INIT) level again, to three. The system starts to guide the dialogue more closely.
U: Tim's message please.	ASR output = "John's message first"
S: Sorry, I didn't understand. You can refer to a message by its number, its sender's names, and its relative position in the message list. Do you want to choose the message by sender or by number?	The system can't make sense of the ASR output. INIT is raised to the highest level, and the system walks the user forwards stage by stage.
U: Sender.	ASR output = "sender"
S: The senders in the current folder Inbox are Abdul, Tim, Jaana, and Horst. Please say the sender's name whose message you would like to hear.	
U: Tim.	ASR output = "tim"
S: A message from Tim about What where. Hi Bat, did you tape the Beckett yesterday? I missed it, darn. Tim. End of message.	The message is played out to the user. The command is completed successfully. If no further ASR problems are detected, the INIT value starts to drop.

4 Expert Evaluations

Prior to usability tests, we have conducted a preliminary qualitative expert evaluation, which has provided some important insights into the design of system utterances in relation to user expertise. We interviewed a group of 5 experts of interactive systems (two women and three men) who had earlier experience in interactive systems and interface design but who were unfamiliar with the current system and with interactive email systems in general. Each interview included three walkthroughs of our system.

All interviewees agreed on one major theme, namely that the system should be as friendly and reassuring as possible towards novices. Dialogue systems can be intimidating to new users, and many people are so afraid of making mistakes that they give up after the first communication failure, regardless of what caused it. Four of the five experts agreed that in an error situation the system should signal the user that the machine is to blame, but that there are things that the user can do in case she wants to help the system in the task. The system should apologize for being imperfect but also ensure that the user doesn't get feelings of guilt of not being able to act in the correct way. For instance, the responses in Example 1 were considered too much accusing the user in this way.

What novice users also need are error messages that do not bother the user with technical matters that concern only the designers. For instance, when ASR errors occur, a novice user doesn't need information about error codes or characteristics of the speech recognizer; but the system can simply talk about not hearing correctly. A reference to a piece of equipment that does the job is unnecessary and the user should not be burdened with it.

Experienced users, on the other hand, wish to hear only the essentials. All our interviewees agreed that at the highest skill level the system prompts should be as terse as possible, to the point of being blunt. Politeness words like *I'm sorry* are not necessary at this level, because the expert's attitude towards the system is very pragmatic: they see it as a tool, know its limitations, and "rudeness" on the part of the system doesn't scare or annoy them anymore. However, it is not clear how this change in politeness when migrating from novice to expert levels actually affects the user's perception of the system; at least the transition should be gradual and not too fast. There may also be cultural differences regarding politeness rules.

Usability issues are easy to overlook when investigating and developing adaptive systems. Badly designed adaptivity decreases usability as it may confuse the user; and it is thus essential that the system is consistent in its use of concepts, and manner of speech.

5 Conclusions

Previous studies concerning user modelling in various interactive applications and dialogue systems have shown the importance of UM in making the interaction with the system more efficient and more enjoyable. In this paper we have focused on the design of an adaptive User Model component and its realization in the AthosMail system. The User Model consists of several components that are meant to support adaptation in interaction, presentation, and search. We provided a more detailed view of the Cooperativity Model which integrates initiative handling and explicitness by combining various parameters and their values in order to provide recommendations to the system about appropriate ways to convey information and control the dialogue. The model is language independent, and it is being integrated into the multilingual AthosMail system.

We have conducted the first user studies to test the Cooperativity model as part of the complete AthosMail system. However, more extensive user studies are needed to evaluate the model's validity and usability in spoken language interfaces. The combined effect of dialogue control and explicitness is complex, and requires careful testing. We also plan to evaluate the system at three different sites using English, Finnish and Swedish users. User tests with the visually impaired are under preparation, too.

Acknowledgements

The research was carried out within the EU-project DUMAS (Dynamic Universal Mobility for Adaptive Speech Interfaces), IST-2000-29452 (http://www.sics.se /dumas). We want to thank all the project participants for cooperation and discussions.

References

1. Chesnais, P., Mucklo, M., Sheena J.A. 1995. The Fishwrap Personalized News System, *IEEE Second International Workshop on Community Networking Integrating Multimedia Services to the Home*. Princeton, NJ, USA.
2. Chin, D. 1989. KNOME: Modeling what the User Knows in UC. In: Kobsa, A., Wahlster, W. (eds.) *User Modeling in Dialogue Systems*. Springer-Verlag Berlin, Heidelberg 74-107
3. Chu-Carroll, J. and Nickerson, J. S. 2000. Evaluating Automatic Dialogue Strategy Adaptation for a Spoken Dialogue System. In *Proceedings of NAACL-00*.
4. Dai, W. and Cohen, R. 2003. Dynamic Personalized TV Recommendation System. *Proceedings of the UM 2003 Workshop on Personalization in Future TV*. Pittsburgh, US, 12-21.
5. Goldberg, D., Nichols, D, Oki, B.M., and Terry, D. 1992. Using collaborative filtering to weave an information tapestry. *Communications of ACM*, 35(12): 51-60.
6. Jokinen, K. 1996. Goal Formulation Based on Communicative Principles. *Proceedings of the 16th International Conference on Computational Linguistics,* Copenhagen, Denmark, 598-603
7. Jokinen, K., Rissanen, J., Keränen, H., and Kanto, K. 2002. Learning Interaction Patterns for Adaptive User Interfaces. In *Adjunct Proceedings of the 7th ERCIM Workshop User Interfaces for all*, Paris, France, 53-58.
8. Jokinen, K., Kanto, K. Rissanen, J., Sahlgren, M. 2003. Prototype user modelling component. Deliverable D6.3. DUMAS IST-2000-29452.
9. Krahmer, E., Swerts, M., Theune, M., Weegels, M. 1999. Problem Spotting in Human-Machine Interaction. In *Proceedings of Eurospeech '99*. Vol. 3. Budapest, Hungary, 1423-1426.
10. Litman, D. and Pan, S. 1999. Empirically Evaluating an Adaptable Spoken Dialogue System. In *Proceedings of the 7th International Conference on User Modeling*, Banff, Canada, 55-64.
11. Malone,T., Grant,K., Turbak, F., Brobst, S. and Cohen, M. 1987. Intelligent information sharing systems. *Communications of the ACM*, (30):390-402.

12. Moukas, A., and Maes, P. 1998. Amalthaea: An evolving Multi-Agen Information Filtering and Discovery System for the WWW. *Autonomous Agents and Multi-Agent Systems*, 1(1):59-88.
13. Oppermann, R. 1994. Adaptively supported Adaptability. *International Journal of Human-Computer Studies*, 40:455-472.
14. Paris, C. 1993. *User Modelling in Text Generation*, Frances Pinter.
15. Sahlgren, M. 2003. Content-based Adaptivity in Multilingual Dialogue Systems. In *Proceedings of the 14th Nordic Conference of Computational Linguistics*, Reykjavík, Iceland.
16. Smith R. W. and Hipp D. R. 1994. *Spoken Natural Language Dialog Systems - A Practical Approach*. Oxford: Oxford University Press.
17. Smith, R. W. 1993. Effective Spoken Natural Language Dialog Requires Variable Initiative Behavior: An Empirical Study. *Proceedings of the 1993 AAAI Fall Symposium on Human-Computer Collaboration: Reconciling Theory, Synthesizing Practice*.
18. Walker, M., Langkilde, I., Wright, J., Gorin, A., and Litman, D. 2000. Learning to Predict Problematic Situations in a Spoken Dialogue System: Experiments with How May I Help You? In *Proceedings of the 1st Meeting of the NAACLs*. Seattle, Washington, USA, 210-217.

A Personalised Interface for Web Directories Based on Cognitive Styles

George D. Magoulas[1], Sherry Y. Chen[2], and Dionisios Dimakopoulos[1],[*]

[1] School of Computer Science and Information Systems, Birkbeck College
University of London, Malet Street, London WC1E 7HX, UK
{gmagoulas,dionisis}@dcs.bbk.ac.uk
[2] Department of Information Systems and Computing, Brunel University
Uxbridge, Middlesex, UB8 3PH, UK
Sherry.Chen@brunel.ac.uk

Abstract. Implementing personalisation in Web Directories depends not only on developing appropriate architectures and equipping Web Directories with adaptation techniques, but also on incorporating human factors considerations at an early design stage. Among a range of human factors this paper explores cognitive styles and their influence on users' preferences. Preferences with respect to the organisation and presentation of the content, and the navigation paths are identified through a small-scale study. The findings are analysed and used to implement a prototype Web Directory Browser, gearing interface features to cognitive style-related preferences.

Keywords: Personalisation, User Interfaces, Web-based Information Retrieval, Cognitive Styles.

1 Introduction

The importance of personalisation has been demonstrated by research works in several areas, where human factors, such as level of knowledge, cognitive characteristics, purpose and goals have been shown playing import role in providing successful personalisation [1, 10]. In the context of Web-based Information Retrieval (IR), a number of previous works [2,6,7,8] have indicated that personalisation can support users performance in information seeking. Nevertheless, users of Web-based IR systems still encounter a number of challenging situations: (a) search results are not clearly interpretable and relevant to users' individual preferences; (b) there is a lack of appropriate navigation support for users with different needs; and (c) search options and format presentations are not flexible enough to align with different users' tasks, behaviours, and experience. One possible explanation is that most current search engines do not take into account human factors and serve all users in the same manner using an index of "global" importance based on the linkage structure of the web, such as in Google's PageRank algorithm. In addition, browsing information organised in structured hierarchies, such as those offered by the Web Directories of search en-

---

[*] The authors gratefully acknowledge support by the UK's Engineering and Physical Sciences Research Council (E.P.S.R.C. Grant References: GR/R57737/01 and GR/R92554/01).

C. Stary and C. Stephanidis (Eds.): UI4All 2004, LNCS 3196, pp. 159–166, 2004.
© Springer-Verlag Berlin Heidelberg 2004

gines, also does not help many users: browsing is an inherently interactive activity, and relies on users constructing both a mental model of the information structure and the knowledge to be assimilated [3]. Some users face difficulties in forming a cognitive model or map of the structure and consequently they become lost in the information space [9]. Therefore, it is important to "learn" the underlying cognitive processes of the mental model in order to obtain a holistic view about the user's behaviour [11,12].

Along these lines, this paper focuses on cognitive styles which are particularly influential in forming a mental model, as they relate to an individual's preferred and habitual approach to organising and representing information [12]. The paper starts with a theoretical discussion on cognitive styles and then develops a new model of users' profiling in Web Directories based on relationships identified between cognitive styles and content, structure and presentation aspects of Web Directories. Lastly, a prototype personalised interface is implemented.

2   Exploring the Preferences of the Cognitive Style Groups

Cognitive styles are described as general tendencies of individuals to process information in particular ways. Within the area of cognitive styles, *Witkin's Field Dependence* has been extensively studied, because it reflects the degree to which a user's perception or comprehension of information is affected by the surrounding perceptual or contextual field: *Field Dependent* (FD) individuals tend to perceive objects as a whole, whereas *Field Independent* (FI) individuals focus on each part of the object [14].

Previous research has revealed that users' cognitive styles significantly influence their reaction to the user interface in terms of formats [5], accessibility [4,12], and structure [3]. Results from these studies suggest that different cognitive style groups favour different interface features provided by web-based applications. Therefore, one may hypothesize:

- FI users are less affected by external format/structure, whereas FD user are easily influenced by external format/structure;
- FI users adopt an active approach in locating information, whereas FD users adopt a passive approach in locating information;
- FI users tend to focus on detailed aspects of information space, whereas FD users tend to see a global picture of information space.

A small-scale study was conducted with a sample of 57 computer science students to investigate the above hypotheses. All participants had the basic computing and Internet skills. The research instruments included three Web Directories with different interface features, Cognitive Style Analysis to measure participants' cognitive styles, and an Exit Questionnaire to identify users' perceptions and attitudes towards the interface features of the examined Web Directories. Despite the fact that participants volunteered to take part in the experiment, they were extremely evenly distributed in terms of cognitive styles: 17 were FD (7 female/10 male), 21 were FI (10 female/11 male), and 19 were Intermediate (9 female/10 male).

The experiment used a with-in subject design. Each participant used three specific Web Directories, namely Google, AltaVista and Lycos, in order to cover different types of Web Directories (see Fig. 1a-c). Indeed, these three directories differ in the interface features, content organisation, search results presentation and structure. Google was chosen for its simplicity in terms of interface design, whereas Lycos was chosen for its complexity. Furthermore, AltaVista adopts a design that comes in-between the other two designs.

In order to identify users' real perceptions, participants were allocated one hour to perform a practical task, designed to focus on users' browsing through the content of each Web Directory and on content presentation. The content presented in each Directory varies, and this is reflected in the task activities shown in Fig. 1d; nevertheless all the activities are of the same nature, putting emphasis on analysis and synthesis. For example, analysis of the activity "[find] bingo software to play with friends", may lead a participant to identify the keyword "bingo" and synthesise this keyword with the term "software" and with the requirement the software should allow multi players at the same time.

The Cognitive Styles Analysis (CSA) by Riding was selected as the instrument to measure the cognitive style dimension investigated in this study because it allows Field Dependent competence to be positively measured rather than inferred from poor Field Independent capability. In addition, the CSA offers computerized administration and scoring. It measures what the authors refer to as a *Wholist/Analytic* (WA) dimension, considering it equivalent to Field Dependence [13].

A paper-based questionnaire was applied to collect participants' perceptions and attitudes towards the Web Directories. Three open-ended questions were related to users' opinions about strengths and weaknesses of each Web Directory as well as problems encountered. Thirty closed questions with a range of predetermined replies attempted to identify perceptions towards interface features; questionnaires were filled in in 15 minutes.

Data collected from closed statements of the questionnaire were coded for analysis using SPSS 10.0. The participants' cognitive style was the independent variable and their choices from a range of options were the dependent variable. The analysis used frequency tables in order to find differences among the three cognitive style groups. Data obtained from the Exit Questionnaire were used to identify participants' most relevant preferences with respect to features of Web Directories. Among 30 closed statements, 10 items have shown significant meaning in our context and used for further processing. The preferences identified are explained in more detail in the statistical analysis presented in the following section.

3   Identifying Preferences and Relations to Interface Features

The analysis of the user responses identified similarities in preferences of contents organisation, search results presentation, and navigation structure. In terms of the organisation of the information space, FD and FI users showed different preferences as far as the number of main categories and sub-categories are concerned. 11 FD users (65%) prefer contents organised in many main categories and fewer sub-categories, while FI users (N=15, 71%) favour a small number of main categories with many more sub-categories. This may be interpreted as a tendency of FD users to obtain a global view of the information space; in direct matching with the holistic strategies they use. Conversely, FI users take a serialistic approach concentrating on procedural details. In addition, FI and FD users also favoured different ways for the directories' categories organisation. FI users (N=13, 62%) consider alphabetical order as the most effective way, whilst FD users (N=11, 65%) appreciate an organisation on the basis of relevance. This behaviour of FI users maybe indicate preference to active strategies for information seeking; deciding on their own path [14]. FD users' behaviour, in contrast, tend to be more passive, as they rely on the level of relevance to guide them in finding out the meaningful information [14].

(a) Google Interface Design	(b) Lycos Interface Design

(c) Lycos Interface Design	(d) Task Activities

Directory	Activities
Google	-Web sites on chinese music. -Bingo software to play with friends. -Instructions on writing CVs
LYCOS	-Description of Manchester Library and its Information Services
altavista	-Personal data of Van Gogh. -Glossary of theological terms

Fig. 1. Web directories and information seeking activities used in the experiments.

With respect to the presentation of search results, FI users prefer an alphabetical arrangement (N=12, 57%), considering understandable headings and sub-headings as the most important thing in finding information quickly (N=11, 52%). They are very goal-oriented, and seem to exhibit strong ability in performing perceptual and conceptual tasks and actively segmenting information into relevant parts. By contrary, FD users (N=10, 59%) prefer the extra support offered when results are presented on the basis of their relevance. It was revealed that the holistic/serialistic strategies adopted by FD/FI users also influence their preferences of results presentation with respect to the sub-categories. Listing the sub-categories first, followed by the corresponding search results can help a FD user to get an overview of the relevant information space and available resources (N=11, 65%). On the contrary FI users adopt a serialistic strategy: seeing the results first followed by the sub-categories allows them to access their targets directly (N=15, 71%).

In terms of navigation, the findings show that FI users prefer a depth-first navigation path, while FD users outperform in a breadth-first path. 11 FD users (65%) prefer main categories and their relevant sub-categories on different pages. Conversely, 16 FI users (76%) would appreciate the main categories and sub-categories to be presented on the same page, and 10 FI users (48%) prefer the sub-categories to be placed under the main categories. Furthermore, 15 FI users (71%) would like the subject categories are arranged vertically (from top to bottom), whilst 11 FD users (65%) favour that the subject categories are arranged horizontally (from left to right). These results imply that a FD user needs clear, planned *structure* and reinforcement in the use of Web Directories. Thus the system should provide them with authoritative *guidance* to restructure their personal information space, as the presence of massive information and the absence of external structure may delay FD users' information seeking. However, the structure of the Web Directories does not interfere with FI users, whose cognitive skill is good in restructuring.

4   A Personalised Interface for Web Directories

It has been made clear from the above analysis that FD/|FI groups' preferences differ with regards to contents organisation. Fig. 2a presents an implementation example based on our Prototype Web Directory Browser (PWDB). Most populated second-level sub-categories are placed under the main subject categories (FI users' preference), whilst an overview of the sub-categories space is also provided through the sub-categories menu (FD users' preference).

As far as search results presentation is concerned, one of the solutions to accommodate different cognitive style groups' preferences is to allow the users to see both the results and sub-categories at the same time by using multiple frames. Multiple frames can provide navigation controls in one frame that always stay visible, even if the contents of another frame change. Fig.2b shows how the PWDB accommodates the needs of FI and FD users. Two frames are used to present information. The left frame lists the sub-categories for FD users to see all of the available resources, and the right frame allows FI users to examine the results directly. When the users click on a relevant result from the right frame, the corresponding web page is presented; the left frame remains unaltered in order to let users see all of the available resources. The resources shown in the right frame of Fig. 2b are arranged in order of relevance. Clicking on "View in alphabetical order" allows FI users to see the resources in alphabetical order.

In terms of personalising the navigation structure, FD and FI users favour different paths to navigate through the space. In the PWDB, the pop-up window in Fig. 3 allows users' access to the content through a sub-category's hyperlink (this aligns with the preferences of FD users), whilst at the same time the top three resources-rich sub-categories are shown under the main categories.

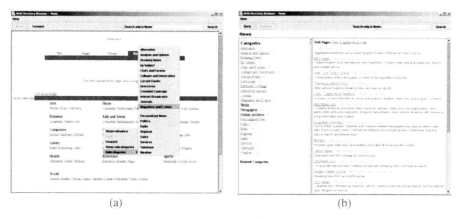

(a)   (b)

Fig. 2. (a) Contents organisation for FI/FD users using multiple menus. (b) Presentation of results in terms of relevance to Field Independent/Dependent users using multiple frames.

Fig. 3. Presentation of sub-categories to Field Dependent users using pop-up.

Our study also indicates that FI and FD users favour different ways to organise the subject categories. Fig. 4a shows an example of interface design that adopts alphabetical order (FI users preference). Moreover, FD users can get additional support by first right-clicking on the main category of interest and then on the "Show relevance" menu item. Subsequently, the relevant subject categories, such as for example "Games", "Recreation" and "Sports", are highlighted with the same colours (see Fig. 4b).

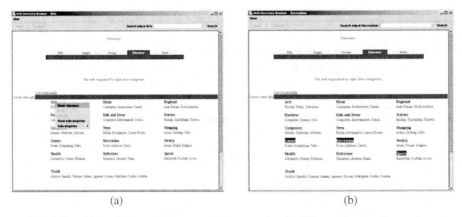

(a)   (b)

Fig. 4. Providing additional support to FD users using the "Show relevance" menu item.

5 Conclusions

Web Directories let users decide their searching and browsing strategies by themselves. In this context, the user interface becomes the major channel to convey information: a well designed and friendly enough interface is thus the key element in helping users to get the best results quickly. This paper identified the interface preferences
of three cognitive style groups by means of a small-scale study, and implemented a
prototype Web Directory browser that accommodates their needs in terms of personalising the content, structure, and presentation.

References

1. Benyon D. and Höök K. Navigation in Information Spaces: supporting the individual. In
   Human-Computer Interaction: INTERACT'97, S. Howard, J. Hammond and G. Lindgaard
   (Eds), London: Chapman and Hall, 39-46, 1997.
2. Borgman, C. L. Why are Online Catalogs Still Hard to Use. Journal of the American Society for Information Science, 47(7), 493-503, 1996.
3. Chen H., Houston A., Sewell R. and Schatz B. Internet browsing and searching: user
   evaluations of category map and concept space techniques, Journal of American Society of
   Information Science 49, 582-603, 1998.
4. Chen, S. Y. and Ford, N. J. Modelling User Navigation Behaviours in a Hypermedia-Based
   Learning System: An Individual Differences Approach. Int. J. of Knowledge Organization,
   25, 67-78, 1998.
5. Chuang, Y-R. Teaching in a Multimedia Computer Environment: A study of effects of
   learning style, gender, and math achievement. Interactive Multimedia Electronic Journal of
   Computer-Enhanced Learning, 1, 1, 1999. [http://imej.wfu.edu/articles/1999/1/10/].
6. Esichaikul, V., Smith, R. D., and Madely, G. R. The impact of learning style on problem-
   solving performance in a hypertext environment. Hypermedia, 6, 2, 101-111, 1994.
7. Ford, N. and Miller, D. Gender Differences in Internet Perceptions and Use. Aslib Proceedings, 48, 183-192, 1996.

8. Hicks, D. L. Tochterman, K. Eich, S., and Rose, T. Using Metadata to support customisation. Proceedings of the third IEEE Metadata Conference, Bethesda, MD (USA), 1999.

9. McDonald S. and Stevenson R. (1998) Navigation in Hyperspace: An evaluation of navigational tools and subject matter expertise on browsing and information retrieval in hypertext, Interacting with Computers 10(2), 129-142.

10. Magoulas G.D., Papanikolaou K.A., and Grigoriadou M. Adaptive web-based learning: accommodating individual differences through system's adaptation. British J. of Educational Technology, 34, 511–527, 2003.

11. Nahl, D. Information counselling inventory of affective and cognitive reactions while learning the Internet. Internet Reference Services Quarterly 2(2/3), 11–33, 1997.

12. Palmquist, R. A. and Kim, K.-S. Cognitive style and on-line database search experience as predictors of Web search performance. J. of the American Society for Information Science, 51, 6, 558-66, 2000.

13. Riding, R. J. Cognitive Styles Analysis. Learning and Training Technology, Birmingham, 1991.

14. Witkin, H. A., Moore, C. A., Goodenough, D. R., and Cox, P. W. Field-dependent and field independent cognitive styles and their educational implications. Review of Educational Research, 47, 1, 1-64, 1977.

Framework for User Interface Adaptation

Jing-Hua Ye and John Herbert

Department of Computer Science
University College Cork
College Road
Cork, Republic of Ireland
jhy1@student.cs.ucc.ie, j.herbert@cs.ucc.ie

Abstract. This paper presents research efforts targeted at the development of a generic framework providing support for automated user interface (UI) adaptation. We have developed a generic java-based adaptation framework that combines the advantages of manual and automated adaptation. This framework supports the addition and removal of modular adaptation mechanisms. The framework is based on a generic UI markup language (XUL) allowing the manual addition of semantic meta-information at design time. Users may add various adaptive transformations as well as making use of various built-in modules. The framework supports transformation in both SAX and DOM. In addition a supplied fragmentation mechanism automates the decomposition of UIs into UI pages that fit device specific resource limits. The framework has been evaluated on simple case studies doing various experiments, for example, cost of fragmentation and speed comparison of SAX and DOM transformations.

1 Introduction

With the advent of the mobile computing paradigm, a wide range of mobile computing devices has emerged (e.g. PDAs, smart phones, handheld computers etc). It has been predicted that within two years there will be over one billion mobile devices with access to services and information through the Internet. Due to the proliferation of new classes of device accessing services on the web, the design of the UI has become one of the major challenges for these devices. The main reason for restricting UIs that are to be implemented for these mobile devices is that they share some common constraints: small display, limited input devices, low bandwidth, slow processors, small memories, limited power. Even as mobile devices improve (e.g. with expanded memory and faster processors), the process of developing an application targeting wireless devices will be substantially decelerated if the UI must be completely redesigned and re-implemented from scratch for each device.

This paper presents generic software architecture for an adaptive UI development system. This system is based on a standard abstract UI description language, XUL, which is shared among different platforms. The main functionality of this system is the tailoring and transforming of UIs.

2 Overview of Related Work

Various approaches have been proposed and developed to allow different devices access a single server-side implementation. A specialized gateway can automatically

C. Stary and C. Stephanidis (Eds.): UI4All 2004, LNCS 3196, pp. 167–174, 2004.

translate HTML content to WML content for WAP devices [3, 7]. This approach allows developers to ignore the device the interface will be rendered on and instead focus on producing high quality UIs. The W3C consortium has also been looking at different means of characterizing diverse display devices, for instance CC/PP descriptions using RDF [13] and DIA [14]. These approaches intend to support accurate and appropriate dynamic UI adaptation.

Traditional UI languages were mostly designed with a specific environment in mind. The design of a UI in an abstract language and the explicit mapping to a concrete UI language is more flexible and provides a more future-proof solution. There are several existing or developing XML-based UI specification languages, for example, UIML [4, 2] is a high-level representation for presentation and dialog data. But it is not capable of describing the design rationale of a UI. XForms [11] is the next generation of HTML forms and provides some level of separation between the actual data and its presentation. However, it is not powerful enough to serve as a universal interchange representation.

XUL [12, 6] is an XML-compliant presentation specification for creating light weight, cross-platform, device-independent UIs. It uses templates in combination with RDF data sources to generate dynamic UIs. The main attractiveness of XUL lies in the fact that one language can serve a multitude of target languages. The layout and look-and-feel of XUL applications can be altered independently of the XUL application definition and logic due to the fact that it provides a clear separation between the client application definition and programming logic, presentation and language specific widgets. The limitation of using XUL is that it is more limited in scope than XIML or UIML. It is an XML based grammar for specifying static GUIs. It lacks a way of describing UIs not defined by distinct graphical objects (e.g. voice, speech).

We choose to use XUL, a standard descriptive language for UI design, instead of inventing a new kind of description language because this description language offers us re-usability, portability and extensibility properties.

3   Software Architecture for Adaptation

Figure 1 shows the main architectural components of this framework. The general philosophy in this model is to form a generic architecture for providing thin client interfaces (that run in the client devices, not the server). Furthermore, this framework makes use of the Xalan-XSLT-processor [1] by the Apache group and the JAXP [9] package from Sun.

3.1   Client Inputs

The XUL, XML and the associated XSL specifications, are created by the clients at design time with a normal text editor, and are the required inputs to this system:

UI Specication: developers specify UIs using XUL based on the logical structure of the UI. It is prudent for developers to explicitly specify whether each XUL element can be split or not by giving a yes/no value to the 'breakable' attribute of each element.

Device Specication: all physical constraints on the target device (i.e. memory capacity, screen size, resolution etc) on which the UI will be displayed are specified in standard XML format.

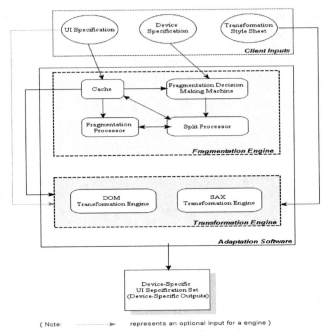

Fig. 1. Generic Architecture for adaptive Uis.

Transformation Style Sheet: all generic XUL interface elements in the UI specification can be transformed to a device-specific default format by applying the transformation rules that are specified in XSL. Each type of device possesses its own style sheet. Currently we have implemented default style sheets for HTML and XHTML for experimental purposes. The selection of a style sheet is based on the client's preferences.

3.2 Fragmentation Engine

The fragmentation engine (fig.1) manages the fragmentation process which paginates a single UI into a set of coherent UIs, each of which is capable of being displayed on the target device. The UI specification is forwarded to a cache that manages the caching of UI fragments. The fragmentation decision-making machine compares the size of a UI that is specified in the UI specification with the display size of the target device, which is specified in the device specification via SAX filters. If the size of the UI exceeds the display size of the target device, the fragmentation processor will be triggered to decide how many fragments need to be formed. Once the number of fragments is determined, each UI fragment can be formed by using the split processor, which fetches the device properties from the fragmentation decision making machine and employs the SAX parser or SAXWriter to write the UI elements into the corresponding files in terms of XUL element tags. Finally, each written fragment is stored in the cache until the completion of the fragmentation process. Further details of the new fragmentation approach that has been adopted by this component is covered in [5].

3.3 Transformation Engine

The transformation engine (fig.1) takes responsibility for transforming either each fragmented page or the UI specification to a device-specific one. Our transformation engine encompasses both the DOM transformation engine and SAX transformation engine, with the DOM transformation engine being set as the default engine. Internally, this component comprises four possible different architectures:

1. Using a DOM transformation engine to transform each fragmented page. In this case, the following constituents are obtained:

   DOM Builder: It is responsible for constructing a DOM tree for each page in memory.

   DOM Navigation Processor: It takes responsibility for adding navigation links as nodes on the DOM tree of each page.

   DOM Parallel Transformation Engine: Each page can be transformed to the device-specific format in parallel by DOM transformers.

2. Using a SAX transformation engine to transform each fragmented page. In this case, two subcomponents are supplied:

   SAX Navigation Processor: It takes responsibility for adding navigation links by means of using SAXWriter or SAX parser to write additional <link> elements to each page. Each <link> element contains a "src" attribute that points to the destination page.

   SAX Parallel Transformation Processor: Each page can be transformed to the device-specific format in parallel by SAX transformers.

3. Using a DOM transformation engine to transform the UI specification explicitly. In this scenario, the UI specification is parsed by the DOM parser, which constructs the corresponding DOM tree in memory. Subsequently, the result of the DOM parser will be transformed by the DOM transformer with supplied transformation style sheet to a device-specific UI specification.

4. Using a SAX transformation engine to transform the UI specification explicitly. The SAX transformation engine exploits filter pipelined architecture. The UI specification and a reader are encapsulated as a Source object. The transformer sets up an internal object as the content handler for filter2, and tells it to parse the input source; filter2, in turns, sets up as the content handler for filter1, and tells it to parse the input source; filter1, in turns, tells the SAX parser to parse the input source. The SAX parser does so, generating SAX events which it passes to filter1; filter1, acting in its capacity as a content handler, processes the events and does its transformations. Then, acting in its capacity as a SAX reader (XMLReader), it sends SAX events to filter2; filter2 does the same, sending its events to the transformer's content handler, which generates the output stream.

4 Evaluation

A simple college book online ordering demo has been developed to demonstrate the adaptation capabilities of our generic framework. A small Mozilla application for this demo rendered on a PDA and a desktop computer (HTML) is shown in the appendix. A one-page PC presentation is paginated into a 6-page PDA presentation. The entry point to the dialog flow of the PDA is the main index page after transforming those fragmented pages into HTML. Navigation to the main index page is done by using the "main index page" link inserted by the framework for each fragment. A user can navigate between the fragments by means of "previous page" and "next page" links inserted by the adaptation system. In addition, this generic architecture offers several conveniences to UI developers:

1. The ability to use component-reuse techniques to update or create a new UI for a new application on the fly. Users can just paginate a single UI into a set of fragments, and then each newly formed fragmentation specification can be regarded as a single standalone component.

2. It offers a great deal of flexibility to the users during the transcoding process. Users can either transcode the un-paginated UI explicitly or render each fragmented page for wireless devices. It also meets the needs of different users. For advanced users, they can select a DOM transformation engine or a SAX one, or create their own transformation engine without too much difficulty. For novices, who have no knowledge of UI development, the default engine can simply be used.

3. In addition to the added flexibilities, this system allows great extensibility as well. Additional functionality can be easily added by pipelining extra engines with the required functionality. For instance, users can customize those UIs (e.g. remove images for target devices that have low resolution or apply reduction-transformations to reduce the resolution of images so that they are displayable on the target device) by supplying additional filter chains with suitable XSL style sheets before the transformation process.

4. Users can learn XUL easily and quickly since it is a declarative language with a simple syntax and semantics. The low learning curve allows a wide range of people to start writing UIs without intensive study.

4.1 Evaluation of the SAX and DOM Transformation Engines

The evaluation of the architecture has consisted of measuring the performance for processing the college book ordering application. The following notations will be used for evaluating the performance of this framework:

SAX-SAX: Using the SAX engine to transform each fragmented page.
SAX-DOM: Using the DOM engine to transform each fragmented page.
Single DOM: Using the DOM engine to transform the UI specification explicitly.
Single SAX: Using the SAX engine to transform the UI specification explicitly.

The simulation for this simple case study was conducted under the following conditions:

- A 2.4GHz Pentium 4 processor DELL PC running SUSE 8.0
- Using the Xalan-XSLT-Processor to perform the transcoding process
- Compiled with the J2SE1.4.2 compiler
- used the JAXP1.2.4 package
- used the Mozilla 1.6 web browser to illustrate the results of this simulation

The total processing time for each possible process is:

SAX-SAX: 0.6618 second
SAX-DOM: 0.6567 second
Single SAX: 0.1431 second
Single DOM: 0.1165 second

These results are the average of 1000 simulations. The above experimental results have shown that:

1. Even though SAX-DOM is faster than SAX-SAX by 0.0051 second, using a standard method of estimating statistical significance, the t-test [10] value(t=0.511) indicates that the difference between them is not statistically significant. After fragmentation, users can choose either DOM transformation or SAX transformation. SAX-DOM spent 88.58% of its time in the transformation out of total processing time. and SAX-SAX spent 88.82% of its time in the transformation out of total processing time. These figures have shown that SAX-SAX and SAX-DOM have spent most of the time on the transformation. Further optimization of the transcoding will lead to a significant speed-up while preserving the advantages of flexibility.
2. Comparing transformation without fragmentation and transforming with fragmentation shows that there is a significant difference between them. This indicates that fragmentation slows down the entire process of adaptation. How to avoid fragmentation during the process of adapting the UI and how to shrink a UI for wireless devices efficiently is a topic that needs further exploration.

5   Conclusions and Future Work

In this paper we presented a generic adaptation framework for building thin client UIs that adapt to multiple display devices. This framework processes XUL descriptions to generate device specific UIs. Furthermore, we introduced a new fragmentation methodology using the SAX API. This framework will reduce memory consumption during the pagination process due to the nature of the SAX parser which means that it does not need to build the whole logical tree structure of the UI in memory in advance. Using DOM to fragment a very sophisticated UI, the size of whose tree exceeds the amount of free memory, will not succeed. This case is unlikely to occur in this framework. The evaluation of this framework has revealed that there is no significant speed difference between the SAX and DOM transformation engines after pagination. Inevitably, the speed of transforming a single page without fragmentation is much faster than with fragmentation.

Ongoing developments include a "dynamic UI validation" and "UI migration" mechanisms. Integrating additional mechanism into the existing architecture can be done easily by introducing new engines due to the extensibility of this architecture.

Acknowledgements

The authors acknowledge the helpful suggestions of the referees.

References

1. The Apache Software Foundation: Xalan-Java version 2.6.0. (Feb 18th 2002)
   http://xml.apache.org/xalan-j/
2. C.Phanouri: UIML:An Appliance-Independent XML User Interface Language. PHD Thesis Computer Science, Virginia Tech (2000)

3. Fox, A., Gribble, S., Chawathe, Y., and Breuer, E.: Adapting to Network and Client Variation using Infrastructural Proxies: lessons and perspectives. IEEE Personal Communications, 5(4), P10–P19
4. Harmonia, Inc.: User Interface Markup Language (UIML) v3.0 Draft Specification. (2000) http://www.uiml.org/
5. Jing-Hua Ye and John Herbert: User Interface Tailoring for Mobile Computing Devices. In: 8th ERCIM Workshop "User Interfaces For All" 2004 (to appear)
6. Lori MacVittie: Conjure Up XUL for Browser Flexibility. Business Applications workshop (March 5 2001) http://www.networkcomputing.com/1205/1205ws4.html
7. Palm Corp: Web Clipping Services. http://www.palm.com
8. Pedro Azevedo,Roland Merrik: OVID to AUIML-User-Oriented Interface Modelling. In: IBM technical report (2000)
9. Sun, Inc.: The JavaTM Web Service Tutorial v1.2.4. In: (2003) http://java.sun.com/
10. TexaSoft Org: Statistics Tutorial: Comparing Two Groups In: tutorial, (2004) http://www.texasoft.com/2groups.html
11. T.V.Raman: XForms:XML Powered Web Forms. publisher: Addison Wesley (September 2003)
12. Vaughn Bullard,Kevin T.Smith: Essential XUL programming. publisher: John Wiley & Sons, Inc. (2001)
13. W3C: Composite Capabilities/Preferences Profile. http://www.w3.org/Mobile/CCPP/
14. W3C: Device Independence Activity: Working towards Seamless Web access and authoring. http://www.w3.org/2001/di/

A College Book Ordering Online Demo Application

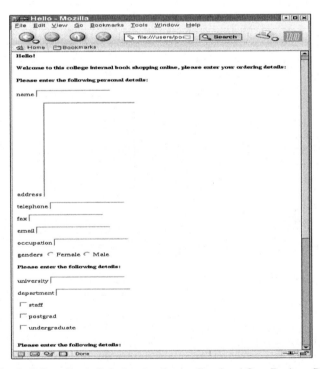

Fig. 2. College Book Ordering Application Rendered On a Desktop PC.

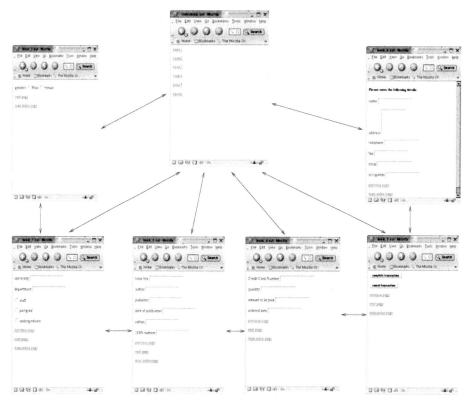

Fig. 3. College Book Ordering Application Rendered On a PDA.

Interface Tailoring for Mobile Computing Devices

Jing-Hua Ye and John Herbert

Department of Computer Science
University College Cork
College Road
Cork, Republic of Ireland
jhy1@student.cs.ucc.ie, j.herbert@cs.ucc.ie

Abstract. One of the major challenges in user interface (UI) development is device heterogeneity. Currently, devices such as smart phones, PDAs, and PCs are already capable of providing ubiquitous access to the Internet. In the near future, we are expecting other devices to support the same capabilities. As the number of these devices proliferates, the conventional approach of developing a UI for each device results in too much redundant effort. To meet this challenge, we propose a new fragmentation methodology using a general indexing technique. It allows users to fragment a UI into a number of fragments for the target device. This innovative fragmentation methodology has been evaluated in terms of processing time, and a comprehensive comparison made between the processing time of adaptation with fragmentation and the processing time of adaptation without fragmentation.

1   Introduction

The market for mobile computing devices is growing two times faster than the market for traditional PCs. As mobile devices have become more and more popular and their physical capabilities have considerably improved, there is a huge demand for adapting UIs rapidly. The new variety of devices available has had a profound influence on the way UIs are built. The aim of UI adaptation is to reduce the effort needed by UI developers to develop similar UIs for different devices. One feasible solution is to split a single UI into a set of manageable UIs that satisfy the constraints of target devices, for example, small display size, low bandwidth network, slow processors and so on.

This paper presents a novel UI fragmentation technique that is embedded in the UI adaptation process. The UI adaptation process contains two sub-processes, one is a UI fragmentation process, and the other is a UI transformation process. The entire UI adaptation process is based on an abstract, generic UI description, XUL, which is an essential component for the fragmentation engine that was proposed in [4]. This newly developed UI fragmentation technique paginates the UI to minimize the mismatch between its presentation and the device's capability to present it.

2   Overview of Related Work

Several techniques and tools have been developed for constructing usable UIs for multiple devices. One approach is design by graceful degradation. This approach employs a priority ordering to preserve a maximal continuity between the platform specific versions of the UI, and is based on an original set of rules, which are de-

C. Stary and C. Stephanidis (Eds.): UI4All 2004, LNCS 3196, pp. 175–182, 2004.

scribed and classified in a model-based framework [2]. Another approach is the model-based transformational approach – the scalable web technique [9]. This technique addresses the problem of device heterogeneity in web development by building a presentation model at design time. This model is submitted to two adaptation processes: a pagination process and a control transformation. This approach offers a guarantee of continuity between the system versions and the adaptation of the UI to the specific targets. However, only a limited set of transformation rules has been provided. Other approaches include Covigo [5] that has developed a system for paginating the content of web pages by pattern or by size, and XWeb [6], which needs to be operated on a specific XWEB server and using a browser tuned to how the particular interactive platform communicates with the XTP protocol.

Besides these techniques there are two additional approaches fro paginating a UI that is to be presented in other devices: a heuristic fragmentation algorithm for web-based dialogs [7] and a hybrid approach that re-models the widgets of a window into a new composition of "small" windows with a reasonable flow of transition between them [3]. In the heuristic fragmentation algorithm, a dialog is considered to be a tree with container parts as inner nodes and non-container parts as leaves. This approach can be implemented using standard DOM APIs, which means that the entire tree structure of a dialog resides in memory. The drawback of this approach is that constructing such a tree is time-consuming and so will likely run out of memory (i.e. requiring larger and larger consumption of memory as the tree grows in size). The latter approach is based on a strategy that links two hierarchies of graphs. This adaptation process dynamically re-models a presentation model to better fit into the current platform model. The shortcoming of this approach is that it is not straightforward enough for the users to easily comprehend.

The analysis of existing approaches to fragmentation algorithms for adaptive UIs has led to a new method for tailoring the UI that is described in the following section. Beyond the basic fragmentation functions, the motivation of the fragmentation methods is to minimize the use of computing resources. Therefore comprehensive evaluation of the new fragmentation method is carried out.

3   User Interface Fragmentation Method

The main difficulty in presenting UIs on multiple heterogeneous devices is the presence of a wide variation in display and memory sizes. A conventional desktop PC can usually display a sophisticated UI in high resolution immediately, but a PDA or smart phone may require the fragmentation of the UI due to its small screen size, limited memory size and low resolution. Fragmentation must not be performed arbitrarily and also must not break the logical structure of the UI. For instance, a text field must not be separated from its description label. In order to preserve this property during the fragmentation process, every generic XUL interface element must have an additional "breakable" attribute to clarify whether it can be split or not.

3.1   Atomic Units of Fragmentation Process

UI compounds are atomic units of the fragmentation process. Figure 1 shows the structure of a UI compound consists of four constituent parts:

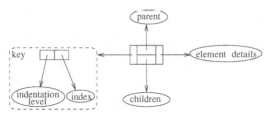

Fig. 1. A UI compound structure.

Keys: This is the unique identifier of each UI compound, and each key has two parts:

Indentation Level: By the nature of the XML-compliant UI specification, the parent-child relationship between two compounds has to be reflected in terms of the indentation level of each generic XUL interface element specified in the UI specification.

Index: Two sibling compounds can be distinguished by their indexes. In other words, when two compounds share the same indentation level, they can be distinguished by their indexes.

Parent: This refers to a group of UI compounds that are the parents of a specific UI compound.

Child: This refers to a collection of UI compounds that are children of this one.

Element Details: This refers to the corresponding generic XUL interface element in the UI specification.

3.2 Fragmentation Process

The process of tailoring a UI has been divided into the following phases (the notations are summarized in table 1):

Indexing Phase: Proper keys and element details are assigned for each UI compound while each generic XUL interface element specified in the UI specification has been read by the SAX parser. In general, a UI can only have one top-level container, in XUL terms this top-level container is a <window> element. The indentation level and index for the root container of a UI are always 1. After all the UI compounds have been allocated with proper keys and element details, each one of them is cached into the UI compound store. A simple "Hello World" example is shown in the Appendix.

Classifying Phase: Starts by retrieving an individual UI compound stored in the compound store and classifies it according to the following criteria:

A UI compound is a breakable UI compound if its "breakable" attribute has a yes value. If the value of the "breakable" attribute for a UI compound is no, then two different scenarios can arise: it is an atomic UI compound group if it shares the same indentation level with other unbreakable UI compounds, otherwise, it will be a standalone unbreakable UI compound.

Redundant Breakable Compounds Removal Phase: When BCs (i.e. containers) are nested within each other, those redundant containers can be eliminated by applying the following redundancy rule:

Assume that there are two BCs X and Y, X is redundant if and only if $l_x <$ l_y and $i_x = \text{prefix}(i_y)$.

After those redundant BCs are identified by applying the above rule, each one of them has to be removed from the group of breakable compounds.

Table 1. Summary of notations.

Notations	
l_X	indentation level for UI compound X
i_X	index for UI compound X
$\text{prefix}(i_X)$	prefix of index of UI compound X
(l_X, i_X)	key of UI compound X
children(x)	children of UI compound X
parent(x)	parent of UI compound X
UBC	unbreakable UI compound
ACG	atomic UI compound groups
BC	breakable UI compound
num(UBC)	number of unbreakable UI compounds
num(ACG)	number of atomic UI compound groups
num(frag)	number of fragments
SAX-SAX	Using the SAX transformation engine to transform each fragmented page
SAX-DOM	Using the DOM transformation engine to transform each fragmented page

Linking Phase: After the removal of redundant BCs, the parent-child relationship can be established properly by applying the following mapping rule:

Assume there is one UBC X, one BC Y, and one ACG Z, if $\text{prefix}(i_z) = i_x$, then children(X) → Z and parent(Z) → X; if $\text{prefix}(i_y) = i_x$, then children(X) → Y and parent(Y) → X.

Fig. 2. Outcome of the mapping rule

The established relationship can be illustrated in figure 2. In order to clarify the meaning of this rule, this rule can be interpreted into simple pseudocode as follows:

if $\text{prefix}(i_z)$ equals i_x then
 the children of UI compound X are the elements of the ACG Z;
 the parent of each element in the ACG Z is X;
if $\text{prefix}(i_y)$ equals i_x then
 the children of UI compound X is the UBC Y;
 the parent of UBC Y is X;

We step through each UI compound in the BC group, and for each one, compare the current prefix of the index of BC with each UBC and then with each ACG by applying the mapping rule.

Number of Fragments Determination Phase: To determine the number of fragments that needs to be formed. The number of fragments is calculated using the equation:

$$num(frag) \rightarrow num(UBC) + num(ACG) \tag{1}$$

This means that the number of fragments equals the sum of the number of UBCs and the number of ACGs.

Writing Phase: While walking through the UBCs and ACGs, the elements details each of these, including the referencing parents and children of each, are written to the file corresponding to that particular fragment in XUL by the SAX writer. The formed file is called the fragmentation specification.

To sum up, properly indexing each UI compound is a vital step in the fragmentation process, because the subsequent steps mainly rely on the index of each UI compound. The index of a UI compound plays an important role in the process. Due to the importance of the index of each UI compound, he fragmentation process has adopted a general indexing technique.

4 Evaluation

In order to evaluate our newly developed fragmentation process we have measured the performance of this process via the following experiment:

Conditions:
- This experiment is performed on a DELL PC with 2.4 GHz Pentium IV processor, 256MB DDR RAM and 40GB Hard drive running SUSE 8.0.
- We used the architecture that we have built previously [4], which is built with the JAXPv1.2.4 package [8] and with Xalan-XSLT-Processor [1], to run our experiment.
- This simulation is executed with the standard J2SE1.4.2 java compiler.

Methods:
1. Design small elements: each small element contains a various number of generic XUL interface components (i.e. XUL UI element tags), the number being in the range from 1 to 70. In this experiment, 26 small elements have been designed for the purpose of this experiment.
2. Design basic components: this experiment makes use of 26 small elements, some of them arre randomly combined together to form a single basic component according to the number of fragments needed.
3. Fragment: the basic component is fragmented, and then each fragment is transformed by the DOM or SAX transformation engine. The number of fragments is increased in increments of 5 (i.e. 5 fragments, 10 fragments, 15 fragments and so on) until the computer stops the process automatically.

4. Establish a control group: the basic elements under identical experimental conditions (e.g. with the same increments in the number of fragments) are not fragmented, but are transformed with DOM and SAX transformation engines separately.

Results:

1. Figure 3 demonstrates that the processing time of pagination increases as the number of fragments grows. The processing time of fragmentation and the number of fragments have a direct proportional relationship.
2. Figure 4 shows that the time consumed on the fragmentation process is roughly 10% of the entire adaptation process time.
3. In this experiment, SAX-DOM (using the DOM transformation engine to transform each fragment) has successfully sliced a UI into 160 fragments and each fragment is transformed into a concrete UI. Likewise, SAX-SAX (using the SAX transformation engine to transform each fragment) has fragmented a UI into 170 fragments and each one is transformed into a concrete UI. By way of comparison, a UI containing 600 fragments (non-sliced) can still be transformed into a concrete UI for the desktop PC. This indicates that the adaptation process with fragmentation consumes 3.5 times more space than the one without fragmentation.
4. Figure 5 shows that the time spent on the adaptation process with fragmentation is much longer than the time spent on the adaptation process without fragmentation.

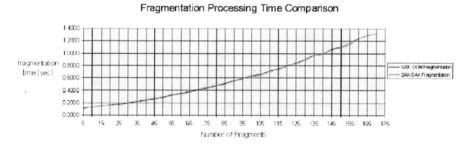

Fig. 3. Comparing the fragmentation time between SAX-DOM and SAX-SAX.

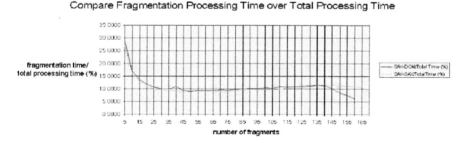

Fig. 4. Comparing the fragmentation time over total processing time.

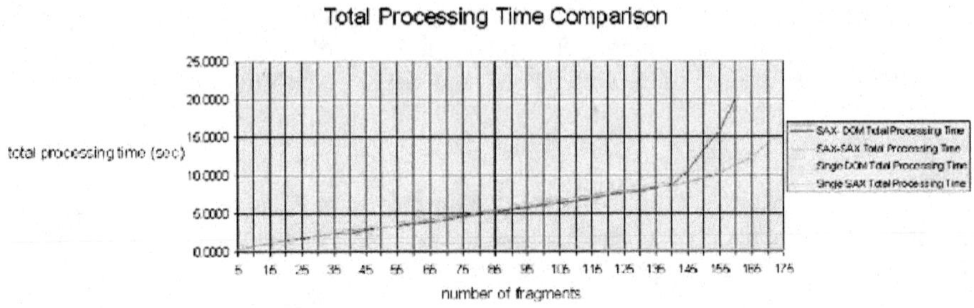

Total Processing Time Comparison

Fig. 5. Total processing time comparison.

5   Discussion and Conclusion

We have developed a new fragmentation method that fragments a sophisticated UI by using SAX APIs to index each abstract XUL interface component so that it can be displayed on the wireless devices. This fragmentation process provides UI developers with the convenience of UI development for multiple-devices. By the nature of the SAX API, this technique can save memory consumption during the UI adaptation process. Clearly there are costs involved in fragmentation and our experiments have quantified these costs. The evaluation has shown that the fragmentation process consumes a certain amount of time and memory resources, slowing down the UI adaptation process. The new fragmentation method and its assessment is complementary to other research on avoiding fragmentation during the UI adaptation process and efficiently shrinking a UI for wireless devices.

Acknowledgements

The authors acknowledge the helpful suggestions of the referees.

References

1. The Apache Software Foundation: Xalan-Java Version 2.6.0 (Feb 18th 2002) http://xml.apache.org/xalan-j/
2. Murille Florins, Jean Vanderdonckt: Graceful Degradation of User Interfaces as a Design Method for Multi-platform Systems. In: Proc. Of 8th ACM Int. Conf. on Intelligent User Interfaces IUT'2004, ACM Press, New York, 2004, p140-p147
3. Guido Menkhaus, Wolfgang Pree: A Hybrid Approach to Adaptive User Interface Generation. In: Journal of Computing and Information Technology (CIT), 10(3), 2002
4. Jing-Hua Ye and John Herbert: Framework for User Interface Adaptation. In: 8th ERCIM Workshop "User Interfaces for All" 2004 (to appear)
5. Mandyam, S., Vedati, K., Kuo, C., Wang, W.: User Interface Adaptations: Indispensable for Single Authoring. In: Proc. of W3C Workshop on Device Independent Authoring Techniques 2002
6. Olsen, D.R.,Jefferies.,S.,Nielsen,T.,Moyes,P. and Fredrickson,P.: Cross Modal Interaction using XWEB. In: Proc. of the 13th annual ACM symposium on User Interface Software and Technology UIST 2000 p191-p200

7. Stedd Gobel, Sven Buchholz: Device Independent Representation of Web-based dialogs and contents. In: Proc. of the IEEE YUFORIC 01 2001
8. Sun, In.: The Java^TM Web Service Tutorial v 1.2.4. In: http://java.sun.com/ (2003)
9. Wong C., ChuH.H. and Katagiri M.A: Single-Authoring Technique for Building Device Independent Authoring Techniques. In: Proc. of W3C Workshop on Device Independetn Authoring Techniques 2002, accessible at http://www.w3.org/2002/DIAT/posn/docomo.pdf

A Indexing Phase for "Hello World" Example

Program A.1 shows how to assign keys for each generic XUL interface component in the "Hello World" UI Specification. Symbol (x,y) represents a key, in which x is the indentation level of the key and y is the index of the key.

Program A.1 "Hello World" XUL UI Specification

```
<?xml version="1.0"?>
<?xml-stylesheet href="skin/morden/global/global.cs" type="text/css"?>
<?xml-stylesheet href="skin/morden/global/samplel.cs" type="text/css"?>
<window  xmlns="http://www.w3.org/keymaster/gatekeeper/there.is.only.xul"
         xmlns:html="http://www.w3.org/1999/html"
         title="hello" width="300" height="215">          (1, 1)
         <box breakable="yes">                            (2, 1.1)
           <vbox breakable="yes">                         (3, 1.1.1)
            <label value="hello" breakable="no">          (4, 1.1.1.1)
            <label value="world" breakable="no">          (4, 1.1.1.2)
           </vbox>
           <label value="hello world" breakable="no">     (3, 1.1.2)
         </box>
</window>
```

Towards Guidelines for Usability
of e-Learning Applications

Carmelo Ardito[1], Maria Francesca Costabile[1], Marilena De Marsico[2],
Rosa Lanzilotti[1], Stefano Levialdi[2], Paola Plantamura[1],
Teresa Roselli[1], Veronica Rossano[1], and Manuela Tersigni[2]

[1] Dipartimento di Informatica – Università di Bari
{ardito,costabile,lanzilotti,pplantamura,roselli,rossano}
@di.uniba.it
[2] Dipartimento di Informatica – Università di Roma "La Sapienza"
{demarsico,levialdi,tersigni}@dsi.uniroma1.it

Abstract. One present goal of researchers and developers is to design software tools that make learning materials available online in an educationally effective manner. We face the twofold challenge of implementing advanced e-learning functionalities, though designing their interface so as to provide an easy interaction grasping the students' interest. A poorly designed interface makes students spend more time in learning it than in mastering the provided knowledge, so becoming a barrier to effective learning. In this context, both User-Centered Design (UCD) and Learner-Centered Design (LCD) guidelines are needed; it is also important to devise suited evaluation tools, able to help in identifying usability, and, more in general, accessibility flaws. Such tools must be designed bearing in mind the specific characteristics of e-learning applications. Traditional heuristic evaluation appears too general and subjective. In this paper, we propose a set of guidelines and criteria for e-learning platforms (containers) and for educational modules (contents), to be used within the SUE (Systematic Usability Evaluation) inspection. We point out that human factors experts can primarily evaluate "syntactic" aspects of applications. Experts of education science and domain experts are to be involved for a more comprehensive evaluation.

1 Introduction

In the age of the new Information and Communication Technology, it should be possible to learn not only by a locally available electronic support, i.e. an interactive CD-Rom, but even "far away" from the teaching source. One challenge for designers and HCI researchers is to develop software tools able to engage novice learners and to support their learning even at distance. Aside from User-Centered Design (UCD) methods [7] for developing usable and accessible tools, we need Learner-Centered Design (LCD) methods [17] in order to make new learning domains accessible in an educationally effective manner. Because of the specific context in which an e-learning application is used, it is necessary to evaluate the application usability, but also the didactic effectiveness of the courseware.

This kind of evaluation must be related to all aspects of didactic design of the courseware such as the *analysis and definition of learning needs*, the *definition of learning goals*, the methodology used for *didactic content organization*, and last but not least the selection and implementation of the *learning assessment strategies*.

C. Stary and C. Stephanidis (Eds.): UI4All 2004, LNCS 3196, pp. 185–202, 2004.
© Springer-Verlag Berlin Heidelberg 2004

Thus, in the evaluation of an e-learning application it is important to involve both education science and domain experts with their own professional skills.

More questions arise depending on the new "vehicle" exploited in the learning process. Both content and teaching strategies must undergo re-purposing, in order to fully exploit the new technologies, adapting to each learner profile. We face a twofold challenge. Effective e-learning applications should include advanced functions, yet their interface should hide their complexity to learners, providing an easy, flexible and satisfying interaction grasping the students' interest. Despite of this, what we often find is a mere electronic transposition of traditional material, provided through rigid interaction schemes and awkward interfaces.

The interaction between learners and computers is a neglected topic in the field of Web-based training. When learners complain about Web-based training or express a preference for classroom-based instruction, it's often not the training, but rather the confusing menus, unclear buttons, or illogical links that scare them off. The success of any training program is largely dependent on the student's motivation and attitude. If a poorly designed interface makes them feeling lost, confused, or frustrated, it will become a barrier to effective learning and information retention [10].

Accessibility is another neglected topic in the e-learning context. Accessibility implies the requirement for access to information by individuals with different abilities, background and preferences, in a variety of contexts of use [23]. To deliver accessible e-learning material, an opportunity worth exploring is personalization of digital material presentation in accordance with users' needs or preferences. Most of the existing efforts for supporting the preparation and delivery of accessible e-learning material [4, 6, 11] propose guidelines directed to technical accessibility aspects, such as the format and navigation of learning materials. Nevertheless, this approach does not take into account the didactic effectiveness of innovative e-learning methods for users with different abilities.

In this work, we argue that ensuring usability should be one of the main challenges of e-learning application developers, as well as a prerequisite that should allow learners to profitably exploit such applications. We also point out that computer scientists can primarily evaluate "syntactic" aspects of applications. Experts of education science and domain experts are to be involved for a more comprehensive evaluation. A cost-effective technique to evaluate usability is the heuristic evaluation originally proposed by Nielsen [14, 15]. It prescribes to have a small set of experts inspecting the system, and evaluating its interface against a list of recognised usability principles – the heuristics. Experts can be usability specialists, experts of the specific domain of the application to be evaluated, or (preferably) double experts, with both usability and domain experience.

Heuristic evaluation has however a number of drawbacks. As highlighted in [5, 8, 9], the major one is its high dependence upon the skills and experiences of the evaluators. Moreover heuristics, as formulated by Nielsen, are basically generic and unable to appropriately drive the evaluator's activity. This problem is pointed out by various researchers who have therefore developed more specific guidelines for particular system classes [1, 12, 23]. In order to provide a more robust evaluation method, SUE (Systematic Usability Evaluation) inspection has been introduced [13]. It uses evaluation patterns, called Abstract Tasks (ATs), describing how to estimate compliance of application components with a set of attributes and guidelines, which are preliminarily identified for a particular system class. ATs guide the inspector's activity, precisely describing which objects of the application to look for, and which actions to perform in order to analyse such objects. In this way, even less experienced evaluators are able to come out with more complete and precise results.

In this paper, we first dwell upon the difference between attributes for platforms (containers) and for educational modules (contents), provided by a platform or apart. We then propose a preliminary set of guidelines and criteria to be exploited for designing usable e-learning applications. More specifically, the paper is organized as follows. Section 2 describes the current scenario of usability of e-learning systems. Section 3 outlines the SUE inspection. In Section 4 we define usability guidelines for e-learning platforms and e-learning modules. E-learning usability evaluation is refined in Section 5 by giving a list of abstract Tasks to verify compliance with identified guidelines. Finally, Section 6 provides conclusions and highlights future works that will take into account the didactic effectiveness of e-learning applications.

2   Usability Issues in e-Learning

In any system, all the more if it is remote such as an e-learning system, usability plays a vital role for its success. If an e-learning system is not much usable, it obstructs the student's learning. So s/he is forced to spend much more time to understand software functionality, rather than to understand learning content. Moreover, if the e-learning interface is rigid, slow and unpleasant, people are just as like to go away and forget about it. As a matter of fact, one of the main goals of a learning system is to avoid any distraction to keep all the content fresh in learners' minds as they accommodate new and foreign concepts.

In the specific case of e-learning, designing a "usable" interface means to put together interaction metaphors, images and concepts used to address functions and concepts on the screen in only one design, to create an interactive system that doesn't confuse learners.

A formative product should represent a rewarding experience for the learner. Norman [16] asserts that this kind of product should:

- be interactive and provide feedback
- have specific goals
- motivate, communicating a continuous sensation of challenge
- provide suitable tools
- avoid distractions and factors of nuisance interrupting the learning stream.

Moreover, it should be pedagogically suitable, though attractive and engaging. Using new technologies does not mean to reject traditional and successful teaching strategies, e.g. simulation systems, problem-based learning, and direct manipulation. So, a learning system should allow integrating such strategies.

As already stated, a system providing new and flexible functionalities, supporting new strategies and allowing the integration with successful traditional techniques, could still suffer for poor usability. The need arises for a clear and coherent interface, able to involve the user in the learning process without overwhelming her/him. Forcing students to spend longer time understanding poorly usable interfaces than understanding learning content, is disruptive: distraction disturbs accommodation of new concepts and overall retention of what is being learnt. Learning interfaces have to give a comprehensive idea of content organization and of system functionalities, simple and efficient navigation, advanced personalization of contents and learning, clear exit. In other words, an efficient and motivating educational strategy must be devised and then suitably mapped onto an interface, concentrating on the needs and goals of the learners.

The key to develop a system conforming to the above usability criteria is to adopt a Learner-Centered (LC) methodology. Whereas User-Centered Design (UCD) assumes users' common culture and similar experiences in the application domain, in LCD a variety of learners' categories must be considered, because of personal learning strategies, different experience in the learning domain, different motivations in affording the learning task. In general, learners are not particularly experienced in the learning domain. In particular, they could not even know the learning domain they are approaching, or know it only partially, or even have a wrong idea of it. Moreover, students are not all stimulated by the same motivation in affording a task, rather, a student's motivation can be greatly influenced by the success rate experienced in learning; it will then be necessary to pay particular attention to aids that are provided (i.e. to the way scaffolding is managed) and to the acknowledgement of the improvements attained.

While for UCD the user's effort only concerns the comprehension of a new tool to perform a well known task, in LCD the gulf of expertise between the learner and the learning domain must be considered [17]. The goal of LCD can be defined as to fill up this gulf, making the learner acquire all the knowledge and tools connected to a given subject. In the case of LCD, then, we have to take the learner, through a tool s/he doesn't know how to use, to learn something s/he doesn't know: the problem doubles. Think for example of teaching a child to write using Microsoft Word.

Besides considering technological issues, it is necessary to rely on an educational theory somehow driving the designer in developing suitable tools. At present, constructivist theory is almost universally adopted. Learning is recognized as an active process, where "learning by doing" strategy takes the learner to cognitively manipulate the new learning material, to create cognitive links between it and prior knowledge. For this approach to be effective, a task must be always included in an actual and collaborative context, to make the learner understand the motivation and the final goal of the task itself, also by facing other learners' opinions (socio-constructivist principle) [22].

From all the previous considerations, it comes out that heuristics defined for UC (User-Centered) applications are not well suited to evaluate LC applications. The specific features required from e-learning tools highlight the need to evaluate the usability of this kind of systems in a specific way. In fact, ensuring usability of e-learning systems is an ongoing challenge for software developers. Various usability evaluation techniques exist, choosing among them is a trade-off between cost and effectiveness. Some methods, like heuristic evaluation, are easier to administer and less costly, but there are problems with using such method. These problems come from applying a small set of principles, the heuristics, to a wide range of systems. Indeed, generic guidelines are not readily applicable to all systems. This is pointed out by various researchers, who have then developed more specific guidelines for particular system classes [1, 12, 23]. For example, heuristics for the usability evaluation of groupware systems [1], and for systems with large display, as those used for fairs or other expositions [23], have been identified. It would be suitable to provide specific guidelines in order to evaluate usability of e-learning systems as well. In the next section, we describe our approach to the evaluation of usability through a technique that solves the drawbacks of heuristic evaluation, and systematizes the work of inspectors. We then present in the successive section a set of usability guidelines specifically defined for e-learning applications.

3 The SUE Inspection

Usability inspection refers to a set of methods through which evaluators examine usability-related aspects of an application and provide judgements based on their knowledge. With respect to other usability evaluation methods, such as user-based evaluation, usability inspection methods are more subjective. They are strongly dependent upon the inspector skills, and therefore it may happen that different inspectors produce non comparable outcomes. However, usability inspection methods "save users" [8], and do not require special equipment, nor lab facilities.

Examples of usability inspection methods are heuristic evaluation, cognitive walkthrough, guideline review, and formal usability inspection [15]. The most commonly used is heuristic evaluation [14, 15]. However, as highlighted in [5, 8, 9], its major drawback is again its high dependence upon the skills and experiences of the evaluators. In order to overcome this problem, the SUE (Systematic Usability Evaluation) inspection technique has been introduced [13]. It uses evaluation patterns, called Abstract Tasks (ATs), for guiding the inspector's activity. ATs precisely describe which objects of the application to look for, and which actions the evaluators must perform in order to analyse such objects. In this way, also less experienced evaluators, with lack of expertise in usability and/or application domain, are able to come out whit more complete and precise results.

SUE inspection framework also provides a solution to the specialization of usability evaluation, mentioned in the previous section. To this aim, the framework provides a list of detailed heuristics that are specific for a class of applications. In the first place general usability principles are decomposed into finer-grained criteria, that can be better analysed. Then heuristics are obtained by specialising such criteria through usability attributes specific for the particular domain. In accordance with the suggestion given in [15], namely to develop category-specific heuristics, we have therefore defined a set of usability attributes, able to capture the peculiar features of e-learning systems.

As stated above, ATs include a detailed description of the activities to be performed by evaluators during inspection [13], in order to detect possible violations of the identified heuristics. They are formulated precisely by means of a template providing a consistent format, that includes the following items:

- *AT Classification Code and Title*: univocally identify the AT, and succinctly convey its essence.
- *Focus of Action*: shortly describes the context, or focus, of the AT, by listing the application components that are the evaluation entities.
- *Intent*: describes the problem addressed by the AT and its rationale, trying to make clear which is the specific goal to be achieved through the AT application.
- *Activity Description*: describes in detail the activities to be performed during the AT application.
- *Output*: describes the output of the fragment of the inspection the AT refers to.

During the inspection, evaluators analyse the application. During this activity, the different application components, i.e., the objects on which the evaluation must focus on, are identified. Then, having in mind the usability criteria, evaluators apply ATs and produce a report in which the discovered problems are described. The list of ATs provides a systematic guidance to the evaluator on how to inspect an application. Most evaluators are very good in analysing only certain features of interactive applications; however, they often neglect some other features, strictly dependent on the specific application category. Exploiting a set of ATs ready for use allows evaluators with no experience in a particular domain to perform a more accurate evaluation.

We have identified a set of usability attributes and guidelines, able to capture the peculiar features of e-learning applications. According to the SUE inspection, from these usability attributes and guidelines we have derived the ATs for evaluating such applications.

4   Usability Evaluation of e-Learning Applications

While defining usability attributes for e-learning, it is first of all necessary to dwell upon the difference between an e-learning platform (container) and educational modules provided by a platform or even apart (content). In particular, an e-learning platform is a more or less complex environment with a number of integrated tools and services for teaching, learning, communicating and for learning material management. Usability attributes for this environment generally differ from those that can be identified for a specific e-learning product considered as an educational module. These two classes of software artefacts must be approached in parallel and independently, since different features must be considered. However, as we will see later, it is true that some characteristics of the e-learning module provided through a platform are bound to functionalities of the platform itself.

In identifying criteria and attributes for evaluating e-learning tools, we must consider the peculiarity of e-learning, whose primary goal is to allow students to learn the didactic material by devoting the minimum effort to the interaction with the system. The work reported in this paper is grounded on our experience in developing e-learning applications targeted to different types of users [2, 3, 19, 20, 21]. Moreover, we have performed various studies. We have considered recent literature (for sake of space we cannot quote all the interesting material, but see for example ACM E-Learn Magazine, http://www.elearnmag.org/), and performed cognitive walk-through for a number of distance courses available in currently used platforms. Nevertheless, as for other classes of applications, users' feedback is the most valuable tool to find out problems. For this reason we have also adopted the *thinking aloud* technique in an experimental study that involved ten post-graduated students of a Master course at the University of Bari, Italy. It is worth summarizing the obtained results. Students were asked to interact with a DL (Distance Learning) system. Their objective was to learn some new topics by using only the system via Internet. A number of communication tools allowed to exchange information, to ask help and to suggest solutions. Then, interviews were carried out for gathering further information from these students. The basic questions concerned the kind of difficulties met, best ways to organize educational material and services, opinions about the communication tools used (forum, chat, mail).

Both thinking aloud and interviews highlighted a number of problems. A major number of participants experienced disorientation and often reported bewilderment and difficulty to proceed, particularly when following a new learning path or using a service for the first time. Moreover, a number of users complained about the lack of mechanisms to highlight both lesson structure and high priority topics, in particular those scheduled for a particular learning session. Actually, a lot of participants linked to a wrong didactic unit. It comes out that learning material presentation, providing a consistent visual conceptual map for easy navigation, is a relevant aspect for e-learning system usability. It would also be suitable to allow a personalized access to the content. Participants also reported problems searching the educational material to study. Search for documents should instead be facilitated, e.g. by a clear specification of key-words for each subject.

A number of participants showed frustration when they had to start from the beginning due to network temporary disconnection. Therefore, a number of comments stated that it should be possible to use the platform even offline, preserving the reached educational context.

Self-assessment allowed the participants to control their progresses, and this was found very motivating. Participants also expressed a positive opinion on the communication tools, allowing collaborative learning: these tools permit managing of the teaching process for one or more learners, through synchronous and asynchronous interactions.

The overall study confirmed that e-learning usability is a very complex issue. We have to consider presentation aspects, in particular cues helping learning. Moreover, the presence of hypermedia tools requires the possibility to personalize the reading path and the communication through different channels, still permitting orientation. Finally, user's initiative should be encouraged: the participants preferred self-assessment tests to evaluate their progress. The above aspects are related not only to the e-learning environment, but also to the structure of the educational material.

Following our preliminary studies, we have identified four dimensions for our analysis:

A. *Presentation* encompasses exterior features of the interface, highlighting possibilities and tools provided by the platform or by the educational module.
B. *Hypermediality* considers aspects bound to the communication through different channels and following a possibly non-sequential structure, stressing the analysis and the personalization of reading paths.
C. *Application proactivity* takes into account mechanisms and modalities through which the system supports the learner's training, and activities proposed.
D. *User's activity* is focused on learner's rising needs, i.e. on unplanned activities s/he would want to perform, and on how the system copes with them.

We will refer to effectiveness and efficiency as general principles to evaluate each dimension. We relay on ISO definition for such principles. According to [ISO98], usability is defined as the "extent to which a product can be used by specified users to achieve specified goals with effectiveness, efficiency and satisfaction in a specified context of use". Effectiveness is defined as the "accuracy and completeness with which users achieve specified goals". In our case, we consider goals related to learning tasks. Efficiency is defined as the "resources expended in relation to the accuracy and completeness with which users achieve goals". We are especially interested in user's efforts required to achieve learning goals. The aim of an e-learning application should be to facilitate the user in grasping new concepts, by not overwhelming her/him with usage difficulties of the application itself while highlighting the conceptual structure and links of the subject at hand. General principles are further divided in criteria, how we shall describe in the following.

In Sections 4.1 and 4.3 we further discuss the four analysis dimensions, considering respectively e-learning platforms and modules, while in Sections 4.2 and 4.4 we propose the corresponding evaluation criteria along the four dimensions.

4.1   Usability Dimensions for e-Learning Platforms

In the following, we detail elements referred by each dimension for evaluating an e-learning platform.

Presentation Dimension
This dimension concerns all aspects bound to the visual design of tools and elements that set up the e-learning platform. To avoid confusion in interpreting the meaning of this dimension, it is necessary to consider that in this context we only analyze mere visualization. Actually, we ought not to confuse visualization of platform elements, discussed in this dimension, with their structuring and modelling, which pertain to other dimensions. In particular, as regards progress tracking, its clear and understandable visualization is an Efficiency parameter in this dimension, as the actions of the student wanting to verify her/his learning state are simplified; on the other hand, the presence of this element in itself, is an Effectiveness parameter in the Application Proactivity dimension, because learning could result less effective without an overview of student's results and gaps. The same holds for the state of the system. On the one end, its constant visualization is an Efficiency parameter in this dimension, facilitating student's movements; on the other end the presence of this element in itself is an Effectiveness parameter in Hypermediality dimension, as orienting oneself in the context of course subjects helps creating a mental map of the discourse and facilitates understanding and memorization.

It is in the Presentation dimension that we consider the issue of the clarity of presentation of platform tools. It is necessary that the possibilities they provide to users be clear and that errors made using them be highlighted, when not avoided.

It is also important that the student can easily identify in which part of the course s/he is at present, and how to reach a different one. To this aim, course structure should be visualized in a way allowing orientation and easy move among subjects (i.e. through a map or a representation based on the folder metaphor).

As it concerns access technology, this is an issue common with Application Proactivity dimension, and is here considered only from the graphical aspect point of view. For example, it would be necessary to consider that if one wants to access the platform from a palmtop computer, layout of elements on the screen must adapt to its reduced size.

Hypermediality Dimension
If we consider hypermediality from the point of a view of a platform, the presence of hypermedia tools surely appears as a further possibility provided to lecturers and students. As it will be discussed later, this could not be true when evaluating how contents are structured inside single educational modules.

Hypermediality allows to communicate through different channels (audio, video, textual) but even to organize lessons in a not necessarily sequential way, also allowing a student to choose a personalized logical path different from the one suggested by the lecturer. It is just in connection with hypermediality that the student should have no difficulty in orienting herself/himself in the course organization, as discussed with regard to Presentation dimension.

Hypermediality contribute is significant to the achievement of learning. Moreover, it is desirable the possibility to insert one's own links (bookmarks) allowing to further increase flexibility of content organization. To this respect, it is important to notice the poor learning value of non-contextual links, which save references to target pages and documents without reference to the source point, i.e. to the point from which the link conceptually starts. After a small amount of time the student would forget her/his aim when creating such a link: in an educational context, information acquires and maintains meaning just from its framework. Such framework should be maintained even in off-line access: it is not desirable the student be forced to be connected to the network along all her/his learning time.

Application Proactivity Dimension
In defining attributes for this dimension, we tried to follow principles of the socio-constructivistic approach, the educational theory most reliable nowadays. This approach, for example, takes to require from the platform spaces for inserting tools of the learning domain. Such tools should be embedded as much as possible in an actual context of use.

In this dimension we consider platform tools related to learning activities, in particular planned ones. Ease of use of such tools is an aspect to consider in all UCD systems. Nevertheless, it gains an even greater importance in LCD systems, where the user just makes an effort consisting in learning, which is the primary goal. The same considerations take to require that student's errors in using the platform tools should be prevented as much as possible. However, we have not to confuse simplification in the interface with oversimplification in the proposed contents and tasks. Ease of use and error prevention do not apply to the activities performed through the tools strictly bound to learning, in particular the learning domain tools, and to students' assessment tests. Rather, the latter category of errors provides a further learning occasion if they are highlighted by the platform, e.g using graphics (as discussed with regard to Presentation dimension), if places for explanations are provided, and if links to scarcely mastered parts of the course are automatically suggested.

In the case of complex tasks, novice learners should be rather supported in their first approach. Specific tools provided to this aim set up scaffolding activities. An effective scaffolding should be gradually attenuated as student proceeds in learning. We have to consider how such attenuation has to be managed: the lecturer should be able to delegate this task to specific platform automatic mechanisms.

As any other multi-user system, an e-learning platform must allow access to different users' classes. Each of them will hold a specific role inside the educational process: lecturer, student, tutor, and administrator. The platform should then allow to define different typologies of profiles and correspondently provide different views and capabilities. These considerations apply specifically to the repository: lecturers and students are two actors bearing different characteristics and needs, and so different access modes to the repository. Moreover, we have to consider the different languages used by the two figures, which is more appropriate for the lecturer and less precise for the student; the platform should so provide different searching modalities.

User's Activity Dimension

In this dimension we consider all needs of a student/lecturer choosing to learn/teach at a distance and platform tools (e.g. communication tools) not strictly related to planned learning activities. Student's needs are to be able to make assessment tests and to check her/his progress at any time, even when not proposed by the platform, and to annotate and integrate the learning material provided with her/his own documents, autonomously collected. Moreover, the possibility to personalize scaffolding attenuation must be provided, in order to efficiently cope with the two symmetrical situations of a student needing supplementary scaffolding, or needing less of it.

Lecturer's needs must also be considered: for example, even if not possible to evaluate student's engagement merely from observation of her/his activities, it is anyway very useful for the lecturer to have a detailed report from which to verify how much and how her/his course is exploited by students. This could help to understand if the organization chosen needs some update or change, if it is appreciated or not and which problems the students encounter.

4.2   Usability Criteria and Guidelines for e-Learning Platforms

For each dimension we considered the general principles of effectiveness and efficiency that contribute to characterize usability [7], dividing them in criteria:

Effectiveness:

Supportiveness for learning/authoring: how the tools provided by the platform allow to learn and prepare lessons in an effective way.

Supportiveness for communication, personalization and access: how the provided tools satisfy these needs greatly influences the learning effectiveness.

Efficiency:

Structure adequacy: how efficiently the activities the user usually performs are structured and visualized.

Facilities and technology adequacy: efficiency of scaffolding and supplementary supports provided to the user; how the platform adapts to the technology used by the learner to access it.

From the above criteria, a first set of guidelines are derived, as reported in Table 1.

4.3   Usability Dimensions for e-Learning Modules

In the following, we specialize each dimension for evaluating an e-learning module.

Presentation Dimension

This dimension regards the way the lecturer decides to make visualized both lessons and supports to the students (scaffolding) s/he has prepared. A new lesson or an updated one, belonging to the same subject or course, should have the same layout, both for the graphical aspect and content organization.

As reading appears to be more tiring during prolonged interaction with the e-learning system through video, it is opportune to concentrate more important contents at the beginning, eventually highlighting their priority through graphical cues. Even the hierarchical structure of subjects must be highlighted: this is very effective both from the conceptual point of view and to exploit and stimulate student's visual memory.

Hypermediality Dimension

Hypermedia tools are one of the major differences among in-presence (classical model) and on-line education. On the one hand, such tools can be surely considered an advantage. Nevertheless, if misused, they burden the student, instead of facilitating her/him. This happens if sensory channels (sight, hearing, hands) are overloaded, also considering that the student is not expert of the learning domain. For example, auditory and textual channels should not be overlapped: this would take to a symbolic memory overload, unless audio and text are strictly related, as in the case of a sound attracting attention on a particular text message.

Table 1. Usability Criteria and Guidelines for e-Learning Platforms.

Dimensions	General principles	Criteria	Guidelines
Presentation	Effectiveness	Supportiveness for Learning/Authoring	For interface graphical aspects, the same UCD attributes hold
			Errors and cues to avoidance are high lighted
		Supportiveness for communication, personalization and access	It is possible to personalize interface graphics
	Efficiency	Structure adequacy	System state is clearly and constantly Indicated
			Progress tracking is clearly visualized
			Possibilities and commands available are clearly visualized
			Course structure is clearly visualized
		Facilities and technology adequacy	Adaptation of the graphical aspect to the context of use is provided
Hypermediality	Effectiveness	Supportiveness for Learning/Authoring	The lecturer is supported in preparing multimedia material
			Easy movement among subjects is allowed by highlighting cross-references through state and course maps
		Supportiveness for communication, personalization and access	Communication is possible through different media channels
			A personalized access to learning contents is possible
	Efficiency	Structure adequacy	Both lecturer and student can access the repository
		Facilities and technology adequacy	It is possible to create contextualized Bookmarks
			The platform can be used off-line, maintaining tools and learning context

Table 1. (continued)

Dimensions	General principles	Criteria	Guidelines
Application Proactivity	Effective-ness	Supportiveness for Learning/Authoring	It is possible to insert assessment tests in various forms
			Platform automatically updates students' progress tracking
			Platform allows to insert learning domain tools
		Supportiveness for communication, personalization and access	Users profiles are managed
	Efficiency	Structure adequacy	Mechanisms exist to prevent usage errors
			Mechanisms exist for teaching-through-errors
			Lecturer and students access the repository in different modes
			Platform tools are easy to use
		Facilities and technology adequacy	Adaptation of technology to the context of use is provided
			The date of last modification of documents is registered in order to facilitate updating
User's Activity	Effective-ness	Supportiveness for Learning/Authoring	Easy-to-use authoring tools are provided
			Assessment tests to check one's progress at any time are provided
			Reports are managed about atten-dance and usage of a course
			It is possible to use learning tools even when not scheduled
		Supportiveness for communication, personalization and access	Both synchronous and asynchro-nous communication tools are provided
			It is possible to communicate with both students and lecturers
			It is possible to make annotations
			It is possible to integrate the provided material
	Efficiency	Structure adequacy	Mechanisms are provided for search by indexing, key or natural language
		Facilities and technology adequacy	Authoring tools allow to create standard-compliant documents and tests (AICC, IMS, SCORM)
			Authoring tools facilitate docu-ments update and assessment tests editing

Moreover, it is good practice not to overuse hypertextual and/or hypermedial links, as a link causes a change in what the student visualizes. Such changes could bewilder the student, taking to a problem which is common on the web, i.e. to be "lost in hyperspace".

Even if multiple communication and presentation media are provided, one has to carefully choose those more suited to the learning goal, or even to the particular learning domain.

Finally, in order to facilitate both lecture editing and in-depth study, it is necessary that the learning materials be reusable even in contexts different from those for which they have initially been conceived (i.e., they might be used as a deeper insight for one course or as a base subject for a different course).

Application Proactivity Dimension

In this dimension, value of teaching is found in the ability to propose activities, as the use of learning domain tools, capable to form in an effective and efficacious way. One of the principles of socio-constructivistic theory is that learning mainly occurs in an environment where tools reflect the actual context of use: the learning domain must be introduced without oversimplifications since the beginning, eventually providing scaffolding; the student will "learn by doing", and making errors, in order to also awake her/his hidden knowledge. To this aim, it is important that assessment tests be organized in such a way to represent deep-insight occasions for the student. A good tool does not limit itself to make the student realize the error, but explains the cause and helps to focus on key-issues of the subject at hand.

A further evaluation parameter is represented by scaffolding organization. In defining scaffolding, presence and attenuation must be carefully considered. As regards presence, we are in the LCD context: differently from UCD, and regarding learning content, the aim is not to minimize the cognitive effort (for example, through a massive use of scaffolding). On the contrary, this must be stimulated, such that learner's activity is not flattened and oversimplified, with the consequence of diminishing learning persistence. As regards scaffolding attenuation, there are still a number of open questions: Who should attenuate scaffolding? The student, based on her/his needs, or the lecturer, based on the provided learning plan? Is it appropriate to assign this task to the system, which will perform it in an automatic way? Which is the speed at which scaffolding must attenuate? For the time being, each specific situation should be analysed in itself. It would not be significant to define general rules encompassing all cases.

User's Activity Dimension

Here we analyse activities which the student could need to perform, even when not suggested by the module according to the lecturer provided plan. Examples of such needs are customizing media channels, searching from the repository through a careful identification of key-words of each subject, creating personal paths or performing assessment tests when needed.

Moreover, the student could "miss" the traditional in-presence lesson. Choosing to teach through e-learning does not mean to reject in toto traditional teaching, rather it seems better to merge on-line learning with "actually" shared moments. If logistic reasons make this unfeasible, it will be necessary to try to reproduce such situations at one's best, e.g. by a video/audio synchronous communication and shared boards.

4.4 Usability Criteria and Guidelines for e-Learning Modules

In this context, for each dimension we have considered the criteria of effectiveness of teaching/authoring and of efficiency of supports and teaching modalities. Criteria and guidelines referring to them are reported in Table 2.

5 SUE Inspection for e-Learning Applications

As we said in Section 3, SUE inspection is based on the use of Abstract Tasks to drive the evaluators' activities. By taking into account the usability attributes and the guidelines reported in Tables 1 and 2, we have derived some ATs that support the inspector in the evaluation of specific components of e-learning applications.

Table 2. Usability Criteria and Guidelines for e-Learning Modules.

Dimensions	Criteria	Guidelines
Presentation	Effectiveness of teaching/authoring	Content update is consistent
		High priority subjects are highlighted
		Graphic layout does not distract the learner but helps him/her in learning
		Hierarchical structure of course subjects is highlighted
	Efficiency of supports and teaching modalities	Scaffolding are assigned a non-invasive space to not distract the learner
Hypermediality	Effectiveness of teaching/authoring	Used tools are able to plunge the learner in the learning domain context
		Specific communication media are used for each subject and learning goal
	Efficiency of supports and teaching modalities	Communication channels are used in an optimal way
		Hypertextual and hypermedial links are carefully used
		Learning material can be reused and integrated
Application Proactivity	Effectiveness of teaching/authoring	Specific learning domain tools are provided
		The help and number of scaffolding are carefully chosen
		Testing tools are reliable
	Efficiency of supports and teaching modalities	Scaffolding is correctly attenuated (if attenuation is driven by the lecturer)
		The document formats used do not require specific plug-ins
User's Activity	Effectiveness of teaching/authoring	It is possible to limit or choose the media channels
		Blended-learning simulations are provided
	Efficiency of supports and teaching modalities	Search for documents is facilitated by a correct and clear specification of key-words

Specifically, these ATs are grouped in the following categories (see also Table 3):

(1) *Content insertion and content access*: this category includes ATs to evaluate tools that permit and facilitate authoring and permit content search.

(2) *Scaffolding*: this category includes ATs to evaluate mechanisms that support the user in harder tasks.

(3) *Learning window*: this category includes ATs to evaluate the features of the virtual environment for learning, i.e. where the student works, studies, and verifies her/his learning level.

ATs are distinguished in *basic* and *advanced* (AT TYPE column in Table 3); the former are took into consideration during a less specific evaluation: their aim is to give the evaluator a first insight of the system functionalities. Advanced ATs, instead, are used for a more detailed analysis of the characteristics to evaluate. In the last column in Table 3, we indicate P if the AT is defined to evaluate features of the Platform, M if it addresses features of the e-learning Modules.

Table 3. Some ATs for Inspecting e-Learning Applications.

AT CATEGORY	AT TYPE	AT CODE AND TITLE	
Content insertion and content access	basic	C_1: check of authoring tools	P
		C_2: check of the window for requests to repository	P
	advanced	C_3: reuse verification	M
		C_4: check of the different access modalities	P
		C_5: check for support to authoring	P
Scaffolding	basic	S_1: help verification	M
		S_2: graphic layout	M
	advanced	S_3: check of attenuation	P/M
		S_4: check of presence	M ·
Learning Window	basic	LW_1: organization of a course document	M
		LW_2: fruition of a course document	P/M
	advanced	LW_3: check of assessment testing	P/M
		LW_4: check of communication tools	P
		LW_5: usage of communication tools	M
		LW_6: check of learning domain tools	P
		LW_7: adequacy of learning domain tools	M
		LW_8: advanced personalization verification	P

In the following, we report two examples of ATs to evaluate the fruition of a course document: the first refers to the platform aspects (P), the latter to modules (M). The ATs are defined according to the template indicated in Section 3.

LW_2 (P): Fruition of a Course Document

Focus of Action: learning window

Intent: to evaluate modalities, commands, and any mechanisms to access course documents.

Activity Description: given a learning window:

- execute commands to move among the course documents
- execute commands to move among the topics of different courses
- access offline to the document

Output: a description reporting if:

- a personalized content fruition is possible (e.g. modifying a predefined path, through a course map, etc.)
- an interdisciplinary content fruition is possible
- the system status and the student position in the course are always indicated
- it is possible to use the commands to move among courses and topics without leaving the learning environment
- the offline access to document is possible without loosing the learning context.

LW_2 (M): Fruition of a Course Document

Focus of Action: learning window
Intent: to evaluate modalities, commands, and tools to access to course documents.
Activity Description: given a learning window:

- explore a document following different logic learning paths
- open some documents to identify the required plug-ins

Output: a list reporting if:

- the documents structure permits different personalized learning paths
- specific plug-ins are necessary

6 Conclusions and Future Work

We have discussed issues related to the evaluation of e-learning systems. We have defined a set of usability criteria that capture some features of this kind of applications. We have also proposed how to adapt to the e-learning domain the SUE inspection technique, which uses evaluation patterns (Abstract Tasks), to drive the inspectors' activities. We have not performed yet an experimental comparison with traditional heuristics, even because we are still refining the set of ATs, but we expect results similar to those presented in [Mat02].

It is worth mentioning that, as human factor experts, we can only evaluate "syntactic" aspects of e-learning applications. In order to go deeply into aspects concerning pedagogical approach and content semantics, experts of education science and domain experts are to be involved. The evaluation from a pedagogical point of view concerns, for instance, the coherence and the congruence of the learning path design. More specifically, the following must be evaluated:

A. *the analysis of learning needs*: in designing the courseware, has a detailed analysis of the learning needs been performed?
B. *definition of learning goals*: are the learning goals well-organized in terms of cognitive and metacognitive abilities that the learners have to acquire?
C. *selection of the teaching methodologies*: is the teaching methodology selected during the design phase appropriately implemented?
D. *didactic content organization*: is the organization of didactic resources consistent with the organization of defined learning goals?
E. *learning assessment*: are the assessment methods and tools suited for the courseware?

These are the issues we are currently exploring in order to perform a more comprehensive evaluation. We are aware of the difficulties of this objective. However, we hope that the synergy with education experts will allow us to possibly identify specific guidelines for didactic effectiveness to be included in our general evaluation framework.

Finally, another important objective is to evaluate accessibility. Guidelines in literature usually provide high-level/generic indications on alternative forms of didactic content to enable access to it by people with different abilities. Further research is necessary in order to identify techniques and tools to evaluate if the application is not only accessible but usable and didactically effective for the learners.

Acknowledgments

The financial support of Italian MIUR through VICE and WEB-MINDS projects is aknowledged.

References

1. Baker, K., Greenberg, S., and Gutwin, C., Empirical Development of a Heuristics Evaluation Methodology for Shared Workspace Groupware. In *Proceedings of the ACM Conference on Computer Supported Cooperative Work (CSCW '02)* (New Orleans, Lousiana, USA, November 16-20, 2002), 2002, 96-105.
2. Costabile, M.F., De Angeli, A., Roselli, T., Lanzilotti, R., Plantamura, P., *Evaluating the Educational Impact of a Tutoring Hypermedia for Children*, Information Technology in Childhood Educational Annual, 2003, 289-308.
3. Costabile, M.F., De Angeli, A., Roselli, T., Lanzilotti, R., Plantamura, P., *Does Hypermedia Really Work for Tutoring Children?*, IEEE Multimedia, vol. April-June 2003, 65-69.
4. CPB/WGBH National Center for Accessible Media (NCAM)
   http://ncam.wgbh.org/cdrom/guideline/
5. Doubleday, A., Ryan, M., Springett, M., and Sutcliffe, A., A Comparison of Usability Techniques for Evaluating Design. In *Proceedings of DIS'97*, (Amsterdam, NL. August 1997). ACM Press, 1997, 101-110.
6. IMS Guidelines for Developing Accessible Learning Applications, Versione 1.0, White Paper, 2002. http://www.imsproject.org/accessibility/
7. ISO 9241: Ergonomics Requirements for Office Work with Visual Display Terminal (VDT), 1998.
8. Jeffriess, R., Miller, J., Wharton, C., and Uyeda, K.M., User Interface Evaluation in the real world: a comparison of four techniques. In *Proceedings of CHI'91*, (New Orleans, LA, USA, 1991), ACM Press, 1991, 119-124.
9. Kantner, L., and Rosenbaum, S., Usability Studies of WWW sites: Heuristic Evaluation vs Laboratory Testing. In *Proceedings of SIGDOC'97*, (Snowbird, UT, USA, 1997), ACM Press, 1997, 153-160.
10. Kruse, K. (May, 2000). Web rules: effective user interface design.
    http://www.learningcircuits.org/may2000/may2000_webrules.html.
11. The Learning Federation http://www.thelearningfederation.edu.au/repo
12. Mankoff, J., Dey, A., Hsieh, G., Kients, J., Lederer, S., and Ames, M., Heuristic Evaluation of Ambient Display. In *Proceedings of ACM Conference on Human Factors and Computing Systems, (CHI '03)*, (Ft. Lauderdale, FL, USA, April 5-10, 2003). 2003, 169-176.
13. Matera, M., Costabile, M.F., Garzotto, F., and Paolini, P., *SUE Inspection: an Effective Method for Systematic Usability Evaluation of Hypermedia*. IEEE Transactions on Systems, Man and Cybernetics- Part A, 32, 1, 2002, 93-103.

14. Nielsen, J., *Usability Engineering*. Academic Press. Cambridge, MA, 1993.
15. Nielsen, J. and Mack, R.L., *Usability Inspection Methods*. John Wiley & Sons, New York, 1994.
16. Norman, D., Things That Make us Smart: Defending Human Attributes in the Age of the Machine, Perseus Publishing, Cambridge:MA, 1993.
17. Quintana, C., Carra, A., Krajcik, J., and Elliot, S., Learner-Centred Design: Reflections and new Directions. *Human-Computer Interaction in the New Millennium*. In Carroll (Ed.) ACM Press, New York: Addison-Wesley, 2001, 605-626.
18. T. Roselli, Artificial Intelligence Can Improve Hypermedia Instructional Technologies for Learning. ACM Computing Surveys, vol. 27, no. 4, Dec. 1995, pp. 624-626.
19. Roselli, T., Faggiano, E., Rossano, V., A Further Investigation On The Effectiveness Of A WWW Hypermedial System For Cooperative Learning. *In Proceedings of International Conference on Computer in Education (ICCE2003)* (Hong Kong, Cina, December 2003), 2003, pp 440-442.
20. Roselli, T., Faggiano, E., Grasso, A., Rossano, V., A Platform for Building and Using Personalized Courseware. *In Proceedings of E-Learn 2003: World conference on E-Learning in Corporate, Government, Healthcare, & Higher Education* (Phoenix, Arizona USA, November 2003), 2003, pp. 141-144.
21. Roselli, T., Faggiano, E., Grasso, A., Pragnell, M.V., A formal model for developing e-learning software, *In Proceedings of IEEE International Convention (Mipro2003)* (Opatija, Croatia, May, 2003), 2003, pp. 70-74.
22. Soloway, E., Jackson, S.L., Kleim, J., Quintana, C., Reed, J., Spitulnik, J., Stratford, S.J., Studer, S., Eng, J., and Scala, N., Learning Theory in Practice: Case Studies in Learner-Centered Design. In *Proceedings of the SIGCHI Conference on Human Factors in Computing Systems (CHI'96)* (Vancouver, British Columbia, Canada, April 1996). ACM Press, New York, NY, USA, 1996, 189-196.
23. Somervell, J., Wahid, S. and McCrickard, D.S., Usability Heuristics for Large Screen Information Exhibits. In *Proceedings of Human-Computer Interaction (Interact '03)* (Zurigo, Svizzera, Sep. 2003), 2003, 904-907.
24. Stephanidis C., Akoumianakis D., Sfyrakis M., Paramythis A., Universal accessibility in HCI: Process-oriented design guidelines and tool requirements. Long Paper of the 4th ERCIM Workshop on "User Interfaces for All", Stockholm, Sweden, 19-21 October 1998.

An Empirical Methodology for Usability Analysis of a Touchscreen-Based Information Kiosk System for African Users with Low Levels of Computer Literacy

Pieter Blignaut

Department of Computer Science and Informatics, University of the Free State,
P.O. Box 339, 9300 Bloemfontein, South Africa
pieterb.sci@mail.uovs.ac.za

Abstract. A set of reliable usability metrics was determined to evaluate touch-screen-based information kiosk systems used by computer-illiterate, low-income, African users. Usability techniques that rely on communication between evaluator and user suffer from a language barrier if the evaluator is not fluent in the language of the typical users. Empirical metrics can be administered so that the effect of the language barrier is minimized. Candidate metrics were identified to measure the usability of a system with regard to learnability, productivity achieved and retention of interface knowledge over time. Three of the candidate metrics for learnability and five metrics for productivity proved to be applicable and reliable. Three of these metrics could also predict the degree to which users retain interface knowledge over time. The reliable metrics were consolidated into a survey form and a methodology is proposed for usability testing.

1 Introduction

In the current study an information kiosk system was developed for a large public transporting company in a third-world community and placed in the foyer of the ticket box complex (Figure 1). The company operates several hundred trips daily in a metropolitan area while transporting people between their homes and workplaces. Depending on the exact area where a person is living and working, it may happen that he or she has to take more than one bus for a one-way trip. Commuters need to be informed about routes, schedules and ticket prices. To date, this information was communicated by means of pamphlets and posters at the terminal building. A touchscreen information kiosk was identified as a way to supplement this medium of communication while also serving to improve the company's image amongst commuters.

Information kiosk systems are computer-based information systems in a publicly accessible place, offering access to information or transactions for an anonymous, constantly varying group of users with typically short dialogue times and a simple user interface [5]. The success of such systems depends largely on the attractiveness of their user interfaces, how easily they allow access to information, and how clearly the information is presented [2].

The system used for this study was developed according to established principles for design of information kiosks [2, 4, 8]. Commuters can obtain information on ticket prices, routes, time tables, etc. from the information kiosk. General company informa-

C. Stary and C. Stephanidis (Eds.): UI4All 2004, LNCS 3196, pp. 203–218, 2004.
© Springer-Verlag Berlin Heidelberg 2004

tion and promotions, as well as advertisements from shops in the centre are displayed on a continuous basis whenever no user activity is registered for 60 seconds. Passers-by or people queuing in front of a ticket box can then follow the presentations which are accompanied by attractive graphical animations, sound, or video clips.

Fig. 1. Touch screen information kiosk at ticket office of large public transporting company.

The goal of this paper is to determine a set of reliable usability metrics to evaluate touchscreen-based information kiosk systems that are used by mainly computer-illiterate, low-income, African users. Often this user-group is excluded from access to computer technology because of geographical, financial or educational reasons. Touchscreen-based information kiosks could bring technology to the people but it is important to determine if the system succeeds in bringing the information to the people. Research has previously been done on the usability of information kiosks [16, 17, 19, 20, 21, 22, 23] but to date no research results could be found for this user group.

Many of the trusted techniques that are currently used to do usability analysis have limited value to assess applications that are intended for African users if the evaluators are not familiar with the cultural background and/or language of the user population. For example, cognitive walkthroughs [3, 10, 15, 24] expects a usability expert to simulate a user's problem solving process – something which is extremely difficult if the expert has a different cultural frame of reference and a level of general literacy that is far higher than the average user. With heuristic evaluations [9, 10, 13, 24] some of the most obvious and common usability problems can be identified, but the culture and language-specific aspects will be difficult to pick up. Pluralistic walkthroughs [10] (scheduled meetings between users, developers and human factor specialists) will be difficult because of the language barrier. Consistency inspection [10, 24] is hardly possible due to the limited applications that are available for the specific African culture. Review-based evaluation [3] is extremely difficult due to the limited availability of literature on systems for African users. Observational techniques such as think-aloud [3, 18] also suffer from the same language barrier, but video recordings [18] can afterwards be analyzed with the aid of an interpreter.

Empirical methods are less dependent on interaction between user and evaluator and can therefore be more applicable to assess user interfaces where evaluators and users have different cultural backgrounds. Data acquired from computer logging [3, 24] can afterwards be analyzed carefully. Questionnaires [3, 24] can be translated into the target language beforehand and administered either personally by a surveyor, or by means of a self-administered on-screen questionnaire [14].

In this study a combination of empirical techniques was used to determine a series of metrics that are reliable and consistent enough to be used for quantifying the usability of a touchscreen-based information system for the intended user population. The IEEE defines a software metric as "a function whose inputs are software data and whose output is a single numerical value that can be interpreted as the degree to which the software possesses a given attribute that affects its quality" [6].

Performance metrics consist of duration measures, count measures, percentage of tasks completed successfully, and quality of output [18]. Duration metrics measure how much time is spent to complete a particular task. Count measures count how many times an event occurs, e.g. how many errors are made. The percentage of tasks that users complete correctly can be measured by carefully setting target goals. This metric is coined by Nielsen [12] as the simplest usability metric since "user success is the bottom line of usability". Subjective measures include oral and written data collected from users regarding their perceptions, opinions, judgments, preferences, and satisfaction regarding the system and their own performance [9].

2 Methodology

Several sources [1, 3, 11, 12, 25, 26, 27] list examples of metrics that can be used to measure the usability of a system. A set of candidate metrics was identified according to which the usability of the touchscreen system was evaluated. The ISO 9241-11 definition of usability [7] and the measurable criteria for usability as identified by Shneiderman [24] were used to categorize the candidate metrics. Usability data was captured by means of surveys as well as real-time observations. This data was analyzed statistically and the results of related metrics were compared to assess the validity and reliability of the metrics for each one of the criteria and types of measures. The proven metrics were consolidated into a survey form and then utilized in a methodology for usability testing of a touchscreen information kiosk.

Two paper-based surveys were conducted over a period of one month six months after the system was implemented. For the first survey users were allowed to use the system spontaneously and perform their own tasks. The surveyors were of the same culture and language group as the user population and mostly succeeded in behaving as a casual onlooker while ensuring that they were near enough to follow the user's actions. A user was only approached with a questionnaire about general user satisfaction when he/she left the kiosk. In this paper these users are referred to as casual users.

The second paper-based survey differed from the first in that users (referred to as selected users) were recruited from the passers-by so that the sample is representative of the population profile with regard to gender, age and level of education. They were asked to perform a predefined and representative set of information search tasks. They were given specific scenarios and asked to find information such as schedules, ticket prices, etc. while the duration of the sessions was recorded. It was accepted that casual users and selected users were different samples of the same population.

During times of surveyor absence, users could complete an on-screen user-satisfaction questionnaire (Figure 2) voluntarily and by own initiative after they had used the system. The nature of the survey was, therefore, the same as that of the paper-based survey for casual users but with the difference that it was not supervised. Results were recorded into an underlying database and analyzed afterwards. The survey screen was specifically designed to accommodate computer-illiterate users. They only had to select from the available alternatives and no navigation or scrolling was expected.

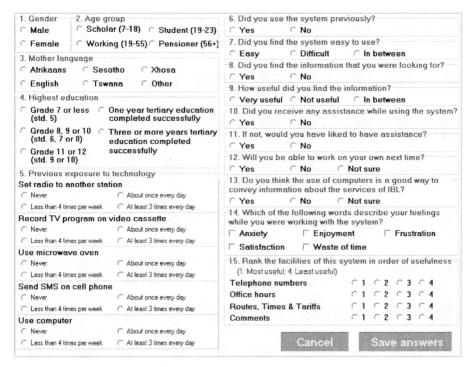

Fig. 2. On-screen survey form.

It was accepted that the paper-based and on-screen surveys were different methodologies to test the same aspects with different samples of the same population. It was, however, possible that extrinsic factors could bias the results of either the paper-based or on-screen surveys. For example, users could be more honest in their responses with the on-screen survey than when confronted by a surveyor. In order to test this possibility, the results obtained with the paper-based survey and those obtained with the on-screen survey were separated and compared statistically.

For the purposes of this paper, users who indicated that they used the system for the first time are referred to as first-time users. Users who indicated that they had used the system at least once before are referred to as follow-up users. It is possible that users can maintain the know-how for a task from a previous session and therefore first-time users and follow-up users could be different populations. In order to test this hypothesis, a Student's t-test or chi-square analysis was done whenever applicable to determine the significance of the observed differences between first-time and follow-up users.

The number of users in each sample is indicated in Table 1. The samples are mutually exclusive, i.e. no user contributed in more than one sample.

Table 1. Number of users per sample group.

	No users
First-time casual users	48
Follow-up casual users	56
First-time selected users	26
Follow-up selected users	42
On-screen surveys first-time users	51
On-screen surveys follow-up users	39
Total	**262**

3 Candidate Metrics

According to the definition of usability of the International Standards Organization [7], usability is "the effectiveness, efficiency and satisfaction with which specified users achieve specified goals in particular environments", where

- effectiveness is "the accuracy and completeness with which specified users can achieve specified goals in particular environments."
- efficiency pertains to "the resources expended in relation to the accuracy and completeness of goals achieved."
- satisfaction pertains to "the comfort and acceptability of the system to its users and other people affected by its use."

Effectiveness can be expressed in terms of metrics that indicate whether a user could do what he/she wanted to do or was expected of him/her and whether he/she was able to complete a task successfully. Efficiency is expressed in terms of metrics that relate to the time it took a user to achieve a task, how much stress he/she had to overcome, how many errors were made while completing the task, or how many possibilities needed to be explored before the required facility was found. Satisfaction can be quantified by means of a subjective response relating to how the user feels about the outcome of a task achieved.

Shneiderman [24] identified some measurable criteria for usability of a computerized information system: learnability, productivity, rate of errors, retention over time, and users' satisfaction.

Candidate metrics for the usability of the touchscreen system were categorized in terms of their applicability to Shneiderman's usability criteria and the ISO types of measure (Table 2). Metrics that apply to the same usability criterion can serve as checks for one another, thereby proving reliability. For example, a user who indicated that the system was easy to use (metric 3) would most probably not express a need for individual assistance (metric 1).

Table 2. Candidate metrics (× indicate *potential* applicability and reliability).

Metric	Usability criterion			Type of measure		
	Learnability	Productivity	Retention	Effectiveness	Efficiency	Satisfaction
1. Need expressed for individual assistance	×		×	×		
2. Searching for information in a structured way	×		×		×	
3. Users' subjective response regarding ease of use	×		×			×
4. User's emotions	×		×			×
5. Users found what they have been looking for		×	×	×		
6. Percentage of users giving up searches before desired information is obtained		×	×	×		
7. Percentage of items found correctly		×	×	×		
8. Subjective comparison of time spent to obtain information with time spent by an average user		×			×	
9. User's subjective responses on the usefulness of the information obtained		×				×
10. Time to find information		×	×		×	
11. Percentage of users who are confident that they will be able to cope with the system without assistance at a subsequent session.			×			×

4   Metrics for Learnability

Initially four candidate metrics were identified to measure the learnability of the system. The details of these metrics are discussed below, followed by an analysis of their reliability.

Metric 1: The percentage of first-time users who indicate that they need individual assistance can give an indication of the effectiveness with which a system can be learned. The number of users who did not receive any assistance, but indicated that they would have liked assistance was recorded with both the paper-based as well as the on-screen survey forms.

Metric 2: A measure of efficiency with regard to learnability of a system is the learning time thereof. Shneiderman [24] asserts that learning time can be regarded as the time it takes for a typical member of the user community to learn how to use the commands relevant to a set of tasks. In this study it was accepted that a user knew how the system worked and had thus completed the learning process when he/she could manage to search for a specific piece of information in a structured way without fiddling around randomly. Users were carefully observed and usage patterns were recorded.

Metric 3: Satisfaction with regard to learnability of a system can be expressed in terms of users' subjective responses for ease of use. In this study, the questionnaire for selected users as well as the on-screen questionnaire prompted respondents to choose between alternatives "Easy to use", "Moderately easy to use" and "Difficult to use".

Metric 4: Another possible satisfaction metric for learnability is an analysis of users' feelings while working on the system. The questionnaire for casual users expected of the surveyors to subjectively indicate the most appropriate emotion(s) that a user experiences by observing his or her body language. Surveyors could select one or more of the following possibilities: Anxiety, satisfaction, enjoyment, frustration and boredom. Users could also report on their feelings themselves with the on-screen survey.

Users' feedback on each of these metrics for learnability could be categorized as either negative or positive (Table 3).

Table 3. Possible feedbacks on metrics for learnability.

Metric	Positive	Negative
1	User did not need assistance	User needed assistance
2	User could use the system efficiently	User only fiddled around in unstructured way
3	User found system easy or moderately easy	User found system difficult
4	User's body language conveyed positive emotion	User's body language conveyed negative emotion

A chi-square analysis of the contingency table containing the number of first-time users per category for each of the learnability metrics has been done to test the following two null-hypotheses:

- The metric used has no effect on the measure of learnability of the system.
- There is no difference between the results obtained with a paper-based survey and those obtained with an on-screen survey.

The results are shown in Table 4. The overall χ^2 is 23.231 (df=6, p = 0.001). This indicates that the first null-hypothesis above can be rejected on the level of significance of α=0.01. The individual cells' contributions to the overall χ^2 value indicate that metric 1 is mainly responsible for this effect. If metric 1 is ignored, the χ^2 value for the remaining table is 5.081 (df=4, p=0.279). This means that if metric 1 is excluded, the first null-hypothesis cannot be rejected.

Table 4. Contingency table for learnability metrics obtained from first-time users with contributing χ^2 values.

Metric	Number of first-time users (with χ^2)		
	Positive	Negative	Total
1 (Paper-based)	4 (3.358)	10 (7.599)	14 (10.957)
1 (On-screen)	14 (1.512)	14 (3.423)	28 (4.935)
2 (Paper-based)	25 (0.000)	11 (0.000)	36 (0.000)
3 (Paper-based)	22 (0.873)	4 (1.976)	26 (2.849)
3 (On-screen)	32 (0.020)	13 (0.045)	45 (0.065)
4 (Paper-based)	40 (1.352)	8 (3.061)	48 (4.413)
4 (On-screen)	35 (0.004)	16 (0,009)	51 (0.013)

The results for follow-up users confirm the above findings. The χ^2 value for the contingency table with metric 1 included is 36.550 (df=6, p = 0.000). If metric 1 is excluded, the χ^2 value for the table is 5.119 (df=4, p = 0.275). Therefore, there is no evidence for either of the populations to prove that metrics 2, 3, and 4 do not test essentially the same thing. It can therefore be concluded that metrics 2, 3, and 4 may be regarded as reliable indicators of system learnability. Also, there is not enough evidence to reject the second null-hypothesis above since the contingency table above contains the results for both paper-based and on-screen surveys.

A possible reason for the fact that metric 1 seems to be unreliable could be related to the often-observed phenomenon that people prefer to be told how to do something whenever possible rather than to explore and discover or even read the manual. This phenomenon has been observed to be even more so true for African people. It is, therefore, possible that there is a difference between the preference for assistance as subjectively expressed by the user and the real need for assistance in order to complete a task. A change in the wording of the metric from "Would you have *liked* to have assistance?" to "Did you *need* any assistance?" could have solved the problem, but it should be tested in another study.

5   Metrics for Productivity Achieved

Initially six candidate metrics were identified to measure the productivity that users can achieve with the system.

Metric 5: After they used the system, casual users were expected to indicate whether they found the information that they were looking for. These results could be used to evaluate a user's productivity in terms of the effectiveness of search.

Metric 6: An item on the questionnaire for casual users expected of surveyors to indicate subjectively whether they got the impression that users gave up a search before the desired information was obtained.

Metric 7: A more quantitative effectiveness measure of productivity is the number of users who find all items correctly when asked to find a specific set of information. Selected users were asked to search for information on 6 specific items that were representative of the available information.

Metric 8: The surveyors had to make a subjective observation regarding the time it took the user to obtain the information he/she wanted in comparison with an average user. It was thought that these results could be used as an efficiency measure of the productivity that users achieve with the system. The benchmark of the time it would take an average user to complete the same task is not exact, nor is it stable. As the system becomes better known by users, their capabilities will improve, resulting in a moving average. Because the average user is the benchmark, the number of users who perform better than the average user and the number of those who perform worse should always be more or less the same.

Metric 9: Casual users were asked to respond in general on the usefulness of the information that they obtained with the system. Users' subjective responses in this respect were regarded as a satisfaction metric for the productivity that users can achieve with the system overall.

Metric 10: A more quantitative efficiency measure of productivity is the average time in seconds that it takes users to complete a specific set of tasks. With metric 7 users were requested to search for information on 6 specific items that were representative of the available information. The surveyors also timed the users with a stop watch while they were doing so. This metric can give a good indication of users' productivity, provided a previously defined benchmark and acceptable boundaries.

Users' feedback on metrics 5 through 10 could be categorized as either negative or positive with regard to the productivity that they achieved with the system (Table 5).

Table 5. Possible feedbacks on metrics for productivity.

Metric	Positive	Negative
5	User indicated that he found what he was looking for	User indicated that he did not find what he was looking for
6	User was observed to continue search until he found what he was looking for	User was observed to give up search before he found what he was looking for
7	User found all requested items correctly	User did not find all requested items correctly
8	User spent less or equal time than average user to find information	User spent more time than average user to find information
9	User found information useful or very useful	User found information to be not useful or only moderately useful
10	User spent less or equal time to find information than is accepted as benchmark	User spent more time to find information than is accepted as benchmark

A chi-square analysis of the contingency table containing the number of first-time users per category for each of the metrics for productivity has been done to test the following two null-hypotheses:

- The metric used has no effect on the measure of productivity that a user can achieve with the system.
- There is no difference between the results obtained with a paper-based survey and those obtained with an on-screen survey.

For metric 10, a benchmark had to be chosen that represents an acceptable upper limit. The choice of this benchmark is largely arbitrary and can have an influence on the results. Therefore, this metric was disregarded in the analysis.

The results are shown in Table 6. The overall χ^2 is 17.34 (df=6, p = 0.008). This indicates that the first null-hypothesis above can be rejected on the level of significance of α=0.01. The individual cells' contributions to the overall χ^2 value indicate that the on-screen version of metric 5 is mainly responsible for this effect. If this metric is ignored the χ^2 value for the remaining table is 3.697 (df=5, p=0.594). This means that if metric 5 is excluded, the first null-hypothesis cannot be rejected. Also, there is not enough evidence to reject the second null-hypothesis above since the contingency table contains the results for both paper-based and on-screen surveys.

The results for follow-up users confirm the above findings to a large extent. The χ^2 value for the entire contingency table for follow-up users (including the on-screen version of metric 5) is 7.873 (df=6, p = 0.248).

Table 6. Contingency table for productivity metrics obtained from first-time users with contributing χ^2 values.

Metric	Number of first-time users (with χ^2)		
	Positive	Negative	Total
5 (Paper-based)	24 (0.675)	7 (1.281)	31 (1.956)
5 (On-screen)	17 (4.009)	25 (7.603)	42 (11.612)
6 (Paper-based)	25 (0.025)	12 (0.047)	37 (0.072)
7 (Paper-based)	17 (0.026)	10 (0.049)	27 (0.075)
8 (Paper-based)	24 (0.002)	13 (0.004)	37 (0.006)
9 (Paper-based)	28 (1.128)	7 (2.139)	35 (3.267)
9 (On-screen)	30 (0.121)	13 (0.229)	43 (0.350)

A possible reason for the perceived difference between the results for paper-based and on-screen surveys for first-time users on metric 5 could be because users were ignorant about the intentions of the system. Some users commented that they would have liked to buy their tickets from the machine rather than to stand in the queues. This was not the intention of the system and was explained to them while they completed the paper-based questionnaires. Users who completed the on-screen survey only realized this during follow-up sessions.

To conclude, metrics 5 – 9 may be regarded as reliable indicators of the overall productivity that users achieve with the system, provided that users are thoroughly aware of the intentions of the system.

6   Metrics for Retention over Time

Several of the metrics discussed thus far are also applicable to the usability criterion for a system's ability to allow users to retain the interface knowledge that they have gained from a previous session. One metric that is not applicable to any of the other usability criteria is described here, followed by a discussion on the reliability of each of the candidate metrics for this criterion.

Metric 11: Both the questionnaires for casual users and selected users, as well as the on-screen survey, included an item where users had to give a subjective indication of whether they thought that they would be able to manage with the system without assistance during a next session. Respondents had to select from the possibilities "Yes", "No", and "Not sure". This metric was regarded as satisfaction metric to determine the amount to which the system allows users to retain the interface knowledge acquired.

With the paper-based survey 63.5% of first-time users and 82.8% follow-up users were confident that they would be able to manage without assistance in a next session. Similar results were obtained with the on-screen survey where the figures were 64.4% and 86.5% respectively.

To determine a system's ability to allow users to retain interface knowledge from one session to another, first-time users and follow-up users were regarded as separate populations for each one of the candidate metrics for this usability criterion. A Student's t-test or chi-square analysis was done to test this null-hypothesis for each metric:

- There is no difference in usability between the first-time users and follow-up users.

If a non-significant difference between the two user groups was observed with a specific metric, it can either mean that the system is inadequate in so far it allows users to retain interface know-how, or the metric is unable to pick up the difference.

The results of the respective t-tests or chi-square tests are summarized in Table 7 for each of the applicable metrics. The fact that there are at least some of the metrics that indicated a significant difference between the user groups suggests that the system did allow users to retain what they have learnt from previous sessions.

The candidate metrics in Table 7 for which no significant difference between the user groups was found can be regarded as inadequate to pick up the system's ability to allow users to retain interface knowledge over time. In some cases this result is due to inherent problems with the metric itself. Examples are the probable biased answering of metric 1 and the moving average problem of metric 8.

In other cases, first-time users performed very well from scratch and there was not much room for improvement, e.g. metrics 4 and 9 and the paper-based versions of metrics 3 and 5. It is possible that these metrics could show a significant difference between the user groups if they were applied on a system with usability problems that users could only overcome after some experience. This possibility will have to be confirmed in another study.

The on-screen version of metric 5 has to be disqualified as metric for retention, despite the perceived significant difference between the user groups. This difference was probably due to another effect, namely users' ignorance regarding the intended capabilities of the system.

Metrics 2, 6 and 11 can be regarded as reliable indicators of the system's ability to allow users to retain interface knowledge over time.

7 Proposed Methodology for Usability Study

The initial questionnaires for casual users and selected users were consolidated into a single survey form to include only those items that were found reliable in the analyses above (Appendix A). The specific metric to which an item in the survey is applicable, is indicated in brackets in the right margin with every item. Specific instructions or notes to the researchers or surveyors are included in italics and preceded by ∗. These may be omitted on the forms that are distributed to the users.

Passers-by must be allowed to use the system spontaneously. A user's body language must be observed for satisfaction indicators (Section A on Appendix A). When the user shows an intention of leaving the kiosk, he/she must be presented with a survey form. The surveyor should then ask the general feedback questions in section B. The user must then be requested to spend another few minutes to search for a set of representative items while he/she is timed (Section C).

The usability of a system can then be calculated by tabulating the number of users for each of the metrics and proceed as indicated in the "Notes" column in Table 8. Users' feedback is categorized into "Positive" and "Negative" in the same way as was done earlier (Tables 3 and 5). Since an information kiosk system must be usable by occasional users, the outcome for learnability and productivity criteria are determined by dividing the number of positive feedbacks by the total number of feedbacks from

Table 7. Summary of metrics and their ability to indicate that users retain commands over time.

Candidate metric	χ^2	t	p	Significant improvement from first-time to follow-up use ($\alpha=0.05$)?
1 (Paper-based)	0.903		0.342	No
1 (On-screen)	0.031		0.859	No
2	5.29		0.021	Yes
3 (Paper-based)	3.85		0.050	No
3 (On-screen)	1.83		0.176	No
4 (Paper-based)	1.36		0.244	No
4 (On-screen)	0.04		0.848	No
5 (Paper-based)	2.38		0.123	No
5 (On-screen)	8.03		0.005	Yes (Disqualify)
6	5.88		0.015	Yes
7	3.72		0.054	No
8	2.22		0.136	No
9 (Paper-based)	0.16		0.688	No
9 (On-screen)	3.76		0.052	No
10		0.414	0.682	No
11 (Paper-based)	6.04		0.014	Yes
11 (On-screen)	5.18		0.023	Yes

first-time users only. The criteria for retention of interface knowledge over time are calculated by dividing the improvement from first-time users to follow-up users by the available room for improvement. The overall usability of the system is calculated by getting the average of all the individual metrics.

A calculation of system usability like this will, of course, be of most value when the same method is used for several versions of a system or for several systems. An isolated value does not tell much of the system's usability, but should be seen in perspective after some experience.

8 Summary

The goal of this study was to determine a set of reliable usability metrics to evaluate touchscreen-based information kiosk systems that are used by mainly computer-illiterate, low-income, African users. Techniques such as cognitive walkthroughs, heuristic evaluations, usability inspections and live observations suffer from a language barrier if the analyst is not fluent in the language of the typical users. Empirical metrics utilize data acquired from computer logging as well as paper-based and on-screen surveys, which can be administered in such a way that the effect of the language barrier is minimized.

Several candidate metrics were identified to measure the learnability of a system, the productivity that a user can achieve with a system and the degree to which a system allows a user to utilize the interface knowledge he has gained on first-use at follow-up sessions. It was found that some of the candidate metrics were not applicable

Table 8. Calculation of system usability.

	First-time / Follow-up	# of users		Percentage (pos*100/ (pos+neg))	Notes
		Pos	Neg		
M21	1st	25	11	69.4	Metric 2, first-time users
M3	1st	22	4	84.6	
M4	1st	40	8	83.3	
Learnability				79.1	Average for learnability (M21, M3 & M4)
M5	1st	24	7	77.4	
M61	1st	25	12	67.6	Metric 6, first-time users
M7	1st	17	10	63.0	
M8	1st	24	13	64.9	
M9	1st	28	7	80.0	
Productivity				70.6	Average for productivity (M5, M61, M7, M8, M9)
M22	f/u	37	4	90.2	Metric 2, follow-up users
R2				68.0	Improvement on metric 2 (M22-M21)*100/(100-M21)
M62	f/u	36	4	90.0	Metric 6, follow-up users
R6				69.1	Improvement on metric 6 (M62-M61)*100/(100-M61)
M111	1st	40	23	63.5	Metric 11, first-time users
M112	f/u	53	11	82.8	Metric 11, follow-up users
R11				52.9	Improvement on metric 11 (M112-M111)*100/(100-M111)
Retention				63.3	Average for retention over time (R2, R6 & R11)
Total				71.0	Average of Learnability, Productivity & Retention over time

due to problems with the metrics themselves, while others presented problems that originated probably from cultural characteristics of the typical user profile. Three of the candidate metrics for learnability and five metrics for productivity proved to be applicable and reliable. When these metrics were applied separately for first-time users and follow-up users, it was found that three of them could also predict the degree to which users retain interface knowledge over time.

The paper concludes with a proposed methodology for the analysis of a touch-screen information kiosk for African users with low levels of computer literacy, utilizing a consolidated survey form.

9 Future Research

The methodology proposed in this paper was proven to be reliable for touchscreen-based systems used by African users with relative low computer literacy levels. It is possible; however, that this methodology and the resulting survey form can be applicable to other types of systems intended for a similar or even different user profile. This has to be tested in another study.

Metric 1 was found not to be a reliable measure of learnability of a system. A general human preference for assistance above exploring and discovering and/or the way in which the metric was worded, were offered as possible reasons for this result. Another study with a different wording could be undertaken to clarify this issue.

It was mentioned above that metrics 4 and 9, and the paper-based versions of metrics 3 and 5 could serve as indicator to highlight usability problems. This possibility must be explored in another study.

Acknowledgements

This work would not have been possible without the commitment of the staff and management of Interstate Bus Lines. Their cooperation is highly appreciated. The inputs of my colleagues, Drs. De Wet and McDonald, are also greatly appreciated.

References

1. Bonharme, E., White, I. Evaluation Techniques: Usability Metrics. http://www.dcs.napier.ac.uk/marble/ UsabilityMetrics.html
2. Borchers, J., Deussen, O. & Knörzer, C. Getting it across: Layout issues for Kiosk Systems. SIGCHI Bulletin, October 1995. 27(4), 68-74
3. Dix, A., Finlay, J., Abowd, G., Beale, R. Human-Computer Interaction. 2nd edition. Prentice Hall (1998)
4. ELO Touch systems. Keys to a successful Kiosk Application. http://www.elotouch.com
5. Holfelder, W. & Hehmann, D. A Networked Multimedia Retrieval Management System for Distributed Kiosk Applications. In Proceedings of the 1994 IEEE International Conference on Multimedia Computing and Systems
6. IEEE Std. 1061. IEEE Std. 1061 (1998), Software Quality Metrics Methodology
7. ISO/DIS 9241-11. Guidance on usability. Ergonomic Requirements for Office Work with Visual Display Terminals
8. Maguire, M. A review of user-interface design guidelines for public information kiosks. HUSAT Research Institute. http://www.lboro.ac.uk/eusc/ g_design_kiosks.html
9. Mandel, T. The Elements of User Interface Design. John Wiley & Sons (1997)
10. Nielsen, J. Heuristic evaluation. In Nielsen, J. and Mack, R.L. (Eds.), Usability Inspection Methods. John Wiley & Sons (1994)
11. Nielsen, J. (1). Usability metrics. http://www.useit.com/ alertbox/20010121.html
12. Nielsen, J. (2). Success rate: The simplest usability metric. http://www.useit.com/alertbox/20010218.html
13. Nielsen, J., Molich, R. Heuristic evaluation of user interfaces. In Proceedings of the ACM CHI'90 Conference, 249-256
14. Norman, K.L., Friedman, Z., Norman, K., Stevenson, R. Navigational issues in the design of online self-administered questionnaires. Behavior & Information Technology, 2001. 20(1), 37-45
15. Polson, P., Lewis, C., Rieman, J., Wharton, C. Cognitive walkthroughs: A method for theory-based evaluation of user interfaces. International Journal of Man-Machine Studies, 1992. 36:741-773
16. Potter, R.L., Weldon, L.J. & Shneiderman, B. Improving the accuracy of touchscreens: An experimental evaluation of three strategies. In Proceedings of the Conference on Human Factors in Computing Systems, 1988, 27-32

17. Plaisant, C., & Sears, A. Touchscreen interfaces for alphanumeric data entry. In Proceedings of the Human factors Society–36th Annual Meeting, '92, Vol. 1, 293-297
18. Preece, J., Rogers, Y., Sharp, H., Benyon, D., Holland, S. & Carey, T. Human-Computer Interaction. Addison-Wesley (1994)
19. Sears, A. Improving touchscreen keyboards: design issues and a comparison with other devices. Interacting with Computers, 1991. 3(3), 253-269
20. Sears, A., Kochavy, Y., Shneiderman, B. Touchscreen field specification for public access database queries: let your fingers do the walking. In Proceedings of the ACM Computer Science Conference '90, 1-7
21. Sears, A. & Shneiderman, B. High precision touchscreens: Design strategies and comparisons with a mouse. In International Journal of Man-Machine Studies, 1991. 34(4), 593-613
22. Shneiderman, B. Touchscreens now offer compelling uses. IEEE Software, 1991. 8(2), 93-94 & 107
23. Shneiderman, B., Brethauer, D., Plaisant, C., Potter, R. Evaluating three museum installations of a hypertext. Journal of the American Society for Information Science, 1989. 40(3), 172-182
24. Shneiderman, B. Designing the User Interface: Strategies for Effective Human-Computer Interaction. Third edition. Addison-Wesley (1998)
25. Usability Website. Learning from usability metrics and statistics. http://www.usabilitywebsite.com/usabilitymetrics.htm
26. Whiteside, J., Bennett, J., Holtzblatt, K. Usability engineering: Our experience and evolution. In Helander, M. (ed.) Handbook of Human-Computer Interaction, North-Holland (1988)
27. Zdralek, J. Clarifying the Metrics of Usability. http://www.deziner.com/site/dezine/words/ text/usability_metrics.htm

Appendix A: Consolidated Questionnaire for Usability Testing of Touchscreen Based Information Kiosks for African Users with Low Levels of Computer Literacy

Section A

Surveyor: Observe silently

A1. Did the user find the use of the system intuitive?   (M2)
Select one of the following:
☐ The user only fiddled around with the system in an unstructured way.
☐ The user fiddled around at first and then carried on in a structured way.
☐ The user found the system intuitive enough so that he/she could work in a structured way from the start.

A2. The user's body language conveyed: (M4)
(You may select more than one option)
☐ Anxiety   ☐ Satisfaction   ☐ Enjoyment   ☐ Frustration   ☐ Boredom

A3. Did you get the impression that the user searched for something but gave up the search before the desired information was obtained?   (M6)
☐ Yes   ☐ No

A4. How long did the user take to obtain the information he/she wanted?   (M8)
☐ Longer than the average user
☐ The same as an average user
☐ Less than the average user

Section B: General

Surveyor: Approach user and request him/her to assist with this research. Discuss the following questions with the user

B1. Is this the first time that you use this system?
☐ Yes   ☐ No

B2. Did you find the system   (M3)
☐ Easy to use   ☐ Moderately easy to use   ☐ Difficult to use

B3. Did you find the information that you were looking for?   (M5)
☐ Yes   ☐ No

B4. How useful did you find the information?   (M9)
☐ Very useful   ☐ Useful   ☐ Moderately useful   ☐ Not useful

B5. Do you think you will be able to use the system on your own next time? (M11)
☐ Yes   ☐ No   ☐ Not sure

Section C: Search for Specific Items

Surveyor: Ask user to search for the listed items. Item C1 may be used to get the user familiar with the system if necessary.

C1. Comprehension / Knowledge gained (with assistance)
*(*Researcher: Select a number of representative items that the user must search for. The following is an example taken from the system used in this study.)*

How many trips does IBL undertake daily, Monday to Friday?

☐ 203   ☐ 422   ☐ 691   ☐ 702   ☐ 845

*(*Researcher: Add representative items so that a novice user will know what is expected from him/her)*

C2. Comprehension / Knowledge gained (without assistance)   (M7 & M10)
*(* Surveyor: Start stopwatch. You may explain the questions, but you you may not provide any help with the system)*
*(*Researcher: Select a number of representative items that the user must search for. The following is an example taken from the system used in this study.)*

How many buses does IBL have?

☐ 95   ☐ 152   ☐ 190   ☐ 201

*(*Researcher: Add representative items so that a conversant user will take approximately 3 minutes to find the information)*
*(*Surveyor: Stop stopwatch.)*
_____ (mm:ss)

Using Automatic Tools in Accessibility and Usability Assurance Processes

Giorgio Brajnik[*]

Dip. di Matematica e Informatica
Università di Udine, Italy
Tel: +39 0432 558445
www.dimi.uniud.it/giorgio

Abstract. The paper claims that processes for monitoring, assessing and ensuring appropriate levels of accessibility and usability have to be adopted by web development and maintenance teams. Secondarily it argues that automatic tools for accessibility and usability are a necessary component of these processes. The paper presents first an analysis of web development and maintenance activities that highlights the reasons why accessibility and usability are so poorly achieved. It then suggests which processes, borrowed from the domain of software quality assurance, should be established to improve production and maintenance of web sites. The paper finally shows how automatic tools could fit in those processes and actually improve them, while being cost-effective.

1 Introduction

There are many books and other published material that present a wealth of information on what to do, and what to avoid, when designing, developing or maintaining a web site, like for example [Lynch and Horton, 02]. They discuss typography on the web, dealing with issues like alignment, capitalization, typefaces, etc. Although extremely educational and useful, this written knowledge is obviously not sufficient, considering the low quality level of existing web sites. In order to improve the quality of sites a web developer has to study this material, has to extract useful guidelines from it and has to decide which principles to apply to the specific case, how to apply them, and when.

A better start is by looking at compiled lists of web usability guidelines [Nielsen, 04; Nielsen, 99; NCI, 02]. But also in this case the web developer has to study this material to figure out which guideline is relevant for the specific situation at hand, and to apply it.

A crucial decision is which principles to apply, as different situations and contexts call for different choices. In order to determine which principles are relevant to a specific situation a web developer has to (i) detect failures of the site, (ii) diagnose them and identify their causes, (iii) prioritize them in terms of importance, (iv) determine how to repair them, and (v) estimate benefits and costs of these changes.

The rapid pace and tight deadlines at which development and maintenance of web sites proceed severely hinder the ability to perform processes (i) to (v) in an effective, reliable and cost-effective manner.

---

[*] Scientific advisor for UsableNet Inc., manufacturer of LIFT tools that are mentioned in the paper.

C. Stary and C. Stephanidis (Eds.): UI4All 2004, LNCS 3196, pp. 219–234, 2004.

On the other hand, processes (i) to (v) are necessary if the site is bound to match a certain level of quality since accessibility and usability are playing an increasingly important role in the game of achieving and maintaining a successful web site.

The claim of the paper is twofold. First, in order to improve accessibility and usability levels of web sites developers and maintainers have to establish assurance processes that are similar to those currently adopted for ensuring software quality. Second, due to the nature of accessibility and usability failures, the adoption of automatic tools supporting these assurance processes appears to be inevitable.

2   Low Accessibility and Usability Levels

The current demand for accessible and usable web sites (as witnessed also by the large number of books published on the subject in the last years: [Nielsen, 93; Mayhew, 99; Nielsen, 99; Nielsen and Tahir, 01; Thatcher et al., 02; Holzschlag and Lawson, 02; Rosson and Carrol, 02; Slatin and Rush, 03] to name a few) stems from the fact that the vast majority of existing web sites suffer from chronically low accessibility and/or usability levels. The trend is improving, thanks to legislation [USDOJ, 01], public awareness and market pressure [Ramasastry, 02].

2.1   Reasons

Even simple changes to web sites like adding a couple of new pages may lead to reduced accessibility and/or usability (A&U). The most relevant reasons are:

- Lack of resources. Lack of time, money or skilled persons hinder any effort aiming at improving quality of the web site. Of the three, by far the biggest problem is lack of skills because if A&U are thought of during design phases (rather than being retrofitted once the web site has already been produced) then their cost becomes much smaller.
- Release cycles of web sites are extremely fast. Changes to a web site may be conceived, designed, implemented and released in a matter of hours. This is due to the informative nature common to many web sites. It is also supported by the flexibility of the medium (changing something in HTML is in general much easier than in any programming language) and by the low distribution barrier (once the modified pages are published then their message is automatically delivered to web visitors).
- Detailed, accurate and complete specifications are missing. When a web site has to be changed, unless the change is a significant redefinition or revamp of the site, often no analysis and specification steps have been carried out. At least not in full detail and accuracy. This implies that the change is implemented sooner than it should, with a number of uninformed decisions being taken.
- Web browsing technologies are quickly evolving. The change to the web site may occur well after the web site has been designed for the first time, and since then the technologies and standards may have evolved. For example, assistive technologies may have evolved in such a way that the choices which were made when the web site had been designed are now obsolete. This means that changing the web site without considering this evolution is likely to worsen its A&U.

- Not all web architects, web designers, web masters and web programmers (in short the persons that are required to design and implement the change) are A&U savvy. Certain apparently trivial design or implementation decisions (f.e. typographic choices like font face and size and their implementation in HTML) may lead to solutions that violate accessibility standards or usability guidelines.

3   Usability and Accessibility Assurance Processes

3.1   Web Site Development Processes

In general a site development and maintenance team includes at least the following roles (potentially carried out by the same persons): web architects, web programmers, web designers, web content producers, accessibility and usability engineers, web masters, project managers.

These job roles are involved in a number of processes, covering the following activities: elicitation of clients' and users' goals, definition of sites' purposes, analysis of users jobs and work flows, definition of task models, choice of technologies, definition of the information architecture and of the look and feel of the site, definition of web site style guides, of page layout, of the site launching activities, and of the site maintenance processes; implementation of the site, graphical design, page debugging, multimedia production, site launch, bug fixing [Hackos and Redish, 98; Lynch and Horton, 02; Goto and Cotler, 02; Holzschlag and Lawson, 02].

3.2   Developing Web Sites vs. Packaged Software

Developing a web site is, in many ways, like developing an interactive software system, as in the latter case the processes being involved are very similar to the one listed above.

However, the specific nature of web sites leads to the following major differences , each one requiring more specific and demanding A&U assurance processes.

- Broader user audience: thus there are more user goals, user tasks and user contexts to cope with, which makes the design of effective sites more difficult.
- Less control on technologies used by web visitors and potential conflicts between standards, browsers, plug-ins, assistive technologies, web site implementations. Which further complicate the user interface of the web site.
- Less experienced users: in few cases a web designer can assume that the users of the site are already experienced in using it. In most of the cases visitors have to learn how to use a web site while trying to get a job done.
- More emphasis on user interface issues, as most of the decisions concern the content, information architecture, interaction structure or look and feel aspects, that are all components of the user interface of the web site.

For these reasons it is important that every design and implementation decision that may affect the user interface (i.e. anything that manifests in DHTML coding of the pages) is validated as soon as possible. *Validation* means to make sure that the adopted design or implementation is indeed something that solves the right problem.

3.3 Difficult Decisions

Achievement of appropriate A&U levels should not be seen as a target, but as a process. A&U assurance is just like cleaning a house: one has to decide which rooms should be cleaned at which level of hygiene (which depends on who will be using the rooms, and why), how to determine if they are clean, how frequently they have to be cleaned, who and with what kind of tools will be cleaning them.

When carrying out these processes, and especially assurance ones, a number of difficult managerial and technical decisions have to be taken (see the glossary in the appendix for some of the more technical terms).

1. Determining the goal of the assurance process.
2. Determining which guidelines to adopt.
3. Determining how to resolve conflicts between competing guidelines.

Discussion. Determining the goal of the assurance process requires that somebody decides which part of the site has to be assessed, and against which level of A&U. One has to decide if this level should be based on existing guidelines (official ones [USDOJ, 01; W3C/WAI, 99] or unofficial but well known ones [Nielsen, 04; NCI, 02; NNG, 01; Nielsen, 99] or if in-house guidelines should be developed for use within the organization. The advantage of adopting existing guidelines stems from the fact that guidelines embody the results of investigations carried out by others which may be relevant also to the specific case. However it may happen that guidelines need to be adapted to fit to specific situations.

For example, putting navigation bars to the right of the page improves accessibility (even though they are repeated in many pages, a screen reader user does not have to hear them over and over *before* getting the page content). However, sighted visitors might be required to horizontally scroll the page to see the navigation bar, which is a known usability hindrance.

4. Choosing the assessment methods.
5. Determining how to detect failures.

Discussion. Choosing the methods affects the effectiveness of the process and its efficiency. One has to decide when to run user testing sessions, comparative usability investigations, expert reviews or walkthroughs for accessibility or usability, or when to use automatic tools. And in any case general principles stated in the guidelines have to be made operational so that it is possible to determine if a web site satisfies the guideline or not.

For example even an apparently simple principle like "provide equivalent alternative textual descriptions for images" requires an ad-hoc standard to be defined regarding different kinds of images (spacers, decorative images, buttons, technical diagrams, etc.), regarding the actual phrasing of alternative texts (are they to be the same as captions, when figure captions exists? are they to be used solely for detecting existence of an image, or should they attempt to provide a concise description of the image?), regarding the way in which the image is embedded in the page (what should the alternative text be for images that are appropriately described by the text already shown in the page?) and regarding the implementation of the solution (should the IMG/ALT tag and attribute be used or would it be better to use the OBJECT tag, perhaps because it supports multilingual alternative text to be attached to the image?).

6. Deciding which guidelines to apply at which stage of the development process.
7. Determining how to prevent errors.

Discussion. Certain methods and guidelines should be applied to early deliverables of the development process. For example, some accessibility failures are due to bad design decisions: the use of frames, putting navigation bars to the left of the page, laying out the page content with fixed-size tables, or implementing menus with roll-overs. These decisions are taken when the page layout is designed, at a stage that occurs earlier than production of content. But, unless a careful assessment of the page template has been carried out *when the template is produced*, the consequences of these choices show up only when content is produced. Leading, for example, to pages where skip-to-contents links have to be added, navigation bars have to be moved to the right, a new implementation of the table layout has to be done in order to yield the correct reading order, and navigation options implemented through rollovers have to be made redundant with other mechanisms. The problem is that fixing a seemingly simple defect requires a reassessment of page design, and it is likely that a change in many of the pages is needed. The later this is done, the more costly it is.

On the other hand, violation of other guidelines can be spotted at later times (say, after content is produced) without incurring in significantly larger costs. For example, figuring out that images are not labeled (with the ALT attribute) is a problem which requires a localized fix that does not impact on other parts of the site. However, doing it afterward still requires a systematic, tedious activity of locating all image occurrences, labeling them and then making sure that labels are all consistent.

8. Determining how to estimate the cost, and the *Return on Investment* of the entire assurance process.

Discussion. A quality cost model used for software quality [Black, 02] could be applied to web development as well.

According to the model the cost of quality (C_q) is the sum of the *cost of conformance* (C_c) and the *cost of non-conformance* (C_{nc}). C_q includes any expenditure for preventing defects (e.g. training, tools, process establishment and tuning) (C_p) and the cost of appraising the current quality level through planning and running verifications (personnel, setting the test environment, running the verifications, reporting results) (C_a). C_p is basically a fixed cost incurred initially, while C_a is a cost that depends on the number of defects that are found (and fixed, which requires repeated verifications). C_{nc} includes the economic effects of bugs discovered by the development team or by users after release. At the very least, C_{nc} includes the costs for the infrastructure, time and effort needed for reporting, replicating, isolating, fixing, verifying each of the bugs reported by web visitors (C_{direct}). In addition it includes also less tangible costs like delays, slowdowns, customer alienation, uncompleted transactions, reduced traffic, reduced sales, reduced customers acquisition, conversion, retention ($C_{indirect}$).

This leads to

$$C_q = C_c + C_{nc} = C_p + C_a(N) + C_{direct}(M) + C_{indirect}(M+K)$$

where N and M are the number of defects found and fixed prior to (and respectively after the) release; K is the number of defects experienced by web visitors but not reported to the technical support team.

This cost model, imported from software engineering, could be applied also to web site development and maintenance. However, for web sites the proportion of defects that are reported by visitors is smaller than for software. Most visitors will not complain and simply will move away from the site after facing one or more A&U failures. Therefore C_{direct} will be small, because of the small number of reported bugs. However $C_{indirect}$ is likely to soar. Only when it reaches certain levels, management might be willing to launch some investigations to determine why the web site is not yielding the expected business results (in terms of visitor reach, acquisition, conversion, retention). These investigations increase C_{direct}. When a number of defects have been found (usability and accessibility ones, perhaps dealing with a poor information architecture, poor task support or poor presentation) they have to be fixed, yielding another increase in C_{direct}.

Little expenditures on C_c will apparently lower the overall cost, but C_{direct} and especially $C_{indirect}$ will increase. The latter will happen without explicit warnings since no monitoring is in place. Only effective assurance processes can avoid this hidden increase in non conformance costs.

The return on investment has to be viewed as a reduction of non-conformance costs, and especially for the intangible costs. Since these costs are affected by many other factors (like usefulness of the web site, popularity of the web site and the organization owning it, their credibility), this explains why it is difficult to accurately characterize the ROI of A&U efforts and why they are often perceived mainly as a cost source.

3.4 GQM: A General Framework for Assessments

The *Goal, Questions and Metrics* (GQM) approach [Basili and Weiss, 84] can be helpful to frame many of the decisions discussed above. It is very likely that each organization has to develop and establish its own means for answering those questions. Generality of guidelines and principles, and specificity of the organization and its work processes are the primary reasons for this state of affairs. Therefore appropriate methods have to be deployed to investigate those questions. The GQM approach supports this. It is based on the following steps, described here in the context of web site analysis:

Establish the goals of the analysis. Possible goals include: to detect and remove usability obstacles that hinder an online sale procedure; to learn whether the site conveys trust to the intended user population; to compare two designs of a site to determine which one is more usable; to determine performance bottlenecks in the web site and its back-end implementation.
Goals can be normally defined by understanding the situation of concern, which is the reason for performing the analysis. Which actions will be taken as a result of the quality assessment? What do we need to know in order to take these actions?

Develop questions of interest whose answers would be sufficient to decide on the appropriate course of actions. For example, a question related to the online sale obstacles goal mentioned above could be "how many users are able to buy product X in less than 3 minutes and with no mistakes?". Another question related to the same goal might be "are we using too many font faces on those forms?". Questions of interest constitute a bridge between goals of the analysis and measurable properties that are used for data collection. Questions also lead to sharper definition of the goals. They can be used to filter out inappropriate goals: goals for which questions cannot be formulated and goals for which there are no measurable properties. Questions can also be evaluated to determine if they completely cover their goal and if they refer to measurable properties. In addition certain questions will be more important than others in fulfilling a goal.

Published guidelines are useful since they suggest relevant questions. For example a guideline requiring to use white space to separate links in navbars suggests questions like "are links too close to each other?", "how will the space between links change if font size is increased?", "how many visitors will be affected by violations of this guideline?", "what are the possible consequences on visitors' tasks if this violation occurs?".

Establish measurement methods (i.e. metrics) to be used to collect and organize data to answer the questions of interest. A measurement method (see [Fenton and Lawrence Pfleeger, 97] for additional details) should include at least:

1. a description of how the data have to be elicited. For example via user testing with a given task description; or by automatically inspecting HTML sources of online pages to learn how links are organized.
2. a description of how data are identified. For example, what does "successfully completed task" mean in a user testing session?; how is "time to complete the task" going to be measured?; what constitutes a link in a web page (i.e. which HTML tags should be considered: A, AREA, IMG, BLOCKQUOTE, ...)?; what constitutes a local link to a web site (e.g. same server, same sub-domain, or same path)?
3. a description of how data are going to be categorized. For example, what are the different kinds of mistakes that users might get involved in, how can the "completion time" be broken down into different phases, if there are different categories of local links: links to images, videos, HTML files, etc. Measurement methods sharpen and refine the questions of interest.

   Even though some A&U guideline is sufficiently precise and specific to suggest the appropriate measurement method, it is often the case that in order to be operational guidelines need to be specialized yielding an internally defined standard.

Accessibility metrics may include the number of violations of a certain guideline/checkpoint, once the guideline or checkpoint have been made sufficiently specific and operational.

3.5 Defect Flow Model

A fundamental assumption of any quality assurance activity is that the artifact being evaluated is rarely free of defects. The purpose of the quality assurance activity is to understand which defects and how many of them are included in the artifact.

Now consider how defects flow in and out of the web site. Defects are inserted into and removed from the web site as an effect of the overall development and maintenance process (see figure 1). More specifically, the following subprocesses can be identified:

Defect insertion: this occurs during web site development and maintenance, at any stage. Defects may be due to errors in implementation decisions (like forgetting to label correctly controls of a form) or in design decisions (like relying on colors to convey information) or during analysis (like not providing the appropriate navigation path to support a given information task). In the majority of the cases this happens implicitly, without notice. Sometimes errors simply occur because somebody has thought of doing something, but then it's been forgotten. Other times they occur because of misjudgment (f.e. deciding that a certain accessibility requirement is not so important) or because of ignorance. Finally there are situations where defects are known to be included in the design, because alternative correct solutions are too expensive to be developed.

Defect removal: this happens after defects have been discovered, have been analyzed and their removal has been planned. Web developers design one or more solutions, rank them, plan their execution, and finally implement them. Usually, after executing a solution, a subsequent verification step takes place making sure that the defect has been removed, and that applied changes do not perturb the rest of the site (*regression testing*).
Defect removal is a process informed by *defect triage*, since the latter provides priorities and schedules for defect removals.

Defect elicitation: this occurs when A&U failures are detected and traced back to their causes: the defects. This may happen when web site visitors complain about the site or when explicit verification activities are carried out and they identify the defects.
During this process several elicitation techniques may be used: user testing, heuristic evaluations, accessibility inspections, accessibility "sniff tests", automated analysis, analysis of web server logs, code inspections.
Defect elicitation is guided by *A&U monitoring* and by *A&U assurance plan definition*: the former triggers elicitation, the latter determines which part of the site has to be tested, why, how and when.

Defect triage: is the process of determining if observed defects have been already dealt with in the past, which defects should be removed, to schedule their removal and to track their evolution in the site. *Defect triage* evaluates reported defects so that most critical ones are treated first [McCarthy, 95]. A complex step, especially with highly changing web sites, is to determine if a defect just being reported has been already managed in the past (for example, it was decided that it was not a violation of some guideline, or that its solution should be deferred).
"Failure Mode and Effects Analysis" [Black, 02] is a way for computing criticality of a defect within a formal approach. In any case, criticality of a defect depends on the following factors, whose importance depends on the specific organization running the assurance processes:

> **Violation on required standards:** for example a failure by a U.S. federal web site that does not satisfy *Section 508* accessibility requirements is a good candidate for a high level of criticality.

> **Individual impact:** (or *severity*) the impact of the failure with respect to an individual user who has to face it. This estimation may be formulated in terms of user inability to successfully complete the task that s/he intended to do, in terms of the importance of the task and importance of that kind of user.

Affected audience: (or *likelihood*) the fraction of the intended user population of the web site that is affected by the failure. The likelihood of a failure in turns depends on (i) how frequently the pages causing it are shown to visitors and (ii) which proportion of those visitors will actually experience the failure.

A defect located on the home page will be more critical than the same defect located on a secondary page, which will be visited by a smaller proportion of visitors. Web server logs can also be used to determine the frequency of display of given pages. On the other hand, determining the proportion of visitors that will experience the failure depends on assumptions, like knowing how many visitors use the page in the contexts leading to the failure. For example, only visually impaired visitors using JAWS on Windows 98 clicking on a certain link might experience the failure.

Symbolic impact: the failure might be perceived by the audience as a symbolic quality problem; it could be an embarrassing bug that requires a prompt treatment, even though its impact and likelihood are low.

Removal costs: in order to remove a bug a number of activities have to performed: (i) to diagnose the failures and determining their causes (i.e. the defect), (ii) to determine one or more possible solutions (i.e. alternative treatments), (iii) to estimate their requirements in terms of persons, skills, and infrastructure, (iv) to implement one solution, (v) to verify that the defect has disappeared, and finally (vi) to estimate time and money needed for all these activities. Fixing a defect like a missing ALT is a relatively easy task (easy to spot, to plan, to implement, and to verify), whereas changing a page layout that is based on fixed size tables so that it becomes CSS based with floating elements is much more complex. More complex to plan and to devise a solution, to implement, and especially to verify on all the pages with all the possible dynamic content that is available on the web site.

Instability of the site: fixing a defect requires changing some part of the web site, and these changes may propagate to other pages across the site. For example, fixing a usability defect by replacing a label of a link appears to be an easy and localized change of a page. But a deeper analysis may indicate that the same label was used in a global navigation bar, in the heading of an entire sub site and also in the URLs of the pages. What appeared to be an easy change has become a very destabilizing activity on a large fraction of the site.

A&U assurance plan definition: the plan should describe:

- what parts of the web site should be evaluated. For example, all the pages at a depth up to 2 from the home page; or all the pages that have a request rate, as gathered from web server logs, higher than 10% of the total.
- which criteria should be used to evaluate them and what levels of A&U should be reached. For example aiming at AA conformance level for accessibility as specified by the Web Content Accessibility Guidelines [W3C/WAI, 99].
- when these evaluations should take place. For example, a global accessibility evaluation should take place whenever any page template is changed. Or a link checking evaluation should be run every day to identify dead links pointing to web resources that have disappeared.

A&U monitoring: it is the process of managing methods, tools and roles for alerting when a failure has occurred and therefore triggering the *defect elicitation* process.

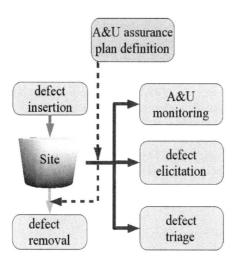

Fig. 1. The defect flow model: the web site is seen as a container of defects. Monitoring, elicitation, triage processes, guided by an assurance plan definition, can lead to effective defect removal.

4   Impact of Automatic Tools on Assurance Processes

In software engineering the deployment of several kinds of tools has been functional to the advance of the discipline. Tools are used to develop code and documentation, to define test cases, to run tests, to categorize and manage defects. Without these kinds of tools, software quality processes would be more demanding in resources than they are now, and would yield lower levels of quality. The same thing is to be expected for web development.

4.1 Automatic Tools

There are several flavors of web testing tools [Brink and Hofer, 02; Brajnik, 00]:

- tools for accessibility testing and repair, like Bobby, A-Prompt, 508Accessibility Suite, Site Valet, AccVerify, LIFT, etc. The metrics implemented by these tools correspond (more or less accurately) to official (W3C or Section 508) accessibility criteria.
- tools for usability testing (e.g. WebXM, LIFT, WebCriteria) that are based on usability guidelines.
- tools for performance testing (e.g. TOPAZ)
- tools for security testing (e.g. WebCPO)
- tools for analyzing web servers logs;
- tools for classifying a web site after learning the classification criteria from other web sites (e.g. WebTango [Sinha et al., 01]);

- tools for analyzing the content structure in a site (e.g. *Information Foraging* theories and models [Chi et al., 00]).

These tools cover a large set of tests for A&U. For example, usability tests can be grouped under the following factors (for more details see [Brajnik, 00]):

- consistency of presentation and controls (e.g. link labels, email labels, color consistency, navbar consistency, link colors)
- adequate feedback (e.g. freshness of information, authorship of pages)
- contextual navigation (e.g. NOFRAMES with equivalent content, links to home, breadcrumbs, skip-links, self-referential pages, frame titles, table summary)
- efficient navigation (e.g. table cells sizes, image sizes, download time, hidden elements, recycled graphics)
- clear and meaningful labels (e.g. page titles, link labels and titles, form labels)
- robustness (e.g. browser compatibility, safe colors, appropriate color contrast, standard font faces, no color-coding of information)
- flexibility (e.g. image ALT, auto refresh and redirect, font and page resizing, optional form fields)
- maintainability (e.g. relative URLs, use of CSS).

Obviously, automatic tools cannot assess all sorts of properties. In particular, anything that requires interpretation (e.g. usage of natural and concise language) or that requires assessment of relevance (e.g. ALT text of an image is equivalent to the image itself) is out of reach. Nevertheless these tools can highlight a number of issues that have to be later inspected by humans and can avoid highlighting them when there is reasonably certainty that the issue is not a problem. For example, a non-empty ALT can contain placeholder text (like the filename of the image); it is possible to write heuristic programs that can detect such a pattern and flag such an issue only when appropriate - and be able not to flag it if the ALT contains other text.

4.2 How Tools Support Assurance Processes

No tool can be expected to directly provide answers to the questions discussed in section 3.1. However tools can support those decisions, by better informing the decision maker and by providing functionalities that can foster certain processes and decisions.

Similarly no tool can be expected to do all the work by itself. To effectively deploy a tool, persons have to be trained on A&U methods and issues, on how to use effectively the tools, on how to establish appropriate processes that fit or improve the existing work flows.

A quick analysis of tools like LIFT (produced by UsableNet Inc., see www.usablenet.com) can highlight its impact on the A&U assurance processes. LIFT is in fact a family of tools including:

- *LIFT for Dreamweaver - Nielsen Norman edition* (LFD): a plug-in for the Macromedia Dreamweaver authoring environment that does evaluation and repairs with respect to accessibility guidelines (W3C/WCAG priority 1 and 2 [W3C/WAI, 99], and Section 508 [USDOJ, 01]) and with respect to usability guidelines for disabled persons developed by Nielsen Norman Group [NNG, 01];

- *LIFT Machine* (LM): a multi-user server-based tool for quality assurance that does evaluation of public web pages with respect to standard accessibility guide-lines and usability guidelines related to some of the usability factors mentioned above.

Impact on Defect Insertion

Automatic tools can affect the *Defect insertion* process.

LFD and LM, for example, come with a rich description of what an accessibility problem is (i.e. the failure and the possible defect), why it is important to fix it (i.e. the consequences of the failure), where you can learn more about it, and how you could fix it (i.e. how to remove the defect). This description can be used to recall a specific guideline to an experienced developer or to train novices, an important re-quirement as many U.S. federal agencies hire external contractors to retrofit accessi-bility on their web sites, as required by Section 508; these contractors are not always selected on the basis of their experience in accessibility.

In addition, being LFD embedded in the authoring environment, this information is readily available while developing the site. And actually through the familiar user interface of the development environment.

Thirdly, LFD has a monitoring function that continuously evaluates the page as it is developed, highlighting the potential defects. This can therefore alert the developer as soon as the defect is inserted in the site so that it can be removed as early as possi-ble.

Finally, both LFD and LM offer page previewers that help to debug a page, right when it is being developed or when it is being assessed. Previewers display the page with colors turned off (to discover if there is information that is color coded) or with linearized content (to check reading order) or in text mode.

Impact on Defect Elicitation

Automatic tools can improve the effectiveness of the defect elicitation process. They are systematic, do not get tired or bored, and are fast.

LFD and especially LM can scan a large number of local or live pages (up to sev-eral thousands) and apply a large (140+) set of tests on them.

Obviously, only certain kinds of properties can be tested in an automatic way. Us-ability and accessibility are *external* properties [Fenton and Lawrence Pfleeger, 97], since they can be evaluated only when a web site is being used by somebody. On the other hand, tools mainly look at static properties of the web site (their coding) to see if certain violation patterns arise. In general everything that has to do with human interpretation and context of use is likely to be poorly machine testable.

If heuristic tests are adopted (which often is the case since accessibility and usabil-ity are properties that seldom can be reduced to easy clear-cut decisions), the tools may produce false positives (i.e. they report potential failures in cases where there is no defect). LFD and LM reduce the number of false positives by guessing the role that images and tables play in a page. On the basis of image size and type, and its location in the page, LFD and LM are able to guess with good accuracy if the image is a spacer, a decoration, a banner, a button, or something else. And therefore they can offer a more specific diagnosis of the problem and suggestions for a solution. See [Brajnik, 04] for a description of an assessment method of tools and some preliminary results about effectiveness of LM with respect to accessibility.

[Lang, 03] discusses criteria to be used to compare different A&U evaluation methods. The same criteria can be used to compare the ability of different tools to elicit defects: ability to detect problems (called *completeness* in [Brajnik, 04]); accuracy and quality of results (called *correctness* in [Brajnik, 04]); time, effort and cost effectiveness; usefulness of results and who can use the results; generality of results.

Impact of Defect Triage

Tools like defect tracking systems are fundamental in this area. These tools have to support the development team in (i) entering defect descriptions, making sure that there are no duplicates, (ii) document possible interactions among defects (for example one defect may mask a different one; a defect may show up only when a different one occurs), (iii) track their evolution over time, and (iv) support triage processes. Bugzilla [Bugzilla.org, 04] is an example of such a tool, used for tracking software bugs.

Tracking defects on web sites is different, and more complex, than for software. In fact it is not easy, in general, to determine if a defect that has just shown up is exactly the same as the one that was seen one week ago. Consider for example that a single web page may show several hundreds of accessibility guidelines violations. And if the content of the page has changed, in principle no two violations are the same.

Secondly, especially for web pages that are dynamic, it is not easy to determine which files or components have to be fixed in order to remove a defect. The wrong code may be part of a template, of an included piece of code processed at compile-time, of content that is pulled out of a database or back-end application. If it is part of a template, or of content that is re-used elsewhere, then the same defect will cause several failures.

LM offers several different views of the list of failures that it detected on a web site, but it does not support defect triage.

Impact on Defect Removal

Tools can improve also the removal process, at least for certain kinds of defects.

LFD and LM offer, whenever possible, examples of good solutions (like fragments of Javascript code for correctly handling events causing new browser windows to be opened) that can be copied into the page being developed.

In addition, LFD offers *Fix Wizards* that allow a user to fix a problem without having to manually edit DHTML code. Which again is convenient for users who are not experienced or not used to work with HTML or Javascript. For example, fix wizards for data tables (i.e. TABLE tags used to display tabular information) that allow to markup correctly table cells so that they refer to table headers.

Finally, the *ALT Editor* of LFD supports a global analysis and fix of the ALT attributes of all the images found in the site. This is useful to ensure consistency among these image labels.

Impact on Monitoring

Tools can support the monitoring process.

For example, LM can schedule evaluations on a live site over time; they are run in an unsupervised mode and when ready an email is sent to the person that requested them.

While LM provides means for getting an overview of the status of a web site, this is limited to pages that have been tested within a single run of the LM. It does not directly support integration of results regarding different runs. For example, users cannot practically see the status of large web sites (10000+ pages) unless they first attempt to run a test on all of them.

[NCAM, 03] describes STEP508, a free tool that uses data produced by accessibility evaluation tools and identifies the defects that are most critical to fix and tracks the progress of the accessibility repair processes. STEP508 support the monitoring process since it can be used to integrate and compare different evaluations. It also supports other processes: by prioritizing defects it supports *Defect triage*; by tracking the progress it supports monitoring *the assurance processes themselves* rather than monitoring the A&U of the web site.

Impact on Plan Definition
Tools can support the definition of the test plan.

For example, LFD and especially LM allow the user to enable/disable individual tests, groups of tests and to define and use named guidelines profiles. In this way the user has a fine control on which tests are applied.

Secondly, the behavior of many tests is affected by parameters whose value can be changed by the user. For example, to determine if a site has a "text only" version, LFD and LM look for links containing words like "text only", "text version", etc. By changing the value of this parameter the user can customize the behavior of the test.

Impact on ROI
Tools affect the cost of A&U assurance in two ways. They contribute to increase fixed costs for the infrastructure and training: cost of the tool itself, of training and of tuning of work processes (C_p). However, if appropriately deployed they are likely to reduce the running costs of appraisal (C_a), to reduce the number of defects that are uncaught by the development team and the direct costs ($C_{direct}(M)$), and to reduce the indirect costs because fewer defects will be experienced by users.

5   Conclusion

While there are differences between development and maintenance of web sites and of software, it is likely that the same assurance processes adopted for software can be deployed for web sites. And, as a consequence, also automated tools for supporting A&U assurance can play a significant and positive role.

They can address the issues raised in section 2.1:

- lack of resources: appropriately deployed tools lead to a positive ROI and save time. Tools are likely to improve effectiveness and productivity of the team and, *at the same time*, increase the quality level that can be achieved.
- Fast release cycles: tools are systematic, fast and reliable. They can be routinely used also within short cycles. In certain cases only automatic testing is viable.
- Lack of specifications: a tool may be used to define in-house guidelines, to make them practical and be easily enforced. Tools can also help in the prevention of errors.
- Evolving technologies: tools can be updated and can reflect the state of the art of the available technology.

- Ignorance: tools are powerful training and reminding vehicles. They can deliver guidelines at the fingertips of those needing them.

At the moment adoption of tools is still limited. In my view this is due to several factors, including a limited awareness of the benefits of a high-quality (high accessibility and usability, to be more precise) web site and absence of established methods for comparing tools and their results. [Brajnik, 2004] is a preliminary step towards such a direction.

6 Glossary

The following terminology has been used in the paper:

bug: a generic term for referring to a misbehavior of the system and its causes.

failure: the manifestation of a misbehavior of the system. For example, when a web visitor using a screen reader gets the content of the page read in an incorrect order. Notice that in case of a usability and accessibility failure of a web site, misbehavior has to encompass the behavior of: the site, the web server, the browser, browser's plug-ins, any assistive technology, and the operating system used by the visitor.

failure mode: the category of failures that share the same kind of misbehavior. A failure mode is the set of symptoms; these symptoms may show up during a specific failure, and are caused by one or more defects (i.e. the disease).

defect: or *fault*, the reason why a failure may show up. Typically, for web usability and accessibility, a defect is rooted in some fragment of code implementing the site (HTML, Javascript, CSS). In the previous example, the defect associated with the incorrect reading order might be a bad use of the TABLE tag to layout the page.

error: is the misbehavior of the developer causing a defect that is inserted into the site.

References

[Basili and Weiss, 84] V. Basili and D. Weiss. A methodology for collecting valid software engineering data. *IEEE Trans. on Software Engineering*, 10(6):728-738, 1984.

[Black, 02] R. Black. *Managing the testing process*. Wiley Publishing Inc., 2002.

[Brajnik, 00] G. Brajnik. Automatic web usability evaluation: what needs to be done? In *Proc. Human Factors and the Web, 6th Conference*, Austin TX, June 2000. www.dimi.uniud.it/giorgio/papers/hfweb00.html.

[Brajnik, 04] G. Brajnik. Comparing accessibility evaluation tools: a method for tool effectiveness. *Universal Access in the Information Society*, 2004. To appear.

[Brink and Hofer, 02] T. Brink and E. Hofer. Automatically evaluating web usability. CHI 2002 Workshop, April 2002.

[Bugzilla.org, 04] Bugzilla.org. Bugzilla - bug tracking system. www.bugzilla.org/about.html, Feb 2004.

[Chi et al., 00] E. Chi, P. Pirolli, and J. Pitkow. The scent of a site: a system for analyzing and predicting information scent, usage and usability of a web site. In ACM, editor, *Proceedings of CHI 2000*, 2000.

[Fenton and Lawrence Pfleeger, 97] N. Fenton and S. Lawrence Pfleeger. *Software metrics*. International Thompson Publishing Company, 2nd edition, 1997.

[Goto and Cotler, 02] K. Goto and E. Cotler. *Web redesign: workflow that works*. New Riders Publishing, 2002.

[Hackos and Redish, 98] J. Hackos and J. Redish. *User and task analysis for interface design.* Wiley Computer Publishing, 1998.

[Holzschlag and Lawson, 02] M. Holzschlag and B. Lawson, editors. *Usability: the site speaks for itself.* Glasshouse Ltd., 2002.

[Lynch and Horton, 02] P. Lynch and S. Horton. *Web Style Guide.* Yale University, 2nd edition, 2002.

[Lang, 03] Lang T. *Comparing website accessibility evaluation methods and learnings from usability evaluation methods.* Peak Usability. www.peakusability.com.au/articles. 2003.

[Mayhew, 99] D. Mayhew. *The Usability Engineering Lifecycle: A Practitioner's Handbook for User Interface Design.* Morgan Kaufmann, 1999.

[McCarthy, 95] J. McCarthy. *Dynamics of software development.* Microsoft Press, 1995.

[NCI, 02] National Cancer Institute. Usability.gov. www.usability.gov, 2002.

[NCAM, 03] National Center for Accessible Media. STEP508. www.section508.gov/step. 2003.

[Nielsen, 93] J. Nielsen. *Usability engineering.* Academic Press, 1993.

[Nielsen, 99] J. Nielsen. *Designing Web Usability: the practice of simplicity.* New Riders Publishing, 1999.

[Nielsen, 04] J. Nielsen. Alertbox. www.useit.com/alertbox/, 2004.

[Nielsen and Tahir, 01] J. Nielsen and M. Tahir. *Homepage usability: 50 websites deconstructed.* New Riders, 2001.

[NNG, 01] Nielsen Norman Group. Beyond ALT Text: Making the Web Easy to Use for Users with Disabilities. www.nngroup.com/reports/accessibility/, Oct 2001.

[Ramasastry, 02] A. Ramasastry. Should web-only businesses be required to be disabled-accessible? www.cnn.com/2002/LAW/11/07/findlaw.analysis.ramasastry.disabled/index.html, Nov 7, 2002.

[Rosson and Carrol, 02] M. Rosson and J. Carrol. *Usability Engineering.* Morgan Kaufmann, 2002.

[Sinha et al., 01] R. Sinha, M. Hearst, M. Ivory, and M. Draisin. Content or graphics? an empirical analysis of criteria for award-winning websites. In *Proc. Human Factors and the Web, 7th Conference,*, Madison, WI, June 2001.

[Slatin and Rush, 03] J. Slatin and S. Rush. *Maximum Accessibility: Making Your Web Site More Usable for Everyone.* Addison-Wesley, 2003.

[Thatcher et al., 02] J. Thatcher, C. Waddell, S. Henry, S. Swierenga, M. Urban, M. Burks, B. Regan, and P. Bohman. *Constructing Accessible Web Sites.* Glasshouse Ltd., 2002.

[USDOJ, 01] U.S. Dept. of Justice. Section 508 of the rehabilitation act. www.access-board.gov/sec508/guide/1194.22.htm, 2001.

[W3C/WAI, 99] World Wide Web Consortium - Web Accessibility Initiative. Web content accessibility guidelines 1.0. www.w3.org/TR/WCAG10, May 1999.

Accessibility in the Field of Education

Laura Burzagli, Pier Luigi Emiliani, and Paola Graziani

Italian National Research Council Institute for Applied Physics "Nello Carrara",
Via Panciatichi, 64 50127 Firenze, Italy
{L.Burzagli,P.L.Emiliani,P.Graziani}@ifac.cnr.it
http://www.ifac.cnr.it

Abstract. Accessibility of documents in electronic format is an important element of the e-inclusion process. An aspect that needs further investigation is the connection between the general problem of accessibility and the specific application domains. An interesting example is represented by Education, because an intense use of the ICT is foreseen in it. By means of the use of scenarios, a description of the relationships between technologies for Education and Accessibility is analyzed in three different situations: a current class with typically employed technologies, a class where all existing technologies are used and a third scenario in which the learning environment is an intelligent environment. The comparison highlights in particular the differences between technologies, accessibility problems and approaches for their solution.

1 Introduction

The accessibility of documents in electronic format is an important element of the e-inclusion process stated by the most important political organizations, such as the American Congress and the European Union Commission.

During the first phase of study of this problem, a large number of aspects had to be identified, such as the specific barriers introduced for disabled persons, the variety of possible solutions, and the connection between accessibility, programming languages and communication protocols. At the end of this first phase, at present, basic rules of accessibility have been created and the WCAG [1], as technical rules, the 508 Rehabilitation Act[2], and the recent Italian law on accessibility [3], as legal rules, are some of the more meaningful results.

However, this great effort to identify, create and apply the rules has not produced an impact at the same level of importance, because a large percentage of web sites and electronic applications still present serious accessibility problems. This implies that a set of relevant elements has been overlooked and will have to be considered in this second phase of study.

The aforementioned set of rules, which are both technical and legal, are effective for all types of electronic documents. Their general character implies the lack of any reference to specific domains of application.

Therefore, an aspect that needs further investigation is the connection between the general problem of accessibility and the specific application domain. The analysis of the problem in different domains, such as the Public Administration, Health Care, etc., leads to the discovery that the presence of specific elements in a particular sector requires a different approach to the problem. In other words, the context becomes an essential component for an effective application of accessibility.

C. Stary and C. Stephanidis (Eds.): UI4All 2004, LNCS 3196, pp. 235–241, 2004.
© Springer-Verlag Berlin Heidelberg 2004

2   A Specific Domain: Education

At the moment, a domain of particular interest is Education, because intense use of the ICT is foreseen here within. Therefore, the presence of accessibility barriers can damage the process of learning for a large number of persons and for a long period (at least 10 years), while this process represents a key element in the life of each person. A specific experiment has been developed for this domain within the framework of the IST SEN-IST-NET project [4]. It addressed the problem of certain groups of learners who are at risk of not being fully involved in new ways of learning, either because of their social disadvantages or their disability. Problems may arise because of both current instruments and future instruments.

The analysis is complex, because the term "Education" embraces many different experiences, from primary school to "Adult education" or "long-life education", which comprises, for example, all the activities related to professional updating.

Differences can also be found in instruments, which may vary from a common computer such as a school aid, or a book in electronic format, instead of a book in paper format, up to the most sophisticated instruments for e-learning.

3   Use of Scenarios

The intricacy of this domain has required the adoption of a flexible instrument that makes possible a correct and concise overview. The scenario seems appropriate for this purpose, because it can synthesize an effective and exhaustive description of this variety of contexts. This methodology can generally be defined as a description of one or more persons who interact with a system. Within the framework of the SEN-IST-NET project, this methodology has also been considered to be a useful tool for eliciting discussions, since the description of a possible context in which the different components of the multidisciplinary group (teachers involved in special-needs education, assistive technology developers, students and their parents) can have a comprehensible picture of possible developments and express their ideas. This description does not only consider the individual needs for a disable student , but also how the entire educational environment will probably change due to the introduction of technology. It places the problems of the new educational environment within the framework of the development of the Information Society, with its emphasis on the accessibility of the system within a community of users, such as a classroom.

In the framework of the IST SEN-IST-NET project, our activity has led to the writing of three different scenarios: a first scenario is related to the current situation, a second scenario describes the possibilities of available technologies; and a third scenario, for 2010, produced by ISTAG, introduces a different concept of school, learning, and teaching.

A history lesson constitutes the common reference.

In each of these scenarios, a set of parameters can describe the accessibility that is related not only to the device or to the document, but also, for example, to different learning paths. The following is the list of parameters:

- Electronic devices and equipments used by disabled people and by classes.
- Accessibility barriers.

- The identification of solutions by means of the adoption of assistive technology or a customized setting of the common applications.
- Additional problems faced by the class and the teacher.

4 First Scenario: Today Situation

The first scenario describes the event of a blind girl who attends to Secondary School. She has already acquired the skills necessary in order to use her PC confidently, first of all in the DOS environment and afterwards with the GUI interfaces, such as Windows. She uses her PC in the classroom essentially as an aid for reading and writing and at home for communicating with many able and disabled friends. From a certain point of view, the computer represents for her a technological interface between her alternative way of reading/writing and the class environment. For example, she writes homework by controlling the word processor by means of the Braille display, and then produces printed materials for the teachers. Unfortunately, this is not possible for all subjects. Mathematics and scientific subjects present difficulties with the computer. For this reason, she also needs traditional tools such as a Perkins Braille writer.

She has discovered interesting new utilisations for her PC, in addition to the educational support, and now, with the Internet connection, her computer has become an aid for communicating worldwide. She discovered this enormous possibility: a way of finding new friends and acquiring a new cultural overview.

Electronic devices: the equipment is represented by the set of assistive technology devices : computer, screen reader, scanner. A more general instrument is the connection to Internet.

Computers are not frequently used in the classroom and her classmates spend only a few hours a week in a special room equipped with PCs for computer science lessons (this is the current situation in the Italian secondary school).

Accessibility barriers: in this scenario, the accessibility landscape is well defined, because problems can be introduced only by the electronic formats of the texts used by the girl and in the applications for the Internet connection.

The identification of solutions by means of assistive technology or a customized setting of the common applications.

If the electronic applications, such as the history book, have been written by following the aforementioned accessibility rules published by WAI, most problems are eliminated. Nowadays this kind of problems can be easily resolved from a technical point of view, because a correct application of accessibility guidelines allows authors to write accessible documents. Incidentally, we could observe that, in reality, the electronic versions of books are not generally available in accessible format. For example, in Italy at times, some publishers provide such a version on request, but it is usually in the form of files for the publishing software of the printing house, which are neither accessible nor compatible with a common word processor or a browser. Alternatively, the electronic version of a book has to be produced by means of a scanner and an OCR program, starting from the printed version. In both cases, an usable and accessible electronic book must be produced by converting and editing one of the aforementioned sources. In any case, since the original book is conceived for sighted students, this process involves an accurate analysis of the contents. This means that, if the book contains just text, the accessible version can easily be produced; however, if it contains formulas and/or graphical representations, the alternative electronic version requires a complete re-writing which involves a specific interpretation of accessibility guidelines for the subject. Also a history book, even if most of it is represented by text, can contain images, drawings and tables, which require suitable alternative representations. This means that a general purpose set of accessibility guidelines is not sufficient to ensure a good result.

Additional problems, faced by the class and the teacher
Since the PC is used only by one person and with a sound rendering (speech synthesizer), two main problems arise for the class: the noise introduced by this device, which can disturb classmates, and the difference from the educational instruments used by the other students. The first problem is overcome with the use of a Braille display, which is even more expensive than a voice synthesizer, or by means of the use of headphones, which can exclude the student from the activities of the class. Moreover, the teacher(s) must be able to use these technologies and support the student, and this is not a common condition.

5 Second Scenario: Possible Evolution

The second scenario describes a classroom of a secondary school, with the presence of a blind student.

The scenario is divided into two parts: the first considers homework assignments, and the second considers the school activities.

The assignment: a group of student is given the task of preparing a report on several Roman emperors, which is to be presented and harmonised with the work of the other groups at school. During this first phase, a group of students is connected in a virtual environment for their home-based study activities. The blind student collaborates with a sighted student: he writes the text, while a classmate inserts the images with a textual comment, using a tool for collaborative work.

The activity at school is completely different, because it involves activities, such as downloading multimedia presentations to the class. Additional activities are implemented such as a virtual museum visit using a videoconference system, or access to the museum information system. The activities also include a virtual reality trip to sites of ancient Rome.

Here, the use of Information and Communication Technologies for the history lesson is not considered as a support for disabled students only, but is a current instrument for the work of the entire class.

Electronic devices:
The use of technologies is now completely different, because the students use interpersonal communications, access to information, such as a school library or the web. The school is also connected with broadband services (e.g. video conferences), and is equipped with information technology (e.g. virtual reality equipment).

Accessibility barriers:
In this situation, accessibility assumes a more important role and the presence of accessibility barriers implies an exclusion of the disabled student from the current activities of the class. Barriers come not only from specific documents, but also from

different applications, such as electronic mail. Moreover, particular activities, such as virtual trips, require specific abilities, that are not possessed by every one.

The identification of solutions by means of assistive technology or a customized setting of the common applications:
In this situation the accessibility of documents in electronic format is not sufficient, and services such as electronic mail must also be considered. Some solutions are very easy, such as the use of messages in plain text, rather than in HTML text, but other groups of solutions must be studied. In this situation of cooperative activities, accessibility must be introduced at the level of the application and networking environment adaptations have to be considered since the creation of the network system.

However, a scenario like this one provides the teacher with different choices: for example the virtual tour of ancient Rome, or the teleconference with a museum site. The different choices could contain problems of accessibility, because some of them require specific abilities. The different perspective shows that alternatives could be followed. This implies a severe impact on the teaching methodologies, because they require personalizing. It involves social dynamics in both the classroom and the external environments. Many abilities need to be integrated, with obvious advantages and disadvantages. The use of common educational materials in multimedia format means that such materials have to be produced by taking into account a different set of guidelines, depending on the technologies utilized for their production (for example, Web contents, interactive software, audio and video records).

Additional problems, faced by the class and the teacher:
This perspective involves a strong impact on the teaching methodologies. The most meaningful example is the need for a personalisation activity. This requires the teacher to acquire knowledge of both the electronic system and the specific abilities of their students. S/he has to prepare different learning paths for the same subject, depending on abilities, preferences and context situation. At this level, accessibility becomes a basic aspect of the educational process. However, this personalization process does not concern only disabled students, but represents a possibility for every student to better utilize his/her resources.

6 Third Scenario: ISTAG Scenario

The third scenario comes from an IST Advisory Group (ISTAG) document. The role of this group is to provide the European Commission with independent advice concerning the strategy, content and direction of research work to be carried out under the IST Programme.

The selected scenario is called "Annette and Salomon – Ambient for social learning" and a complete description of it can be found at the address:
http://www.cordis.lu/ist/istag-reports.htm.

It describes the learning environment as an intelligent environment, integrated within a network of intelligent environments, and presents a restructuring of the learning space.

Some key elements are:
– A definition of the general topic of discussion and main lines;
– A free aggregation of groups for examining different aspects of the problem;

- A free aggregation in the space – the environment is reconfigured in order to obtain the required facilities (communications and access to information);
- The role of the teacher as moderator of group activities and of integration within a coherent scheme;
- An environment which can be reconfigured for purposes of general discussion and integration.

The scenario is complex and does not consider the specific presence of a disable member in the group. Application of the previous analysis structures, (consisting of a definition of the electronic devices and equipment used by disabled persons and by the class, the accessibility barriers; an identification of solutions by means of the adoption of assistive technology or a customized setting of common applications; and the additional problems, for the class and for the teacher) does not find a correspondence here, because a set of innovative circumstances is present.

For example, the official document, states the specific technologies needed:

- Recognition (tracing and identification) of individuals, groups and objects;
- Interactive commitment aids for negotiating targets and challenges (goal synchronisation);
- Natural language and speech interfaces and dialogue modelling;
- Projection facilities for light and soundfields (visualisation, virtual reality and holographic representation), including perception-based technologies such as psychoacoustics;
- Tangible/tactile and sensorial interfacing (including direct brain interfaces);
- Reflexive learning systems (adaptable, customisable) to build aids for reviewing experiences;
- Content design facilities, simulation and visualisation aids;
- Knowledge management tools to build community memory.

In this list, many new technologies have been introduced and these need an indepth analysis in order to discover new potential barriers. The vast majority have not yet reached product level, but are still in the prototypal stage. This type of integrated system could offer a whole new perspective for the disabled, but its study is only at the beginning.

Different input and output interaction systems are considered, for example brain interfaces or perceptual interfaces, which must still be considered from an accessibility point of view.

Within this framework, Design for All can constitute a good approach, as, in accordance with its principles, it embraces user needs and preferences, devices and contexts of use in a common operative platform.

7 Conclusions

Application of the accessibility principles in the specific domain of Education leads to a consideration of different environments, for both now and the future. From the analysis of the previous three scenarios, important differences appear in the approach to accessibility between the current situation and the situation foreseen for the future.

For the current scenario it is quite sufficient to consider some kinds of adaptations to the technologies normally used by disable students. The process can include different levels of complexity, but most of the problems are at least in principle solvable.

On the contrary, the last scenario shows a completely different situation, for both the technologies and the methodologies. The education environment will be redesigned, and this process will also involve its accessibility. In this sense vast research will prove necessary. The scenario shows a lot of new applications, some of which are still closer to an idea rather than to a product. In this sense it is important that the properties of any new kind of interfaces are studied, with the aim of defining both barriers and opportunities.

But this phase of study concerning applications is not sufficient. A second level of research is equally necessary and regards new methodologies of education. It is no longer true that the same learning path will be adopted for all students. This condition can also lead to the creation of a customized path for disable people, which must satisfy all special needs and personal preferences. At this level a specific approach for accessibility has to be set up. And again in this case in depth research proves to be essential.

This paper has considered the evolution of accessibility concept in the specific field of Education. However, some conclusions can be generalized, because the technological development concerns any application field. This development involves a different organization of activities in which the personalization assumes a key role. New problems arise, so that it is required a new approach for accessibility guidelines, which could interpret a more flexible and personalized interaction between human and ICT merged in the environment.

References

1. W3C Web Content Accessibility Guidelines,1.0, http://www.w3.org/TR/WCAG10/
2. Electronic and Information Technology Accessibility Standards, http://www.access-board.gov/sec508/508standards.htm
3. Provisions to support the access to information technologies for the disabled, http://www.pubbliaccesso.it/normative/law_20040109_n4.htm
4. IST-2000-26449, European Network of Excellence in Information Society Technologies for Special Educational Needs, http://www.senist.net

Supporting Web Usability for Vision Impaired Users

Francesco Correani, Barbara Leporini, and Fabio Paternò

ISTI - C.N.R.
56124 - Pisa, Italy
{francesco.correani,barbara.leporini,fabio.paterno}@isti.cnr.it

Abstract. The aim of this work is to provide designers and developers of Web applications with support to obtain systems that are usable for vision-impaired users. To this end, we have defined a number of design criteria to improve Web site navigation through screen readers or other similar devices. A test of navigation by blind and vision-impaired subjects showed that our criteria improved Web site usability both qualitatively and quantitatively. Subsequently, an inspection-based tool was developed to ease application of such criteria. Its main features are presented along with a discussion of some of the first application results.

1 Introduction

In recent years there has been increasing interest in accessibility and usability issues, since it is more and more important that the information on the Internet be easily reached by all categories of users. However, these issues are often addressed by two separate communities with two different focuses, one on usability and the other on accessibility. Indeed, the W3C consortium has developed guidelines only for accessibility, whereas in the human-computer interaction area many methods aim to evaluate only usability aspects. Vision-impaired users need to have both accessible and usable applications. Recently, designers and developers are becoming aware that there is a need for integrating these two aspects in order to obtain Web sites for a wide variety of users, including those with disabilities. Indeed, if such integration is lacking then it is possible to obtain usable sites with low accessibility (sites easy to use but not accessible for users with disabilities) or vice versa accessible sites but with low usability (where even users with disabilities can perform their tasks but with difficulty or at least not easily as it could be).

When only accessibility guidelines are applied a number of navigational problems can be found when using a screen reader or magnifier:

- *Lack of context* – reading through the screen reader or a magnifier the user may lose the overall context of the current page and read only small portions of texts. For example, when skipping from link to link with the tab key, a blind user reads the link text on the braille display or hears it from the synthesizer (e.g. ".pdf", "more details", etc.), but not what is written before and after.

- *Information overloading* – The static portions of the page (links, frames with banners, etc.) may overload the reading through a screen reader, because the user has to read every thing almost every time, thus slowing down the navigation.

C. Stary and C. Stephanidis (Eds.): UI4All 2004, LNCS 3196, pp. 242–253, 2004.
© Springer-Verlag Berlin Heidelberg 2004

- *Excessive sequencing in reading the information* – the command for navigating and reading can constrain the user to follow the page content sequentially. Thus, it is important to introduce mechanisms to ease the identification of precise parts in the page. An example of this is the result page generated by a search engine. Usually, in the top of such pages, there are several links, advertisements, the search fields and buttons, and so on, and then the search results begin.

To overcome these problems, we have developed a number of criteria [5] aiming at identifying the meaning of usability when Web sites are accessed by users with disabilities through screen readers. In this paper we present a tool that provides support for designers and developers interested in applying such criteria.

In the following sections, after discussing related work we present the proposed criteria, then we introduce the tool developed to support designers and developers interested in applying such criteria. Lastly, some concluding remarks are drawn along with indications for future work.

2 Background

2.1 Related Work

Well-defined criteria and guidelines must be provided to guide designers in the development process of more usable and accessible Web sites. Up to now, usability and accessibility guidelines have usually been proposed separately, whereas we propose an integrated approach. Many detailed usability guidelines have been formulated for both general user interfaces and Web page design. Most accessibility issues are taken into account especially by W3C (World Wide Web Consortium) in the Web Accessibility Initiative (WAI), in which a set of specific guidelines and recommendations has been defined: "Web Content Accessibility Guidelines 1.0" (WCAG 1.0) [15]. Currently, a new version 2.0 of Web Content Accessibility Guidelines as a Recommendation is in progress [16]. A number of tools (for example, BOBBY [3], LIFT [13], and WebSat [8]) have been proposed to identify accessibility problems mostly following the guidelines of Section 508 and W3C. LIFT and WebSat also support usability criteria for users without disabilities but do not support specific usability criteria for users accessing through screen readers.

There are various international projects involving accessibility and usability of user interfaces for people with special needs [7]. Stephanidis' group has long been working on user interfaces for all, elaborating methods and tools allowing the development of unified user interfaces [10]. In the AVANTI project, a "Unified Web Browser" has been developed: it employs adaptability and adaptivity techniques, in order to provide accessibility and high-quality interaction to users with different abilities and needs (e.g., blind users or those with other disabilities). In particular, for vision-impaired people, it incorporates techniques for the generation of a list of large push buttons containing the links of a page. However, apart from this feature, which is similar to some checkpoints of the criteria proposed in our work, the AVANTI browser focuses on accessibility issues, but does not specifically address navigation usability through screen readers. The analysis of Web site accessibility and usability by means of guidelines, similarly to other inspection methods used in usability/accessibility assessment, requires observing, analysing and interpreting the Web site characteristics themselves. Since those activities involve high costs in terms of time and effort, there is a great interest in developing tools that automate the process of registration, analysis and interpretation of these accessibility data. Ivory & Hearts [4] distinguish between automatic capture, analysis and critique tools. Automatic capture tools assist the process of collecting relevant user and system information. Examples of such tools are Web server logging tools and client-side logging tools (e.g. WebRemUsine [9]), and so on.

Many automatic evaluation tools were developed to assist evaluators with guidelines review by automatically detecting and reporting violations and in some cases making suggestions for fixing them. EvalIris [1] is an example of tool that allows designers and evaluators to easily incorporate new additional accessibility guidelines. The tool proposed herein aims at working on the basis of the checkpoints associated with the criteria, in order to evaluate and repair Web sites through an interactive process with the evaluator/developer.

Regarding usability of Web site navigation from the perspective of users with disabilities, Barnicle [2] reports on some first usability testing of GUI applications for blind and vision-impaired users interacting through screen readers. However, despite progress in screen reader development, blind users of GUI applications still face many obstacles when using these applications. In [12] a study about usability of Web site navigation through screen readers is discussed. In particular, this work addresses accessibility supported in the 508 standard [11]. Indeed, through a user testing conducted with 16 blind users, they showed the lack of support of usability criteria according to the 508 standard guidelines. From the empirical evaluation, they suggested 32 guidelines aimed at improving usability for blind users. Some of those guidelines are furnished for Web site developers and others for screen reader developers. As a result, an unstructured and unorganised list of guidelines was proposed. Such list appears difficult to use as reference by developers because of the lack of a clear structure and organization of the guidelines. In contrast to their approach, we have sought to formulate general principles according to the three main properties of usability of its standard definition. In addition, we have classified the criteria on the basis of their impact on the Web user interface. Furthermore, although further investigations are in progress, at the moment the guidelines proposed in [12] refer only to blind users and do not consider low vision users. Besides, some important aspects for blind users are not considered, such as "messages and dynamic data management", "sound usage", "appropriate names for frames or tables", etc. Considering how their guidelines are expressed, it is likely to be difficult to perform automatic evaluation of them. Moreover, no indication is given about the development of a tool for their automatic support.

2.2 The Proposed Criteria

The usability of a Web site depends on many aspects. In order to improve the navigability through a screen reader, we propose 19 criteria [5] that we have divided into three subsets according to different aspects of usability indicated by the standard usability definition (ISO 9241): "effectiveness" criteria (5) ensure the accomplishment of the task, for example using a logical partition of interface elements or ensuring a proper link content, "efficiency" criteria (10) shorten the time required to complete that task, for example using proper names for frames, tables and images or providing importance levels for the elements or identifying the main page content; "satisfaction" criteria (4) provide Web pages with minor additional characteristics (addressed to improve the navigation) without the need to use specific commands.

The other parameter that we have used to classify the criteria is the user interface aspect involved: presentation criteria are indicated by an "a" and those related to the user interface dialogue by a "b". Table 1 shows the list of the proposed 19 criteria. To identify each criterion we used the format I.J.L where: I denotes the usability aspect addressed, that is 1 for effectiveness, 2 for efficiency, or 3 for satisfaction; J is a progressive index number to enumerate the criteria ($j=1..N_i=5|10|4$); L can be a (presentation) or b (dialogue) to indicate the aspect type on which the criterion has an effect.

Table 1. List of the proposed criteria.

Effectiveness	1.1.b Logical partition of interface elements
	1.2.a Proper link content
	1.3.b Messages and dynamic data management
	1.4.a Proper style sheets
	1.5.b Layout and Terminological Consistency
Efficiency	2.1.b Number of links and frames
	2.2.b Proper name for frames, tables and images
	2.3.a Location of the navigation bar
	2.4.b Importance levels of elements
	2.5.b Keyboard shortcuts
	2.6.a Proper form use
	2.7.b Specific sections
	2.8.b Indexing of contents
	2.9.b Navigation links
	2.10.b Identifying the main page content
Satisfaction	3.1.b Addition of short sounds
	3.2.a Colour of text and background
	3.3.a Magnifying at passing by mouse
	3.4.a Page information

The 19 formulated criteria address usability issues of Web interfaces when a screen reader is used. The criteria intend to be general principles that should be considered by Web designers/developers during the development phases of a Web site. Such principles are aimed at structuring user interface elements and content of the page, as well as providing additional features, which can help users to move about better in the Web site through a screen reader. Some possible examples of criteria application are: appropriately marking the navigation bar and side-menu; logically spreading out the content in the page; using meaningful names and labels for textual/graphical links and buttons; keeping consistency among pages. Many criteria affect visually the Web interface (e.g. coloured areas or element magnifications), whereas others are detected only by the screen reader (e.g. hidden labels or names of frames).

To facilitate their application by Web site developers, we have suggested 54 technical checkpoints. A checkpoint is a specific construct in a language for Web page development that, when provided, it supports the application of a given criterion. For each criterion, we provide a number of different technical solutions to support it, taking into account developers' choices in building the Web site (e.g., frames,

JavaScripts, etc.). Thus, usability aspects are addressed in terms of associated criteria, while the technical solutions in terms of checkpoints. For instance, the criterion "proper form usage" has four checkpoints related to: (1) button labels, (2) groups of control elements, (3) Onchange event (to be avoided), (4) matching labels and input elements; whereas, the criterion "Loading suitable style sheets" has three checkpoints referring to different devices: (1) voice synthesizer, (2) display and (3) printer Braille device.

In spite of the effort of providing an objective classification of the criteria, the inclusion of some of them in one group rather than in another may be somewhat open to personal interpretation although this is rarely significant.

2.3   Empirical Testing of the Criteria

In order to estimate the impact of our proposed criteria on the user interface for visually-impaired users, a user testing was conducted [6]. Usability testing provides an evaluator with direct information regarding the way people use applications and the problems they encounter when they use the tested interface. In our case, the test was conducted with two groups of users: twenty blind and visual impaired people were recruited for the testing. All the participants had been using Windows 98/ME and Jaws (as screen reading application) for at least one year at the moment of the testing. Thus, it could safely be assumed that they were adept at using the combination of a screen reader and Windows with the Internet Explorer browser.

Half of the participants were blind and the other half had a partial vision deficit: in any case, no-one could spot elements on the screen without an auxiliary support. The experience with the screen reader was extremely different within the group of participants, their level ranging from beginner to expert. The testing procedure adopted was based on two remote evaluation techniques (remote logging complemented with a remote questionnaire) and was performed by using two Web site prototypes and two tests, each one composed of 7 assigned tasks. The remote evaluation was used for capturing objective data: participants used the system to complete a pre-determined set of tasks while the system recorded (via log files) the results of participants' interaction (i.e. time spent), whereas through the questionnaire subjective information on navigation quality were collected from users (e.g. opinions about sound usage, colour contrast, shortcut preference, tasks more difficult, and other personal considerations), and other qualitative data not obtainable by the logging tool were collected.

For our testing, we considered a Web site containing specific information about the "The Tuscan Association for the Blind" (Unione Italiana Ciechi – Regione Toscana). This testing site was chosen with the intent of putting blind people in a comfortable situation by providing them with familiar information, thus reducing navigation difficulties.

Two versions of the same Web site prototype were considered: a "control version" implemented without applying our criteria (used as control in our testing protocol) and an "implemented version" created according to our 19 criteria. Practically, in the "implemented version" we applied all the proposed criteria analysing how to apply one checkpoint instead of another (e.g. heading levels rather than frames for logical partition). However, we tried to cover most checkpoints by applying various solutions for different pages (remember that one criterion can be applied through several checkpoints). Half of the participants were asked to start from the "control version" and the other half from the "implemented version". The testing procedure was conducted through two sessions driven automatically: "*test0*" (control version) and "*test1*" (implemented version). A Wizard was implemented with the purpose of indicating the assigned sequence of tasks to perform (necessary for the subsequent evaluation) to the users without constraining participants' behaviour. Each participant was asked to carry out a set of seven tasks per test (from easier to more difficult), in the two Web sites. The time required for performing the tasks was recorded in both cases. The tasks included common navigation operations, such as page opening, content reading, and information search. *Test0* and *test1* included the same types of tasks, which differed only in some minor aspects (e.g. the file to download, the information to find, etc.).

During both testing procedures, the main interaction activities performed by each user were captured and logged. The log files contained a wide variety of user actions (such as mouse clicks, text typing, link selections…) as well as browsing behaviour, such as page loading start and end. In particular, the tool logged the time when each specific interaction was performed. Consequently, it was possible to compute the time spent for carrying out each task as the difference between the times corresponding to the beginning and the end of the task. Thus, all data gathered through the testing procedure were analysed in order to evaluate the overall improvement of the Web site after the application of our criteria. Such improvement was measured in terms of navigation time saved by users in accomplishing given tasks.

At the end of the testing procedures, two log files per users were available. Each log file contained a set of couple <event type / performing time>, which allowed to compute the time spent per task. The difference between the time spent performing each task in *test0* and *test1* ("control site" and "implemented site" respectively) was used to verify if and to what extent the application of our criteria had improved navigability. So, the time saved by users was taken as an indicator of Web site improvement.

In order to assess the statistical significance of the data analysed, non-parametric statistic tests were applied to raw data: α was fixed at 0.05 (significance) and 0.01 (high significance). We found a significant difference between the total time spent by all users performing each task in *test0* and *test1* (Wilcoxon matched pairs test). For each task, the total time was calculated by summing the time spent by each user (twenty users). We also found a highly significant difference between the total time spent by each user performing all the given tasks in *test0* and *test1* (Wilcoxon matched pairs test). For each user, the total time required in *test0* and *test1* was computed by summing the time required for each task. The time analysis revealed a wide range of differences for tasks and users, possibly due to the different ability of users/difficulty of tasks. However, on average, application of our criteria to the Web site has led to a significant time saving for all users and tasks.

Among the seven tasks, the task "looking for information in a long page" turned out to be the most influenced by our criteria. This is likely due the fact that low vision users could considerably reduce their navigation time by using the side submenus (e.g. local links or list boxes) to move quickly to a specific section of the page, while blind users cut navigation time thanks to the list of heading levels generated by the screen reader commands.

In conclusion, our results showed that both blind and low vision users benefited from application of our criteria, which saved them around 40% in terms of navigation time.

3 NAUTICUS: A Tool Supporting Usability Criteria

Basing on the encouraging feedback from the testing, we decided to create automatic support for our criteria, especially addressed to developers who want to make their Web sites usable for vision-impaired users. Current tools only support accessibility (e.g. Bobby) or usability evaluation (e.g. WebSAT) but not both of them when users access through a screen reader.

3.1 The Tool Goals

The NAUTICUS tool (New Accessibility and Usability Tool for Interactive Control in Universal Sites) has been developed with the intent of checking whether a Web site is usable for users interacting through screen readers. To this end, the tool checks how satisfactorily our criteria are applied to the code of Web pages. This is obtained through automatic identification of the checkpoints associated with each criterion and analysis of the associated constructs and attributes to check whether they provide the necessary information.

The tool is not limited to checking whether the criteria are supported but, in case of failure, it also provides support in modifying the code in order to make the resulting Web site more usable and accessible. Thus, it points out what parts of the code are problematic and provides support for corrections indicating what elements have to be modified or added. The process is not completely automatic because in some cases the tool requires designers to provide some information that cannot be generated automatically. Examples of criteria that require the designer's intervention are:

1.2.a Proper link content, in this case the tools asks the designer to provide meaningful text for the link;

1.4.a Proper style sheets, in this case the tool requires an indication of the file containing the external style sheets:

2.2.b Proper names for frames, tables and images; here the designer may have to provide the value for the summary attribute for tables or for the alt attribute associated with images. This can also happen for frame titles and names. In the event the two values are different, then the tool makes them consistent and provides the designer with the possibility of modifying the resulting value.

3.2 The Tool User Interface

The main layout of the tool user interface is structured into three main areas:

(1) *Criteria*, which provides access to the supported criteria;
(2) *Report*, with the results of the selected page analysis;
(3) *Source Code*, which shows the source code of the loaded page;

Supported criteria are grouped depending on the main usability aspect to which they refer and they are visualized using a tabbed pane providing access to the various groups. The designer can select the application of all or only part of them through check-boxes.

In the report, blue labels are used to indicate the criteria analysed, while the elements that do not satisfy the criteria are highlighted in red, and the black parts are

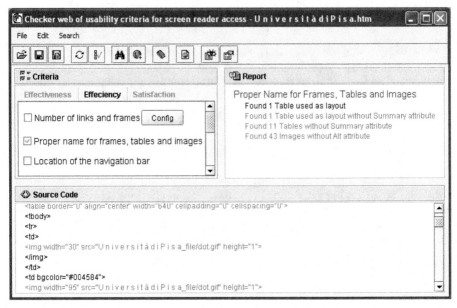

Fig. 2. Tool output related to a criteria-based evaluation.

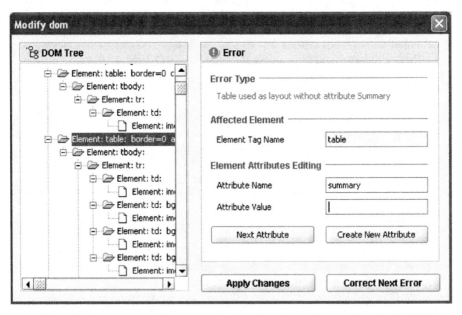

Fig. 1. Tool-support identification and repair of problematic parts through the DOM.

considered to satisfy the criteria. In the case of Figure 1, the criterion regarding proper name for frames, tables and images has been selected and the report with the corresponding list of issues is displayed.

For each issue, the number of occurrences is indicated as well. The code can be corrected either through the DOM (Document Object Model) [14] or by editing the page. The Document Object Model is a platform- and language-neutral interface that allows programs and scripts to dynamically access and update the content, structure and style of Web documents. The document can be further processed and the results of that processing can be incorporated back into the presented page. Our tool supports direct access to the DOM: the designer has to select a criterion and then activate the analysis and ask for correction. At this point, the tool shows the corresponding interface (see an example in Figure 2). In the left part there is a tree representing the DOM elements of the current page, where it is possible to distinguish the elements from the attributes and texts.

The right part displays useful information to identify and repair the problematic parts of the tags currently under analysis. It shows the error type, the affected element and its associated attributes and values.

Through the *"Correct Next Error"* button it is possible to access the next tag that raises an error according to the current criterion. The left part displays the hierarchical structure of the DOM with the possibility of folding/unfolding elements. In addition, through the controls, it is possible to scroll and modify the attributes of the selected element or create new ones. The modifications made can be saved in order to immediately apply them to the DOM. It is also possible to automatically search for the next error. In Figure 2 we can see how the tool immediately identifies the first element that does not satisfy the selected criterion (proper use of frames, tables and images). In the example it is a table. Then, the designer can edit it, for example by adding a summary attribute.

In order to perform an evaluation about the names of frames, appropriate links, adequate summaries for tables and so on, a complete objective evaluation can not be done. So, for this purpose we defined a set of dictionary files in which a list of "wrong terms" or "appropriate potential terms" are stored. For example, terms such as "click here", "here", "pdf", "more information", and so on, are stored as inappropriate text for links; or names such as "left", "central", "sx", etc., are listed as frame names to be avoided.

All these files can be updated and modified, so that evaluators can customize them. In addition, the use of such dictionaries allows designers to change languages. Therefore, changing a language implies changing the dictionary used for evaluating / repairing.

3.3 The Tool Architecture

The tool has been implemented in Java. It first checks through the Tidy library whether the page is well-formed and then corrects any syntactical errors. Then, for each evaluation criterion there is a class implementing the associated algorithm to check its application. It mainly analyses the DOM to see whether the associated constructs are provided along with the necessary attributes.

The architecture is structured in a number of modules implemented through the Java packages:

- Effectiveness: this package contains all the classes implementing the effectiveness criteria;

- Efficiency: this package contains all the classes implementing the efficiency criteria;
- Satisfaction: this package contains all the classes implementing the satisfaction criteria;
- Gui: this package contains all the classes implementing the graphical user interface of the tool;
- Utility: this package contains frequently used classes   such as text analyzers, DOM manipulation, …
- Configuration: this package contains classes that handle the files that are loaded at the beginning of the application, such as dictionaries and images.
- Exception: this package contains the classes handling the exceptions of Tidy, the HTML parser.
- Org: this package contains the DOM and Tidy classes.

4   Example of Tool Application

The tool has been applied to the University of Pisa Web site (see Figure 3) and a number of problems were immediately detected: no style sheets specific for vocal synthesizers, lack of alt attributes for images used as background and in the layout, lack of summary attributes to comment the many tables used in the document. There was no use of tabindex and accessKey, which are very useful for blind users to quickly go through the Web pages.

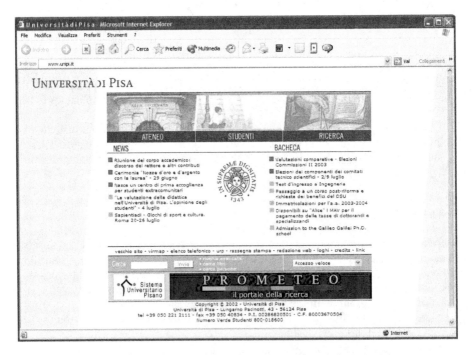

Fig. 2. The Web site considered for the tool application.

One of the most serious problems was that the access to some university services can be achieved only through the use of a <select> tag with a Javascript associated with the OnChange attribute. If the link were accessible through a text or an image, there would be no problem, but the OnChange attribute creates many difficulties. A blind user often uses the keyboard for navigation and the TAB key to move from one element to the next. When they reach the <select> element, since an onChange attribute has been defined, then the first associated link is automatically selected. In order to avoid this problem it would have been sufficient to consider the OnClick event instead of the OnChange, thus the link would have been selected only after an explicit link selection from the user. This aspect is checked through the criterion 2.6.a (proper form use).

5   Conclusions

In this paper, we have discussed a set of usability criteria to improve Web navigation for vision impaired people. Then, we have presented an automatic tool supporting such criteria and report on its application to a case study.

The tool provides interactive support for checking the application of our criteria and help designers to improve their Web sites in case it detects problems. We are extending the tool in order to support evaluation of Web sites obtained through dynamic pages.

Future work will be dedicated to further extending the evaluation tool in order to integrate it with assessment performed through other methods (such as automatic log analysis) and to support designers even in the development phase.

Acknowledgments

We thank Francesco Conversano for his help in the development of the tool and Domenico Natale (SOGEI) for useful discussions on the topics of this paper.

References

1. Abascal J., Arrue M., Fajardo I., Garay N., Tomás J., *Use of Guidelines to automatically verify Web accessibility*. Universal Access in the Information Society, special Issue on "Guidelines, standards, methods and processes for software accessibility", Springer Verlag, Vol.3, N.1, 2004, pp. 71-79.
2. Barnicle, K. *Usability Testing with Screen Reading Technology in a Windows Environment*. Proceedings of the 2000 Conference on Universal Usability (CUU-00), pp. 102-109, ACM Press, November 16-17 2000.
3. Clarck D., Dardailler D. (1999) *Accessibility on the Web: Evaluation and repair tools to make it possible*. In proceedings of the CSUN Technology and Persons with disabilities Conferences, Los Angeles, CA. Available at http://www.cast.org/bobby.
4. Ivory, M. and Hearts, M. (2001) The State of the Art in Automating Usability Evaluation of User Interfaces. ACM Computing Surveys, Vol, 33, No 4: 470-516.
5. Leporini, B., Paternò, F. (2004). *Increasing Usability when Interacting through Screen Readers*, International Journal Universal Access in the Information Society (UAIS), special Issue on "Guidelines, standards, methods and processes for software accessibility", Springer Verlag, Vol.3, N.1, pp. 57-70.

6. Leporini, B., Paternò, F. Testing the effects of web usability criteria for vision impaired users. ISTI-CNR Technical report, January 2004, Submitted paper.
7. Nicolle, C., Abascal J. *Inclusive design guidelines for HCI*, p. 285, Taylor & Francis, 2001.
8. Nist Web Metrics: http://zing.ncsl.nist.gov/WebTools/ tech.HTML
9. Paternò, F., Paganelli, L., 2001. *Remote evaluation of Web sites based on task models and browser Monitoring*. Proceedings of CHI'01, Extended Abstracts, (Seattle, WA, USA, April 2001), pp 283-284
10. Stephanidis, C., Paramythis, A., Karagiannidis, C., Savidis, A. *Supporting Interface Adaptation: the AVANTI Web-Browser*. 3rd ERCIM Workshop on "User Interfaces for All", Strasbourg, France, November 3-4, 1997.
11. Section 508 standards. http://www.section508.gov
12. Theofanos, M.F., Redish, J (2003). Bridging the gap: between accessibility and usability. ACM Interactions magazine, New York: ACM Press, Nov.-Dec. 2003 issue, pp.36-51
13. USABLE NET (2000) LIFT ON LINE. Available at http://www.usablenet.com/
14. W3C Document Object Model (DOM) http://www.w3.org/DOM/
15. Web Accessibility Guidelines 1.0. Web Accessibility Initiative, W3C Recommendation 5-May-1999. Accessible at http://www.w3.org/WAI/GL/WCAG10/
16. Web Content Accessibility Guidelines 2.0, W3C Working Draft 1 March 2004available at http://www.w3.org/WAI/GL/WCAG20/

Disability as a Vehicle for Identifying Hidden Aspects of Human Activity: Inclusive Design and Dyslexia in Educational Software Development

Mark Dixon

University of Plymouth, School of Computing Communications and Electronics,
Drake Circus, Plymouth, Devon, UK
mark.dixon@plymouth.ac.uk

Abstract. Dyslexia accounts for the largest proportion of UK higher education students identifying themselves as disabled, and recent widening participation initiatives mean that numbers are likely to rise. Static media (slides, books, handouts) cannot express the temporal aspects of computer programming concepts, and require narratives, which are difficult to follow, especially for dyslexic students.
Code-memory diagrams show changes to memory that individual instructions make over time, and can facilitate deeper and quicker understanding. However, they are error prone and time consuming. An animation software tool could address this. Furthermore, inclusive design would be essential to ensure accessibility to the widest range of students.
This paper focuses on inclusive design aspects of such a tool. The software helped enhance learning for all students, but dyslexic students to a greater degree. It showed that disabled people can identify subtle hidden aspects of human activity, that the target user population is unable to articulate.

1 Introduction

1.1 Dyslexia in Higher Education

According to the Higher Education Statistics Agency (HESA) during the 2001-2002 academic year, dyslexia accounted for just over 31% of UK higher education (HE) first year students identifying themselves as disabled [5]. It seems likely that this is also the case internationally (especially in the USA and Australia).

Also, recent changes aimed at widening participation in HE mean that the number of disabled students entering higher education is likely to rise at a higher rate that other student groups. The most recent of these changes was the special educational needs and disabilities act 2001 [12], which introduced the right for disabled students not to be discriminated against in education (with effect from 1 September 2002).

1.2 Nature and Difficulty of Teaching Stage One Computer Programming

Computer programming concepts are complex, have both practical and conceptual elements, and are highly inter-related with many critical dependencies. Individual concepts cannot be taught in isolation, and the sequence in which topics are covered is critical. Also, a selection of concepts are recognised as being particularly difficult. For

C. Stary and C. Stephanidis (Eds.): UI4All 2004, LNCS 3196, pp. 254–261, 2004.

example, in a recent study [9] recursion, pointers, and passing parameters by reference were rated the three most difficult, stage one, procedural programming concepts – more difficult than some, stage two concepts.

Undergraduate computing degrees differ from other disciplines (such as biology) in that they admit students with no prior experience of computing directly into stage one. Hence, the students exhibit an unusually diverse range of subject specific prior experience. This situation has been complicated by the recent move across all UK HE disciplines toward increasingly larger (especially first stage) class sizes [1].

These factors combine to put very high demands on the lecturer's time during tutorials, which reduces the time spent with individual students. This is especially problematic for dyslexic students, who greatly benefit from smaller group sizes [2].

The effectiveness of narrative explanation of diagrams in computer programming text books and lecture slides is limited. This failure may be due to an incompatibility between a key characteristic of books/slides (where the information displayed is fixed) and a key characteristic of programming, which involves concepts relating to things changing over time. It is very difficult to explain these dynamic concepts using a static medium. To demonstrate these concepts adequately requires animation.

1.3   Code-Memory Diagrams

The author has used code-memory diagrams (CMD) in tutorials (drawn on paper or white boards) to display a simulation of the program code being executed in context with a diagram representing the storage of variables in computer memory. Figure 1 shows a code memory diagram used to explain passing parameters by reference. Specifically, it shows the formal parameter (x) being created at the same memory address (1139) as the actual parameter (y).

Fig. 1. Code-memory diagram to explain passing parameters by reference.

Personal experience provided anecdotal evidence suggesting that this can allow rapid understanding of programming concepts and techniques beyond the capabilities of static media. However, drawing the diagrams was difficult, time consuming, and error prone. Therefore, a purpose built CMD animation software tool could have significant potential to assist the lecturer enhance student learning.

2   Method

The work is in line with work done over the last 10 years that uses social science methodology in the software development process [6, 13]. A mixed methods approach was taken: integrating qualitative and quantitative methods to triangulate one another.

The software was not targeted specifically at dyslexic students. However, they represented a significant proportion of the target population, and their inclusion in the design process was therefore regarded as critical. There was no attempt to deliberately identify dyslexic students, consequently the exact number of dyslexic participants involved was unknown (other participants may have been dyslexic, but either were unaware of it or preferred not to disclose it). However, 2 participants voluntarily disclosed their dyslexia. In general these students were treated no differently to the other participants, although their dyslexia was discussed where relevant.

Keates et al [7] describes a 5-level inclusive design approach. Although this was not deliberately adhered to, the activities undertaken corresponded to all levels except level 4 (user motor function) as physical disability was not applicable.

Phase 1 of this project was completed during the last academic year (2002-2003), and constituted an initial formal evaluation in revision sessions [4]. Phase 2 is currently in progress and involves the modification and use of the software in initial teaching sessions, as an integral part of an entire year-long module. It uses continuous participant observation, and occasional informal interviews with students.

2.1 Phase 1

Development of Initial Solution: Software was developed using Microsoft Visual BASIC (a programming language specially suited to rapid application development).

Solution Review and Modification: A series of formative trial sessions were then conducted, to prepare the software for the summative evaluation. The software was demonstrated individually to students and staff. During the sessions, participants were asked to 'think-aloud' [10], to yield feedback which inspired modifications to the software.

Evaluation: Once the software tool had reached an acceptable standard, a summative evaluation was conducted. A stage one computer programming module delivered by the author was selected for use in the evaluation on the basis of availability and it typifying stage one computer programming modules in general. The evaluation was undertaken during revision sessions conducted the week before the examination. Four sessions were conducted (one per tutorial group) each lasting one hour. The software was used by the lecturer to present material to the class, and by the students to view the demonstration at their own pace with lecturer support.

A single animation for each of the following revision topics was presented to the students: variables, arrays, passing parameters by reference in procedures, functions, and structures. The following data collection methods were used:

- A questionnaire to elicit perceptions of software use from a larger number of students. The questions were worded to avoid common problems (guided by [11]), such as ambiguity, prestige bias, variation in meaning, complexity, and double-barrelled.
- Participant observation (the lecturer reflecting on the tutorial) to elicit perceptions of software use from the lecturer, without bringing in another observer, which could have changed student/lecturer behaviour (hawthorn effect).
- Video recording of a small number of students using the software, to elicit details of student-software-lecturer interaction, and the impact on student understanding.

Analysis of Results: The analysis followed the principal of conclusions being grounded in the data, which is common across many quantitative studies and especially in line with grounded theory. Simple statistical analysis of quantitative closed questionnaire questions was performed. The video recording was transcribed, and recurrent themes identified from this and the responses to the qualitative questions (often referred to as coding or classification). This approach to the analysis of qualitative data derives from the field of qualitative data analysis [8]. The themes were emergent from the data rather than being pre-determined, hence this process was exploratory rather than confirmatory. The themes were explicitly linked back to the data via paragraph number (a method used in [3]).

3   Code-Memory Diagram Animation Software Tool

3.1   Modes of Operation

Potentially, the software tool could be used in three situations:

1. during lectures by the lecturer as a presentation aid to demonstrate a concept or algorithm to a large group of students,
2. during tutorials by students to allow them to view the demonstration at their own pace, but with the opportunity of immediate assistance from the lecturer, or
3. outside formal contact hours, possibly away from the university (for example at home) as a remote learning tool, without the support of a lecturer.

This project focused on the first two situations. The software was designed to enhance the lecturer's teaching process, rather than eliminate lecturer involvement. The last situation would require a far more sophisticated system that would operate without lecturer supervision.

3.2   Functionality

Figure 2 shows animation 1 (used to explain variable declaration and assignment). The dropdown list box (A) shows the names of all animations in the database.

Once an animation is selected, its code is displayed on the left hand side of the window. The run button (B) can then be clicked to start simulated execution of the code. A small arrow, representing the program counter (C), appears above the line of code that will be executed next. The next button (D) can then be clicked to execute a single line at a time. Every time a line of code is executed:

1. the changes that it makes to variables in memory are shown in the memory diagram to the left of the code text (M),
2. a grey arrow is drawn between it and the memory location that it changed (only one grey arrow is shown at a time to avoid making the diagram too complex),
3. a small tick is added to the left of the code to explicitly show that it has been executed (these ticks persist for the duration of the execution cycle, so that it is easy to see which lines have been executed), and
4. the program counter arrow is moved to the next line to be executed.

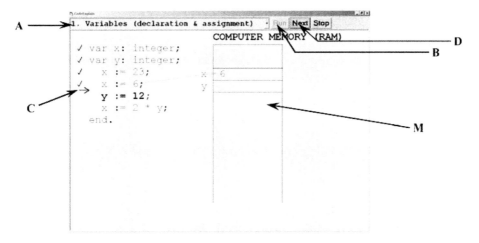

Fig. 2. Example 1, which was used to explain variable declaration and assignment.

At the point in time shown by figure 2, the 'x := 6;' line has just been executed as a result of the user clicking the next button. This placed a tick to the left of that line, drew a grey arrow between that line and variable x's value (which was changed to 6), and moved the program counter (C) on 1 line to sit above the line 'y := 12;'.

The software is language independent, because it displays the code and follows a set of instructions supplied by the lecturer (it does not interpret the code in any way).

3.3 Dyslexia Related Design Considerations

Several suggestions were implemented specifically to provide access to dyslexic students (such as increased font size, and the colour scheme avoiding black on white). Probably the most significant modification was the inclusion of the tick, which came about as a direct result of interaction between a dyslexic student and the software developer/researcher.

4 Results

The revision sessions were attended by a total of 26 students (sessions 1, 2, 3, and 4 by 11, 1, 12 , and 2 students respectively). A total of 25 students completed the questionnaire. One student expressed a desire not to complete the questionnaire (although they still participated fully in the revision session). Two students gave permission for their individual use of the software to be video recorded.

Questionnaire: No drop in understanding was reported for any topic by any student. Across all topics and all students, 47.54% of responses indicated that understanding remained the same, 41.80% of responses indicated that understanding increased by 1 category, 10.66% of responses indicated that understanding increased by 2 categories, and no students for any topic reported an increase in understanding of 3 categories or more. Twenty three students indicated that the software helped their understanding. The two who did not, said that they already understood the material. The students indicated that they thought of the concepts in terms of the end result – 'most people think the computer just does it', and that the 'step by step', 'visual' nature of the software showed the 'hidden ... internal workings' of 'how the computer' did it, which made the concepts 'clearer'. One student indicated that this may be of particular benefit to students with dyslexia.

Video observation: The following sequence was observed:

- Students described what they expected to happen ('that should add 23 in there', 'I would expect 23 to go in there', and 'you think 4, 5, and 6').
- At times this was different from what actually happened ('Oh, of course it increments [the variable] i to 2', 'Oh, hang on, it's 6', and 'I was surprised by it going to 6'). Sometimes, the student was able to explain this. At other times the lecturer offered an explanatory narrative.
- Following this, the students reported gaining a better understanding ('I see, it does make sense now') or articulated something indicative of better understanding ('Occupy the same space. OK, then that would set both x and y to zero').

The students indicated that the use of the software helped their understanding ('it puts it into perspective more, you sort of take it in better'), because it made details of how the code works visible ('you know what happens, you don't think about it actually happening, because it's invisible', 'when you think about loops ... you don't really think about how it works ... it [the software] helps, you can actually see it incrementing') and provides an explicit visual model ('this is how I remember it now, and it's more visual').

Participant observation: From the lecturer's perspective the software was very useful. It made the concepts much easier to explain, and the students seemed to understand them better. It relieved the lecturer of the mundane mechanistic drawing tasks required to produce code-memory diagrams. These tasks take the lecturer's attention away from the students and the concept being explained, and increase the chances of the lecturer making small errors. This allowed the lecturer to work at a more controlled pace, and made more time available for oral explanation, answering student questions, and maintaining student eye contact. Hence, the sessions were more interactive, with a greater number of gaps in student understanding being identified and resolved. It was easier to discuss what was going on, as the diagram gave a common concrete visual point of reference.

The software provided a level of drawing that was not possible manually (such as the program counter, code line execution ticks, and arrow showing element in memory last affected by previous line), which aided understanding.

Informal interview with dyslexic student: The student identified several areas where dyslexia impacted on learning. They described the following problems:

- losing position when jumping around in blocks of text (program code), as very common and 'much easier [more common] for dyslexics' especially when working from a white board, as there was no way to mark position.
- the speed of delivery ('if you [the lecturer] just slowed down ever so slightly – its just so much easier to take it all in').
- suffering from information overload to a greater degree and sooner than others.

They also described two solutions:

- working on a one to one basis (also described by another student during phase 2 participant observation) allowed them to control the flow of information, and
- high levels of repetition.

Finally, they described how the software helped:

- the diagram being linked explicitly 'shows what it actually does', this was easier to follow than describing the code orally 'much much much easier – no end easier'.
- the ticks and program counter helping to maintain position,
- reducing the volume of and slowing the narrative given by the lecturer
- making it easier to repeat the process
- being able to predict what happens next, gives very interactive formative feedback (this 'works like flash cards – builds confidence').

Overall the software had the same type of impact as per other students, just to a much greater degree, thereby helping them to 'close the gap'.

5 Conclusions

There was no evidence of the tool inhibiting student learning. There was evidence that the tool moderately enhanced student learning (questionnaire data and the qualitative comments). During the video observation students reported that the software made things clearer, and there was direct evidence of student understanding improving. The lecturer indicated that the software made the explanation of programming concepts easier and more effective.

The code-memory diagrams provided students with an explicit detailed visual model of how the concepts and the code underpinning them work. Without this students generate their own model, which may be vague, incomplete, and inaccurate. Also, the software provided a common point of reference that supported the interactive 'scaffolding' process between the student and the lecturer.

The software had the same effect for dyslexic students as for other students. However, this effect was to a greater degree. Hence the software acted as an equaliser – raising the performance of both students, but dyslexic students to a greater degree, thus closing the gap.

Disability as a vehicle for identifying hidden aspects of human activity: Dyslexic students (one in particular) seemed to be far more consciously aware of difficulties and subtle aspects of human learning activity, aspects that others took for granted. This suggests that user testing with dyslexic (and possibly disabled people in general) when they do not constitute part or all of the target group, may be a means of identifying and understanding significant yet hidden usability issues that apply to non-disabled target-users. This contrasts with other inclusive design work which focuses on the inclusion of disabled users for their own benefit.

Further Work: This study has shown the potential for the use of a code-memory diagram animation software tool to enhance student understanding. However, the software needs to be evaluated by more lecturers. Further improvements to the animation editing facilities are required to facilitate this. It has also shown the potential for disabled users to yield detailed insights into hidden aspects of human activity. Further work could consider the deliberate realisation of this potential.

References

1. Biggs, J.: Teaching for Quality Learning at University. Open University Press (1999)
2. Cairns, Moss,: Students with specific learning difficulties/dyslexia in higher education: a research report. Goldsmiths College, University of London (1995)
3. Dixon, M.: User-centred methods in the analysis and design of software tools to support management consultants. PhD Thesis, University of Plymouth (2000)
4. Dixon, M.: Code-memory diagram animation software tool: towards on-line use. Proceedings of the IASTED International Conference on Web-based education, Innsbruck, Austria, 14th –16th February (2004)
5. HESA,: Students in higher education institutions 2001/2002. Higher education statistics agency (2003)
6. Hughes, J., Sommerville, I., Bentley, R., Randall, D.: Designing with ethnography: making work visible. Interacting with Computers, 5 (2), (1993) 239-253.
7. Keates, S., Clarkson, P., Robinson, P.: Developing a practical inclusive interface design approach. Interacting with Computers, 14 (4), (2002) 271-299.
8. Miles, M. B., Huberman, M.: Qualitative Data Analysis: an expanded sourcebook. Sage Publications Limited (1994)
9. Milne, I., Rowe, G.: Difficulties in Learning and Teaching Programming – views of students and tutors. Education and Information Technologies, 7 (1), (2002) 55-66.
10. Nielsen, J., Mack, R.: Usability Inspection Methods. John Wiley and Sons, Inc (1994).
11. Oppenheim, A. N.: Questionnaire design, interviewing and attitude measurement. Pinter (1992).
12. SENDA: The special educational needs and disabilities act. Stationary Office Ltd (2001)
13. Sommerville, I., Rodden, T., Sawyer, P., Bentley, R.: Sociologists can be Surprisingly Useful in Interactive Systems Design. In Monk, A.; Diaper, D.; and Harrison, M. (eds.) People and Computers VII: proceedings of HCI'92, York, September 1992. Cambridge University Press (1992)

Designing Web-Applications for Mobile Computers: Experiences with Applications to Medicine

Andreas Holzinger and Maximilian Errath

Institute for Medical Informatics, Statistics & Documentation (IMI),
Medical University of Graz, Auenbruggerplatz 2,
A-8036 Graz, Austria
{andreas.holzinger,maximilian.errath}@meduni-graz.at

Abstract. Designing Web-applications is considerably different for handhelds than for desktop computers. Screen size is limited, browsers further limit the visible content area and users interact differently. Detecting handheld-browsers on the server side and delivering pages optimized for a small client form factor is inevitable. The authors discuss their experiences during the design and development of an application for medical research which was designed for both handhelds and desktops. It is important to include mobile computing design considerations into "User Interfaces for All" [1], [2].

Keywords: Information Interfaces and Representation, Life and Medical Sciences, Internet Applications, Mobile Computing

> *"The old computing is about what computers can do,*
> *the new computing is about what people can do" Shneiderman (2002), [3].*

Introduction

Mobile computers, also known as Handheld computers (also referred to as Personal Digital Assistants or PDAs) presents a number of challenges in Human-Computer Interaction (HCI) including the tension between the appropriate user interface design and the device and the social context of the device's use [4]. Handhelds are used often together with desktops (PCs) [5] and subsequently support nomadic and ubiquitous computing. This is of tremendous interest for physicians and healthcare professionals who are generally highly mobile within a hospital moving frequently between clinics, diagnostic departments, operating theatres and their offices [6], [7].

As it is difficult to make devices with small displays usable, there is also the fundamental challenge of **making them useful.** To achieve both goals particularly for these new devices it is strongly recommended to apply a User-Centered Design (UCD) approach [8]. UCD evolved in the field of HCI and was first articulated as such in User Centered System Design [9] and focuses strongly on the intended End-Users [10].

Some key principles of UCD methods include understanding the users and analyzing their tasks; setting measurable goals and involving the users from the very beginning. Based on the experiences within this project and on previous work [11], [12],

C. Stary and C. Stephanidis (Eds.): UI4All 2004, LNCS 3196, pp. 262–267, 2004.
© Springer-Verlag Berlin Heidelberg 2004

[13] we found again that UCD is of particular importance to realize usable and useful software, especially for mobile devices and in an application area such as Medicine. According to Stephanidis & Savidis (2001) simple, cheap and easy-to-use solutions in information technology (IT) can be a step further to the information society for all where all people can have access to relevant information [2]. Exactly the accessibility is considered to be of paramount importance for the success of the emerging information society [14].

The Medical Problem to Be Solved: Randomized Clinical Trials

In medical research, the randomized clinical trial is the preferred scientific standard for assessing treatment effects (see for example [15]). Randomization, in this context, means that patients are allocated to treatments by chance. For example, in a trial of a new treatment versus an existing treatment, random treatment allocation ensures that each patient has the same chance of receiving either the new or the existing treatment.

There are two main reasons why randomization is used with our devices. Firstly, we want to reduce bias, that is, we want to be able to conclude that observed differences between the treatment groups are due to differences in the treatments alone. Without randomization, the comparison of treatments may be prejudiced by selection of participants of a particular kind to receive a particular treatment. Random allocation does not guarantee that the groups will be identical apart from the treatment given, but it does ensure that differences between them are due to chance alone. Secondly, randomization leads to treatment groups that are random samples of the population and thus statistical tests based on probability theory can be used.

In most clinical trials randomization is performed using pre-printed randomization lists, sealed envelopes, or in large and multi-center clinical trials (i.e. trials where multiple centers are contributing patients) a commercial third party, the trial coordination center, is responsible for patient registration, data collection and randomization. These tasks are traditionally accomplished using faxes and forms filled out by hand or via telephone.

Our WEB-Based Solution

Performing randomization and trial data collection via the Internet using Web-based applications has several advantages over the traditional telephone-based services, particularly in multi-center trials. Using the web reduces communication delays and expenses, provides a worldwide 24-hour-service, reduces transcription errors, supports better auditing due to comprehensive logging of each transaction, and saves the researchers time.

Finally, yet most importantly, a web-based solution also facilitates communication between the trial users (investigators, statisticians, trial coordinators, etc.). For example, the latest version of the trial handbook or a directory of trial users' email addresses can be stored on the central website used for randomization and downloaded by trial users on demand.

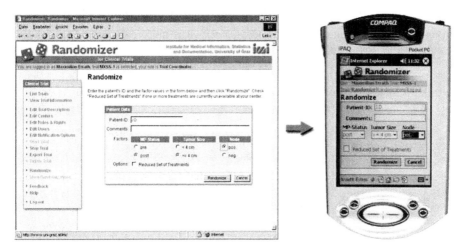

Fig. 1. The randomization software offers patient randomization and trial management features using a standard web-interface designed for desktops. Core functionality (i.e. randomization) is also available via web pages optimized for PDAs.

Our Web-Based Mobile Solution

We have now implemented such a web-based solution for randomization in multi-center clinical trials, the so called **Randomizer.** To make the core functionality of this software – i.e. randomization of new patients – available in places without a computer- or network infrastructure, we considered using handheld equipped with cell phone (GSM) or WLAN modules. This offers a rapid solution for physicians who work with existing healthcare practice habits and flows with the healthcare professionals' daily routine (see figure 1).

Lessons Learned: Designing Web-Applications for Handhelds

Developing Web-applications for handhelds is considerably different than for desktop computers [16], [17], [18], [19] Screen size is limited, for example a typical handheld, including the Hewlett Packard iPAQ, comes with a 240 x 320 pixel display. With Microsoft's Pocket Internet Explorer (Pocket IE), browser decoration (scroll bars, address line, title bar, etc.) further limits the visible content area to 229 x 255 pixels. Our first experiment – using the standard web-interface designed for desktop machines – did not lead to useful results. Users simply got lost whilst scrolling horizontally and vertically through the pages. Pocket IE's "Fit to Screen" feature did not help since our page layout is too complex for reformatting to such a small screen resolution. Moreover, our page design depends on cascading stylesheets (CSS) and Pocket IE is basically a HTML 3.2 browser (Pocket IE identifies itself as MSIE 3.02) and has no CSS-support built in (XSL stylesheets can be used, however). Therefore, detecting PDA-browsers on the server side and delivering pages optimized for a small client form factor is inevitable.

Moreover, users **interact differently** with handheld devices than with PCs (see for example [20], [21], [16], [22], [8], [23], [24]). For example, where it is acceptable to require keyboard input on desktop machines, typing on a PDA's soft-keyboard becomes getting burdensome. With handheld devices it is much easier to select values from a list rather than enter text in an input field. During the design of this interface and according to our experiments (methodological based on task analysis, video analysis, cognitive walkthroughs and thinking aloud sessions, N = 12) we were able to learn the following lessons which we present here in the form of condensed guidelines:

- Keep things simple. Handheld devices have limited resources in terms of memory, screen size, and bandwidth. A simple, mainly text-based interface with few small images not only saves resources, but makes the browser's reformatting algorithm more likely to succeed. For low bandwidth connections (e.g. via cell phone modules), consider using online compression on the server side (for example using mod_gzip for the Apache web server).
- Preferably use a single-column layout. Pages should be designed to allow dynamic resizing, fixed-size designs (e.g. using tables and transparent images for sizing table columns). Pages that need horizontal scrolling should be avoided. We realized that most of the users simply overlook the fact that there is more to view in horizontal direction. Scrolling can simplest be reduced by strictly focusing on the content task.
- Preferably use selection over direct keyboard input.
- Use narrative texts sparingly. Introductory texts, instructions or other narrative texts, when placed near the top of the web page, push relevant content (e.g. input forms) out of the visible area so users are more likely to miss it.

Involving the End-Users!

Involving the end-users in our design process was also in this "mobile project" a primary concern, to understand how our users work (and in what context) and to provide a system, which is easy and pleasant to operate, with no or at least little learning effort. Our aims were in close compliance with the research agenda of the European sixth framework programme wherein the topic Human-Computer Interaction gains a steadily increasing importance [14].

Conclusion

Applications for mobile computers are mostly the "mobile part" of a larger non mobile Web application. However, the mobile solution must be particularly designed for a quick and short interaction "on the way". This was of particular importance for our highly mobile group of end-users including medical doctors and healthcare professionals within an University Hospital setting. We noticed that the availability of a mobile solution raised the acceptance for the main system in the sense of "ubiquitous usability". Concerning such "mobile interfaces" it is important to consider the highly restricted resources of Input and Output when using mobile computers. With respect to the interface design the structure of the whole Web application, the kind of the data input as well as the amount of output information is to consider. Mainly "flat menu hierarchies" and simple "single column" layouts proved to be appropriate. Quick and easy navigation for frequent functionalities are an absolute necessity. Our experimental results emphasized again that extensive text entry is to avoid as well as the priority of shortlists opposite of direct input is important. User Centered Design (UCD) proved to be an appropriate design technique also for this kind of mobile computer interface design and finally led to a simple and easy to use interface, according to the proverb: *less is more.*

References

1. Stephanidis, C., et al., *Toward an Information Society for All: HCI challenges and R&D recommendations.* International Journal of Human-Computer Interaction, 1999. **11**(1): p. 1-28.
2. Stephanidis, C. and A. Savidis, *Universal Access in the Information Society: Methods, Tools and Interaction Technologies.* Universal Access in the Information Society, 2001. **1**(1): p. 40-55.
3. Shneiderman, B., *Leonardo's Laptop: Human Needs and the New Computing Technologies.* 2002, Boston (MA): MIT Press.
4. Myers, B., et al., *Strategic directions in human-computer interaction.* ACM Computing Surveys (CSUR), 1996. **28**(4): p. 794-809.
5. Myers, B.A., *Using handhelds and PCs together.* Communications of the ACM, 2001. **44**(11): p. 34-41.
6. Bludau, H.-B. and A. Koop, *Mobile Computing in Medicine, Lecture Notes of Informatics.* 2002, Heidelberg: GI.
7. Hameed, K., *The application of mobile computing and technology to health care services.* Telematics and Informatics, 2003. **20**(2): p. 99-106.
8. Marcus, A. and E. Chen, *Designing the PDA of the future.* interactions, 2002. **9**(1): p. 34-44.
9. Norman, D.A. and S. Draper, *User Centered System Design.* 1986, Hillsdale (NY): Erlbaum.
10. Sutcliffe, A., *User-Centred Requirements Engineering: Theory & Practice.* 2002, Berlin, Heidelberg, New York: Spinger.
11. Holzinger, A., *User-Centered Interface Design for disabled and elderly people: Experiences with designing a patient communication system (PACOSY),* in *Lecture Notes in Computer Science. Vol 2398,* K. Miesenberger, J. Klaus, W. Zagler, Eds. 2002, Springer: Berlin, p. 34-41.
12. Holzinger, A., *Experiences with User Centered Development (UCD) for the Front End of the Virtual Medical Campus Graz,* in *Human-Computer Interaction, Theory and Practice,* J.A. Jacko and C. Stephanidis, Editors. 2003, Lawrence Erlbaum: Mahwah (NJ). p. 123-127.
13. Holzinger, A., *Application of Rapid Prototyping to the User Interface Development for a Virtual Campus.* IEEE Software, 2004. **21**(1): p. 92-99.
14. Emiliani, L.P. and C. Stephanidis:. *From Adaptations to User Interfaces for All.* in *6th ERCIM Workshop "User Interfaces for All".* 2000. Florence, Italy.
15. Field, D. and D. Elbourne, *The randomized controlled trial.* Current Paediatrics, 2003. **13**(1): p. 53-57.
16. Weiss, S., *Handheld Usability.* 2002, New York: John Wiley and Sons. 292.
17. Karampelas, P., D. Akoumianakis, and C. Stephanidis, eds. *User Interface Design for PDAs: Lessons and Experiences with the WARD-IN-HAND prototype.* User Interfaces for All. Lecture Notes of Computer Science Vol. 2615, ed. N. Carbonell and C. Stephanidis. 2003, Springer: Berlin, 474-485.
18. Buchanan, G., et al. *Improving mobile internet usability.* in *International World Wide Web Conference.* 2001. Hong Kong.

19. Holzinger, A., *Multimedia Basics, Volume 3: Design. Developmental Fundamentals of multimedial Information Systems*. 2002, New Delhi: Laxmi Publications (www.basiswissen-multimedia.at)

20. Chittaro, L.E. *Human-Computer Interaction with Mobile Devices and Services*. in *5th International Symposium, Mobile HCI 2003, Lecture Notes in Computer Science, Vol. 2795*. 2003. Udine, Italy.

21. Waycott, J., A. Kukulska-Hulme, *Students' experiences with PDAs for reading course materials*. Personal & Ubiquitous Comp., 2003. **7**(1): 30-43.

22. Sears, A. and R. Arora, *Data entry for mobile devices: an empirical comparison of novice performance with Jot and Graffiti*. Interacting with Computers, 2002. **14**(5): p. 413-433.

23. Jessup, L.M. and D. Robey, *Issues and challenges in mobile computing: The relevance of social issues in ubiquitous computing environments*. 2002. **45**(12): p. 88-91.

24. Brewster, S., *Overcoming the Lack of Screen Space on Mobile Computers*. Personal and Ubiquitous Computing, 2002. **6**(3): p. 188-205.

Empirical Performance Analysis of Web Accessibility in Ubiquitous Information Network

Yung Bok Kim[1] and Young-Han Kim[2]

[1] Department of Computer Engineering, Sejong University
KunJa-Dong, Kwang-jin-ku, Seoul, Korea
yungbkim@sejong.ac.kr
[2] School of EE, Soongsil University
1-1 Sangdo-Dong, Seoul, Korea
yhkim@dcn.ssu.ac.kr

Abstract. Beyond the computer networking, the wired Internet and mobile Internet penetrate deeply in various applications based on the ubiquitous computing and networking. We need to consider the Web-based information services with ubiquitous information portal and client devices for convenient accessibility without any gap of the Digital Divide. Web accessibility for unified and ubiquitous information portal becomes important for real-time ubiquitous information networking in the milieu of ubiquitous computing. We studied the empirical performance analysis of Web accessibility in ubiquitous information network based on wired and mobile Internet.

1 Introduction

Web server is the appropriate as a role center for unified information service, and the client mobile devices become very important for Web accessibility in ubiquitous computing environment. For the objective of user interface for unified information portal in the ubiquitous information network, we considered several aspects about the Web accessibility, as follows.

Uskela [1] discussed the mobility management in mobile Internet, and introduced two different approaches for technical realization, personal mobility and device mobility. The personal mobility is the ubiquitous reach-ability for user, irrespective of the wired or mobile devices. We should consider some unified concept for personal mobility in business model independent from the devices, e.g. PC, PDA, other hand-held mobile devices operated by many different telecommunication operators as well as by many different mobile phone manufacturers.

The real-time mobile applications with mobile devices have been proliferating world-widely. The performance of the unified and ubiquitous portal, for all users in the wired Internet and mobile Internet, is important to provide services in unified way, in ubiquitous way and in cost-effective way. For small sized file or web page, the sever load for the information processing is the major factor for performance, therefore the server should be dedicated for single purpose Web server, i.e. information Web server in our case. This concept is important to design applications running in the unified information portal and in the mobile client devices, while considering the performance of user interface for Web accessibility with various mobile phones.

Universal access implies the accessibility and usability of Information Society Technologies (IST) by anyone, anywhere, anytime. It is important that we should take

C. Stary and C. Stephanidis (Eds.): UI4All 2004, LNCS 3196, pp. 268–274, 2004.
© Springer-Verlag Berlin Heidelberg 2004

into account the needs of the broadest possible end-user population in the early design phases of new products and services. Universal Design in the Information Society has been defined as the conscious and systematic effort to proactively apply principles, methods and tools, in order to develop IST products and services that are accessible and usable by all, thus avoiding the need for a posteriori adaptations or specialized design [2]. Donnelly and Magennis [3] introduced their research for making accessibility guidelines usable. Moreover, Leporini and Paterno [4] studied the criteria for usability of accessible Web sites, beyond the accessibility.

We considered the performance of Web server and mobile devices for information processing in wired and mobile Internet environment, especially in terms of the accessibility and usability. We studied new performance analysis of Web accessibility for unified and ubiquitous information portal, at the user's perspective, i.e. at the customer's viewpoint about the services for information access in this ubiquitous computing environment. We introduce the empirical performance analysis of Web accessibility in ubiquitous information network, for worldwide information network. We will discuss the user interface with the results from real implementation of a unified and ubiquitous portal for real-time ubiquitous information network, e.g. Korean information network as an example of a ubiquitous information network using PCs as well as hand-held phones.

2   Mobile User Interface for Web Accessibility

In many countries, a better access to Web services and Web administration is becoming an important issue; and a few action lines of improvement for the Web Content Accessibility Guidelines are suggested [5]. New approaches and related instruments are necessary for capturing human requirements in the new reality. Appropriate architectural framework and development tools will need to be elaborate in the age of disappearing computer [6]. The development of highly efficient and effective user interfaces, which matched to the user needs and abilities, was discussed for the successful application of Assistive Technology [7].

The unified Web server for information processing should have the capability of showing the appropriate contents, i.e. the HTML contents for wired Internet as well as the mobile contents for many different kinds of mobile devices, e.g. WML, mHTML, etc. We implemented the unified and ubiquitous information portal for Korean information networking with wired Internet for PC as well as with wireless Internet for mobile devices. We used single Web server as a unified and ubiquitous portal for the simplicity of management and the cost-effectiveness of information access. This method gives the effectiveness and efficiency for the notification of information and utilization of resources, in terms of the bandwidth for communication and the size of required disk storage for information DB.

For information access, the text entry with PC or mobile phone is an important basic-step to consider the user interface. Soukoreff and MacKenzie [8] studied and introduced metrics for text entry, i.e. evaluation of MSD (Minimum String Distance) and KSPC (Keystrokes per Character), and a new unified error metric. This study was focusing only on the QWERT keyboard. With the mobile phone, the error rate for text entry becomes more serious, and we should keep in mind for the following discussion.

To access the unified portal pervasively in the real-time ubiquitous information network, the user interface for all users should be as convenient as possible even for typing-in the domain names or URL. Because the first step for Web service with wired/mobile Internet (especially, mobile case) is typing-in the URL of the Web site offering the requested information. Based on the assumption of using single-character; the performance of keystroke number is analyzed at the user's point of view. For writing of notification information in real-time way, the user's typing speed of character is one of important performance factors, especially for Web accessibility with mobile phones.

The English domain name is at least consisted of several alphabet characters; that means the averaged keypad-stroke number for English domain names, being composed of several alphabets, will be the multiple of the single keypad-stroke number, whose average is around 2.15. For example, to type-in our unified portal site 'ktrip.net', the actual keypad-stroke number with the LG-i1500 model is around 20 including the mode change from Korean mode to the English mode; in the case of the portal site 'yahoo.com', the keypad-stroke number is around 22. The number of key-pad-stroke for '.net' itself is 6 and the keypad-stroke number for '.com' itself is 8 for both models by LG, a Korean major manufacturer of mobile phones.

For user interface in the real-time information network, even the input of characters becomes important for retrieval of information or registration of information, especially with keypads in the mobile phone for the disabled and elderly people. To access the unified portal ubiquitously, the user interface even for the elderly people in the Silver Society should be as convenient as possible even for typing-in the domain names or URLs, or information with mobile phones. For writing the information in real-time way, the user's typing speed of characters, e.g. Korean characters, is one of important performance factors, especially with the mobile phone. Over 4 keypad-stroke numbers, even for typing-in simplest Korean character composed of one consonant and one vowel, is required, that means inconvenient keypad-stroke is unnecessarily required to the mobile phone users. Therefore, we need to consider the convenient mobile user interface for Web accessibility in the milieu of ubiquitous computing and networking.

3   Performance Analysis of Web Accessibility

The performance analysis at the user's viewpoint may be different from the conventional analysis methodology. We need this type of new approach, because the environment has changed quite a lot, especially in terms of the interactivity of customers with mobile devices in the milieu of ubiquitous computing. In this paper, we studied the new performance analysis at the user's viewpoint; and this approach might give rather realistic insight for Web accessibility. We will consider the real-time application, getting required information as well as writing information in the wired Internet and mobile Internet environment, for all users.

We studied the important performance metric, delay, for Web accessibility at the user's perspective, to shorten the gap of the Digital Divide. We studied the performance metric, not only with the time in the network and server but also with the spent time by user, e.g. input time with keypads for URL or information for notification.

For example, referring to the Fig. 1 for the mobile user, we assume that the random variables, the round-trip response time for user's single interaction in a session, from user to the contents in DB through wired/mobile Internet before next interaction with mobile phone is R. That is composed of the preparation time for any users to get mobile device (e.g. hand-held phone, etc) in his hand is U. The time spent by the user with mobile phone to do appropriate action for service is D. The aggregate time to the Web server after the mobile device through wired/mobile Internet for mobile service is S (the conventional network time is embedded here). The time depending upon mobile contents is C.

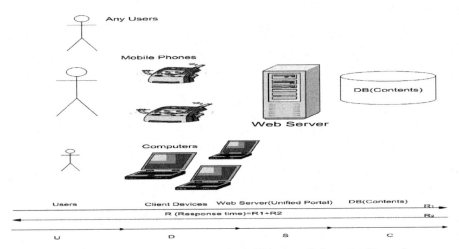

Fig. 1. Aggregate Performance Metrics in Ubiquitous Information Network.

The session time may be dependent on this content retrieval or registration, and there may be several back and forth iterations. The returning round trip time, from the content retrieval time to the requesting user through Web server and wired/mobile Internet using mobile device, is **R_2**.

Among the above random variables, i.e. the performance metrics, (U, D, S, C) for mobile user and PC user, the most dominating factor, i.e. the random variable, may be different from person to person. At first, for the fair comparison, we assume that the same person is using the same content in the same server with the same device. Then, we can order the dominating random variables, after estimation with an implementation for information network with the unified server, http://ktrip.net [9].

The previous works for computer networking have been mainly focused on the analysis of the time, S, but we suggest the overall performance metric, delay, i.e. the response time R, instead of the partial and minor delay S, for all users in the real-time ubiquitous information network beyond the computer networking. The user's preparation time or ubiquity metric, U will be decreasing depending upon the proliferation of ubiquitous computing and networking environment.

We should consider the average of the keypad-stroke number for the case of Korean handheld phone model, discussed before, and it affects the device time, D. For writing the information in real-time way, the user's typing speed of Korean character is one of important performance factors in any mobile Internet services for any user with mobile phone. For example with the simplest Korean character composed of one consonant and one vowel, several Korean hand-phone models showed that the average number of keypad-stroke is around 4~5 for the mentioned single Korean character and around 2~3 for single English alphabet, including shift key for next character. Because the device time D is proportional to the number of keypad-stroke for any applications. This is also serious dominating factor related to the device time D, especially for writing contents of information with mobile phone.

4 Empirical Results and Discussion

The real-time information network for the ubiquitous information services, here Korean information network, as an example, is based on wired or mobile Internet, many single Korean character domains for fast access of the required Korean domain name with simple single character. The required information or advertisement can be registered in any time and any place using wired or mobile Internet in the unified Web server for ubiquitous information service, i.e. the 'ktrip.net' [9]. As we discussed already, we considered the size of web page for unified service below 1.5Kbyte, i.e. between 500Bytes and 1.5Kbytes of compiled WAP binary, to minimize the dependency of the overall performance to the shared and stochastically varying network traffic. The Web server is dedicated to minimize the server load, and dedicated for the unified portal of Korean information network as an example. For the cost-effectiveness, we chose the most common and inexpensive server available, and the E1 line as one of most common communication channels for Web service in Korea.

The speed of real-time registration of any advertisement as well as the speed of access of special information for various communities is fast enough for real application for ubiquitous information services. Moreover, we can expect the effectiveness and efficiency of storage for advertisement and information, if we consider rather efficient way instead of inefficient applications, e.g. various community sites, home pages for small companies, or inconvenient notification bulletin boards, as far as the consumed disk storage, operation and administration are concerned.

Considering the performance of the unified portal, we can make the processing time deterministic in the web server for contents, where the deterministic time is possible with the deterministic size of packet, below around 1.5Kbytes, i.e. below one WML deck size for the old models of mobile phone.

With the statistical analysis for the mean and standard deviation of 100 samples, we can observe that the response time at wired PC is fastest and stable with little deviation. The averaged response time with mobile phone Internet is around 12 seconds with about 2 second standard deviation, the other two cases with wired PC via the intermediate server in domain registrar office show that depending upon the intermediate server the mean and deviation of the response time become very different. The size of one web page for wired Internet is around 25Kbytes. The size of web page for the wired Internet accessed by the domain name ktrip.net is about 5 Kbytes, and the size of the mobile web page about 1Kbytes after converted to WAP binary file.

We could observe that the network and server response time for Ping command is much shorter than the content retrieval time in the server. The mobile 1.5Kbyte content retrieval time with mobile Internet is about 10 seconds longer than the wired (PC) 5Kbyte content retrieval time because of the elapsed time with the gateway, and this time is related to the network time (in WAP gateway and in mobile system) instead of time in server.

With the PC using wired Internet, the time S may be considered rather short period (around 5~30 msec with Ping, which is related to S; but with 5Kbytes web page for PC the response time is around 2~3 seconds, which is related to the S and C, here C is much larger than S). With PC, for larger contents (over 20Kbytes, in our case), the server time is longer than the shorter packet (below 5Kbytes).

With recent mobile phone using mobile Internet (for short packets below 1.5Kbytes and even around 5Kbytes), the response time is around 12 seconds with little deviation through the WAP gateway; therefore the time S is longer than C, where S includes the elapsed time at the gateway in the mobile Internet.

We may order the dominating factors in the overall performance at the user's perspective as follows. In general, in the previous Fig.1, the relationship for wired Internet with PC could be $U>D>C>S$; and the relationship for mobile Internet with mobile phone could be $U>D>S>C$. Here, we need to decrease the major times, U and D, as well as the network and server (minor) time S (or C).

Empirical performance with various mobile phones by 50 students, the average of D (the typing time of a URL, i.e. ktrip.net) is about 30 seconds with Standard Deviation (14.3 seconds). The average of $S_{(ktrip.net)}$ is about 9 seconds with Standard Deviation (6.4 seconds), the average of $S_{(operator's\ portal)}$ is about 7.9 seconds with Standard Deviation (5.8 seconds). The average time of reading-content is about 6.8 seconds with Standard Deviation (7.3 seconds).

We need to try continuously to decrease the times U and D; as Internet URLs for the unified and ubiquitous portal in the ubiquitous information network, we used around 1000 single Korean character.net as URLs to find information as well as to notify information in real-time way and ubiquitously. We can also consider speech technology to decrease the time D. The Pen Phone introduced by Siemens during CeBit 2004 can also reduce the device time D. Standardization for UI (User Interface) of mobile phone is important, and service providers and manufacturers of mobile phones are doing the effort for standardization in Korea. UIs for standardization are about positioning of keypads and menus, etc. This will be also helpful to reduce the device time D.

There are some other examples using speech applications as follow. The maturity of speech technologies represents a great opportunity for people working with other or/and with a piece of information through Interactive Voice Systems; and the research with the VoiceXML technology was considered for the universal access paradigm by speech for the new generation of interactive systems [10]. Raynal and Serrurier [11] studied an HTML browser for visually impaired people with the comparison between VoiceXML approach and structural approach.

5   Conclusions and Future Works

We studied the empirical performance analysis for Web accessibility, considering the effective response time with efficient investment, for unified and ubiquitous information portal in the milieu of ubiquitous computing and networking. We studied especially the overall performance analysis for Web accessibility in real-time ubiquitous information network at the customer's perspective for assuring the real-time requirement with the unified portal, including the statistical analysis based on the empirical results. With more ubiquitous network environment (i.e. the decrease of the ubiquity time, U), the time in the device, D will become more critical, thus we need more efficient user interface for all users, especially using mobile Internet with mobile devices like handheld phones. For future works, we will include the voice application in the ubiquitous information network for the real-time retrieval of information as well as for real-time registration of information or advertisement to reduce the dominating times, i.e. the discussed user time and device time, as the aggregate performance metric, round-trip delay in session time. In the milieu of pervasive and ubiquitous computing, e.g. even in the driving car as well as during overseas-travel, the disabled can retrieve information as well as notifying information in real-time way with the suggested unified and ubiquitous information portal in the ubiquitous information network. We will study also the guidelines for standardization of mobile phones and services.

Acknowledgements

This work was supported in part by the Korean National Center of Excellence in Ubiquitous Computing and Networking.

References

1. S. Uskela. Mobility Management in Mobile Internet. 3G Mobile Communication Technologies, pp. 8-10 May 2002, Conference Publication No. 489, IEE 2002.
2. Constantine Stephanidis and Pier Luigi Emiliani. Universal Access to Information Society Technologies: Opportunities for People with Disabilities. ICCHP 2002, LNCS 2398, pp.8-10, 2002.
3. Alexis Donnelly and Mark Magennis. Making Accessibility Guidelines Usable. User Interface for All, LNCS 2615, pp. 56-67, 2003.
4. Barbara Leporini and Fabio Paterno. Criteria for Usability of Accessible Web Sites. User Interface for All, LNCS 2615, pp.43-55, 2003.
5. Sylvie Duchateau, Denis Boulay, Claudine Tchang-Ayo, and Dominique Burger. A Strategy to Achieve the Accessability of Public Web Sites. ICCHP 2002, LNCS 2398, pp.58-60, 2002.
6. Constantine Stephanidis. The Disappearing Computer: Emerging Opportunities and Challenges for Disables and Elderly People. ICCHP 2002, LNCS 2398, pp.41-48, 2002.
7. Wolfgang L. Zagler. Matching Typing Person and Intelligent Interfaces. ICCHP 2002, LNCS 2398, pp.241-242, 2002.
8. R. William Soukoreff and I. Scott Mackenzie. Metrics for text entry research: An Evaluation of MSD and KSPC, and a new unified error metric. Ft. Lauderdale, Florida, USA, April 5-10, CHI 2003.
9. Ubiquitous Information Network Site (test site), Korean Information Network Web site: http://ktrip.net
10. Regis Privat, Nadine Vigouroux, Philippe Truillet, and Bernard Oriola. Accessibility and Affordance for Voice Interactive Systems with VoiceXML Technology. ICCHP 2002, LNCS 2398, pp.61-63, 2002.
11. Mathieu Raynal and Mathieu Serrurier. CYNTHIA: An HTML Browser for Visually Handicapped People. ICCHP 2002, LNCS 2398, pp.353-359, 2002.

Designing and Implementing a Paradigm of Interactive and Communicative Cultural Playspaces in an On-Line Language Learning Program

Dimitris Tolias[1], George Exadaktylos[1], and Diana Slattery[2]

[1] Hellenic American Union, Athens, Greece
{dtolias,gexadaktilos}@hau.gr
[2] Academy of Electronic Media, Rensselaer Polytechnic Institute,
Troy, New York, USA
slattd@rpi.edu

Abstract. Since 2000, the Hellenic American Union (Greece) and the Academy of Electronic Media at Rensselaer Polytechnic Institute (USA) have been involved in the development of Hellas Alive©, an on-line language and culture learning program for Greek as a Foreign or Second Language. Users of Hellas Alive© work in a virtual environment, which supports autonomous exploration, simulation, representation and collaboration, and are provided with multiple learning opportunities in the form of an immersive 3D world, rich multimedia content, synchronous and asynchronous learning tools, and interactive cultural playspaces. The aim of these playspaces is two-fold: On the one hand, they promote language learning in a variety of realistic contexts and in a way consonant with current educational communicative methodology. On the other hand, they raise the user's cultural awareness. Thus, the playspaces address a broad audience that encompasses not only ordinary language learners, but also those who are intrigued by the idea of cultural information, contact and awareness. Both objectives are implemented with a very high degree of interactivity. Eight types of playspaces have been developed so far: How To, Art Exploration, Documentary, Maps and Directions, Meet the Parea, Word Games, Let's Talk Greek, and Scavenger Hunt.

1 Introduction

1.1 Background Information

The Hellas Alive© project is the result of ongoing cooperation between two teams from the Hellenic American Union (HAU) in Greece and the Academy of Electronic Media at Rensselaer Polytechnic Institute (RPI) in the U.S.A. Working towards its design and implementation since 2000, there is a team of five programmers and media experts from RPI and another team of six content developers and language experts from the HAU.

C. Stary and C. Stephanidis (Eds.): UI4All 2004, LNCS 3196, pp. 275–286, 2004.
© Springer-Verlag Berlin Heidelberg 2004

Hellas Alive© comprises the "Workspace" component[1], the "3D World"[2] component, and the playspaces component. At its present phase, the project aims at teaching Modern Greek as a second or foreign language within its associated cultural context, in 15 units, each including 4 lessons. The targeted audience of this stage (level one) is one of beginners to intermediate learners.

It should be noted though that the project is language-free by nature; all its components have been designed with a view to be adaptable to other languages as well.

1.2 The Purpose of the Playspaces

No natural language can be separated from the culture that has created it. Therefore, be it on-line or on-site, when language is taught, relevant culture must be presented as well. In the Hellas Alive© project, language teaching is mostly handled by the Workspace. Immersion of Hellas Alive© users into the culture of the language taught is mainly handled by the project's eight playspaces. The playspaces serve their cultural purpose in three ways: they create understanding for the target culture and build on-line user communities; they adhere to the communicative educational methodology; they are attractive to users due to their high degree of interactivity and multimedia usage.

2 The Communicative Approach

2.1 Definition

According to contemporary teaching methodology, learners should be able to "transfer knowledge and skills developed in the rather artificial environment of the classroom [in the particular case of Hellas Alive©, the digital on-line environment can be considered a 'classroom'] to new contexts and situations in the world outside" (Nunan, 1988, p. 78). Labeled as "communicative", such methodology indicates a cluster of approaches, "all of which characterize language learning as the development of communication skills" (Nunan, 1988, p. 78). To this end, truly communicative activities focus on tasks rather than on plain exercises. These tasks are authentic, set within a realistic context and situated in discourse. Furthermore, communicative activities center on the learners' needs and are explicitly designed to promote learning. Finally, they follow course objectives and are sources of comprehensible input in a recursive and sequential manner.

The playspaces developed within the framework of the Hellas Alive© project – even though they are not considered language-teaching tools per se and are by their

---

[1] The "Workspace" simulates a complete learning environment with students and tutor. Its interface provides users with a clickable list of its contents; it allows them to watch a video, slideshow or image; to record, type and submit material to their designated tutor; to chat with other users; to perform 18 different types of interactive, self-corrected language exercises; to access links with text and media information on related grammar and vocabulary; to access the 3D World.

[2] The "3D World" is accessed through the Workspace and represents a virtual cityscape. Users can navigate around it and, through various hotspots, hear and read in Greek names of stores and businesses and enter the playspaces.

generic nature language-free – adhere to the principles of the communicative approach.

2.2 The Communicative Approach and the Playspaces

The playspaces are:

Task-oriented: Users are exposed to and are encouraged to use language with a real world outcome. To this end, they focus not on specific linguistic phenomena but on the use of these phenomena to communicate in real situations.

Needs-based: The playspaces have been designed and implemented only after extensive research had profiled potential users and identified their needs.

Learning-centered: Language is exploited to the fullest and users are exposed to all major language levels[3].

Contextualized and aligned with instructional objectives: The playspaces relate to the users' experience or to situations that may become part of such an experience. Also, activities within each playspace interact with each other either through the achievement of the common playspace objectives or by having all activities in the same context.

Authentic: Language is presented as it naturally appears in discourse and in various types of communicative events, suitable for a variety of user learning styles and strategies.

Situated in discourse: Language is presented without being isolated from the behaviors, conventions, roles, and practices that accompany it.

Sources of comprehensible input: No playspace "talks about language" and all language-oriented activities are structured to encourage active language use.

Recursive: Linguistic input is reintroduced in and throughout each playspace.

Sequenced: Materials are organized to move from discovery (induction) to explanation and application (deduction). The scenarios involve activities that shift from acquisition activities to learning activities, either in the case of language structures or of cultural practices.

3 Cultural Awareness

3.1 Levels

As all contemporary learning tools do, the Hellas Alive© project attempts to raise the cultural awareness of its users. The playspaces are the project's most powerful instrument to do this.

Hanvey (1976) recognizes four levels of cross-cultural awareness: The first level involves using information about the "other" culture (in this case, contemporary

---

[3] Beginner, lower intermediate, intermediate, upper intermediate and advanced.

Greek culture) to create superficial stereotypes about it. The second level involves having a better knowledge of the "other" culture, focusing on its differences and the difficulties this presents. In the third level there is acceptance of the "other" culture at an intellectual level and an attempt to understand it. At the fourth level, there is empathy of the "other" culture through direct experience with it.

3.2 Cultural Awareness Through the Playspaces

The playspaces aim at meeting levels three and four in a variety of ways:

a. Contemporary language usage is made in a variety of areas, such as the Arts, geopolitics, everyday activities, popular culture, the media, politics, youth, education, language, family, employment, and, in general, every aspect of social behavior.
b. The high degrees of interactivity, in combination with the attractive and multiple interfaces, enhance users' interest in actively engaging with the scenarios presented and realistically experiencing contemporary culture.
c. Certain playspaces encourage direct communication with an assigned Hellas Alive© administrator, responsible for the playspaces, thus providing users with immediate feedback to their input.
d. All playspaces strengthen users' cultural characteristics by transforming them into a community of learners and enabling them to communicate with one another and engage in sociolinguistic activities. This is achieved by allowing users to contribute their own material (media and/or text), which can be inserted into any of the playspace types and shared by other users.

4 Interactivity

4.1 Definition

Current literature does not provide one standard definition of interactivity.

Campbell (1999) identifies various levels of interactivity in interactive programs, the simplest being a point-and-click operation. Selnow (in: Sims, 1998) argues that an interactive activity involves two-way communication and, therefore, messages have to be receiver-specific, message exchanges have to be response-contingent and the channel of communication should accommodate feedback through a two-way information flow. According to Villiers (1999), communication in interactive programs needs to be "individualized, adaptive, and remedial". Borsook and Higginbotham-Wheat (in: Sims, 1998) propose a set of interactivity elements which would not only classify a program as interactive but also help the learner: responses should be immediate; access to information should be non-sequential; programs should be adaptable, provide feedback and options to the end-user; programs should allow for bi-directional communication and should be characterized by a short presentation sequence, thus enhancing interactivity. Also, according to Weller (in: Sims, 1998), laborious instructional design adds to the degree of interactivity. Fenrich (in: Sims, 1998) suggests that interactive programs should involve operations that enhance users' interaction with technology. Allen adds that users should also risk and "suffer the consequences", should they make a mistake. Lastly, Sims (in: Villiers 1999) claims that the degree of interactivity is proportional to "the extent to which the learner is working with the content" and to the availability of options for "accessing and navigating through the content structure".

4.2 Interactivity and the Playspaces

The playspaces in Hellas Alive© meet the following interactivity criteria:

Responses: All playspaces provide immediate response to users' actions, with clues and prompts that help learners use the material and answer questions. Where needed, prompts are provided with explanation of "errors", and interactive buttons provide users with the results of their actions.

Feedback: Users do not have access to answers until they produce their own. Correct answers are provided and reinforced with positive comments. Where needed, answers are evaluated and explained by the software itself, and interactive buttons provide users with the results of their actions.

Adaptability: The generic nature of the playspaces allows for easy and fast adaptation by the administrator to users' individual needs and styles. This enables users to contribute their own material (media and/or text), which can be inserted in any of the playspaces. A core of instructional design principles has been consistently applied throughout all the playspaces and users have a wide choice among various types of presentation (with the exception of animation). Users cannot modify any of the interface aesthetic features, but can opt for one working language (e.g. in prompts, feedback, comments, instructions) or the other (in the case of the particular eight playspaces, Modern Greek and English).

Bi-directional communication: All playspaces encourage "dialoguing" between users and program.

Length of presentation sequence: In all playspaces, the length of presentation is kept to a minimum.

Active learning: All playspaces allow users to "discover" their content and encourage them to contribute with their experiences and skills. Different input types are requested, only where necessary. Users can opt among various paths (read or watch or listen) and length of media is kept to the minimum required. Where needed, users risk and "suffer the consequences", should they make a mistake. Through the playspaces themselves, there is no direct access to Internet resources or on-line areas (chatrooms, discussion forums, networks); nonetheless, users can access such paths indirectly, through the Hellas Alive© main interface of which the playspaces are a component.

Content engagement and users' control: Interface and overall program design encourage users' involvement with playspace content and provide them with control of activities.

5   Description of Playspaces

5.1   How To

This playspace presents users with instructions to make or do something which is culturally relevant (e.g. a traditional recipe, the building of a kite, etc.)

In the opening screen with general instructions, users select one of the available scenarios and enter the relevant area. Users may watch a video with information on the content of the scenario, look at images with ingredients (for the making of food), objects (for the making of an object), or activities (for a custom). Then, they read and listen to the instructions and the items or processes involved, perform the same process virtually and, in general, become familiar with it.

At the end, users are prompted to actively re-enact the process observed and send a media and/or text file with this information to the Hellas Alive© administrator who is responsible for the playspaces. The playspace combines bilingual text and media.

To the present, one scenario has been implemented; it demonstrates how to make a traditional Greek kite.

5.2   Art Exploration

The aim of this playspace is to introduce users to different forms of Art (architecture, sculpture, painting, literature, theater, and cinema). The opening screen offers an overview of the various forms of Art. Users select one and receive information about an artist or a specific work of Art, through a combination of media and bilingual text. At the end, users are prompted to play a "trivia" game with multiple-choice questions on what they have explored.

To the present, one scenario has been implemented; it presents the life of the Greek writer and philosopher Nikos Kazantzakis and his novel <u>Zorba the Greek</u>.

5.3   Dialogue: Interaction with Software

This playspace offers users the chance to familiarize themselves with particular language structures used in respective communicative contexts. Therefore, this playspace can serve as a miniature survival-language guide for foreigners who visit the country for the first time. The opening screen provides users with a set of various social situations (to select from) in which they may find themselves in the new environment. From there, users can choose to actively engage in a dialogue, which is accompanied by media and text. Explanations are provided for wrong answers and correct answers are praised. At the end, users can visualize the complete dialogue through an automatic, system-generated presentation. The playspace combines bilingual text and media.

To the present, one scenario has been implemented; users assume the role of taxi-passenger and engage in a typical dialogue with a Greek taxi driver.

5.4   Word Games

This playspace acquaints users with forms and structures of the language and tests their knowledge of this material in the form of a language game. Varieties of games like scrabble, crossword, hangman, find-the- hidden-word, trivial pursuit, write-the-word, and match-the-words are included in the multiple scenarios of this playspace.

To the present, one scenario has been implemented: using drag-and-drop, users are asked to unscramble letters or syllables of words which form the ingredients of *baklava*, a traditional Greek sweet; with each word forming correctly, is formed the category of sweets to which baklava belongs.

5.5 Documentary

This playspace aims to familiarize users with culturally relevant topics such as history, folklore, archaeological sites, and tourist destinations. In the opening screen, users may select among the following categories: People, Places, Events, Culture, and Social Life. Users receive information through a combination of media and bilingual text. At the end, users are prompted to play a "trivia" game with multiple-choice questions on the content they have explored.

To the present, under the category "People", one scenario with four sub-scenarios has been implemented; it presents the lives and work of four Greeks who have excelled in the U.S.A., namely Stamatios M. "Tom" Krimigis, Dimitris Mitropoulos, George Papanikolaou, and Katina Paxinou.

5.6 Meet the Parea

This entirely anthropocentric playspace involves users in realistic daily situations by presenting the life of a group of young friends (in Modern Greek, this group is called a *parea*) who meet and discuss their daily program and general plans. In the opening screen, users receive a complete personal profile of each of these young persons. Automatically, users enter subsequent sub-scenarios where they try to match those persons' needs with the available resources and make decisions based on the profiles and the information provided. The playspace combines bilingual text and media.

To the present, one scenario with three sub-scenarios has been implemented; it presents five members of a *parea* who have to decide what film to watch at the cinema, what food to order, and where to go during the weekend.

5.7 Maps and Directions

This playspace engages users in discovering information about various geographical locations. The opening screen provides an initial clue for locating an imaginary person. Automatically generated subsequent screens provide clues as to this person's whereabouts, and users have to follow and eventually learn about the locations and their characteristics, until they finally locate the person. An interactive map is used to enhance the navigation process and make the trip more intriguing. Image, video, and bilingual text are provided as clues.

To the present, one scenario has been implemented; it presents a Greek-American who is visiting Greece; users have to locate him by following clues given in cards that he sends them; an interactive map of Greece provides image/text descriptions of the locations (Santorini, Mykonos, Thessaloniki, Aegina, Olympia, Rhodes, Zakynthos).

5.8 Scavenger Hunt

This playspace immerses users in the social and language-specific context of purchasing. Users enter a virtual shopping area with different types of shops and see/read instructions as to what products are needed for a specific occasion. Given an allotted time and/or budget (which they risk losing), users are prompted to visit the appropriate shops and buy the necessary items which are priced. Items are accompanied by image, audio, and bilingual text. Scenarios vary in level of difficulty.

To the present, the shopping area includes 28 stores fully operational with audio, image and text. One scenario has been implemented, whereby users have to buy the indicated items necessary for a friend's birthday celebration at an allotted time and budget.

6   Conclusion

With its present phase fully developed, the Hellas Alive© project will comprise the following:

- Five levels of teaching Modern Greek
- The above described eight playspace types enriched with more scenarios
- At least eight more different playspace types

At a later phase, the project and its components will be modified so as to accommodate for other languages, as well.

The project is estimated to be available on line upon completion of the user testing that is currently taking place.

References

1. Campbell, K. (1999). The Web: Design for Active Learning. Retrieved February 10, 2004, from the World Wide Web: http://www.atl.ualberta.ca/articles/idesign/activel.cfm
2. Hanvey, R. (1976). An Attainable Global Perspective. Denver: The Center for Teaching International Relations, University of Denver.
3. Nunan, D. (1988). The learner-centred curriculum. U.K.: Cambridge University Press.
4. Sims, R. (1998). Interactivity for effective educational communication and engagement during technology based and online learning. In C. McBeath and R. Atkinson (Eds), Planning for Progress, Partnership and Profit. Proceedings EdTech'98. Perth: Australian Society for Educational Technology. Retrieved February 7, 2004, from the World Wide Web: http://www.aset.org.au/confs/edtech98/pubs/articles/sims1.html
5. Villiers, de G. (1999). Criteria for evaluating the quality of Interaction in educational programs or web sites. Retrieved February 2, 2004, from the World Wide Web: http://hagar.up.ac.za/catts/learner/rbo1999/bda/eel/interact.html

Appendix

Images from Playspaces

How To

Fig. 1. Opening Screen.

Fig. 2. Activity Screen on How to Make a Greek Kite.

Fig. 3. Activities Screens on How to Make a Greek Kite.

Art Exploration

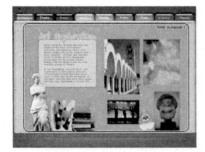

Fig. 4. Opening Screen.

Fig. 5. Information about Nikos Kazantzakis and Zorba the Greek.

Fig. 6. Trivia Game Screen.

Dialogue: Interaction with Software

Fig. 7. Opening Screen.

Fig. 8. Activity Screen with Dialogue in a Taxi.

Word Games

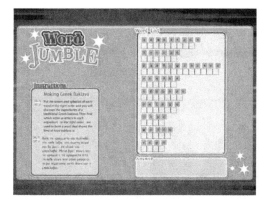

Fig. 9. Unscrambling the Ingredients of a Greek Sweet.

Documentary

Fig. 10. Opening Screen.

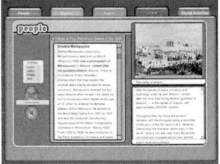

Fig. 11. Information about Four Famous Greeks.

Fig. 12. Trivia Game Screen.

Meet the Parea

Fig. 13. Opening Screen.

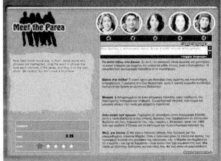

Fig. 14. Activity Screen.

Maps and Directions

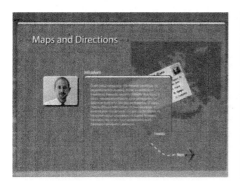

Fig. 15. Opening Screen.

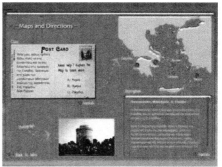

Fig. 16. Activity Screen.

Scavenger Hunt

Fig. 17. Opening Screen.

Fig. 18. Activity Screen.

User Needs and e-Government Accessibility: The Future Impact of WCAG 2.0

Shane Anderson[1], Paul R. Bohman[1], Oliver K. Burmeister[2], and Gian Sampson-Wild[3]

[1] WebAIM (Web Accessibility in Mind), Center for Persons with Disabilities
Utah State University, USA
Shane@cpd2.usu.edu, paulb@cc.usu.edu
[2] Swinburne Computer-Human Interaction Laboratory,
School of Information Technology, Swinburne University of Technology,
and PhD student, Charles Sturt University, Australia
oburmeister@it.swin.edu.au
[3] Member of the W3C Web Content Accessibility Guidelines Working Group,
and Accessibility Consultant/Managing Director, PurpleTop, Australia
gian@purpletop.com.au

Abstract. Governments in many countries require that government Web content adhere to international accessibility standards, in addition to specific national standards. The Web Content Accessibility Guidelines (WCAG) version 2.0 will set a new standard for Web accessibility. The implications of WCAG 2.0 for eGovernment sites in two nations, the United States of America and Australia, are considered. While the needs of all users are important when determining accessibility and usability requirements of sites, the particular needs of people with cognitive impairments are considered in greater detail, as an example to designers that people with disabilities are a heterogeneous group, where one solution does not fit all.

Keywords: Accessibility, W3C, Web, disability, guidelines.

1 Introduction

Universal usability recognizes that people with disabilities account for a significant proportion of the general population. In Australia 19% of the population have some form of disability [14]. Kaye [8] reported on longitudinal research following the Web practices of people in 48,070 US *households*. Of these 21.8% (10,480) households had at least one member of the household who was "work disabled." He says that the most common reasons cited by people with disabilities for using the Internet were virtually identical to the reasons given by people without disabilities.

Governments around the world have created legislation to ensure equity of access to participation in the information society. In many countries the legislation is limited in terms of the types of organizations that are required to comply. Most countries with Web accessibility laws require that government Web sites be made accessible, but compliance requirements vary from one country to another and even within some countries. The level of enforcement of standards also varies.

Designing for inclusion requires a commitment to involve users from the intended audience. In the case of eGovernment Web sites, rather than alienate people with

C. Stary and C. Stephanidis (Eds.): UI4All 2004, LNCS 3196, pp. 289–304, 2004.

disabilities, various co-operative design methodologies have been proposed, for example Buhler [2]. However, the focus of this paper is not on the design aspects per se, but rather on compliance issues and changes to those with the introduction of the soon to be released Web Content Accessibility Guidelines (WCAG) version 2.0. Using these, Web developers can better work towards ensuring an inclusive design process.

Yet there is more to accessibility of government than just complying with legislation. Sites need to incorporate into issues of usability, those of accessibility; referred to as *universal usability* by the Human-Computer Interaction (HCI) community [15]. Developing for accessibility means ensuring that the information or functionality present is available to all user groups, regardless of how the information is accessed. Often people with disabilities access information via different methods, for example, by over-riding style sheets, enlarging text, changing font, and/or by using a screen-reader, on-screen keyboard, a pointer, a magnifier, or other assistive technologies. Accessibility for the different user groups of a particular Web site should be ensured through the design process. However, it is important to remember that designing for accessibility does not mean sacrificing dynamic sites in favor of text only sites. Instead it involves the creation of accessible dynamic Web sites.

This paper begins with a review of the needs of people with various types of disabilities, and cognitive disabilities in particular. This focus on cognitive disabilities was chosen partly because it is so often neglected in Web accessibility literature, and partly because of an increased focus on cognitive disabilities in the forthcoming Web Content Accessibility Guidelines (WCAG) 2.0. This second generation of Web accessibility guidelines is discussed in detail, in terms of philosophical and practical differences compared to WCAG 1.0. The paper finishes with an examination of the legal situation in Australia and the United States, including case studies of selected eGovernment sites in Australia and the United States. The implications for Web site design are then drawn together.

2   User Needs

The authors of WCAG 1.0 state that: "The primary goal of these guidelines is to promote accessibility. However, following them will also make Web content more available to *all* users, whatever user agent they are using (e.g., desktop browser, voice browser, mobile phone, automobile-based personal computer, etc.) or constraints they may be operating under (e.g., noisy surroundings, under- or over-illuminated rooms, in a hands-free environment, etc.)." [19, p 1]

The aim is to promote inclusiveness. Inherent in these guidelines is the fact that not all people with disabilities are the same. They are a diverse, heterogeneous group. For example, the World Wide Web Consortium (W3C) defines users with access difficulties as follows [19, p 4]:

- "They may not be able to see, hear, move, or may not be able to process some types of information easily or at all.
- They may have difficulty reading or comprehending text.
- They may not have or be able to use a keyboard or mouse.
- They may have a text-only screen, a small screen, or a slow Internet connection.
- They may not speak or understand fluently the language in which the document is written.

- They may be in a situation where their eyes, ears, or hands are busy or interfered with (e.g., driving to work, working in a loud environment, etc.).
- They may have an early version of a browser, a different browser entirely, a voice browser, or a different operating system."

Similarly, in describing the needs of users for WCAG 2.0, the W3C have used the following scenarios to show access difficulties experienced by different users [20, p 9]:

- "Someone who cannot hear will want to see the information normally presented via sound.
- Someone who cannot see will want to hear or read through Braille information that is usually presented visually.
- Someone who does not have the strength to move quickly or easily will want to use as little movement as possible and have as much time as they need when operating Web interfaces.
- Someone who does not read well may want to hear the information read aloud."

The above lists show the heterogeneity of the population of people with access difficulties. As Powlik and Karshmer [12] put it, there is not one accessibility audience, but rather there are multiple audiences. However, it is also inadequate to simply group disabilities into categories and then to treat people within such a category as belonging to a homogeneous group. Thus categories like hearing impaired, visually impaired, and cognitively impaired are inadequate. For a start, many older adults experience functional disabilities that arise with aging. They might suffer hearing loss, as well as a physical impairment, such as arthritis in the hand, making mouse usage difficult. But aside from combinations of functional disabilities, there is also the problem of sub-groups within a category. For example, in visual impairment, that could be total blindness, color blindness or any of a great number of partial vision problems.

2.1 Cognitive Disabilities

Though all types of disabilities are considered in this paper, special attention is given to the oft-neglected category of cognitive disabilities (also described as intellectual impairment in the literature; see for example [18]). Doing so illustrates that, even within a disability category, the people involved can be very different in terms of their functional capabilities.

The IMS guidelines [6] say that the category of cognitive disability is one of the most diverse. "It includes individuals with general processing difficulties (mental retardation, brain injury, etc), people with specific types of deficits (short term memory, inability to remember proper names, etc.) learning disabilities, language delays, and more" [6, p 11]. In addition, as with other disabilities, severity differs amongst people.

Cognitive disabilities can stem from a variety of causes, such as Down's syndrome or cerebral palsy, which means it is at times also accompanied by physical impairments. One advantage for designers is that because cognitive disabilities frequently involve print disabilities, accessibility increases where screen reading software functions well. So design for visual impairment can also assist with cognitive disabilities.

To some the diversity of access difficulties amongst users with various types of cognitive disabilities may appear daunting. But it is worth remembering that "A degree in cognitive psychology is not required to be effective; rather, the process begins with attentive understanding" [12, p 219].

3   Implications of Adopting WCAG 2.0 for e-Government

With WCAG 1.0, the goal was to create content accessible to people with disabilities. The creation of this document by an international committee in 1999 was a significant step toward making the Internet more accessible to people with disabilities. However, there are significant weaknesses in WCAG 1.0 that are in the process of being addressed by the WCAG Working Group [17]. These weaknesses necessitated fundamental changes in the document. For the purposes of this paper, these changes have been categorized as 1) conceptual differences, 2) the requirement that conformance be verifiable, 3) differences in conformance criteria, 4) an increased focus on usability, and 5) an increased recognition of non-(X)HTML technologies.

Although WCAG 1.0 is still the current official document of the WAI, designers should be aware of the changes that WCAG 2.0 will bring in the future. WCAG 2.0 is still a document under development, so it is still subject to future revisions, but it has remained steady in the major areas, despite changes that have been introduced since the work began. The comments in this paper reflect the status of the latest internal draft of WCAG 2.0 at the time of this writing, dated February 14, 2004.

3.1   Conceptual Differences

On a practical level, some of the changes in WCAG 2.0 are subtle. For example, images will still require alternative text. Web developers who currently design accessible Web sites will not have to change their habits much. On the other hand, WCAG 2.0 represents a substantial shift in philosophy. Rather than focus exclusively on the specific do's and don'ts of (X)HTML techniques, as WCAG 1.0 does, WCAG 2.0 is written on the conceptual level, so that it can be applied to multiple technologies, and not just to (X)HTML. This makes WCAG 2.0 more relevant to developers who create content in PDF format, Flash, Java, Video, and other forms of non-(X)HTML media. Whereas WCAG 1.0 implores developers to avoid non-(X)HTML technologies, WCAG 2.0 allows the use of any technology, as long as developers can make the content accessible to people with disabilities.

The HTML-centric design of WCAG 1.0 is evident in such concepts as accessible tables. In WCAG 1.0, the overarching guideline specifically mentions tables: "Create tables that transform gracefully." The checkpoints beneath this guideline include such phrases as "use TD to identify data cells and TH to identify headers" and "use THEAD, TFOOT, and TBODY to group rows, COL and COLGROUP to group columns, and the 'axis', 'scope', and 'headers' attributes, to describe more complex relationships among data." In contrast, the corresponding overarching principle in WCAG 2.0 is "Content must be perceivable." Beneath this principle, the guideline states that developers should "ensure that information, functionality, and structure are separable from presentation." The word "table" is not used at all until one level deeper (the success criteria), which states that "associations between table cells and their headers" should be able to "be derived programmatically...through a markup or data model." Nothing else is said about tables at all in the document. The specific techniques (using TH, THEAD, TFOOT, etc.) will be included in a separate "techniques" document. Other techniques documents will explain how to accomplish the same success criteria within other technologies. The emphasis has unmistakably shifted away from technology-specific language within the guidelines, in order to ensure that the guidelines can be applied in a wide range of current and future technologies. The techniques documents will expand as new techniques become available and entirely new techniques documents will be created when new Web technologies are created. The hope is that the guidelines will be robust enough to be useful and applicable on a long-term basis, rather than suffer obsolescence in the face of the rapidly-changing Internet technology landscape.

The shift from technique-driven guidelines to concept-driven guidelines resulted in a reduced number of top level ideas, or *principles*. WCAG 1.0 had fourteen principles at the top level. WCAG 2.0 places only four principles at the top level under which more specific guidelines are organized. These four principles can each be referred to by a single keyword:

- Perceivable,
- Operable,
- Understandable, and
- Robust.

Content must be made available to users in a format that they can *perceive* with at least one of their senses (i.e. sight, hearing, touch). It must be presented in a way that they can interact with or *operate* it with either standard or adaptive devices. It must be presented in a way that the user can *understand* or comprehend. Finally, content must be presented using technologies and interfaces that are *robust* enough to allow for disability access, whether natively or in alternative technologies and interfaces. Together these principles address all areas of accessibility, at least in broad conceptual strokes.

3.2 The Requirement That Conformance Be Verifiable

One of the key areas of weakness in WCAG 1.0 is that some of the requirements are somewhat ambiguous, leaving them open to interpretation. In terms of implementing WCAG 1.0, this means that one developer's method of complying with a particular checkpoint could be quite different from that of another developer. WCAG 2.0 does much to fix this problem, by requiring that all minimum checkpoints be *normative*. The Working Group defines normative as meaning that compliance with a checkpoint can be unambiguously verified. This verification can be performed either through an automated, algorithm-based process or through human testing. Automated processes can verify the existence or absence of certain required elements, such as the "alt" attribute for images. Human testing requires a process that can be performed with high inter-rater reliability, for example by having 9 out of 10 trained individuals reaching the same conclusion about the element in question.

WCAG 2.0 contains a paradigm shift that relates to the underlying philosophy of minimum compliance. In WCAG 1.0, minimum compliance is on what is required by the user in order to access the information in the site. WCAG 1.0 defines minimum compliance (Level A) by saying: "A Web content developer must satisfy this checkpoint. Otherwise, one or more groups will find it impossible to access information in the document. Satisfying this checkpoint is a basic requirement for some groups to be able to use Web documents" [19].

In contrast, WCAG 2.0 [20] requires that checkpoints in the minimum compliance area:

- Achieve a minimum level of accessibility through markup, scripting, or other technologies that interact with user agents, including assistive technologies,
- Are reasonably applicable to all Web sites.
- Are testable (machine or reliably human).

The requirement of minimum accessibility is similar to the WCAG 1.0 approach, but the addition of applicability across Web sites and testability are a reflection of the needs of designers and policy makers. WCAG Working Group decided upon this change in philosophy hoping that it would ensure more sites would attempt accessibility compliance by overcoming the myths of "accessible sites must be text only," which is narrowly applicable and subjective.

3.3 Difference in Conformance Criteria

One of the most obvious differences between WCAG 1.0 and WCAG 2.0 is the method of claiming conformance. One problem with WCAG 1.0 has been that if a site was unable to comply to a particular checkpoint, there was no incentive to attempt other checkpoints in the same conformance level. WCAG 2.0 allows for sites to specify the exact criteria they have met in a particular priority level, however exactly how this will be achieved is still to be decided.

Every checkpoint in WCAG 2.0 has a *minimum* requirement, without which it is impossible to claim conformance to the guidelines. This minimum requirement is equivalent to the definition of WCAG 1.0 Level A; implementing this checkpoint will offer substantial benefit to people with disabilities by removing barriers that would otherwise make it difficult or impossible to access the content.

In WCAG 1.0, conformance was broken into three levels: A, AA and AAA. In WCAG 2.0, conformance had been broken down differently in recent drafts, but there is disagreement as to what the new breakdown ought to be. This is reflected in the current internal draft: "As we publish this Working Draft of WCAG 2.0, the WCAG WG is in the midst of significantly changing the conformance scheme from previous drafts." [20, p 6]

It is anticipated that changing conformance criteria will encourage sites to comply with more checkpoints. Current discussion in the Working Group has focused on how a site can identify exactly which checkpoints it has complied with. One suggestion has been to provide this information in the metadata of each page. This would allow a specific search engine to search for sites that conform to particular accessibility criteria and this may also encourage sites to increase the number of checkpoints they comply with.

3.4 An Increased Focus on Usability

Another major difference is that WCAG 2.0 focuses more on the usability aspects of Web accessibility. All users, with or without disabilities, benefit from this increased focus on usability. Perhaps those that will benefit most are users with cognitive disabilities. One of the major criticisms of WCAG 1.0 is that it did not include many guidelines that specifically benefited users with cognitive disabilities, and those guidelines that were specific to cognitive disabilities were relegated to Level Triple-A. Some may still argue that WCAG 2.0 does not focus sufficiently on this group, but it does represent a step forward in that direction. One of the guidelines under the key-word "operable," for example, instructs developers to "Make it easy for users to browse the resource, to know their place in it, and to find information they need." This guideline is solidly aligned with general usability principles that cut across all abilities. As another example, the principle about understandability explains that "content and controls should be understandable to as many users as possible." This means that it is not sufficient to make sure that the site is merely available, or that the controls are merely functional. Users must be able to understand both the content and the controls that are necessary to interact with that content. In other words, the site must be intuitive.

3.5 Increased Recognition of Non-(X)HTML Technologies

Due to the evolving nature of the WCAG 2.0 document, it is difficult at this point to identify a list of all of the specific techniques that Web developers will have to follow in order to comply with the WCAG 2.0 recommendations. Nevertheless, it is possible to look forward and anticipate the general nature of these techniques.

First of all, developers will not be limited to (X)HTML alone when writing Web content. The wording of WCAG 2.0 allows them to use any technology that satisfies the criteria set forth in the document. Of course, this does not imply that (X)HTML should be abandoned or that developers should seek out new and untested technologies. On the contrary, WCAG 2.0 requires that developers be very selective in terms of the technologies used and the way in which they are used. Since the list of accessible Web technologies is currently a short list, (X)HTML will still figure prominently in future accessible Web development.

Lastly, developers will need to pay closer attention to the human-computer interaction implications of their Web content. They will need to test their site for usability and understandability. They will need to consider the ways in which people with various types of disabilities interact with the computer. Users with cognitive disabilities, visual disabilities, hearing loss, and motor disabilities all have specific needs and methods of interacting with Web content. Some of these needs and methods are common among all of these groups. Others are specific to certain types of disabilities. It will no longer be enough to follow checklists. Rather, developers will need to consider the human side of disability access to the Web. Thinking optimistically, this focus gives users with disabilities reason to hope that developers will include users with disabilities in their planning process, thus leading to a more universal user-centered design paradigm.

4 Accessibility in e-Government

e-Government Accessibility in Australia

Thirty-two Commonwealth departments and agencies have created Disability Actions Plans (DAPs) with the Human Rights and Equal Opportunity Commission; thirty-seven state government agencies and one hundred and three local governments have also created DAPs. All Commonwealth Government agencies are also required to address accessibility in their online action plans developed to meet the Commonwealth Government's commitment to eGovernment. These online action plans can usually be located on the individual Commonwealth agency's Web site.

Senior Ministers from State, Territory and local governments meet twice a year to discuss policy issues related to the information economy. In June 2000 they adopted the W3C Web Content Accessibility Guidelines as the common best practice standard for Australian government Web sites to "promote the confidence of users in online services, and the accessibility of online government information and services" [10].

The Victorian state government was the first to produce best practice guidelines in 1999 to mandating the use of the W3C Web Content Accessibility Guidelines 1.0 when developing Victorian Government sites [16]. The Victorian state Government also has extensive information on accessibility, including an accessibility toolkit and FAQs. However, other states have their own state level guidelines.

In Australia the legislation says government sites must comply with world best practice [13], which for several years has been interpreted as compliance with WCAG 1.0. That means that eGovernment practice will soon undergo changes in regards to accessibility, as the W3C move their draft second version (WCAG 2.0) to the status of stable reference document, as is the case with their first version (WCAG 1.0).

e-Government Accessibility in the United States

The United States federal government is required to make Web content accessible to people with disabilities by virtue of Section 508 of the Rehabilitation Act [1]. Though there are other laws regarding disability rights, Section 508 is the only place anywhere in US law that provides a checklist of accessibility requirements for Web accessibility. The scope of Section 508 is actually broad enough to encompass all electronic information technologies, such as telephones, fax machines and copiers. All federal government entities are required to abide by the guidelines in Section 508. Interestingly, though Section 508 technically only applies to the federal government, some states have chosen to adopt Section 508 guidelines as their standard for Web accessibility. Even states that have not adopted the Section 508 are required to provide equal access to individuals with disabilities, though, without the Section 508 guidelines as a standard, the actual definition of accessibility is a bit vaguer in these states.

Section 508 itself was patterned after WCAG 1.0. The main difference is that Section 508 is much more limited in scope. It does not contain any guidelines that specifically benefit people with disabilities, for example, and the amount of support for all types of disabilities is more limited than in WCAG 1.0. Another difference is that Section 508 was written to more easily testable than WCAG 1.0. The testability of this law makes compliance easier to verify and easier to codify into law. The testability of Section 508 will provide a relatively smooth transition into the guidelines of WCAG 2.0, except for the fact that Section 508 is a small subset of the WCAG guidelines.

Other laws that play an important role in the United States are the Americans with Disabilities Act (ADA) and Section 504 of the Rehabilitation Act. Both of these are anti-discrimination laws. Among other things, the ADA requires that public buildings and other public spaces be made accessible to people with disabilities, with elevators, access ramps, and so on. It can be argued that the Web is a public place as well, even if it is in a virtual space rather than a physical space. Still, neither the ADA nor Section 504 provides developers with a specific set of checklist items as does Section 508.

It will be interesting to see how the US Access Board, the organization that created the Section 508 guidelines, reacts to WCAG 2.0 when it is released. Since the Web requirements of Section 508 were so heavily based on WCAG 1.0, the Section 508 guidelines will need to adapt to the changes in WCAG 2.0 in order to not fall badly behind. If the Access Board does not respond to the changes in the field of Web accessibility, the end result may be that Web developers continue to abide by out-of-date standards even as the Web continues to evolve. People with disabilities will be the ones to suffer as a result.

5 Cases

These cases have been chosen because they represent current practice in regards to accessibility compliance. They also serve to illustrate the similarities and differences between Australia and the US in regards to accessibility. In these cases the needs of users with disabilities have been considered and provided for. However, as the above discussion on WCAG 2.0 illustrates, the needs of users with disabilities can be more comprehensively met. World's best practice needs to change. The implications of those changes for eGovernment generally are explored in these cases.

5.1 Australian Cases

www.gov.au
The www.gov.au Web site is a small site that provides summary information on the state and territory Governments in Australia. It has been 'developed with usability and accessibility principles as the main drivers for design' [5], although the site does not claim any particular accessibility conformance. The site boasts a text-only version, however this appears where the accessibility of the site begins and ends, which is unfortunate as people with cognitive disabilities often have greatest difficulties with reams of text. On first glance, the site appears to be consistent with a number of visual cues that could assist people with disabilities, especially cognitive disabilities. However, noting that some people with cognitive disabilities use screen readers to assist in reading a site, the inappropriate use of alt tags is problematic. There are a number of images in the site without alt tags, however there are eleven instances on the homepage alone where the alt tag is "spacer", and a further eight instances where the alt tag is "#". All these images are spacer images which could all be removed if the site were designed with style sheets instead of images.

Another concerning aspect of the site is the provision of information available only via mouseover. When hovering over a state or territory in the left hand menu, the southern cross image in the top left hand corner changes to an image of that state or territory's official emblem. This information is not provided elsewhere on the site.

Each state and territory page is set out in a similar fashion – including a map of Australia indicating the position of the state or territory and a screenshot of the appropriate site. Unfortunately, the location of the state or territory is indicated by a change in color (the state or territory is colored magenta whereas all other areas are blue), and this information is not indicated in the alt tags or elsewhere. This is a clear violation of WCAG 1.0 Checkpoint 2.1 – ensure that all information is provided without reliance on color. Interestingly this would be a violation of the WCAG 2.0 Checkpoint 1.3: "any emphasis can be derived programmatically from the content without requiring interpretation of presentation" [20]. Thus, providing an indicative alt tag would mean compliance with the WCAG 2.0 Checkpoint 1.3, but not with WCAG 1.0 Checkpoint 2.1.

www.companioncard.org.au

The Companion Card [3] site is a Disability Services Division initiative aimed at people with significant disabilities and their companions to provide information on the 'Companion Card' initiative, which allows people who require a companion to accompany them, to have this companion admitted without charge to a range of venues and events in Victoria. The site is run and funded by the Victorian State Department of Human Services.

The site complies with WCAG 1.0 Level Triple-A, although full testing will not be completed until mid-May. The site offers a number of features specific to people with cognitive disabilities, such as visual cues, anchor links and nested headings.

Companion Card uses icons in conjunction with style sheet manipulated text to identify major navigational items. These icons are specific to a particular navigational section, for example, the Home section icon is a house, and the icon for Sitemap is a flowchart. When in a particular section of the site, the relevant navigation section is colored orange (instead of blue) and sub-navigation items are provided directly underneath the relevant item. Further use of icons in the site includes downward arrows next to anchors, indicating links that link further down the same page, and double browser windows to indicate links which open in a new window.

Another feature of the Companion Card is the range of documents available for downloading. Taking into account that tagged PDFs are often larger than their non-tagged counterparts, Companion Card provides two versions of each PDF: an untagged version purely for printing purposes, and a tagged version for people using screen readers or requiring additional accessibility features. Documents are also available as Word and RTF documents for people that do not have access to Adobe Acrobat or would prefer these versions. The Companion Card documents are also available in Easy English and a variety of languages and formats can be sent out at no charge by contacting the Companion Card Information Line. Recorded information is also available in a variety of languages.

The Companion Card Web site is a best-practice example of how a site can be visually attractive and comply with the highest accessibility requirements. The site complies with Triple-A checkpoints of WCAG 1.0, but has also included a variety of other accessibility features.

5.2   US Cases

www.firstgov.gov

Firstgov.gov [4] is the US government's main portal for all information within the US government. As such, it has been highly publicized and marketed to US citizens as the place to go for government information. The high profile of this site underscores the importance of making it accessible to all US citizens, including to those with disabilities.

An initial analysis of the Web site reveals that the developers of this site have paid attention to issues of Web accessibility. All of the images have alt text, for example, and there are links at the top of the page which allow users to skip to the main content or to other important areas of the page.

Upon closer examination, however, it is apparent that the developers are not Web accessibility experts, though they may have had good intentions. For example, the form elements have labels, as they should, but none of the labels are coded correctly. The developers clearly did not understand the basic technique, and have applied it in a way that is useless to users with disabilities. Similarly, the "skip to content" link is completely non-functional. When users select the link, nothing happens. This is an error that is easy to correct, but which has been left neglected, probably due to a lack of careful coding and quality control. In fact, the site's (X)HTML is woefully out of compliance with standardized (X)HTML markup protocols.

The designers of the firstgov.gov site face a daunting task in terms of usability. They must organize hundreds, if not thousands, of different government agencies, offices, and Web sites into understandable categories that are easy to navigate. Considering the enormity of the task, the designers are to be commended for the way in which they have organized all of the content. They provide four top level categories based on user characteristics: "for citizens," "for businesses and nonprofits," "for federal employees," and "government-to-government." In addition to these main tabs, other lists offer "information by topic," "by audience," "consumer help," "contact your government," and others. This scheme for organizing information seems intuitive enough, though some users will undoubtedly still have to search through these categories in order to find the specific information that they are searching for.

One limitation to their overall organization scheme is that it is geared mostly toward visual users. The bold colors of the main tabs in the design suggest to users that these are the principle divisions of the site. Users who cannot see the colors are not given any indication that these are the main tabs. The links are there, and the links are accessible, but the links are stripped of their context, and are likely to blend in with all of the other 70+ links on the page. In order to provide more of an understandable interface to people using screen readers – in the spirit of WCAG 2.0 – the developers would need to provide textual cues that convey the importance of the links in the main tabs. The text could say "start main site navigation" before the tabs begin, and then "end main site navigation" after the last tab. Another technique that could benefit firstgov.gov would be to use headings and other semantic markup. These are simple techniques, but they would position the site more in line with the recommendations in WCAG 2.0.

www.irs.gov
Like firstgov.gov, the irs.gov Web site [7] is another huge undertaking that demands a high level of user-centered design and information categorization. This is the Web site of the Internal Revenue Service, which is the office in charge of collecting taxes from US citizens. With such a distasteful topic, it is apparent that the irs.gov designers attempted to make the site as friendly and non-threatening as possible.

The site features a clean design, with photographs of people smiling as if they actually enjoyed paying taxes. The home page features links that are focused on user wants and needs, rather than those of the government agency. For example, the most prominent link tells users to "start here for free online filing [of taxes]." Other links include "find what you need, fast," and "where's my refund?" All of these links are intuitive from the perspective of the American tax payer, and seem to follow the philosophy of putting the customer first, even if it is a bit of a stretch to call taxpayers "customers." Though outside of the scope of disability access, another evidence of the focus on user needs is the existence of a Spanish version of the site.

In contrast to the firstgov.gov site, the main navigation of the irs.gov site is easily interpreted by screen reader users as the main navigation. The number of links on the home page are much fewer, and the main navigation appears right after the government agency's title and logo, which is a logical place for the main navigation to appear. One criticism is that the main navigation text is small and the contrast with the background is not as good as it could be.

The irs.gov Web site features hundreds of forms. Nearly all of these forms are in PDF format, which is usually problematic for screen reader users. However, the designers of irs.gov have gone to great lengths to provide many ways of accessing these forms. The forms are available in tagged PDF format (which is compatible with some screen readers), in PDF forms that can be filled out directly using a screen reader, and in alternative text versions. In light of WCAG 2.0, the use of accessible PDF files would not be a problem, as long as they truly are accessible. Still, even WCAG 2.0 advocates for the robustness of Web content, which often means providing a text alternative to non-(X)HTML technologies. The designers of irs.gov have done well in this regard.

There is still room for improvement on the site. For example, the developers could validate their (X)HTML markup against the accepted standard. Like firstgov.gov, the code behind irs.gov is sloppy and haphazard. The site could also benefit from more semantic markup, such as the use of headings.

In terms of cognitive disabilities, the site could use more graphics and illustrations. The site may be a clean design, but it is definitely text-centric, and could be intimidating to some users.

www.mbda.gov

The mbda.gov Web site [9] is where US citizens can find information about the Minority Business Development Agency, though it's hard to tell what the acronym stands for, because the expanded version is not featured prominently on the site. A graphic at the top of the page simply says "MBDA," without offering any kind of explanation. In this regard, screen reader users actually have a slight advantage over visual users, because they can hear the screen reader read the title of the page to them, which says "Minority Business Development." However, that is where the screen reader advantages end. In all other ways, this site is an accessibility nightmare to screen reader users.

The main navigation of the site is a group of five tabs, none of which have alternative text. In an ironic twist, the site is overrun by alt text for unimportant images, which serve only to confuse screen reader users. Image after image has such meaningless alt text as "spacer," "space," "clear space," and "arrow." The lists on this site are all pseudo lists. None of them were created using the standard (X)HTML tags for bulleted or numbered lists. These lists are not recognized as such by screen readers, leaving users to guess as to the semantic structure of the content.

Users with cognitive disabilities do not fare much better on this site. Upon clicking on the "who we are" link, for example, it appears that nothing at all has changed on the page. All of the content that was on the home page is still there. The one difference is that a new submenu option has appeared under the "who we are" link, but users may not notice this change at all. It is a subtle change, and the text is small, with poor contrast against the background. Users with or without cognitive disabilities are likely to feel disoriented on this site.

One further consideration is the lack of usability for people with access difficulties, cognitive and other. Powlik and Karshmer [12, p 218] ask "does simply getting one inside the door really make the resource usable?" They argue that simply complying with accessibility guidelines does not make a site usable. The designers of sites such as the mbda.gov site need to consider not only meeting the minimal accessibility standards, but also how well it works for those needing to use it.

Perhaps the most serious and cruel form of irony is that people with disabilities are part of the target audience of the site: minorities. From a political perspective in the United States, people with disabilities are often a forgotten minority. Much emphasis has been placed on minority races, and on gender disparities, but a proportionally small amount of emphasis has been placed on people with disabilities. That people with disabilities would be unable to access a Web site intended to serve minorities is a travesty, and makes a mockery of the reason for the Web site's very existence.

http://nihseniorhealth.gov

The Senior Health Web site of the US National Institutes of Health is one of the few US government Web sites designed specifically to accommodate people with disabilities. The main reason for this focus is that the target audience is senior citizens, many of whom have one or more disabilities due to age-related processes.

The disability features on this site are prominent and intuitive. In fact, the first four links are disability-related. These are "skip navigation," "enlarge text," "high contrast," and "turn speech on." The "skip navigation" link takes the user to the beginning of the main content. The "Enlarge text" link increases the font size substantially for the benefit of people with low vision. The "high contrast" option turns the background black and the text white, also for the benefit of people with low vision. The "turn speech on" button provides an uncommon, but useful, feature that can benefit users with cognitive disabilities as well as those with low vision. When this button is activated, a java applet is activated in a popup window in the background which begins to read the Web page out loud. The Web site designers use this applet to stream the sound of a voice synthesizer reading the page's contents. Users are able to control what is read by clicking on the content they want to hear. The reader reads one paragraph at a time.

The use of a site-specific synthesized reader is not a technique that should be applied across all Web sites, because most users who need voiced output will need this output for their entire computer, not just for certain Web sites. They need full-featured screen readers. The NIH Senior Health Web site is a bit different though. Most elderly individuals do not have extensive experience on the computer, and most feel at least somewhat intimidated by the prospect of using a computer at all. Chances are low that these individuals would have full-featured screen readers at their disposal, even if they would find this functionality useful. It makes sense then to include this functionality in the Web site itself for this specific audience and on this specific site. The designers have made a special effort to accommodate their target audience.

The designers have also made a concerted effort to construct a site that is very simple and well-organized for the benefit of those with cognitive disabilities or memory loss. The amount of text on each page is minimal, with plenty of white space, resulting in content that is easy to read. Longer passages of text are split up across multiple pages, and the "next page" buttons are clearly marked, in both text and graphic format, with a large arrow pointing to the right. All of these techniques facilitate navigation and increase comprehension for people with cognitive disabilities and reduce cognitive load for all users.

The site also features several video clips, used to explain concepts. This is also in line with the idea of providing assistance to users with cognitive disabilities. In order to accommodate users with hearing loss, the videos are captioned and text transcripts are provided.

In many ways, this is a model site in terms of accessibility. Not only have the designers made sure to "obey the rules" of Web accessibility by conforming to the existing standards, but they have extended the accessibility of the site by catering specifically to those with disabilities. The site is not only *accessible* to people with disabilities, but *usable* to them as well. This site is well positioned for the changes that WCAG 2.0 will bring.

6 Conclusion

All people, with or without disabilities, have a right to access government information on the Web. In many countries, such as in Australia and in the United States, this right is written into law. Though the specifics of these laws differ, they all have the same goal in mind: to make government information accessible to all citizens.

Though separate national standards exist in the US and although there are some additional requirements in Australia in the form of commonwealth and state based guidelines, the dominant standards in the area of eGovernment accessibility for people with disabilities has been and continues to be set by the W3C. In Australia, additional commonwealth and state-based guidelines are effectively attempts to deal with these standards within the confines of the Australian legal system. Similarly Section 508 in the US is in large part a reinterpretation of WCAG 1.0, in terms of legislative requirements in that country.

As WCAG 2.0 moves closer to being the official document of the W3C on Web content accessibility, governments should take the opportunity to anticipate the changes that this document will bring. With a greater focus on usability for people with disabilities, WCAG 2.0 can serve as a catalyst to cause developers to consider the user's perspective more seriously. It is not enough to merely provide access. The information must also be useful and usable. With WCAG 2.0 allowing the use of accessible non-(X)HTML technologies, this opens up a realm of possibilities that many in the Web accessibility community previously shunned. This is an exciting development in terms of the possibilities for multi-modal engagement that can benefit all users, especially those with cognitive disabilities. The caveat, of course, is that these non-(X)HTML technologies must be accessible to a broad range of users, and not just to those with specific abilities or disabilities, unless equivalent alternatives are provided. Also, with impending changes in the verifiability of conformance, WCAG guidelines and changes in conformance criteria, Web developers will need to adapt their processes for testing the accessibility of their creations. This requires new protocols in the quality control process.

The review of the six sites above reveals some common areas that designers need to address. There is the general principle of user-centered design, that the users need to be considered. Not all people with disabilities have the same needs. Even within a disability sub-group, such as cognitive disabilities, the type and severity of disability can vary and the functional capabilities of users can therefore vary. The best approach then is to include representatives from the target user populations in the design process. Where this has been done from the start, the additional cost of accessibility considerations in site designs has been shown to be minimal [11].

All these sites have some implementation of accessibility guidelines, with the better ones showing that, in many areas, a great deal of effort was made to conform to the guidelines. Nonetheless, those better sites are still inconsistent in the way in which they implement the guidelines. Aside from implementing the guidelines per se, there is also the inconsistent use of standard (X)HTML. These types of inconsistencies should be picked up through a quality control process. One form such a quality control process could take is that of an accessibility audit. The W3C provides extensive instructions on how to evaluate a site for accessibility compliance [19, 20]. It is important to consider universal usability throughout the Web development life cycle. Leaving such considerations until the last phase of development can result in the need for significant redesign and a much greater increase in cost, than if universal usability had been considered from the concept phase.

When all things are considered, making Web content – especially government Web content – accessible to people with disabilities is a matter of basic human rights. This is the answer to the question of *why* this important. It is not enough to merely be aware of *what* to do or *how* to do it. With this in mind, the most important thing for developers to remember when designing accessible Web content is that they are designing it for real people with real needs, and not just to satisfy a checklist of guidelines.

References

1. Access Board (2001). Section 508 of the Rehabilitation Act, www.section508.gov, accessed February 28, 2004.
2. Buhler, C. (2001), Empowered participation of users with disabilities in universal design, Universal Access in the Information Society, Vol 1. No 2. Oct, 85-90.
3. Companion Card (2004) www.companioncard.org.au, accessed 1 March 2004.
4. Firstgov (2004) US government portal for all information within the US government, www.firstgov.gov, accessed 1 March 2004.
5. Gov (2004) Australian whole-of-government single point of access (portal), www.gov.au, accessed 28th February 2004.
6. IMS (2001) IMS Guidelines for Developing Accessible Learning Applications, Version 0.6 White Paper, IMS Global Learning Consortium, Inc., 19 October.
7. IRS (2004) Internal Revenue Service, www.irs.gov, accessed 1 March 2004.
8. Kaye, H.S. (2000) Computer and Internet Use Among People with Disabilities, Disability Statistics Report (13), Washington DC: U.S. Department of Education, National Institute on Disability and Rehabilitation Research.
9. MBDA (2004) Minority Business Development Agency, www.mbda.gov, accessed 1 March 2004.

10. Online Council (2000) Joint Media Statement, www.dcita.gov.au/Article/0,,0_1-2_1-4_15092,00.html, accessed 1 March 2004.
11. Pedlow, R., Mirabella, M, and Chow, C. (2001) Universal access in HCI: Towards an information society for all, Proceedings of HCI International 2001, Ed. C. Stephanidis, New Jersey, Aug, Vol 3, 714-718.
12. Powlik, J.J. and Karshmer, A.J. (2002) When accessibility meets usability, Universal Access in the Information Society, Vol 1, No 3, 217-222.
13. Sampson-Wild, G. and Burmeister, O. K. (2001) The Continuing Evolution Of Best Practice Principles In Designing For Web Accessibility, Proceedings of OZCHI2001 Usability and usefulness for knowledge economics, Nov, 122-127.
14. Smith, P.D. and Brien, A.O. 2000. Universal Design from Policy to Practice - The Western Australian Experience. Proceedings, Designing for the 21st Century II: An International Conference on Universal Design. http://www.adaptenv.org/21century/proceedings.asp, accessed 28 February 2004.
15. Schneiderman, B. (2001) CUU: bridging the digital divide with universal usability, ACM Interactions, Vol 8(2), 11-15.
16. Vic eGov (2003) IT&T 39 – Accessibility Policy, http://www.mmv.vic.gov.au/accessibility, accessed 28th February 2004.
17. WCAG (2004) Web Content Accessibility Guidelines 2.0, http://www.w3.org/WAI/GL/, Web Content Accessibility Guidelines Working Group, accessed 28 February 2004.
18. Williamson, K. and Stillman, L. (2000) Online services for people with disabilities in Australian public libraries, Final report for the @ccessAbility Program, DoCITA, Monash University: Melbourne, Sep.
19. W3C (1999) Web Content Accessibility Guidelines 1.0. http://www.w3.org/TR/WAI-WEBCONTENT/, accessed 28 February 2004.
20. W3C (2004) Web Content Accessibility Guidelines 2.0, http://www.w3.org/WAI/GL/WCAG20/, W3C internal Working Draft, 14 February 2004, accessed 28 February 2004.

Inclusive Design in Industry:
Barriers, Drivers and the Business Case

Hua Dong[1], Simeon Keates[2], and P. John Clarkson[1]

[1] Engineering Design Centre, Department of Engineering, University of Cambridge,
Trumpington Street, CB2 1PZ,UK
{hd233,pjc10}@eng.cam.ac.uk
http://www-edc.eng.cam.ac.uk
[2] IBM TJ Watson Research Center, 19 Skyline Drive, Hawthorne, NY 10532, USA
lsk@us.ibm.com

Abstract. Despite increasing discussion in academia, genuinely 'inclusive' design in industry remains the exception rather than the rule. Based on literature reviews and industry surveys, this paper explores the barriers faced by manufacturers, retailers and design consultancies in adopting inclusive design. Drivers for practising inclusive design are also investigated. Using information about such barriers and drivers and linking them to business objectives, a basic framework for the business case for inclusive design is proposed. The paper contributes to the in-depth understanding of industry barriers and motivations for inclusive design and forms the basis for further research into the business case in an inclusive design context. The paper provides an insight into industry practice that is applicable to the design of User Interfaces for All.

1 Introduction

Despite the apparent need, the years of research, the efforts of special interest and lobby groups, the conferences and the recourses available to designers, truly inclusive design products and services remain the exception, not the norm [1]. It seems that barriers to inclusive design come from various parts of the supply chain, for example, design consultancies, manufacturers and retailers. Identifying such barriers is important in developing strategies for implementing inclusive design in industry.

The Universal Design Research Project (funded by the American National Institute on Disability and Rehabilitation Research of the Department of Education) has identified a number of barriers from consumer product manufacturers [2]. These barriers were classified into four categories, namely:

– fears and concerns;
– inadequate training or resources;
– lack of interest; and,
– structural barriers.

The Kyoyo-hin (Universal Design) survey under the Japanese Ministry of International Trade and Industry [3] investigated the motivations/drivers and problems/barriers facing the uptake of Universal Design in companies in Japan. A number

C. Stary and C. Stephanidis (Eds.): UI4All 2004, LNCS 3196, pp. 305–319, 2004.
© Springer-Verlag Berlin Heidelberg 2004

of drivers and barriers were identified. For example, major drivers for Japanese companies to be involved in Universal Design included:

- high demand from consumer and society needs;
- quality improvement/more consumer satisfaction;
- development of a new and expanding market;
- differentiation of own products; and
- drivers from Government such as regulations.

Major barriers to the adoption of Universal Design included:

- technical complexity and lack of cost-effectiveness;
- lack of knowledge and techniques; and
- lack of guidelines.

The UDRP project involved 26 US manufacturers, while the Kyoyo-hin project targeted 1,000 business in Japan, which included five different industry categories (i.e. clothing, domestic appliances, household goods, electric appliances and vehicles, refer to the report available from the Helen Hamlyn Research Centre, Royal College of Art). Although the relevance of these research findings to the UK was unclear, they provided a useful reference to the survey of industry barriers and drivers to inclusive design in the UK. The instructions of the UDRP survey questionnaire [4] were referred when designing the questionnaire for UK industry. Inspired by the Kyoyo-hin project, a rating scale was employed to the UK survey.

2 Methodology

To facilitate comparisons with the US data, this study also involved consumer product manufacturers in the UK.

Early studies helped the researchers form the following hypothesis:

The perceptions of barriers may be related to the type of business, i.e. perceptions of manufacturers may differ from perceptions of retailers or design consultancies.

In order to test the hypothesis, consumer product retailers and design consultancies with consumer product design specialists were also selected.

2.1 Sampling

The selection of companies was based on a simple random sample strategy [5]. Five widely used industry directories, i.e. *Kompass, Applegate, Kelley, Yellow Pages* and the *DTI Company Index* were searched for the selection of manufacturers and retailers. The selection of design consultancies was based on a web search of UK Design Consultancy directories.

Sampling depends on the type of measurements, the nature of the population being studied, the complexity of the survey design and the resources available [5]. For this research, it was hard to determine a truly representative sample because the classification of industry directories various and information often overlaps. In addition, missing data and out-of-date information also presented challenges. However, the researchers managed to select a total of 87 manufacturers, 68 retailers and 177 design consultancies during a two-week period. The common criteria used for sampling were the accuracy of the company addresses (cross-checked using different directories) and the potential availability for the research (making phone calls to confirm this in advance). The numbers of each type of business were determined by the manageable size for a two-week intensive web search.

2.2 Questionnaire Design

Two sets of questionnaires were designed based on the researchers' knowledge of manufacturers and design consultancies. The one for manufacturers and retailers followed the instructions of the UDRP survey, and the other (for design consultancies) was based on the initial findings of the potential barriers from interviews with nine UK design consultancies, which were presented at the 7th ERCIM workshop [6].

Manufacturers and retailers shared the same questionnaire as they both can be design commissioners. The fact that a different set of questionnaire was used for design consultancies might make it difficult for cross-business comparisons, but this was regarded as less important than getting an insight into design consultancies regarding their detailed requirements for the development of a practical support for inclusive design. In addition, the researchers tried to keep the questionnaire as brief as possible to encourage responses, any choices listed in the questionnaire to manufacturers/retailers that was thought as irrelevant to design consultancies were deleted, thus saving places for more useful questions.

The draft questionnaire to manufacturers and retailers was initially reviewed by two acknowledged experts of inclusive design and revised. Prior to distribution, the revised questionnaires were pilot–tested with ten people familiar with inclusive design concept and further revised. This provided a reference to the draft questionnaire for design consultancies, which was pilot-tested with four colleagues of the researchers before distribution.

In both sets of questionnaires, the same introduction was used, as follows:

Inclusive design is a relatively new concept, also known as 'Universal Design,' and 'Design for All.' It describes a process whereby designers, manufacturers and service providers ensure that their products and services address the needs of the widest possible audience, irrespective of age or ability.

This preamble aimed to make sure that all respondents were aware of the definition of inclusive design used in the questionnaire and avoided any ambiguity resulting from different interpretations of each respondent.

For manufactures and retailers, the definition of inclusive design was followed with a sentence like "However, in spite of the motivations for more inclusive design practices, industry in general has been slow to adopt them..."

What do you think would be effective to encourage companies like yours to adopt an inclusive design approach?

(A list of seven motivations with a 1-7 Likert-type scale, followed by a space for open comments)

What do you think would be effective to support companies like yours to adopt an inclusive design approach?

(A list of 10 incentives with a 1-7 Likert-type scale, followed by a space for open comments)

Note: The contents of the motivations (from inside), and incentives (from outside), later mixed as drivers, are presented in Table 6 and 7.

To what extent do the following issues present a barrier to companies like yours to adopting an inclusive design approach?

(A list of 26 barriers with a 1-7 Likert-type scale, followed by a space for open comments, refer to Table 1,2,3)

For design consultancies, the definition of inclusive design was followed with the following sentence: "A successful inclusive design example could be the OXO 'Good Grips'. However, in spite of the motivations for more inclusive design practices, it has been difficult to find many good inclusive design examples in the market…"

What do you think would be effective incentives for encouraging companies like yours to adopt an inclusive design approach?

Please write down the first couple you immediately think of below:

(a space for comments)

Please rate how effective you consider the following incentives to be.

(a list of seven incentives with a 1-7 Likert-type scale, refer to Table 8)

What do you think are he barriers to companies like yours in adopting an inclusive design approach?

Please describe two or three major barriers briefly:

(a space for comments)

Please rate how significant you consider the following barriers to be.

(a list of 14 barriers with a 1-7 Likert-type scale, refer to Table 4)

Both sets of questionnaire included requests for basic information of the company in question and a space for open comments.

The questionnaires were sent to people in middle or high management level, for example, managing directors, marketing directors or design directors. Reminders were sent to non-respondents within six weeks after the initial distribution of the questionnaire. In total, 18 useful responses were received from manufacturers, 15 from retailers and 35 from design consultancies. The findings are presented in the next section.

3   The Analysis of Barriers

Closed questions were designed to get quantitative information and open questions qualitative information. The barriers were identified and their importance rated. For the analysis of the questionnaire to manufacturers and retailers, the barriers (26 in total) were grouped into three categories, namely:

Table 1. 'Perception barriers' of manufacturers and retailers to inclusive design.

Perception barriers		Manufacturer		Retailer	
		Mean	SD	Mean	SD
a	Lack of awareness of inclusive design	4.2	2.0	4.9	1.9
b	Lack of interest in inclusive design	4.3	2.1	4.4	2.1
c	Lack of motivation for tackling inclusive design	4.1	2.1	3.9	2.0
d	Perception that inclusive design is more expensive	4.1	1.7	5.2	1.8
e	Perception that it can be complex to design inclusively	3.8	1.6	5.2	1.8
f	Perception that inclusive design represents a niche market	4.3	2.0	4.7	1.9
g	Lack of business case	5.0	1.7	4.3	1.9
h	Perception that inclusive design is an unachievable goal	3.9	2.0	4.2	2.1
i	Perceived problems of brand association with disabled/older people	2.9	1.7	3.0	1.2
j	Perceived 'sacrifice' of the aesthetics of the brand	4.6	1.4	3.7	2.0
k	Perceived longer development time to market	3.9	1.7	4.8	1.6
l	Perception that there is no need to practise inclusive design	3.7	2.0	3.7	1.7
m	Perception that inclusive design is contradictory to the diversity of the market	3.8	1.7	4.4	1.9
n	Perception that the social context for inclusive design has not been set	3.4	1.5	4.3	1.9
o	Perception that inclusive design is a passing trend	2.8	1.6	3.5	1.9

'Perception barriers' (barriers that are due to assumptions – can be true or not in reality, e.g. perception that inclusive design is more expensive);

'Technical barriers' (barriers relating to practical difficulties or hindrance of implementation, e.g. lack of time to learn); and

'Organisational barriers' (barriers relating to the nature or culture of the organisation, e.g. lack of risk-taking).

The subjectivity of the grouping was tested by asking a colleague to classify the barriers independently; the consensus rate was 96%.

Compared with the barriers identified in the UPRD project (refer to Section 1), 'perception barriers' involve 'fears and concerns', and 'lack of interest;' 'technical barriers' include 'inadequate training or resources,' and 'organisation barriers' are similar to 'structural barriers.'

3.1 Barriers from Manufacturers and Retailers

'Perception barriers' rated on the 1-7 Likert-type scale (1: least negative/no barrier effect; 7: most negative/much barrier effect) by the 18 manufacturers and the 15 retailers, together with their standard deviation (SD), are shown in Table 1. Note that only for three of the 15 barriers (c, g and j) do the manufacturers have more negative perceptions than the retailers.

Table 2. 'Technical barriers' of manufacturers and retailers to inclusive design.

Technical barriers		Manufacturer		Retailer	
		Mean	SD	Mean	SD
p	Lack of resources/guidance on inclusive design	4.3	1.9	4.8	1.6
q	Time taken to learn the approach	3.9	2.0	4.1	1.7
r	Lack of availability of good design examples	4.3	1.8	4.5	2.0
s	Lack of government regulations	3.7	2.2	3.3	2.0
t	Lack of methods/tools for practicing inclusive design	3.8	1.6	4.3	1.9

Table 3. 'Organisational barriers' of manufacturers and retailers to inclusive design.

Organisational barriers		Manufacturer		Retailer	
		Mean	SD	Mean	SD
u	Difficulty in changing the culture of a business	3.8	1.9	4.1	2.0
v	Lack of company policy on inclusive design	3.7	2.1	3.9	2.2
w	Business is sales-led rather than design-led	4.4	1.9	4.6	2.2
x	Lack of willingness to change	3.7	1.8	2.9	1.8
y	Lack of risk-taking / unwillingness to invest money in a new practice	3.7	2.3	4.1	2.0
z	Working for short-term financial objectives	3.7	2.0	2.9	1.7

'Technical barriers' from both manufacturers and retailers are shown in Table 2. In this case, only for one of the five barriers do the manufacturers have more negative perceptions than the retailers.

Table 3 shows the 'Organisational barriers' rated by the manufacturers and retailers. The table shows that manufacturers have more negative perceptions (reflected by higher scores) for two out of the six barriers.

The respondents were provided with an opportunity to write down additional barriers. None were added by the manufacturers, while retailers suggested two more, namely:

"perception that market place is too small;" and "lack of vision."

The mean scores to individual barriers assigned by manufacturers were compared with those assigned by retailers. It was found that retailers tend to assign a higher level of significance than manufacturers to most of the barriers (19 out of 26). The average rating score regarding the barriers was 4.1 for the retailers and 3.9 for the manufacturers.

The most significant barriers to manufacturers were "lack of business case" (score: 5.0) and "perceived sacrifice of aesthetics" (score: 4.6), while for retailers they were "perception that inclusive design is more expensive" (score: 5.2) and "perception that it can be complex to design inclusively" (score: 5.2). Interestingly, those are barriers that one would normally have expected to be greater concerns for manufacturers rather than retailers. From a psychological standpoint, the retailers surveyed were effectively saying that "we are not doing it, because it is too complex for our suppliers [the manufacturers]".

However, the manufacturers themselves do not share the same concerns. Instead they are focused on how well the inclusively designed products will sell, which one would have expected to have been the retailers' prime concern. So both retailers and manufacturers perceive the most significant barriers to be within the domain of the other party, rather than their own. This naturally leads to the open question as to whether the manufacturers and retailers are actually communicating their concerns with each other.

In general, 'perception barriers' form the majority of the barriers and are rated as most significant, followed by 'technical barriers' and then 'Organisational barriers.' This implies that efforts should be put on raising awareness to overcome perception barriers, and providing supportive tools to overcome technical barriers.

3.2 Barriers from Design Consultancies

The questionnaire to design consultancies was based on a pilot study, i.e. interviews with nine design consultancies. A detailed report of the interviews is available [7]. The results of the survey with design consultancies are summarised in Table 4:

Table 4. Barriers to inclusive design from design consultancies.

Barriers	Average score	Standard deviation
Lack of inclusivity requirements from design commissioners	5.6	1.9
Lack of budget for user research	5.4	1.7
Lack of time for involving users in testing	5.0	1.5
Lack of information on inclusive design	4.6	1.8
Lack of support from company culture	4.6	1.9
Lack of good design examples	4.4	2.0
Lack of time to learn how to design inclusively	4.1	1.8
Lack of methods/skills to design inclusively	3.9	1.8
Manufacturers 'not-invented-here' syndrome	3.7	1.8
Perceived 'sacrifice' of aesthetics	3.6	2.1
Lack of users for testing concepts and prototypes	3.4	1.5
Difficult in changing design process to accommodate inclusive design	2.8	1.8
Perception that inclusive design will not be a lasting trend	2.7	1.4
Perception that inclusive design is a specific skill	2.4	1.1

Table 5. Additional barriers identified by design consultancies.

Types of barriers	Frequency of mentions	Example-of-comments (quotation)
Barriers from clients	16	• [Inclusivity] not in the brief from the client
Time and budget	7	• No funds/time to test design
Lack of knowledge /methods	7	• Lack of experience
Lack of legislation	2	• Lack of legislation
Miscellaneous	1 (for each)	• The market power of the dominant players • Conflicting commercial requirements • Lack of priority – i.e. ongoing things have precedence • Consumers are slow to articulate what they want • Design (only) for representative 'average' user sample • No clear immediate commercial benefits • Some products sell based on their exclusivity • Perception that aesthetics become clumsy • Mere importance • Lack of market intelligence • Definition of 'inclusive' is woolly

Additional barriers added by the respondents are grouped and summarised in Table 5.

Designers' open comments relating to barriers are as follows:

"All good design consultancies will apply inclusive design to some degree. Inclusive design will include all age/user groups and will apply more to ergonomic/user interface products. Assessment on the effectiveness of these designs become more difficult."

"Manufacturers are slow to recognise the shift in demographics. The flower power generation are now pensioners!"

"Do not forget the core needs, aims and objectives of the business and the relationship of this to its currently available resources. Media sources and academic sources have an intrinsic bias and self-justification that is not relevant in the commercial world."

"Inclusive design is a highly academic approach to design practice that will probably find most failure in large organisations seeking to reduce perceived risks. It is likely to result in banal products that wouldn't find favour in design-led organisations."

"Many manufacturers still view inclusive products as excluding the market/trends they wish to pursue - best example - mobile phones as much a bonus to lifestyles for the less able and elderly as us all - but increasingly they are excluded by size, interface and complexity."

"As a consultancy we can raise awareness of inclusive design, but industry does not always recognise design benefits - be it inclusive or not. Companies still largely regard design as spend and not investment. I fear that many regard inclusive design as further spend rather than appropriate investment."

An inspection of the perceptions and comments reveals an interesting fact: the major barriers from design consultancies are concerned with the 'design commissioners,' not the 'design consultancies themselves.'

Ironically, it seems that manufacturers, retailers and design consultancies all consider the major problems are from the other parties. Having discussed the major barriers in general, the next section explores the drivers for inclusive design.

4   Analysis of Drivers for Inclusive Design

Drivers in this paper refer to motivations, incentives and other favourable factors for inclusive design. In the questionnaire, motivations (from inside) and incentives (from outside) for inclusive design were differentiated, as mentioned in section 2.2. This made the flow of questions natural. However, it was found that the differentiation of motivations and incentives was not important for data analyses. It was then decided to integrate the motivations and incentives into 'drivers' and re-group them into 'financial drivers' and 'non-financial drivers.' The subjectivity of the grouping was also tested by asking a colleague to classify the drivers independently. The consensus rate was 87%.

4.1   Drivers for Inclusive Design from Manufacturers and Retailers

The perceptions of drivers from the 18 manufacturers and 15 retailers, computed as the means of the responses on the 1-7 Likert-type scale (1: lest positive/no driver effect; 7: most positive/much driver effect), are shown in Table 6 ('Financial drivers') and Table 7 ('Non-financial drivers').

'Financial drivers' refer to drivers that projects the likely financial results, while 'non-financial drivers' refer to drivers that relates to other business consequences rather than monetary results. Standard deviations were also compared in the tables.

Table 6. Manufacturers and retailers' perceptions of 'financial drivers' for inclusive design.

	Financial drivers	Manufacturer		Retailer	
		Mean	SD	Mean	SD
A	Successful business studies (i.e. those showing commercial success)	4.2	1.6	4.8	1.5
B	Potential market for those currently excluded	6.0	1.1	5.5	1.6
C[*]	New market opportunities by practising inclusive design	5.9	1.2	5.1	2.0
D	Assessment of how many people are excluded	5.2	1.5	5.5	1.5

[*] The questionnaire was modified once during the process of distribution, C in Table 6 was combined with B in the modified version.

Table 7. Manufacturers and retailers' perceptions of 'non-financial drivers' for inclusive design.

	Non-financial drivers	Manufacturer		Retailer	
		Mean	SD	Mean	SD
E	Consumer dissatisfaction with current products	5.7	1.7	5.5	1.6
F	Chances of innovation by practising inclusive design	5.4	1.0	5.4	1.2
G	Analysis of why people are excluded	5.2	1.0	5.0	1.6
H	Public/consumer awareness of inclusive design	3.8	1.7	4.9	1.2
I	Availability of expert consultation on inclusive design	3.9	1.6	4.3	1.9
J	Availability of tools/methods to help the practice of inclusive design	4.0	1.4	4.7	1.5
K	Government regulation/legislation on inclusive design	4.4	2.1	3.1	2.2
L	Users available for testing prototypes during the design process	4.1	1.4	4.8	1.7
M	Availability of training on inclusive design to staff/designers	3.8	1.6	4.6	1.8
N	Chances of improving brand image by practising inclusive design	5.1	1.7	5.3	1.4
O	Champion for inclusive design on company boards	4.1	1.7	4.7	1.9
P	Corporate strategy incorporating inclusive design	4.5	1.7	4.6	1.7
Q	Availability of standards/guidelines on inclusive design	4.0	1.8	4.6	1.5
R*	Major competitor's adoption of inclusive design	–	–	4.4	1.5

* R in Table 7 was added in the modified questionnaire and few responses were received from the manufacturers.

The respondents were provided with an opportunity to write down additional drivers, however none were added.

It was found that the top drivers (B+C: potential market, D: the measure of current exclusion, E: consumer dissatisfaction, F: innovation) were similar between those perceived by manufacturers and retailers. Key drivers for industry (including design consultancies, refer to Section 4.2) involves both financial ones and non-financial ones.

4.2 Drivers for Inclusive Design from Design Consultancies

Designers' perceptions on drivers for inclusive design are summarised in Table 8. In addition to the provided multiple options, designers suggested more drivers (Table 9).

Table 8. Designers' perceptions of 'non-financial drivers' for inclusive design.

Drivers	Average score	Standard deviation
Consumer demand	6.1	1.0
Successful business studies (i.e. those showing commercial success)	5.4	1.5
Chances of innovation	5.2	1.6
Potential market for those currently excluded	5.1	1.3
Legislation requirements / regulation	5.1	1.8
Chances of improving company image	4.5	1.5
Competitor's adoption of inclusive design practice	3.8	1.8

Table 9. Additional drivers identified by design consultancies.

Types of drivers	Frequency of mentions	Example of comments (quotation)
Clients-related motivations	14	• Clients' requirement for inclusive design
Market-related motivations	9	• Larger markets
Awareness and better understanding	7	• The fact that the market is getting older
External support	6	• Easy access to up-to-date data
Examples or case studies	6	• Successful examples
Legal incentives	5	• Legislation requirements are effective but "unnecessary"
Financial incentives	5	• Provide grant incentives for inclusive design projects
Customer demand	2	• More consumer awareness/demands
Miscellaneous	1	• Some sort of product approval
	(for each)	• Ease of implementation
		• Moral incentive
		• Point of difference/design registration/patent ability

Designers' general comments relating to drivers for inclusive design are as follows:

"I expect that consumer demand will drive this forward - demographic trends are that way. However, product manufacturers are not very likely to move until pushed! Perhaps some Third Age organisation should team up with the [UK] Consumer Association! They could add inclusive design in the [Consumer Association] 'Which?' magazine."

"Increasing manufacturers' awareness of the benefits of inclusive design is necessary and is probably best achieved by illustrating the financial benefits rather than the human ones - sad, but gearing education along fiscal lines is the way to make them change."

"If we had data/consultants available we would be adapting a more inclusive approach. Market data would facilitate persuasion of customers of the benefits, which is key. At the end of the day, the client supplies a brief and the client pays the bills, so the designer will often be wary of introducing extra requirements, unless market gain can be demonstrated."

"I believe inspiration is a key requirement for designers to understand how to develop inclusive design standards in a highly creative way, subtly and effectively. I imagine the industry standards and legislation need to develop and exemplify better methods of inspiring companies."

5   The Business Case for Inclusive Design

Making a good business case is key for industry. Business case may be defined as a decision support and planning tool that projects the likely financial results and other business consequences of an action [8].

The exploration of industry barriers to inclusive design and drivers for inclusive design has formed a basis for investigating the business case in an inclusive design context. As one of the designers commented "do not forget the core needs, aims and objectives of the business and the relationship of this to its currently available resources" (refer to Section 3.2). Thus the investigation of the business case should identify the business objectives and link them to currently available resources.

Based on literature reviews [8], [9], [10], the business objectives relating to inclusive design could be:

Product/service-focused objectives:

- to improve performance
- to improve safety
- to achieve greater desirability
- to introduce more competitive products
- to enter new product markets
- to achieve technology leadership
- to improve customer satisfaction ratings
- to provide better quality customer service
- to provide new service offerings
- to permit more customized customer service

Market-focused objectives:

- to increase market share
- to take market leadership
- to improve market position

- to increase repeat business
- to win first-time customers
- to counter competitive threats
- to increase competitive strengths
- to differentiate own products from the competition

Revenue-focused objectives:

- to increase sales revenues
- to increase margins or profits
- to improve earnings per share
- to increase unit sales

Image-focused objectives:

- to be recognised as a technology leader
- to be recognised as a contributor to industry standards or industry cooperation
- to be recognised as a producer of quality products or reliable products
- to be recognised for outstanding customer service
- to be recognised as the performance leader

The measurable indicators or tangible evidence of these objectives of business play an important role in building the business case for inclusive design. For instance, the improved customer satisfaction might appear as fewer complaints, or more repeat business, or even the results of customer satisfaction surveys. Such 'soft benefits' are often the hardest to quantify, but they could be the highest priority objectives of business.

When building the business case, design and process are everything (Schmidt, 2002). An initial structure of building the business case for inclusive design is proposed (see Figure 1), which includes the analysis of barriers and drivers, the identification of indicators of business objectives and the exploration of available resources.

It remains important to be able to address these elements and explain how they were chosen and how they were valued in order to develop strategies for promoting inclusive design in the real world.

6 Conclusions

The focus of this research is inclusive design in industry. Major barriers and drivers relating to the industry practice of inclusive design have been identified based on the survey with consumer product manufacturers, retailers and design consultancies in the UK.

It was found that the perception of barriers is related to the type of business. The top two barriers from manufacturers are 'lack of business case' and 'perceived sacrifice of aesthetics.' The most significant barriers from retailers are 'perception that inclusive design is more expensive' and 'perception that it can be complex to design inclusively.' The most important barriers from design consultancies are 'lack of inclusivity requirements from design commissioners' and 'lack of budget for user research.' The research hypothesis has been proved. More interestingly, it appears that manufacturers, retailers and design consultancies all consider the major barriers are from the other parties rather than from themselves.

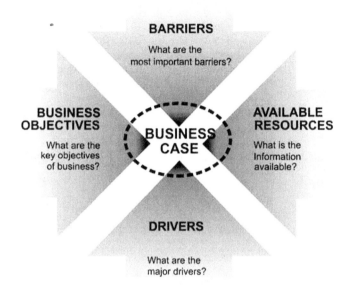

Fig. 1. The framework of the business case for inclusive design.

Both financial drivers and non-financial drivers were found critical to manufacturers, retailers and design consultancies, among which 'potential market,' 'consumer demand,' and 'chances of innovation' were highly rated by all.

The basic framework for building the business case requires analyses of barriers, drivers and the objectives of business, and relating these to the available resources. Future work involves the revision and application of the framework to further case studies and development of convincing business cases for industry.

References

1. Bontoft, M., Pullin, G.: Chapter 30: What is an Inclusive Design Process? In: Clarkson, J., Coleman, R., Keates, S., Lebbon, C. (eds.): Inclusive Design: Design for the Whole Population. Springer-Verlag London Berlin Heidelberg (2003) 520-531
2. Vanderheiden, G., Madison, J. Barriers: Incentives and Facilitators for Adoption of Universal Design Practices by Consumer Product Manufacturers. At: http://www.tracecenter.org/docs/hfes98_barriers/barriers_incentives_facilitators.htm. (1998)

3. Mitsubishi Research Institute: Kyoyo-hin in Japan Survey. Helen Hamlyn Research Centre, Royal College of Art, London (2000)

4. Trace Research Centre: Survey instrument (for the UDRP project). At: http://www.tracecenter.org/docs/univ_design_res_proj/Survey.htm. (1998)

5. Breakwell, M. Hammond, G., S. Fife-Schaw, C. (eds.): Research methods in psychology. Sage publications, London (1995)

6. Dong, H., Keates, S., Clarkson P. J.: Implementing Inclusive Design: the Discrepancy between Theory and Practice. In: Carbonell, N., Stephanidis, C., (eds.): Universal Access: Theoretical Perspectives, Practice, and Experience. 7th ERCIM International Workshop on User Interfaces for All, Paris, France, October 2002, Berlin Heidelberg New York (2002)106-117

7. Dong, H., Cardoso, C. Cassim, J. Keates, S.,Clarkson, P. J.: Inclusive Design: Reflections on Design Practice. CUED/C-EWDC/TR118-June 2002, Cambridge, Engineering Design Centre, Department of Engineering, University of Cambridge, Cambridge (2002)

8. Schmidt, M. J.: The Business Case Guide. Solution Matrix Ltd, Boston (2002)

9. Renfrew Group: The Business Case for 'Inclusive' Design. At: http://www.dpaonthenet.net/editorialextra/prod_extra04.html (2004)

10. Clarkson, P. J., Coleman, R. Keates, S., Lebbon, C. (eds.): Inclusive Design: Design for the Whole Population. Springer-Verlag London Berlin Heidelberg (2003)

The Role of Working Memory and Long Term Memory in Deaf Users' Hypertext Navigation: Review of Guidelines for Web Accessibility

Inmaculada Fajardo[1], Julio Abascal[1], and José J. Cañas[2]

[1] Laboratory of HCI for Special Needs (UPV/EHU)
Manuel Lardizabal 1, E-20018 Donostia
{acbfabri,Julio}@si.ehu.es
[2] Cognitive Ergonomic Group, Granada University
Campus Cartuja, s/n, 18071 Granada
delagado@ugr.es

Abstract. Important tasks performed in hypertext such as information retrieval or comprehension of texts are strongly related to memory process functioning, more exactly, to working memory and long term memory functioning. These two processes work in a peculiar way for deaf users. In this document, we discuss the validity of the existing web accessibility guidelines for people with deafness in contrast to our own empirical work in the web environment with these kinds of users, and according to literature reviews concerning memory process in the deaf and in hypertext interaction.

1 Introduction

On certain occasions, deafness is exclusively considered a sensorial problem, that is, a deficiency characterized by the lack of auditory stimuli processing of the sense of hearing. Consequently, the accessibility guidelines for deaf users are focused on overcoming this sensorial problem, for instance, providing visual information instead of acoustic [1]. However, deafness also influences the functioning of cognitive processes and the representation and organization of knowledge affecting complex tasks such as problem solving or decision making [2]. Nevertheless, these cognitive peculiarities are not always negative and could be exploited by web designers [3].

Almost all web interaction tasks involve cognitive processing [4]. Memory process is one of the most studied processes in this context, mainly the working memory process. Curiously, this process in deaf people has also been intensively studied by Cognitive Psychology. Therefore, we now know that people who are deaf have problems maintaining a set of verbal items in short term memory [5] or reading and understanding a written text [6]. This theoretical background makes formulating predictions about the behaviour of deaf users in the Internet possible and to make a critical review of representative web accessibility guidelines for these users.

Therefore, the question we must consider is if the existing accessibility guidelines for the deaf and hard of hearing are usable and moreover enough. Furthermore, if we consider that deafness affects cognitive processing are the guidelines for cognitively disabled people also applicable to deaf people. Finally, taking that both deafness and usage of sign language can involve certain cognitive advantages for deaf signer people into account, how these particularities could be exploited by web designers.

C. Stary and C. Stephanidis (Eds.): UI4All 2004, LNCS 3196, pp. 320–325, 2004.

2   Review of Web Accessibility Guidelines for Deaf Users Considering the Characteristics of Working Memory and Long Term Memory

The specific accessibility recommendations for deaf users are usually focused on the substitution of sounds for other non-acoustic elements. For example, the guideline 1 of the Web Contents Accessibility Guidelines (WCAG) [7] recommends providing texts equivalent to auditory contents, and authors as [1], propose to substitute environmental sound with visual presentation[1].

On the other hand, as Seeman [8] shows, the WCAG 1 [7] promotes the following checkpoints that benefit the Cognitively Disabled:

- Use simple language to form a high interest/low vocabulary semantic content
- Enable the enlargement and reading of textual content
- Use a clear and correct document structure
- Provide a well illustrated text
- Use consistent navigational techniques
- Keep to commonly used conventions

However, as Seeman [8] admits, these guidelines are too general and, therefore, valid for a wide range of disabilities: "There is a lack, however, of specific checkpoints or techniques that could increase accessibility for specific cognitive impairment." [8]

Therefore, we will then attempt to clear up this gap by answering the questions formulated in the previous section considering the following aspects related to memory process in deaf users as well as web interaction tasks.

With regard to Working Memory in deaf people, the storage and processing of visuospatial information is more efficient than the storage and processing of verbal information (both, written and oral). It seems that this efficiency is mainly related to the use of sign language, the mother language of the majority of people who are born deaf.

The main difference between oral and sign language is the modality of linguistic inputs and outputs, which in sign language is visuo-manual instead of audio-oral. However, in spite of its visuospatial modality, sign language would be processed in the same working memory store as oral language, the Phonological Loop (PL), and not in the visual working memory store, the Visuospatial Sketchpad (VS). The signers PL would have certain special characteristics which would allow them to store and maintain linguistic visuospatial inputs instead of verbal [9]. This means that the VS abilities of deaf people would not be necessarily better than VS abilities of hearing people.

Nevertheless, it has been demonstrated that the use of a visuospatial language improves a number of aspects of other visuospatial tasks directly related to VS, such as the memory for spatial places, the discrimination of faces and the processing of facial characteristics. In spite of this, other visuospatial aspects such as the memory for visual images or the visuo-constructive abilities are not affected by sign language use.

---

[1] It is important to point out that Emiliani cites this adaptation for deaf as a possible solution not exclusively for web environment but for computer-based products and telematic services in general.

Emmorey [9] hypothesizes that these results could mean that there is only an improvement in those aspects of the visuospatial cognition which are important for the comprehension and production of sign language. That is, not all dominions of visuospatial cognition are specially developed in deaf signers.

With regard to Long Term Memory (LTM), there are other findings which induce us to think that differences could exist between deaf and hearing people in the amount and organization of knowledge [2]. For example, deaf people do not perform a top-down process while reading, they do not use the context (that is, they read word for word) and, for this reason, working memory is overloaded. This overload could interfere with comprehension. Along with short term storage, Marschark [2] proposes that the problem could be due to the organization and connection of words or concepts in LTM, where item details are stored, more than the relations among these items. In fact, it has been proved that, in some contexts, deaf people are do not perform as well as their hearing peers in attending and recognizing relational information while reading and in activating the categories related to the exemplars [2].

All things considered, we can say that deaf people are not efficient in verbal task. However, they are especially competent with certain visuo-spatial tasks, both linguistic and non-linguistic. In this case, if memory processes are involved in these tasks implicated in hypertext navigation.

World Wide Web (WWW) is a set of hypertexts with a net structure and could be considered as one of the most extensively hypertext forms used. Within this net, each hypertext consists of a series of information chunks (nodes) connected by links (arcs), offering the user different pathways for navigation. User interaction with hypertext involves, at least, two tasks related to memory process:

A) An Information Retrieval task: the user tries to find text (words, sentences, paragraphs...) and/or images (e.g. pictures, icons...) within or between hypertext nodes. For instances, a user can retrieve information by means of a query engine, a menu bar, a map or, simply, by clicking on node links[2]. Furthermore, during the majority of information retrieval tasks, users have to be orientated, that is, users have to familiarize themselves with the hypertext structure, remember the path followed, know where they are regarding the global hypertext structure and how to arrive to other nodes. For instance, the orientation process could be activated when a user wants to return from a low level node of hypertext to the homepage.

B) A Learning task acquires a profound understanding of the subject matter [11]. The objective of the users is "to carry out meaningful learning by semantically integrating accessible pieces of information" (p.p 388, [12]). For instance, in an instructional context, not only has the user to retrieve information, but also learn this information. According to Rouet [13], there are three relevant verbal components (related to the PL of Working Memory), pre-requisites of the text comprehension processes, which could be involved in information retrieval task of verbal targets: phonological or grapheme representation, representation of words meaning and functions, representation of logical and grammatical structure.

---

[2] Although we have focused on user actions in this document, it is important to distinguish between the retrieval process performed by systems (e.g. a query engine as Google) and by users[10], as the actions of both may be interacting in certain occasions. To characterize both the users´ action and the system actions, terms such as seeking, browsing, searching, etc. have been used.

With regard to the information retrieval task, a recent review of empirical studies concerning this task and its relation with working memory [14], has driven us to the conclusion that information retrieval task is dependant on both, verbal and visuo-spatial resources of users. If deaf and hearing people differ in their process of memory (both, working memory and representations in long term memory), then information retrieval task in hypertext would be enhanced for different characteristics in each kind of user.

On the one hand, as previously explained, deaf people obtain poorer results than hearing people do when working with verbal information; in contrast to that, they obtain better results when working with certain kinds of visuo-spatial information. We must then ask ourselves if the substitution of textual information by visual contents would improve web information retrieval tasks of deaf users. We have empirical data that would support this guideline; however, only partially [15]. Deaf signer users only improve the web searching with visual targets when the search does not imply having a categorical decision, that is, when there are no involved semantic factors in the information retrieval task and the search is based on visual factors as visuo-perceptual speed (related to the visuo-spatial store of working memory).

On the other hand, connected to cited finding, several semantic aspects related to LTM seem fundamental in order to perform information search tasks in a Web Site. Whether users are not able to or, have difficulties in generating the category they are searching for (for instance, a sports category, where users want to find out the news concerning football matches in a digital newspaper), their performance would probably drop. This fact might be applicable to both, verbal and graphical interfaces. In the case of icons, different ways of organizing the knowledge in memory may affect the users´ judgment of semantic distance (or judgment of the relation icon-referent) and, in this manner, the efficiency in the selection of the icon which would open the desired site or would activate the desired function. Currently, [15] deaf signers were found to have more problems than hearing non-signers in finding visual targets in a newspaper website when the targets were in a deeper layer of the web structure and therefore necessary in order to make more categorical decisions for finding them. The authors concluded that the qualitative difference in knowledge organization between deaf and hearing people, found in a previous normative study on semantic distance of icon-targets used in the experiment may be determining the difference in the web information retrieval task.

That is, if we have to use icons, images or pictures for information retrieval task, we have to take into account that all the users do not extract the same meaning from them. This might mediate the applicability of accessibility guidelines for the deaf and cognitively disabled, such as, provide well illustrated texts [7], provide content-related images in pages full of text [7] or provide visual information instead of acoustic[3] [1]. Clark [16] has criticized these guidelines arguing that certain abstract concepts cannot be illustrated by pictures and icons; or that the increasing of downloading times, due to the sizes of images files, would damage usability. In addition, as a conclusion of the revision of theory and several new empirical facts about deaf people

---

[3] It is important here to distinguish between visual stimuli used as targets in a search task, and visual stimuli used as redundant information of text. In the second case, the visual stimuli are generally used to improve the comprehension of texts and users' abilities such as visual memory o visual perceptive speed could not be as relevant as in search task. Anyway, spatial clues could also improve the comprehension of the contents [18].

and web interaction, it is possible to say that the user memory process mediates the efficiency of these guidelines. For this reason, when a search task involves not only visuospatial factors but also semantic ones, the mere substitution of words and sentences by pictures and icons is not recommended without a previous study of aspects related to user memory, especially of the organization of knowledge in LTM such as the semantic distance of icons and the familiarity of users with such visual representations (e.g. [17]).

Finally, let us comment the second most important hypertext task. The learning task is mainly related to the reading comprehension in the web as nowadays, the essence of the Web is text [16]. Although deaf people are able to read, the reading process would consume a large amount of cognitive resources that are unnecessary for hearing as reading is an automatic process. However, deaf people could overcome their verbal deficit in other kinds of hypertext structures such as deep structures, where the verbal information could be distributed and it would become more dependent on visuo-spatial abilities. Users with more visuo-spatial abilities (e.g. deaf signer users) could be more orientated in complex visuo-spatial hypertext structures. They could even take advantage of the spatial clues to improve their comprehension of the contents [18].

In this sense, the checkpoints of the WCAG 1 [7] directed to Cognitively Disabled users (Use simple language to form a high interest/low vocabulary semantic content, Enable the enlargement and reading of textual content and Use a clear and correct document structure) would be perfectly applicable also to deaf people with reading problems. One way of fitting the third cited guideline would be to distribute verbal contents along more layers of nodes along hypertext structures or provide several spatial clues [14]. Although this solution is especially effective for people with high spatial skills, like Deaf Signers, there is empirical evidence showing a beneficial effect of this kind of help in the general population, for instance, by means of colour usage for grouping spatially similar items of verbal information [19].

3   Conclusions

By means of this revision of the cognitive characteristics of deaf users and hypertext environment, we wished to carry out a critical analysis of the existing guidelines for these kinds of users.

It is clear that deafness is not a simple sensorial deficit as it affects cognitive processes, such as memory and language, implicated in web interaction task. In addition, this deficiency does not always affect people in a negative way (e.g. lower memory for verbal items) if not in a positive way (for instance, improving the visuo-spatial abilities in sign language speakers). For this reason, supported by theory and empirical data, we have argued about the validity of certain web accessibility guidelines for deaf users, and about the necessity of also applying accessibility guidelines for the cognitively disabled to deaf users.

The conclusion was that the most developed visuo-spatial abilities of deaf users could be exploited by website designers distributing verbal contents in spatial demanding web structure (with more layers of nodes), which in addition could serve as semantic spatial clues for comprehension. Besides, due to the different organization of knowledge in deaf people LTM, the substitution of verbal information by visual one in web information search task is only recommended with some precautions. It is necessary to consider that icons and words do not necessarily mean the same thing for the deaf as it does for the hearing. Thus a previous study of semantic distance of the potential users of the website would be needed.

References

1. Emiliani, P.L.(2001). Special needs and enabling technologies: and evolving approach to accessibility, in Stephanidis, Constantine (ed.) User interfaces for all, Lawrence Erlbaum Associates: Mahwah, New Jersey, pp. 97-113.
2. Marschark, M. (2003). Cognitive functioning in deaf adults and children. In M. Marschark & P.E. Spencer (Eds.), Oxford handbook of deaf studies, language, and education (pp. 464-477). New York: Oxford University Press.
3. Fajardo, I., Cañas, J.J., Antolí, A., and Salmerón, L. (2002). Accesibilidad Cognitiva de los Sordos a la Web. 3° Congreso Internacional Interacción'2002, Madrid.
4. Kim H. and Hirtle S. C. (1995). Spatial metaphors and disorientation in hypertext browsing. Behaviour and Information Technology, 14(4):239-250.
5. Rollman, S. y Harrison, R.: A comparison of deaf and Hearing subjects in Visual Nonverbal sensitivity and Information 21. Processing. American Annals of the Deaf, (1996), 141 (1): 37-41.
6. Leybaert, J., Alegria, J. y Morais, J. (1982). On automatic reading processes in the deaf. Cahiers de Psychologie Cognitive 2 (2), 185-192.
7. Web Accessibility Initiative –WAI (1999). Web Content Accessibility guidelines 1.0 Available at http://www.w3.org/WAI/.
8. Seeman, L. (2002). Inclusion Of Cognitive Disabilities in the Web Accessibility Movement. Presented at The 11th international World Wide Web Conference, Honolulu, Hawaii, USA
9. Emmorey, K. (2002). Language, Cognition and the Brain. Insights from sign language research. Mahwah, New Jersey: LEA.
10. Toms, E.G. (2000). Understanding and facilitating the browsing of electronic text. International Journal of Human Computer Studies, 52, 423-452.
11. Kintsch, W. (1994). Text comprehension, memory, and learning. American Psychologist, 49, 294-303.
12. Astleitner, H., & Leutner, D. (1995). Learning strategies for unstructured hypermedia. A framework for theory, research, and practice. Journal of Educational Computing Research, 13, 387-400.
13. Rouet, J-F. and Passerault, J-M. (1999). Analyzing learning hypermedia interaction: An overview of on line methods. Journal of Instructional Science, 27:201-219.
14. Fajardo, I., Cañas, J.J., Salmerón, L. & Abascal, J. (2003). Working Memory Architecture and its Implications for Hypertext Design: Insight from Deaf Signer Users Research. Manuscript in revision.
15. Fajardo, Cañas, Salmerón and Abascal (2004). Distancia Semántica e Interacción con Interfaces Web Gráficas. Contribution accepted for being presented in the V Congreso Interacción Persona Ordenador, 3 - 7 de mayo de 2004 Universitat de Lleida (Spain).
16. Clark, (2002). Building accesible websites. Indianapolis, Indiana: New Readers.
17. McDougall, S., Bruijn, O., & Curry, M. (1999). Measuring symbol and icon characteristics: Norms for concreteness, complexity, meaningfulness, familiarity and semantic distance for 239 symbols, Behaviour Research Methods, Instruments & Computers, Vol. 51, No. 3, pp. 487-519.
18. Foltz, P.W. (1996). Comprehension, Coherence, and Strategies in Hypertext and Linear Text. In J.F. Rouet, J.J. Levonen, A. Dillon and Spiro, R. Hypertext and Cognition. Mahwah, New Jersey: LEA. pp. 109-136.
19. Salmerón, L., Cañas, J.J. & Fajardo, I., Gea, M. (2004). Expertise and Semantic Grouping on Hypertext Information Retrieval Tasks. Manuscript submitted for publication.

The Role of the Trust Intermediary in the Information and Knowledge Society

Dino Giuli, Paolo Bussotti, Maria Chiara Pettenati, and Ioana Codoban

Electronics and Telecommunications Department, University of Florence
Via Santa Marta, 3 - 50139 Firenze, Italy
Tel. +39 55 47961, Fax: +39 55 488883
giuli@det.unifi.it
{bussotti,pettenati,codoban}@achille.det.unifi.it

Abstract. The evolution of the Internet encourages us to think that universal and pervasive access is going to be possible in the near future, from the technological point of view. However there are many other problems that we have to address before, in order to bring the Internet to the desired state of an Information and Knowledge Society for all. The incredible widening of possible users is also determining problems for personalization of services. Adaptive interfaces represent one of the solutions, but they need to backed-up by an adequate network architecture. This paper describes and analyses this conceptual architecture.

1 Introduction

In the Information and Knowledge Society ubiquitous and pervasive access to technology and its possibilities becomes a desired goal for everyday activities. Information and Communication Technology (ICT) is expected to be embedded in everyday objects, hopefully connected together within a "Global Network". At present such changes in available technologies and applications are beginning to pervade everyday life, and provoke relevant changes.

If, on one hand, network services are becoming ever more available and globally accessible, on the other hand the number of users and their heterogeneity is growing so fast that targeting them is getting an ever more difficult task to be performed.

This apparently determines a crisis in users-providers relationships as regards the actual access a person can have to the opportunities of technology. Because the same content, navigation or presentation cannot suite everybody's needs, it is hard to imagine an interface that satisfies all users and their requirements. This is why adaptable interfaces seem to be a solution in this context. However, in order to be able to provide such interfaces, structural changes of Network architecture are needed.

In [1] the authors analyze the role of the intermediaries in the Internet, naming them *infomediaries* and state that they have a key role in the network relationship, especially in the one business-to-consumer, because they make a bridge among information demand and offer, where the *information* to be valued are the consumer profiles collected by the Internet. At present there is no network actor that offer this kind of service through the Internet.

C. Stary and C. Stephanidis (Eds.): UI4All 2004, LNCS 3196, pp. 326–331, 2004.
© Springer-Verlag Berlin Heidelberg 2004

The problems underlying the introduction of infomediaries as they are called in [1] or of the *trust intermediaries*, as we prefer to name them, are those privacy-related, derived by the unbalanced relationship among the final user (the consumer or products and services) and the provider.

Information and Communication technologies must serve to the user to increase his control and mastery on his information (or integrated profile), give awareness and offer transparent choices; trust intermediaries can support users offering services to this purpose.

This paper presents a proposal of a conceptually-designed network system that is able to provide the type of interfaces needed in order to reach the point of universal access in the wider framework of instrumental and knowledge-based intermediation of network relation and interaction.

2   Dealing with Individual and Social Factors by Fiduciary Intermediation

Many studies have pointed out a series of problems located at the individual and social level regarding both the fruition of the Internet and the aspects of building relationships in the Internet environments. Currently, some of the most debated issues are privacy and security; negotiability of goals of relation and interaction and how to accomplish them; personalisation of services at an individual level; symmetry of actors from the point of view of availability, control and use of instruments and processes of relation and interaction [1] [2]. These characteristics are to be considered primary requirements of a social-cultural context that is what the Internet is expected to evolve to, the Global Network, conceived as a global and qualitative extension of the traditional environment in all its senses, a social-technical environment. But current Internet architecture poses inherent constraints. It becomes more and more evident that a new approach is needed, an approach that presupposes wider analysis and evaluation of the impact that new technology has on human subjectivity in a specified social and cultural context, not only restricted to the economical context. It is important to correctly identify the requirements corresponding to these factors, and use them to drive the Network evolution, as for applications, organisation and services. We propose a theoretical framework to guide and support future developments and evolutions in the Network environment.

As it is impossible to have one representation of the content that suites all prospective users (having in mind the fact that they are very different from each other not only in terms of age, gender, experience and knowledge of technology, but even in regards to wider aspects like language and culture), the solution of multiple representations seems at hand in a flexible medium like Internet. Until now the tendency was that providers and other enterprises using the Internet develop user representations (profiles) and use them during the interaction with clients and potential clients so as to personalise contents, navigation and presentation. But in order to build a trustful relationship there is the need of a representation of both parts involved in the relationship and the possibility to negotiate services on the basis of reciprocal knowledge. Thus a *profile* of all actors using the network has to be accomplished, as integrated in a common framework providing fiduciary intermediation and support to negotiation therefore acting proactively for the weakest part – the final user - but also providing reputational benefits for providers accepting the proposed negotiation-based approach. At present the relationships developed through Internet are not equilibrated because owners of user information (profiles) could use it for their interest, the problem of trust is nowadays felt as the fundamental requisite. A solution to this problem can be devised: the use of an *trust intermediary* between the two parts involved. Similar solutions can be found also in literature [1] [2] [3]. In this work, the proposed mediator system is indicated as the Instrumental Environment of Trust Intermediary (IETI), as its instrumental functions allow to mediate the relationships between users and between user and technology, in order to improve the process and bring user satisfaction in the wider sense.

The current marketing approach, which is centred on a certain segment of the population, is contemporarily excluding entire social layers and even nations (i.e. digital divide). As opposite, the Information and Knowledge Society is expected to provide access to everybody. This is why a new approach is needed, an approach that addresses Universal Access. In order to overcome the current shortcomings, a strong role is required from Public Administration, as a reference trust subject, for the proposed intermediation framework, the IETI. The management of the IETI also requires the presence of a technologically competent subject in order to provide and guarantee the environment itself. Therefore we may conceive the Trust Intermediary – the trust subject providing the IETI – as a collective subject, which could result from the participation of Public Administration and a private ASP (Application Service Provider).

3   Steps Towards an Information and Knowledge Society

The evolution toward an Information and Knowledge Society involves important changes, especially at the individual and community level. New spaces for interaction and relation between subjects (individuals, communities, public and private organisational contexts), ubiquitous and facilitating new ways of communication and new opportunities and modalities of knowledge transfer and sharing are created. The main changes that will affect the every-day life of individuals and communities should be considered in strict relation to the new open global social-technical system that is based on human subjectivity.

The gap in Internet usage is narrowing between man and women, old and young, but widening between rich and poor and between well and poorly educated. Less documented is the continuing separation between cultural and racial groups, and the low rates of usage by disadvantaged users whose unemployment, homelessness, poor health, or cognitive limitations raise further barriers.

Breakdown of community social systems, alienation of individuals, loss of privacy, expansion of bureaucracies and inadequate attention to potential failures are some of the subjects that necessitate further studies [4].

Prior research has shown that, having free access to technology, users encounter trouble even with the easiest-to-use computer and applications [5].

There is a continuous search for solutions regarding these issues. It is clear that supporting a broad range of hardware, software, and network [4] access is desired. As well as accommodating users with different skills, knowledge, age, gender, disabilities, disabling conditions (mobility, sunlight, noise), literacy, culture, income, and so forth. Bridging the gap between what users know and what they need to know is also one of the main objectives [4].

Some of these goals can be addressed with the help of an adaptive interface [6], that could increase usability (realisation of tasks with more efficacy), satisfaction (subjective reaction towards the interaction) and positive subjective experience (understood as the subjective mirroring of external events at an individual level).

4   The Trust Intermediary Model and Functions

One of the first functions provided by the Trust Intermediary regards the activation of a basic logical infrastructure of the network to be integrated with the physical structure to facilitate service offers and fruition. Such an organisation would bring to a macroarchitecture of the network and would increase contractual and operational power of final users.

The Trust Intermediary is entitled of realising individual and inter-individual knowledge basis composed not only from final users profiles, but also from profiles of providers and form community shared knowledge representation. The shared knowledge spaces fundamentally enable the automation of its intermediation functions and can be also used in order to support and encourage local communities, and communication between users/communities with different backgrounds and characteristics that would have encountered problems communicating otherwise. (ex. Language, cultural differences, etc.)

The main role of the Trust Intermediary is the activation of an instrumental environment located between final users and providers. This environment aims at giving the needed support for interactions and relations realised with the help of the network, from an individual and social point of view; such a development could encourage the evolution of the network towards a global social-technical system. The environment IETI is expected to be widely adopted for the fiduciary value of Trust Intermediary and it is devised to satisfy subjective and social user requisites, thus helping the widespread of technology usage in everyday life. In particular, the instrumental environment provided by the Trust Intermediary promotes the personalization of interaction and relation among individual users, communities/groups of users and service providers.

5   Scenarios for the Trust Intermediary

In the following, the characteristics of the mediator as well as its conceptually-designed network architecture is described through possible scenarios. The aim of this proposal is prospecting a solution – although still at a conceptual level - to overcome the present shortcomings and to offer a possible reference for future studies about the expected network evolution towards an Information and Knowledge Society accessible to all.

The final user, which is also a potential client, should have access to the profile of the service-provider, but this access should be focused on the information relevant to him and to the context of use. In expected new scenarios also a user should have access and be able to manage the information representing himself, limiting possible data violation, for example. The Trust Intermediary not only represents the users but can match the user profile and the service provider profile, so that a personalization of the offer takes place, and this process is determined balanced and equal.

Another activity that the Trust Intermediary can provide is the instrumental support for matching individual user requirements (i.e. intelligent discovery of well - reputed services matching user requirements both from his profile and his direct request to the intermediation system or content-based search for information). During the negotiation between a final user and a service-provider, the Trust Intermediary acts as a moderator allowing the choice of the relation and interaction modalities. The moderator guarantees to respect the privacy of users data, and helps in building a trustful relationship by offering information about the service provider necessary for constructing a "reputation".

Final users can be treated, in certain situations, as communities or groups of users. This approach could give the necessary basis for helping them in their interaction with the network and relations developed. For example, the Trust Intermediary is devised to receive and collect in knowledge bases the opinions of users about experienced services. This provides a basis for constructing a reputation on services and service providers, differently shared within groups of users nonetheless giving to the intermediation system that contractual power enabling a true negotiation process. The decision making process should be thus supported.

As a conclusion, the trust intermediary is an independent actor of the network that facilitates interactions and relations, assuring by this the enlargement of accessibility to the network.

6   Conclusion

The approach described here devises a possible solution for the evolution and development of the network through the introduction of a new network actor: the trust intermerdiary. From this point of view, the requirements of universal usability formulated by [7] could be helpful in evaluating the proposal. Although these requirements target only usability aspects, they can be generalised also to other elements of universal access interfaces.

The first requirement regards the applicability to any target and delivery context aspect. The structure described above is adaptable to any service and context of use, of course some environments are better suited in comparison with others. For example, the e-commerce field would particularly benefit from implementing the Trust Intermediary because it allows users to take advantage of the information about the other party while building the necessary relationship in order to get the desired service. Because it supports a wide knowledge base about users, communities/groups of users and service providers providing them a proper contractual power for negotiation - the personalization of contents, interaction and presentation is therefore enabled and enhanced. On the side of providers the Trust Intermediary can offer them some important targeting information – adequately anonymous – in change of their collaboration in respecting the negotiation terms regarding personalisation and other user requirements. Personalisation is another criterion of [7] satisfied by our proposal.

The Trust Intermediary is flexible and extensible. The "help" it offers to all the actors of the interaction will help its spread and acceptance. Terwin, Zimmermann and Vanderheiden in [7] recommend a simple solution to all this problems. In our opinion, when possible a simple solution is to be preferred. However, understanding individuals and society is undoubtedly an extremely complex problem, and it is our opinion that oversimplifying approaches to the Information and Knowledge Society evolution may not be very effective in dealing with the large context.

Many issues are still open research fields and our proposal must be regarded as an attempt to deal with both social and technological aspects in an interdisciplinary fashion and give some contributions, in the opinion that simplification will only follow the achieved level of understanding on human beings.

References

1. Hagel III, J. , Singer M., Net Worth, Come cambiano i mercati quando i clienti definiscono le regole. Apogeo, 2001.
2. Giuli, D. (2001). From the individual to Technology towards the Global Network, in *Proceedings of the HCI 9th International Conference*, August 5-10, 2001, New Orleans, Lousiana.
3. Trewin, S., Zimmermann, G. & Vancerheiden, G. (2003). Abstract User Interface Representations: How Well do they Support Universal Access?, *ACM CUU'03*, November 10-11, Vancouver, Canada.
4. Bussotti, P., Vannuccini, G., Calenda, D., Pirri, F., Giuli, D. (2001). Subjectivity and Cultural Conventions: the Role of the Tutoring Agent in the Global Network, in *Proceedings of the HCI International 2001*, 9th International Conference on Human-Computer Interaction, August 5-10 2001, New Orleans, Lousiana.
5. Schneiderman, B. (2000). Universal Usability, *Communications of the ACM*, May 2000, vol.43, No.5.
6. Kraut, R., Mukhopadhyay, T., Szczypula, J., Kiesler, S. & Scherlis, W. (1998). Communication and Information: Alternative Uses of Interent in Households, *CHI 98*, 18-23 April.
7. Stephanidis, C., Karagiannidis, Ch. & Koumpis, A. (1997). Decison Making in Intelligent User Interfaces, *ACM*, IUL 97, Orlando Florida USA.
8. Titkov, L., Poslad, S. & Tan, J.J. (2003). Privacy Conscious Brokering in Personalised Location-Aware Applications, *AAMAS'03*, ACM, July 14-18, Melbourne Australia.

Developing BS7000 Part 6 –
Guide to Managing Inclusive Design

Simeon Keates

IBM TJ Watson Research Center, 19 Skyline Drive, Hawthorne, NY10532, USA
lsk@us.ibm.com

Abstract. Companies are increasingly finding themselves having to ensure that their products and services are accessible and inclusive, or else be exposed to the possibility of litigation and damage to their brand reputation. However, the adoption of inclusive design within industry has been patchy at best. While there are undoubtedly companies that have yet to be persuaded of the merits of inclusive design, there is a growing number that want to design inclusively, but do not know how to set about doing so. In response to this need, a new technical guidance Standard is currently being prepared by the British Standards Institute (BSI). The new document, BS 7000-6: 2004 – Guide to managing inclusive design, will form part of the BS 7000 Design Management Systems series. The aim of this paper is to explain the rationale behind the development of the new Standard and an overview of its contents. Due to copyright restrictions, this paper does not attempt to provide a summary of the contents of the new Standard.

1 Introduction

Disability is not a simple consequence of a person's impaired capability, but results from a failure to take proper account of the needs and capabilities of all potential users when designing products and services. Internationally there is a move towards creating a more inclusive society. This move is being encouraged through a mixture of legislation, regulation, incentives and also by changing attitudes within society.

Research has shown that despite the various incentives for adopting inclusive design, many companies have not done so [6]. Prevalent among the barriers cited by those companies are the perception that inclusive design is primarily a niche activity that does not apply to them and also concerns about the knowledge and skills requirements involved [5].

In an attempt to provide guidance on the importance for companies of adopting inclusive design and also on how methods for implementing the adoption, the MS4/10 panel of the British Standards Institute approved a new addition to the BS7000 Design Management System series of technical guidance standards. To date, BS7000 consists of five parts and a glossary of design management terms. The new addition, Part 6: Guide to managing inclusive design [1] forms the sixth part of the series. At the time of writing, it is being sent out for external review by recognised experts in the fields of design, management and accessibility, prior to a final edit. The final publication date is expected before the end of 2004.

C. Stary and C. Stephanidis (Eds.): UI4All 2004, LNCS 3196, pp. 332–339, 2004.
© Springer-Verlag Berlin Heidelberg 2004

1.1 The Aims of BS7000-6

The new Standard aims to help companies not only adopt inclusive design, but to do so in a manner that actively helps their commercial prospects. In particular the five key goals of the Standard are to help companies:

1. to adapt to market changes, such as those due to population ageing, new legislation, technological change and the adoption of inclusive design by competitors;
2. to understand changing consumer expectations and lifestyles;
3. to maintain workforce loyalty, particularly in the context of a longer working life for employees, an ageing population and changing expectations with regard to retirement;
4. to realise user-centred design, through the implementation of ergonomics and human factors principles (and so guard against dissatisfaction due to lack of usability and accessibility); and,
5. to build and sustain corporate reputation in an era of social and technological change.

The emphasis in the management of inclusive design makes this new Standard unique among the many standards that address universal access issues, which typically focus on specific topics such as:

- buildings access – e.g. BS 8300:2001 - Design of buildings and their approaches to meet the needs of disabled people. Code of practice [2];
- assistive technology – e.g. ISO 9999:2002 - Technical aids for persons with disabilities - Classification and terminology [7];
- anthropometric measures – e.g. BS 4467:1997 - Guide to dimensions in designing for elderly people [3]; and even
- standards development – e.g. PD ISO/IEC Guide 71 - Guidelines for standards developers to address the needs of older persons and persons with disabilities [8].

2 The Rationale Behind BS7000-6

The new Standard takes its ideological basis from the argument that inclusive design is not simply a moral duty, but can be highly beneficial for a company if implemented correctly [4]. On the other hand, companies that do not adopt inclusive design when developing new products will find themselves at risk of punitive legal actions and also losing ground to more inclusive products and services from competitors.

Note that BS7000-6 uses the term 'product' in accordance with terminology used in Quality Management Standards (ISO 9000:2000 series), to refer to products, services, processes (including business processes), environments and interfaces.

Inclusive design is defined within BS7000-6 as:

"[The] design of mainstream products ... that are accessible to, and usable by, as many people as reasonably possible on a global basis, in a wide variety of situations and to the greatest extent possible without the need for special adaptation or specialized design." [1]

This definition recognises that it is not always possible or economically viable to design one product for all. Thus the rationale adopted by the document is that of countering design exclusion [9]. This rationale advocates the systematic identification of the capability demands placed upon a user by a product or service. Where those demands exceed the capabilities of the target users, then the feature responsible for the demands should be re-designed, wherever possible, to remove the cause of the exclusion.

For example, consider a newspaper that is printed using a very small font. A proportion of the potential readership will be unable to read the newspaper because the vision capability demanded of them by the small font is greater than they posses. In other words, their eyesight is simply not good enough to read such a small font. So the choice of font size has excluded them. The solution is therefore straightforward – to increase the font size. Doing so would remove the source of exclusion and include many more users. The newspaper will have become more inclusive.

However, if the font size is continually increased, then the newspaper will eventually become bigger and bulkier, thus making it more expensive to produce (more paper needed) and also potentially more exclusionary as the readers require greater dexterity skills to manipulate the larger and more numerous pages. This leads to the inclusion of the caveat "as reasonably possible" in the definition used in BS7000-6.

Companies are encouraged to consider solutions across the entire brand and not just on a product-by-product basis. For example, companies could try to develop all of their products to be as inclusive as possible (along the lines of one product for all). Alternatively, they could consider adding more inclusive products to their existing ranges, design add-ons to improvement the accessibility of their current products or develop completely new ranges of products.

3   The Structure of BS7000-6

Following the approaches taken with the other five parts of BS7000, Part 6 recognises that there are three distinct levels of hierarchy within companies and that each has a different role to play in the adoption of inclusive design.

3.1 Organisational Level

At the top of the organisational tree are the 'Principals', here defined as owner-managers, partners, board directors and other top executives in private sector, as well as executive officers in public sector and not-for-profit organizations.

The Standard places the ultimate responsibility for the adoption of inclusive design squarely on the principals of the company. They are obligated to ensure that an appropriate culture of inclusivity is adopted throughout the company.

Specific activities for the company senior management are divided into four main groupings:

1. Explore potential / assess demands and commitment / finalise proposition
2. Establish foundation / get into gear

3. Implement changes / determine impact
4. Consolidate expertise and benefits / Refine approach

Each of these activity groupings have explicit supporting activities associated with them. For example, the first grouping, "Explore potential, etc." has the can be broken down into:

- Acknowledge and assign inclusive design responsibilities
- Research opportunities, key issues; augment knowledge and seek guidance on inclusive design
- Undertake audit of what is and what could be regarding inclusive design
- Finalise and communicate business case for change

Similarly, "Establish foundation, etc." comprises:

- Craft mission statement relating to inclusive design
- Formulate inclusive design philosophy, objectives and strategies
- Plan corporate campaign to introduce new orientation to inclusive design
- Communicate essence of philosophy, objectives and change programme
- Promote nurturing culture for inclusive design

The third grouping, "Implement changes / determine impact" consists of:

- Introduce infrastructure to manage inclusive design
- Draw up master programme of inclusive design work
- Bring together and develop inclusive design expertise
- Implement programme and support new orientation to inclusive design
- Evaluate progress and contribution of programme

Finally, "Consolidate expertise, etc." entails:

- Build distinctive competencies and competitive advantage through inclusive design
- Document, share, publicise and celebrate inclusive design achievements
- Enhance corporate reputation through inclusive design
- Review and refine inclusive design approach

3.2 Project Management Level

Below the principals, but above the designers involved in the day-to-day design process are the middle level executives who typically commission and administer the product development projects. The Standard aims to provide them with the material to establish more inclusive briefs and also provide mechanisms for reviewing the progress of the product inclusivity and keeping the design teams focused and motivated.

4 The Design Process

The BS7000 design process, common across each to the six parts, is split into five phases, each with between one and four component stages, as shown in Table 1.

Table 1. The BS7000 design process.

PRE-PROJECT PHASE	Define problem and plan project
	• Stage 1: First awareness and understanding of opportunity
	• Stage 2: Feasibility / Clarify opportunity and prepare context
PROJECT PHASE	Design and development
	• Stage 3: Design origination – Identify/generate options to solve set problems
	• Stage 4: Design origination – Develop preferred solution(s)
	• Stage 5: Design development – Detail design
	• Stage 6: Design implementation – Realise complete product for delivery
PROJECT PHASE	Deliver to market and support
	• Stage 7: Launch product
	• Stage 8: Sustain product in market through periodic augmentation, improvements and updates
PROJECT PHASE	Extract maximum value from market
	• Stage 9: Create range / develop integrated system of products to extend market reach
	• Stage 10: Withdraw product/service from market(s)
POST-PROJECT PHASE	Build effectively on whole experience
	• Stage 11: 'Lifetime' review of project and product experience

An important feature of this approach is the enforced use of strict gateways at the end of each stage. The gateways are effectively review stages with a number of potential outcomes, ranging from approval to proceed to the next stage through to referring back to an earlier stage for re-working or even stopping the project completely.

The decision whether to proceed or not is based on a review of the work in that stage, and earlier stages where appropriate, confirmation that the inclusivity properties have not been compromised and that the business context is still intact.

4.1 Putting Inclusive Design into the Design Process

So far the design process described is generic and could be applied to all product development. To help companies implement inclusive design, the Standard deconstructs each of the stages into distinct components. These are shown in Table 2 which shows the breakdown of Stage 1.

5 Summary

The development of BS7000-6 represents a first UK attempt at standardising an approach not only to the adoption of inclusive design by companies, but also to the recognition that management has a key role to play in ensuring that inclusive design becomes the norm rather than the exception [4].

Central to the approach advocated by the new Standard is the concept that inclusive design is not simply a bolt-on activity that is the responsibility of the designers.

Instead, it needs to become a corporate ethos, with a company-wide culture of the promotion of inclusive design practice.

Table 2. An illustration of the component breakdown of Stage 1.

STAGE NAME	STAGE 1 - FIRST AWARENESS / TRIGGER(S)
	• Preliminary groundwork to understand problems, needs issues and context
OVERVIEW (the purpose of the stage)	• Getting to grips with the opportunity presented • Gaining greater understanding of target customers, users and other stakeholders, their needs and aspirations
GENERIC TASKS (the tasks relevant to any design activity at this stage)	• First stab at defining problem(s) to be addressed • Distil critical aims, priority targets and distinctive factors presented by opportunity • Build preliminary vision of experienced reality of implemented solution (when problems are solved) • Formulate outline brief ('design the problem') • Formulate preliminary business case
INCLUSIVE DESIGN TASKS (additions to the generic tasks to facilitate inclusive design)	• Undertake background research • Collate comprehensive information on 'inclusive design dimension' of problem (identified research, user tests, case studies, data, etc.) • Determine legislation, regulations and standards to comply with • Identify, hold exploratory discussions with, and recommend appointment of inclusive design specialists and 'expert' users • Identify and estimate excluded markets, as well as resource requirements of a more inclusive approach • Re-define new market priorities and opportunities, then develop clearer profiles of target users • Check against company's inclusive design mission, objectives and master programme • Assess project life-span and start date
TOOLS AND TECHNIQUES (specific tools and techniques that could be applied to generate an inclusive design)	• Market surveys, product range reviews, competitor analyses, user observations, focus groups, risk-opportunity analyses and brainstorming
KEY OUTPUTS (what the stage should generate)	• Body of knowledge / reference material on market • Preliminary grasp of problem to be addressed
STAGE GATEWAY (the decision process for deciding whether to proceed or not)	• Authorisation of further groundwork leading to the formulation of a comprehensive project proposal with the allocation of appropriate resources

This is achieved as much top-down through the company hierarchy as it is bottom-up. Companies adhering to the Standard are encouraged to take steps such as developing corporate inclusive design mission statements and appointing a principal as the inclusive design champion.

The Standard also promotes keeping written records of all decisions made that affect the final inclusivity of the product. The aim is to develop a paper trail so that in the case that a company is subject to litigation, documentary evidence of the rationales behind the decisions is easy to obtain. The presence of the paper trail also encourages companies to ensure that users are only excluded where there is a real, substantive and justifiable reason that they could defend in court, otherwise their own paper trail could condemn them as easily as it could exonerate them. It is in their interests to be as inclusive as possible.

As discussed earlier, at the time of writing the latest draft is about to be sent out for review, before final amendments are made. The deadline for feedback is April, 2004. This will then be followed by a process of finalising the text for submission to MS4/10 in September, 2004. It is anticipated that the final version of the Standard will be published in December, 2004.

Once the Standard has been published, it is intended to perform follow-up research to examine the impact that the Standard has when companies adopt it. This will involve 'before and after' comparisons of product developed without the Standard (most likely an existing model) and one developed using the new recommendations.

The follow-up activities will also examine the paper trails generated to identify which inclusive design features found favour with the management, and which did not. This information could then be used to build more compelling business case arguments to use with companies that have not adopted inclusive design.

Acknowledgements

The development of the draft Standard was undertaken by a sub-committee of the MS4/10 panel, including representatives from user groups, academia and industry. Particularly active and instrumental in the development of the draft were Alan Topalian of ALTO Design Management and Roger Coleman of the Royal College of Art.

References

1. BSI (2004) BS7000 Part 6: Design Management Systems – Guide to managing inclusive design (latest draft). British Standards Institute, London, UK
2. BSI (2001) BS 8300 Design of buildings and their approaches to meet the needs of disabled people. Code of practice. British Standards Institute, London, UK
3. BSI (1997) BS 4467 - Guide to dimensions in designing for elderly people. British Standards Institute, London, UK
4. Coleman, R. (2001) Living longer: the new context for design. The Design Council, London, UK.

5. Dong, H., Keates, S., Clarkson, P.J. and Cassim, J. (2002) Implementing inclusive design: the discrepancy between theory and practice. In Proceedings of the 7th ERCIM Workshop "User interfaces for all". Special Theme: "Universal Access", Paris (Chantilly), France, 173-185

6. DTI (2000) A study on the difficulties disabled people have when using everyday consumer products, Government Consumer Safety Research Department of Trade and Industry, London, UK.

7. ISO(2002) ISO 9999 : Technical aids for persons with disabilities - Classification and terminology. International Organization for Standardisation (ISO), Geneva, Switzerland.

8. ISO/IEC (2001) PD ISO/IEC Guide 71 - Guidelines for standards developers to address the needs of older persons and persons with disabilities. International Organization for Standardisation (ISO), Geneva, Switzerland.

9. Keates, S. and Clarkson, P.J. (2003) Countering design exclusion: An introduction to inclusive design. Springer-Verlag, London, UK

Investigating the Inclusivity
of Digital Television Set-Top Boxes

Simeon Keates

IBM TJ Watson Research Center, 19 Skyline Drive, Hawthorne, NY 10532, USA
lsk@us.ibm.com

Abstract. The aim of this study was to investigate the accessibility of digital television (DTV) technology available in the UK, focusing on the current generation of set-top boxes (STBs) which provide 'free to view' services. Specifically, the objective of the study was to identify specific causes of concern with regard to user interaction with DTV that might lead to exclusion, i.e. situations where users may be unable to use the new technology. In particular interest was the identification of new challenges presented to users by DTV that are not found when using the current analogue equivalent. The number of STBs is increasing rapidly. Hence, for the purposes of this study, efforts were focused on looking at three set-top boxes (STB1, 2 and 3). STB1 was selected because it was being marketed as 'easy to use'; STB2 because it was the market leader at the time; and STB3 was a satellite-based television service.

1 Introduction

The objective of this study was to identify specific causes of potential user exclusion with regard to current DTV services. The STB, satellite or cable box and its remote form only a part of a larger system, which also includes the TV and service provider.

In assessing DTV it is important to understand the contribution of each of the elements to the potential for exclusion. The system must therefore be tested as a whole and in a way that represents 'normal' use. It is also important to remember that 'use' starts with the purchasing and commissioning of the system. As a result, a number of use scenarios were used to investigate the accessibility of DTV focusing on the purchasing, installation and use of STBs. These included:

Scenario 1	System selection – deciding which STB to buy
Scenario 2	System set-up requirements – e.g. which aerial to buy?
Scenario 3	Installation instructions – how easy to read and understand
Scenario 4	System installation – e.g. how easy to plug in the cables?
Scenario 5	System tuning – how easy to understand and to physically perform
Scenario 6	Setting 'favourites' – programming the STB
Scenario 7	Channel selection (on/off) – changing channels
Scenario 8	Subtitles – switching subtitles (closed captioning) on and off
Scenario 9	Teletext operation (on/surf/off)
Scenario 10	Interactive operation (on/surf/off)

C. Stary and C. Stephanidis (Eds.): UI4All 2004, LNCS 3196, pp. 340–359, 2004.

The investigation focused on identifying the broad steps involved in the interaction between the user and the STBs. The aim was to identify the potential causes of exclusion that may prevent users from interacting with the STBs effectively. Typical approaches to such accessibility studies include expert assessment (using systematic analyses), simulation, user observations and user trials [9, 11].

It was decided that the best approach for this study was to use a combination of methods to ensure adequate identification of potential sources of difficulty. There was also a need for both quantitative and qualitative investigation, where generally the latter is necessary before attempting the former.

It was appropriate to use a human-computer interaction (HCI) type model as a basis for assessment as this allows a focus on the key elements of user interaction. For example, the Model Human Processor approach identifies perception, cognition and motor functions as the building blocks for any interaction [1]. These may be further decomposed into basic elements:

- Perception (sensory) – vision and hearing;
- Cognition – communication and intellectual functioning;
- Motion – locomotion, reach and stretch, and dexterity.

The advantage of this approach was that it also facilitated quantitative and qualitative investigation. The basic elements of interaction could be observed and data would become available for the identification of the prevalence of such characteristics in the general population. Three key techniques were identified as core to the assessment of DTV:

1. Expert assessment – the analysis of the accessibility of DTV systems by researchers with experience of other such assessments;
2. Exclusion analysis – the estimation of the levels of exclusion when using DTV;
3. User observations – the observation of individual users undertaking a range of specified tasks using DTV.

The use of these three methods of assessment maximised the chances of identifying the principal areas of difficulty when interacting with an STB and, where possible, of providing estimates of the levels of exclusion to be expected. The purpose here was not to ensure complete coverage of all scenarios by each method of assessment, rather to assess those scenarios most suited to the methods of assessment. For example, whilst 'channel selection' was evaluated using each approach, 'setting favourites' was found to be too difficult for the participants in the user observation sessions.

Wherever appropriate, comparative assessments with analogue televisions were performed, to provide a baseline comparison for the levels of exclusion associated with the STBs. The assertion made was that any additional exclusion over and above that of the analogue televisions represented existing users who would be disadvantaged, and perhaps denied access to the new digital television services, by the design of the DTV systems.

Note: the assessments were performed over the period April to June, 2003, and thus all comments expressed within this paper are derived from the services available during that time period. With the continually evolving nature of DTV, some of the interaction details will have changed by the time that this paper is published.

2 Expert Assessment

The accessibility of DTV systems was analysed by researchers with experience of other such assessments. The purpose was to provide an indication of where users may have difficulty interacting with a typical DTV system. The qualitative assessment involved a simulation of the activities involved in installing and operating the STBs. Purchasing the STBs was not simulated in detail, however, supporting purchases, such as a new aerial, were included.

Four users participated in mock user observation sessions. Two were experienced usability practitioners with extensive DTV knowledge and the other two were experienced usability engineers, but digital television novices.

2.1 Results from Expert Assessment

In terms of summarising what was learnt, the following summary points provide a list of key challenges encountered when assessing the three DTV systems. Particular attention has been given to identifying general problems that will limit accessibility to DTV, rather than problems specific to an individual system. Following analysis of the expert assessment, a list of points of comment or concern was prepared:

Installation and Set-Up

1. Set-up requirements – retailers appear to have inadequate knowledge of installation requirements (signal coverage/strength, need for aerial etc.) and the necessary additional equipment is not always available at the point of purchase of the STB. There is also then an additional cost required to complete installation. This is not a problem for equipment which is 'installed' for the user as part of the purchased package (e.g. with STB3).
2. Set-up instructions – these are critically important for the users who attempt to self-install their STB. The instructions need to be clear and up to date (e.g. not referring to an earlier model of remote control as was the case with STB2). Graphical instructions, if done well, can be particularly helpful if they identify buttons on the remote control and elements on the display that the user has to interact with. A complementary combination of graphical and written instructions minimises the potential for exclusion.
3. Tuning – the initiation of the tuning of the STB must be straightforward, both in terms of when it must be done and how it must be done. Clear instructions must be provided on both these points.
4. Battery replacement – remote controls use batteries, therefore it is important that access to the battery compartment is straightforward without compromising the safety of small children. The need to reactivate the remote after replacing batteries should also be avoided since this is unnecessary and uncommon practice.

Operation

5. Operating modes – there is potential for confusion regarding STB and TV modes and the buttons required to switch between them. Simpler operation and clearer instructions are required.

6. Volume controls – the presence of direct TV volume controls on the remote control is ambiguous. On only one of the remotes used did this feature actually work. In practice, this would be a very useful feature, allowing channel selection and volume adjustment from the same remote control.

7. Response times – the delay between pressing buttons on the remote and seeing a response on the TV screen is unacceptably long and is likely to lead to much confusion. Unless the user is familiar with the system and has the confidence that it will respond, many actions are interrupted by the user because no feedback has been provided that the user request has been received. Good practice is to ensure that the user is provided with direct and immediate feedback in response to an action (e.g. by using an hour-glass symbol).

8. On-screen menus – the use of on-screen menus must be done in such a way as to be intuitive for inexperienced users. The selection of highlighted options provides a particular cause of confusion since it is not immediately clear if the default selected item (usually at the top of the list) is a heading or a member of the list of options. This is particularly ambiguous for novice users and those unfamiliar with menu-driven systems.

9. Subtitles – the accessibility of subtitles is important. Expecting users to navigate multiple menu layers with ambiguous names (e.g. 'language') is not acceptable. A single button press is better.

Remote Controls

10. Nomenclature – there is a lack of consistency in the use of nomenclature by the various providers of digital television. This, coupled to the use of different on-screen navigation paradigms, leads to unnecessary confusion. Some menu systems require navigation using cursor keys and a SELECT/OK button, others rely on selection by number. The latter is preferable for those without experience of menu-driven systems.

11. Labelling – appropriate fonts of appropriate sizes in appropriate colours should be used for labelling on the remote control. There is much guidance available in this area from a number of sources, e.g. the Royal National Institute for the Blind.

12. Layout – care needs to be taken that commonly used keys on the remote are not so close together as to invite the user to inadvertently select the wrong function. In addition, the legends used need to be informative to those without general experience of such devices. Confusion can arise between cursor control keys that are often unmarked and the keys used for programme selection that are often marked with 'up' and 'down' arrows.

13. Sourcing – the use of 'off-the-shelf' remotes can provide buttons that are not used and layouts that are not suited to the system they should control. A remote designed in conjunction with the system it controls is likely to be better suited to the task.

3 Exclusion Analysis

Unlike the qualitative assessment, which focused on expert opinions and user observations to identify possible sources of difficulty when interacting with the STBs, the quantitative assessment focused on evaluating the number of people who are likely to experience those difficulties.

3.1 Introduction to the Analysis Process

The first step in examining any interaction is to expand the use scenario into its component steps to enable a systematic assessment to be performed. As with all studies of this type, there are many possible interaction paths, so assumptions have to be made about the context of the use. For example, it was assumed for this study that the STB was to be used in conjunction with a TV and a video recorder (VCR) that were already mounted on some kind of storage/display cabinet.

In general, it is helpful to split the interaction into high-, medium- and low-level activities. Each of these can be assessed individually to build up an overall picture of the interaction process. The demands made by the product on the user for each interaction step are estimated. The number of people unable to meet such demands is then evaluated, where the demands are expressed in terms of the user capability required to interact with the product. The total number of people excluded from the interaction can be estimated by taking the maximum demands made by the product during the complete interaction.

Note that in this paper, the focus is primarily on the user capabilities demanded by the product for successful interaction. In other words, the user must have this level of capability to accomplish that task. Reduced levels of capability can arise from many causes. These include congenital medical conditions such as Cerebral Palsy, acquired medical conditions such as strokes and Parkinson's Disease, trauma (accidents) and the process of ageing. No attempt is made to distinguish between any of these causes, as it is the effects of the symptoms, i.e. the reduced capabilities of the user, that are of principal importance when interacting with the STBs.

The levels of exclusion are calculated from the 1997 Disability Follow-up Survey [5] to the 1996/7 Family Resources Survey [10] available from the UK Office of National Statistics (ONS). Table 1 summarises the number of adults in Great Britain with a loss of capability, as defined by the ONS.

Each of the motion, sensory and cognitive scales represents the total level of exclusion from the relevant capability scales used in the ONS data set [8]. The scales are comprised as follows:

- Motion: consists of Locomotion, Reach & Stretch, Dexterity
- Sensory: consists of Vision, Hearing
- Cognitive: consists of Intellectual Functioning, Communication

The levels of exclusion have been calculated by identifying the bottlenecks in the interaction associated with each of the ONS scales (Locomotion, Reach & Stretch, etc.). These levels of exclusion are summed to produce a total level of exclusion for each of the motion, sensory and cognitive scales, after correcting for multiple counting (because some people will have multiple capability losses).

Table 1. Estimate of number of people in Great Britain with some loss of capability.

Age	Motion		Sensory		Cognitive		Total	
bands	,000s	%	000s	%	000s	%	000s	%
16-49	1484	5.4	617	2.3	862	3.2	1975	7.2
50-64	1940	20.9	968	10.4	752	8.1	2234	24.0
65-74	1317	27.0	792	16.2	393	8.0	1475	30.2
75+	1970	47.2	1603	38.4	615	14.7	2442	58.5
16+	6710	14.7	3979	8.7	2622	5.7	8126	17.8

3.2 Interpreting the Results

It is important to note that the levels of exclusion calculated for each of the use scenarios are based solely on users with functional impairments. It does not include users with learning difficulties, as they are not typically classified as disabled under the ONS definitions.

As such, the estimated levels of exclusion for this study can be considered to be significantly conservative since the ONS data is based on self-reporting (which is most often conservative) and represents only those living in private homes and with functional impairments. It does not include users who may be excluded through simple lack of experience or familiarity with the interaction paradigms, or the technical knowledge to differentiate one cable from another, for example.

It is obviously difficult to provide accurate estimates of how the exclusion will increase beyond the members of the population included in the ONS database. However, the best estimate is that the exclusion associated with the cognitive demand may need to be scaled up by perhaps as much as an order of magnitude.

One of the principal causes for this increase in exclusion associated with the cognitive demand is that the user is unlikely to have a clear mental model of how to interact with the STB.

For example, as noted in the qualitative analyses, there are inconsistencies between the on-screen display (OSD) and the remote controls. There appears to be a merging of both web-browsing and traditional analogue television interaction paradigms, and it is not always clear which one is being used at any particular point in the interaction. What is needed is a clear 'cause and effect' relationship that ideally matches the user's preconceptions of what the STB should be doing.

3.3 The Levels of Exclusion

For brevity the full systematic breakdowns of the interactions are not provided, as these would be very lengthy per task. A summary of the exclusion analysis results is given in Figure 1a for all users over 16 years of age. The black column represents the base reference of all those people with some form of functional impairment and, for comparison between analogue and DTV, the cross-hatched column shows the level of exclusion expected for channel-hopping by an expert user with an analogue TV. Figure 1b shows a similar graph for those over 75. Note the different scales at the right hand edge of the graphs, the absolute level of exclusion for those over 75 is less than a third of the level of those over 16. However, the percentage exclusion for those over 75 is more than three times higher than for those over 16. Hence, although the absolute numbers for those over 75 are lower than for those over 16, the relative numbers (proportions) are higher.

Each of the scenarios begins to highlight the many possible sources of difficulty with interaction that users of all capabilities and experience levels may encounter. Of course, users with functional impairments or reduced capabilities are almost certain to experience either increased frequency or increased severity of difficulty than their able-bodied counterparts.

In terms of summarising what has been learned, the following provides a list of key observations made when analysing the three DTV systems. First, it is interesting to note which of the users' capabilities have most impact on user interaction:

- **Locomotion** – only an issue during purchasing, installation and 're-tuning' if this required access to a button on the STB;
- **Reach and stretch** – only an issue during purchasing, installation and 're-tuning' if this required access to a button on the STB;
- **Dexterity** – an issue at almost all stages – exclusion greatly influenced by small changes to size and layout of the remote control;
- **Seeing** – an issue at all stages, including when having to look for buttons, having to read on-screen text and shifting focus between the screen and the remote control – exclusion greatly influenced by small changes to labelling, size and layout of the remote control;
- **Hearing** – primarily an issue during purchasing and installation of the STB;
- **Communication** – primarily an issue during purchasing of the STB, and also whenever seeking help, such as from a call centre;
- **Intellectual functioning** – exclusion greatly influenced by the experience of the user and the complexity of the interaction.

Note that the sources of difficulty for each capability are for first-order effects only. In other words, they relate to those stages of interaction that are dependent upon those capabilities. However, it must be borne in mind that many users with any of these individual capability losses may also have associated second-order difficulties. For example, the exclusion predicted for 'intellectual functioning' is restricted to the capabilities measured by the ONS and does not account for the experience of the user.

The differences shown in Figure 1 for the 'novice' and 'expert' relate only to those users recorded by the ONS as having some disability. The effect of different levels of experience in the able-bodied population will be much greater. Another example is that while loss of hearing does not appear to be a major concern for most of the scenarios considered, many people with hearing loss from birth also have an associated increase in difficulty with communication.

The exclusion analysis performed was therefore conservative in terms of the estimates generated.

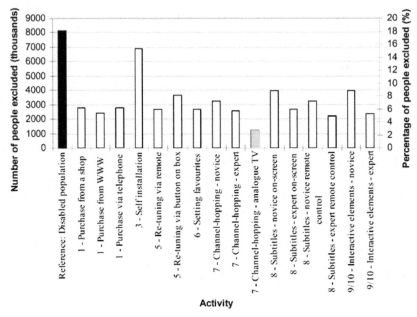

Fig. 1a. The levels of exclusion in the 16+ GB population.

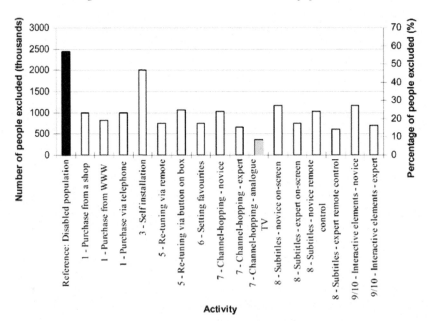

Fig. 1b. The levels of exclusion in the 75+ GB population.

With regard to the specific scenarios investigated, the following may be observed:

- **Purchasing** – users may not be physically excluded any more than for other similar products, however, they are unlikely to be fully 'informed' purchasers;
- **Installation** – results in the highest levels of exclusion with nearly 15% of all users predicted to be excluded (nearly 50% over 75) – the ability to purchase an 'installed' system is attractive;
- **Set-up/tuning** – is easier to do via a remote control when the on-screen instructions are clear and the process is straightforward;
- **Channel selection** – using an on-screen electronic programme guide (EPG) can add a considerable load to novice users, here experience makes a difference; a traditional search may be easier;
- **Interactive TV** – adds a significant cognitive load and can add to the sensory load even for the expert users – a greater need for understanding of the underlying interaction paradigm and a need to use more buttons contributes to this load.

In comparing the different STBs it is clear that small changes can have a large impact on the levels of exclusion predicted. Larger, better-spaced buttons reduce the load on the user's dexterity; fonts and colours affect the load on seeing; and the interaction design greatly affects cognitive load. The STB3 remote control, specifically designed for purpose, excluded fewer users than the other two devices.

4   User Observations

To verify the results of the earlier assessments, a series of user observation sessions were conducted. User observations are an invaluable tool when assessing both the usability and accessibility of a product.

4.1   User Selection

A total of thirteen users were recruited and the observation took place over a period of six days in two locations. These were the offices of Scientific Generics in Harston (just outside Cambridge) and the Hester Adrian Centre in Cambridge – a day-care centre for both older adults and younger adults with severe functional impairments.

The users were identified based on a number of criteria, primarily focused around whether they were strong candidates for being edge-cases in terms of their ability to interact with STBs. Based on the results of the earlier assessments, it was decided to focus on recruiting older adults not living in residential care. More extreme users could have been selected for the user group, however, the level of information that can be obtained is then limited.

Older adults typically exhibit a range of different kinds of capability loss and are more likely to show multiple minor impairments. This is important because most assistive technology is predominantly aimed at single major impairments and thus users with multiple minor impairments are less likely to be able to find assistive technology to aid them should they encounter severe difficulty interacting with a product.

Older adults as a whole are also more numerous than younger disabled ones [8, 3]. Thus if it was shown that older users generally experienced difficulty interacting with the STBs, irrespective of their capability losses, then this equates to a much higher level of exclusion within the general population.

The decision to select users still living in private homes, rather than residential care was based on the desire to have users who still have enough functional capability to support independent living to some degree [2]. They should therefore be able to perform tasks such as operating a television on their own. If they experienced significant difficulty, then it could be argued that the STBs are causing undue exclusion. As a comparison, a younger user with a more severe impairment was also recruited to highlight whether a more extreme user would also encounter the difficulties experienced by the older adults.

During the recruitment process efforts were made to ensure that the users exhibited a range of capabilities. For example, it was known that those with arthritis would exhibit a loss of dexterity, that many older users would exhibit macular degeneration or loss of hearing, and that it would be very likely that a range of intellectual functioning capability would be observed. Care was taken not to skew the sample towards any particular capability loss, rather to provide a balanced representation of motion, sensory and cognitive losses.

User 1 was a retired academic. He had limited locomotion capability, and walked with frequent, short steps, using a walking stick for support. This user also had a slight, but constant tremor in his hands, making activities involving hand-eye co-ordination difficult. He also wore spectacles and a hearing aid on one ear.

User 2 was a retired civil servant. She self-reported only a mild hearing impairment, but had difficulty following many of the instructions during the course of the observation session. She also exhibited a tendency to forget things and occasionally lost track during conversations. Otherwise she exhibited no signs of capability loss, beyond being slightly slower in her physical movements than would be expected for a younger person.

User 3 had a range of minor impairments, covering all of the motion, sensory and cognitive capabilities. This user led an active life, including cooking lunch for other members of her day-care group. She appeared to be nervous around high-technology. She had tried to learn to use a computer in the past, but gave up on it because, in her own words, her "memory isn't very good."

User 4 was a retired nurse and a wheelchair user. Her only other noticeable impairment was a need to wear reading glasses to read small print. She regarded many high-technology products with disdain, proudly declaring her house to be "a computer-free zone."

User 5 was a retired member of the clergy, who exhibited a strong affinity for high-technology products. This user exhibited mild capability loss in all three categories, i.e. sensory, motion and cognitive. As with many of the other users, there was no apparent medical cause for these losses and so were attributed to the ageing process.

User 6 was a retired deputy-head teacher, who only exhibited a mild loss of cognitive capability. She also displayed a fear of high-technology products, often relying on her husband or children to operate the STB that she had at home.

User 7 was also a retired deputy-head teacher, who was a self-professed fan of high-technology products. He did not appear to exhibit any capability loss, beyond a mild hearing impairment.

User 8, despite being a computer manager during his working life, did not consider himself to be very adept with high-technology products. However, he showed himself to be willing to try and learn new things, even though he did not rate his chances of success as terribly high. He exhibited no obvious capability loss.

User 9 was a wheelchair user who exhibited moderate to severe loss of motion capability, including the inability to use one hand through arthritis. This user needed to use distance glasses to read on-screen text, but reading glasses to read button legends on the remote control. Thus, she had to keep changing between two remote controls and two pairs of glasses, while having the use of only one hand. Although she did not self-report any, she appeared to exhibit a degree of loss of cognitive capability as well and had difficulty understanding sections of the user observation sessions.

User 10 had no discernible impairment beyond having an artificial eye, although she had a number of severe illnesses in the year or so before participating in these user observation sessions. She was very dismissive of high-technology and frequently repeated that she was too old to be learning new things and that she probably "would not be around" when analogue television was switched off.

User 11 exhibited a range of mild sensory and moderate motion capability losses. However, she was a very active individual and along with user 3, frequently prepared lunch for the other members of the day-care group.

User 12 was a wheelchair user with moderate cognitive and mild vision capability loss. However, on the day of the user observation session, she forgot to bring her distance glasses, and so had to use her reading glasses throughout. This resulted in difficulty read the on-screen text, and so all such text had to be read aloud to her.

User 13 was the youngest participant in the trials by approximately 35 years. He exhibited the most severe sensory loss, being registered as having a severe and permanent loss of sight, and being eligible for legal classification as blind. His particular visual condition was congenital, and primarily involved loss of central field of view. Otherwise he was fully able. He was also a PhD student in Computer Science and thus had a strong affinity for high-technology products.

It is worth noting that a range of user capabilities was observed. Two users showed no obvious impairment on the ONS data scales, four showed single impairments and the remaining seven exhibited multiple impairments. Three of the users reported a loss of dexterity at levels likely to cause difficulties using DTV. Five of the users reported a loss of intellectual functioning, where three were at levels that might also be likely to cause difficulties.

Table 2 summarises the users selected to participate in the user observation sessions. To maintain consistency with the earlier STB assessments the users were asked to self-report their own assessments of their capabilities, from which their scale points were deduced. This is the same approach as the ONS adopted in the collection of the data used in the exclusion analyses. However research has shown that older adults find it difficult to assess their own levels of capability [6]. A number of PC-literate and DTV users were recruited to investigate the effect of prior experience of DTV and PC-based menu systems on the use of otherwise unfamiliar STBs.

Table 2. The user observation participants.

User	Age	Gender	DTV owner?	No. of hours TV watched per day	PC user?
1	85	Male	No	<1	Yes
2	82	Female	No	1 to 2	No
3	65-69	Female	No	2 to 4	No
4	80-84	Female	No – analogue cable	>4	No
5	69	Male	Yes – STB	1 to 2	Yes
6	62	Female	Yes – STB	1 to 2	Yes
7	65-69	Male	Yes – satellite	>4	Yes
8	65-69	Male	Yes – integrated DTV (iDTV)	1 to 2	Yes
9	60	Female	No – analogue cable	2 to 4+	Yes
10	70-74	Female	No	2 to 4	No
11	70-74	Female	No	>4	No
12	70-74	Female	No	>4	No
13	24	Male	No	<1	Yes

4.2 Methodology

The user observation sessions were organised to be a subset of the usage scenarios used in the earlier assessments. Each user session was limited to 2 hours to ensure that user fatigue was kept to a minimum. Thus the user activities were restricted to those operations that could be considered fundamental to watching television, such as the ability to change channels, and also to those advanced features that could be explored within the available timeframe. 2 STBs were assessed (STB1 and STB2). The STBs selected for the trial reflected different design approaches, with one focused on ease-of-use and the other on functionality.

Initially the users were interviewed for 30 minutes to find out their capability profiles and also background information on their attitudes towards television use and exposure to DTV. Two or three observers attended each interview, each recording the user responses. Following the interview, the users began an equipment trial. This began with a familiarisation exercise with the analogue television set being used. All users used the same television and remote control. The users were asked to perform basic operations, such as changing channel and volume. They were also asked to use teletext services and to call up subtitles.

The users were then asked to choose which of the two STBs being assessed they would prefer to buy. This involved showing them the external packaging and then the STBs themselves. Again, the same STBs were used for all of the observation sessions [Scenario 1 – Purchasing]. The next stage was to provide the users with the installation instructions for their chosen STB and to ask whether they would install the box themselves. Those users who felt up to doing so were encouraged to connect up the

STB to the television. For those users who declined to do so, the STB was connected for them [Scenario 2 – Installation]. This was followed by simple television operations such as changing channels and channel-hopping. Users were encouraged to use the on-screen electronic programme guide (EPG) for one of the channel hops [Scenario 5 – Finding out what's on and selecting]. The more advanced interaction activities included finding weather and television programme guide information from both Teletext and BBCi (the BBC's new interactive digital service) [Scenario 7 – Interactive elements], as well as calling up subtitles [Scenario 6 – Using subtitles/altering settings].

The equipment trial took an average of one hour to complete. Finally, a closing debrief session was held, that lasted approximately 15 minutes. During this session, the users were asked what they thought of their experience with the STBs. Table 3 provides a summary of the incidence of difficulties experienced by the users. The following text reiterates these numbers and provides further explanation as to the likely cause of the difficulties. In many cases there are a number of reasons why problems arie, sometimes more than one for any particular user.

Table 3. The distribution of causes of difficulty.

	Activity	No. of users having difficulty	Types of problems encountered			No. of unique problems
			Motion	Sensory	Cognitive	
Analogue TV	Switching on	8	1	-	1	2
	Changing to a specified channel	1	1	-	-	1
	Channel-hopping	-	-	-	-	-
	Changing volume	-	-	-	-	-
	Using teletext	6	1	3	3	7
	Using subtitles	-	-	-	-	-
Digital TV STB	Connecting up the STBs	4 (out of 6)	1	-	1	2
	Switching on the television	1	1	-	-	1
	Switching on STB	6	-	1	2	3
	Changing DTV channels	3	-	1	2	3
	Changing volume	7	-	-	1	1
	Changing to a high channel number	10	2	2	2	6
	Changing channel via the EPG	13	3	4	6	13
	Teletext	13	2	4	12	18
	Subtitles – button (STB1)	6	-	1	1	2
	Subtitles – menu (STB2)	13	-	1	4	5
	BBCi	13	2	6	6	9
	Switching off	5	-	-	2	2

4.3 Results from User Observations

The difficulties recorded during the user observation sessions correspond closely to those predicted during the earlier assessments. The most notable additions identified through the user sessions were problems such as:

- time-outs (using the EPG and channel-hopping) – *dexterity;*
- arrow button overshooting (e.g. on menus) – *dexterity;*
- switching between distant and close reading (different spectacles) – *vision.*

As predicted in the earlier assessments, the majority of difficulties encountered were cognitive in origin, unlike for the analogue television, where the sources of difficulties were evenly distributed. Table 4 shows the spread of causes of difficulty.

Table 4. The distribution of causes of difficulty.

	Vision	Dexterity	Cognitive
Analogue (out of 10)	3/10 (30%)	3/10 (30%)	4/10 (40%)
STBs (out of 65)	15/65 (23%)	11/65 (17%)	39/65 (60%)

Many of the cognitive difficulties experienced were not directly attributable to any kind of 'medical model' impairment. Instead, lack of experience with, and mental model of, the interaction paradigms used in digital television was the principal cause of the difficulties encountered.

5 Countering User Exclusion

For the case of STBs, a number of key areas for re-design can be identified. Several of these are shown in Table 5. This is not a complete list; it is intended to highlight the origins of some of the common problems and how they may be countered.

Table 5. Key areas for re-design.

Category	Problem
High-level understanding:	1: Poor user mental model of interaction
	2: Inconsistent language/labelling
Performing interaction:	3: Poor accessibility of remote control
	4: Multiple modes
	5: Use of OK/SELECT button (on remote control)
	6: STB times out on user input
	7: Delay in responding to user input
	8: Switching on subtitles via menus
Instructions:	9: Unclear set-up instructions
	10: Unclear instructions for use

Having identified the most prominent problems encountered by the users, the next step is to propose potential solutions in a format that designers can readily use and interpret [7]. Tables 6 and 7 show examples of how information about the problems and their potential solutions could be presented to designers.

Table 6. Problem 6: STB times out on user input.

Symptoms:
• STB only responds to part of the input from the user
Encountered:
• When changing channel, ending up on channel 04 instead of channel 40
Result:
Channel changing
• Impairment of ability to change channels
• Tendency to end up on wrong channel
• Reinforces concept of DTV 'being difficult'
Causes:
Principal cause
• Time-outs almost certainly based on model of young, able-bodied user
Exacerbated by
• Checking the screen to see that the previous input has been recognised (e.g. showing "4-" when trying to go to channel 40) – even further exacerbated if this involves a change in spectacles from reading to distance pairs
• Finding the next button to press (e.g. the '0' on the STB1 remote is not in the standard position)
• Deciding on the next button to press (e.g. the OK/SELECT button)
Possible fixes:
• Extend time-out periods to allow for 'slower' users
• Use of warning-style dialogue boxes before dropping a user out back at the start of a process ("You have not selected an option – do you wish to do so or leave the menu?" – then press appropriate button) – problem: this may get annoying if you keep encountering it
• Use of buttons such as the "-/--" button on Sony remote controls for specifying "I am doing a two-digit input now" – problem with this: not many users understand what this button does
• Reducing the 'exacerbating' features – e.g. having an LCD display on the remote control show the user the input created (saves having to swap between the TV and the remote control) – ensuring 'standardised' layout of remote controls to reduce hunting for buttons – fixing the OK/SELECT problem

A study of the possible fixes (e.g. those in Tables 6 and 7) show that many are complementary and that some solutions may benefit more than one problem. For example, the use of appropriate affordances [4] could aid the user's mental model of the interaction, at the same time as providing reminders to use the OK/SELECT button.

Table 7. Problem 7: Delay in responding to user input.

Symptoms:
User presses a button and either nothing seems to happen or the screen goes blank

Encountered:
- Changing channel (initial black screen from inherent DTV lag on channel change, no indication of which channel moved to)
- Calling up interactive elements (e.g. BBCi)
- Calling up subtitles

Result:
- User believing that certain functionality is not available
- User repeatedly pressing button (potential for ending up somewhere unexpected, damaging user mental model of interaction)
- User frustration

Causes:
- Download time for system to update screen

Possible fixes:
- Clear, unambiguous feedback from the STB that the input has been recognised – e.g. Teletext page "loading" legend

6 Overall Summary

This paper has presented the results of 3 assessments – expert assessment, exclusion analysis and user observation sessions – of the accessibility and usability of 3 digital television set-top boxes. It has shown that the use of complementary methods of assessing accessibility can provide a comprehensive overview of the problems encountered by a diverse range of users.

1 – Expert assessment: The expert (systematic) assessment provided rapid identification of the expected areas of difficulty, allowing subsequent assessment methods to be targeted efficiently. It involved a qualitative assessment through simulation of the activities involved in installing and operating three typical STBs by two experienced assessors.

2 – Exclusion analysis: The exclusion analysis focused on quantitatively evaluating the number of people who are likely to experience difficulties when interacting with the STBs. It provided the basis of a line of argument for the DTI to take to STB manufacturers to show that their boxes were excluding too many people and needed to be re-designed.

3 – User observation: Finally, the user observation sessions involved studying 13 users interacting with two of the STBs and provided validation of the difficulties observed/predicted by the other assessment methods, along with highlighting new additional difficulties, especially regarding the users' mental models of the interaction.

6.1 Common Problems Seen

Throughout this paper, interaction has been considered in terms of the sensory, cognitive and motor demands placed on the users. Common sensory problems included finding/reading buttons on the remote controls, reading on-screen text, and swapping between the two (especially for users with distance and reading glasses). These problems are made worse in comparison to analogue television because of the increased functionality leading to the need for more (and hence smaller) buttons and also increased use of on-screen text displays. Users with hearing impairments would find the dedicated subtitle button on the remote control approach of STB1 very useful, but would be disadvantaged by the on-screen menu approaches of STB2 and STB3.

The most common source of motor difficulties was pressing the buttons on the remote control. Again, while this is a common task for both analogue television and the STBs, it is made more difficult for the latter by the need for more (and hence smaller) buttons and also increased levels of user interaction.

However, while there was an increase in both the vision and dexterity demands made upon the users, by far the biggest cause of exclusion noted during the user observation sessions was the cognitive demands. The inherent increase in user cognitive effort associated with having to use two remote controls (or a single remote control with multiple modes) rather than a single remote control is further exacerbated by the mismatch between the users' mental models of the interaction and the interaction paradigms adopted.

For example, users are familiar with the concept that pressing a button on a television remote control has an immediate effect on what they see on the screen. For example, pressing a channel number button causes the television to immediately tune to that channel. Thus a strong link between cause and effect is observed, and a solid user mental model of the interaction is developed. The STBs, though, present the users with numerous new interaction paradigms, such as pop-up menus, combined with weakened cause and effect.

For example, nothing happens when an item is highlighted on a pop-up menu until the OK/SELECT button is pressed (another new concept). The situation is worsened further by the seemingly arbitrary inconsistencies in language and interaction between similar purpose entities of the interface. For example, in BBCi the 'menu' option is called 'menu', whereas in Teletext it is called 'control'. On one remote control the SELECT button was called just that, whereas on the other it was denoted OK. To enter BBCi, the user has to press the RED button, while for Teletext it is the TEXT button. These inconsistencies present unnecessary usability hurdles to the users. These differences breach one of the central tenets of usability theory, namely that of the need for consistency.

The prevalence of the cognitive difficulties encountered by users with no discernible loss of cognitive capability reinforces the estimation made during the exclusion analyses, that the levels of population exclusion predicted using the ONS data alone are demonstrably conservative.

6.2 Comparing STBs to Analogue Television

One of the aims of this study was to examine whether the users found STBs to be more difficult to use than traditional analogue television sets. All three of the assessments performed showed that interacting with the STBs was indeed more difficult than interacting with traditional analogue television services. In fact, the typical digital system is likely to exclude at least twice as many users as the typical analogue system for basic operations such as channel selection. Thus the STBs are excluding potential users who at the moment are able to access and use the available television services.

The additional exclusion arose from two principal causes. First, the basic operations, such as changing channel or volume, are all made fundamentally more complex by the presence of either two remote controls, or a single remote control with multiple modes of operation. Second, digital television offers increased functionality and thus places additional burdens on the user who attempts to access this.

Looking at the basic operations, e.g. changing channel, on an analogue television, the user only has the option of using a single remote control. This limits the amount of cognitive effort required by the user, as no decision as to which remote control to use is required.

However, when an STB is present, the user is faced with the additional decision of which remote control to use. This presents a fundamental additional cognitive load on the user, as well as an additional motion requirement to keep swapping between the two remote controls. Some STB manufacturers have responded to this difficulty by supporting both television and STB operation into a single remote control that operates in dual modes. Unless some kind of affordance is provided indicating which mode the remote control is in (STB or television), the user can only find out by pressing a button and then seeing and interpreting the response. If the response was not the desired one, then the user needs to undo the action, change the mode and then perform the desired action a second time.

Consequently, STBs will only cease to exclude more people than analogue televisions when their operation is completely transparent from the user's point of view. Integrated digital televisions, for example, appear to manage to achieve this level of transparency for basic functions by using only a single remote control with minimal need for mode changes.

However, even iDTVs exclude more people than analogue televisions when considering the full range of operation. Put simply, digital television offers more functionality, and thus requires more cognitive effort to learn and operate.

For example, if a user wishes to use the full functionality of DTV, then there is a greater need to be able to read the on-screen display and to swap to reading the remote control (vision demand). Similarly, the users need to be able to operate the arrow buttons and SELECT/OK, rather than just the channel numbers. The increase in number of channels means that users have to enter more double-figure channel numbers, with the inherent time-out limitations increasing the dexterity demand still further.

Only if all of the additional functionality is as accessible and usable as interacting with an analogue television, will digital television not be more excluding than analogue. This is a tough target to aim for, but a necessary one unless it is to be accepted that not all users will have access to all of the digital services.

6.3 Further Work

The predominance of exclusion arising from the differences between the users' mental models and the interaction paradigms within the interface affects far more users than those that would typically be classed as a stereotypical 'special needs user'. This is well illustrated by the comparative lack of difficulty with the interaction experienced by the youngest participant who had the most severe vision impairment of any of the users, but who nonetheless experienced little difficulty completing the tasks, most probably because of his wide experience with high-technology products. Consequently, manufacturers should be encouraged to look beyond the stereotypes of young, severely, impaired people when considering who may have difficulty using their STBs and to also consider the needs of older adults and those who may not be familiar with the interaction paradigms used. There is also a clear need to standardise within those paradigms to minimise the cognitive demand placed on the users and to make interaction with the STBs as transparent as possible. Ultimately, what is being advocated is not special purpose design for a small market sector, but rather good 'design for all'.

Acknowledgements

This study was funded by the Department of Trade and Industry and was performed in conjunction with the Inclusive Design group of the Engineering Design Centre at the University of Cambridge and also The Generics Group.

References

1. Card SK, Moran TP, Newell AF (1983) The Psychology of Human-Computer Interaction. Lawrence Erlbaum Associates, Hillsdale, NJ, USA
2. DTI (2000) A study on the difficulties disabled people have when using everyday consumer products. Government Consumer Safety Research, Department of Trade and Industry, London, UK
3. GAD (2001) National population projections: 2000-based. Office for National Statistics, London, UK
4. Gibson JJ (1977). The theory of affordances. In: Perceiving, Acting, and Knowing (eds. RE Shaw and J Bransford), Lawrence Erlbaum Associates, Hillsdale, NJ, USA
5. Grundy E, Ahlburg D, Ali M, Breeze E, Sloggett A (1999) Disability in Great Britain. Department of Social Security, Corporate Document Services, London, UK

6. Hirsch T, Forlizzi J, Hyder E, Goetz J, Stroback J, Kurtz C (2000) The Elder project: so-cial, emotional and environmental factors in the design of eldercare technologies. Proceed-ings of the 1st international Conference on Universal Usability, ACM Press, New York, NY, USA, 72-79

7. Keates S, Clarkson PJ (2003) Countering Design Exclusion. Springer-Verlag, London, UK

8. Martin J, Meltzer H, Elliot D (1988) The prevalence of disability among adults, HMSO, London, UK

9. Popovic V (1999) Product evaluation methods and their importance in designing interactive artefacts. In: Human Factors in Product Design (eds. P Jordan and WS Green), Taylor and Francis, London, UK, 26-35

10. Semmence J, Gault S, Hussain M, Hall P, Stanborough J, Pickering E (1998) Family re-sources survey - Great Britain 1996-97. Department of Social Security, Corporate Docu-ment Services, London, UK

11. Stanton N, Young M (1998) Is utility in the eye of the beholder – a study of ergonomic methods. Applied Ergonomics, 29(1): 41-54

Methodological Approaches to Identify Honorable Best Practice in Barrier-Free Web Design

Examples from Germany's 1st BIENE Award Competition

Michael Pieper[1], Renate Anderweit[1], Beate Schulte[2], Ulrike Peter[2],
Jutta Croll[3], and Iris Cornelssen [4]

[1] Fraunhofer Institute for Applied Information Technology – FIT
Schloss Birlinghoven, 53754 Sankt Augustin, Germany
{Michael.pieper,renate.anderweit}@fit.fraunhofer.de
[2] Institut für Informationsmanagement (ifib)
Am Fallturm 1, 28359 Bremen, Germany
{bschulte,upeter}@ifib.de
[3] Stiftung Digitale Chancen, Am Fallturm 1,
28359 Bremen, Germany
jcroll@digitale-chancen.de
[4] Aktion Mensch, Heinemannstr. 36,
53175 Bonn, Germany
Iris.cornelssen@aktion-mensch.de

Abstract. In the European Year of People with Disabilities 2003 the major German social organisation "Aktion Mensch" (German Association for the Care of the Disabled) and the "Stiftung Digitale Chancen" (Digital Opportunities Foundation) have for the first time jointly initiated a competition for the design of barrier-free websites. The so-called BIENE-Award is meant to honour the best barrier-free web sites in the German language and to present them as best practice examples. BIENE[1] stressing the objectives of promoting communication, joint action and productive cooperation. This article refers upon the methodological approach underlying the evaluation of competitive award contributions.

1 Germany's BIENE Award for German Language Websites

The BIENE Award has the objective of acknowledging best practice, therefore contributing to increase the winner designers' reputation. Only for operators of non-commercial websites of public interest, such as public associations or self-help groups, several promotion prizes up to € 2,500 have been assigned.

The application time period lasted from the 5th of May 2003, which was the European protest day of equal opportunities for People with Disabilities, until the 1st of September 2003. The award ceremony took place in Berlin on the 3rd of December 2003. Announcement documents and further information have previously been made publicly available on the website www.biene-award.de.

---

[1] In this context, the acronym BIENE (in its original German language meaning the insect "bee") stands for "Barrierefreies Internet eröffnet neue Einsichten" ("barrier-free internet reveals new insights").

C. Stary and C. Stephanidis (Eds.): UI4All 2004, LNCS 3196, pp. 360–372, 2004.
© Springer-Verlag Berlin Heidelberg 2004

The initiators of the competition, "Aktion Mensch" (German Association for the Care of the Disabled) and "Stiftung Digitale Chancen" (Digital Opportunities Foundation) pursued three aims of equivalent importance:

1. Increase of the amount of barrier-free Internet sites and accordingly increase of usability and usefulness of the World Wide Web for people with disabilities.
2. Create public consciousness for the topic of barrier-free communication and information technology.
3. Exemplify a collection of best-practice-examples.

Since its foundation in 1964 "Aktion Mensch"[2] (www.aktion-mensch.de, www.einfach-fuer-alle.de) has been one of the most successful social organizations in German society. It is orientated towards the ideas of humanity and solidarity and the strive for social equality, as well as the right of self-determination and equal participation in social life.

It pursues this mission essentially in a twofold way: Firstly by sponsoring projects and institutions which support and help handicapped people, thereby favoring especially self-help organizations in which handicapped people help themselves. Since 2003 Aktion Mensch has also been sponsoring projects and institutions for children and the help for young people. Secondly "Aktion Mensch" temporarily organizes extensive information campaigns aiming at creating awareness and a positive atmosphere for these social issues in society.

The "Stiftung Digitale Chancen" (Digital Opportunities Foundation, www.digitale-chancen.de) emerged from the project network "Digital opportunities", under the leadership of the University of Bremen, and was established on behalf of the German Federal Department of Economics and Labour as a public private partnership in January 2002. Original founders were the University of Bremen and AOL Germany. This public private partnership could lately be extended to the consulting enterprise Accenture and the "Burda Academy for the 3rd Century" as co-founders[3]. The foundation's basic mission is to set up an information system to provide instruments for overcoming the Digital Divide in Germany, in accordance with the demands of the "Barrierefreie Informationstechnik Verordnung - BITV" (Barrier-free Information Technology regulation) as part of the most recent general Federal Equal Opportunities Legislation in Germany[4].

1.1 Professional Advisory Board, Jury, and Representatives of End-Users

A professional advisory board supervised the selection of competitive comparison criteria for submitted contest contributions, and the corresponding evaluation process. The board consisted of about 25 representatives of organizations of handicapped people in Germany and other experts in the field of web-accessibility. The board agreed upon a tentative rank ordered proposal list for award assignments. For the irrevocable

---

[2] Formerly "Aktion Sorgenkind".

[3] The Burda academy to the 3rd millennium (www.akademie3000.de/index.htm) is an institution of the Hubert Burda foundation (www.hubert-burda-stiftung is). It is a forum for researchers, philosophers and visionaries of most diverse scientific disciplines and social areas. In international conferences, discussions, presentations and publications it unites experts dealing with central questions of present and future societal developments.

[4] English version at: www.einfach-fuer-alle.de/artikel/bitv_english/

final selection of prize winners[5], this list was presented to a jury consisting of important representatives from private and public media, education media, media design agencies, and commercial internet providers.

1.2 Competition Categories

Since contents, size, target user groups and design requirements vary in different application domains, and the evaluation procedure also varies accordingly , the BIENE–Award for best barrier-free web sites in the German language was announced for different categories of web services, ranging from e-Commerce, e-Government (federal -, state -, and community services), culture and society, science and research, and media (print and broadcast media).

Special prizes have been dedicated to exceptional and innovative solutions addressing the needs of single user groups, e.g., web sites for children, web sites for deaf people who use sign language, and web sites for people with learning disabilities.

1.3 Participation Prerequisites

Contributions to the competition had to be in the German language, and publicly available on the World Wide Web at the time of submission. It was requested that contest submissions, besides pure information transfer, provided some support for elementary interaction with targeted end-users, e.g., e-mail inquiries for requesting additional content-related services. The submitters had to specify in which of the contest categories mentioned above they wanted their submissions to be evaluated. It was also possible to submit only a subsection of a more comprehensive website in one of the dedicated competition categories.

Competition applicants had to fill in an application form and a short description (approx. two to three pages) of the basic concepts and instruments underlying the development of their barrier free website.

2 Evaluation Procedure

The evaluation process was developed and carried out by the "Institut für Informationsmanagement Bremen" (ifib). The team has been working in the field of accessibility for several years now and is well known in Germany. During the whole process the above-mentioned professional advisory board accompanied the ifib team. This very constructive co-operation helped to overcome lots of problems and questions that came up during the contest. Especially because representatives of concerned end-user groups were requested to actively participate in the advisory board, the acceptance of the BIENE competition in the public grew notably.

In total, 173 contributions have been submitted for the competition. Because four contributions out of this total number of 173 either presented contents in non-German language or were not any longer available in the web at the time of the contest's evaluation period, finally only 169 entitled for the competition.

---

[5] Winners in the 5 categories and exceptional prizes are available at:
http://www.einfach-fuer-alle.de/award/gewinner

Fig. 1. The test crew.

Table 1. Entitled and qualified Contributions.

Categories	Entitled Contributions	qualified contributions	qualified contributions for the practice test
E-Commerce	26	10	3
E-Government	42	12	6
Culture and Society	81	34	4
Science and Research	15	4	2
Media	5	1	1
total	**169**	**61**	**16**

According to the overall evaluation procedure first of all inappropriate contributions could be sorted out from the competition by a so-called exclusion-test. Subsequently 61 remaining contributions, which sufficiently passed the exclusion procedure, had to undergo a so-called fine test. Out of this fine-test 16 best contributions, which were identified under additional consideration of their different complexity, qualified for final practice tests with concerned end-users with different disabilities.

Out of this practice tests, the advisory board nominated 12 candidates to the jury. It was their task to check the candidates on the quality of content. They also had an eye on attractive web design. Finally the jury devoted the BIENE Award to 11 candidates.

2.1 Legislative Frameworks

The evaluation of competitive award contributions took into account the regulatory demands of the "Barrierefreie Informationstechnik Verordnung - BITV" (Barrier-free Information Technology regulation). As part of the most recent Federal Equal Opportunities Legislation in Germany this ordinance was issued by the Federal Ministry of the Interior, in agreement with the Federal Ministry of Labor and Social Affairs as being effective of July 17, 2002. It is based on section 11(1) sentence 2 of the German Federal Act on Equal Opportunities for Disabled Persons of April 27. 2002[6].

2.2 Ergonomic Frameworks

The five principles for accessibility from WCAG 2.0 (Web Content Aceesibility Guidelines) Working Draft 24 april 2003[7] served as a basis for the BIENE evaluation. These principles have been verified by the results of a survey amongst 180 associations out of the community of the disabled in Germany with the request to estimate on a scale of 1–5 the importance of respective ergonomic principles for the special needs of the special reference groups of disabled people represented by each of them. Based on this survey it should be determined whether the criteria of the five general ergonomic principles should be weighted differently. The result of the inquiry however revealed no significant variance but a more or less even distribution. Thus five equally important basic ergonomic principles for improved accessibility served as a conceptual framework for the overall evaluation procedure:

- **Perceptibility**
  All website information and functions must be presented in such a way that they can be perceived by each user regardless of certain impairments or handicaps, e.g., pictures for blind - and sounds for hearing-impaired end-users have to be supplemented by circumscribing texts (Alt-Text). Individually adjustable font sizes and colour, as well as contrast, facilitate perception for visually impaired persons.

- **Operability**
  All elements that are required to access website contents, e.g., buttons, menu bars and input fields, must be controllable by each user. End-users with certain motor impairments may have problems to adequately operate and position a computer mouse. They might be dependent on navigating websites completely by (special) keyboards.
  Moreover, websites should allow for individually different utilization speeds without time restrictions that may invoke automatic discontinuance of usage processes.

- **Orientation**
  To be able to navigate efficiently within large websites, end users should be able to orient themselves quickly and simply. A prerequisite for that is a strict separation of content and function (e.g., navigation tools), as well as a meaningful and consistent user interface design which satisfies users' expectations derived from previous experiences.

- **Understandability**
  Textual information and textual descriptions should be short and simple. This is not only of advantage for end-users with a learning disability, but also for deaf people who frequently have to communicate textual information by sign language. Intelligible graphic elements can add meaning to written information.

---

[6] Federal Law Gazette I p. 1467
[7] See http://www.w3.org/TR/2003/WD-WCAG20-20030429/

- **Robustness**

  Quite often disabled end-users use alternative browsers and special needs access technologies, e.g., enlargement software, screenreader software or speech recognition. In this respect, websites have to be compatible with current and future special needs technologies and alternative browsers.

2.2.1 Checkpoint Operationalization

Both the exclusion-test was as well as the fine test were operationalized in terms of checkpoint-criteria relating to these basic ergonomic principles for improved accessibility.

A further demand was that the checkpoint-criteria should comprehensively cover special needs requirements from the entirety of impairments to be taken into account. Moreover the single checkpoints had to be easily examinable.

2.2.1.1 Exclusion Criteria

The exclusion procedure was based on 16 criteria with 29 single test steps which were especially operationalized to serve as a first rough filter to identify contributions with serious shortcomings.

Nearly none of the contributions fulfilled all criteria of the exclusion test. Thus the evaluation team decided in agreement with the advisory board to accept contributions for the fine-test in spite of minor defects. Nevertheless, a contribution was not accepted for the fine-test if the defects all emerged in one of the five testing areas, circumscribed by the five basic accessibility principles mentioned above.

Certain test criteria revealed most common accessibility flaws in the evaluation of each of the five accessibility principles by, e.g. links did not have consistent and meaningful names, especially within listings (deficient *orientation*), sometimes ALT-tags were empty or were far from giving the information of the associated pictures (deficient *perceptibility*). The HTML-source code on the home pages was very often much better and closer to WCAG-conformity then it was on the following pages (deficient *robustness*).

2.2.1.2 Fine Test Rank-Order Criteria

In the end, 61 competition contributions were identified for the fine-testing. The fine-test consisted of 80 criteria with 205 steps.

While the criteria for the exclusion test were based on the common accessibility guidelines, the fine-test criteria covered a broader spectrum. They have additionally been derived from international standards concerning software ergonomics (DIN/ EN/ ISO 9241-10/11 and ISO TS 16071) from guidelines dealing with data security, protection of data privacy, e-Government and e-Commerce. As the criteria about understandability and easy language are defined only roughly in the common accessibility guidelines, we added the guidelines for dyslexia and for use of easy language ("Plain German").

2.2.2 Evaluation Methodologies

Methodologically the overall evaluation procedure combined different forms of expert validation with participative end user involvement. Expert validation comprised classical guideline oriented approaches based on the exclusion and rank order criteria circumscribed above, the application of software supported validation and repair tools for accessibility checking and an inspection whether competitive website contributions were compatible with widespread used assistive technologies.

2.2.2.1 Guideline-Oriented Expert Evaluation

In the exclusion test, only two pages, which previously had been selected as being representative for the submitted overall website were validated by experts. In general this was the homepage and a page that offered complex interaction functionality, which might be at least a form or a questionnaire. The exclusion test procedure served as a first rough filter to identify contributions with serious shortcomings. It took about 60 to 80 minutes to do one test. To guarantee reliability of the results each test was done twice by different experts. According to this expert validation approach all contributions were tested based on 16 exclusion criteria, in 29 single test steps.

Table 2. Examples from the lists of exclusion criteria with testing steps.

Criterion: Every part of the site can also be reached in a logical order by exclusively using the keyboard.
Step 1:
Check in the browser if all functions can be reached with thxe tab.
Step 2:
Assess, if there is a logical tab order through links, form controls, and objects.
Criterion: Several navigation mechanisms are available.
Step 1:
Check in the browser, if navigation bars are provided
Step 2:
Check in the browser, if a sitemap is provided. (This step is not applicable with low complexity).

Two different task-oriented scenarios were defined for *fine testing* each contribution, to make sufficiently sure that a broad as possible view of the whole site was considered. During scenario based task accomplishment, all five accessibility principles had similarly to the exclusion test to be checked by 80 fine-test criteria in 205 single test steps at previously selected checkpoints. Additionally, one test-run was re-checked. A single test-run took 4 to 6 hours depending on the complexity of the site. This meant that a complete test for a single site took about 12 hours.

The basic test environment for both the exclusion test and the fine test consisted of operating system Windows 2000 and standardbrowser MS Explorer 5.5.

2.2.2.2 Assistive Technologies Compatibility Check

Additionally certain test programs had to be available to check for "robustness", i.e. checking whether websites are compatible with current and future special needs technologies (e.g. enlargement software, screenreader software or speech ycognition) and alternative special needs browsers. Thus the basic test environment was extended by auxiliary special needs technology including Webformator 1.31, IBM HPR, JAWS 4.5, Opera 7.0, and Lynx. The Webformator was for example used to examine whether sites, which contain frames or tables can be converted into a linearized read sequence representing a logically meaningful arrangement of frame – or table based contents, i.e. to what degree logical linear read sequences support "perceptibility".

2.2.2.3 Software Tools for Accessibility Checking

Carrying out the exclusion test required some technical preconditions, amongst them the application of software supported validation and repair tools for accessibility checking. In this context amongst other tools the self-developed BIENE tool was used, e.g. to confirm proper use of ALT-text, frame- and table-tags for improved perceptibility. Additionally conventional public domain accessibility checkers like Vischeck and Adobe plug-in were applied.

2.2.2.4 Participative End User Evaluation

The 16 contributions with the best results in the fine-tests went into participative end user evaluation The Internet competence of involved end users varied from beginners to experts.

The tests were done with 8 women and 8 men, aged 16 to 55. The test persons had different kinds of disabilities; several suffer from more than one impairment. The tests were carried out at the working places or homes of the test persons and took about 4 hours.

User tests relied on scenario based task accomplishment. Statements and impressions during task completion were recorded in writing. When a task was successfully concluded or aborted, the test person had to answer a standardized questionnaire. When the test person had done all tests within one competition category (e.g. e-Government, media etc.) s/he was asked to decorate the most favoured contributions amongst the tested websites with medals (gold, silver, bronze).

Fig. 2. Test person working with Braille.

One evident result of the tests was that accessibility cannot be reduced to technical issues. This is just the first step: All test persons regardless of their disabilities stranded on sites with an inadequate structure or with too much complexity. Furthermore it became very obvious that also the degree of Internet competence was a very crucial aspect whether a task could be completed or not.

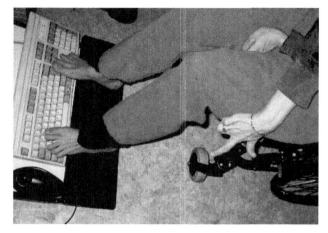

Fig. 3. Test person using her feed for navigation.

2.3 Exceptional Awards

Next to the awards for the regular competition categories (e-Commerce, e-Government, culture and society, science and research, and print and broadcast media) three additional competition categories were awarded special prices for outstanding website contributions focussing on the special needs of *deaf end users* accustomed to using sign language, *end users with learning disabilities* and *children*. Whereas for the regular competition categories conceptually the contest explicitly avoided to focus on needs of particular groups these exceptional prices in contrast explicitly aimed at drawing attention on disabled end user groups that are almost unidentified with regard to their special IT accessibility needs in public.

Four contributions offered special services for deaf people, e.g. sign language videos. Four more contributions offered especially designed contents and service for people with learning disabilities. Unfortunately all website contributions focussing on children lacked appropriately designed accessibility for that special target group.

The evaluation of the contributions for the three special prices was carried out by human factors experts with particular awareness for the special needs of the concerned target groups. This expert evaluation was complemented- by participatory end user evaluation (see above) with concerned end users and concluding interviews, partially supported by sign language interpreters.

3   Conclusion and Outlook

Concluding remarks about results and experiences from the exclusion-, fine- and finally the participatory end user evaluation aim at showing how to improve the overall evaluation procedure, so that it will be easier to identify best practice examples in the upcoming 2nd BIENE-competition 2004.

3.1 Variation in Number of Applicable Testing Steps

The tests showed that many test criteria could only be applied on sites with enhanced diversity and complex transactions. Thus some tests were much more voluminous than tests that were done on sites which simply offered plain information. The number of testing steps that could be used varied between 90 and 190.

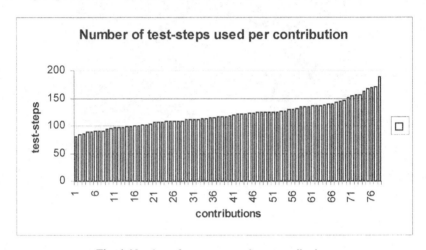

Fig. 4. Number of test-steps used per contribution.

These enormous variations made it difficult to compare the results. As a consequence the criteria catalogue will be restructured for the next BIENE-contest in 2004. Furthermore the complexity of a site with regard to functionality and amount of information will be included in the general concept.

3.2 Subjective Evaluation

Although trying hard to operationalize the criteria for objective testing, the fine-tests showed that the competition contributions were of such a wide range and variety that in many cases the evaluation experts had to decide subjectively. This was necessary for questions concerning the adequacy of a function or the means of realization (e.g. should there be a sitemap or a glossary on the page or not).

These kinds of questions were discussed by the whole testing crew for each individual case.

3.3 Weighting

When the evaluation process was defined, the ifib methodology development team explicitly did not differently weigh certain testing areas or criteria. This decision was the result of the above mentioned survey amongst 180 associations out of the community of the disabled in Germany and organizations of handicapped people. As already mentioned the results of that survey revealed that the planned testing areas perceptibility, operability, orientation, understandability and robustness had almost the same relevance.

One more reason is to be found within the concept of accessibility itself: Each single barrier may prevent a handicapped person from reaching his or her individual goal within a website with equal relevance.

Certain test results and the need of ranking the contributions anyway showed that one cannot abandon weighting. It is for example difficult to compare a criterion concerning the accessibility of navigation mechanisms to a criterion concerning the accessibility of mechanisms to protect data privacy.

As a consequence a weighting system will be introduced for the next BIENE contest 2004.

3.4   Use of Future Technologies

When the criteria catalogue for the overall evaluation was developed there was a strong interest not only to take into account well-known HTML-techniques, but also technologies that are recommended by W3C and not common yet. Most recent "leading edge technologies" cannot per se be recommended from the perspective of accessibility, but there may be reasons that are worth thinking about, e.g. the need for high-risk security standards. A very high number of contest contributions was based on plain HTML. Hopefully this picture will change in the next BIENE 2004 award, as there are lots of web sites around that make use of other technologies.

3.5   Feedback to Contest Presenters

All the contest participants received a review of their results in the weeks after the prize awarding. As the results of the evaluations were extremely voluminous, the results were summarized: The report contained every criterion, which was not or only partly ok. This feedback was meant as a motivation to continue the work on accessibility and to understand accessibility as an integral quality criterion of a website.

References

1. Balzert, H.: Software Ergonomie. Teubner, Stuttgart (1991)
2. Clark, J.: Building accessible websites. New Riders, Indianapolis (2003)
3. Dzida, W.: Qualitätssicherung durch software-ergonomische Normen. In: Eberleh, Oberquelle, Oppermann (ed.): Einführung in die Software-Ergonomie. deGryuter, Berlin (1994) 373-406
4. Dzida, W. et. al.: Gebrauchstauglichkeit von Software, ErgoNorm: Ein Verfahren zur Konformitätsprüfung von Software auf der Grundlage von DIN EN ISO 9241 Teile 10 und 11; Schriftenreihe der Bundesanstalt für Arbeitsschutz und Arbeitsmedizin, (2001)
5. DIN EN ISO 9241 Ergonomische Anforderungen für Bürotätigkeiten mit Bildschirmgeräten, Teil 10: Grundsätze der Dialoggestaltung, Teil 12: Informationsdarstellung
6. Goffman, E.: Behavior in Public Places: Notes on the Social Organization of Gatherings. The Free Press, New York, NY (1963)

7. Goffman, E.: The Presentation of Self in Everyday Life. Garden City, NY (1969)
8. Heath, C. and LUFF, P.: Technology in Action. Cambridge University Press, Cambridge, MA (2000)
9. Hill, W. and Hollan, J.: History enriched data objects: Prototypes and Policy Issues, in: Information Society 10 (2001)
10. ISO/TS 16071: Ergonomics of human-system interaction – Guidance on accessibility for human-computer interfaces
11. Kishi, N., Kinoe: Assessing Usability Evaluation Methods in a Software Development Process. In: H.-J. Bulinger (ed.): Human Aspects in Computing: Design and Use of Interactive Systems and Work with Terminals. Chichester: Elsevier Science Publishers (1991) 597-601
12. Kubicek, H., Taube, W.: Der gelegentliche Nutzer als Herausforderung für die Systementwicklung. In: Informatik Spektrum (1994) 347-356
13. Maaß, S.: Software-Ergonomie. In: J. Friedrich et.all. (ed.) Informatik und Gesellschaft, Spektrum Akademischer Verlag Heidelberg, Berlin, Oxford (1995)
14. Mead, G.H.: Mind, Self and Society from the perspective of a behaviorist. Chicago: University of Chicago Press (1934)
15. Nielsen, J.: Designing Web Usability: The practice of simplicity. Indianapolis (IN): New Riders Publishing (2000)
16. Oppermann, R: Individualisierung von Benutzungsschnittstellen. In: Eberleh, Oberquelle, Oppermann (ed.): Einführung in die Software-Ergonomie. deGryuter, Berlin (1994) 235-269
17. Oppermann, R.; Reiterer, H.: Software-ergonomische Evaluation. In: Eberleh, Oberquelle, Oppermann (ed.): Einführung in die Software-Ergonomie. deGryuter, Berlin, (1994) 335-371
18. Ostrom, E.: Governing the Commons: The Evolution of Institutions for Collective Action. Cambridge University Press, New York (1990)
19. Pieper, M.: 'Calling the Blind' is 'Watched by the Deaf'- Directions for Multimodal CSCW-Adaptations to Receptive Disabilities, in: Proceedings of the 1st ERCIM-Workshop 'User Interfaces for ALL', Heraklion, Greece, FORTH - Institute of Computer Science (1995)
20. Pieper, M.: Sociological Issues in HCI Design, in: Stephanidis, C. (ed.), User Interfaces for All - Concepts, Methods, Tools, chapter 11, pp. 203 – 221, Mahwah (NJ), London, Lawrence Erlbaum Associates (2001)
21. Preece, J.: Online Communities: Designing Usability, Supporting Sociability. John Wiley, Chichester, U.K. (2000)
22. Preece, J.: Supporting Community and Building Social Capital, in: Communications of the ACM, April 2002, Vol. 45, (2002) pp. 36
23. Smith, M.: Tools for Navgating large Social Cyberspaces, in: Communications of the ACM, April 2002, Vol. 45, (2002) pp. 51
24. Spiegel, D.S.: Coterie: A Visualization of the Conversational Dynamics within IRC, Massachusetts Institute of Technology (School of Architecture and Planning), Cambridge, MA (2001)
25. Stephanidis, C.: User Interfaces for All: Concepts, Methods, and Tools. Lawrence Erlbaum Associates; Mahwah, New Jersey (2001)
26. Thatcher J. et.al.: Accessible Web Sites, glasshaus (2002)
27. Warschauer, M.: Social Capital and Access. University of California, Irvine (Dept. of Education and Dept. of Computer Science), (2002) unpubl. man.
28. Whittaker, S., Terveen L., Hill, W. and Cherny, L.: The Dynamics of Mass Interaction, in: Proceedings of CSCW ´98, ACM Press, New York (1998)
29. Whyte, W.H.: City: Return to the Center, Doubleday, New York (NY) (1988)
30. Xiong, R. and Donath J. (1999): PeopleGarden: Creating Data Portraits for Users, in: Proceedings of UIST (1999)

Internet-Links

- Informationen zum barrierefreien Webdesign. Eine Initiative der Aktion Mensch e.V.:
  http://www.einfach-fuer-alle.de (12.8.2003)
- Gesetz zur Gleichstellung behinderter Menschen (BGG):
  http://www.bmgs.bund.de/download/gesetze/behinderung/gleichstellung.pdf
  (12.8.2003)
- Web Accessibility Initiative (WAI) (2003)
  (W3C): http://www.w3.org/WAI (12.8.2003)
- BSI, Bundesamt für Sicherheit in der Informationstechnologie: e-Government-Handbuch
  http://www.bsi.de/fachthem/egov/3.htm (28.4.2004)
- ILSMH, Europäische Richtlinie für die Erstellung von leicht lesbaren Informationen
  www.inclusion-europe.org/documents/SAD66EETRDE.pdf
- NCAM SALT (Specifications for Accessible Learning Technologies) Guideline:
  http://ncam.wgbh.org/salt/guidelines/
- TechDis: Dyslexic Perspective on e-Content Accessibility, Peter Rainger 20/01/03
  http://www.techdis.ac.uk/seven/papers
- National Audit Office UK: Progress in making e-services accessible to all,
  http://www.nao.gov.uk/pn/02-03/0203428.htm

A Supportive Multimodal Mobile Robot for the Home

Lynne Baillie, Michael Pucher, and Marián Képesi

Forschungszentrum Telekommunikation Wien (FTW.),
Donau-City-Strasse, 1220, Vienna, Austria
{baillie,Pucher,Kepesi}@ftw.at

Abstract. This paper explores how multimodality and robotics can aid us to support users in their homes. We describe how our work attempts to tackle issues such as privacy, control of personal space and fun within the home. In an ever increasingly ageing society, we realize that certain information gathering or support may be required by users in their homes. However, we strongly believe that we should preserve a user's privacy in their home and ensure that any artifact we propose is seen as fun, aesthetically pleasing and most importantly non-stigmatizing. We describe in this paper how a multimodal mobile robot can assist in the monitoring of a home in a fun and unobtrusive way.

1 Introduction

At *ftw.* we develop and investigate multimodal interfaces for mobile devices for next generation telecommunications. The solution we are offering for low-level home monitoring[1], i.e. the multimodal mobile robot, we feel, brings together a combination of experience and knowledge of people in their homes. We believe (in the same vein as Norman, [16]) that any proposal should be part polemic, part science, part serious and part fun. In this paper we outline some previous pertinent studies of users in their homes and the issues these studies raised such as control, privacy and our relationship with artifacts. We introduce our multimodal mobile robot as a possible fun solution to some of these issues, in this arena, in the multimodal robot section. We are not suggesting that the robot becomes a pet (for information on the benefits or problems with this see: Arkin et al [2]; Friedman, et al., [10]), what we are suggesting is that the multimodal robot is a way of making very light home monitoring non-stigmatizing and less obvious. Nor do we foresee this application being useful to people who have medium or high care needs this can be done much better with a system of the type suggested by Dewsbury [8].We conclude the paper with a short discussion and an outline of our future work.

2 Background

In this section we discuss some of the relevant research which has been carried out in the home in the areas of Telemonitoring, Ambient Intelligence, and home technology.

---

[1] Low level-monitoring: a system that provides information such as, whether the lights are on or off, what the temperature is in certain rooms.

C. Stary and C. Stephanidis (Eds.): UI4All 2004, LNCS 3196, pp. 375–383, 2004.
© Springer-Verlag Berlin Heidelberg 2004

We conclude the section by highlighting some of the issues we think are important to consider when designing a technology for the home.

2.1 Telemonitoring

Telemonitoring[2] is an area of growing interest because of the western worlds ageing society. We will talk about the telemonitoring area only briefly as we feel the work is of great value, but not directly relevant to this paper. The reason for this is that the raison d'etre of most telemonitoring projects has been to support patients and care workers in the monitoring of life threatening (Benatar, et al., [5]) or chronic illness (Giraldo, et al., [11]). We did not design the multimodal robot application for telemonitoring purposes but as a useful and fun device to have in the home that sprung from suggestions made to us by our home study participants (see Section 3). One of the main issues in telemonitoring, related to this work is that telemonitoring systems require multiple devices, monitors, and complex database set-ups (Lukowicz et al, [14]; Sachpazidis, [19]). A benefit can clearly be seen for this complex set-up when the purpose is to monitor patients who have chronic diseases. However, a device along the lines of the multimodal mobile robot may be more appropriate when very low level monitoring is required.

2.2 Ambient Intelligence

The concept of ambient intelligence is of growing importance in the home sphere. Ambient intelligence refers to a world in which people are surrounded with electronic environments that are sensitive and responsive to people (Aarts, et al. [1]). The central issue here is to remember that surrounding should not mean swamping people. People can become anxious and worried at the thought of technology surrounding them and invading their home environment. We should be aware that, in the main, a technology is meant to merge harmoniously into the background of the home and support the user in undertaking tasks. The technology should not cause conflicts over the control of the home space.

2.3 Technology and the Home

We believe that we should think carefully about the artifacts we introduce into the home space. This is because our background research has led us to believe that there are two main issues that designers should consider when designing artifacts for the home:

1. That any artifacts provided, along with all the usual usability goals, should be aesthetically pleasing and fun to interact with.

---

[2] Telemonitoring is when a patient's chronic condition is monitored in the home via a specifically set up system. The results can then be sent via a mobile phone, fax or to another remote system.

2. The user should feel a sense of privacy and control over any artifacts proposed for their home space.

We, therefore, discuss aesthetics, privacy and control in the following subsections.

2.3.1 Aesthetics

The attachment we have to artifacts in our homes, and how this can affect use, has been highlighted by Csikszentmihalyi and Rochberg-Halton [7]. They found that three modes mediate the relationship between an artifact and a person: aesthetics, attention and goal. The importance of aesthetics has also been found in other studies of the home, for example, Hirsch et al [12] conducted a study of the elderly and their use of artifacts in a retirement village in the United States. They found that artifacts such as rails to help elderly users in their bathrooms were being used as towel racks, as the users did not want to be viewed in a certain way. They also found that motorized wheelchairs were being shunned in favor of motorized buggies. Why, because buggies were associated with 'golf and leisure pursuits' and wheelchairs with creeping old age. We would, therefore, submit that having something fun like a robot undertaking surveillance of the home may be seen as more fun, aesthetically pleasing and less obtrusive than other artifacts, such as: video cameras, monitors and sensors on the walls.

2.3.2 Control

The issue of privacy and control of space is of importance in the home, indeed, it has been commented that architects often forget the importance of spaces in the home and the roles they play. Rosselin [18] gives the example of the apartment of a young student that had no hallway. The student placed a carpet of one square meter on the floor, to suggest a hallway, where guests had to leave their shoes, therefore, making what was one space, the living room, into two spaces, the hallway and living room. How can this ownership and control of space impact on our use of our artifacts? Silverstone and Hirsch [21] thought that artifacts in the home posed a whole set of control problems for households, such as regulation and control of space. In another study, feelings of control or lack-of control, were found to be an important indicator of the participants' feelings towards certain spaces in their homes and the artifacts they contained (Baillie, [4]). This issue of control can present itself in surprising ways, for example, an elderly lady commented that she was unhappy with the way in which the housing association, which owned her home, decided, without consultation, to place sockets in her kitchen. The resulting inappropriate placement of sockets meant that she had to change the layout of her kitchen space.

2.3.3 Privacy

Do the assitive technologies and devices that are being proposed for people with disabilities or elders, take into account feelings of loss of control? Also, how do they tackle the issue of privacy? It would seem that people may be willing to give up some of their privacy, in order to gain tangible benefits. We were aware, as designers, that by putting intelligent devices into peoples' homes, we are opening up the possibility for people to be monitored remotely. Rather than hide this information gathering from the users we would propose that it would seem a much more reasonable step to take to be open about this aspect of the device and let the user control it. The reason for this is that it has been found that people are aware that these devices collect information about them (O'Brien et al., [17]; Baillie, [4]) and are happy to let them do so in certain circumstances e.g. to summon help in an emergency.

3 Homes Studies

Five households in central Scotland agreed to take part in a series of home-based workshop sessions (a full description of the study and its results can be seen in Baillie, [4]). The households that volunteered for the study ranged from a family with two young children to a single woman of eighty-four (see Table 1 for a full list of the participants). The families represented a good cross-section of society, with some of the participants living in affluent areas while others occupied modest public-sector accommodation. The educational attainment was varied with some still at school, some having left school at sixteen and some with a higher degree. All the families gave permission for the data collected as a result of the workshops to be published. To preserve anonymity, pseudonyms have been used.

Table 1. The families who took part in the Home Workshop Sessions (Baillie, [4], p85).

Identifier	Who		Age	Occupation
Cook	Robert	Father	50	Lecturer
	Sue	Mother	45	Housewife
	Dianne	Daughter	10	School Pupil
	Tarquin	Son	7	School Pupil
Petric & Naysmith	Catherine	Partner	25	Recruitment Consultant
	Gordon	Partner	29	Admin. Officer
Suttons	Emily	Wife	70	Retired teacher
	Peter	Husband	72	Semi-retired builder
Smiths	Mike	Father	46	Joiner
	Barbara	Mother	44	Catering Assistant
	Simon	Son	15	School Pupil
Reilly	Agnes	Widow	84	Retired Cook

The study focused on what technology the households currently used but also went further and tried to discover what they wanted for the future. The format of the workshop can be seen in Table 2.

In session two the participants were asked to envision a future device in the form of a sketch. A very small selection of the sketches and comments made by the participants are presented in this section. We hope to show from this that it was not just our ideas, as designers and technologists, that led us to make the suggestions that we do, but that the concepts and ideas actually came from people who were sketching and explaining these ideas in the context of their own homes.

In the sketches the privacy issue seemed to be elucidated by the participants wanting to know more about what was going on in their home and who was in them when they weren't there. The concept of security and privacy spanned further than the security of the home from burglars, but also encompassed the well being of family members and the ability to contact the emergency services. For example, Agnes wanted her device to be used in the event of a fire or an emergency she anticipated that the system could be accessed by the emergency services to let them know who, if anyone, is in the building (see Fig. 1).

Table 2. The methods and focus for each of the Home Workshop Sessions (Baillie, [4], p88).

	Focus	Methods
Session One	Investigate current problems and Future Possibilities	1. Technology Tour 2. Representations of emerging technologies 3. Scenarios
Inter-session activities	*Collecting data in-between sessions*	*EU(exploring use) notes*
Session Two	Contextualising ideas for the home in the future and daily life	1. Informal interview 2. Materializing ideas for future technologies
Session Three	1. Sharing ideas across families 2. Modifying and elaborating designs	1. Critique 2. Redesign

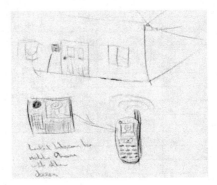

Fig. 1. Agnes Reilly's Remote Home Monitoring Device.

Agnes also wanted her device to be able to see and monitor her home when she was not present. The idea of the device came to her because of her frustration about just this issue, when she went on a holiday to the United States. She had to ask a neighbor to regularly go into her home and check that all was well. She thought that this could be made much simpler if she could check for herself from her mobile phone. Additionally, she thought that checking herself would be less intrusive as she did not have to give a set of keys to her home to someone else. Another participant wanted a device that would alert him if he had left devices on in a room e.g. television, cooker or lights. He mentioned that he was becoming forgetful and that he would find a device of this type very useful. He felt very strongly that he did not want an artifact taking up space and dominating his home. Peter also remarked that if the other houses in his street were wired up to this system, they could have a communal warning and message system to aid communication. Some researchers have also suggested that people may benefit in unanticipated ways from linking up homes and private spaces in this way. For example, Blythe et al., [6] suggested that social connections, which have been lost over time, could be reactivated by using local on-line street maps that would help householders to keep in touch with their local surroundings, and chat with neighbors. The fact that a senior citizen designed a device, which would help him as he grows more infirm and forgetful is of interest, as many researchers at the moment are looking at building 'smart homes' and trying to understand what senior citizens would want from this type of home.

The conclusions we drew from our studies led us to believe that a device which would provide some level of home monitoring would be more welcomed by users if it had the following attributes:

- It could be accessed and controlled remotely, either via a mobile device or via the internet;
- It was unobtrusive and did not take up space in their home or affect it's fixtures or fittings;
- And, finally, privacy and control should rest with the householder. The householder should be the only one to relinquish this privacy and control, should they wish to do so.

We thought of many devices and concepts, however, none could be said to offer all of the wishes expressed by the householders. Ultimately, and quite surprisingly, we found that an intelligent multi-modal robot that could be controlled via a web browser (this would enable someone to access the robot interface either via a PC, Digital Television, or a web enabled mobile device e.g. a Pocket PC or a Smart Phone) could provide a way in which to monitor a home remotely in an unobtrusive manner. By enabling the user to access the robot from many different devices we would avoid the situation highlighted by Deswbury [8]. He found that if an elderly person is offered a communication aid that they cannot fit into a pocket then, they may choose not to carry it. The second point was that the device should be unobtrusive, we discovered from previous research (Friedman [10]) that people felt comfortable ignoring robots and similar devices. The device suggested should also not affect the fixtures or fittings: our robot can be easily picked up and put in a cupboard. Finally, control of the multimodal robot would, of course, rest with the householder or whomever they decide to give access to. We hoped that householders would view the robot as being aesthetically pleasing, fun and protective of their privacy, while at the same time providing unobtrusive support.

4 Multimodal Robot

Multimodality promises natural user interaction with devices and applications. Because human communication is multimodal, multimodal communication is perceived as natural and intelligent. These properties are relevant to build easy and fun to use interfaces and applications. Presented in Fig. 2 are two pictures of the robot we used as the basis for our application.

Fig. 2. The multimodal robot.

The robot was built using the Lego Mindstorms kit [15]. It can drive around and has a touch sensor and a simulated temperature and vision sensor. To enable communication between the Webserver and the robot we installed the Lejos Java Virtual Machine [13]. The behavior of the robot, including the navigation, was implemented according to the behavior control theory from Bagnall, [3]. We developed a web interface that a user can use to control the robot using a multimodal user interface. The interface shows a map of the rooms in the home and where the robot is located. It is possible to send the robot around the home (this can be done via a PC or a mobile device with internet access, which supports SALT) and let it fulfill different tasks e.g. measuring the temperature, checking if the windows are closed, or if the lights are on or off. Dewsbury [8] comments that these types of sensors would provide support to someone who needs a low level of care, and that someone with this level of needs probably does not need a full scale smart home technology.

4.1 Multimodal Interaction

The user can ask the robot, via the web interface, about its functionality or control the robot remotely. The robot "answers" questions posed by the user using the system Text To Speech (A Text to Speech system converts a given text to synthesized speech [22]). A user can verbally tell the robot to move to a point on the map e.g. a user can ask: "What's the temperature in the living room?" The robot would then proceed to the living room, if it is not already there, and measure the temperature. While the recognition process is running the user can see a progress bar showing the voice energy on the screen. When the recognition ends with an error (which can mean silence, no recognition, or error) then the recognition starts again, otherwise, the page is submitted, calling a JSP (Java Server Page) which generates a new SALT page. The temperature of the room is then displayed on the web interface.

5   Studies at FTW and Future Work

We undertook a small study at the research center premises. The study investigated, in the first instance, whether or not the robot could in fact be manipulated using voice commands and if these voice commands were carried out effectively i.e. if the user told the robot to 'go forward' did the robot indeed go forward as commanded. The second part of the study focused on the multimodal robots ability to negotiate around a mock-up of an apartment. The robot, at the moment, moves around a mock-up of one of the participants homes, therefore, it is not moving in a real environment e.g. the robot moves to a place we have called the living room. The robot was able to successfully negotiate around the mock-up of the apartment. We realized that this is not ideal as in a real home the robot would encounter obstacles in its path around the home, but it was an appropriate experiment to undertake at such an early stage of development.

We have not as yet undertaken field studies, the reason for this is that in order to place the robot in people's apartments it was necessary to add a sophisticated navigation module to the robot and replace the dummy sensors in our robot with real sensors. Also we needed to develop a configuration interface for the robot. With this interface it is possible to name the robot and define custom speech commands, thus making it easier for us to place the robot in the more realistic environment of a participant's home. We have now completed these tasks and our next step is to recruitment some households for the next stage of our study.

6 Conclusion

We were, of course, wary of whether or not the robot we were proposing would be adopted by users. Is adoption more unlikely with certain groups? The elderly have been found to adopt new innovations when the technology met their needs and the benefits to using it were effectively communicated [9]. Therefore, it could be concluded that there is no reason to believe that a multimodal robot would be unacceptable to this user group. Further, our home studies demonstrated to us that the elderly were quite capable of coming up with new and interesting ways in which their homes could be monitored, without the need to install permanent cameras and sensors, which could be seen as obtrusive and not in harmony with the aesthetics of the home. Such utilitarian devices could in fact intrude in a negative way into the home space.

We discussed in this paper the importance of privacy in the home and how this may affect, on the one hand, the user and, on the other, their use and interaction with an artifact. We also introduced the concept of 'fun' in this environment, in that we do not need to always design solutions which are work based or utilitarian, but can think of using devices which have been developed for fun and amusement and put them to a more utilitarian use. We also explained how we built a nontrivial multimodal interface using standardized components. There are and will be many different types of mobile support devices, therefore, it is crucial that the community that these artifacts are built for should be designing and contributing to the discussion of what assitive technologies there should be in the home. Our study found that including ideas from participants in the design led to more fun and unusual suggestions being included in the discussion of how to support people in their homes.

Acknowledgments. This paper is dedicated in loving memory of Janette M Archibald one of the participants of the home studies.

References

1. Aarts, E., Collier, R., Loenen, E., Ruyter, B. Ambient Intelligence. Proc. First European Symposium, EUSAI 2003, 5-6.
2. Arkin, R.C., Fujita, M., Tokagi, T., Hasegawa, R. An ethological and emotional basis for human robot interaction. Robotics and Autonomous Systems. Elsevier, 42, 191-201, 2003.
3. Bagnall, B. Core Lego Mindstorms Programming. Prentice Hall, New Jersey, 2002.
4. Baillie, L. The Home Workshop: A Method for Investigating the Home. PhD Thesis, Napier University, Edinburgh. 2002.
5. Benatar, D., Bondmass, J., Ghitelman, J., and Avitall, B. Outcomes of Chronic Heart Failure. *International Medicine*. 16, 347-352, 2003.
6. Blythe, M., Monk, A., Park, J. Technology Biographies: Field Study Techniques for Home Use Product Development. Proc. CHI 2002, 658-659.
7. Csikszentmihalyi, M., E. Rochberg-Halton. The Meaning of Things: Domestic Symbols and the Self. Cambridge University Press, New York, 1981.
8. Dewsbury, G., Taylor, B., and Edge, M. Designing Safe Smart Home Systems for Vulnerable People. In Proctor R, and Rouncefield M, (Eds) In proceedings Dependability in Healthcare Informatics, Lancaster University, 2001, pp.65-70.
9. Dunphy, S., Herbig, P. Acceptance of Innovations: The Customer is the key! *The Journal of High Technology Management Research*, 6, 2, 1995, 193-209.
10. Friedman, B., Kahn, P.H., Hagman, J. Hardware Companions? – what online AIBO discussion forums reveal about the human robotic relationship. In Proceedings of CHI 2003. Ft Lauderdale, USA, 273-280.
11. Giraldo, C., Helal, S., and Mann, W. mPCA A Mobile Patient Care-Giving Assistant for Alzheimer Patients. Proc. First International Workshop on Ubiquitous Computing for Cognitive Aids, Sweden, 2002.
12. Hirsch, T., Forlizzi, J., Hyder, E., Goetz, J., Stroback, J., & Kurtz. C. The Elder Project: Social, Emotional, and Environmental Factors in the Design of Eldercare Technologies. Proc. CUU'00, ACM Press, 2000, 72-79.
13. Lejos – Java for the RCX, http://www.lejos.org/
14. Lukowicz, P., Anliker, U., Ward, J., Troster, G., Hirt, E., and Neufeld, C. AMON: A Wearable Medical Computer for High Risk Patients. Proc. Sixth International Symposium on Wearable Computers, 2002.
15. Mindstorms - Robotics Invention System 2.0, http://www.mindstorms.com/
16. Norman, D. The Design of Everyday Things. Doubleday: New York, 1988.
17. O'Brien, J., Rodden, T., Rouncefield, M., Hughes, J. At Home with the Technology: An Ethnographic Study if a Set-Top-Box Trial. *ACM Transactions on Computer-Human-Interaction*, 6, 3, 1999, 282-308.
18. Rosselin, C. The Ins and Outs of the Hall: A Parisian Example. In Cieraad, I (Ed.) At Home: An Anthropology of Domestic Space. (53-59) New York: Syracuse University Press, 1999.
19. Sachpazidis, I. @Home: A Modular Telemedicine System. Proc. Mobile Computing in Medicine. Heidelberg, Germany, 2002.
20. SALTFORUM: Speech Application Language Tags, http://www.saltforum.org
21. Silverstone, R., & Hirsch, E. Consuming Technologies: Media and Information in Domestic Spaces. Routledge, London, 1992.
22. W3C: Multimodal requirements for Voice Mark-up Languages. Working draft 10. July, 2000, http://www.w3.org/TR/multimodal-req

Multimodal Interaction
in Architectural Design Applications

Lou Boves[1], Andre Neumann[1], Louis Vuurpijl[1], Louis ten Bosch[1],
Stéphane Rossignol[1], Ralf Engel[2], and Norbert Pfleger[2]

[1] NICI, Nijmegen, The Netherlands
[2] DFKI, Saarbrücken, Germany

Abstract. In this paper we report on ongoing experiments with an advanced multimodal system for applications in architectural design. The system supports uninformed users in entering the relevant data about a bathroom that must be re-furnished, and is tested with 28 subjects. First, we describe the IST project COMIC, which is the context of the research. We explain how the work in COMIC goes beyond previous research in multimodal interaction for *e*Work and *e*Commerce applications that combine speech and pen input with speech and graphics output: in design applications one cannot assume that uninformed users know what they must do to satisfy the system's expectations. Conse-quently, substantial system guidance is necessary, which in its turn creates the need to design a system architecture and an interaction strategy that allow the system to control and guide the interaction. The results of the user tests show that the appreciation of the system is mainly determined by the accuracy of the pen and speech input recognisers. In addition, the turn taking protocol needs to be improved.

1 Introduction

Research in multimodal interaction tends to divide into two categories that have little in common. One field focuses on applications where users interact with some kind of map, or complete some kind of form using a combination of speech and pen for input. More often than not, the pen can only be used as a pointing device. For entering al-phanumeric input with the pen, a soft keyboard must be used, or the user must write isolated characters in a dedicated field on the screen. Examples of projects in this category are SmartKom [1] and MUST [2]. The other category addresses virtual real-ity applications, where the user can move around freely, while the system interprets all speech and gestures that are relevant for the completion of a specific task [3]. In the ongoing IST project COMIC[1] [4] we intend to narrow the gap between the two categories, by extending the input and output capabilities of an application in the first category. At the output side the COMIC system features a talking head, displaying naturalistic turn taking behaviour, expressed by means of speech prosody, eye contact and gaze. At the input side the COMIC system supports pen input processing, in addi-tion to automatic speech recognition.

Projects in multimodal interaction differ in yet another aspect. Many projects aim at a fundamental investigation of how several input and output modalities can be combined in human-system interaction. Here, the focus is on experiments with proce-

---

[1] http://www.hcrc.ed.ac.uk/comic/

C. Stary and C. Stephanidis (Eds.): UI4All 2004, LNCS 3196, pp. 384–390, 2004.
© Springer-Verlag Berlin Heidelberg 2004

dures to interpret multimodal input, and methods for rendering information in parallel output channels. Another category of projects aims at developing operational multimodal services, often in digital telecommunication networks, but also desktop applications for non-expert users. Projects in this category focus – by necessity – on developing interfaces that can be implemented and maintained cost-effectively, yet are easy to use for a broad range of customers. It is well known that there is a large difference between customers who pay for using a service and subjects who are paid for participating in experiments. Perhaps it is less well appreciated that the difference between computer scientists who have developed their own multimodal interfaces and uninformed users (be they subjects or customers) is at least as large.

In COMIC, we move one step beyond the conventional map and form filling applications, by addressing an architectural design task, instantiated in the form of bathroom design. In this paper we first introduce the COMIC project in more detail. In section 3 we explain the fundamental problems that must be solved to enable natural human-system interaction in architectural design. Section 4 describes the system that we built for entering a blueprint of a bathroom, and section 5 reports on an experiment in which uninformed subjects tried to use the system. Section 6 completes the paper with conclusions and recommendations.

2   The COMIC Project

COMIC [4] is an FP5 project in Key Action 2, in the area of Long Term, High Risk Research. COMIC combines software and system development with experiments in human-human and human-computer interaction in language-centric multimodal environments. The experiments are based on a scenario that can be controlled experimentally, but that at the same time is relevant for *e*Commerce and *e*Work applications. The bathroom design application has speech and pen input recognition at the input side (cf. Fig. 1). In addition, users can point at objects on the screen, such as bathtubs, basins, faucets, etc., and ask the system to shown alternative designs. The system can explain advantages and disadvantages of specific designs. In doing so, it takes into account a dynamically evolving model of the preferences, likes and dislikes of the user. In addition to the tablet screen, where designs and drawings can be shown, the system features a second screen that displays a highly realistic talking head. To enhance the naturalness of the interaction this 'avatar' is able to express the moods and attitudes that a customer expects from an expert sales consultant (but the automatic system will always stay polite and will never show irritation). A schematic image of the layout of the application during the phase when the shape and dimensions of the room is being entered is shown in Fig. 1. The avatar guides the user through the application by explaining what it is expecting and by asking questions if the input is ambiguous. The user can simultaneously draw or write and speak.

Fig. 1. Overview of the bathroom design application. The tablet is used for pen input to enter size and dimension of the bathroom.

The interaction starts with the user entering the blue print of the room, including the position of the door(s) and windows, the opening direction of the door and the height and width of the windows, since these determine feasible layouts of sanitary ware and additional bathroom furniture. After the ground plan of the room is entered, it can be decorated with tiles and sanitary equipment. Subsequently, the user can move through a 3D image of the design, and discuss possible changes. However, the present paper only addresses the process of entering the shape and size of the room.

3 Issues in Multimodal Interaction in Design Applications

In order to get an impression of how naive subjects go about entering the shape and dimensions of a room into a computer system with human-like capabilities, we conducted an experiment in which we asked several people to perform the task. They were told that they could draw, write and speak freely. The experimenter provided backchannel feedback to encourage the subjects to speak as if they were addressing a person, and asked clarification questions if he did not understand the information. In addition, the experimenter prompted the subjects to provide all the information that they were instructed to give. Figure 2 shows a representative example of the resulting pen input [see also 5]. The problems that the experimenter experienced in interpreting the sketches and the verbal explanations given by the subjects are very similar to the issues addressed in [11], where it is shown that there is no fixed and predictable relation between sketches and speech: in some cases verbal expressions can only be interpreted with the support of a sketch, while in other cases sketches can only be interpreted with the help of verbal explanations.

From Fig. 2 it is clear that unconstrained pen and speech input pose recognition problems that are insurmountable with existing technology. In addition, it appeared that all subjects needed substantial guidance and help from the experimenter to complete the task of specifying a complete bathroom. Virtually all subjects needed help in devising ways for expressing the opening direction of a door and the height of a window and a window sill. In Fig. 2 it can be seen that this subject tried to solve the latter problem by drawing a side view of the wall containing the windows. To avoid insurmountable problems for subjects trying to interact with an automatic system, we decided to design a much more structured interaction strategy. To simplify the task for on-line pen and speech input recognition as much as possible, we opted for a system driven interaction style, in which the system prompts the user to enter individual information elements, such as the position and the length of the walls, the position and opening direction of the doors, and the position, height and widths of the windows.

4 The COMIC System for Entering Blueprints

Fig. 3 shows the architecture of the system that we built for conducting a Human Factors experiment to investigate whether uninformed subjects are able to enter the blueprint of a bathroom using pen and speech as input channels. The system is built using the MultiPlatform environment for implementing multimodal applications that was developed in the Verbmobil and SmartKom projects [6] and that is now publicly available[2]. The present implementation of the system is a simplified version of the

---

[2] http://sourceforge.net/projects/multiplatform/

eventual COMIC system in that it does not yet include the Dialogue and Action Management (DAM), Fission and Output modules that are described in [4]. The task of the DAM is taken over by a Wizard, who essentially decides whether or not a user input can be interpreted, and triggers the appropriate system response. System outputs consist of spoken prompts requesting the user to enter an information element and feedback about the interpretation of the user input in the form of graphical output on the Wacom Cintiq LCD Tablet. The recognition of walls, doors and windows is echoed by 'beautifying' the user's pen input: it is overlaid by straight lines for the walls, and standardised graphics for doors and windows. Lengths and measures are echoed as printed characters on the tablet. Users can erase wrongly recognized input by means of spoken utterances ("*No, I meant three meters and thirty centimetres*"), or by erasing the system output with the upper end of the pen (that doubles as an eraser).

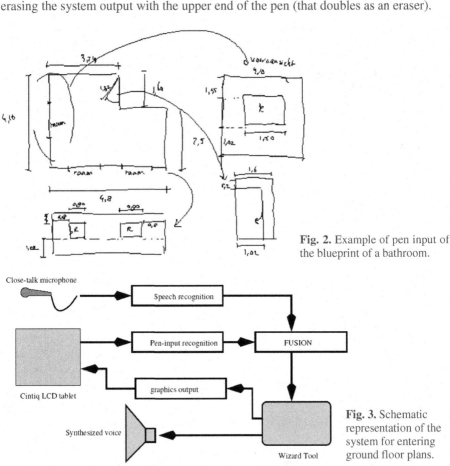

Fig. 2. Example of pen input of the blueprint of a bathroom.

Fig. 3. Schematic representation of the system for entering ground floor plans.

Speech recognition is implemented with the HTK toolkit, adapted for interactive usage [7]. Context dependent phone models were trained using the German Speech-Dat database [8]. The language model was inferred from recordings in pilot experiments, and extended with the intuitions of the experimenters about plausible types of expressions. Pen input recognition is implemented with algorithms developed in the

NICI. Fusion is implemented on the basis of the procedures and software developed at DFKI in the framework of the SmartKom project. The Dialog Management protocol followed by the wizard is presently being automated, taking due account of the experience gained in the Human factors experiments reported in this paper. The data recorded in this experiment were processed using a tool developed in the NICI [9].

The first fully operational version of the system depicted in Fig. 3 did not implement a strict definition of 'turn' and turn taking, allowing for fully asynchronous, full-duplex interactions. This asynchrony caused severe misunderstandings between subjects and wizard, and the lack of a mutually agreed communication protocol caused the partners to run out-of-sync. Therefore, we were obliged to define a strict turn taking protocol that boils down to half duplex communication in which speech and pen input were confined to a fixed time window following the end of a system prompt. The moment when the subject could start writing and speaking was indicated by a green square that appeared in the left upper corner of the tablet. At the end-of-turn that square turned red, after which input would not be processed.

5 Experiment and Results

We have conducted a large scale experiment in which 28 subjects (8 male, 20 female) aged between 20 and 37 (median 23) have used the system to enter ground floor plans of three bathrooms. All subjects had a university level education, but no computer science background; more importantly, none of the subjects was familiar with the research project. However, most reported to have substantial computer experience, but very little experience using speech recognition systems and even less using pen tablets. At the start of the experiment subjects were given a short explanation of what was going to happen. Next, they were requested to specify three bathrooms, their own, that in their parents' house, and a third one of their choice. During this phase they could freely speak and draw and become acquainted with writing on the tablet and using the head mounted microphone. The experimenter would ensure that all data were given (including doors and windows) and suggest ways for expressing specific information elements when needed. Hardcopies of the ground plans were then made and given to the subject to serve as a mnemonic during the next part, in which they had to copy the information into the 'automatic' system, one room at a time. Before starting with the first room subjects saw a short instruction video that explained how the system would show what it had recognised, and how they could correct recognition errors. After completing the third room subjects were asked to fill out a questionnaire comprising 26 Likert scales; a score of 1 corresponded with 'I disagree completely', whereas a score of 5 meant 'I fully agree'. Below we present the results of the analysis of the objective interaction data that were logged during the experiments, the subjective scores on the Likert scales, and interesting correlations between the objective and subjective measures.

From the scores on the Likert scales it appears that subjects had no difficulty understanding the task: mean score is 4.09. It was less clear what to do while using the system (3.43), although the prompts were clear (4.36), and it was easy to understand the way in which the system showed its recognition result (4.14). In general, subjects knew what to do to correct recognition errors (3.59). Despite the fact that they did understand the task, subjects said that they found it rather difficult to use the system (2.68) and that it was not very efficient (2.59). As a consequence, they said that they needed to concentrate hard (3.82), and that it took long to enter all information (3.91). Also, they did not find themselves in control (2.18), the system was not seen as very reliable (2.14), and it definitely needs improvement (4.18). Several subjects found it difficult to wait for the green square to appear on the tablet, and to react within the time window. Also, subjects did not always understand how they had to correct recognition errors in numbers and dimensions. If subjects said or wrote the equivalent of 3.25 m, and the system recognised 2.25 m (i.e., substituting the '3' in the number by a '2'), they could only erase the complete string (both the number and the dimension) and they had to re-enter both. Quite a number of subjects wanted to erase or to re-enter only the digit that was misrecognised. Although on average subjects disagreed with the statement that the system was too fast (mean score 2.64), we observed that a substantial proportion of the input utterances were truncated because they exceeded the maximum allotted time window. With respect to the input modalities subjects reported that they found the pen easy to use (3.55); the use of the eraser was even simpler (4.27). The combination of pen and speech was easy (3.5), the naturalness of the interaction was assessed as almost neutral (3.09). Only a small proportion of user utterances contained simultaneous and related pen and speech input. However, as is apparent from the Likert scales, subjects appreciated the possibility to choose between pen and speech (4.05).

Although the performance of the pen recogniser was substantially higher than that of ASR, subjects tended to first try and speak the answer to prompts about sizes and dimensions. Only after repeated misrecognitions they switched to writing. However, subjects for whom ASR performed worst changed their behaviour during the course of the experiment: especially while entering the third room they tended to avoid speech and used the pen exclusively. Natural Language Processing and Fusion could do little to improve recognition accuracy, since subjects hardly ever combined pen and speech to enter size and dimension.

While the major cause of the ASR errors is mostly related to robustness of ASR against out-of-grammar utterances, most of the errors in handwriting recognition can be traced back to the fact that many subjects used a comma as the 'decimal point', whereas the recogniser was trained with a bias towards the Anglo-Saxon use of the full stop for that purpose. The mediocre recognition performance is the major explanation of the finding that the subjects were not very happy with the system. Objective data about recognition performance explain more than 50% of the variance in the (negative) scores on the Likert scales. However, several subjects said that the system would have been easy to use if the recognition performance had been better.

6 Conclusions and Recommendations

The positive scores on the Likert scales addressing the transparency of the task show that the overall design of our system is sound from a Human Factors point of view. However, it is also evident that substantial technical development and improvement is needed before uninformed subjects are able to use the system in an easy and transparent manner. Both input recognisers must be improved substantially, to enable them to handle the behavior of subjects who are task oriented, instead of focusing on human-system interaction per se. In addition, we have found that – although the system driven interaction strategy did not frustrate our subjects – the turn taking protocol needs to be improved. Subjects' inputs should not be constrained to fixed duration time windows, the start of which is determined by the end of the system prompt.

Our data confirm previous results that show that subjects tend to stick to a given input mode, despite the fact that this may not be the most effective one [10]. Moreover, our results suggest that the subjects' preferred mode is heavily influenced by the mode used by the system to address its user: in our design all system prompts are spoken, eliciting spoken replies whenever that is feasible.

Multimodal interaction combining pen and speech input in a system driven interaction can support non-experts in performing a complex task that would be very difficult to perform without substantial guidance of the system. Yet, the turn taking paradigm should be made more flexible than was the case in our system. Most importantly, the accuracy of the input recognisers needs to be improved. It is important to investigate methods for error correction that allow subjects to repair only those parts of a complex expression that were recognised incorrectly, without having to re-enter the parts that were correctly recognised in the first place.

Acknowledgement. This research is partially funded by the European Commission, under the 5th Framework Programme, project number IST-2001-32311.

References

1. W. Wahlster, "SmartKom: Fusion and Fission of Speech, Gestures, and Facial Expressions". *Proc. First International Workshop on Man-Machine Symbiotic Systems*, Kyoto, Japan, 2002, pp. 213-225.
2. L.Almeida et al., "User-friendly Multimodal Services - A MUST for UMTS. Going the Multimodal route: making and evaluating a multimodal tourist guide service". *Proc. EUESCOM Summit*, 2001.
3. T. W. Bickmore, and J. Cassell, "Relational Agents: A Model and Implementation of Building User Trust". *CHI 2001*, Seattle, WA.
4. E. den Os and L. Boves, "Towards Ambient Intelligence: Multimodal computers that understand our intentions". *Proc. eChallenges*, Bologna, October 2003.
5. S. Rossignol, L. ten Bosch, L. Vuurpijl, A. Neumann, L. Boves, E. den Os, and J.P. de Ruiter, "Human Factors issues in multi-modal interaction in complex design tasks". *Proceedings HCI International* 2003.
6. G. Herzog, H. Kirchmann and P. Poller, "MULTIPLATFORM Testbed: An Integration Platform for Multimodal Dialog Systems". *HLT-NAACL'03 Workshop Software Engineering and Architecture of Language Technology Systems*, 2003.
7. S. Young, G. Evermann, D. Kershaw, G. Moore, J. Odell, D. Ollason, D. Povey, V. Valtchev and P. Woodland, *The HTK Book (for HTK Version 3.2)*, Cambridge University, Cambridge, UK, 1997.
8. H. Hoege, C. Draxler, H. van den Heuvel, F.T. Johansen, E. Sanders & H.S. Tropf, "Speechdat multilingual speech databases for teleservices: across the finish line". *Proc. EUROSPEECH'99*, Budapest, Hungary, 5-9 Sep. 1999, pp. 2699-2702
9. L. Vuurpijl, L. ten Bosch, S. Rossignol, A. Neumann, N. Pfleger and R. Engel, Evaluation of multimodal dialog systems, *LREC Workshop Multimodal Corpora and Evaluation*, Lisbon 2004.
10. Oviatt, S. and VanGent, R., "Error resolution during multimodal human-computer interaction". *Proc ICSLP 1996*, pp. 204-207.
11. Lee, J. "Words and pictures – Goodman revisited". In: R. Paton and I. Neilson, Visual Representations and Interpretations, London: Springer-Verlag, 1999, pp. 21-31

Audio Rendering of Mathematical Formulae Using MathML and AudioMath

Helder Ferreira and Diamantino Freitas

Faculty of Engineering University of Porto
DEEC, LPF-ESI, Portugal
{hfilipe,dfreitas}@fe.up.pt

Abstract. Technical, scientific or even simple documents presented online that involve mathematical expressions, issue a big problem with accessibility regarding visually impaired persons. One possible solution is to parse and interpret the mathematical contents and convert them into an audio format. This is a complex and multidisciplinary problem, which AudioMath [1], a work in progress at LPF-ESI [2], studies and aims to contribute to solve. AudioMath provides conversions from mathematical expressions in W3C's MathML [3][4] format into plain text, something that a capable text-to-speech (TTS) engine would "understand" and read-out. This paper reviews the state of the art in publishing mathematical documents in the Internet, and introduces the AudioMath prototype and its working mechanisms, as an accessibility tool for use together with a TTS engine or to use as a standalone application, with great advantages for visual impaired persons. The main scientific and technical challenges, specifically at the levels of interpretation of the content of the MathML coded expressions and conversion into spoken form, are considered and the current status of the work is described.

Keywords: Accessibility, Audio Rendering of Mathematical Expressions, Text-to-Speech, MathML, Conversion of mathematical formulae into text.

1 Publishing Scientific Documents with Mathematics in the Internet

"How hard can it be to communicate about math on the Internet? The truth is, it's a fairly difficult task. [5]". The publication of scientific documents containing mathematical formulae is extremely demanding. The appearance of the TeX [6] system developed by Donald Knuth solved the majority of problems with printed documents. Then WYSIWYG (*What You See Is What You Get*) editors, and subsequently mark-up languages, for Internet appeared, such as HTML (*Hypertext Mark-up Language*). However, HTML *per se* doesn't allow the use of a mathematical description language directly into the document. So being, alternatives were developed, as described in the following.

1.1 Images Containing Mathematical Contents

This is the approach used by software like LaTeX2HTML [7] and TeX4ht [8]. The process consists in converting TeX or LaTeX documents to HTML, where the mathematical contents are converted into GIF objects. There are two main disadvan-

C. Stary and C. Stephanidis (Eds.): UI4All 2004, LNCS 3196, pp. 391–399, 2004.

tages in this process: the low resolution of images and the creation of an accessibility problem, once these images will have to contain a text description (ALT) [9] that allows the mathematical expression to be read-out, otherwise the only possibility is to interpret the image contents. The main advantage is that the user doesn't need to install any special plug-in because the browser can present the information easily.

1.2   Alternative Formats, Such as: PDF, TeX, Postscript, Word or RTF

Most of the times, documents containing mathematical expressions are saved in formats such as: PDF (*Portable Document Format*), TeX, Postscript, Microsoft Word or RTF (*Rich Text Format*), and placed as links in online documents. The visualization of those documents is only possible if the browser provides plug-ins for each type of format, or if the user edits the document after downloading it. There are two main disadvantages in the use of these alternative formats: the need to have a plug-in installed, and the lack of accessibility in reading those documents, once they open inside the browser. However some efforts have been made to provide more accessibility features; this is the case of Adobe PDF [10]. The main advantage of this approach resides in the fact that these formats are widely spread and most users or browsers support them for visual rendering.

1.3   Applets to Create Graphical Representations of Mathematical Contents

This approach is used by WebEQ [11], which consists in an applet server that receives a mark-up language defining a mathematical expression. Currently, WebEQ understands WebTeX (mark-up language that can be included in a HTML document). This approach has the same disadvantages and advantages than the use of images to represent mathematical content. However, the applet download makes the rendering a little slower.

1.4   Plug-Ins to Create Visual Rendering of Mathematical Contents

The use of plug-ins is identical to the use of Java applets; however, using a plug-in requires that the user has already installed it in the browser, since the application runs at the client instead of at the server. TechExplorer [12] from IBM and MathPlayer [13] from Design Science are examples belonging to this approach. Both applications have some support to W3C's MathML language.

1.5   HTML and Symbol Fonts

This approach supplies the simplest documents; however, it compromises the aesthetic form of the document. Translator TtH [14] (TeX to HTML) is an example. It uses special HTML supported fonts and symbols to represent mathematical glyphs, and HTML mark-up to structure the mathematical expression representation. The main advantages are simplicity and swiftness of download. The downsides are the accessibility limitations introduced, since the mathematical expression is geometrically structured using tables [9].

1.6 Use of XHTML and CSS

This is a relatively recent approach to render mathematical expressions online. The main disadvantages are: the rather complex learning of the mark-up languages, and the fact that not all the browsers support XHTML [15] and CSS (Cascading Style Sheets) [16]. As a main disadvantage, the range of mathematical expressions capable to be expressed in XHTML and CSS is limited. The main advantages are: simplicity (once you know the mark-up), swiftness in rendering and the fact that the user doesn't need any additional plug-in in the browser.

1.7 Mark-Up Languages Such as: MINSE, MathML, SVG and Others

Currently there are several mark-up languages that allow the publication of scientific documents in the internet; however the majority are still in a development phase. Some examples of mark-up languages that can be used to publish mathematical contents in the Internet are: MINSE [17], MathML, SVG [18], WebTeX, TeX and HyperLaTeX [19]. The future of the publication of scientific and technical documents resides in these mark-up languages, specially, in MathML. However there's still a long way to go, once not all the browsers support them.

1.8 Creating the Documents

Several authoring software packages allow a relatively easy composition and edition of mathematical expressions for inclusion in web documents:

- MathType, from DesignScience, an evolution of Microsoft Equation Editor, produces documents in HTML+GIF or HTML+MathML formats. The MathPlayer plug-in is required for visualization. The code produced is MathML Presentation Markup [4].
- WebEQ also from DesignScience is composed of two packages, WebEQ Editor and WebEQ Publisher. They produce documents in the formats HTML+GIF, HTML+Java Applet or HTML+MathML. This code is either MathML Presentation Markup or MathML Content Markup [4].
- Mathematica and Publicon, from Wolfram Research, produce documents in the formats XHTML+MathML, XML (NotebookML), XML (NotebookML+MathML), TeX, HTML or TechExplorer. The resulting code is MathML Content Markup.
- Scientific Word, from Mackichan Software, produces documents in the formats HTML+MathML and LaTeX. The output code is MathML Presentation Markup.
- Amaya, from W3C is a free browser with built-in editor producing documents in the formats HTML, XHTML, XML, Text, MathML, CSS and SVG. The output code is MathML Presentation Markup.
- EZMath from David Ragget, is a free mathematical expressions editor with a special notation and browser plug-in. Output code blocks can be embedded in HTML and XHTML documents. The code is MathML Content Markup.
- For TeX or LaTeX users there are tools like:
  - Itex2mml that converts ITeX coded formulas into XHTML+MathML and the output code is MathML Presentation Markup.

- TeX2MML, an online converter from LaTeX to MathML Presentation Markup.
- TeX4ht that converts LaTeX and TeX into HTML. By default produces GIF images for formulas, but can also produce HTML+MathML in the MathML Presentation Markup.
- TtM converts LaTeX or TeX documents in HTML+MathML and the code is MathML Presentation Markup.
- LaTeX2HTML converts LaTeX into HTML.

As can be seen the MathML Presentation Markup dominates relatively to the MathML Content Markup, amongst authoring software.

2 The AudioMath Project

2.1 Introduction

The *AudioMath Project* is an initiative of the Laboratory of Speech Processing, Electro Acoustics, Signals and Instrumentation. The main aim of this project is to produce a tool, either standalone or for integration in a TSS engine, that does the parsing, interpretation and conversion into European Portuguese (EP) plaintext form, of text or mark-up elements (MathML) not directly "understandable" by a regular TTS engine. This tool, under development, is called **AudioMath** and is, as far as we know, the first published application in the world that speaks mathematical expressions in the *MathML Presentation Mark-up* format in European Portuguese.

In its current form *AudioMath* is an ActiveX *dynamic link library* (DLL) that can be used by any program through internal calls. It has been developed in Perl and Microsoft Windows 9x/ME/2K/XP. The tests and refinement were made with help of a specifically developed console (see in figure 1 a screenshot of the program GUI). Text or text files can be retrieved or an Internet web page be opened for reading, and be subsequently processed, converted and read through the selected TTS engine.

Fig. 1. Screen shot from AudioMath Test and Development Application.

AudioMath can be used mainly for:

- Reading of technical and scientific documents online in an accessible way, with particular benefit for vision impaired persons.
- Teaching or learning how to read mathematical formulae [20].
- Enhancing general accessibility to computer-based applications, when applied to a TTS engine.

2.2   MathML – Mathematical Mark-Up Language

MathML is an XML application for the publication of mathematical contents over the Internet. This mark-up language has a simple and concise syntax that codes either the notation (*MathML Presentation Mark-up*) or the meaning (*MathML Content Mark-up*) of a mathematical expression. The *AudioMath Project* has chosen MathML for the following reasons:

- The mark-up language was developed by W3C and will eventually become an ISO standard.
- A rapidly growing use by several relevant organizations associated with the teaching and learning of mathematical contents, such as the *American Mathematical Society* [21] and *The OpenMath Group* [22], as well as the involvement of software houses like *Design Science, HP, IBM, Microsoft* and *Wolfram Research*.
- Emergence of editors and applications that create and manipulate MathML documents.
- Existence of conversion tools for the main publishing formats.
- The fact that it is a mark-up language allows its parsing, interpretation and conversion to other formats, and consequently a higher accessibility, portability and platform independence.

2.3   MathML Presentation Mark-Up vs. MathML Content Markup

The representation of mathematical formulae and other mathematical contents is perceived by two distinct aspects: the visual structure or notation of the mathematical expression, and the concept or meaning that it conveys [23]. For example: the same concept of "*division of a by b*" can have the different notations: a/b, $a \div b$, $\dfrac{a}{b}$ or ab^{-1}. The mapping from notation into concept can be ambiguous as well, for instance, the notation A_2^3 can have the meanings: "*square of A_2*" or "*permutations of 3 elements 2 at a time*".

The two sets of MathML mark-up address separately both modalities:

- MathML Presentation Mark-up:
  - Aimed to the visual presentation of a mathematical expression
  - Doesn't differentiate the meaning of the mathematical expression
  - Not intended to (but possible) audio rendering of mathematics
  - The conversion of Presentation Mark-up into Content Mark-up is not advised.

- MathML Content Mark-up:
  - Aimed to represent the meaning of a mathematical expression
  - Used to transfer MathML between applications
  - Doesn't differentiate the mathematical notation
  - Ideal for audio rendering of mathematical representations
  - Can be converted into Presentation Mark-up
  - Limited only by the mathematical operators and functions it supports.

Although *Content Mark-up* is recommended to be used in audio rendering of mathematical expressions [24] (once it preserves the meaning of the formulae) it has some limitations concerning the list of mathematical operators and functions it supports presently. The OpenMath Group, for example, offers a lot bigger dictionary. Moreover, most current editors are WYSIWYG and code the mathematical contents into *Presentation Mark-up* instead of *Content Mark-up*. Therefore the online documents that contain MathML expressions are almost all coded in *Presentation Mark-up*. For these reasons, *AudioMath* selected *MathML Presentation Mark-up*. However this introduces several difficulties to the interpretation of the formulae ambiguities. These difficulties can, in principle be overcome by contextual information or "intelligence".

2.4   The AudioMath Process

AudioMath was built in a modular, extensible and configurable architecture, in Perl. Therefore, the support for new target languages, the update of dictionaries and of algorithms can be done quite easily. Currently only the European Portuguese language is supported.

Text Analysis

A technical document can contain several elements such as: acronyms, abbreviations, numbers and similar expressions and mathematical expressions. Also, it is probably to come with special Unicode characters and math glyphs. Therefore the first step is to clean up the text, converting Unicode to Latin1 (in this case to support European Portuguese characters). Next step is an auto-discovery process that recognizes types of elements and makes calls to the modules that convert the element into a full written form. For example: if "det." is detected, it should be converted into *"determinant (of)"*. To speed up the process the document should be divided into blocks of text, splitting the MathML Mark-up from the rest of the text.

Parsing and Interpreting MathML

The MathML Markup is parsed using the Perl module: *XML::Parser* [25] which acts as a SAX parser type (event-based), supporting Encoding ISO-8859-1 and discarding XML Namespaces.

Since *AudioMath* uses *MathML Presentation Mark-up*, a big effort and computation is needed on the interpretation of the mathematical expression. This is done using a process of raising flags each time a starting or ending tag is detected. By knowing the history of the mark-up the function or operation under parsing can be guessed and therefore information retrieved to understand the structure of the math expression and do its conversion.

Converting and Speaking Mathematical Contents

"No standard protocol exists for articulating mathematical expressions as it does for articulating the words of an English sentence." [26]. Except for a few significant works [27] [28], currently there is an almost complete lack of studies or research on how should a mathematical expression be read. The authors don't know any work of the kind for Portuguese.

The conversion of the MathML tree to text form is done according to a database of rules that was built based on a collection of materials written by experienced professors.

Note that the bigger the expression the more complex the interpretation and conversion process become. The same happens during audio output time. The listener will hardly handle a full complex formula. A solution would be to introduce navigational mechanisms to browse inside the expression.

The objective of automatically speaking mathematical contents has to deal besides the non-trivial issues of text generation and phrasing, with the generation of the prosody to impose over the synthetic speech.

For example, consider the simple mathematical expression: $\sqrt{a^2 + b^2}$. This could be rendered more or less ambiguously as:

- Square root of a squared plus b squared, end of radicand.
- Square root of a taken to power two, plus, b taken to power two, end of radicand.
- Square root of power base a exponent two, end of power, plus power base b exponent two, end of radicand.

Which of these forms is more correct, not ambiguous and efficient? Now consider the following expressions: $\sqrt{a^{2+b^2}}$, $\sqrt{(a^{2+b})^2}$ and $\sqrt{(a^2 + b)^2}$. Taking in account the text forms presented before, how should we read these expressions?

One could do the experience of speaking the texts monotonically to someone that is not looking to the expression and ask for a written version after the dictation. If one is not careful enough they'll all sound much a like, and quite ambiguous, so identification of the right formula them can easily become very difficult.

The solution must pass by the adoption of formal ways of text generation that keep the right structure information of the formula.

How do things happen in speech communication then? Let's go back to the first example of text rendering of the first expression and consider the sample spoken version, whose waveform, f0 contour (intonation) and text labelling are depicted in figure 2, from top to bottom (the picture was obtained with the PRAAT [29] software).

As can be seen in figure 2, there are two distinct large pauses and a smaller optional pause between *"á ao quadrado=a squared"* and *"mais bê ao quadrado=plus b squared"*.

Another immediately apparent aspect in the middle waveform is the existence of rising and falling movements of f0 in the speaker's intonation intended to provide classification of the boundaries introduced by the pauses. A rising tone is used when a lower hierarchical level is starting (see at the end of *"quadrado de"*) and a falling tone is used when this level is ended (see at the end of *"bê ao quadrado"*) while a rising tone associated to a down tone are used to classify the smaller separating pause between identical elements, so indicating a continuation. Finally the emphatic falling

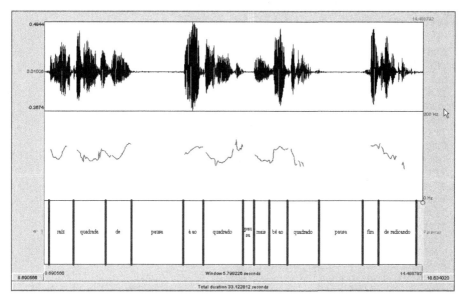

Fig. 2. "Square root of a square plus b square, end of radicand" in European Portuguese.

f0 movement at *"fim de radicando=end of radicand"* signals the end of the expression.

The rules already defined in the present development phase of the project are implemented at conversion time by tagging the text with prosodic marks, to command the TTS device in order to produce the required pauses and f0 modulations.

Although this research is being carried out for European Portuguese, the authors believe that it can be substantially extrapolated to many other languages.

3   Conclusions and Trends of Future Work

Providing mathematical contents on-line, that is, in digital format, allows a greater access to information than before. However, problems do exist in reading those contents, in particular for blind persons that don't have access to graphical representations. It is known that the difficulties for blind persons rise and accessibility diminishes with the increase of technical level in documents [30]. More efforts are therefore needed in order to provide more means to achieve the full accessibility of technical documents in the Internet. *AudioMath* is, without doubt for the authors, a valuable contribution to the increase of accessibility in reading on-line documents with mathematical contents.

However it is a work in progress and plenty still needs to be done, such as: – complete the support to *MathML Presentation Markup* and add support to *MathML Content Markup*; – develop modules that support HTML, XHTML, XML [31] and SSML [32]; – add support for new languages; – continue to develop the study on the prosody of reading mathematical formulae; – provide mechanisms for navigating inside more complex mathematical formulae.

References

1. AudioMath for European Portuguese – http://lpf-esi.fe.up.pt/~audiomath .
2. LPF-ESI – Laboratory for Speech Processing, Electro acoustics, Signals and Instrumentation at the Faculty of Engineering University of Porto – http://lpf-esi.fe.up.pt .
3. W3C – World Wide Web Consortium – http://www.w3c.org .
4. MathML – Mathematical Markup Language – http://www.w3.org/Math .
5. Math Typesetting for the Internet. The Math Forum - http://mathforum.org/typesetting .
6. TeX Users Group (TUG) Homepage - http://www.tug.org .
7. Latex2HTML Homepage - http://saftsack.fs.uni-bayreuth.de/~latex2ht/ .
8. TeX4ht Homepage - http://www.cis.ohio-state.edu/~gurari/TeX4ht/mn.html .
9. Web Content Accessibility Guidelines 1.0, W3C - http://www.w3.org/TR/WCAG10/ .
10. Accessibility in PDF - http://www.adobe.com/products/acrobat/access_overview.html .
11. WebEQ Homepage - http://www.dessi.com/en/products/webeq/default.htm .
12. TechExplorer Homepage - http://www-3.ibm.com/software/network/techexplorer .
13. MathPlayer Homepage - http://www.dessi.com/en/products/mathplayer/ .
14. Translator Tth Homepage - http://hutchinson.belmont.ma.us/tth .
15. XHTML 1.1 - http://www.w3.org/TR/xhtml11/ .
16. CSS 2.0 - http://www.w3.org/TR/REC-CSS2 .
17. The MINSE Project - http://lfw.org/math/top.html .
18. SVG - Scalar Vector Graphics - http://www.w3c.org/Graphics/SVG/ .
19. The HyperLatex Package - http://www.cs.uu.nl/~otfried/Hyperlatex .
20. Freitas, Diamantino. Ferreira, Helder. Et al. *A prototype application for helping to teach how to read numbers.* HCII2003 Proceedings. Volume I.
21. AMS - American Mathematical Society - http://www.ams.org .
22. The OpenMath Group – http://www.openmath.org/coccon/openmath/index.html .
23. Pierce, John. *An Introduction to Information Theory. Symbols. Signals and Noise.* Dover Publications Inc. New York. 1961.
24. Sandhu, Pavi. *The MathML Handbook.* Charles River Media. 2002.
25. XML::Parser - http://search.cpan.org/dist/XML-Parser/Parser.pm .
26. The MathSpeak Project - http://www.rit.edu/~easi/easisem/talkmath.htm (by A. Nemeth).
27. Karshmer, Arthur. *How Well Can We Read Equations to Blind Mathematic Students?* HCII2003 Proceedings. Volume 4.
28. T.V. Raman. *Audio System For Technical Readings.* Dissertation to the Faculty of the Graduate School of Cornell University. 1994.
29. PRAAT: Doing Phonetics by computer, http://www.fon.hum.uva.nl/praat/.
30. Monaghan, Alex. Fitzpatrick, Donal. *Browsing Technical Documents: Document Modelling And User Interface Design.* BULAG 1999.
31. Mark-up languages from W3C used to publishing documents in Internet.
32. SSML - Speech Synthesis Markup Language – http://www.w3.org/TR/speech-synthesis .

A Comparison of Prediction Techniques to Enhance the Communication Rate

Nestor Garay-Vitoria and Julio Abascal

Laboratory of Human-Computer Interaction for Special Needs, Informatika Fakultatea,
Euskal Herriko Unibertsitatea, Manuel Lardizabal, 1, E-20018 Donostia
Tel: + 34 943 018000, Fax: + 34 943 015590
{nestor,julio.abascal}@si.ehu.es

Abstract. Prediction is one of the most extended techniques to enhance the rate of communication for people with motor and speech impairments who use Augmentative and Alternative Communication systems. There is an enormous diversity of prediction methods and techniques mentioned in the literature. Therefore, the designer finds tremendous difficulties in understanding and comparing them in order to decide the most convenient technique for a specific design. This paper presents a survey on prediction techniques applied to communicators with the intention of helping them to understand this field. Prediction applications and related features, such as block size, dictionary structure, prediction method, interface, special features, measurement and results, are detailed. Systems found in the literature are studied and described. Finally, a discussion is carried out on the possible comparison among the different methods.

1 Introduction

Over the last few years, several computerised systems have been designed to assist people with disabilities for personal communication purposes. Thanks to these systems, people who cannot speak, obtain alternative means of communication. This is the case of a large group of people with speech and motor disabilities provided with alternative input systems in order to overcome their limitations. For instance, the scanning of a set of options selected by using a single key is a very appropriate method for people with poor control of hand movement. For this input system, only a residual voluntary controlled movement is required in order to input each character. Nevertheless, scanning-based communication devices are extremely slow, and only few words per minute can be composed with their use. Several authors have estimated this speed up to 10 words per minute[1] [4]). This leads to embarrassing situations where disabled people cannot participate in normal conversations, and, therefore, become socially excluded.

1.1 Precedents of the Prediction

Prior to the appearance of communicators, a number of people used to point to a board with a matrix of characters in order to communicate. The interlocutor would

---

[1] In a normal conversation some 180-200 words/minute are said, whereas a disabled person using a scanning-based input device can only type around 2-10 words/minute. This difference may cause practical problems for maintaining a conversation and psychological effects on the users [2].

C. Stary and C. Stephanidis (Eds.): UI4All 2004, LNCS 3196, pp. 400–417, 2004.
© Springer-Verlag Berlin Heidelberg 2004

look at the character pointed by the user and reconstruct the sentence. Observing this process, one can frequently detect, the user did not need to finish the word, as the interlocutor was able to predict the remaining letters. To do this, the interlocutor used their knowledge about the structure of the language (morphologic and syntactic levels), and about the context of the conversation (semantic level). This prediction ability produced a considerable increase in the speed of communication, and a feeling of integration in both speakers. Therefore, the challenge for human interface designers is whether a computer is able to reproduce this behaviour, proposing sensible predictions based on the available information about the language and context.

1.2 Users of Prediction Methods

As previously mentioned, predictors are included in communication aids and try to increase the user's rate of communication. Therefore, these predictors benefit people with severe motor and oral disabilities such as cerebral palsy, hemiplexia, etc., under the condition they are able to use them. According to [43], users of prediction systems require a certain phonetic spelling ability. They also need to be able to distinguish words which look similar in prediction lists and they must also be able to flexibly shift their attention back and forth between the input device and the prediction lists. Even if prediction methods have been firstly studied to be applied in order to solve the needs of people with disabilities, anybody can benefit from prediction techniques if they are adequately integrated into the interface. See, for instance, the Reactive Keyboard [15, 28].

1.3 Diversity of Prediction Methods

Several research teams have reported diverse works on prediction over the last few years. A number of systems developed are commercially available, whereas others have only reached the prototype phase. Different algorithms, dictionary organisations and interfaces have been designed. They are based on diverse features of language and the number of offered options; the selection method is also very varied. Their performance can hardly be compared as the measurements offered by authors are based on heterogeneous parameters, not always clearly described. Even if all these differences make the comparison difficult, we have found surveying known prediction methods useful to obtain an idea on the state of the art in this area. We are aware of the fact that some of the interesting systems commercially available are not included. Several authors, such as [27, 31], have compared commercial products. This survey is limited to those methods that have been sufficiently described in technical papers we have found.

2 Analysis of Prediction Systems

Focusing on the assistive communication field, a predictor is a system which tries to anticipate the next block of characters (letters, syllables, words, sentences, etc.) the user wants to express. In general, the prediction is based on the previously produced blocks. The main aims of a predictor are to reduce the effort and message-elaboration time. In order to reduce the effort, it tries to decrease the number of keystrokes needed to compose a message. To decrease the needed time, the predictor offers blocks with more characters than the block the user can normally select from (the system predicts the user wants to say/write).

There are two main concepts to bear in mind when analysing communication systems, *articulacy* and *fluency* [30]. *Articulacy* means there is always at least one option that can be selected among all the offered proposals. That is to say, the option the user wants to write is always among those offered by the system. The fluency, also called the communication rate, is the number of characters produced by a time unit.

Articulacy and fluency are opposite concepts, as the increase of one usually causes a decrease in the other. A system that only offers the alphabet to the user is an example of a very articulate but fluently poor system. When using this system, a choice can be always selected; however, the communication rate is slow. A very fluent but not very articulate system is the one that offers several common words or sentences. If one of the options is selected, the communication rate is greater than having to compose words letter by letter. Nevertheless, it is also possible that the required option may not appear.

The aim of a communication-aid device is to maximise and balance both *articulacy* and fluency. When trying to obtain a high level of *articulacy*, all the possible characters are offered. In the case of fluency, in addition to the alphabet characters, various options longer than one character should be proposed. If these options are frequently selected, the fluency increases while *articulacy* remains of a high standard as, at least, one of the shown options may be selected each time.

Diverse criteria can be used to measure the quality of a predictor. A predictor can be considered adequate if it has a high hit ratio. In order to obtain a better hit ratio, designers can increase the number of options, consequently increasing the time required to select an option. This happens as the user is required to read all the options in order to decide if one is valid. A good design requires a balance between the hit ratio and the required selection time.

In the next sections, a number of important factors related to prediction systems are described. These factors are: block size, dictionary structure, prediction method, influence of the interface, special features, prediction measurement and prediction results.

2.1 Block Size

The choice of the predictable blocks is a very important factor as the keystroke rate and time saving depends on the size of the anticipated block. Therefore, the possible savings are a function of the block size and the hit rate of the predictor [26]. In this paper we will only consider blocks composed of alphabetic characters (other symbols and pictograms are not taken into account).

For pure texts, the minimum block size is a character. Each character has a different frequency of appearance. A first prediction method may propose all the letters sorted by frequency, without taking the preceding composed text (that is, with zero memory) into account. In this way, the proposals are always the same, independent to the previous characters. It is evident this method does not produce any keystroke savings as it requires the same number of keystrokes to accept the proposals and to write these characters, in the case of success. Nevertheless, the information of the character frequencies is useful in the scan-based interfaces to minimise the average time access [40, 53]. Hence, the options are distributed depending on their frequencies for a speedier access to the most frequent ones.

Predicting just one character produces very poor results; therefore, higher blocks must be treated. To make the use of the statistic information possible, which can be given by knowing the precedent text, *n-grams* (that is, blocks of *n* characters) are used. If the frequencies of the n-grams are stored, depending on the *(n-1)* precedent characters, the following may then be tried to be guessed [15, 28, 40]. A number of strings can be predicted, taking less than the *(n-1)* precedent characters into account. Depending on the number *n*, both the hit rate and the keystroke savings may be very high. The information related to n-grams is used to display dynamic scanning matrixes where, depending on the last selected characters, the most probable are placed near to the top-left place in the matrix. Lesher carried out a study related to this type of prediction and compared it with a word prediction method presented later in this paper [40].

Traditionally, the maximum length of the n-grams has been four (tetra-grams), mainly due to computational and storage limitations [40]. However, with reference to Shannon's studies, it has been estimated that adequate predictions only require the knowledge of few characters and there are no significant improvements in the achieved results when knowing more than eight previous characters [48].

A special case is *k-grams*, which are n-grams whose first character is the start of a word. N-grams are independent to their position within a word whereas k-grams take advantage of the positioning [40].

Syllables and morphemes have interesting linguistic properties that are very predictable. However, they produce low keystrokes savings. In this line of approach, the word is considered as a very adequate block due to its linguistic properties and average length. The idea is to guess the word the user is trying to write by taking the first character(s), already written, into account in order to obtain optimum keystroke savings and hit rate.

Another option is to try more than one word. Taking the last composed words(s) into account, the system then tries to anticipate the following words. In case of guessing correctly, the keystroke and time savings would be very high; however, the hit rate for more than one word is very low as the frequencies of sets of words are not very relevant except in a few common sentences, as in filler remarks, greetings and farewells [4, 21].

Among all the possible blocks, the word usually selected is due to its optimum relationship between the hit rate and the keystroke savings. Furthermore, the addition of morphologic, syntactic and/or semantic information may enhance the hit rate and the keystroke savings. Therefore, the word is the most used predictive block [10, 13, 17, 22, 31, 32, 33, 36, 49, 51, 55]. Nevertheless, there are studies that work with n-grams [28, 40] and morphemes [7, 23, 35].

2.2 Dictionary Structure

The character and n-grams predictors only need a table to store the blocks and their frequencies. Nevertheless, word prediction systems store the information they require in dictionaries or lexicons (that is, each word and all its related information) [24]. Predictors, which treat units longer than one word, have larger storage requirements. With each sentence, they may have to store information relative to the context, block type, frequency, type of conversation, etc. [4, 21].

To select the lexicon structure, the following factors must be taken into account [49]: Speed of operation (either access or modification), Facility of modification,

Price of storage, Storage simplicity and backup charge/discharge. The possibility of compressing files must also be taken into account.

Adaptability of the dictionary. It is usual to consider that initially the lexicon is common to the entire user population (that is to say, the lexicon is general and impersonal). This lexicon may be fixed or adaptable. In the last case, al least the original frequencies are being modified with the use of the system (the lexicon is personalised) [19, 33, 49]. The personalisation of the dictionaries creates a few problems related to their size and to management. A complete study related to this feature may be found in [24, 26].

Dictionary organisation. Another factor is the method by which the lexicon is organised [49]. This may be a linear list where items (that is, words and their related information) are stored sequentially. The order where items are stored may be ascendant or descendant, alphabetically (taking the words into account) or by frequencies [24]. This organisation is very simple: it is easy to carry out searches and modifications. However, the main disadvantage is that it is very slow: the accesses are mainly sequential, therefore, in highly sized lexicons, obtaining access to the last items requires a long time.

In contrast to the linear list organisation, a number of lexicons have a tree structure. In these dictionaries, the searches are faster; however, the structure and the management of the lexicon are more complicated. Moreover, in cases where adding a new element may cause changes in the entire lexicon structure.

Number of dictionaries. The number of dictionaries is another important factor. It is possible to have only one lexicon that stores all the items or to have diverse lexicons to distribute all the items. The first option may have a higher accessing time associated but a simpler management. The second option may have a faster access associated but complicating the management due to the number of dictionaries to be treated. In this way, the management of the small lexicons may be especially complex and the treatment of all the items may then become slower than in the case of having only one lexicon.

2.3 Prediction Method

Diverse strategies may be used to make predictions. This section focuses on word prediction methods. Nevertheless, these methods may also be applied, with subtle variations, to the case of the morphemes.

Prediction using frequencies. The simplest predictors take the words and their frequencies[2] into account [19, 30, 33, 49, 52]. When the user has written the beginning of a word, the system offers the **n** most probable words beginning with the same character(s). The user may then accept one of the proposals or may continue writing the word (if the desired word is not among the options given by the system). The system may automatically adapt to the user lexicon by simply updating the frequencies of the used words. If a new word is added to the system, an initial frequency is assigned.

---

[2] Standard frequencies from dictionaries are usually taken. If it is possible, it is much better to use the actual frequencies of the words used by each user. Additionally, there are studies related to the frequencies of the words for different populations: For instance, [8] gives a list of the most probable English words used by people with disabilities.

In order to enhance the results of this approach, it is possible to take the last time a word was used into account, that is, the recency of use. In this case, the system offers the words most recently used, selected among the most probable words that begin with the character(s) written by the user. A *recency* field is stored in the dictionary with each word along with its frequency. Although the results obtained with this method are better than the previous ones [49], they require more information and an increased computational complexity.

Prediction using word probability tables. Another possibility is to consider the probability of each word to appear after the one previously composed. A two dimensional table where the probability of the word W_j after the word W_i is built. If therefore, the system has N words, there are N^2 entries in this table, most of them zero or nearly zero. By using this strategy, the system may offer predictions even before writing a character. These results may be enhanced if the recency is also taken into account. The main problem with this method is the difficulty of adaptation to the user's vocabulary when the dimensions of the table are fixed. Therefore, this approach is normally restricted. For example, several authors only use this approach with the most probable word-pairs [33].

Syntactic prediction using probability tables. This approach takes the syntactic information inherent to natural languages into account. With this purpose, two statistical data types are used, the probability of appearance of each word and the relative probability of every syntactic category to appear after each syntactic category. These systems offer the words with the most probable categories at this point of the sentence. The results are usually better than the ones obtained with the previously shown strategies.

A word in the dictionary is associated to its syntactic category and its frequency of appearance. For words with ambiguous categories, diverse strategies are discussed in Garay et al [22]. The most common are either to create a new category related to each possible ambiguity or to associate a list of categories to each word.

A two-dimensional table stores the probabilities of the categories to appear after each category. Its dimensions are fixed before the predictive system is built. This table is much smaller than the one in the previously presented approach and the number of probabilities that are nearly zero is also lower. The adaptation of these systems is made by updating the probabilities of the table and the frequencies in the lexicon. If new words are added, they may be included in the dictionary with a provisional category. There is then a need to manually give the correct definite category to the new words. It is possible to add morphological information in order to offer the words with the most appropriate morphological characteristics. This may cause an enhancement in the results achieved. Several systems in the references implement this strategy [19, 50].

Syntactic prediction using grammars. Sentences are analysed using grammars and applying Natural Language Processing techniques that come from the Artificial Intelligence area in order to obtain the categories that have the highest probability of appearance. Methods to analyse the sentences may be either top-down [51] or bottom-up [20, 22]. To do this, the set of syntactic rules of a given language is fundamental. These rules usually have the following structure:

$$\text{LEFT} \leftarrow [\text{RIGHT}]^+ . \tag{1}$$

This means that the category on the left of the rule may be decomposed in the sequence of categories on the right of the rule in the same order as they appear. At least one category has to appear on the right and all the categories are defined in the system. For example, if NP represents a Noun Phrase, PP a Prepositional Phrase, Noun a noun and Prep a preposition, the following rules:

$$NP \leftarrow Noun\ PP\ . \tag{2}$$
$$PP \leftarrow Prep\ NP\ . \tag{3}$$

may be expanded to give following:

$$NP \leftarrow Noun\ Prep\ NP\ . \tag{4}$$

Therefore, recursive application of the rules is possible. In addition, it is possible to define a number of grammatical agreements (such as the number) amongst the categories on the right of a rule. In this way, it is possible to offer a few proposals taking their most appropriate morphological characteristics into account.

The used dictionary is very similar to the one in the previous approach, in addition to the required morphological information to make the grammatical agreements possible. These systems have a higher computational complexity than the previous, mainly due to the fact that they take the entire beginning of the sentence into account (while the previous systems take at the most, the last entirely composed word). These types of systems may be adapted by updating the word probabilities and weights of the syntactic rules. To add new words to the dictionary, the solutions that can be taken in the previous approach may also be used here [34, 55].

Semantic prediction. These methods are not commonly used as the results they achieve are very similar to syntactic approaches with much higher computational complexity. The easiest way to make this type of prediction is by semantically analysing the sentences as they are being composed. In this way, each word has a semantic category (or a set of semantic categories) associated, similarly to the syntactic categories of previous approaches. The remaining characteristics (working method, complexity, dictionary structure, adaptations, etc.) are very similar to the syntactic approach using grammars. However, the biggest difficulty is to a semantic category to each word. Several authors propose to carry out the categorisation "by hand" [34]. There are a number of automatic allocation methods which use semantic information [20, 33]; nevertheless, they are quite complex and it is difficult to implement them in a real-time system. The time they require to make predictions is the main reason why they are normally academic approaches (not implemented in the real world).

2.4 The Influence of Language in Predictions

Most of the references related to prediction, analyse non-inflected languages such as the English. In this paper, we will also consider inflected languages such as Basque, Finnish, German, Swedish, etc. A language is inflected (or better still, highly inflected) when it is possible to produce a large number of inflections starting from a root or lemma. In contrast, we consider a language as not being inflected (or better still, poorly inflected) when only a small number of inflections may be obtained by starting from a root (as in the cases of English, French or Spanish, for example) [24, 25].

In non-inflected languages, inflections are mainly derived from the number (and, in some cases, the gender). The root is the part representing the main idea of the word and remains unchanged in every word of the same semantic family. Inflections are added to obtain diverse meanings. For instance, the number may be singular or plural (*house/houses*, *spy/spies*, etc.). In some languages (French, Spanish, etc.), the gender may be masculine or feminine: *voisin/voisine*.

When the variations of a word are only few, it is possible to store all in the used dictionary in order to make the predictions. However, inflected languages produce many inflections; therefore, it may be difficult to store all of them[3]. This is the main reason for the search of new prediction methods to be used in languages with a wide use of prefixes, infixes and suffixes. Work related to this field can be found in [7, 10, 23, 24, 35].

Morpho-syntactic correctness. Another interesting feature of word prediction is the possibility of showing the proposals in the most adequate morpho-syntactic inflection. It is also possible to automatically correct the resulting text after accepting a proposal in order to obtain the most adequate form [58].

When the system does not have any type of correction, the user has to manually adapt the suffixes of the accepted proposal. For example, if the user wishes to write "houses" and the system only proposes "house" he or she must add an "s". This occurs as the context of the sentence is not taken into account, as in the case of prediction using frequencies (see section 2.3). For non-inflected languages, this may be a perfectly valid approach. However, in inflected languages, the number of possible suffixes is very high and a great physical (and possibly cognitive) effort is needed to add the appropriate suffix to the base form. In order to solve this problem, several authors propose dividing the prediction of a word into *root* and *suffix* [7, 23]. In this way, the root is firstly composed and then a list of suffixes is proposed to create the adequate form. In general, a two-step process is needed to compose a word entirely (there may be a few exceptions) and a post-processing of the system may be necessary (for example, to create the irregular cases starting from a root and a suffix). Therefore, there is a need to have at least two lexicons, each one related to each part of the word taken into account [25]. Nevertheless, there may be a number of cases where roots and suffixes may be concatenated to provide entire words as proposals [24].

2.5 Influence of the Interface

There is a large number of factors related to the interface that may have an influence on the results a predictive system may have. A number of them also affect the acceptation a system achieves in the user population. These factors are slightly shown in this section, as they are presented in greater detail in several references [24, 26].

Number of proposals. A large number of proposals produce better prediction results [11, 13, 19, 33, 37, 40, 49], measured as hit ratio and keystroke savings. However, the required time to read the proposals [37] and the difficulty in putting all of these pro-

---

[3] In the case of Basque language, starting from a given root, 62 basic inflections may be obtained. Suffixes may be recursively concatenated (as it is an agglutinated language) increasing the number of possible inflections. With a two-level recursion, it has been estimated that a noun may reach 458,683 variations [1]. While prefixes and infixes are possible in Basque, in our studies relative to the prediction, we have included them within the roots as their probabilities are not very significant.

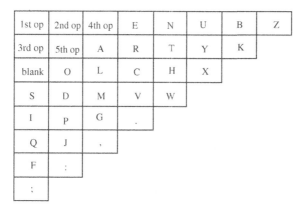

1st op	2nd op	4th op	E	N	U	B	Z
3rd op	5th op	A	R	T	Y	K	
blank	O	L	C	H	X		
S	D	M	V	W			
I	P	G	.				
Q	J	,					
F	:						
;							

Fig. 1. Example of a triangular matrix.

1st option		blank	E	O	R	U	Q	G
2nd option		A	S	L	T	B	J	X
3rd option		N	D	C	Y	F	W	:
4th option		I	M	H	Z	.	;	)
5th option		P	V	K	,	(	+	-

Fig. 2. Example of the grouped access for a scan-based interface.

posals within an interface [24] causes the number to be normally restricted in real systems up to between five and seven [31, 49].

Layout of the proposals. Vertical lists of proposals are better appreciated than horizontal lists as they require less effort to see and process [45, 49]. A number of authors suggest sorting the proposals alphabetically instead of probabilistically [37]. Others suggest allocating fixed places to the proposals in order to facilitate the memorising of the locations and automate their use [37, 40].

Acceptation or rejection protocol. A number of systems oblige the user to select one of the proposals or to explicitly reject them (if none are valid) in order to continue the input of text. An adequate strategy to enhance the message composition speed is to implicitly reject all the proposals by writing a new character of the word.

Layout of the selection set. In scan-based interfaces, the layout of the proposals must be carefully analysed. Triangular matrixes (Figure 1) give the best average access time [5]; however, they are difficult to present on a screen. There is also the possibility of distributing the options between more than one matrix, as shown in Figure 2, known as grouped access [40]. In both Figures, "nth option" (or "nth op") are proposals given by the predictor (usually ordered by probabilities), "blank" is the space character, and the remaining characters are letters and punctuation signs. For instance, in Figure 1, scanning may start highlighting rows top-down. When a row is selected, its elements are scanned from left to right until one is selected. In Figure 2, the block is first selected (either the list of predictor proposals on the left or either a matrix with the characters on the right). If the left block is selected, the desired word is directly incorporated to the text. While if the right block is selected, two more keystrokes are needed (one for the row and another for the column) to choose the following character the user wishes to write.

Required time for the prediction. Highly complex prediction algorithms may lead to inefficient systems. Large lexicons may also increase search time. There is a need to find a balance between algorithm complexity, dictionary size and response time.

Minimum size of the options. With very small blocks, the achieved keystroke savings are not very significant in the case of hit. It is convenient to stop predictions if the number of saved keystrokes is not enough.

Usability. There is a need to make a number of intelligent decisions in order to provide adequate dimension to anticipatory systems [45] and decrease the required cognitive and physical effort needed by the users. User preferences must also be taken into account to enhance the efficiency and to decrease fatigue. For instance, the including of proposals and keyboard characters in a touch screen may decrease the physical effort needed to use a prediction system, as they are in the same visual plane [26]. In a similar way, [54] tests the functionality and usability of a word prediction prototype.

Adaptation. Adaptable systems may enhance the achieved results if, for example, the words most used in the system are promoted in relation to words not used, even if the last initially have a higher frequency of appearance. Adaptation may be well appreciated by users who see their vocabulary becoming more approximate to the system with use; however, other users may prefer the system not to be adapted in order to memorise the locations of the options.

2.6   Special Features

In the literature, there are prediction systems with particular features not present in other predictors. In this section, we review the most relevant features found.

For example, the dictionary of the PAL (Predictive Adaptive Lexicon) system developed in the University of Dundee [49] has a tree structure. In this structure, each node can be the prefix of the words contained in its sub-tree. It is necessary to store two pointers with each node: one points to the sub-list based on the common prefix and the other points to a sub-list which takes the current node as its prefix. A flag is associated to each node in order to distinguish a node containing a word and another containing a prefix. This structure proves to be extremely useful to gain access to the lexicon; however, the storage size and the management of the dictionary increase. Another factor also studied by this research team is the possibility of making remote prediction by using the client-server model and showing the interface in the local machine [6]. The minimum bandwidth required for this objective is estimated 9,600 bauds. With a lower bandwidth, the prediction list requires a long time to arrive and the user tend to ignore it.

The script technique to make predictions is also studied [45]. These scripts capture the essence of stereotyped situations and allow taking constancy of what it is happening and predicting what is going to happen next. The Script Talker system uses a scene-based interface to guide users through common dialogues.

There is a remarkable effort devoted to product *speech acts* in a competent way, instead of enhancing the production of letters, words or specific sentences [2, 3, 4]. A speech act is a phrase or a sentence that has a particular purpose in dialogue. The CHAT (Conversation Helped by Automatic Talk) prototype is based on the patterns found in a non-restricted dialogue. The main purposes of this technique are to increase the communication speed, to express the user's personality and form of communication and to minimize silences. The best results of this system have been obtained at the start and at the end of the conversation, as they are very regular. However, in the main discussion, and taking all the possible themes into account, the hit ratio decreases.

The COHORT programme, described by [33], is especially designed for people with aphasia. This system tries to reconstruct the current word from phonemes, phonetic components or stressed syllables. The list of proposals includes the pronunciation elements that have been used in the same order they appear; however, they are not necessarily consecutive. The proposals may be presented on the computer screen or by means of synthesised voice.

The PROFET system applied to Swedish, a highly inflected language, can make the prediction of a word in two steps: one for the word-root and the other for the suffix [7]. PROFET II includes syntactic and semantic information and uses Markov models to consider the previous last two words and their frequencies [10, 11, 42].

There are several works focused on n-gram prediction. For example, the Reactive Keyboard system is devoted to predict text written in any natural language, programming language, command interpreter, etc. [15, 28]. Predictions are generated from an adaptive model obtained from previously written text. It uses a "click and drag" interface, which makes extensive use of the mouse.

Lesher et al. study k-gram, n-gram and word prediction strategies in order to include them in scan-based interfaces [40]. Square matrixes are used to lay out the selection set. The predictor's proposals are located in these matrixes. These authors also present quantified human word prediction in order to estimate the desirable performance [41].

Several systems make syntactic predictions using an X' grammar based probabilistic ATN parser [51]. They analyse sentences top-down which are expanded by level instead of by depth.

Claypool et al. [12] present a statistic predictor based on word tri-grams (series of three words) applied to Gaelic, within a project relative to various European languages such as English, French, German, Spanish, etc. This predictor is called PredictAbility and its results are evaluated by programmes and stored in files compatible with MATLAB.

Wood et al. use a Grammar Description Language (GDL) to describe an aspect of English grammar and apply it to word prediction [55]. Based on this idea, they have also developed a prototype called WindMill [56].

The VITIPI (Versatile Interpretation of Text Input by Persons with Impairments) presented by Boissiere [9] is a word predictor that, when no proposal may be presented, tries to infer certain analogies or even alter strings in order to present one.

Laine et al. distinguish between manual (written) and oral (by speech recognition) word prediction and study where to apply each one [38, 39].

In [47], artificial neural networks are used to make predictions for Spanish. They implement a network using 130 neurones (100 in the input layer, 10 in the hidden layer and 20 in the output layer), which obtains the probabilities of the 20 categories of POS (Part Of Speech) categorisation.

Even if most systems are designed for the Windows environment [29], there are several for other platforms. For instance, Gaiarin [18] present a method for Linux operating system and Worthylake [57] refers to a platform-independent system built in Java.

Garay et al. [20] present a chart bottom-up parser, which may be used in syntactic word prediction for Spanish. The results obtained with this technique (comparing with the prediction using frequencies) suggested its application to a highly inflected language, such as Basque [24], in a two-step process to complete the words.

To conclude several prediction systems allow for abbreviation expansion, topic-specific lists, word modifications and even speech features [43].

2.7 Measurement of the Prediction

In general, it has been considered a predictor is adequate if its hit ratio is high as the required number of selections decreases (as seen in [13, 19, 33, 40, 49]). A high hit ratio may be achieved by giving the appropriate choosing criteria to the predictor.

The hit ratio is the probability of guessing in prediction and it may be expressed as the quotient between the number of times the words are guessed and the number of written words (that is, it is the probability of guessing the word before completely writing it):

$$\text{hit ratio} = \text{no of times the word is guessed} / \text{no of written words} . \tag{5}$$

However, the hit ratio is not enough to evaluate the quality of a predictor, as it is possible for the valid guesses occur at the end of the word and then the keystroke savings are very low. This is the reason for including several parameters to measure this feature. Therefore, the keystroke savings are defined as:

$$\text{keystroke savings} = 1 - \text{no of written keystrokes} / \text{total no of keystrokes} . \tag{6}$$

In direct selection, a keystroke gives a character as the result and this equation will easily be adapted to obtain the character savings.

Time savings are also defined in a similar way:

$$\text{time savings} = 1 - \text{used time} / \text{necessary total time} . \tag{7}$$

This last measurement is more difficult to evaluate, as there are various factors that depend on the user's characteristics. For this reason, the time savings are usually estimated as a factor proportional to the keystroke savings.

All these measurements are taken with the supposition that only one proposal is offered each time. It is evident the hit ratio is enhanced when presenting a number of options instead of only one. However, after a given number of options, the hit ratio grows very slowly (it presents an asymptote) [13, 24]. Moreover, by incrementing the number of options, the probability of guessing sooner grows. Nevertheless, the required time to select among them is also incremented. Therefore, it is not very useful to increase the number of options as the delay in selecting the adequate option compensates the advantages of the prediction.

There are other methods to evaluate the quality of the predictors. For instance, Greenberg et al. present the potential savings as the difference between the cost using predictions and the cost of entering standard events, as seen in Table 1 [28]. In both costs (using predictions and entering standard events), there is a time required to decide and further time required to execute its relative actions. Even Zohar et al. [17] use the Word Error Rate and the Errors in the Focus of Attention (that is, when the correct word and its category are not guessed) to measure the systems.

Table 1. Potential savings using prediction.

Savings = Cost of using predictions - Cost of entering standard events
Cost of using predictions = Visual scan time to search predictions + Cognitive time to decide on prediction + Physical movement time to select prediction
Cost of entering standard events = Cognitive time required to formulate next event + Physical movement required to enter next event

Expressing the results. Generally, the anticipatory methods found in the literature express their results in terms of the savings they achieve. For example, most of the anticipators have been evaluated showing the keystroke savings they obtain [19, 20, 33, 34, 49, 50]. There are others which show the message composition time saved, which is directly associated with the keystroke savings [13, 36]. The hit ratio may also be shown [24], as previously noted.

A rigorous comparison among the different methods appearing in the literature would require a standard workbench to establish a corpus from where to obtain the dictionaries, the trial texts to write and the type of measurements to obtain [24]. As this workbench does currently not exist up, the results authors present are very heterogeneous and practically impossible to reproduce (as the description of the used algorithms is usually superficial). Therefore, the comparisons among them are purely estimative and do not have evidential value.

Obtaining the results. In the literature related to prediction, there are two main methods to evaluate the presented systems. The first, automatic, uses a programme which tries to write several trial texts, emulating human behaviour. This system makes use of a communication programme that reproduces the predictor behaviour. The second method, manual, takes a set of real users who try to write given texts into account.

By using simulations, the best results in terms of keystroke savings may be achieved. Furthermore, the best communication speed that can be achieved to a given text may be calculated. Nevertheless, this method of evaluating has the disadvantage that it does not take human features into account such as fatigue and the errors a real user may produce. Nevertheless, this method is relatively objective and it is useful to take a number of design decisions. Many authors show the results when using this evaluation method [11, 19, 32, 33, 49, 56].

On the other hand, the empirical evaluation with users allows for the obtaining of more reliable data with regard to the message composition speed as the test includes human factors such as error rate, fatigue, learning time, the likelihood of the system, etc. Moreover, it is possible to measure how the system is used (for example, if the user reads all the proposals the system gives before making a selection), whether the system and its interface copes with the user's objectives (that is, if it is easy to learn and use, if a faster message composition is achieved, if a better orthography is achieved, and so on). Data related to user's preferences may also be obtained. Therefore, several authors prefer to perform tests with real users [11, 36, 44, 52].

In our opinion, the second method is the best to obtain a validation of the design in real conditions; however, it presents the difficulty of finding a set of people who may represent the entire population of possible users of the system. Moreover, the confidentiality of the results may also prove to be a problem [14] and there are authors who suggest this type of study may be very limited and confined to individual case studies [16]. This is the reason why in the design phase (testing and selecting the different characteristics of the system) predictors are frequently evaluated by simulations in order to compare their characteristics in an objective way.

2.8 Prediction Results

Not all the authors present the obtained results with the methods they use. In addition, as previously indicated, the lack of a standard workbench makes it impossible to compare each approach with the others. In this section we are going to present the most relevant results the developers show in the references we have found.

Firstly, the results achieved with the PAL system and the SYNTAX PAL (as shown in [49, 50]) are presented. With an initially empty lexicon, the keystroke savings vary between 29% and 41% by only using statistical information. With pre-built lexicons, results may vary between 50% and 55%. Adding certain syntactical information, the results are enhanced between 0.5% and 2.0% with regard to the purely statistical version. Taking only syntactical information into account (without statistical data), the authors note the results are enhanced between 4.3% and 6.4%. In all the studies, the number of proposed words is one, five or ten and that from five proposals onwards, there is no significant enhancement of the results. The authors also state they have obtained a 69.48% for keystroke savings, which is very near the theoretical maximum.

With the CHAT system [2, 3, 4], the authors suggest the achieved communication speed is between 12 and 85 words/minute, still far from the 150-200 words/minute of natural oral conversations; however, better than the 2-10 words/minute achieved with the use of typical communication devices.

In the studies related to the PROFET programme, they have studied a statistical approach in comparison to the addition of syntactic or semantic information [33, 34]. The authors have found the addition of syntactic information enhances between 2.6% and 5.1% the results of a purely statistic approach (taking from one to six proposals into account). Surprisingly, they have also found the addition of semantic information does not enhance these results. With relation to the studies devoted to PROFET II [11], the grammatical monograms enhance the results of the statistical approach by 3.1%. The grammatical bi grams enhance by 7.4% the monogram approach and a tri-grammatic approach enhances by 1% the bi-grammatic one. The new version achieves a 47% in keystroke savings in comparison with the 35% achieved by the older version; nevertheless, the keystroke saving are nearby 50% with a greater lexicon.

A number of different predictive programmes are evaluated by using the same trial tests in [32]. These systems are EZ Keys, Predictive Linguistic Programme (PLP), Write 100, Words Strategy and Generic Encoding Technology (GET). Several tests with 20 texts of 500 word-length are composed by some scholars without disabilities. The keystroke savings vary between 31% (GET) and 45% (EZ Keys). The vocabulary covered by these methods is also mentioned and varies from the 45% in Write 100 to the 91% in EZ Keys.

The results of the Messenger programme presented by [52] with an initial lexicon having 903 words and showing up to 15 proposals for the user are: the keystroke savings are 49.1%, the 88% of the words are predicted and the time needed to compose the messages is greater when using prediction than without (in a proportion of 1.057 to 1.0).

The studies carried out by Lesher et al. related to prediction applied to scanning-based interfaces show that with n-grams and k-grams, the keystroke savings are up to 40.5% while the word prediction achieves up to 38.8%, presenting seven proposals [40]. The authors conclude by saying it is easier to guess one out of 26 characters than one out of 50000 words.

The WindMill system achieves up to 56.33% in keystroke savings taking both statistical and syntactic information into account [56] and nearly 100% in hit rate after entering the initial three letters of a word.

In the VITIPI system presented by Boissiere [9], the keystroke savings the system achieves are up to 29.3% for French (with a 5930 word lexicon), up to 35.3% for English (with 2566 words in the lexicon) and up to 44.3% for German (with 5835 words). They also claim the communication speed is incremented and the quality of the composed text is better than the HandiWord system, which is one of the systems compared to VITIPI.

The Predice and PredictAbility systems are evaluated by using a number of multilingual trial texts (in English, French, German, Italian and Spanish) published by the European Union [46]. With five proposals, the keystroke savings obtained by PredictAbility vary between 30% and 37%. They suggest if several of the particular characteristics of the languages are born in mind, these results may be enhanced (for example, up to 48.21% in the case of Spanish).

The systems designed and implemented in the Laboratory of Human-Computer Interaction for Special Needs are presented and evaluated in [24]. The results for the Spanish language are up to 52.22% in keystroke savings and 97.26% of the words may be predicted (with one, five and ten proposals). The results for the Basque language (an inflected one) are, with maximum of ten proposals, up to 52. 52% in keystroke savings and 90.09% of the words may be predicted. The keystroke savings are similar to both languages with different hit ratios mainly due to the fact that the average length of the words in Basque is higher than in Spanish.

3   Conclusions

In this paper, a study on the prediction of alphanumeric blocks and their related factors has been presented. The factors analysed are block size, dictionary features, prediction method, language, interface, adaptability, and other special features.

The diverse prediction measurement and their results have been shown, both objectively (using programmes emulating the user's behaviour) and subjectively (by means of users tests). The results are expressed by the keystroke savings; however, other factors such as the hit ratio may be used. The most relevant results found in the literature have been compared.

The need of a standard workbench has been expressed in order to compare the different techniques in an appropriate way. While this test is not set, the comparisons made are merely informative and not provable, and they cannot be used to express whether one approach is better than another.

Acknowledgements

This work has been financed by the Basque Government, the Department of Economy of the local administration Gipuzkoako Foru Aldundia, the University of the Basque Country and the PITER Program, supported by the CICYT and IMSERSO.

References

1. Agirre E, Alegria I, Arregi X, Artola X, Diaz De Ilarraza A, Maritxalar M, Sarasola K, Urkia M. 1992. Xuxen: A Spelling Checker/Corrector for Basque Based On Two-Level Morphology. Proceedings of the 3rd Conference on Applied Natural Language Processing. Association for Computational Linguistics. 119-125
2. Alm N, Arnott J L, Newell A. 1989. Discourse Analysis and Pragmatics in the Design of Conversation Prosthesis. *Journal of Medical Eng. and Technology* 13, Number 1/2. 10-12
3. Alm N, Newell A, Arnott J. 1989. Revolutionary Communication System to Aid Non-Speakers. *Speech Therapy in Practice Update*. March, VII-VIII
4. Alm N, Arnott J L, Newell A F. 1992. Prediction and Conversational Momentum in an Augmentative Communication System. *Communications of the ACM* 35, Number 5. 46-57
5. Arruabarrena A, G. Abascal J. 1988. Comunicadores y Emuladores de Teclado. *Tecnologías de la Información y Discapacidad*. Fundesco, Madrid. 133-156
6. Beattie W, Hine N, Arnott J. 1998. Distributed Assistive Communication Devices For Non-Speaking Users. *Proceedings of the Isaac Conference*, Dublin (Ireland), August. 447-448
7. Bertenstam J, Hunnicutt S. 1995. Adding Morphology to a Word Predictor. *The European Context for Assistive Technology (Proceedings of the 2nd Tide Congress)*. IOS Press/Ohmsa, Bruselas. 312-315
8. Beukelman D R, Yorkston K M, Poblete M, Naranjo C. 1984. Frequency of Word Occurrence in Communication Samples Produced By Adult Communication Aid. *Journal of Speech and Hearing Disorders* 49. 360- 367
9. Boissiere P, Dours D. 1996. VITIPI: Versatile Interpretation of Text Input by Persons with Impairments. *Interdisciplinary Aspects on Computers Helping People with Special Needs: 5th International Conference (ICCHP'96)*. Oldenbourg, Linz (Austria). 165-172
10. Carlberger J. 1997. Design and Implementation of a Probabilistic Word Prediction Program. *Master's Thesis in Computer Science*, Nada, KTH, Stockholm (Sweden). http://www.speech.kth.se/~Johanc/Thesis/Thesis.doc
11. Carlberger A., Carlberger J., Magnuson T., Hunnicutt M. S., Palazuelos-Cagigas S. E., Aguilera Navarro S. 1997. Profet, a New Generation of Word Prediction: An Evaluation Study. *Procs. of the Natural Language Processing for Communication Aids Workshop*. Association for Computational Linguistics. 23-28
12. Claypool T., Ricketts I., Gregor P., Booth L., Palazuelos S. 1998. Learning Rates of a Tri-Gram Based Gaelic Word Predictor. *Procs. of ISAAC Conference*, Dublin (Ireland). 178-9
13. Copestake A. 1997. Augmented and Alternative NLP Techniques for Augmentative and Alternative Communication. *Proceedings of the Natural Language Processing For Communication Aids Workshop*. Association for Computational Linguistics. 37-42
14. Copestake A, Flickinger D. 1998. Evaluation of NLP Technology for AAC Using Logged Data. *Isaac 98 Research Symposium Proceedings*, London. Whurr Publishers. http://www-csli.stanford.edu/~Aac/Evaluation-Dsp1.htm
15. Darragh J J, Witten I H, James M L. 1990. The Reactive Keyboard: A Predictive Typing Aid. *Computer*, 23. No. 11. 41-49
16. Digiovanni J M. 1996. Word Prediction Software as a Tool to Improve Writing Literacy. http://san183.sang.wmich.edu/Sped603fall96/Digiovannipaper.html
17. Even-Zohar Y, Roth D. 2000. A Classification Approach to Word Prediction. *Proceedings of the Naacl'00*. http://l2r.cs.uiuc.edu/~Evenzoha/Papers/Classificationapproach.Ps

18. Gaiarin M. 1999. Un Sistema di Predizione Sintattica per Gnu/Linux. *Tesi Di Laurea.* Università Degli Studi Di Padova. http://www.dei.unipd.it/~Gaio/Tesi/Favele.Ps.Gz
19. Garay N, Abascal J. 1994. Using Statistical and Syntactic Information in Word Prediction for Input Speed Enhancement. *Information Systems Design and Hypermedia.* Cépaduès-Éditions, Toulouse (France). 223-230
20. Garay-Vitoria N, Abascal J. 1994. Application of Artificial Intelligence Methods in a Word-Prediction Aid. *Computers for Handicapped Persons.* Springer-Verlag, Berlin. 363-370
21. Garay-Vitoria N, Abascal J, Urigoitia-Bengoa S. 1995. Application of the Human Conversation Modelling In a Telephonic Aid. *Procs. of the 15th International Symposium on Human Factors in Telecommunications (HFT'95),* Melbourne (Australia). 131-138
22. Garay-Vitoria N, Abascal J. 1997. Intelligent Word-Prediction to Enhance Text Input Rate. *Procs. of the Intelligent User Interfaces 97 Congress.* ACM Press, New York. 241-244
23. Garay-Vitoria N, Abascal J. 1997. Word Prediction for Inflected Languages. Application to Basque Language. *Proceedings of the Natural Language Processing for Communication Aids Workshop.* Association for Computational Linguistics. 29-36
24. Garay-Vitoria, N. 2001. Sistemas de Predicción Lingüística. Aplicación a Idiomas con Alto y Bajo Grado de Flexión, en el Ámbito de la Comunicación Alternativa y Aumentativa. *Servicio Editorial de la Universidad del País Vasco,* Leioa (Spain)
25. Garay, N, Abascal, J, Gardeazabal L. 2002. Evaluation of Prediction Methods Applied to an Inflected Language. *Proceedings of the 5th International Conference Text, Speech and Dialogue TSD2002.* Springer-Verlag, Berlin (Germany). 397-403
26. Garay-Vitoria, N, Abascal, J. 2004. User interface factors related to word prediction systems. *Proceedings of the 7th International Conference on Work With Computing Systems WWCS2004.* Kuala Lumpur (Malaysia)
27. Gillette Y., Hoffman J. L. 1995. Getting to Word Prediction: Developmental Literacy and AAC. *Proceedings of the Tenth Annual International Conference, Technology and Persons with Disabilities.* Northridge, California. Taken From [43]
28. Greenberg S., Darragh J. J., Maulsby D., Witten I. H. 1995. Predictive Interfaces: What Will They Think of Next? *Extra-Ordinary Human-Computer Interaction. Interfaces For Users With Disabilities,* Edwards A. D. N. (Ed.). Cambridge University Press. 103-140
29. Hecht J., Heinisch B. 1997. A Comparative Overview of Word Prediction Software for Windows 95. http://www.southernct.edu/Departments/Cat/Wordpred.html
30. Heckathorne C. W., Childress D S. 1983. Applying Anticipatory Text Selection in a Writing Aid for People with Severe Motor Impairment. *IEEE Micro.* 17-23
31. Heinisch B., Hecht J. 1993. Predictive Word Processors: A Comparison of Six Programs. *Tam Newsletter, 8,* 4-9
32. Higginbotham D. 1992. Evaluation of Keystroke Savings Across Five Assistive Communication Technologies. *Augmentative and Alternative Communication,* 8. 258-272
33. Hunnicutt S. 1987. Input and Output Alternatives in Word Prediction. *STL/QPRS 2-3/1987.* 15-29
34. Hunnicutt S. 1989. Using Syntactic and Semantic Information in a Word Prediction Aid. *Procs of the European Conference on Speech Comm. and Technology* 1, Paris. 191-3
35. Hunnicutt S, Nozadze N, Chikoidze G. 2003. Russian Word Prediction with Morphological Support. *5th Int. Symposium on Language, Logic and Computation,* Tbilisi, Georgia
36. Koester H. H., Levine S. P. 1994. Modeling the Speed of Text Entry with a Word Prediction Interface. *IEEE Transactions On Rehabilitation Engineering* 2, Number 3. 177-187
37. Koester H. H., Levine S. P. 1998. Model Simulations of User Performance with Word Prediction. *Augmentative and Alternative Communication* 14, 25-35
38. Laine C. J. 1998. Using Word-Prediction Technology to Improve the Writing of Low-Functioning Children and Adults. *Proc. Of The Australian Computers in Education Conference.* http://www.cegsa.sa.edu.au/Acec98/Papers/P-Laine.html
39. Laine C. J., Bristow T. 1999. Using Manual Word-Prediction Technology to Cue Student's Writing: Does It Really Help? CSUN99. http://www.dinf.org/Csun_99/Session0067.html

40. Lesher G. W., Moulton B. J., Higginbotham D. J. 1998. Techniques for Augmenting Scanning Communication. *Augmentative and Alternative Communication*, 14. 81-101
41. Lesher G. W., Moulton B. J., Higginbotham D. J., Alsofrom B. 2002. Limits of Human Word Prediction Performance. *2002 Technology and Persons with Disabilities Conference*, California State University Northridge
42. Magnuson T. 1998. Linguistic Evaluation of PROPHET II: A Pilot Project. *Proceedings of the Isaac Conference*, Dublin (Ireland), August. 479-480
43. National Center to Improve Practice. NCIP Library. http://www2.edc.org/Ncip/Library/Toc.htm
44. Newell A F, Arnott J, Waller A. 1992. On The Validity Of User Modeling In AAC: Comments on Horstmann and Levine (1990). *AAC*, 8. 89-92
45. Newell A. F., Arnott J. L., Booth L., Beattie W., Brophy B., Ricketts I. W. 1992. Effect of the "Pal" Word Prediction System on the Quality and Quantity of Text Generation. *AAC*, 8. 304-311
46. Palazuelos-Cagigas S., Aguilera S., Claypool T., Ricketts I., Gregor P. 1998. Comparison of Two Word Prediction Systems Using Five European Languages. *Proceedings of the Isaac Conference*, Dublin (Ireland), August. 192-193
47. Palazuelos-Cagigas S., Aguilera S., Ricketts I. W., Gregor P., Claypool T. 1998. Artificial Neural Networks Applied to Improving Linguistic Word Prediction. *Proceedings of the ISAAC Conference*, Dublin (Ireland), August. 194-195
48. Shannon C E. 1951. Prediction and Entropy of Printed English. *Bell System Technical Journal*. 50-64
49. Swiffin A. L., Arnott J. L., Pickering J. A., Newell A. F. 1987. Adaptive and Predictive Techniques in a Communication Prosthesis. *AAC*, 3. 181-191
50. Swiffin A. L., Arnott J. L., Newell A. F. 1987. The Use of Syntax in a Predictive Communication Aid for the Physically Handicapped. *RESNA 10th Annual Conference*, San Jose (California). 124-126
51. Van Dyke J. A. 1991. Word Prediction for Disabled Users: Applying Natural Language Processing To Enhance Communication. *Thesis Submitted For The Degree Of Honors Bachelor of Arts In Cognitive Studies*. University of Delaware
52. Venkatagiri H. S. 1993. Efficiency of Lexical Prediction as a Communication Acceleration Technique. *Augmentative and Alternative Communication*, 9. 161-167
53. Venkatagiri, H. S. 1999. Efficient Keyboard Layouts for Sequential Access in Augmentative and Alternative Communication. *AAC*, 15. 126-134
54. Wester M. 2003. User Evaluation of a Word Prediction System. *Master's Thesis in Computational Linguistics*, Uppsala University, Uppsala (Finland). http://stp.ling.uu.se/~matsd/thesis/arch/2003_wester.pdf
55. Wood M. E. J. and Lewis E. 1993. Grammatical Recognition in Computer Aided Conversation. *Proceedings of the European Speech Communication Association Workshop on Speech and Language Technology for Disabled People*. Stockholm (Sweden). 115-118
56. Wood M. E. J. 1996. Syntactic Pre-Processing In Single-Word Prediction for Disabled People. *PhD Thesis of the Department Of Computer Science*. University of Bristol, June
57. Worthylake K. 2000. A Platform-Independent Word Prediction Editor. *Honours Thesis Defence*. Acadia University, March. http://cs.acadiau.ca/Seminars/Previous/ Kevinworthylake.html
58. Zordell J. 1990. The Use of Word Prediction and Spelling Correction Software with Mildly Handicapped Students. *Closing the Gap*, 9(1). 10-11. Taken From [43]

A Framework for Context-Sensitive Coordination of Human Interruptions in Human-Computer Interaction

Sonja Gievska and John Sibert

Department of Computer Science, The George Washington University,
Washington D.C. 200052, USA
{sonjag,sibert}@gwu.edu

Abstract. Recent trends in software development directed toward intelligence, distribution, and mobility need to be followed by an increased sophistication in user interface design. Employment of theoretically sound methods for managing and coordinating complex information, and supporting graceful switching between tasks is especially critical for information-intensive and safety-critical tasks. This paper presents a framework for computer-mediated coordination of human interruptions. As a basis for the framework a new Interruption Taxonomy is outlined to categorize a variety of traceable information needed to exhaustively describe the context space. An exploratory user study is underway to calibrate the kind of benefit gained with the formulated Interruption Model. The expressiveness of the proposed Interruption Model is demonstrated by concretizing the general approach using the particularities of the selected problem domain. The initial results have shown that taxonomy-based coordination of interruption resulted in statistically significant improvement of the primary task resumption time.

1 Introduction

Any information presented to a user while she is working on a task could be considered interruption of her current endeavor. Given the frequency of presenting information in today's computer systems and the relative scarcity of humans, it is not surprising that some of these interruptions will have disruptive consequences on the human activity being interrupted. Interruption of one task in order to carry out another task very often leads to an increased error rate, hesitation and delay in making decisions, and in general, people are less effective when exposed to interruptions [1], [2], [3], and [7]. When repeated and numerous interruptions arise, increased attentional demand occurs because of the effort required to evaluate the significance of, and decide on appropriate responses to, multiple concurrent events [5]. Persistent and repeated interruptions may affect a person's attitude toward the entire situation, very often leading to a non-optimal behavior.

Computer outputs are very often generated in isolation from the context in which the interaction occurs. Presenting any kind of information to the user occurs for a reason, and that reason in relation to the current context in a broader sense of view, should ground the relevance and timing of the presentation. Employment of "intelligent" software that knows more about individuals with whom it is interacting and the

C. Stary and C. Stephanidis (Eds.): UI4All 2004, LNCS 3196, pp. 418–425, 2004.
© Springer-Verlag Berlin Heidelberg 2004

context of the situation in which the interaction occurs, can help computer systems augment humans' capabilities in the context of interruptions.

The motivation behind this research is the belief that effective coordination of interruption in human-computer interaction (HCI) cannot be accomplished without an appropriate interruption model. The proposed conceptual model is based on the new Interruption Taxonomy and uses Bayesian Belief Networks as a decision-support aid for mediating interruptions. Our first exploratory study is underway and the initial results confirm the hypothesized performance advantage of taxonomy-based coordination of interruption compared to the case with no coordination.

2 Interruption Taxonomy

It seems reasonable to establish a taxonomy of important characteristics relevant to the process of coordinating human interruption. The Interruption Taxonomy includes a set of abstractions that helps unify the issues previously considered by other researchers in a variety of different disciplines, proposes new ones, and suggests avenues for further exploration. The interruption-related information (i.e., categories) is categorized according to context: Task Context, User Context, and Environment Context. Each of the dimensions is consistent with a well-established tradition in HCI, which captures the three essential aspects of HCI. A graphical representation of the taxonomy three-dimensional interruption space is presented in Fig.1.

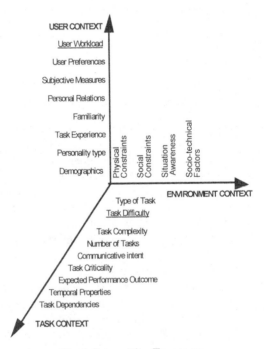

Fig. 1. Interruption Taxonomy.

Task-related context knowledge is crucial in disambiguating the meaning and the relevance of the interruption task in regard to the current user endeavor. Interruption requires a coordination of human behavior, and since coordination is "a process of managing dependencies among activities" [6], an important aspect of interruption coordination involves an identification of the relevant task interdependencies.

The user-related categories of the taxonomy are included to support representation of and reasoning about a particular situation as the user views it. Finding solutions to the problems associated with interruptions that are effective with respect to some objective criteria (i.e., task characteristics) is necessary but not sufficient. Coordination solutions must also be acceptable to a user's subjective criteria which may constrain the space of solutions and possible ways of handling interruption.

The Environment Context dimension extends the system context knowledge with information that captures the physicality and the dynamics of the working space. The inclusion of the environment-related categories attributes substantially greater sensitivity to the system, namely, the ability to adapt to a social setting, physical and organizational constraints, or the particularity of a given situation.

There are two theoretical constructs in the Taxonomy, namely Task Difficulty and User Workload. This framework proposes mapping these categories to other context variables that belong to all three taxonomy dimensions, and include: (1) factors that are used to portray the "objective" difficulty/workload based on what is known about that task in general, (2) characteristics to account for the individual differences and user's perspectives on how difficult/demanding a task is, and (3) environmental influences.

It is our hope that by beginning with the identification and categorization of interruption-relevant context information, this research has in some small way explicated the complex and multidimensional aspects of human interruptions and has attempted to present a way to capture it.

3   Conceptual Framework

The conceptual framework for a computer-supported coordination of human interruptions is based on the Interruption Taxonomy. This framework is not an attempt to build a deep psychological model of human behavior under interruptions, but rather an attempt to augment the machine's "intelligence" with a variety of contextual information, and appropriate reasoning machinery that will help the system decide when and in what manner to interrupt users when presenting tasks, messages, alerts and other information. This framework approaches the interruption problem by analyzing how people use the circumstances to evaluate the significance of an interruption and plan the most appropriate time to switch between tasks.

Augmenting machine's "intelligence" with a variety of contextual information, and appropriate reasoning machinery can help a system decide *when* and *in what manner* to interrupt users when presenting information. Inferential techniques must be applied to provide context-sensitive actions that are responsive to a particular state of interaction. We have adopted an approach based on Bayesian Belief Networks (BBNs) to represent the causal relationship between different pieces of information and to integrate rules for how to use, maintain, and reason with interruption-related knowledge. BBNs have proved suitable for making predictions and decisions from incomplete and uncertain data [4]. For our first exploratory study, the constructed BBN shown in Fig. 2 was initialized and trained off-line. Its outcomes were used as a basis for implementing the taxonomy-based mediated control of interruptions in our experimental environment.

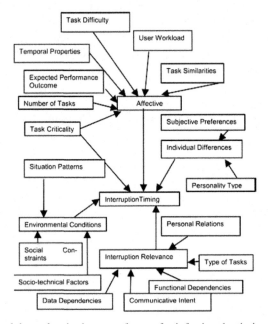

Fig. 2. High-level dependencies between factors for inferring the timing of interruption.

4 Exploratory User Study

Our major priority at the moment is to gather some evidence to evaluate the adequacy of the proposed approach and the utility of the taxonomy. To demonstrate the scope and the utility of the Interruption Taxonomy, an exploratory user study is underway. Our goal is to demonstrate the expressiveness of the Taxonomy by applying it in a particular interruption environment. In addition, we examined the effectiveness of taxonomy-based mediated control of interruptions compared to condition with no interruption control (i.e., interruptions were presented immediately at random-generated points).

As a test-bed application, we are using a two-task experimental system developed at the US Naval Research Laboratory (NRL) in Washington D.C that has already been used for interruption-related studies. The primary (interrupted) task is a resource-allocation task named Three-Strike (TS). The objective is to attack and destroy three destinations utilizing available resources, ten heavy and ten light tanks and a certain amount of fuel and munitions. On their missions, users are encountering resistance from differing locales and different kinds of obstacles based on a stochastic model of the TS task. User's interactions are limited to mouse point-and-click events with several dialog-box style windows.

The interrupting task is Tactical Assessment (TA) task presented to a user at random points while she is performing the primary task. In this task, the user plays the role of a fighter aircraft pilot looking at a radar-screen-like display where three types of objects appear. The objective is to indicate whether the approaching object is hostile or neutral. The decision of the "pilot" is assisted by an intelligent-automated component that colors the objects as red (hostile), blue (neutral) or yellow (when the assessment can not be made). The user is to confirm the red/blue indications or give the appropriate classification for the yellow objects based on a set of rules. User's interactions consist of two keystrokes per object using the right-hand numeric key pad. The first keystroke is the object classification (5-neutral, 6-hostile) and the second is the track number that appears next to each object.

The complex structure of the primary (TS) task was divided into a set of subtasks with different sensitivity to interruption (e.g., outfitting tanks, allocating tanks to mission, planning a mission, carry out a mission and review the mission report). We have conducted a pilot study to help us identify the subtasks particularly sensitive to interruption and distinguish the interruption points that were denoted as obtrusive or during the pilot study and domain-specific knowledge were used as a basis for coupling and chunking the TS task structure. The results had implications for selection of taxonomic factors relevant in our experimental environment and for initialization and off-line training of the constructed BBN.

We would like to note that our exploratory study was also used as a first step in refining the interruption model and putting the emphasis on the task-related taxonomy categories. For this particular experiment the timing of the interruption was mapped and coded to a certain interruption point within subtask (e.g., before or after a particular interaction event). The system keeps records of the times and contexts of all relevant interaction events. Each time the specified situation arises (i.e., sequence of interaction events), the system infers the user's goals based on the context of her interaction before and at the time of the interruption. The system adjusts in such a way that a user is not interrupted during interruption points sensitive to interruptions, deferring the interruption task for the next opportune moment.

4.1 Pilot Study

Fifteen volunteers participated in the pilot study using the same scenarios as experimental trials. Primary task resumption time defined as time from completing the interrupting task (restoring the TS window) to resuming the primary task was chosen as an appropriate measure in this study. Subjective preferences and perceptions were collected, but they were not considered as a factor in our implementation of the interruption coordination. Subjective preferences were generally inclined toward choosing the end of a subtask as the most opportune interruption point within each subtask. Not surprisingly, subjective preferences were not supported by actual objective measures. To the contrary, an interruption point placed at the end of a subtask led to longer resumption times partially because of the effort to decide on what to do next. Subjective preferences should not be neglected when designing user interfaces that give equal priority to user's satisfaction and comfort as to other performance measures.

Pilot study users were asked to rate the relative difficulty level of each subtask. The cognitive complexity/demand scale ranged from 1 (neglective) to 5 (very high). "Planning a mission" was rated as the most complex 4.5, while "allocating a task to a mission" was rated as a subtask with almost neglective cognitive demand 1.3. Objective measures have confirmed that "planning a mission" subtask was most sensitive to interruptions. This subtask consists of three activities, reviewing the map, reviewing the destination status and selecting a destination. The results showed that interrupting a user during this subtask leads to prolonged resumption time, several times longer than the user's average inter-click time. The severe degree of disruption during the "planning" block was expected because of its complexity and user's cognitive load associated with it. What was perhaps more informative for our design was that interruptions at the beginning of subtasks subsequent to the "planning" block caused lengthy resumption times as well. The likeliest explanation could be that the user was still maintaining the "planning" goal state as a basis for subsequent actions (e.g., outfitting a tank depended on users' strategy and plans established during the "planning" stage).

This finding is in line with, but also somewhat contradictory to the results and suggestions presented in [1], [3] and [7]. Their results showed that interruption coming at the beginning of a task is less disruptive than those presented at later points. The contradictory results may be due to differences in our experimental designs, especially the types of tasks that were used. Their suggestions that the most opportune moment for interruptions could be the moments associated with a start of a task could be generalized to tasks similar to their experimental tasks. In general, relatively simple tasks without any interleaving and inter-relationships were used, namely simple VCR programming tasks in [7], sequence of independent web-search tasks in [1], and [3]. Real-life task are not necessarily independent of each other and domain specific knowledge impacts interaction in profound way that have to be incorporated in the mechanisms for coordinating interruptions.

4.2 Experiment in Progress

A more formal experiment is currently underway. Twenty four participants were run through the experiment and the results presented in this section represent the initial data results. Each participant was instructed and trained on the primary and the interruption task, independently, followed by a 20 min. practice trial in the context of interruptions. The practice session lasted for approximately 1 hour including the time for completing the background questionnaire. After short break, the participants concluded four 15-minute trials of the TS task interrupted by a number of times, either 8 or 12, by the interruption task. The data were analyzed with a 2 (immediate and mediated interruption control) x 2 (8 and 12 number of interruptions during 15 min. session) within-subject Analysis of Variance (ANOVA). We analyzed the within-subject difference in task performance between the condition with immediate and computer-mediated coordination of interruption. An effort was made to control the number and the type of situations in which an interruption occurs keeping the frequency of interruptions randomly distributed across condition. Dependent variables were primary task resumption time, and accuracy on the interrupting task (i.e., percentage of correct object classifications).

Initial results have showed that resumption time for the interrupted task is sensitive to mediated coordination of interruption. Resumption times averaged at 5.5 sec for immediate condition to 4.7 sec for mediated coordination of interruptions. Fig. 3 contains mean resumption times separated by condition.

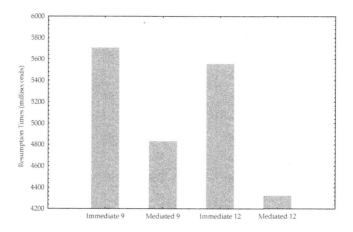

Fig. 3. Means of resumption times separated by condition.

Significant main effects were observed both for coordination method of interruption, $F (1, 23) = 48.707$, $p < 0.00001$, and frequency of interruptions $F (1, 23) = 9.85$, $p = 0.0046$. No reliable interaction between coordination method and frequency of interruption was found. The results confirm the hypothesized performance advantage of taxonomy-based mediation of interruption resulting in resumption times compared to condition with immediate coordination method. We found no significance effect of coordination method of interruption and the frequency of interruption on user's accuracy when performing the interrupting task.

Subjective exit questionnaires were distributed at the end of the experimental trials to measure the subjective level of stress and anxiety experienced by a user at specific interruption points. Subsequent analysis will assess the effects of individual differences and any potential correlation between subjective and objective measures.

5   Conclusions

In this paper, we presented a taxonomy-based conceptual framework for a computer-supported coordination of human interruptions in HCI. The outlined Interruption Taxonomy, which synthesizes various kinds of interruption-related context information served as a basis for implementing graceful coordination of interruption. An exploratory user study is underway to show the expressiveness and the effectiveness of the proposed framework. The initial results support the hypothesized performance advantage of taxonomy-based mediation of interruption to lessen the disruptive consequences of interruptions reflected in shorter resumption times compared to condition with immediate coordination method.

References

1. Bailey, B.P., Konstan J.A. and Carlis J.V.: The effects of interruptions on task performance, annoyance, and anxiety in the user interface. In: Proc. of Human-Computer Interaction – INTERACT 2001. IOS Press, (2001) 593-601
2. Cellier, J-M., and Eyrolle, H.: Interference between switched tasks. Ergonomics, Vol. 35, No. 1, (1992) 25-36
3. Cutrell E. B., Czerwinski M. and Horvitz E.: Effects of instant messaging interruptions on computing tasks. In: Proc. of Conference on Human factors in computing systems - CHI 2000, ACM Press New York (2000) 99-100
4. Horvitz, E., Jacobs, A., and Hove, D.: Attention-sensitive alerting. In: Proc. of UAI '99, ACM Press (1999) 305-313
5. Kirmeyer, S.: Coping with competing demands: Interruption and the type a pattern. Journal of Applied Psychology, Vol. 73, No. 4 (1988) 621-629
6. Malone, T., and Crowston, K.: The interdisciplinary study of coordination. ACM Computing Surveys, Vol. 26, No. 1 (1994) 87-119
7. Monk C. A., Boehm-Davis D. A. and Trafton J. G.: The attentional costs of interrupting task performance at various stages. In: Proc. of 46th Annual Meeting of the Human Factors and Ergonomics Society, HFES (2002) 1824-1828

A Method to Extend Functionality of Pointer Input Devices

Oleg Gusyatin[1,2], Mikhail Urinson[3], and Margrit Betke[1]

[1] Department of Computer Science, Boston University, Boston, MA 02215
{gusyatin,betke}@bu.edu
http://www.cs.bu.edu/~betke
[2] Department of Cognitive and Neural Systems, Boston University, Boston, MA 02215
gusyatin@cns.bu.edu
[3] Department of Computer Science, Tufts University, Medford, MA 02155
Mikhail.Urinson@tufts.edu

Abstract. We describe a general method for extending any pointer input device with an arbitrary set of commands. The proposed interface can be trained by the user to recognize certain cursor movement patterns and interpret them as special input events. Methods for extraction and recognition of such patterns are general enough to work with low-precision pointing devices, and they can be adjusted to provide computer access for people with disabilities. The core of the system is a trainable classifier, in the current implementation an artificial neural network. The architecture of the neural network automatically adjusts according to complexity of the classification task. The system demonstrated good accuracy and responsiveness during extensive experiments. Some tests included a severely motion-impaired individual.

1 Introduction

As miniature computers, such as personal digital assistants (PDAs), tablet and wearable computers gain popularity, more people face the problem of finding a mobile alternative for the traditional keyboard. While most portable devices offer a comfortable way to perform pointer input, their keyboard substitutes often have significant drawbacks. On-screen keyboard and graffiti symbol recognition software are among the most common keyboard alternatives for portable computers with pointer input. The disadvantage of on-screen keyboard is that it occupies valuable screen space. The graffiti symbol recognition method (sometimes it also employs a special area, but this can be avoided) is usually very inflexible: the user has to learn predefined symbols that might only slightly resemble real letters and digits. Accuracy of recognition and speed of input depends on the user's experience with this symbol language, which will take time to learn. Furthermore, users of traditional desktop and notebook computers, who employ wireless pointing input devices, such as camera-based [1], eye-gaze [9] and gyroscopic mice, often find keyboards, even wireless keyboards, inconvenient, for example, during a presentation. For many tasks, being able to access quickly and accurately even a small number of keys and key combinations could be very helpful. PDAs and advanced mice address this by having a few customizable

C. Stary and C. Stephanidis (Eds.): UI4All 2004, LNCS 3196, pp. 426–439, 2004.

buttons. Similarly, a small number of commands can be recognized by camera-based interfaces, for example, using eye blinks or eyebrow raises [6].

Some alternative pointer input techniques can be employed by people with disabilities to communicate with the computer. Vision-based human-computer interfaces allow users with limited range of voluntary motions to control the cursor using head, eye, or tongue movements [1]. From a more general point of view, the problem of adding an accessible keyboard to the computer with pointer input is similar to the problem of developing a convenient keyboard under mobility constraints.

To summarize all the above: several groups of people can benefit from an interface that allows to quickly access an arbitrary set of commands (keyboard keys and key combinations, internet browser commands, customizable "shortcut"-like functions, macros) on a computing device designed for pointer input. This interface should require minimum resources (no screen space, no additional hardware, small amount of processor time) and should not demand high precision of cursor control. Finally, rather than asking the user to memorize or practice predefined symbols, the interface should "learn" and adjust to "understand" the user's own commands. This is particularly important to people with severe motion impairments because with the proposed system they can design symbols according to their physical abilities.

In this paper we describe a general mechanism that extends pointer input functionality with an arbitrary set of commands. The core of the system is a trainable classifier, in the current implementation, an Artificial Neural Network (ANN), that is used to recognize user-defined Spatio-Temporal Patterns (STPs) produced by the cursor. The classifier has an adaptive architecture that enables it to automatically and efficiently adjust to accommodate the necessary number of classes. We attempted to make as few assumptions about potential STPs and user abilities and preferences as possible. As a result, the system can be used with different pointer input devices, and it can be modified to provide computer access for people with disabilities.

2 System Overview

The system consists of three major components: a preprocessor, a classifier, and an interpreter as shown in Figure 1. It takes an STP produced by the pointer input device and produces an operating system event.

Fig. 1. General System Overview.

In our approach, the collection of STPs used by the system, the alphabet, is completely determined by the user. As a result, the interface is general and can be conveniently used for many different tasks. However, the fact that no a priori information is available about the alphabet and its elements makes the classification problem difficult. In particular, the classifier has to be able to efficiently distinguish between an unknown number of classes of unknown appearance and structure. In addition, we want to allow the user to change the alphabet, i.e. add and remove elements at any moment. Hence, the choice of classifier is limited to models that can dynamically adjust their architectures without loosing the data that was already computed. A static classifier is not an option for three reasons. First, its potential, the number of classes it can distinguish, has an upper bound that may limit the size of alphabet. Second, among classifiers with enough potential to distinguish between members of a user-defined alphabet, we want to choose the smallest one for performance reasons. Third, the alphabet size may change during run time if the user decides to add or delete symbols. Instead of a static classifier, we use a dynamic one, namely, a neural network with an adaptive architecture as described in Section 4.

As mentioned above, we employ spatio-temporal patterns as alphabet elements. Simply speaking, an STP is a path produced by the cursor. The temporal component, mouse events interarrival times, plays secondary role in recognition and its analysis is described in the next section. The spatial component constituted by path points is what the classifier actually learns to recognize. In our system, we attempted to minimize the restrictions on path configuration and to let the user decide which patterns are to be remembered and reproduced easily. However, it was necessary to limit the path complexity from both below and above. The former was needed because primitive patterns (lines, arcs etc) often emerge during cursor movements and would result in frequent false recognitions. The upper bound for the path complexity is set indirectly by two parameters, input buffer length and maximum position age, which can be adjusted for optimal performance (as described in the next section).

STPs undergo only minor preprocessing before being fed to the classifier. The system does not employ any sophisticated feature extraction algorithms, for example, path direction is omitted. However, if poor input quality due to noise, low precision of pointing device and/or human factors is expected, it might be necessary to employ a more elaborate preprocessing scheme. In particular, we conducted a number of experiments to record and analyze input patterns produced by severely disabled people using the Camera Mouse [1] as the pointer input device. To solve the problem of poor input quality, we attempted to extract regions to which the cursor seemed to converge. We will return to this issue in the discussion section. Let us now describe the primary components of the system: the high-level recognition procedure and the low-level classifier.

3   Recognition System

This section describes how input data is preprocessed before being supplied to the classifier and how the classifier's output is analyzed and interpreted. These procedures require both intensive processing and close interaction with the input hardware. A simple but effective scheme is employed to ensure efficient use of computational resources as well as responsiveness of the system. A recognition pipeline overview is given in Figure 2.

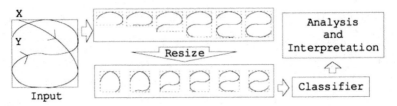

Fig. 2. Recognition System: The input pattern, drawn from X to Y, is shown processed in segments (top row). Each segment includes the previous segment plus additional cursor positions on the input path. The bounding boxes of the segments are resized (bottom row, magnified for visualization purposes) to fit a fixed size rectangle. The pixels of this rectangle constitute the classifier input.

3.1   Input Acquisition and Buffering

The system employs two buffers. The main buffer stores the current input segment processed by the system. The preliminary buffer is necessary to store cursor positions that do not introduce significant changes to the pointer path in the main buffer. When the preliminary buffer accumulates enough data, its contents are appended to the main buffer and recognition is restarted. The purpose of having this temporary buffer is to prevent interruption of the recognition process due to minor (perhaps, involuntary) cursor motion. After the main buffer is updated with the new path segment, some of the old pointer positions are removed from it to ensure it does not exceed its length limit. Moreover, all positions whose age is older than a certain maximum (typically 1 sec) are also removed. The main buffer length limit and maximum cursor position age are determined based on the trained STP's complexity and cursor movement speed. Their main purpose is to aid the classifier's operation under the real-time constraints.

3.2   Cursor Path Segmentation and Processing

Because recognition is done continuously and there are no special rules for entering STPs (unlike graffiti interfaces), the system expects that a pattern may start with any cursor position (stored in the buffer) and must end with the most recent position in the buffer. If exhaustive processing of the accumulated input were performed after each buffer update (which includes path segmentation, multiple scaling operations and multiple classifier evaluations), a heavy load of computational resources would result, which would be unacceptable for an interface. To reduce computation time, the recognition process is suspended until cursor motion reduces, which results in a smaller rate of buffer reads. Consequently, the time-consuming recognition process usually runs after all input, which may contain a valid STP, has been acquired, while the buffer is kept up to date at all times. Furthermore, this allows controlling an acceptable processor load by adjusting the preliminary buffer length and the main buffer update-rate threshold.

When the system decides that the current buffer update rate gives it enough time to process the accumulated input, recognition is initiated. First, the system finds all cursor path segments that can potentially be recognized as valid STPs. Each segment starts with the most recent position in the buffer. The bounding box of the minimal segment has to have an area that is at least as large as the classifier input size and it must be more complex than a line segment. Each following segment contains the previous one plus enough cursor positions to allow resizing of the bounding box (see Figure 2). Resizing is necessary to equate the area of the segment bounding box to the classifier's input size. The fact that the original segments are usually much larger than their resized versions allows us to grow segments several pointer positions at a time.

Each resized segment is evaluated by the classifier whose output is stored for analysis. This operation ends a single processing cycle (segment extraction, resizing, and evaluation). At this point, the recognition process might be forced to halt until the interpretation of a command is completed. In this case, the system either interprets information collected so far, or discards it. Otherwise, a new segment is extracted and processed. The next section describes how the processing results are analyzed and interpreted in each case.

3.3 Classifier Output Analysis and Interpretation

As described in the previous part, input path segments are extracted and processed in order of their length starting from the shortest. As a result, simple STPs, which can represent frequently used commands (mouse clicks, browse back/forward etc.) are recognized almost instantly. Very often, however, simple patterns emerge within more complex ones. A circle, for example, is a very convenient pattern to use, but it is a part of many digits and letters. For this reason, it is necessary to complete all processing cycles even if one of the first segments was positively recognized by the classifier.

In case the system succeeds in recognizing one of the early segments, but then is interrupted, it has to quickly decide what to do with the recognized STP and start processing more up-to-date input. It turns out that the best way to make this decision depends on the user's proficiency with the system and the currently performed task. Experienced users who trained the classifier to accurately recognize their input usually do not need feedback on one command before they can start entering the next one. During text processing, for example, one can enter letters with only small delays between each two. On the other hand, an inexperienced user makes more pronounced delays before starting an STP and after ending it. Moreover, certain tasks, like web browsing, usually require feedback on one action before the next one can be performed. Hence, in all cases, the time stamps that are stored with all cursor positions provide the final piece of information necessary to positively identify STPs. If the endpoints of some input path segment correspond to peaks in the interarrival time of input events (see Figure 3, bottom), the system can be confident that it did, in fact, recognize a valid STP. This method significantly increases the system responsiveness. However, this method is inappropriate during early stages of training and in cases of bad control and/or poor precision of the input device. If no good segment candidate was found by the time recognition is interrupted, the collected data is discarded. Otherwise, the best candidate has to be interpreted, as discussed in the last paragraph of this section.

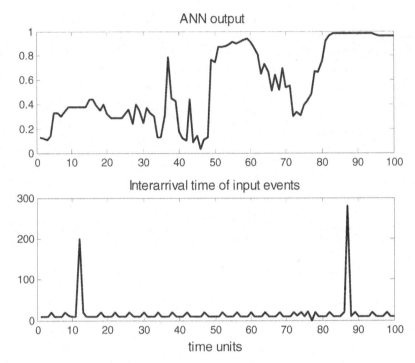

Fig. 3. Using the rate of input events to choose an STP. Top: ANN output over a period of 100 time units. Bottom: Interarrival time of input events over a period of 100 time units. At time t=12, a significant pause in cursor movement was registered, but no candidate STP was recognized by the ANN at that time. At time t=60, the ANN recognized a candidate STP, but no cursor pause was registered. At time t=88, the ANN recognized a candidate STP and a cursor pause was registered. Only in the last case does the system output that this candidate STP is a valid STP.

If two or more overlapping input path segments are recognized by the classifier (Figure 3, top), the one that correlates in time with the peak in input event interarrival time is the true STP. The reason why this works is that the speed of the cursor movement is usually rather stable when a valid pattern is being drawn. Tests showed that this assertion is true in the great majority of cases. STP candidates are compared in this fashion after all segments have been processed. The best candidate (if there is one) is then interpreted as described in the next paragraph.

The user can associate each STP with an input event. Any event that an operating system can process can be chosen, for example, keyboard keys, combination of keys pressed, mouse clicks, special buttons like back, forward, refresh etc. When the system positively recognizes an STP, it generates the corresponding event. In case of mouse clicks, the exact position of each click event occurrence is determined using the position of a predefined "hot-spot" relative to the pattern's bounding box. The default location of the hot-spot is the center of the bounding box, but any point within the box can be chosen. Note that it is possible to associate series of events or macros with STPs, which may be convenient in some applications.

4   Artificial Neural Network

The current implementation of the system employs an ANN as an STP classifier. As described in the overview section, we had two primary requirements for the choice of the classifier: real-time performance and an adaptive architecture. Although training an ANN can take a significant amount of time, the evaluation complexity of even large networks is rather low. In fact, some real-time applications utilize ensembles of neural networks and still meet all the deadlines. On the other hand, fulfilling the requirement of an adaptive architecture is somewhat problematic because most neural networks are used with static architectures. In this section we describe a simple neural network that dynamically changes its architecture to distinguish between an arbitrary number of classes efficiently. For this problem, we turn to supervised classification methods using a multi-layer perceptron (MLP) [4] as a base classifier. It is possible to use supervised classifiers because the alphabet is predefined by the user and constitutes the set of training as well as teaching inputs. We now proceed to discuss the network architecture, training set acquisition and training methods that we used with the ANN.

4.1   Adaptive Architecture

The neural network receives the scaled pointer path image pixels as input. Thus, the size of the input layer equals the resolution of the scaled image, which is a parameter to the system (16x16 was chosen experimentally). Higher resolution can represent more complex patters, but takes longer to evaluate. The resolution should be chosen according to alphabet size and input device precision.

The number of nodes in the output layer equals the number of classes defined by the user. It changes when the user adds or deletes commands to the alphabet. Note that adding or deleting a node does not result in the loss of data (e.g. weights) that was already computed for other nodes.

The size of the hidden layer (only one layer is used), on the other hand, is a parameter that can be adjusted, and is critical for the network performance and potential. From the performance point of view, the number of hidden nodes has to be minimized. Unfortunately, there is no simple relation between the network potential and the number of nodes and/or weights. As a result, neural network parameters are usually selected through experimentation rather than computed from strict rules and formulas. To optimize the architecture and the training of our neural network, we employ a combination of a method to automatically choose the size of the hidden layer and a probabilistic technique to assess the likelihood of training convergence.

Given the dimensionality of a classification task, one can estimate the sufficient number of hidden nodes in a two-layer (one hidden layer) fully connected feed-forward neural network by bounding the number of weights N_w [7,11]:

$$\frac{N_y N_p}{1 + \log_2(N_p)} \leq N_w \leq N_y \left(\frac{N_p}{N_x} + 1 \right) (N_x + N_y + 1) + N_y \tag{1}$$

where N_x denotes the number of input nodes, N_y denotes the number of output nodes, and N_p denote the size of the training set. Number of hidden nodes N_z is then given by:

$$N_z = \frac{N_w}{N_x + N_y} \qquad (2)$$

Figure 4 shows minimum, maximum and average N_z values as given in Eq. (2). The best and worst cases correspond to "easy" classification tasks (close to linear) and "hard" ones (highly non-linear) respectively. Because no a priori information is available about pattern configurations, it is reasonable to guess that the actual value lies somewhere in the middle. We initialized the number of hidden nodes to the average of maximum and minimum N_z values.

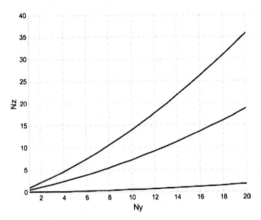

Fig. 4. Minimum, maximum and average number of hidden nodes N_z for 1–20 classes N_y, 10 examples per class and 256 input nodes N_x.

Slightly overestimating the network potential proved to be not harmful, whereas a far more complex problem arises if the potential associated with the size of the hidden layer is not sufficient to accommodate all classes. This can happen if either the initial guess is too small or if the user adds more classes (commands) to the existing network. In such case, it will be impossible to train the network to produce the desired classification. The main difficulty comes from the fact that one cannot tell what compromises the training procedure: it might just get stuck in a local minimum, or there might not be a suitable minimum at all. In the first case, training should just be restarted with random weights, while in the second case, the number of hidden nodes should be increased – otherwise training may not converge. Taking a probabilistic approach to this problem, one can estimate the number of training attempts that should be made before one establishes the inability of the training procedure to converge for a given network state by computing [8]:

$$N = \frac{\ln(1 - F_W(a))}{\ln(1 - F_X(a))} \tag{3}$$

Here N is the number of training attempts taken before changing the architecture, X is the sum of squared errors on any individual attempt, W is the best (lowest) value for X, $F_X(a)$ is the fraction of attempts which would result in a value of X less than or equal to a, a confidence threshold, and $F_W(a)$ is the fraction of X values that result in a value of W less than or equal to a. Once N attempts to converge have been made, the number of hidden nodes should be increased.

We must note the principal difference between our approach and the approach of a modified Cascade Correlation network (CasCor) [5,10]. Although a CasCor network implements a dynamical architecture by sequentially increasing (cascading) the number of hidden layers, it was shown that the potential of such network can be utilized only with a large (unfeasible in this case) number of training examples [10]. Expanding on this idea, architecture with one hidden layer to which nodes are sequentially added was later introduced [10]. The resulting network performed at least as well as the original CasCor on a set of benchmark problems [12]. Although seemingly efficient, the modified CasCor architecture does not take into account a priori information about the problem at hand, for example, input dimensionality. In our approach, the size of the hidden layer is selected according to the complexity of the classification task without resorting to traverse architectures which are unlikely to deliver the potential required for the given task.

4.2 Training

Neural network training proceeds in two stages (see Figure 5). During the first stage, which we call basic training, the network is presented with only few examples of each pattern (usually five). In rare cases, these examples are sufficient to train the network to stably recognize a pattern. However, most STPs require larger training sets to ensure correct classification. Basic training provides the network with a rough estimate of the classification task, so the error rate might be high due to partially learned decision boundaries of certain classes. In other words, the neural network was not presented with enough examples of one or more classes to be able to distinguish between all accurately. The system identifies problematic classes by assigning a confidence value to each member of the alphabet. Initially, all classes have the same value.

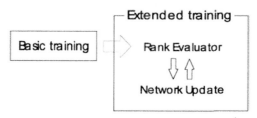

Fig. 5. Training overview.

In the second stage, which we call extended training, the user can start experimenting with the system. During this experimentation, the recognition error rate is usually still high. The user is asked to notify the system about its mistakes in order to update the confidence values of the alphabet elements to reflect their recognition error rates. The confidence values are increased for every correct classification and decreased for every incorrect one. To speed up the training, the user is asked to provide additional examples for alphabet elements. The chance of an element being selected is proportional to its confidence value. As a result, STPs that were recognized poorly after basic training are emphasized during extended training. Each new sample STP is added to the training set if the current network does not recognize it correctly and is discarded otherwise. In addition, for each new sample STP, the system continues to adjust confidence values. The network is updated after each time an additional STP is entered by the user. This procedure, if continued long enough, typically results in a sufficient number of examples for each class. In practice, it takes about 5 minutes to decrease the classification error rate to a point where the system can be used reliably. The purpose of dividing training into two stages is to ensure that correct classification will be produced by the network trained on as few examples as possible, hence minimizing training time.

We employ a standard back-propagation training algorithm with gradient descent and conjugate gradient descent methods [3]. To increase the speed of training and reduce the likelihood of converging into local minima, we employed different training modes (stochastic, batch), a momentum term and a variable learning rate [3]. The first few examples of an alphabet member are trained sequentially in batch mode, which is quite robust for small training sets. Then training switches to a stochastic mode, which is more robust for large training sets. Such a combination of training modes and the techniques mentioned above resulted in rapid convergence.

5 Testing

In this section we describe the methodology and results of the quantitative experiments. In the next section we describe our experiences working with a subject with severe disabilities and discuss possible extensions of our system.

5.1 Participants

Formal testing was conducted with participation of twenty subjects. The first ten subjects (Group A) were sophomore year college students with above average computer literacy. The next ten subjects (Group B) were individuals with average computer skills. None of the subjects was previously exposed to the system.

5.2 Methods and Apparatus

The testing procedure consisted of two tasks designed to test both the usability and the accuracy of the system. In the first task, which targeted primarily usability, subjects were asked to use the system to create an alphabet of five commands by mapping four arbitrary symbols to the following standard internet browser functions: "back", "forward", "stop", and "favorites", respectively. Subjects were asked to map the last symbol in the alphabet to the mouse single-click event. Upon completion of this configuration step, subjects were asked to perform basic training and proceed to interact with the system in its recognition mode to acquire alphabet rankings. After a period of interaction, subjects were asked to conduct an extended training step for 3 minutes. In this step, the subjects were asked to open an internet browser and, using only the five newly created symbols, browse the internet in a natural way with the mouse as the input device.

The second task required subjects to expand an existing alphabet to include ten symbols to be mapped to keyboard events that correspond to digits 0 through 9 and the last symbol to the mouse single-click event. The training procedure was the same as in the first task. Subjects were then asked to launch a word processor and produce all ten digits in a consecutive order using the mouse as a pointing device.

Note that access to the keyboard and full mouse functionality was allowed only during the configuration and training stages in both tasks. Results reflecting accuracy of the system (Recognition Accuracy) were recorded during the actual recognition stage and consisted of percent of correctly performed actions out of all attempted. The numbers of attempts were 50 for Task 1 and 10 for Task 2. As a measure of usability, the time it took each subject to configure the system (Average Adjustment Time) for each task was recorded. Another parameter that was recorded across all subjects was the average processing time of one symbol (Response Time) during the session.

All tests were conducted on Pentium IV 1.4 GHz machines running the Windows XP operating system.

Table 1. Average recognition accuracy of the system and the average adjustment time as measure of usability for two groups of 10 subjects each performing Task 1 50 times and Task 2 10 times.

Subject Groups	Average Recognition Accuracy		Average Adjustment Time	
	Task 1	Task 2	Task 1	Task 2
A (subjects with above average computer skills)	95 %	87 %	3 min	12 min
B (subjects with average computer skills)	85 %	75 %	6 min	18 min

5.3 Results

The results indicate that both groups of users were able to successfully complete the tasks assigned during testing (see Table 1). Although it is evident that individuals with less computer experience (Group B) took longer to adjust to the interface, high average recognition accuracy was achieved for both groups. Recognition accuracy depended directly on the duration of the extended training procedure, which was here limited to 3 minutes (importance of prolonged extended training is discussed in Section 4.2). Samples of symbols created by users are shown in Figures 6 and 7.

Results show that an average user as well as a more advanced user can configure this interface in a relatively short time (see Table 1). At the end of the second testing task, subjects were capable of using such tools as a calculator user interface without resorting to a keyboard and using a mouse merely as a pointer input device. The system proved to be robust with the average response time under 600 milliseconds.

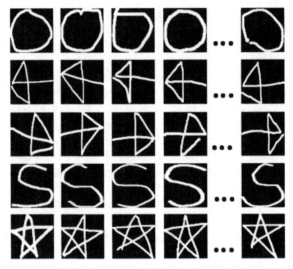

Fig. 6. Instances of five symbols as produced by a user in Group B in Task 1.

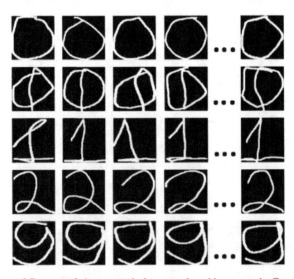

Fig. 7. Instances of five out of eleven symbols as produced by a user in Group B in Task 2.

6 Discussion

The system described in this paper is a general interface for communication with the computer. Since it does not need information about the type of pointer device used to control the cursor, it provides a general extension to the device's capabilities. The system was designed to be modular: each of the main components – input processor, classifier, and interpreter – can be changed or completely altered to fit particular tasks and input devices.

The system is intended to replace the functionality of the mouse input device and some functionality of the keyboard input device. For this purpose, the number of commands (order of 10-20) and the number of instances of training patterns for each command (20-30) used in the testing phase were appropriate. The system can potentially be expanded to handle a larger number of commands, for example, fully replacing the functionality of the keyboard. Such expansion, however, will raise the computational demands of the system requiring a redesign of its major components.

The two major approaches to improve input processing are feature extraction (reduces input dimensionality) and to use additional input characteristics (cursor movement direction, speed etc). Feature extraction is beneficial if input characteristics that emphasize differences between classes can be identified and no significant computational costs are associated with their extraction. As for using additional input characteristics, this can only be justified if the readily available spatio-temporal information is not a sufficient representation of the user's input. We did not choose to extract additional information because the STPs used carried sufficient information for symbol classification.

The fact that the system performed well during testing, and that users quickly became comfortable with it, encouraged us to tackle a more difficult problem. Taking into account the constraints placed on the input devices that can be used by disabled individuals we examined how to modify it to work with camera-based human-computer interfaces (in particular, the Camera Mouse [1]) to provide an accessibility solution for these individuals. The major difficulty about recognizing input produced by motion-impaired users is that, in most cases, the cursor path is significantly distorted by involuntary movements [2]. In other words, a subject can move the cursor sooner or later to a desired screen position, but the cursor's trajectory on the way to the target point is difficult for the subject to reproduce. To address this problem we explored the idea to discretize the input signal further in order to extract "pivot points," i.e., points or regions that the cursor's path must travel through. The neural network would then be utilized to classify patterns constituted by pivot points. We conducted preliminary experiments with a motion-impaired user due to severe cerebral palsy, showing that pivot points can indeed be detected and analyzed for classification. This approach is a subject of a future investigation.

Acknowledgements. We wish to thank John J. Magee, Rick Hoydt, and the students of the Boston University Video Game Creators Consortium for assistance. The work was supported by the National Science Foundation, grants IIS-0093367, IIS-0308213, IIS-0329009, and EIA-0202067.

References

1. Betke, M., Gips J., Fleming P.: The Camera Mouse: Visual Tracking of Body Features to Provide Computer Access for People With Severe Disabilities. IEEE Transactions on Neural Systems and Rehabilitation Engineering, vol. 10, no. 1 (2002)
2. Cloud, R.L., Betke, M., Gips, J.: "Experiments with a Camera-Based Human-Computer Interface System." Proceedings of the 7th ERCIM Workshop "User Interfaces for All," UI4ALL 2002, pp. 103-110, Paris, France, October 2002.
3. Cun, Y. L., Bottou, L., Orr, G., Muller, K.: Efficient BackProp, Neural Networks: Tricks of the trade. Springer Lecture Notes in Computer Sciences 1524, pp.5-50 (1998)
4. Duda, R.O., Hart, P.E., Stork, D.G.: Pattern Classification. New York: Wiley Interscience (2001)
5. Fahlman, S.E., Lebiere, C.: The Cascade-Correlation learning architecture. Technical Report CMU-CS-90-100, School of Computer Science, Carnegie Mellon University, Pittsburg PA (1991)
6. Grauman, K., Betke, J., Lombardi, J., Gips, J., Bradski, G.: Communication via Eye Blinks and Eyebrow Raises: Video-Based Human-Computer Interfaces. Universal Access in the Information Society, 2(4), pp. 359-373 (2003)
7. Hecht-Nielsen, R.: Kolmogorov's Mapping Neural Network Existence Theorem. Proceedings of IEEE First Annual Int. Conf. on Neural Networks, San Diego, Vol. 3, pp. 11-13 (1987)
8. Iyer, M.S., Rhinehart, R.R.: A Method to Determine the Required Number of Neural Network Training Repetitions. Proceedings of IEEE Transactions on Neural Networks, vol. 10, no. 2, pp 427-432 (1999)
9. Kim, K.-N., Ramakrishna, R.S.: Vision-Based Eye-Gaze Tracking for Human Interface. IEEE International Conf. on Systems, Man, and Cybernetics, Tokyo, Japan (1999)
10. Sjogaard, S.: A Conceptual Approach to Generalization in Dynamic Neural Networks. Ph.D. Thesis, Aarhus University, Aarhus, Denmark (1991)
11. Widrow, B., Lehr, M.A.: 30 Years of Adaptive Neural Networks: Perceptron, Madaline, and Backpropagation. Proceedings of the IEEE, vol. 78, No. 9, pp. 1415-1442 (1990)
12. Yeung, D.-Y.: Node Splitting: A Constructive Algorithm for Feed-Forward Neural Networks. In Moody, J.E., Hanson, S.J., Lippman, R.P. (eds.) Advances in Neural Information Processing Systems 4, San Mateo, CA. Morgan Kaufman Publishers, pp. 1072-1079 (1991)

A New Visualization Concept for Navigation Systems

Wolfgang Narzt[1], Gustav Pomberger[1], Alois Ferscha[1], Dieter Kolb[2], Reiner Müller[2],
Jan Wieghardt[2], Horst Hörtner[3], and Christopher Lindinger[3]

[1] Johannes Kepler University Linz, Altenbergerstr. 69, A-4040 Linz, Austria
{wolfgang.narzt,gustav.pomberger,alois.ferscha}@jku.at
[2] Siemens AG, Otto-Hahn Ring 6, D-81730 Munich, Germany
{kolb.dieter,reiner.e.mueller,jan.wieghardt}@siemens.com
[3] Ars Electronica Future Lab, Hauptstr. 2, A-4040 Linz, Austria
{horst.hoertner,christopher.lindinger}@aec.at

Abstract. At present, various types of car navigation systems are progressively
entering the market. Simultaneously, mobile outdoor navigation systems for pe-
destrians and electronic tourist guides are already available on handheld computers. Although, the depiction of the geographical information on these appliances has increasingly improved during the past years, users are still
handicapped having to interpret an abstract metaphor on the navigation display
and translate it to their real world.
This paper introduces an innovative visual paradigm for (mobile) navigation
systems, embodied within an application framework that contributes to the ease
of perception of navigation information by its users through mixed reality.

Introduction

Modern navigation systems follow up different approaches of presenting geographical
information to their users. Whereas the constitution of information may either be
verbal or spatial, the presentation can be visual or auditory [6], [19] (see Fig. 1).

	visual	auditory
verbal	text message: "turn left"	spoken message: "turn left"
spatial	←	tone to the left of the driver

Fig. 1. How to present navigation information.

The combination of those characteristics builds up the basis for the man-machine-
interface of current navigation systems: So called turn-by-turn systems display a simple, flat arrow indicating a turn or pointing to the desired direction (spatial, visual)
together with a dynamically changing designation for the distance to the next maneuver point (verbal, visual) (see upper part of Fig. 2). A built-in voice enhances this
information by instructing the driver where to go next (verbal, auditory). A two-
dimensional bird's eye view showing a geographical map and the driver's current
position and orientation on it is just another state of the art method for illustrating
navigation data to the users (Fig. 2, lower part).

However, all these attempts of an adequate visualization method face one common
problem: There is an abstraction gap between the provided information and the mapping of these data to the real world. Even though a car navigation system displays an
arrow to the left and a voice additionally directs the driver to turn left in 100 meters,

C. Stary and C. Stephanidis (Eds.): UI4All 2004, LNCS 3196, pp. 440–451, 2004.
© Springer-Verlag Berlin Heidelberg 2004

the driver still has to determine the distance of 100 meters. It is even harder for a two-dimensional geographical map: The driver has to handle a vast quantity of data within just one glimpse to the navigation display while driving. In addition, he is not capable of recognizing possible hazards on the street during this time.

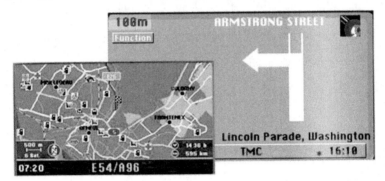

Fig. 2. Current visualization techniques.

Consequently, we cannot consider these types of visualization methods as adequate for safety reasons and urge for a secure navigation guide that defeats the problems concerning the man-machine-interface.

A Novel Paradigm for Visualization

The navigation information shall easily be accessible to the drivers in an intuitive and natural way, thus maximizing the degree of perception. To support the drivers in perceiving navigation data, we propose a see-through-based theatre experience of visual perception, seamlessly merging the components of the real and the digital world. Every car's windshield can transact the allegory of the see-through-based theatre and be used to superimpose the navigation information in front of the real world outside the car. So, we extend the characteristics for the constitution of navigation information by annotated reality and mark the route in a translucent color (see left part of Fig. 3).

The advantages should be obvious by viewing the picture: By virtually painting the road in a semi-transparent color the new paradigm eliminates ambiguity which may arise at conventional navigation systems when the driver is requested to turn left with two junctions back to back. This visualization concept even enables a driver to recognize junctions, which are hidden to his eyes in the real world, because other vehicles or blind summits restrict the driver's view (right part of Fig. 3).

No more counting of exit ways out of traffic circles is necessary in order to get off at the designated exit (Fig. 4, left). Furthermore, the driver always surveys the road ahead, because he is no longer handicapped by a constrained view of the current traffic and driving situation (Fig. 4, right).

As a consequence, we consider this paradigm to be a self-explanatory and easy to understand visualization method, which helps to avoid indistinctness concerning maneuver instructions, and conspicuously increases safety aspects. In the course of a three years project, we (i.e. the University of Linz, Austria, Siemens Corporate Technology in Munich, Germany, and the Ars Electronica Futurelab in Linz, Austria) have developed a software architecture that engages this new visualization concept. The main principles and the prototypical implementations of this idea are described in the following sections.

Fig. 3. Translucent path for navigation.

Fig. 4. Roundabout and Safety Aspects.

Approach

Present head-up displays [7] using the windshield are not yet maturely conceived to be used as a see-though window as originally intended. Instead, the annotation of the route is superimposed on a live-stream video showing the road ahead on the navigation display. Accordingly, augmented reality is our technical instrument for the realization of the new concept, which is also reflected in the name of our navigation system: INSTAR – Information and Navigation System Through Augmented Reality.

The first obvious approach for calculating the virtually colored route – the use of picture recognition algorithms [20], [27] – would be insufficient, as those algorithms are poorly conceived. They are too complex, too expensive and, by the way, could not cope with the entanglement of the streets in large cities. The INSTAR system follows a different strategy: It simply uses the data coming from a conventional navigation system (the current GPS position and orientation, the maps, the topography information and the route) and calculates a three-dimensional depiction of the street as it may look from the driver's perspective (see Fig. 5).

This technical approach is also advantageous in terms of daylight conditions, for, it only visualizes pure, measured data and does not utilize picture recognition algorithms, which would be dependent on weather and lighting situations.

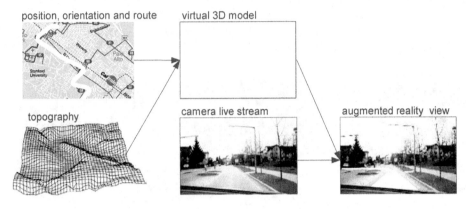

Fig. 5. Thought model of AR view.

System Architecture

In order to receive the required data from the navigation system the INSTAR software has to provide a variety of input interfaces (see Fig. 6): Most car navigation systems are equipped with a GPS receiver and in some cases additionally keep track of the car using wheel sensors when GPS is not constantly available, e.g., within city areas. However, the system is also prepared for alternative tracking technologies, like indoor tracking systems (ITS) and other wireless positioning approaches. Usually, the orientation of a car comes from the GPS signal, but the generic system architecture of the INSTAR kernel facilitates different orientation trackers (compasses, gyros, etc.) as input sensors, as well. Static model data (i.e., 2D and 3D maps typically stored on a compact disc), dynamic model data (i.e., ongoing road works and accidents) and the route planning algorithm finally enable the INSTAR kernel system to compute the virtual 3D road image. The video interface for transferring the live-stream from the camera completes this list of interface components.

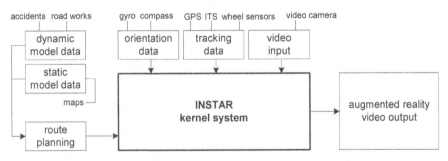

Fig. 6. The system as a black box.

Fig. 5 outlines the interaction of all input components in a simplified way. Naturally, the algorithms behind this thought model must handle a challenging and complex problem. Just to give an idea of what is meant by this assertion, consider the following scenario: Depending on the current position and pitch of a car and the topography of the street ahead, the augmentation to the next maneuver-point differs in its length even if the distance from the car to the maneuver-point is the same (compare the two driving situations illustrated in Fig. 7). Actually, the virtual arrow may grow in its length even if the car is continuously approaching the maneuver-point.

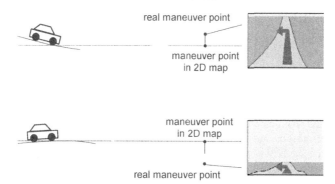

Fig. 7. Characteristics of AR view.

To go into detail, the route from the navigation component is provided through a dynamically changing sequence of geographical points in the three-dimensional space (see left part of Fig. 8). A distinction is drawn between shape points tagging the route in front of the car and maneuver points indicating upcoming navigation maneuvers.

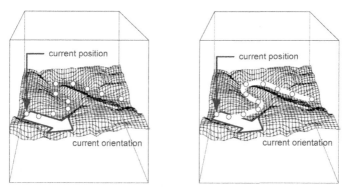

Fig. 8. 3D shape points tag the route.

The catenation of those points (e.g., through a cubic spline or by nurbs [23]) results in the desired virtual path (see right part of Fig. 8). Accordingly, the static topography information (as denoted in Fig. 5) is not directly retrieved from the three-dimensional maps of the navigation computer but considered indirectly by the spline.

So, the INSTAR system calculates a virtual three-dimensional model of the spline relative to a fictive origin within a virtual space. Corresponding matrix transformations rotate, shift, and zoom this model regarding the current position and orientation of the car (and also several other parameters like the current speed, wheel sensor data, etc.) so that the spline finally looks as if it was a colored part of the street viewed from the driver's perspective (see Fig. 9).

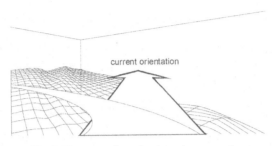

Fig. 9. The route from the driver's perspective.

The calculated 3D-path is stored in an appropriate data structure, a scenegraph, which is detached from any graphical library or operating system needed to illustrate the routing information. As the scenegraph approach for storing three-dimensional graphics is used by many popular 3D renderers [13], it has also been used within the software design of the INSTAR framework. A traversal of the graphical objects and transformation nodes stored in the scenegraph finally initiates the augmented reality-drawing process, with several customer-dependent implementation variants for differ-ent operating systems and graphic libraries already contained in the framework (ex-pressed by the hashed square below the AR renderer in Fig. 10).

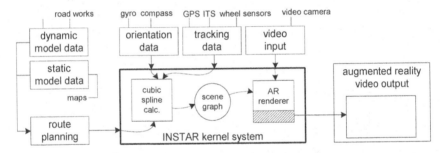

Fig. 10. Generic AR data calculation and storage.

This architecture enables users to arbitrarily exchange navigation devices. The ge-neric scenegraph data structure can be processed by several different graphic render-ers, which allow the output to be displayed on notebooks, handheld computers, and, of course, on conventional navigation displays, as well. The INSTAR navigation system is beyond this capable of dealing with various tracking systems, which enables users to take the navigation system out of the car and use it as a mobile pedestrian navigator [22].

Results

The INSTAR-framework has been developed by using a self-made simulation envi-ronment. All the navigation data coming from a commercially available car naviga-tion system were recorded synchronously together with a video stream from a digital camera mounted inside a test car. These data repetitively served as the simulation input for the initial INSTAR system running on a personal computer. The software was written in C++ and developed for the operating systems Windows 2000/XP and Windows CE. At the back-end, OpenGL and PocketGL were used to combine the computed 3D route and the video stream to an augmented reality navigation view. Fig. 11 shows an OpenGL window in front of the simulation environment with a semitransparent yellow path guiding the way. The borders of the path are kept in diverse colors in order to denote different purposes: Red indicates a left turn and green indicates a right turn. You can also clearly recognize the shape points and the already covered distance in the backward simulation control window.

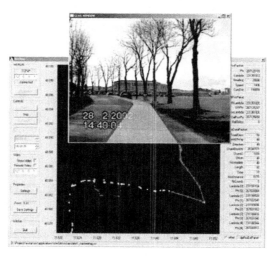

Fig. 11. INSTAR simulation.

When the implementations for the simulation environment had been finished, the INSTAR system started migrating into a test car. Initially, the system was still executed on a laptop computer, but already connected to the built-in Siemens VDO navigation system via a serial port. A digital firewire camera mounted behind the rearview mirror provided the live stream of the scene in front of the car. For the premier time, the new visualization concept could be experienced in a real testing environment. The left part of Fig. 12 shows a picture of our first real world experiment in March 2002.

Due to the restriction that the INSTAR navigation system has been undisclosed until now, and that it is only available in one test car, no empirical research has been done, so far, to formally evaluate the acceptance of the new human-machine interaction method. However, the developer crew has acknowledged the intuitive way of perception of the navigation information in several test runs in the city of Munich.

As the INSTAR system was running properly within the test car, the exchangeability aspect of the navigation display could be validated. Therefore, the kernel of the framework moved onto a handheld using PocketGL as the graphic renderer. In the same way as in the laptop version, the handheld was directly connected to the car navigation computer (see right part of Fig. 12) and additionally plugged into a video jacket in order to receive the video signals from the camera. The successful port of the software to a handheld device can be considered as the first step towards facilitating the mobility aspect of navigation systems [22].

Fig. 12. Augmented reality car navigation system.

Future Work

The prototypical implementations have demonstrated the applicability of the INSTAR framework for navigation systems since the beginning of 2002. They ubiquitously retrieve tracking and navigation data and display an intuitive, augmented reality view of the route on exchangeable devices.

We believe the utility of our navigation system being even better exploited when it is presented in a more adequate manner than shown so far. So, we are also carrying out design studies on the augmentation of the digital information. One promising modification could arise when we ask the most natural question on the subject of navigation systems: What is the easiest way to find a desired destination? Answer: Follow somebody who knows the way. This idea leads to an alternative augmentation variant showing a virtual car in front of one's own car, blinking, braking and accelerating (see left part of Fig. 13), making the navigation aspect in cars natural as possible.

Fig. 13. Alternative augmentation methods.

A few manufacturers have recently started offering colored head-up displays [28] within their cars, using a small part of the wind shield to display important data, like the current speed, the fuel gage, but also conventional depictions of navigation information. With this technology emerging, we could also (e.g., by a command from the steering wheel) display the augmentation of the route directly in the front shield. The driver will not have to avert his eyes from the street, anymore (Fig. 13, right).

The INSTAR system may furthermore be extended by context-sensitive services: In coordination with external sensors or smart devices [4] it calls attention to points of interest located along the route. The left picture in Fig. 14 explains this idea where the system e.g., considers the refuelling indicator of a car and (when crucial) displays the location of the nearest gas station along the route (and maybe further information, e.g., about the price, when available within a pervasive computing environment [10], [12]).

Fig. 14. Additional location based AR information.

Hooks for further location-based services in the framework architecture extend the area of applicability of the framework, which until now only considers navigation aspects. Persons, things and places [18], expressed by positions, names (IDs), profiles, etc, could also be processed and displayed in an augmented reality manner to the users. Tourist information could then be added in the same way as security aspects or adventure games for the fun generation. The right picture in Fig. 14 illustrates just one example of these ideas, where a digital post-it displayed on a PDA provides location-bound information for private issues.

Related Work

The university of Nottingham focuses on human factors design issues in general, and also on human factors of in-car technology [8], [9]. The researchers present established and funded work as well as innovative and creative design issues concerning the perception of navigation information. However, they do not consider augmented reality as an alternative visual offer of information.

The research community for augmented reality proposes ideas for easily comprehensible, innovative augmented reality user interfaces for location-based services. As an example, the MARS project [14], [15], [16] (Mobile Augmented Reality System) presents an approach where augmented reality is used for path finding and orientation. Equipped with a huge backpack including a GPS receiver for position determination and a head mounted display, users are guided within a delimited area by textual location-based denotations and a graphical route displayed as a pipe system. This system, though, narrows the user's freedom of movement significantly, and a head mounted display is also far from being considered a natural interaction instrument, thus letting our prototypical implementation appear to be fairly applicable.

The university of Graz in Austria presents a hybrid positioning technique for an augmented reality outdoor tracking system using a wearable apparatus [24], [25]. However, the methods for locating and identifying points and objects in the real world by coordinating dissimilar positioning techniques represents the main focus of their research area. The augmented reality view seems to be just a means to an end for illustrating the results of their calculations.

Several other research projects in this area deal with human interaction factors, augmented reality views and the growing range of divergent positioning techniques [1], [2], [3], [5], [11], [17], [21], [26], [29]. Nevertheless, none of the approaches developed so far enhances the navigation information by simply coloring the route to the destination and therefore decreases the level of abstraction at the user interface to a minimum, thus making navigation intuitive and natural.

Conclusion

We consider the novel concept for visualizing navigation information by means of augmented reality to be an advancement in the man-machine-interface of navigation systems and have therefore applied the ideas for patents. The new paradigm appears natural to its users and helps to enhance traffic safety, for, the driver perceives navigation information quickly and intuitively and is always aware of the current traffic situation ahead. Even while looking at the navigation display he is able to keep his attention to the street ahead and to other road users.

The new navigation system also unifies diverse methods for acquiring tracking and orientation data, provides generic implementations for graphical output on different displays and different operating platforms, and consequently enables the users to arbitrarily exchange navigation systems, using an indoor navigation handheld as a car navigation system and vice versa. The applicability of the visualization concept has been demonstrated within this paper by presenting prototypical implementations.

A prospect of our visions reveals of one single mobile device as the navigation system, small enough to be easily kept in one's pocket and used wherever it is needed. The INSTAR framework can be considered as a first step in this direction of future navigation systems.

References

1. R.T. Azuma et al., "Tracking in Unprepared Environments for Augmented Reality Systems", Computers and Graphics, vol. 23, no. 6, Dec. 1999, pp. 787-793.
2. J. Baus, C. Kray, A. Kruger, W. Wahlster; "A Resource-Adaptive Mobile Navigation System", Proceedings of the International Workshop on IPNMD, Verona, Italy, 2001.
3. R. Behringer, C. Tam, J. McGee, S. Sundareswaran, M. Vassiliou, "A wearable augmented reality testbed for navigation and control, built solely with commercial-off-the-shelf (COTS) hardware", IEEE & ACM International Symp. on Augmented Reality ISAR, Munich, Germany, 2000.
4. M. Beigl, H.-W. Gellersen, "Smart-Its: An embedded platform for Smart Objects", Smart Objects Conference, Grenoble, France, 2003.
5. D. Benyon, B. Wilmes, "The Application of Urban Design Principles to Navigation of Information Spaces", Proceedings of the HCI Int. Conference, ISBN: 1-85233-766-4, Bath, GB 2003.
6. G. E. Burnett, "Usable Vehicle Navigation Systems: Are We There Yet?", Vehicle Electronic Systems 2000 - European conference and exhibition, ERA Technology, Ltd, 29-30 June 2000, pp. 3.1.1-3.1.11, ISBN 0 7008 0695 4.

7. G. E. Burnett, "A Road-Based Evaluation of a Head-Up Display for Presenting Navigation Information", Proceedings of HCI International Conference, Crete, 2003.

8. G. E. Burnett, S. M. Joyner, "An Investigation on the Man Machine Interfaces to Existing Route Guidance Systems", Proceedings of the IEEE-IEE Vehicle Navigation and Information Systems Conference, VNIS '93, Ottawa, Canada, 1993, pp 395-400, ISBN 0 7803 1235 X.

9. G. E. Burnett, S. M. Joyner, "Vehicle Navigation Systems - Getting It Right From the Driver's Perspective", Proceedings of the Mapping and the Display of Navigation Information Conference, Royal Institute of Navigation, "Nav 95", London, 7-9 November, 1995, pp201-209.

10. G. E. Burnett, J. M. Porter, "Ubiquitous computing within cars: Designing controls for non-visual use", International Journal of Human-Computer Studies, 55(4) 2001, 521-531

11. K. Cheverst, N. Davies, K. Mitchell, A. Friday, C. Efstratiou, "Developing a Context-Aware Electronic Tourist Guide: Some Issues and Experiences", Proceedings of CHI 2000, Netherlands, April 2000.

12. N. Davies, H.-W. Gellerseb: "Beyond Prototype: Challenges in Deploying Ubiquitous Systems", IEEE Pervasive Computing, Vol. 1, 26-35, 2002.

13. V. Ferrari, T. Tuytelaars, L. Van Gool, "Markerless Augmented Reality with A Real-Time Affine Region Tracker" Proceedings of the IEEE and ACM Int'l Symposium on Augmented Reality, vol. I, IEEE CS Press, Los Alamitos, CA., 2001, pp. 87-96.

14. T. Höllerer, S. Feiner, D. Hallaway, B. Bell, "User Interface Management Techniques for Collaborative Mobile Augmented Reality", Computers and Graphics 25(5), Elsevier Science Ltd, Oct. 2001, pp. 799-810.

15. T. Höllerer, S. Feiner, J. Pavlik, " Situated Documentaries: Embedding Multimedia Presentations in the Real World", IEEE Proceedings of ISWC '99 (International Symposium on Wearable Computers), San Francisco, CA, October 18–19, 1999, pp. 79–86.

16. T. Höllerer, S. Feiner, T. Terauchi, G. Rashid, D. Hallaway, "Exploring MARS: Developing Indoor and Outdoor User Interfaces to a Mobile Augmented Reality System", Computer and Graphics, 23, 6 (1999).

17. B. Jiang, U. Neumann, "Extendible Tracking by Line Auto-calibration", Proceedings of the IEEE and ACM Int'l Symposium on Augmented Reality, IEEE CS Press, Los Alamitos, CA., 2001, pp. 97-103.

18. T. Kindberg, et al., "People, Places, Things: Web Presence for the Real World", Technical Report HPL-2000-16, Internet and Mobile Systems Laboratory, HP Laboratories Palo Alto, 2000.

19. G. Labiale, "In-car road information: Comparisons of auditory and visual perception", Proceedings of the Human Factors and Ergonomics Society, 34th Annual Meeting, Santa Monica, CA, 1990.

20. C.P. Lu, G.D. Hager, E. Mjolsness, "Fast and Globally Convergent Pose Estimation from Video Images", IEEE Trans. Pattern Analysis and Machine Intelligence, 22 (2000) 6, pp. 610-622.

21. A. Müller, S. Conrad, E. Kruijff, "Multifaceted Interaction with a Virtual Engineering Environment Using a Scenegraph-Oriented Approach", Proceedings of the 11th International Conference in Central Europe on Computer Graphics, Visualization and Computer Vision'2003, Czech Republic, 2003

22. W. Narzt, G. Pomberger, A. Ferscha, D. Kolb, R. Müller, J. Wieghardt, H. Hörtner, C. Lindinger, "Pervasive Information Acquisition for Mobile AR-Navigation Systems", 5th IEEE Workshop on Mobile Computing Systems & Applications, Monterey, California, USA, October 2003.

23. L.Piegl, W.Tiller, "The Nurbs Book", Springer Verlag, ISBN:3-540-55069-0, London, UK, 1995.

24. A. Pinz, "Consistent Visual Information Processing Applied to Object Recognition", Landmark Definition, and Real-Time Tracking. VMV'01, Stuttgart, Germany, 2001.

25. M. Ribo, P. Lang, H. Ganster, M. Brandner, C. Stock, A. Pinz, "Hybrid Tracking for Outdoor Augmented Reality Applications", IEEE Computer Graphics and Applications, Nov./Dec. 2002.
26. K. Satoh et al., "A Hybrid Registration Method for Outdoor Augmented Reality", Proceedings of the Int'l Symposium on Augmented Reality, IEEE Computer Soc. Press, Los Alamitos, CA., 2001, pp. 67-76.
27. J. Steinwendner, W. Schneider, R. Bartl, "Subpixel Analysis of Remotely Sensed Images", Digital Image Analysis: Selected Techniques and Applications, chap. 12.2, W.G. Kropatsch and H. Bischof, eds., Springer-Verlag, New York, 2001, pp. 346-350.
28. Siemens VDO Automitive AG, "Head-up Display Module", Information Systems Passenger Cars, http://www.siemensvdo.com/.
29. L. Tijerina, E. Palmer, M. J. Goodman, "Driver workload assessment of route guidance system destination entry while driving", (Tech. Rep. No. UMTRI-96-30). Ann Arbor, MI: The University of Michigan Transportation Research Institute, 1998.

Haptic and Spatial Audio Based Navigation of Visually Impaired Users in Virtual Environment Using Low Cost Devices

Vladislav Nemec, Adam J. Sporka, and Pavel Slavik

Czech Technical University in Prague, Faculty of Electrical Engineering
Department of Computer Science and Engineering
Karlovo náměstí 13, 12135 Praha 2, Czech Republic
{sporkaa,nemec,slavik}@fel.cvut.cz

Abstract. The use of haptic peripherals to mediate spatial information to visually impaired users is a problem which has recently been examined thoroughly, however the main issue of almost all current approaches is the use of custom made peripheral devices, the high cost of which renders their massive deployment infeasible. We have focused on using low-cost haptic devices to allow visually impaired users to navigate in and inspect a virtual environment. In this paper we describe our approach to navigation in virtual environments by using force feedback joystick and haptic mouse. We also employ the spatial sound to enhance the information perception. We discuss two different navigation modes of avatar in the virtual environment (joystick and mouse based) and several information mediation techniques. Numerous tests have also been performed. Results show that the efficiency and usability of our solution is comparable with tactile exploration of physical paper models of an environment.

1 Introduction

Personal computers (and mainly adoption of the Internet as a new information channel) have given the visually impaired people the possibility to reach the information which used to be almost inaccessible. Currently, most of the visually impaired computer users use a screen reader combined with synthetic speech and/or a Braille display. This gives them access to text on the screen, but not to the graphics [1].

The use of the haptic peripherals to mediate the graphic information to the visually impaired users is rather obvious (and already well implemented) idea, but the actual deployment of this approach could not be done without the massive production of low-cost haptic devices. These devices exist, but are not originally intended to be used by the users with disabilities. Common low-cost haptic devices are focused on computer games sector and used to increase the immersive factor of gaming experience – for example force feedback joysticks, steering wheels etc.

Most of existing solutions focused on haptic (tactile) interfaces use special devices (such as PHANTOM [2]). There are many known, implemented, and published approaches how to use these as peripherals for the visually impaired – for example [3] or [4]. However – because of their price – these devices are not affordable to most of the end users and therefore their common use is not probable.

There were only few attempts to employ low-cost force feedback devices – for example Dillon et al. [5] describes system simulating surface of the fabric by using haptic mouse. He discusses several interesting issues that emerged during testing of

C. Stary and C. Stephanidis (Eds.): UI4All 2004, LNCS 3196, pp. 452–459, 2004.
© Springer-Verlag Berlin Heidelberg 2004

his system – we take into account his suggestions when designing our solution. Sjöström in [1] describes number of experiments held on Lund University that were examining various different approaches to haptic interfaces.

Our research activities are focused on applications and systems allowing visually impaired users to explore virtual environments. We have started with the project examining the possibilities of the navigation and movement in 3D space without visual feedback (using text to speech system, TTS) [6] and then extended abilities of the system by adding spatial sound, simulated sound of cane tapping etc. [7].

Our current effort is to incorporate the haptic modality. We have focused on low-cost haptic devices and their (currently underestimated) abilities to mediate various types of spatial information. We employ two modalities allowing accessing the scene – the tactile (haptic) modality (using force feedback and other haptic devices) and acoustic modality taking (the spatial sound and the TTS.)

In this paper, we focus on our novel approach to the induction of a mental model of virtual environments by means of combination of spatial audio and low-cost haptic (kinesthetic) devices allowing its direct exploration. Currently, we limit our goal to the presentation of maps of flat (2D) environments only, such as the layout of an apartment or and office floor.

2   The Background

In this section we will briefly describe two technologies used as a basis of our solution – haptic devices and spatial sound.

2.1   Haptic Devices

Appelle [8] defines haptic sensing as "the use of motor behaviors in combination with touch to identify objects". Most haptic devices provide force feedback to the actions performed by user – resulting effects influence user's muscles and movement of user's hands/arms/fingers rather than tactile receptors in skin (what the world haptic would imply – as it is derived from Greek "haptesthai" meaning "to touch").

We are using two devices that together combine both ways of haptic information providing – force feedback joystick and haptic mouse.

The **force feedback joystick** is a device allowing – aside from measurement of depression and twist of its stick – the users to feel force of magnitude and direction specified by the application employing it. In our experiments, we were making use of the Logitech Wingman StrikeForce 3D joystick.

The **haptic mouse** (usable also as a common pointing device) contains small generators of vibrations that may be perceived by the user as he or she rests the hand on it. Although this mouse is optical one, the generators are able to evoke the feeling of moving the mouse over rough surface. We have used the Logitech iFeel mouse TouchSense API [9] for our experiments.

2.2   Spatial Sound

The spatial audio is based on simulation of sound distribution phenomena that affect the sound emitted from its source. As a result of interaction of the sound and the environment, the sound received by human auditory system contains spatial information on the position of the sound source and also the surrounding environment.

From various auditory cues (IID, ITD, band attenuation [10]), the human auditory system is capable to extract the information on the direction of the sound received. The positional audio is a sound output in which these effects are synthesized. This way, the sound stimuli may be located "around" the user's head.

The length and timbre of the reverberation of a room gives user information on the approximate size and nature of the environment – as described in [10] or [11] and also serves as the *memoria loci* – personalized reminder of the place or event.

3   Navigation in Environment

In this section, we describe basic concepts of our navigation method. We consider the navigation of avatar (representation of user in virtual environment) consisting of two components: The control of the avatar's motion in which the users drive their avatars around the scene, and the environment sensing through which the users may check their position in the scene and also to get acquainted with the scene.

In the following two sections, we describe our approach to both mentioned components of the navigation.

3.1   Avatar Movement

We have implemented two methods of the motion control: The mouse based and the joystick based. We assumed that the position of the avatar in the scene could be described by its location and heading.

In the **mouse based motion control**, the motion of avatar is tied to the motion of the mouse. Velocity of the mouse movement is interpreted as the velocity of the avatar in the environment. The avatar's heading is controlled by the mouse buttons as shown in Fig. 1 (left for left turn by 45 degrees, right for right turn), however the heading is usually fixed to the North.

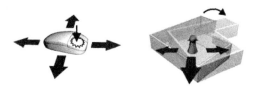

Fig. 1. Mouse-driven motion control.

In the **joystick based motion control**, the avatar may move forward or backward (upon the appropriate depression of the stick). Its heading is controlled by the joystick handle twist (the Z-axis), as shown in Fig. 2.

3.2   Environment Sensing

The Table 1 summarizes the components of the environment description we made available to the user for simultaneous use, and also the peripheral devices (mediators) we used to implement them.

Fig. 2. Joystick-driven motion control.

Table 1. Types of information mediated by different modules of the system (M = haptic mouse, J = force feedback joystick, S = sound output, *), **), ***) – see section 5.3).

Information Component	Content of Information	Mediator		
		M	J	S
Location description	Name of the room or region	–	–	TTS *)
Size of the room	Approximate size of the surrounding environment	–	–	Reverberation *)
Floor material	Characteristics of the surface, sound of the footsteps	Haptic texture	–	Footsteps
Avatar's heading	Direction to the North	–	–	Positional audio
Scene topology	Location of the neighboring doors	–	–	Positional audio (TTS) *)
Collisions	Direction of the motion that caused collision, textual description of the event	Vibration *)	Force pulse	TTS *)
Remote obstacles	Positions of the obstacles in vicinity of the avatar	–	Haptar **)	Sonar ***)

Sonar. Using the spatial audio, the sonar allows the user to "hear" the surrounding obstacles. Every visible obstacle is represented by a virtual sound source that produces a short beep. Different stimuli are assigned to different types of obstacles in order to facilitate the user their recognition. When requested from the user, the virtual sound sources produce the beeps sequentially in counter-clockwise order as shows Fig. 3. The beep of a door is followed by the TTS that announces the name of the room on their other side.

Haptar. The haptar allows the user to touch the surrounding environment using the force feedback joystick. The force that is transmitted to the stick is dependent on the distance to the closest obstacle in the direction in which the user depresses the stick (see Fig. 4). When fully depressed, the TTS describes the closest obstacle in that direction.

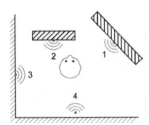

Fig. 3. Principle of sonar - the numbers denote the order in which the virtual sources sound.

4   Testing

We have performed several tests (using system prototype) that should evaluate usability of individual navigation and information providing concepts.

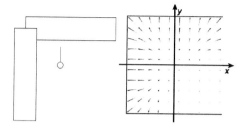

Fig. 4. Principle of *haptar* - an example of layout of the obstacles and appropriate diagram of forces cast upon the deflection of the stick in the device coordinate system (x, y).

4.1 Usability of Different Navigation Methods

Four different users participated in this experiment. Its aim was to receive an initial feedback from the users concerning the usability of the two navigation modes. All users were asked to judge which navigation mode was more acceptable for them to browse through a simple scene (up to three different rooms). All of them responded that the joystick based navigation is very confusing as they lost their sense of position very quickly and even the supplementary sensing components (such as the environment description, or the avatar's heading) did not supply enough information to regain it. However, they felt very comfortable with the mouse based navigation, therefore we concentrated on it in our subsequent tests.

4.2 Haptar Evaluation

The same group of users was asked to try to use the haptar sensing component to "touch around" a few simple scenes and then to draw the layout on a sheet of paper. The table 2 shows the results of this experiment. We may see that for the contiguous

Table 2. The haptar evaluation experiment results. ✓ = correct identification. The incorrect answer is either shown in drawing or as a rephrased user's comment.

Scene layout and avatar's position					
	1	**2**	**3**	**4**	**5**
Participant #1	✓	✓	✓	✓	"Unable to identify"
Participant #2	✓	✓	"Same as layout 2"	"I can't step back"	"Unable to identify"
Participant #3	✓	*(drawing)*	"Same as layout 2"	*(drawing)*	*(drawing)*
Participant #4	*(drawing)*	✓	*(drawing)*	*(drawing)*	*(drawing)*

wall layouts, the users were mostly capable to identify the correct topology of the scene. However, the shape identification often led to more or less serious misinterpretations, especially in the scenes 3 and 4. In the scene 5, most users were not capable to identify the gap in the wall. Therefore, we have concluded that our haptar is usable only as a rough mediator of the scene topology.

4.3 Evaluation of the Mouse Based Navigation

In this experiment we have evaluated the usability of the mouse based navigation enhanced by the spatial audio. There were five participants of age from 25 to 45 and all of them were experienced computer users.

For the purposes of this experiment, the participants were blindfolded at the beginning of their sessions. Their task was to create a mental model of different flat layouts (4 rooms, and 3 or 4 doors in one scene) presented using the mouse based navigation (used standalone or enhanced by the sonar or haptar) and then to reproduce it by sketching a map. The following presentation methods were used:

1. *Direct tactile exploration*, in which a paper model was presented to the participants to test their capabilities to memorize and reproduce a model of an environment.
2. *Mouse based navigation and spatial audio.* We have used the combination of the sensing components and the mediators marked with *) in the Table 1.
3. *All the components from the previous point, enhanced with the sonar.* The combination of items marked *) and **) in the Table 1 was used.
4. *All the components from point 3, enhanced with the haptar.* The combination of items marked *) and ***) in the Table 1 was used.

We evaluated the correctness of the participants' responses from the following three points of view: the scene topology (the neighborhood and interconnectedness of rooms), the room names, and the room shapes.

During the direct tactile exploration, the participants were able to quickly acquire mental models of the presented environments. The mean time was approximately 2 minutes.

Even though the number of participants is not enough to make a statistically valid conclusion, the results indicate that using the haptic mouse navigation together with the spatial audio enhancements the participants yielded the mental models of the equal precision as in the direct tactile exploration, and this process took approximately one minute longer.

The sonar and haptar enhancement brought no improvement to the plain mouse based navigation.

5 Conclusion

In this paper, we have shown the problem of the presentation of the graphic information to the visually impaired users and its possible resolution by means of combination of the audio and haptic peripheral devices. We have described our approach to this problem and an implementation of the pilot version of the browser of the maps of the flat indoor environments.

Our experiments have shown high usability of our method of navigation by means of combination of the haptic mouse and the spatial audio. They have shown that the users were capable to acquire the mental model of an environment with the same precision and in comparable time as with the tactile exploration of the physical models.

The force feedback joystick did not prove efficient for these purposes – according to users' comments it is very difficult to determine the centre of the stick movement because the force pulses are non-linear and "contain hysteresis". Nevertheless we have found that it may be employed in the local haptic explorations of the scene.

In our future work, we would like to extend our concept especially in the following ways: a) to implement the navigation in the full 3D environments and b) to modify the existing system to be able to mediate different types of structured information that may be visualized in 2D, such as the oriented graphs, or electric circuits.

References

1. Sjöström, C.: Using Haptics in Computer Interfaces for Blind People. In Proceedings of the Conference on Human Factors in Computing Systems (CHI2001), ACM press, Seattle, USA, 2001.
2. PHANTOM Overview, on-line product presentation. http://www.sensable.com/ products/phantom_ghost/phantom.asp.
3. Jansson, G., Fanger, J., Konig, H, Billberger, K.: Visually Impaired Person's use of the PHANToM for Information about texture and 3D form of Virtual Objects, Proceedings of the Third PHANToM Users Group Workshop, Cambridge, MA: Massachusetts Institute of Technology, 1998.
4. Colwell, C., Petrie, H., Kornbrot, D., Hardwick, A., Furner, S.: Use of haptic device by blind and sighted people: perception of virtual textures and objects. In I. Placencia-Porrero and E. Ballabio (Eds.), Improving the quality of life for the European citizen: technology for inclusive design and equality. Amsterdam: IOS Press, 1998.
5. Dillon, P., Moody, W., Bartlett, R., Scully, P., Morgan R., James C.: Sensing the Fabric: To Simulate Sensation through Sensory Evaluation and in Response to Standard Acceptable Properties of Specific Materials when Viewed as a Digital Image. Proceedings of the First International Workshop on Haptic Human-Computer Interaction, LNCS 2058, 2000. pp. 205–218.
6. Nemec, V., Mikovec Z., Slavik P. Adaptive Navigation of Visually Impaired Users in Virtual Environment on the World Wide Web. In: Universal Access: Theoretical Perspectives, Practice, and Experience, 7th ERCIM International Workshop on User Interfaces for All, Paris, France, October 24-25, 2002, Revised Papers. LNCS 2615, Springer 2003, pp. 68–79.
7. Nemec, V., Sporka, A., Slavik, P.: Interaction of Visually Impaired Users in Virtual Environment with Spatial Sound Enhancement. In: Universal Access in HCI: Inclusive Design in the Information Society. Mahwah, New Jersey : Lawrence Erlbaum Associates, Publishers, 2003, pp. 1310–1314.
8. Appelle, S.: Haptic perception of form: Activity and stimulus attributes. In The Psychology of Touch, M. Heller and W. Schiff, Eds. Lawrence Erlbaum Associates Inc., Hillsdale, NJ, 1991, pp. 169–188.
9. Immersion TouchSenseTM Fundamentals. http://www.immersion.com/developer/ downloads/ImmFundamentals/HTML/ImmFundamentals.htm.
10. Kurniawan, S. H., Sporka, A., N mec, V., Slavík, P.: Design and Evaluation of Computer-Simulated Spatial Sound. To appear in the proceedings of 2nd Cambridge Workshop on Universal Access and Assistive Technology, Design for a more inclusive world, Springer Verlag (London), 2004.

11. Funkhouser, T., Jot, J.-M., Tsingos, N.: Sounds Good to Me!. Computational Sound for Graphics, Virtual Reality, and Interactive Systems, SIGGRAPH 2002 Course Notes, ACM Press, 2002.
12. Lokki, T., Grohn M., Savioja, L., and Takala T.: A Case Study of Auditory Navigation in Virtual Acoustic Environments, in: Proceedings of the 6th International Conference on Auditory Display (ICAD'2000), Atlanta, Georgia, USA, 2000, pp. 145–150.
13. Zikovsky, P., Slavik, P. Systems for Training Audio Perception. In: Proceedings of the 1st Cambridge Workshop on Universal Access and Assistive Technology. Cambridge: Cambridge University Press, 2002, p. 133–137.

Data Entry on the Move:
An Examination of Nomadic Speech-Based Text Entry

Kathleen J. Price[1], Min Lin[1], Jinjuan Feng[1], Rich Goldman[1],
Andrew Sears[1], and Julie A. Jacko[2]

[1] UMBC, Information Systems Department, Interactive Systems Research Center,
1000 Hilltop Circle, Baltimore, MD 21250, USA
{kprice1,mlin4,jfeng2,rich1,asears}@umbc.edu
[2] Georgia Institute of Technology, School of Industrial & Systems Engineering,
765 Ferst Drive, Atlanta, GA 30332-0205, USA
jacko@isye.gatech.edu

Abstract. Desktop interaction solutions are often inappropriate for mobile devices due to small screen size and portability needs. Speech recognition can improve interactions by providing a relatively hands-free solution that can be used in various situations. While mobile systems are designed to be transportable, few have examined the effects of motion on mobile interactions. We investigated the effect of motion on automatic speech recognition (ASR) input for mobile devices. We examined speech recognition error rates (RER) with subjects walking or seated, while performing text input tasks and the effect of ASR enrollment conditions on RER. RER were significantly lower for seated conditions. There was a significant interaction between enrollment and task conditions. When users enrolled while seated, but completed walking tasks, RER increased. In contrast, when users enrolled while walking, but completed seated tasks, RER decreased. These results suggest changes in user training of ASR systems for mobile and seated usage.

1 Introduction

The intent behind the development of mobile and hand-held devices is to produce portable electronic devices that can be used when away from traditional desktop computing equipment. As described by Johnson [1], mobile devices have the potential to provide access to an abundance of computer resources in a variety of settings; but the capabilities will never be fully realized without effective interface design. In some instances, poor mobile device design may create safety issues such as concerns with mobile phone use while driving. In other situations, poor design may simply render a device difficult to use and therefore unpopular with consumers. In one recent study, researchers questioned health care workers about their use of personal digital assistants (PDA). They found that users liked PDAs and utilized them in a number of daily functions, but also described several issues with their use including difficulty with currently available data entry techniques and complaints about small screen size [2].

It may be possible to improve mobile device interfaces through the implementation of speech interaction. Speech input provides a relatively hands-free solution for data entry, as well as command-and-control tasks, which can render a mobile device more functional in a greater variety of situations. There are a number of factors to be considered during the development of speech interfaces for mobile devices and some have been addressed in previous research. Speech recognition is inherently computa-

C. Stary and C. Stephanidis (Eds.): UI4All 2004, LNCS 3196, pp. 460–471, 2004.

tionally intensive especially in large vocabulary applications [3]. This has important implications given the limited computational capabilities of many mobile devices. Further, accuracy and error correction techniques play a large role in speech recognition usability and acceptance [4, 5, 6, 7, & 8]. Given the limited computational resources and inferior interaction solutions available with current mobile technologies, developing effective speech-based solutions may prove challenging. These issues are explored in more detail below.

While mobile systems are designed to be mobile, few researchers have examined the effects of motion on interactions with mobile devices. The motivation for this study is to examine the effect of motion on the use of automatic speech recognition as an input technique for mobile devices. To date, such nomadic speech-based interactions have received little to no attention in the literature.

2 Background Literature

An interest in the design of mobile devices has recently emerged with researchers examining the best techniques to design and develop mobile technology. Users desire access to necessary information regardless of their location, the environment, or the device they are using. Therefore, it is up to human-computer interaction experts to design interfaces that can support the desired activities [9]. Research has been undertaken with user participation through envisioning and enacting real-life use scenarios to provide a better understanding of the challenges of mobile design [10]. Dahlbom and Ljungberg [11] suggest that mobile systems have unique qualities that cannot be addressed using traditional design techniques utilized for stationary desktop workstations. Mobile Informatics, the challenge of providing users with effective access to information under mobile conditions, must address issues such as what type of work occurs in a mobile context and what technologies will best support the identified mobile work.

Researchers have begun to examine the use of mobile devices in field studies to determine issues such as device preference and how those devices are used [12]. Others are investigating characteristics of mobile work to determine important factors related to field work such as accessing remote information and colleagues [13]. Mobile design issues have been summed up in two statements: Mobile devices must tolerate a broad range of external conditions and technology must be adaptable to deal with changing external conditions [14]. Several studies have examined systems solutions for mobile users such as systems which can be used in an eyes-free manner, not using the standard GUI interface found on most desktop systems [15]; a minimal attention user interface which is specifically designed for field workers [16]; and speech and audio interaction with mobile devices [17].

One unique feature of mobile devices that needs further research is the ability to use the device while the user is in motion. We call this context of use "nomadic usage", as it requires the capability to enter data and retrieve information in a variety of situations such as in a moving vehicle or while walking. Current data entry techniques for mobile devices are not always conducive to use while in motion. Interfaces requiring the use of a small keyboard, a stylus with character writing, or a stylus and soft keyboard are visually intensive and not easy to use while in motion.

One potential solution for the challenges that come with mobile data entry could be data entry using ASR. Some researchers believe that user actions with ASR are inherently error prone [18]. While we acknowledge speech recognition errors as problematic in speech interface design, we maintain that much can be done to decrease the number of recognition errors or increase the ease of error correction thus making speech interfaces more reliable and functional. As the concept of speech data entry has become more realistic due to improvements in the underlying speech recognition algorithms and error correction mechanisms as well as increased computational capabilities of both mobile and desktop systems, researchers have begun to examine the efficacy of speech data entry. Ward and Novick [19] describe speech as an attractive choice for data input into mobile devices as it enables users to move around their environment. Others have argued that spoken computer interactions can be useful when a user's hands and eyes are busy, if a keyboard is not feasible or when screen size is limited or nonexistent [20 & 21]. Researchers are also investigating architecture features for the use of small-vocabulary real-time speech recognition on handheld devices, describe speech input as a desirable approach used to overcome challenges such as difficulty typing on a small keyboard while in motion during travel [22]. However, they did not discuss the effect of motion on ASR.

One study has examined the use of a portable medical documentation system utilizing a speaker-independent ASR system as the mode of data entry. The researcher evaluated the effects of noise, such as that produced by wind, but did not discuss the possible effects of motion on the system efficacy [23]. One group of researchers did examine the effect of physical exertion on ASR, finding that recognition accuracy decreased with increased exertion. The study required participants to read a newspaper article for the speech data entry task. However, the study was conducted after the participants stopped exercising; therefore researchers were able to assess the physiological effects of exercise, but they were not able to assess ASR during actual motion and exertion [24]. Entwistle (p137) presented several research questions for future studies. Namely, "if a participant completes enrollment while lightly exerted, would accuracy rates improve for that participant when dictating under the conditions of light or hard exertion?" Enrollment refers to ASR system enrollment by having the user read predefined text aloud into the computer via a microphone. This allows the system to develop customized models of the individual user's speech patterns thus improving speech recognition rates. Entwistle also asks, "does enrolling during exertion negatively impact rested accuracy rates in the same way that enrolling while rested and reading during exertion negatively impacted accuracy?" The current study directly addresses both of the above questions.

Further, our research extends the activities described above by studying the effects of walking motion on speech data entry by examining the efficacy of the speaker-dependent ASR system while participants are actually walking. In addition, we use composition tasks as opposed to the previously used reading tasks to simulate activities that are closer to real-world usage.

3   Research Objectives and Measures

This study examines the effectiveness of speech text entry for data entry into a mobile device while walking. The research objectives are to analyze the effect of exertion/motion and ASR enrollment condition (seated vs. walking) on speech recognition accuracy. The dependent variable for this study is the speech recognition error rate. Word recognition error rate, or as described by us RER, is a commonly used measure of speech recognition accuracy. RER is defined as the number of recognition errors divided by the number of words spoken. Recognition errors include substitution, deletion and insertion errors [25]. The independent variables are task condition (seated vs. walking) and enrollment condition (also seated vs. walking).

Perceived workload was rated by users immediately after each task condition using the NASA Task Load Index (NASA TLX) [26& 27]. This workload measurement tool has been commonly used by researchers to collect subjective assessment of user workload. The NASA-TLX is a multidimensional measurement tool for the subjective assessment of mental workload by human users/operators during task performance or use of a system. The most regularly cited version of the NASA-TLX entails the use of numerical scales and a weighting system based on six workload subscales (mental demands, physical demands, temporal demands, effort, frustration and performance) to collect information about user-perceived workload resulting from a particular task or set of conditions. This measurement tool provides subjective user ratings of the relative impact of each of these subscales on their task-induced workload, as well as a composite workload score [28]. The composite workload score is weighted based on each individual user's determination of the relative importance of each subscale during task performance. The weighting is achieved through user evaluation of a number of pairwise comparisons between the subscales. A demographic survey was also administered to gather background information about the participants.

The following research questions were examined:

- Does exertion and motion (task condition) result in significantly degraded recognition accuracy?
- Does enrollment condition result in a significant affect on recognition accuracy?
- Does decreased task length result in significantly degraded recognition accuracy?
- Is there a significant difference in the perceived workload of seated vs. walking study tasks?

4   Methodology

A within-subjects repeated measures design was used to examine the effect of motion on recognition error rates with all subjects completing tasks in both the seated and walking conditions. The effect of enrollment was observed using a between-subjects design with half of the participants completing enrollment while seated (without motion) while the other half enrolled in the ASR system while walking. As described in a previous section, enrollment involves reading predefined text. In this study, enrollment involved reading 57 sentences and required approximately 10 to 15 minutes. Participants were randomly assigned to perform enrollment either while seated or walking. The possible effects of noise, introduced by the treadmill during walking conditions, was negated by introducing equivalent noise during seated tasks as discussed below.

4.1 Participants

Thirty-two participants were recruited via a student announcement listserv at UMBC including 18 females and 14 males with an average age of 21. Participants' college majors or career fields varied across a wide range of subjects. All participants had multiple years of computer experience and reported frequent e-mail use. Subjects were all native English speakers with no previous speech recognition experience.

4.2 Equipment and Software

The equipment used in the study is intended to simulate the use of ASR with a mobile device, such as a PDA, while walking. Speech input occurred via a headset with microphone attached to a laptop computer. Speech data was collected via TK Talk II v2.0, a software application developed in the Interactive Systems Research Center (ISRC) at UMBC for collection and correction of speech recognition data. Since the goal was to measure recognition error rates, we wanted a pure measure of recognition accuracy. Therefore, we did not want participants to change the way they were speaking as a result of recognition errors. Thus, participants were not allowed to view the resulting speech output and were not asked to perform correction of recognition errors. Since participants were not aware of the quality of the subsequent output, they were not asked to rate satisfaction with the performance of the system. The ASR engine used for this study was IBM Via Voice® Pro USB Edition, Release 10. Custom analysis software, LISDLogger, was used for coding and analysis of speech recognition data.

Subjects used a treadmill when completing walking enrollment and tasks. During the completion of both the seated enrollment and tasks, prerecorded treadmill noise was introduced at the same level as it occurred during treadmill usage, via speakers to rule out noise as a confounding factor. Consequently, all recognition error rates result from conditions in the presence of background noise. Participants were instructed to choose a comfortable walking pace while reading a paragraph of text projected on a large screen. We found that pilot subjects often chose a speed that was not a comfortable walking pace, so for safety reasons we decreased the user-chosen treadmill speed by 20% during enrollment and study trials.

Respiratory rates were obtained using a gas pressure sensor belt for the purpose of assessing when users returned to a resting state after each task. During walking tasks, participants were asked to hold a Palm Pilot PDA with an accelerometer attached for the purpose of documenting motion during the walking condition. The PDA with the accelerometer was not held by participants, but instead was set on a table during seated conditions. Both the accelerometer and gas pressure (respiration) sensor collected data via a Vernier LabPro® interface system that enabled the data to be transferred to a desktop computer. The data collection software used with the LabPro® consisted of a real-time sensor display software developed in the ISRC. The accelerometer and gas pressure output was monitored during the experiment, but more detailed analysis was not relevant to the current discussion and is not reported below.

4.3 Procedure

Upon arrival, participants were screened for eligibility and signed the necessary consent form. The gas pressure sensor belt was attached and a baseline respiratory rate was obtained. The original, resting respiration rate, prior to any exertion was used as a baseline. In pilot studies we compared our resting respiratory rates, based on measurements from the gas pressure sensor belt, with health care standards and determined that our sensor-based rates were closely aligned with established health care standards

[29]. In previous research, respiratory rates have been demonstrated to decrease during speech with exertion (walking). This occurs as a side effect of controlling air flow for speech production [30 & 31]. Therefore, we used our sensor display software to determine when participants had returned to their original resting respiratory rate between tasks. More specifically, our software displays a green light to indicate that the participant has been at their resting respiratory rate for one minute. On occasion the green indicator did not light due to extraneous motion affecting the respiratory count. In those instances a trained health care professional manually counted the respiratory rate.

Subjects were oriented to the treadmill and they chose their treadmill speed. Treadmill speeds selected by participants (with the 20% decrease) ranged between 1 – 1.9 miles per hour. Participants were randomly assigned to an enrollment condition (seated or walking) and enrollment in the ASR software was completed. Subjects were required to rest by sitting quietly between each activity to allow their respiratory rate to return to their baseline rate as monitored by the sensor display software. Participants were then ready to complete study tasks. Condition (seated or walking) and Task length (short, medium, or long) were randomized for each participant.

Study tasks were composition in nature, answers in response to questions projected on a large screen in front of the participant. Participants were given three practice tasks one of each task length, prior to completing each trial condition. Tasks for each condition included 25 short phrases of 2 – 3 words, 10 medium phrases of 1 sentence, and 5 long phrases of 3 – 5 sentences each.

Sample Tasks:

- Short Task: Dictate a task you need to accomplish this week in 2 to 3 words.
- Medium Task: Describe your clothing in one sentence.
- Long Task: Discuss what you like to do during leisure time in 3 to 5 sentences.

Users were instructed to answer with a specific length response based on the given instructions for each task. Speech was digitally recorded to enable later analysis. Participants completed the TLX workload survey after each task condition. At the completion of all study trials, participants answered demographic questions in order to gather background information on the study sample population.

5 Results

Means and standard deviations are reported for RER in Table 1. A two-way ANOVA with repeated measures for task completion condition and task length was used to assess the effect of enrollment condition on RER. As illustrated in Figure 1, the examination of the effect of task conditions yielded significant results ($F(1,31) = 4.545$, $p<0.05$). Recognition error rates were significantly lower for seated conditions.

Table 1. Recognition Error Rates means and standard deviations.

Enrollment Condition	Recognition Error Rates			
	Seated Task		Walking Task	
	Mean	SD	Mean	SD
Seated Enrollment	0.38	0.17	0.44	0.20
Walking Enrollment	0.33	0.12	0.40	0.15

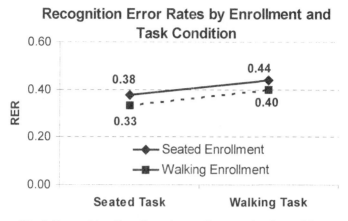

Fig. 1. Recognition Error Rates by enrollment and task condition.

Table 2 presents means and standard deviations for RER by task length and condition. Within both the seated and walking conditions, it is interesting to note that RERs decreased as task length increased. The seated long task condition had the lowest RER at 33%.

Table 2. Recognition Error Rates by task length and condition.

Task Condition	Recognition Error Rates					
	Short Task Length		Medium Task Length		Long Task Length	
	Mean	SD	Mean	SD	Mean	SD
Seated	0.37	0.18	0.36	0.15	0.33	0.15
Walking	0.48	0.25	0.39	0.20	0.38	0.18

The repeated measures ANOVA also confirmed that task length had a significant effect on RER ($F(1,31) = 4.912$, $p<0.05$) (see Figure 2). However, the effect of enrollment was not statistically significant ($F(1,31) = 0.735$, n.s.).

To address the question raised by Entwistle (2003), we also computed the difference in RER between task conditions as follows: $RER_\Delta = RER_{Diff} - RER_{Match}$ with RER_{Diff} representing the mean RER when the task condition differs from enrollment and the RER_{Match} for the mean RER when task condition is the same as enrollment. An analysis of RER_Δ then allows us to determine if similar task conditions result in improved recognition accuracy as opposed to differing task conditions.

A t-test was used to compare RER_Δ scores for the seated vs. walking enrollment conditions resulting in a statistically significant difference ($t(30) = 2.132$, $p<0.05$). When users enrolled while seated, but completed the tasks when walking, RER increased by 6.0% as compared to the seated task condition. In contrast, when users enrolled while walking, but completed the tasks when seated, RER decreased by 6.4% when compared to the walking condition.

Mean Recognition Error Rate by Task Length and Condition

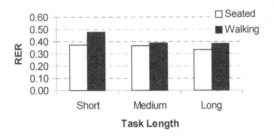

Fig. 2. Recognition Error Rates by task length and condition.

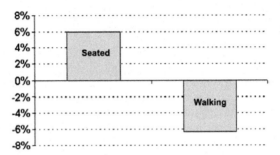

Fig. 3. Percent change in Recognition Error Rates, by enrollment condition, when moving from a task condition that matches enrollment to a task condition that differs from the enrollment condition.

5.1 Workload Index Results

A log transformation was used to normalize the TLX workload data. All TLX sub-scale scores as well as the overall weighted scores were examined. These data were then analyzed using paired t-tests. As illustrated in Table 3, each subscale as well as the overall weighted scores resulted in large standard deviations. As a result, the only significant finding was that physical demand was higher for the walking vs. seated conditions (t(30)= 8.368, p<0.001).

6   Conclusions

In this paper we discuss research on ASR and associated errors during nomadic conditions using variable length text composition tasks. Since participants completed both stationary (seated) tasks as well as tasks while walking, this research provided the opportunity to examine the effects of motion on the reliability of ASR systems. In order to develop ASR systems which are more efficient, it is necessary to decrease the RER thereby improving usability and decreasing user frustration. Currently, mobile device designers are looking for ways to improve the usability and promote safe use of their products. An interface which demands less attention would assist users with the integration of mobile devices into their everyday activities. This research was completed towards meeting the above noted goals of improving the use of ASR with nomadic systems.

Table 3. Results from NASA TLX questionnaire by task condition.

TLX Subscales	NASA TLX Workload Scores			
	Task Condition			
	Seated		Walking	
	Mean	SD	Mean	SD
Mental	37.81	23.45	35.16	21.61
Physical	8.44	7.23	27.10	20.03
Temporal	35.94	21.76	39.06	22.01
Effort	37.19	20.40	35.47	18.11
Frustration	24.69	20.12	22.34	19.30
Performance	31.72	21.24	34.06	21.27
Overall	36.44	16.31	37.81	15.34

Our earlier studies, using the same recognition engine with various tasks, resulted in RER ranging from 10 to 19% [e.g., 32, 33, & 3]. We suggest that the substantially higher RER observed in the current study (e.g., 33-44%) is due, at least in part, to the addition of background noise. Unlike our earlier studies which used transcription tasks [e.g., 3], our current results indicate that RER decreases as phrases get longer. This is likely due to the additional contextual information, provided by other words in the phrase, that is available to the speech engine.

We also confirmed that walking does indeed have an effect on speech recognition error rates. Recognition errors increased when participants were walking, but the effect may be mitigated by changing the conditions under which the users complete the enrollment process. Interesting results were obtained when investigating the relationship between enrollment and task conditions. When users enrolled under less demanding conditions (i.e., seated) accuracy decreased when performing tasks under different, more demanding, conditions (i.e., walking). Interestingly, users enrolled under demanding conditions (i.e., walking) accuracy increased when they completed tasks under different, less demanding, conditions (i.e., seated).

The most intriguing possibility presents itself when comparing overall recognition error rates for both enrollment and task conditions. In the current study, enrollment was a between-group variable making it more difficult to evaluate differences between conditions, especially when using a technology like speech recognition where large individual differences are common. However, it is interesting to observe that users who enrolled when walking experienced a 33% RER when completing tasks in the seated condition, but those users who enrolled when seated experienced a 38% RER when completing the tasks in the seated condition. This difference was not statistically significant in the current study, perhaps due to the large individual differences and the between-group treatment of enrollment condition, but it is interesting. If these differences are reliable, this would suggest that performance could be improved, even for less demanding conditions, by having users complete the enrollment process under more demanding conditions.

Our research results demonstrate intriguing outcomes that may lead to future changes in the design and use of ASR interfaces. Our results raise interesting questions regarding the most effective approaches for completing the standard enrollment process for ASR systems. More specifically, our data suggest that ASR output may be improved by having users complete the enrollment process under more stressful conditions than will be experienced during actual usage. Further research is needed to build on the findings in this study. We are planning a follow-up study, treating enrollment condition as a within-subject factor to explore the issue of the interaction between enrollment and task condition in greater detail. If our initial results are supported by additional studies, one could confidently recommend that enrollment be completed under conditions which are more challenging for the recognition engine as this would result in improved recognition accuracy under both challenging, and less challenging, conditions. Whether this trend exists only when physical exertion is involved, or is also evident when noise is introduced, is an issue that needs to be investigated. Studies would also be necessary to determine how challenging the enrollment conditions could be made without negating this potential benefit by developing user profiles that are no longer useful. When the optimal enrollment process is determined, it would be beneficial to test the findings on limited vocabulary systems in an attempt to improve their reliability as well. Previous research describes the effects of noise on ASR and the user's manner of speaking, suggesting that users often change their manner of speaking in noisy situations which causes a degradation in RER [34]. For this reason, it would also be interesting to replicate the study in a manner which removes the added noise characteristic to determine if there is an improvement in RERs without this confounding factor. Finally, it may prove interesting to further evaluate the accuracy of ASR output, including the specific nature of the errors encountered, when enrollment is completed under varying conditions. For example, researchers have explored the impact of combining the output from multiple ASR engines to reduce RER. Similarly, it may prove interesting to explore the potential benefits of combining the output produced when using multiple enrollment profiles with a single ASR engine. Users of ASR systems will benefit greatly from the increased system reliability gained from the results of the proposed research. In addition, users of mobile systems will also benefit from the enhanced system interaction made possible through the use of advanced ASR.

Acknowledgements

This material is based upon work supported by the National Science Foundation (NSF) under Grant Nos. IIS-0121570 and IIS-0328391. Any opinions, findings and conclusions or recommendations expressed in this material are those of the authors and do not necessarily reflect the views of the NSF. Numerous colleagues in the ISRC were instrumental in the completion of this research including Liwei Dai who performed analysis and coding of speech data. We would also like to thank the anonymous reviewers for their thoughtful feedback which lead to several improvements in this paper.

References

1. Johnson, P.: Usability and mobility; Interactions on the move. Retrieved August 20, 03, from Department of Computer Science Web Site: http://www.dcs.gla.ac.uk/~johnson/papers/mobile/HCIMD1.html (1998)

2. Lu, Y-C, Xiao, Y., Sears, A., & Jacko, J.: An observational and interview study on personal digital assistant (PDA) uses by clinicians in different contexts. In D. Harris, V. Duffy, M. Smith & Stephanidis, C. (Eds.): Human-centred computing: Cognitive, social and ergonomic aspects. Mahwah, NJ: Lawrence Erlbaum Associates. (2003) 93-97

3. Price, K. J., & Sears, A.: Speech-based text entry for mobile devices. In C. Stephanidis & J. Jacko (Eds.): Human-computer interaction: Theory and practice (Part II) Lawrence Erlbaum Associates, Mahwah, NJ (2003) 766-770

4. Karat, C-M, Halverson, C., Karat, J., & Horn, D.: Patterns of entry and correction in large vocabulary continuous speech recognition systems. In Proceedings of CHI '99 New York: ACM Press. (1999) 568-575

5. Noyes, J. M., & Frankish, C. R.: Errors and error correction in automatic speech recognition systems. Ergonomics, Vol. 37 (1994) 1943-1957

6. Price, K. J., & Sears, A.: Speech-based data entry for handheld devices: Speed of entry and error correction techniques (Information Systems Department Technical Report). Baltimore, MD: UMBC. (2002) 1-8

7. Sears, A., Feng, J., Oseitutu, K., & Karat, C-M.: Hands-free, speech-based navigation during dictation: Difficulties, consequences, and solutions. Human-Computer Interaction, 18 (2003) 229-257

8. McCormick, J.: Speech Recognition. Government Computer News, Vol. 22(22), (2003) 24-28

9. Paterno, F. Understanding interaction with mobile devices. Interacting With Computers, 15, (2003) 473-478

10. Iacucci, G., Kuutti, K., & Ranta, M.: On the move with a magic thing: Role playing in concept design of mobile services and devices. In (Ed.): Proceedings of the conference on designing interactive systems: Processes, practices, methods, and techniques. New York: ACM Press. (2000) 193-202

11. Dahlbom, B., & Ljungberg, F.: Mobile informatics. Scandinavian Journal of Information Systems, Vol. 10(1 & 2), (1998) 227-234

12. Brodie, J., & Perry, M. Designing for mobility, collaboration and information use by blue-collar workers. SIGGROUP Bulletin, Vol. 22(3), (2001) 22-27

13. Perry, M., O'Hara, K., Sellen, A., Brown, B., & Harper, R.: Dealing with mobility: Understanding access anytime, anywhere. ACM Transactions on Computer-Human Interaction, Vol. 8(4), (2001) 323-347

14. Satyanarayanan, M.: Fundamental challenges in mobile computing. In Proceedings of the fifteenth annual ACM symposium on principles of distributed computing ACM Press, New York: (1996) 1-7

15. Brewster, S., Lumsden, J., Bell, M., Hall, M., & Tasker, S.: Multi-modal 'eyes-free' interaction techniques for wearable devices. Letters to CHI, Vol. 5(1), (2003) 473-480

16. Pascoe, J., Ryan, N., & Morse, D. Using while moving: HCI issues in fieldwork environments. ACM Transactions on Computer-Human Interaction, Vol. 7(3), (2000) 417-437

17. Sawhney, N., & Schmandt, C.: Nomadic Radio: Speech and audio interaction for contextual messaging in nomadic environments. ACM Transactions on Computer-Human Interactions, Vol. 7(3), (2000) 353-383

18. Bradford, J. H.: The human factors of speech-based interfaces. SIGCHI Bulletin, Vol. 27(2), (1995) 61-67

19. Ward, K., & Novick, D. G.: Accessibility: Hands-free documentation. In (Ed.): Proceedings of the 21st annual international conference on documentation. ACM Press, New York (2003) 147-154

20. Cohen, P. R., & Oviatt, S. L.: The role of voice in human-machine communication. In D.B. Roe & J. Wilpon (Eds.): Human-Computer Interaction by Voice. National Academy of Sciences Press, Washington, DC (1993) 1-36
21. Shneiderman, B.: The limits of speech recognition. Communications of the ACM, Vol. 43(9), (2000) 63-65
22. Hagen, A., Connors, D. A., & Pellom, B. L.: The analysis and design of architecture systems for speech recognition on modern handheld-computing devices. In (Ed.): Proceedings of the international symposium on systems synthesis ACM Press, New York (2003) 65-70
23. Holzman, T. G.: Speech-audio interface for medical information management in field environments. International Journal of Speech Technology, 4, (2001) 209-226
24. Entwistle, M. S.: The performance of automated speech recognition systems under adverse conditions of human exertion. International Journal of Human-Computer Interaction, Vol. 16(2), (2003) 127-140
25. Fiscus, J. G., Fisher, W. M., Martin, A. F., Przybocki, M. A., & Pallett, D. S.: 2000 NIST evaluation of conversational speech recognition over the telephone: English and Mandarin performance results. Retrieved February 28, 2004, from http://www.nist.gov/speech/publications/tw00/pdf/cts10.pdf (2000)
26. Hart, S. G., & Staveland, L. E.: Development of NASA-TLX (Task Load Index): Results of empirical and theoretical research. In P.A. Hancock & N. Meshkati (Eds.): Human mental workload, Elsevier Science Publishers B.V., Amsterdam (1988) 139-183
27. NASA Ames Research Center: NASA Human Performance Research Group Task Load Index (NASA-TLX) instruction manual [Brochure]. Moffett Field, CA: (1987)
28. Emery, V. K., Moloney, K. P., Jacko, J. A., & Sainfort, F.: Assessing workload in the context of human-computer interactions: Is the NASA-TLX a suitable measurement tool? (200401). Laboratory for Human-Computer Interaction and Health Care Informatics, Georgia Institute of Technology, Atlanta, Georgia (February, 2004)
29. Chandrasekhar, A.: Respiratory rate and pattern of breathing: To evaluate one of the vital signs. Retrieved October 14, 2003, from Loyola University Medical Education Network Web Site: http://www.meddean.luc.edu/lumen/meded/medicine/pulmonar/pd/step73a.htm (n.d.)
30. Doust, J. H., & Patrick, J. M.: The limitation of exercise ventilation during speech. Respiration Physiology, Vol. 46, (1981) 137-147
31. Meckel, Y., Rotstein, A., & Inbar, O.: The effects of speech production on physiologic responses during submaximal exercise. Medicine and Science in Sports and Exercise, Vol. 34(8), (2002) 1337-1343
32. Feng, J., Sears, A., & Karat, C-M.: A longitudinal evaluation of hands-free speech-based navigation during dictation (Information Systems Department Technical Report). UMBC, Information Systems Department, ISRC, Baltimore, MD (2004)
33. Feng, J., & Sears, A.: Using confidence scores to improve hands-free speech-based navigation. In C. Stephanidis & J. Jacko (Eds.): Human-Computer Interaction: Theory and Practice (Volume 2) Lawrence Erlbaum Associates, Mahwah, NJ (2003) 641-645
34. Rollins, A. M.: Speech recognition and manner of speaking in noise and in quiet. In (Ed.): CHI '85 Proceedings. ACM Press, New York (1985) 197-199

Whistling User Interface (U³I)

Adam J. Sporka[1], Sri Hastuti Kurniawan[2], and Pavel Slavik[1]

[1] Department of Computer Science, Czech Technical University in Prague
Faculty of Electrical Engineering, Karlovo náměstí 13 Praha 2, 12135 Czech Republic
{sporkaa,slavik}@fel.cvut.cz
[2] Department of Computation, UMIST
PO Box 88, Manchester, M60 1QD, United Kingdom
s.kurniawan@co.umist.ac.uk

Abstract. The paper describes the design, implementation and user evaluation of a system that allows a user to control a mouse pointer through whistling or humming. The pointer can be controlled in two ways: orthogonally (the pointer can only move with variable speed either horizontally or vertically at a time) and melodically (the pointer can move with fixed speed in any direction). The user study indicates that the users thought the orthogonal control was easier to operate than the melodic control. The orthogonal control was considered useful for controlling mouse movement while the melodic control was more useful for entertainment purposes. Humming was considered less tiring than whistling. This study makes several contributions to the field. First, it is perhaps the first published study investigating the use of whistling to operate a mouse pointer. Second, the system can be used as a low-cost alternative pointing device for people with motor disabilities.

Keywords: Pointing devices, motor disabilities, acoustic input, assistive technologies.

1 Introduction

Throughout recent years, much effort has been put to the development of alternative input user interfaces for computer users with motor disabilities. Some common approaches include the addition of speech recognition software or additional devices such as an eye-tracker or various breath controllers (such as the sip-and-puff controller [4].) Speech recognition software had been reported to be particularly useful for entering text [1] while the additional devices are usually used as a pointing device (to control the mouse pointer) [2]. However, the availability of these devices and software is very limited and they usually cost much more than a standard input device such as a mouse and a keyboard.

This paper presents a novel approach of operating a pointing device without additional hardware or expensive software. The system allows the users to control on-screen mouse pointer through whistling, humming or singing any sound of different pitches. Because whistling, humming and singing operate the system exactly the same way, throughout the paper only whistling as the input mechanism will be explained. The system can be implemented on a standard PC or a PDA device for mobile applications and does not require any hardware other than a microphone and a sound card capable to sample the input audio signal.

The paper consists of two main topics: an overview of the method employed to implement the system and the results of a small user study.

C. Stary and C. Stephanidis (Eds.): UI4All 2004, LNCS 3196, pp. 472–478, 2004.
© Springer-Verlag Berlin Heidelberg 2004

2 The Input Method

The overview of the input method is shown in Figure 1. When a user whistles, the sound of whistling is received by the microphone and digitized by the sound card. The digitized sound is processed in frames 1024 samples long.

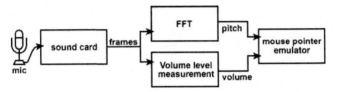

Fig. 1. Block diagram of the system.

Using the Fast Fourier Transform (FFT), the melody of the whistling is tracked. In this method, the melody is defined as the development of the pitch of the tone of whistling over time. The frequency at which there is most energy transferred is considered the pitch of the tone. The volume level of a frame is determined as a simple sum of the absolute values of the samples of the frame.

A sound is recognized as a tone if it exceeds user-defined threshold of the volume level. No other processing has been implemented at this point of study. For environments with the background noise of a constant volume level, the user study (which will be described in more detail later) showed that this method is sufficient. The designed system interprets the melody in two different modes when controlling the mouse pointer: orthogonally and melodically.

Orthogonal Control Mode

In this mode, the mouse pointer is controlled either horizontally or vertically at a time. The direction of the pointer's motion is determined by the pitch of the tone at its beginning (the initial pitch). The velocity is controlled by changing the pitch of the tone. If the user starts a tone below a specified threshold f_t, the mouse pointer will move only to the left and to the right. Similarly, if a tone is started above f_t, the pointer will move only up or down. The actual direction and speed of motion at any given time is determined from the difference of the current and the initial pitch. The bigger than the initial the current pitch is, the faster the cursor moves up (or to the right), and the lower pitch, the faster cursor's motion down (or to the left). The click of the left button is emulated when the user only makes a short tone. Some control tones are shown in Figure 2.

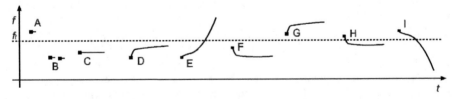

Fig. 2. Examples of control tones. t – time, f – pitch, ft – threshold pitch; A – click, B – double click, C – no motion, D – motion to the right, E – fast motion to the right, F – motion to the left, G – motion up, H – motion down, I – fast motion down.

The state diagram of this control mode is shown in Figure 3a. As mentioned, the cursor can only be controlled by whistles which last more than a threshold length t_t (typically 0.2 seconds). If the pitch f_s of a tone at its start is greater than the threshold t_f, the cursor would move vertically, otherwise it would move horizontally (transitions 2-3 and 2-4 respectively). As the whistle changes its frequency f_s, the cursor changes its velocity in appropriate direction. When the tone disappears, the system returns to the initial state and another mouse click may be emulated or another cursor motion may be started. An example of this control mode is shown in Figure 5a.

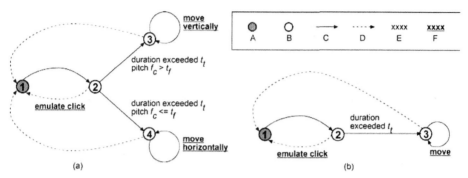

Fig. 3. Functionality described by means of state diagrams. (a) Orthogonal (b) Melodic modes. Key to the legend in the box above: A – initial state, B – other state, C – transition when there is a sound on input, D – transition when no sound is being received, E – additional condition of a transition, F – action initiated upon a transition.

Melodic Control Mode

In this mode, the cursor can move in any direction with a constant speed. There are two input parameters to this mode: the speed of the cursor and the pitch of the base tone. The left mouse button click is emulated in the same way as in the orthogonal control. If a longer tone than the threshold t_t is detected (Figure 3b, transition 2-3), the cursor pointer starts to move. The direction of motion varies with the pitch of the whistling tone. The pitch of the tone may be any from the control octave: <base tone, base tone + 12 semitones>.

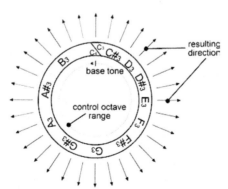

Fig. 4. The assignment of directions of cursor's motion to different pitches within the control octave.

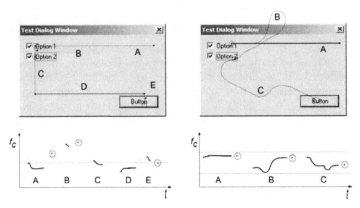

Fig. 5. The orthogonal and melodic modes in operation. Individual movements are indicated with letters and start with small squares. Mouse clicks are marked with circles. (a) The orthogonal mode, the trace of the mouse pointer is shown above, the melody of whistling is shown below; the dotted line represents the threshold pitch ft, (b) the similar pictures for the melodic mode; the pitches in control octave are localized between the dotted lines.

However, the range of possible pitches is continuous – i.e. it is not limited only to the octave's semitones. Figure 4 shows the assignment of directions when the C3 note (approx. 1050 Hz) is chosen for the base tone pitch. An example of this control mode is shown in Figure 5b.

3   The Implementation

The designed system runs as an independent application (EXE) and requires a Microsoft Windows 98 or newer operating system. The system was written in Microsoft Visual C++ (ver.6.0). The application is available for download from [3]. A snapshot of the application is provided in Figure 6.

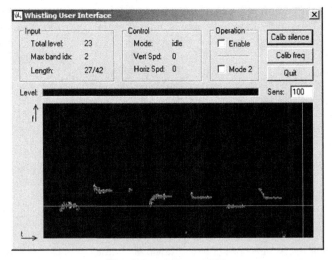

Fig. 6. A snapshot of U3I.

4 The User Study

The designed system was tested in two separate sessions by four regular computer users (defined as people who use computers at least 5 hours a week) whose data are listed in Table 1. The participants were asked to control the mouse through whistling in the first session and through hissing/humming in the second session. All participants either had no visual impairment or wore corrective lenses at the time of the experiment. In both sessions, a Pentium-4 1.7 GHz PC running Windows XP with a 17" monitor set at 1024 by 768 pixels resolution and a standard blank (blue) background was used. Each participant tested the system in a quiet room accompanied only by the experimenter. To minimize the noise interference from the surrounding environment, the participants wore headsets throughout the sessions. Participants' mouse movements were recorded using Camtasia Studio 2 screen capture software.

Table 1. Participants' data.

Subjects	S1	S2	S3	S4
Gender	M	M	F	F
Motor disability	Missing fingers (accident)	None	Arthritis (cannot move her finger joints well)	None
Age	40	23	67	19
Average weekly computer use	>20 hrs	10-20 hrs	5-10 hrs	>20 hrs

The First Session

At the beginning of this session the experimenter informed the participants that the purpose of the study was to investigate how easy it was for them to control the mouse pointer through whistling and not to measure their performance in using the system. The experimenter then introduced the participant to the two control modes. The participants were then given 5 minutes to try the system out after being reminded that any noise they made might affect the mouse pointer movement.

The participants were then given an instruction sheet to move the pointer to various objects on the screen and to click some icons (5 tasks per control mode). The participants were allowed to take breaks of any time length between tasks to prevent fatigue affecting their performance. The tasks varied in the directions and angles of pointer's movement while the distances from the current pointer to the next target were kept fairly constant. The icons were standard Windows icons displaying folders numbered 1-5 (the number allows the participants to see the sequence of targets to click).

Two participants (S1 and S4) tested the orthogonal control first and the other two (S2 and S3) tested the melodic control. This experimental design was aimed at balancing the control mode, gender, age or disability.

Even though there were only four participants (hence a statistical analysis could not be performed), the results indicate that in average the participants took twice as long to arrive to an icon and click it when using the melodic control (an average of 2.6s, the standard deviation is not reported because there are only four participants) than when using the orthogonal control (1.4s). When the screen capture was analyzed, it showed that all participants overshot the target when using the melodic control.

In the post-session interviews, the participants mentioned that they felt they could control the pointer much better using the orthogonal control than using the melodic control, comments that were correlated with the objective performance results (i.e., the time taken to finish the tasks). When asked how they thought these control modes would be useful for them, all participants answered that the orthogonal mode would be useful as a way to control the mouse. Three answered that the melodic mode would be "a fun way to move the mouse on the screen" or "may be good for drawing". One said that she could not think of how this mode would be useful for her. All said that they felt comfortable using the system even though this was the first time they were exposed to it and were certain that they would master both control modes if they were given enough exposure.

The Second Session

The same four people did the second session one month later. Testing the system with the same group of participants allows a comparison of the ease of whistling and of the other two types of input sound, i.e. hissing and humming. The same setup and equipment was used. However, the stimuli (the locations of the icons) were changed to minimize the familiarity, although the one month gap between the first and second sessions might ameliorate the familiarity problem. In this session, S1 and S4 tested the melodic control first and S2 and S3 tested the orthogonal control first to balance the experimental design.

There were some major problems with operating the system through hissing. Two participants were unable to hiss properly. The other two could finish the tasks in the orthogonal mode (albeit with a lot of difficulty) through hissing. However, these two participants were unable to even home in on the first target in the melodic mode.

The participants were then instructed to redo the tasks through humming or singing the tones. All participants were successful in finishing the tasks in both modes. However, they took slightly longer compared to the times they took in the first session (1.8s for the orthogonal mode and 3s for the melodic mode). The analyzed screen capture indicated that all participants overshot the target when using the melodic control. Examining the u3i screen, it was apparent that humming and singing produced signals that were less pure than whistling. Therefore, the control was not as good as the one performed through whistling. The participants still thought that the orthogonal mode was easier to control and operate than the melodic mode.

In the post-session interview, three participants indicated that they preferred to control the mouse through humming or singing rather than whistling. When asked why, they mentioned that whistling was more tiring. The last participant said that he preferred whistling because he felt that this way he could control the mouse better.

5 Conclusion and Future Work

The paper reports on the design and evaluation of a whistle-operated pointing device. The key benefits of this system include: low computation power needed (especially suitable for mobile devices), short learning curve (as indicated from the user study), easy installation, and no special device is required.

The results of the user study indicated that the orthogonal control was easier to perform than the melodic control. However, in both control modes, the users were able to complete the tasks. The users reported that they felt comfortable to use our system. Most participants indicated that humming or singing was less tiring than whistling.

Currently, our system is a working prototype. However, since no noise detection and filtering routines were implemented, the system is very sensitive to acoustic interferences. In order to be able to use our system in everyday situations, the system must be built more robust.

The user study only involved four participants. A study of a larger scale would allow statistical analysis of the results.

References

1. Basson, S. Speech Recognition and Accessible Education. Speech Technology Magazine 7(4) [On-Line], 2002. Available at: http://www.speechtechmag.com/issues/7_4/avios/.
2. Sibert, L. E., Jacob, R. J. K. Evaluation of Eye Gaze Interaction, in Proceedings of CHI'00, (The Hague, The Netherlands, April 2000), ACM Press, 281-288.
3. Sporka, A. Whistling User Interface [On-Line], 2003. Available at: http://cs.felk.cvut.cz/~sporkaa/index.php?page=u3i.
4. Kitto, K. L. Development of a low-cost Sip and Puff Mouse, in Proceedings of 16th Annual Conference of RESNA, pages 452-454, USA, Las Vegas, 1993.

Use of Force Feedback Pointing Devices for Blind Users

Bertrand Tornil and Nadine Baptiste-Jessel

IRIT, Université Paul Sabatier, 118, Route de Narbonne
31062 Toulouse Cedex 4, France
{tornil,baptiste}@irit.fr
http://www.irit.fr

Abstract. We discuss in this paper the possible uses of force feedback pointing devices for a blind user. We use the Wingman Force Feedback Mouse® and the PHANTOM®, associated with a sound feedback. First, we set the definitions of the gesture interaction and we propose the interaction loop relative to these devices. Related works enable us to raise the limit of their use and to specify an adapted framework : the relative localization. The applications that we are developing are based on this applicative context. We present our application of geography which shows the relative positions of the areas on a map. We finish with a presentation of our 3-dimensional application prototype, which shows the relative position of the human body elements. In order to automate the treatment as much as possible, we have based our applications on XML data files : the SVG for the geographical maps and the X3D will be retained for the format of the forms in 3D.

1 Introduction

In front of a computer, a blind user uses the keyboard to operate the machine which answers him by a voice synthesis and/or a braille display. The text processing is well adapted to these methods. However, a graphic document will be presented to him by long and tiresome descriptions. The force feedback devices are used within the framework of the accessibility for the blind users because they authorize a more direct interaction based on sensory capacities.

We will first set the main definitions of the gestural interaction and will locate the perceptual mechanisms needed in order to use these devices. Here, we concentrate more specifically on force feedback pointing devices like the mouse. While reviewing related works within the framework of the accessibility for the blind users, as well as the limits observed, we propose a specific context of use for these devices: relative localization. Then, we present two applications of the relative localization. In 2D, it is a program of reading of geographical maps which allows a better accessibility for the blind users; and in 3D, our prototype makes it possible to a blind user to deduce the position from a human body model displayed on the screen. Lastly, we will conclude by presenting the outlooks which we consider.

2 Gestural Interaction

We set the general standards which relate to the gestural interaction between the user and the machine. Then, an action-reaction loop (or interaction loop) could be defined in our applicative context.

C. Stary and C. Stephanidis (Eds.): UI4All 2004, LNCS 3196, pp. 479–485, 2004.
© Springer-Verlag Berlin Heidelberg 2004

2.1 Human Gesture

The tactilo-kinesthetic or "haptic" [1] system is the synthesis of the movements of exploration of the motor system and of perceptions of the tactile system. The haptic sense is thus both effector and receptor. [2] classified these two aspects in the following way:

1. movements of exploration of the hand:
   (a) side friction (movement on both sides of the surface of an object)
   (b) envelopment
   (c) the static contact (positioning of the palm of the hand on the surface of an object)
   (d) the following of contours
   (e) the pressure (regular force applied to a given place of the object)
   (f) the rising of an object
2. sensory capacities related to the gestural modality:
   (a) the cutaneous sense: it is the touch sense. It allows to feel the temperature, the pressure or the pain, and is relayed by sensory receptors located under the skin.
   (b) the kinesthetic sense: it is the sense related on the position and the movements of the body. It enables us for example to know the weight of an object we're handling and its position. It is relayed by receptors based in the muscles, the tendons and the articulations.

All these human capacities must have their equivalent on the machine, in order to accomplish the interaction loop. We will see further which sensory and exploratory capacities are stimulated according to the devices that we use.

2.2 Computer "Gesture"

There are numerous force feedback and/or tactile devices.

In our study, we focused more specifically on the force feedback pointing devices. These devices handle only one pointer in the virtual space of the machine: the position of the device is translated into a couple of coordinates (X,y) in 2D or a triplet (X,y,Z) in 3D.

The devices we use are the Wingman Force Feedback Mouse® for the 2D and the PHANToM® for the 3D.

The Wingman Forces Feedback Mouse ® (figure 1), was created by Immersion Corporation and marketed by Logitech.The mouse is interdependent of its base. The effective surface of work is of 1.9 X 2.5 cm and the forces can reach 1N in peak. Formerly, the Wingman® was a game device, but its use was diverted toward research on the accessibility.

The PHANToM® device (figure 2) was created and is marketed by Sensable Technology. It is the most popular device in research on the haptic interaction. The volume of work is of 13 X 16 X 13cm and the force feedback can reach 8.5N.

2.3 Interaction Loop for the Pointing

The handling of these two pointing devices makes use of the movements of exploration of the arm. Articulations of the shoulder, the elbow and the wrist, and their associated muscles are stimulated. The feedback operates on the same parts of the body.

Thus, it is the kinesthetic perception related to the arm via the shoulder, the elbow and the wrist which is requested.

Fig. 1. Wingman Force Feedback Mouse.

Fig. 2. PHANToM.

3 Force Feedback for Blind Users

3.1 Related Works

The use of the force feedback for blind users aims to make up, as much as reasonably possible, for the absence of the visual channel. Several approaches exist.

1. Haptic feedback of a graphic interface. Thanks to force feedback mice, [3] and [4] transcribed the the graphic interactors of the interface in force feedback.
2. Haptic feedback of the contents and the layout of a document. The translation of mathematical figures or tables was studied by [5]. Finally, [6] carried out a haptic system of visualization based on the PHANToM® for people with visual handicap. [7] developed a programming library making it possible to identify the layout of a document and to guide the hand of the user on this document.
3. Description of graphic documents. [8] studied the possibilities of a force feedback on VRML (Virtual Reality Markup Language), a 3D file format on the Web. [9] used the SVG (Scalable Vector Graphics) to enable blind users to read geographical maps.
4. Apprehension of shapes or textures. [5] worked on the synthesis of haptic textures. [10] used the Impulse Engine 3000 to study perception by the blind users of textures and virtual shapes. Finally [11] studied the perception of mathematical graphics by blind users using the PHANToM®.

Moreover, [12] showed the interest of the audio-haptic bimodality for blind users. The table 1 indicates the percentage of good answers for three modal situations for 12 sighted users and 12 blind users.

Table 1. Scores in Different Modal Situations.

	Blind Users: 12	Sighted Users: 12	Total:24
Audio	68 %	62 %	64 %
Haptic	78 %	71 %	74 %
Bimodal	83 %	78 %	80 %
Total	76 %	70 %	73 %

3.2 Limits

Limits were raised in the use of force feedback pointing devices for the blind users. As follows:

1. the use of these devices for the perception of textures is inadequate, as pointed [11]. Indeed, the cutaneous receptors of the skin are not stimulated.
2. [13] and [10] pointed that the single contact point of the PHANToM® does not allow the recognition of a three-dimensional complex shape. The gestures of envelopment of the hand would allow such a recognition, but that would need a device activating the kinesthetic feedback on the fingers.

3.3 Relative Localization

The use of force feedback pointing devices must be based on the properties of the kinesthetic interaction of the arm.

Kinesthetic perception related to the arm enables us to visualize the position of the hand in space. Thus, if an haptic event, like a vibration or a shock, occurs during a move of the arm, we can mentally represent the position that the hand had when the event occurred. Associated with a voice synthesis, this approach will allow the rebuilding of a mental image of an object from the relative positions of the elements of this object.

The two applications which we will present use the force feedback in this context.

4 Applications of the Relative Localization

4.1 2D Application: Géogr'Haptic

This application run in a Internet browser. We display a map indicating the American states. A blind user handle the Wingman Force Feedback Mouse® to explore the surface of the screen. When the pointer of the mouse passes on an area, it is "magnetized" toward its center. A sound feedback gives the name of the state, via a screen reader and a voice synthesis. The figure 3 illustrates this operation.

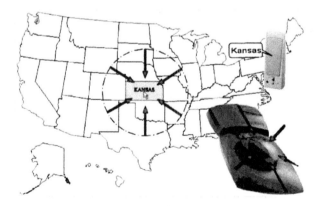

Fig. 3.

Then, it is necessary for the user to force his way out of the area, and either:

1. to fall into a state bordering and to hear the name of this state(figure 4)
2. to leave the map, and then to feel an effect of texture.

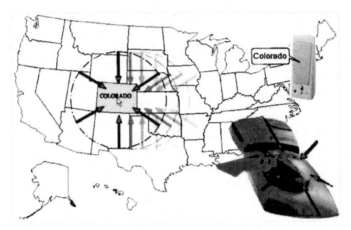

Fig. 4.

The format of the map is the SVG [14] which is the implementation in XML for the vectorial pictures. The interest to use this format is multiple:

1. its contents can be indexed by the search engines on the Web.
2. the SVG supports the DOM (Document Object Model) and is therefore entirely scriptable. Geogr'Haptic is coded in Javascript.
3. graphics in SVG can react to the users events: OnMouseOver() when the mouse passes on an area. OnMouseClic() when the user clicks.
4. the SVG can be displayed perfectly on all platforms, all output resolutions, with various bandwidths.

The first tests which we carried out with blind users are encouraging: they are able to quote the frontier states of Canada. Moreover, they can know which states must be crossed to go from a point A to a point B, which would not be possible by using traditional pictures on the Web.

4.2 3D Application

This application uses the same principle as géogr'Haptic but in three dimensions thanks to the use of the PHANToM®. We plan to base the application on the 3D XML format: the X3D [15]. However, we currently use the POSER® file format[16] for the prototype. It contains some meta-data like the X3D. The figure 5 shows the prototype of the application after the loading of a model of a human skeleton.

When we load the 3D model, the bounding boxes of each element are computed. A 3D cursor moved by the PHANToM® allows to navigate into the 3D scene. A force feedback then attracts the pointer in the center of the nearest bounding box. Then, a voice synthesis reads the name of this element.

Nowadays, our prototype allows to blind user to deduce the 3D model position. For instance, on the figure 5 the model is standing with the arms in cross.

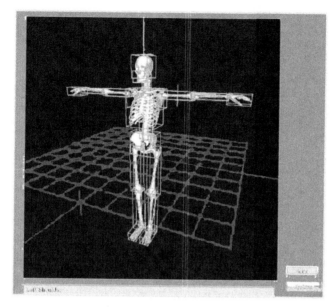

Fig. 5.

5 Outlooks

We should soon propose a test protocol which aims to confront our prototypes with the existing tools of access to the graphic documents for blind people.

The prototype of our 3D application is still in an early stage development. For complex 3D models, our application will have to filter informations to be handled by the force feedback in instance to produce a scene with a good haptic legibility. We're going to use the XML 3D file format for the Web: the X3D [15]. Just like the SVG, the X3D is completely scriptable, and support the DOM, which ena   bles us to consider an exploitation in a Internet browser. Moreover its specifications include the management of the objects displayed by pointing devices. We must also study adjustments of the force feedback, which would be specific with the 3D model loaded: an effect could thus guide the user hand along the elements. The effects could be characteristic of the various parts of the body (the intensity of the effect would be different if we are in a bone or in an organ).

This leads us to our last objective: we are about to build a 3D model of a human body including the organs. The haptic reading of such a model would be useful for blind and sighted users, in a pedagogical context.

Acknowledgments

The authors would like to thank Frederic Gianni for providing the handling libraries of POSER® file, and for it constant support.

References

1. Revesz, G.: Psychology an art of the blind. New York: Longmans (1950)
2. Lederman, S.J., Klatzky, R.L.: Haptic exploration in humans and machines: An initial overview. Technical report, Office of Naval Research (1987)
3. Ramstein, C.: Combining Hpatic and Braille Technologies, Design Issues and Pilot Study. In: ASSET'96, ACM/SIGCAPH. In 2nd Annual ACM Conference on Assistive Technologies, Vancouver, BC, Canada. (1996) 37–44
4. Rosenberg, L.: Feelit mouse: Adding a realistic sense of feel to the computing experience (1997)
5. Fritz, J., Barner, K.: Design of haptic graphing method. In: Proceedings of RESNA-96 Annual Conference, Salt Lake City, USA. (1996) 158–160
6. Fritz, J., Barner, K.: Design of a haptic visualisation system for people with visual impairments. In: IEEE Transactions on Rehabilitaion Engineering. (1999) 372–384
7. Offen, D., Thomlinson, B.: Good vibrations: Using a tactile mouse to convey page layout information to visually impaired computer users. In: Proceedings of CSUN'S Sixteenth Annual International Conference :"Technology and Persons with Disabilities", Los Angeles. (2001)
8. Hardwick, A., Further, S., Rush, J.: Tacile display of virtual reality from the world wide web - a potential access method for blind people. Display **18, Issue 3** (1998) 151–161
9. Gardner, J., Bulatov, V.: Smart figures, svg, and accessible web graphics. In: Proceedings of Technology And Persons With Disabilities Conference 2001, Los Angeles. (2001)
10. Colwell, C., Petrie, H., Kornbrot, D., Hardwick, A., S., F.: Use of a haptic device by blind and sighted people: perception of virtual textures and objects. In: Improving the quality of life for the European citizen: technology for inclusive design and equality. I. placencia-porrero and e. ballabio edn. Amsterdam: IOS Press (1998)
11. Yu, W., Ramloll, R., Brewster, S.: Haptic graphs for blind computer users. Lecture Notes in Computer Science **2058** (2001) 41–? ?
12. Dufresne, A., Martial, O., Ramstein, C.: Multimodal user interface system for blind and 'visually occupied' users: Ergonomic evaluation of the haptic and auditive dimensions. In: Proceedings of IFIP International Conference Interaction'95, Lillehammer, Norway. (1995) 163–168
13. Magnusson, C., Rassmus-Gröhn, K., Sjöström, C., Danielsson, H.: Navigation and recognition in complex haptic environments - reports from an extensive study with blind users. Présenté à EuroHaptics, Edinburgh, UK, July 8-10 (2002)
14. SVG: Scalable vector graphics (svg) 1.1 specification. http://www.w3.org/TR/SVG/ (2003)
15. X3D: X3d working group overview. http://www.web3d.org/x3d.html (2002)
16. Curious Labs: Poser 5. http://www.curiouslabs.com/ (2004)

Author Index